Preparing to Use Algebra

PREPARING TO USE ALGEBRA has been used successfully by students all over the United States. This expanded new edition will benefit two groups of students:

- *Those who are not ready for a first course in algebra.* The book contains all the mathematics content needed for those students to succeed in algebra.
- *Those who may not study algebra but need to master more than minimum mathematics competencies.* PREPARING TO USE ALGEBRA benefits those students through an emphasis on computational skills and practical applications.

──────── Note These Features ────────

Practical, comprehensive content emphasizes:

Numeration
Computational Skills
Problem Solving and Applications
Geometry and Measurement

Algebraic Expressions and Equations
Graphing
Statistics and Probability
(See Table of Contents)

A choice of suggested course levels provides flexibility. (Page T6)

Lessons are concise and easy to follow.

Practice exercises are grouped for oral classwork (A), individual written practice (B), and student discovery and enrichment (C). (Pp. 36, 184-185, 374-376, etc.)

Frequent review and testing assure mastery:

Getting Ready (Pp. 1, 33, 63, etc.)
Quick Quizzes (Pp. 11, 46, 79, etc.)
Chapter Reviews (Pp. 28, 59, 96, etc.)

Chapter Tests (Pp. 30, 61, 99, etc.)
Cumulative Reviews (Pp. 102-103, 230-231, etc.)

Optional special topics apply math skills:

Career Corner (Pp. 100, 464, 558, etc.)
Consumer Corner (Pp. 163, 269, 362, etc.)

Activities (Pp. 32, 101, 342, etc.)
Other Topics (Pp. 84, 95, 533, etc.)

Homework Handbook, in the back of the textbook, gives students valuable help.

Functional Teacher's Edition contains the annotated student's textbook and a complete manual. Included are:

Answers
Suggested class times/assignment guides
Teaching suggestions for every lesson

Performance objectives
Pretests, Posttests, Cumulative Tests,
    End-of-Year Test (all reproducible)

Correlated Supplements give you more help:

- **Practice Book** includes practice for each lesson plus review for each chapter. Accompanied by Answer Key.
- **Blackline Masters: Tests** provide complete chapter pretests and posttests, five cumulative tests, and multiple-choice end-of-year test. Answer Key included.

(For further information on PREPARING TO USE ALGEBRA, see page T3 of this Teacher's Edition.)

PREPARING TO USE ALGEBRA

Fourth Edition

Albert P. Shulte
Director, Mathematics Education
Oakland Schools
Pontiac, Michigan

Robert E. Peterson
Chairman, Mathematics Department
Fraser High School
Fraser, Michigan

LAIDLAW BROTHERS • PUBLISHERS
A Division of Doubleday & Company, Inc.
RIVER FOREST, ILLINOIS
Sacramento, California   Chamblee, Georgia   Dallas, Texas   Toronto, Canada

Project Manager Max V. Lyles / *Senior Editor* Mary E. Fraser
Production Manager Kathleen Kasper / *Production Supervisor* Mary C. Steermann /
Production Staff Christine Brainer Bassindale, Diane L. Bergmann /
Photo Researcher William A. Cassin / *Manager, Art and Design* Gloria J. Muczynski /
Designer Dennis Horan / *Artists* Joann Daley, John D. Firestone & Associates,
George Hamblin, Paul Hazelrigg, Rick Incrocci, Frank Larocco, Donald C. Meighan

Cover Photographer Don Renner / Photo Trends

Teacher's Edition ISBN 0-8445-1851-4

ISBN 0-8445-1850-6

Printed in the United States of America

23456789 10 11 12 13 14 15   2109876

23456789 10 11 12 13 14 15   2109876

CONTENTS

Chapter 1   Symbols and Sentences

Chapter 2   Solving Open Sentences

Chapter 3   Important Properties

Chapter 4 Fractions and Mixed Numbers

Chapter 5 Decimals and Estimating

Chapter 6 Adding and Subtracting Integers

Chapter 15 Statistics and Probability

Chapter 16 Geometry

Chapter 17 More Algebra

This handbook is in the student's text only. It includes answers for the *odd-numbered* items in the "A" and "B" exercises and in the Chapter Reviews, as well as for *all* items in each Quick Quiz and Chapter Test. A model solution is also given for each major exercise type in the text.

Getting Ready for Chapter 1

Assignment Guide GR 1
Written: Min. 1–30
Reg. 1–30

Compute.

1. $\begin{array}{r} 12 \\ +73 \end{array}$ 85

2. $\begin{array}{r} 83 \\ +19 \end{array}$ 102

3. $\begin{array}{r} 95 \\ +8 \end{array}$ 103

4. $\begin{array}{r} 45 \\ +68 \end{array}$ 113

5. $63 + 9$ 72

6. $21 + 46$ 67

7. $7 + 27 + 13$ 47

8. $700 + 6 + 40$ 746

9. $\begin{array}{r} 87 \\ -35 \end{array}$ 52

10. $\begin{array}{r} 24 \\ -3 \end{array}$ 21

11. $\begin{array}{r} 56 \\ -37 \end{array}$ 19

12. $\begin{array}{r} 846 \\ -578 \end{array}$ 268

13. $40 - 27$ 13

14. $20 - 13$ 7

15. $100 - 43$ 57

16. $60 - 19$ 41

17. $\begin{array}{r} 32 \\ \times 3 \end{array}$ 96

18. $\begin{array}{r} 71 \\ \times 4 \end{array}$ 284

19. $\begin{array}{r} 52 \\ \times 21 \end{array}$ 1092

20. $\begin{array}{r} 38 \\ \times 65 \end{array}$ 2470

21. 90×3 270

22. 57×10 570

23. 30×100 3000

24. $3 \times 15 \times 7$ 315

25. $128 \div 4$ 32

26. $96 \div 3$ 32

27. $408 \div 24$ 17

28. $2500 \div 100$ 25

List the numbers in order from smallest to largest.

29. 19, 7, 9   7, 9, 19

30. $5 + 12, 9 \times 3, 18 - 4$ $18 - 4, 5 + 12, 9 \times 3$

Note: The "Getting Ready" page in each chapter reviews material that will be used or extended in the chapter.

Brent Jones

SYMBOLS AND SENTENCES

A good worker learns what each tool is used for, when to use it, and how to use it.

A good problem-solver also needs a set of tools. In this chapter you will learn about such mathematical tools as units of measure, operations, variables, and equations. You will see some things these tools are used for. You will also begin to learn when and how to use them.

Metric Units of Measure

One way to describe something is by stating some of its measurements, such as its height, weight, or temperature. There are several systems of measurement. The one used in most of the world today is the **metric system.** We will use this system often in this book.

The person in the picture at the left is using a *meterstick* (a stick one meter long) to make a measurement. A doorway is usually about two meters high. An outside doorway is a little less than one meter wide.

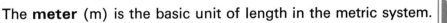

The **meter** (m) is the basic unit of length in the metric system.

Other metric units of length are named by using a prefix with the word *meter*. The meanings of some metric prefixes are shown in the chart. The prefixes used most often are in color.

prefix	symbol	meaning	In this unit	there are this many smaller units.
kilo-	k	thousand	1 kilometer (km)	1000 meters
hecto-	h	hundred	1 hectometer (hm)	100 meters
deka-	da	ten	1 dekameter (dam)	10 meters
deci-	d	tenth	1 meter	10 decimeters (dm)
centi-	c	hundredth	1 meter	100 centimeters (cm)
milli-	m	thousandth	1 meter	1000 millimeters (mm)

The **gram** (g) is a unit of mass (often called *weight*) in the metric system.

In 1 gram there are 1000 milligrams (mg).

In 1 kilogram (kg) there are 1000 grams.

Ed Hoppe Photography

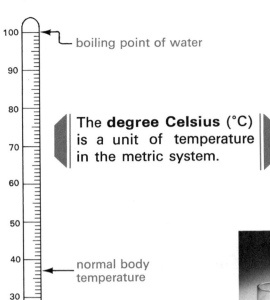

boiling point of water

normal body temperature

recommended room temperature

freezing point of water

The **degree Celsius** (°C) is a unit of temperature in the metric system.

The amount a container will hold is its *capacity.*

The **liter** (L) is a unit of capacity in the metric system.

In 1 liter there are 1000 milliliters (mL).
In 1 kiloliter (kL) there are 1000 liters.

Ed Hoppe Photography

■ Exercises

Assignment Guide 1.1
Oral: 1–10
Written: Min. 11–19
       Reg. 11–19
       Max. 11–21

A **1.** *Kilo-* means (*ten, hundred, thousand*).

2. *Centi-* means (*hundred, hundredth, tenth*).

3. Which is shorter, a centimeter or a millimeter?

4. Which is longer, a kilometer or a meter?

5. Which is heavier, a kilogram or a milligram?

6. Which is more, a liter or a milliliter?

7. What is normal body temperature in degrees Celsius? 37°

8. What does each symbol stand for? **a.** m **b.** km **c.** mm **d.** cm
      a. Meter; **b.** Kilometer; **c.** Millimeter; **d.** Centimeter

9. What does each symbol stand for? **a.** g **b.** mg **c.** kg **d.** L
      a. Gram; **b.** Milligram; **c.** Kilogram; **d.** Liter

10. On the Celsius scale, 0° and 100° are the freezing and boiling points of _____. Water

4

B **11.** Which are more than 1 meter?

    a. a car length   **b.** the length of your foot

    c. the length of this book   **d.** your height

12. Which weigh less than 1 gram?

    a. a feather   **b.** a car

    c. a lettuce seed   **d.** you

13. Which hold more than 1 liter?

    a. an eye dropper   **b.** a cup

    c. a car's gas tank   **d.** a swimming pool

14. Which hold more than 1 kiloliter?

    a. a milk pitcher   **b.** an oil tanker

    c. a car's gas tank   **d.** Lake Erie

15. Which would weigh about 1 gram?

    a. a dog   **b.** a paper clip   **c.** a nickel

16. The temperature of ice is about (*0 °C*, *32 °C*, *20 °C*).

17. The temperature of a person with a fever might be (*37 °C*, *98 °C*, *41 °C*).

18. Most people would wear a sweater or a coat if the air temperature was (*50 °C*, *30 °C*, *10 °C*).

19. How many meters to the next exit?
                                       1000

C **20.** There are 1 000 000 grams in a metric ton. How many kilograms are there in a metric ton? 1000

21. One centimeter contains how many millimeters? 10

NEXT EXIT
1 KILOMETER

1.2　**Order of Operations**

In mathematics, we write a *phrase* (also called an *expression*) by using numbers and operation symbols like $+$, $-$, $\times$, and $\div$. For example, here are some phrases:

$$3 + 1 \qquad 2 \times 5 \qquad 8 - 4 + 1 \qquad 4 + 5 \times 3$$

For a phrase indicating more than one operation, like $4 + 5 \times 3$, you must decide which operation to do first.

If you add first,

$$4 + 5 \times 3$$
$$9 \quad \times 3$$
$$27$$

If you multiply first,

$$4 + 5 \times 3$$
$$4 + \quad 15$$
$$19$$

To make sure that a phrase has only one value, we use the following rule for the order of operations:

> As indicated from left to right,
> 1. First multiply and divide.
> 2. Then add and subtract.

Example 1:　What is the value of each phrase?

a. $4 + 5 \times 3$

$4 + \quad 15$　　Multiply first.

19　　Then add.

b. $18 \div 3 - 2$

$6 \quad - 2$　Divide first.

4　　Then subtract.

c. $8 - 4 + 1$

$4 \quad + 1$　Add and subtract
　　　　　from left to right.
5

d. $5 \times 4 \div 2$

$20 \quad \div 2$　Multiply and divide
　　　　　from left to right.
10

JOHNS

" GOSH! I HOPE THOSE SLIDES WEREN'T
IN ANY PARTICULAR ORDER "

If you want to write a phrase that does not follow the rule for order of operations, you can use parentheses. For example,

$4 + 5 \times 3$ **BUT** $(4 + 5) \times 3$

means to multiply first   means to add first

> Do the operations within the ( ) first. Then use the rule for the order of operations.

Example 2: What is the value of each phrase?

a. $(4 + 5) \times 3$

$9 \quad \times 3$

27

b. $18 \div (3 - 2)$

$18 \div \quad 1$

18

c. $15 \div (3 + 2) - 1$

$15 \div \quad 5 \quad - 1$

$3 \qquad - 1$

2

d. $(9 + 7) \div 4 + (2 \times 3)$

$16 \quad \div 4 + \quad 6$

$4 \quad + \quad 6$

10

■ Exercises

Assignment Guide 1.2
Oral: 1–12
Written: Min. 13–29 odd
     Reg. 13–30
     Max. 13–41 odd

A Which operation should you do first?

1. $7 + 5 - 2$

2. $7 + (5 - 2)$

3. $10 - 3 + 6$

4. $10 - (3 + 6)$

5. $4 \times 6 \div 3$

6. $4 \times (6 \div 3)$

7. $5 \times 2 + 3$

8. $(5 \times 2) + 3$

9. $12 \div 2 + 4$

10. $12 \div (2 + 4)$

11. $14 \div (2 + 5) - 1$

12. $(14 \div 2) + 5 - 1$

B Find each value.

13. $18 - 7 + 5$ 16

14. $23 + 4 - 2$ 25

15. $5 \times 4 + 7$ 27

16. $3 + 6 \times 4$ 27

17. $6 \times 3 \div 2$ 9

18. $12 \div 2 \times 3$ 18

19. $28 \div 4 + 3$ 10

20. $20 + 16 \div 2$ 28

21. $7 \times (6 + 5)$ 77

22. $12 - (2 + 9)$ 1

23. $(10 + 8) \div 6$ 3

24. $42 \div (3 + 4)$ 6

25. $(32 - 12) \div 5$ 4

26. $(5 + 7) \times 3$ 36

27. $(9 \times 4) \div (11 - 5)$ 6

28. $(17 - 9) \times (2 + 7)$ 72

29. $32 \div (6 + 2) \times 5$ 20

30. $14 \times (8 - 5) - 26$ 16

C Find each value. Do the operations in ( ) first. Then do the operations in [ ].

31. $6 + [4 \times (5 - 2)]$ 18

32. $[(14 + 6) \div 4] - 2$ 3

33. $[(21 - 5) + 4] \div 5$ 4

34. $47 - [3 \times (21 \div 7)]$ 38

35. $9 \times [6 + (5 - 4)]$ 63

36. $[(9 + 6) \times 3] + 13$ 58

Insert ( ), or ( ) and [ ], so each phrase has the given value.

	Phrase	*Value*		*Phrase*	*Value*
37.	$48 \div (4 \times 3)$	4	**38.**	$(16 + 11) \div 3$	9
39.	$4 - [3 - (2 - 1)]$	2	**40.**	$(10 + 6) \times 3 + 12$	60
41.	$(4 - 3) - (2 - 1)$	0	**42.**	$(10 + 6) \times (3 + 12)$	240

Variables

Let h represent the number of hours it takes to tune up your car. Then you can write the following phrase for the cost of the tune-up.

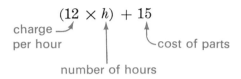

$$(12 \times h) + 15$$

charge per hour →   number of hours ↑   cost of parts

Tune-Up

$12 per hour labor

plus $15 for parts

JIM'S AUTO SERVICE

M. Wannemacher/Taurus Photos

"Twelve times h" can be written in the following ways.

$$12 \times h \qquad 12(h) \qquad 12h$$

For example, the phrase for the cost of the tune-up can be changed to

$$12h + 15.$$

The letter h may be replaced with different numbers. It is an example of a *variable*.

A **variable** is any symbol, like h, x, A, or $\square$, that may be replaced with numbers.

Example 1 :   Suppose it takes 2 hours for the tune-up of your car. To find the cost, replace h with 2 and find the value.

$12h + 15$	
$12\,(2) + 15$	Replace h with 2.
$24 + 15$	Multiply.
39	Add.

NOTE: $12h$ means "12 times h," but 122 does not mean "12 times 2." So we write $12(2)$ or 12×2.

The cost of the tune-up is $39.

Example 2: Find the value of $7 + (x \div 3)$ if x is replaced with 36.

$$7 + (36 \div 3) \qquad \text{Replace } x \text{ with 36.}$$
$$7 + 12 \qquad \text{Divide.}$$
$$19 \qquad \text{Add.}$$

Example 3: Find the value of $16 + n - 5$ if n is replaced with 9.

$$16 + 9 - 5 \qquad \text{Replace } n \text{ with 9.}$$
$$25 - 5 \qquad \text{Add.}$$
$$20 \qquad \text{Subtract.}$$

■ **Exercises**

Assignment Guide 1.3
Oral: 1–9
Written:
Min. 11–31 odd; Quiz, p. 11
Reg. 11–39 odd; Quiz, p. 11
Max. 11–45 odd; Quiz, p. 11

A What is the variable in each phrase?

1. $17 - x$ x **2.** $\square + 31$ $\square$ **3.** $5n + 2$ n

4. $29 - 3r$ r **5.** $3(t + 4)$ t **6.** $13b \div 4$ b

7. $43c$ c **8.** $3d + 7$ d **9.** $6y - 1$ y

B Replace the variable with 4. Find the value of each phrase.

10. $12x$ 48   **11.** $9n + 17$ 53   **12.** $21(\triangle - 1)$ 63

13. $8a - 15$ 17   **14.** $35 \div (3 + y)$ 5   **15.** $16 + 5x$ 36

16. $11x - 20$ 24   **17.** $n \times n$ 16   **18.** $3a + 2a$ 20

Replace the variable with 7. Find the value of each phrase.

19. $31 - x + 5$ 29   **20.** $6y \div 3$ 14   **21.** $4(n + 13)$ 80

22. $82 - 5y$ 47   **23.** $9 \div (x - 4)$ 3   **24.** $17 - 2x + 6$ 9

25. $8x - 3x$ 35   **26.** $y \times y$ 49   **27.** $5a + 4a$ 63

Find all the values of each phrase for the given values of x.

28. $7 + 3x$ values of x: 3, 4, 20, 112   16, 19, 67, 343

29. $9x - 13$ values of x: 6, 2, 10, 27   41, 5, 77, 230

30. $(x + 6) \div 3$ values of x: 9, 3, 30, 93   5, 3, 12, 33

31. $75 \div (x - 2)$ values of x: 7, 5, 17, 27   15, 25, 5, 3

32. $51 + 4x$ values of x: 8, 12, 148, 222   83, 99, 643, 939

Replace the variable in the phrase $\square \times 10$ with the given number of centimeters to find the length in millimeters.

33. 10 cm   **34.** 150 cm   **35.** 230 cm   **36.** 20 cm
100 mm   1500 mm   2300 mm   200 mm

Replace the variable in the phrase $g \div 1000$ with the given number of grams to find the weight in kilograms.

37. 3000 g 3 kg   **38.** 1000 g 1 kg   **39.** 92 000 g 92 kg   **40.** 10 000 g
                                                                                  10 kg

◀ *Note:* Metric measurements with 5 or more digits are usually written with space instead of commas.

C Replace x with 2 and y with 5. Find the value of the phrase.

Example: $3x + y$

$3(2) + 5$ Replace x with 2 and y with 5.

$6 + 5$ Multiply.

11 Add.

41. $x + 7y$ 37   **42.** $4x + y$ 13   **43.** $6x + 3y$ 27

44. $x(y + 8)$ 26   **45.** $7(y - x)$ 21   **46.** $8y - 6x$ 28

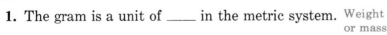

Quick Quiz
Sections 1.1 to 1.3

1. The gram is a unit of _____ in the metric system. Weight or mass

2. The liter is a unit of _____ in the metric system. Capacity *

3. The meter is the basic unit of _____ in the metric system.
Length

* "Volume" is also correct, but this concept has not yet been covered.

Find each value.

4. $7 + 2 \times 3$ 13   **5.** $9 + 6 \div 3$ 11

6. $(8 - 4) \div 2$ 2   **7.** $(3 + 7) \div (5 - 3)$ 5

Find the value if the variable is replaced with 3.

8. $3h + 8$ 17   **9.** $5(n + 2)$ 25

Translating Into Symbols

Which symbols on the sign tell you which way to turn to find gasoline? To find a campsite?

Miller Services Limited

Often you must translate words into symbols in order to solve a problem.

Example 1 : Translate into symbols.

a. six divided by eleven

$$\frac{6}{11} \text{ or } 6 \div 11 \text{ or } 11\overline{)6}$$

b. eight more than nine

$$9 + 8$$

Suggested Class Time

Course	Min.	Reg.	Max.
Days	1	1	1

Here are some possible translations.

WORDS:

add	subtract	multiply	divide
plus	minus	times	divided by
increased by	decreased by	multiplied by	divided into
added to	subtracted from	twice	quotient
sum of	difference	product of	
more than	less than		

SYMBOLS: $+$ $-$ $\times$ other symbols $\div$
                                              or

A number, some number, and *the number of* can be translated as *n, x,* or any other variable.

You need to be careful that the order of terms is correct.

four *subtracted from* a number *n*   from four *subtract* a number *n*

$$n - 4$$ $$4 - n$$

Example 2: Translate into symbols.

    a. three times a number r ⟶ $3r$

    b. five less than some number n ⟶ $n - 5$

    c. the product of two numbers ⟶ xy

    d. ten minus twice a number ⟶ $10 - 2n$

Assignment Guide 1.4
Oral: 1–12
Written: Min. 13–29 odd
        Reg. 13–30
        Max. 13–32

■ Exercises

A Tell what operation is involved in each phrase.

1. $9 + 1$ Add.   **2.** $7 - 3$ Subt.   **3.** 12×3 Mult.   **4.** $8(4)$ Mult.

5. $9 \div 1$ Div.   **6.** $2\overline{)4}$ Div.   **7.** $\frac{8}{4}$ Div.   **8.** $3x$ Mult.

9. $n - 8$ Subt.   **10.** $8 - n$ Subt.   **11.** $7(3)$ Mult.   **12.** ab Mult.

B Translate into symbols.

13. fifty-two minus twenty
    $52 - 20$

14. the sum of four and three $4 + 3$

15. twelve divided by three
    $12 \div 3$ or $3\overline{)12}$ or $\frac{12}{3}$

16. eight multiplied by seven $8(7)$ or 8×7

17. nine more than a number x
    $x + 9$

18. thirty times a number a $30a$ or $30(a)$ or $30 \times a$

19. twice a number B
    $2B$ or $2(B)$ or $2 \times B$

20. four less than a number s $s - 4$

21. six subtracted from some
    number r $r - 6$

22. the product of five and a
    number N $5N$ or $5(N)$ or $5 \times N$

23. a number n increased by two
    $n + 2$

24. seventeen decreased by three $17 - 3$

25. three added to eighty
    $80 + 3$

26. from eight subtract a number x $8 - x$

27. from three times a number c
    subtract four $3c - 4$

28. nine subtracted from the prod-
    uct of five and a number d $5d - 9$

29. the sum of eight and twice
    some number b $8 + 2b$

30. the product of two numbers
    a and b, plus seven $ab + 7$

C **31.** six divided by the sum of
    some number s and nine
            $6 \div (s + 9)$ or $\frac{6}{s + 9}$

32. four times the difference when
    one is subtracted from n $4(n - 1)$

1.5 Sentences

Sentences about numbers are often written entirely in symbols.

Example 1: Use symbols to show that $3 + 1$ and 4 name the same number.

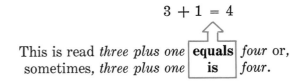

$$3 + 1 = 4$$

This is read *three plus one* **equals** *four* or, sometimes, *three plus one* **is** *four*.

$=$ is used to show that two phrases have the same value.	A sentence using $=$ is called an **equation.**

$<$ and $>$ are used to show that two phrases do not have the same value.	A sentence using $<$ or $>$ is called an **inequality.**

Example 2: Read each sentence.

    a. $2 < 5$ **b.** $3 + x > 3$

Two **is less than** five.   Three plus x **is greater than** three.

Notice that both $<$ and $>$ always point to the name of the smaller number. So any sentence using $<$ or $>$ can be rewritten using the other symbol.

Example 3: Write a sentence using $<$ to show which number is smaller. Then rewrite the sentence using $>$.

    a. $3, 4$ **b.** $8 + 3, 8$

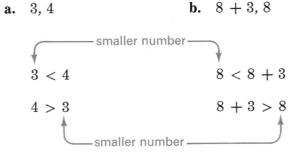

smaller number

$$3 < 4 \qquad\qquad 8 < 8 + 3$$

$$4 > 3 \qquad\qquad 8 + 3 > 8$$

smaller number

■ Exercises

1–9. Variations in reading are possible. For example, = may be read "equals," "is equal to," or "is."

A Tell how to read each sentence.

1. $13 = 12 + 1$ **2.** $24 < 30$ **3.** $15 > 7$

4. $9 = 9$ **5.** $2 \times 7 > 13$ **6.** $x + 2 < 10$

7. $6 \div 3 = 2$ **8.** $5 < 3(2)$ **9.** $4x > 8$

Assignment Guide 1.5
Oral: 1–9
Written:
Min. 11–35 odd
Reg. 11–25 odd; 26–35
Max. 11–25 odd; 26–37

B Write a sentence using $<$ to show which number is smaller. Then rewrite the sentence using $>$.

10. 10, 14 $10 < 14$ $14 > 10$ **11.** 9, 2 $2 < 9$ $9 > 2$ **12.** $4 + 3$, 17 $4 + 3 < 17$ $17 > 4 + 3$

13–25. Answers at right.

13. 91, $82 + 5$ **14.** $7(5)$, 32 **15.** $12 \div 4$, 4

16. $9 + 16$, 22 **17.** $13 - 4$, 10 **18.** 37, $40 - 13$

19. 92, $12(8)$ **20.** 17, $54 \div 3$ **21.** $3(8)$, $5(5)$

22. $17 + 12$, $13 + 15$ **23.** $72 + 10$, $97 - 12$

24. $7(15)$, $24 + 83$ **25.** $75 \div 15$, $22 - 19$

Replace the ? with $=$, $<$, or $>$ to show that the measures are equal or that one is smaller than the other.

26. 1 cm ? 1 m $\overset{<}{}$ **27.** 1 m ? 100 cm $\overset{=}{}$ **28.** 1000 g ? 1 kg $\overset{=}{}$

29. 1 g ? 1 mg $\overset{>}{}$ **30.** 1 mL ? 1 L $\overset{<}{}$ **31.** 1 km ? 1000 m $\overset{=}{}$

Translate into symbols.

32. A number increased by four equals twenty. $n + 4 = 20$

33. Twelve subtracted from twice a number is less than thirty. $2x - 12 < 30$

34. Twenty-five more than a number is one hundred fifty. $a + 25 = 150$

35. A number divided by two is more than forty. $\frac{n}{2} > 40$

C **36.** Ten times the number of centimeters is the number of millimeters. $10c = m$

37. The number of kilograms is the number of grams divided by one thousand. $k = \frac{g}{1000}$

---

13. $82 + 5 < 91$
   $91 > 82 + 5$
14. $32 < 7(5)$
   $7(5) > 32$
15. $12 \div 4 < 4$
   $4 > 12 \div 4$
16. $22 < 9 + 16$
   $9 + 16 > 22$
17. $13 - 4 < 10$
   $10 > 13 - 4$
18. $40 - 13 < 37$
   $37 > 40 - 13$
19. $92 < 12(8)$
   $12(8) > 92$
20. $17 < 54 \div 3$
   $54 \div 3 > 17$
21. $3(8) < 5(5)$
   $5(5) > 3(8)$
22. $13 + 15 < 17 + 12$
   $17 + 12 > 13 + 15$
23. $72 + 10 < 97 - 12$
   $97 - 12 > 72 + 10$
24. $7(15) < 24 + 83$
   $24 + 83 > 7(15)$
25. $22 - 19 < 75 \div 15$
   $75 \div 15 > 22 - 19$

1.6

Open Sentences

Classify each sentence below as *True, False,* or *Can't decide.*

a. Florida is one of the 50 states in the U.S.A.

b. A meter contains 100 millimeters.

c. Little Orphan Annie is a comic-strip character.

d. He won an Olympic gold medal.

e. She was a famous scientist.

f. It is my worst subject.

Why couldn't you decide on sentences **d, e,** and **f?**

If you replace *She* in sentence **e** with *Marie Sklodowska Curie,* most people would mark the sentence *True.* If you replace *She* with *Susan B. Anthony,* most people would mark the sentence *False.*

Classify each sentence below as *True, False,* or *Can't decide.*

g. $3 + 5 = 8$

h. $\square + 6 = 10$

i. $4 + 7 = 9$

j. $1111 \times 9 = 9999$

k. $8 - n > 15$

l. $3a < 9$

Why couldn't you decide on sentences **h, k,** and **l?**

Sentences **h, k,** and **l** are neither true nor false. They are called *open sentences.* If you replace $\square$ with 4 in $\square + 6 = 10$, the sentence is *True.* If you replace $\square$ with 7, the sentence is *False.*

 An **open sentence** contains one or more variables and is neither true nor false.

■ Exercises

Assignment Guide 1.6
Oral: 1–20
Written:
Min. 21–29 odd; Quiz, p. 18
Reg. 21–30; Quiz, p. 18
Max. 21–39 odd; Quiz, p. 18

A Classify each sentence *True, False,* or *Can't decide.*

1. Lake Erie is one of the Great Lakes. T

2. Football is called the national anthem. F

3. It is the smallest state in the U.S.A. Can't dec.

4. Martha Washington invented the light bulb. F

5. A meter contains 100 centimeters. T

6. He is bigger than you. Can't dec.

7. The kilogram is a unit for measuring length. F

8. She is a United States Senator. Can't dec.

9. 20° Celsius is a comfortable room temperature. T

10. Chicago is the largest city in Illinois. T

Classify each sentence *True, False,* or *Open.*

11. $2 \times 2 \times 2 \times 2 \times 2 = 32$ T

12. $8 + \square = 14$ O

13. $7 - n > 3$ O

14. $7 - 5 > 3$ F

15. $7 - 5 < 3$ T

16. $8x = 16$ O

17. $2x + x = 11 + 7$ O

18. $39 = 13 + 13 + 13$ T

19. $81 > 3 \times 20$ T

20. $26 > 2 \times 7$ T

B For each sentence, find a replacement that makes it true. Then find a replacement that makes it false.

21. It is the capital of the U.S.A. Washington, D.C.; *any other city*

22. It is the third letter of the English alphabet. c; *any other letter*

23. He invented the telephone. Alexander Graham Bell; *anyone else*

24. She discovered radium. Marie S. Curie; *anyone else*

17

25. $7 + \square = 19$ *12; any other number*
26. $4 \times \square + 3 = 11$ *2; any other number*
27. $14 > 2n$ *Any number less than 7; any other number*
28. $n \div 5 = 7$ *35; any other number*
29. $3 \times 2 < a$ *Any number greater than 6; any other number*
30. $x - 6 = 13$ *19; any other number*

C Find a number that will make each sentence true.

Example: $3a + a = 32$
— Replace both a's with the same number.

$3(8) + 8 = 32$

$24\ \ + 8 = 32$ Multiply.

$\quad\quad\quad 32 = 32$ Add.

Since $32 = 32$ is true, 8 makes the sentence true.

31. $a + a = 18$ *9*
32. $3x + x < 8$ *Any number less than 2*

33. $x + 2x = 12$ *4*
34. $3a - a > 6$ *Any number greater than 3*

35. $n + 2 = 2 + n$ *Any number*
36. $4x + 2 = 3x + 4$ *2*

Find a pair of numbers that makes each sentence true. Then find a pair of numbers that makes each sentence false.

37–40. *Typical answers.*
Example: $x + y = 10$ $\begin{cases} \text{Let } x = 6 \text{ and } y = 4 \blacktriangleright 6 + 4 = 10 \text{ True} \\ \text{Let } x = 7 \text{ and } y = 1 \blacktriangleright 7 + 1 = 10 \text{ False} \end{cases}$

37. $2x + 3y = 35$ *T: $x = 1$, $y = 11$* *F: $x = 1$, $y = 10$*
38. $y = 2x + 7$ *T: $x = 0$, $y = 7$* *F: $x = 0$, $y = 6$*

39. $x + y = y + x$ *T: Any pair* *F: No pairs*
40. $2x + y > 15$ *T: $x = 0$, $y = 16$* *F: $x = 0$, $y = 15$*

Quick Quiz
Sections 1.4 to 1.6

1. *Translate into symbols:* a number n increased by one *$n + 1$*

Replace the ? with $<$ or $>$ to show which number is smaller.

2. $3 + 12 \overset{>}{\ ?\ } 14$
3. $9(2) \overset{<}{\ ?\ } 24 - 2$
4. $27 \div 3 \overset{<}{\ ?\ } 2(5)$

For each sentence, find a replacement that makes it true.

5. $12 + n = 17$ *5*
6. $15 > 3x$ *Any number less than 5*
7. $16 - r < 13$ *Any number greater than 3*

18

Replacement and Solution Sets

1.7

When the variable in an *open sentence* is replaced by a number, a sentence is formed that is either true or false. In different problems, the replacement numbers may come from different sets.

> The set of numbers that can replace a variable is called the **replacement set**.

Suppose the replacement set for the open sentence $n + 7 = 10$ is $\{1, 2, 3, 4\}$. It may help to think of the open sentence in terms of a "pattern frame" as shown here.

Brent Jones

$1 + 7 = 10$ False

$2 + 7 = 10$ False

$3 + 7 = 10$ True

$4 + 7 = 10$ False

The number three made the sentence true. It was the *only* number that did.

> The set of numbers that makes a sentence true is called the **solution set**.

Each number in the solution set is called a *solution*. To *solve* a sentence means to find its solution(s).

$n + 7 = 10$ $\{1, 2, 3, 4\}$ $\{3\}$ $n = 3$

variable   replacement set   solution set   solution

$$\overbrace{\text{sentence}}^{\displaystyle} \qquad \overbrace{\text{replacement set}}^{\displaystyle}$$

Example 1: Solve $13 = 3x + 4$. Use $\{1, 2, 3, 4\}$.

$13 = 3(1) + 4$ $\qquad\qquad$ $13 = 3(3) + 4$

$13 = 7$ $\qquad$ False $\qquad$ $13 = 13$ $\qquad\qquad$ True

$13 = 3(2) + 4$ $\qquad\qquad$ $13 = 3(4) + 4$

$13 = 10$ $\qquad$ False $\qquad$ $13 = 16$ $\qquad\qquad$ False

The solution set is $\{3\}$; $x = 3$.

Example 2: Solve $2n > 7$. Use $\{0, 1, 2, 3, 4, 5\}$.

$2(0) > 7$ $\qquad\qquad\qquad$ $2(3) > 7$

$0 > 7$ $\quad$ False $\qquad\qquad$ $6 > 7$ $\quad$ False

$2(1) > 7$ $\qquad\qquad\qquad$ $2(4) > 7$

$2 > 7$ $\quad$ False $\qquad\qquad$ $8 > 7$ $\quad$ True

$2(2) > 7$ $\qquad\qquad\qquad$ $2(5) > 7$

$4 > 7$ $\quad$ False $\qquad\qquad$ $10 > 7$ $\quad$ True

The solution set is $\{4, 5\}$.

Example 3: Solve $n + 5 = 12$. Use $\{4, 5, 6\}$.

$4 + 5 = 12$ $\quad$ False $\qquad\qquad$ $6 + 5 = 12$ $\quad$ False

$5 + 5 = 12$ $\quad$ False

There is no solution in the given replacement set.

When no numbers in the given replacement set make a sentence true, as in Example 3 above, the solution set is said to be the **empty set.** $\{\ \}$ and $\varnothing$ are symbols for the empty set.

Example 4: Solve $3(x + 2) = 3x + 6$. Use $\{4, 6, 8, 10\}$.

$$3(4 + 2) = 3(4) + 6$$
$$3(6) = 12 + 6$$
$$18 = 18 \quad \text{True}$$

$$3(6 + 2) = 3(6) + 6$$
$$3(8) = 18 + 6$$
$$24 = 24 \quad \text{True}$$

$$3(8 + 2) = 3(8) + 6$$
$$3(10) = 24 + 6$$
$$30 = 30 \quad \text{True}$$

$$3(10 + 2) = 3(10) + 6$$
$$3(12) = 30 + 6$$
$$36 = 36 \quad \text{True}$$

The replacement set is also the solution set.

Assignment Guide 1.7
Oral: 1–4
Written: Min. 5–23 odd
Reg. 5–29 odd
Max. 5–35 odd

■ Exercises

A For each diagram, state **(a)** the open sentence, **(b)** the replacement set, and **(c)** all sentences that can be formed by replacing the variable.

1.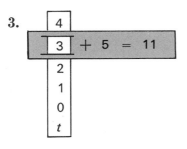

2.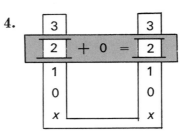

1–4. Answers may be read directly from diagrams at left.

3.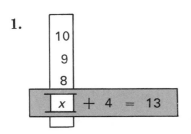

4.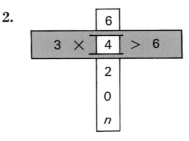

B Use $\{0, 1, 2, 3, 4, 5\}$ as the replacement set. Solve.

5. $n + 8 = 12$ 4

6. $3n = 15$ 5

7. $4x \div 2 = 2x$ 0, 1, 2, 3, 4, 5

8. $8x + 4 = 5$ $\varnothing$

21

9. $n > n + 1$ $\varnothing$

10. $n + 1 > n$ 0, 1, 2, 3, 4, 5

11. $2(x + 1) = 2x + 1$ $\varnothing$

12. $2(x + 1) = 2x + 2$ 0, 1, 2, 3, 4, 5

13. $4x + 3 = 11$ 2

14. $6n - 4 = 20$ 4

Solve. Use the given replacement set.

15. $2n - 2 = 12$ 7   {5, 7, 9, 13}

16. $2n - 3 < 4$ 2, 3   {2, 3, 5, 8, 12}

17. $17 = 2x + 5$ 6   {4, 6, 8, 10}

18. $24 - 3y = 15$ 3   {2, 3, 4, 5, 6}

19. $31 = 7n + 3$ 4   {2, 3, 4, 5}

20. $4x - 8 = 0$ 2   {1, 2, 3, 4}

21. $5(x - 4) = 5x - 20$ 5, 6, 7, 8   {5, 6, 7, 8}

22. $3n + 15 = 3(n + 5)$ 0, 1, 2, 3   {0, 1, 2, 3}

23. $3n > 2n$ 2, 3, 4, 5   {2, 3, 4, 5}

24. $4x = 10$ $\varnothing$ {3, 4, 5, 6}

The replacement set is {50, 51, 52, 53}. Solve.

25. $2x + 7 = 3x - 44$ 51

26. $4x + 4 = 2(2x + 2)$ 50, 51, 52, 53

27. $3n < 156$ 50, 51

28. $5x - 10 = 5(x - 1)$ $\varnothing$

29. $2x - 1 > 103$ 53

30. $n + 19 = 19 + n$ 50, 51, 52, 53

$\boxed{\text{C}}$ Solve. Use the given replacement set.

31. 4 cm = ____ mm   40   {4, 40, 400, 4000}

32. 3000 mL = ____ L   3   {3, 30, 300, 3000}

33. 10 g = ____ mg   10 000   {100, 1000, 10 000, 100 000}

34. 1 km = ____ cm   100 000   {100, 1000, 10 000, 100 000}

35. 10 kg = ____ g   10 000   {10, 100, 1000, 10 000}

Equations on the Balance Beam

1.8

Finding solutions by trying all numbers in a replacement set can take a long time. In fact, it is impossible for replacement sets like the *whole numbers*, {0, 1, 2, 3, $\cdots$}. (The $\cdots$ means "and so on.") Here is another way to solve equations when the replacement set is the whole numbers.

Example 1: Solve $n + 3 = 5$.

Step 1: You can think of the equation on a balance beam.

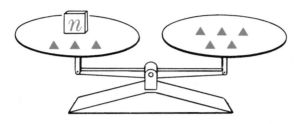

To keep the balance, whatever you do to one side, you must also do to the other side.

Step 2: To get n by itself, take 3 weights off the left side. To keep the balance, also take 3 weights off the right side.

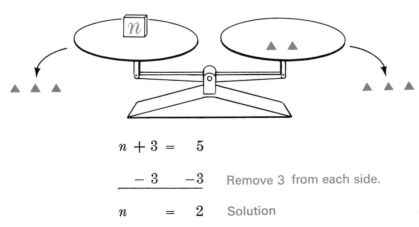

$$n + 3 = 5$$

$$\underline{-3 \quad -3} \quad \text{Remove 3 from each side.}$$

$$n \quad = \quad 2 \quad \text{Solution}$$

Step 3: Always check the solution.

$$\begin{aligned} \text{Check:} \quad n + 3 &= 5 &&\text{Original equation} \\ 2 + 3 &= 5 &&\text{Replace } n \text{ with 2.} \\ 5 &= 5 \ \checkmark &&\text{It checks!} \end{aligned}$$

Example 2 : Solve $12 = n + 7$.

Step 1: Think of the equation on a balance beam.

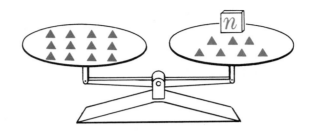

Step 2: Remove 7 weights from each side.

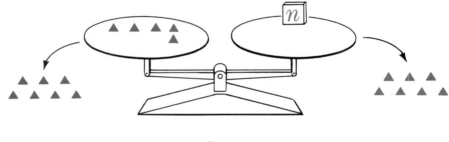

$$12 = n + 7$$

$$\underline{-7 \qquad -7} \qquad \text{Remove 7 from each side.}$$

$$5 = n \qquad \text{Solution (or you can write } n = 5\text{)}$$

Step 3: Check: $12 = n + 7$

Assignment Guide 1.8
Oral: 1–4
Written: Min. 5–21 odd
       Reg. 5–25 odd
       Max. 5–31 odd

$$12 = 5 + 7$$

$$12 = 12 \; \checkmark \; \text{It checks!}$$

◼ Exercises

Ⓐ Solve the equations shown on the balance beams.

1.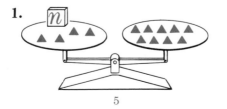

5

2.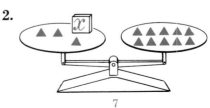

7

3.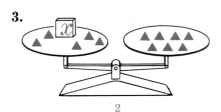

2

4.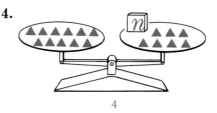

4

B Solve. Be sure to check your solution.

5. $n + 5 = 13$ 8   **6.** $x + 4 = 11$ 7

7. $y + 23 = 39$ 16   **8.** $21 = a + 9$ 12

9. $x + 4 = 14$ 10   **10.** $26 = n + 15$ 11

11. $c + 2 = 7$ 5   **12.** $36 = x + 18$ 18

13. $y + 6 = 19$ 13   **14.** $n + 10 = 43$ 33

15. $33 = x + 11$ 22   **16.** $a + 2 = 9$ 7

17. $56 = n + 21$ 35   **18.** $t + 30 = 72$ 42

19. $308 = x + 105$ 203   **20.** $n + 7 = 10$ 3

21. $y + 46 = 81$ 35   **22.** $a + 55 = 90$ 35

23. $x + 87 = 90$ 3   **24.** $n + 240 = 354$ 114

25. $y + 100 = 579$ 479   **26.** $x + 750 = 1275$ 525

C **27.** $8 + y = 17$ 9   **28.** $64 = 29 + n$ 35

29. $y + (5 + 3) = 39$ 31   **30.** $x + (26 - 12) = 57$ 43

31. $n + 13 = 4(9 + 2)$ 31   **32.** $y + 10 = 16 + (18 \div 3)$ 12

Which Way?

Jon was working on an algebra assignment. Being somewhat absent-minded, he forgot whether he was to add or to multiply the three numbers recorded on his paper. So he decided to do it both ways. Much to his surprise, the answers were the same.

The numbers were three different whole numbers. What were they?

1, 2, 3

1.9 Formulas

A **formula** is a rule or principle written as a mathematical sentence.

The number of meters is the number of centimeters divided by 100.

$$\overset{\text{meters}}{\swarrow} \qquad \overset{\text{centimeters}}{\searrow}$$
$$m = c \div 100$$

Example 1: How many meters equal 300 centimeters?

Step 1:	$m = c \div 100$	**Write the formula.**
Step 2:	$m = 300 \div 100$	**Substitute the given value.**
Step 3:	$m = 3$	**Divide.**
Step 4:	3 meters	**Answer the question. Include the unit of measure if it is needed.**

Suggested Class Time

Course	Min.	Reg.	Max.
Days	1	1	1

The distance traveled is the rate of speed multiplied by the time of travel.

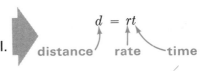

$$d = rt$$
distance   rate   time

Example 2: How far will an object travel in 4 hours at 33 kilometers per hour (also written 33 km/h)?

Step 1:	$d = rt$	**Write the formula.**
Step 2:	$d = 33 \times 4$	**Substitute the given values.**
Step 3:	$d = 132$	**Multiply.**
Step 4:	132 kilometers	**Answer the question.**

Assignment Guide 1.9
Oral: 1–4
Written: Min. 5–19 odd
　　　　 Reg. 5–23 odd
　　　　 Max. 5–17 odd;
　　　　　　 19–26

■ Exercises

A 1. A formula is a rule or principle written as a ——. Mathematical sentence

2. How many variables did we replace to use the formula $m = c \div 100$? One

26

3. What operation does *rt* indicate? Multiplication

4. How many variables did we replace to use the formula $d = rt$? Two

B Find the number of meters equal to the given number of centimeters.

5. 1200 12 m   **6.** 7800 78 m   **7.** 10 000 100 m   **8.** 13 500 135 m

9. 100 000   **10.** 28 700   **11.** 1 320 200   **12.** 3 400 000
       1000 m   287 m   13 202 m   34 000 m

Find the distance for the given rate and time. The following are standard abbreviations: min for *minute(s)*, h for *hour(s)*, wk for *week(s)*.

13. 30 km/h; 6 h 180 km   **14.** 360 cm/h; 3 h 1080 cm

15. 23 m/min; 10 min 230 m   **16.** 3 cm/min; 28 min 84 cm

17. 90 m/wk; 52 wk 4680 m   **18.** 3 km/wk; 8 wk 24 km

Formulas for the perimeters of some geometric figures are shown.

triangle	rectangle	square	regular pentagon

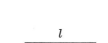
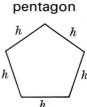

$p = a + b + c$ $p = 2(l + w)$ $p = 4s$ $p = 5h$

Find the perimeter; use one of the formulas above.

19. square; $s = 132$ 528   **20.** rectangle; $l = 20$, $w = 13$ 66

21. rectangle; $l = 23$, $w = 10$ **22.** triangle; $a = 3$, $b = 7$, $c = 5$ 15
              66

23. regular pentagon; $h = 15$ **24.** triangle; $a = 30$, $b = 30$, $c = 30$ 90
             75

C Use a formula from this section to solve each problem.

25. What is the perimeter of a swimming pool 50 m long and 20 m wide? 140 m

26. A truck driver stops to rest every three hours. If the driver averages 80 km/h between stops, how far is it between stops? 240 km

Terms and Symbols Review

Match each term or symbol with the best description.

Suggested Class Time

Course	Min.	Reg.	Max.
Days	1	1	1

1. meter i

2. gram n

3. liter c

4. degree Celsius p

5. kilo- m

6. centi- e

7. cm d

Assignment Guide Rev.
Oral: Terms & Symbols 1–16
Written: 1–29 odd; 30

8. mg j

9. variable f

10. = g

11. < o

12. > l

13. solve a

14. solution set b

15. replacement set h

16. formula k

a. find the solution set

b. all numbers that make a sentence true

c. metric unit of capacity

d. symbol for centimeter(s)

e. prefix meaning "hundredth"

f. n in $5n + 4$

g. shows that phrases have the same value

h. all numbers that can replace the variable

i. metric unit of length

j. symbol for milligram(s)

k. rule written as a mathematical sentence

l. means "is greater than"

m. prefix meaning "thousand"

n. metric unit of weight

o. means "is less than"

p. metric unit of temperature

Chapter 1 Review

1.1 Which is less?

1. your height or <u>1 meter</u>

2. your weight or <u>1 kilogram</u>

3. a bathtubful or <u>1 liter</u>

4. <u>normal body temperature</u> or 50 °C

5. <u>the distance you could throw a ball</u> or 1 kilometer

Find each value.   1.2

6. $7 + 2 \times 4$ 15   **7.** $(5 \times 6) \div (17 - 7)$ 3

8. $21 \div (5 + 2)$ 3   **9.** $24 \div (2 + 6) - 3$ 0

Replace the variable with 5. Find the value of each phrase.   1.3

10. $7y - 20$ 15   **11.** $(n + 7) \times 4$ 48

12. $18 + 2x$ 28   **13.** $65 \div (a + 8)$ 5

Translate into symbols.

14. one more than twice three   **15.** four less than a number n 1.4
$2(3) + 1$ $n - 4$

16. Five increased by nine is the product of two and a number x.   1.5
$5 + 9 = 2x$

17. Eight divided by three is less than the sum of one and a number a.
$8 \div 3 < 1 + a$

18. Five times seven is greater than fifty minus a number b. $5(7) > 50 - b$

Classify each sentence *True, False,* or *Open.*   1.6

19. $12 = 12$ T   **20.** $9 + n = 17$ O

21. $x - 7 = 8$ O   **22.** $87 \div 3 = 26$ F

23. $6 + 7 = 10$ F   **24.** $3 \times 13 < 40$ T

Solve. Use the given replacement set.   1.7

25. $3x - 4 = 5$ 3 $\{1, 2, 3, 4\}$

26. $6y - 5 < 10$ 0, 1, 2 $\{0, 1, 2, 3\}$

27. $4x + 3 > 23$ 6, 7, 8 $\{5, 6, 7, 8\}$

Solve.   1.8

28. $y + 8 = 13$ 5   **29.** $x + 19 = 42$ 23

30. Use the formula $d = rt$ to find the distance run by a long-distance   1.9
runner who runs 13 kilometers per hour for 3 hours.   39 km

Chapter 1 Test

Find each value.

Assignment Guide Test
Written: 1–22

1. $21 - 6 \div 3$ 19

2. $(17 - 8) \div (2 + 1)$ 3

3. $(4 + 5) \times 9$ 81

4. $32 - (6 \times 3) + 7$ 21

Replace the variable with 3. Find the value of each phrase.

5. $14 - 4x$ 2

6. $(a + 6) \times 11$ 99

7. $7y + 8$ 29

8. $72 \div (15 - n)$ 6

Classify each sentence *True*, *False*, or *Open*.

9. $7 + 2 = 9$ T

10. $(x - 4) \times 8 < 22$ O

11. $(3 \times 4) + 5 = 17$ T

12. $64 \div 8 > 8$ F

Solve. Use $\{3, 4, 5, 6, 7, 8, 9\}$ as the replacement set.

13. $x + 7 = 13$ 6

14. $7 > n + 2$ 3, 4

15. $y - 5 > 1$ 7, 8, 9

Solve.

16. $n + 8 = 12$ 4

17. $5 = n + 2$ 3

18. *Translate into symbols:* The product of four and some number x is less than nine decreased by three. $4x < 9 - 3$

What does each stand for?

19. a. mg   Milligram(s)   **b.** km   Kilometer(s)   **c.** L   Liter(s)

20. a. centi-   Hundredths   **b.** milli-   Thousandths   **c.** kilo-   Thousand

Find the distance for the given rate and time.

21. $r = 22$ km/h, $t = 9$ h   198 km

22. $r = 13$ cm/min, $t = 27$ min   351 cm

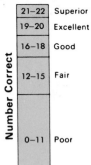

RATE YOURSELF

Number Correct		
21–22	Superior
19–20	Excellent
16–18	Good
12–15	Fair
0–11	Poor

SYMBOLS AT WORK

A symbol is usually easier to see and understand than the words for the same idea. And a symbol can have the same meaning to people who read and speak different languages. The skull and crossbones, for example, means **POISON** the world over. And symbols like $+$, $-$, $\times$, and $\div$ mean the same thing to mathematicians everywhere.

Special symbols are used in many kinds of work. For example, shippers and freight handlers use the symbols below. Can you figure out what they mean?

Handle with care.   Keep dry.   Protect from heat.   Do not stack.

Truck drivers in all countries must understand the symbols shown below. (If you drive a car, you should also know them.) What do they mean?

No trucks.   Filling station   No left turn   Road narrows.

Carpenters, plumbers, and electricians need to be able to read the symbols used on blueprints. Some of these symbols are shown below.

door   window   tub   shower   electrical outlet   fuse

Activity 1

Make a balance beam. You might use two paper cups, a ruler, a round pencil or drinking straw, a paper clamp, and two paper clips as shown. Place the paper-clip hooks at about the 1-inch and 11-inch marks, adjusting the distance to make the beam balance.

Use the balance beam you made to do the following activities:

Activity 2

1. Hang 10 paper clips on each hook.

2. Remove half the paper clips from each hook.

3. Hang 2 more paper clips on each hook.

4. Remove 1 paper clip from each hook.

Did the beam stay balanced at all times?   Yes

Activity 3

1. Hang 4 paper clips on the left hook and hang 7 on the right hook.

2. Remove 2 paper clips from each hook.

3. Double the number of paper clips on each hook.

4. Hang 3 more paper clips on each hook.

Did the beam stay tipped in the same direction at all times?   Yes

Getting Ready for Chapter 2

2

Match each item with the best description.

1. liter   e

a. n is greater than three.

1.1

2. cm   j

b. metric unit of temperature

3. centi-   g

c. three subtracted from some number n

Assignment Guide GR 2
Written: Min. 1–23
      Reg. 1–23

4. degree Celsius   b

d. some number n divided by three

5. $3n$ h

e. metric unit of capacity

1.4

6. $3 + n$ i

f. Three is less than n.

7. $n - 3$ c

g. prefix meaning "hundredth"

8. $\frac{n}{3}$ d

h. three times some number n

9. $3 < n$ f

i. three plus some number n

1.5

10. $n > 3$ a

j. symbol for centimeter(s)

Find each value.

11. $4 \times 2 + 9$ 17   **12.** $(6 + 2) \div 2$ 4   **13.** $6 \div 2 \times 3 - 1$ 8

1.2

14. $n - 8$
   if $n = 19$ 11

15. $5a + 6$
   if $a = 7$ 41

16. $(4n - 3) \div 7$
   if $n = 6$ 3

1.3

Solve. Use the replacement set $\{0, 1, 2, 3, 4\}$.

17. $n + 3 = 7$ 4   **18.** $x - 2 < 1$ 0, 1, 2   **19.** $r + 5 > 6$ 2, 3, 4

1.7

Solve.

20. $5 = x + 3$ 2   **21.** $n + 2 = 8$ 6   **22.** $12 = a + 5$ 7

1.8

23. If a car is driven at 50 kilometers an hour for 3 hours, how far
does it travel? (Use $d = rt$.)   150 km

1.9

SOLVING OPEN SENTENCES

Copyright, 1978, Universal Press Syndicate

Letting out a deep breath undoes taking in that deep breath. Climbing down a ladder undoes climbing up the ladder. And unlocking a door undoes locking the door. But, on the other hand, nothing undoes breaking an egg!

In mathematics, an operation by a number can often be undone by another operation by the same number. In this chapter you will learn how to use this fact to solve equations and inequalities.

Addition, subtraction, multiplication, and division are the four basic operations. Each of them can be undone by another of the four.

Example 1: What operations undo each other?

$$(13 + 5) - 5 = 13$$

L----same----⌐

Subtraction undoes addition.

$$(14 - 2) + 2 = 14$$

L----same----⌐

Addition undoes subtraction.

$$(5 \times 3) \div 3 = 5$$

L---same---⌐

Division undoes multiplication.

$$(12 \div 4) \times 4 = 12$$

L---same---⌐

Multiplication undoes division.

Operations that undo each other are called **inverse operations.**
Addition and subtraction are inverse operations.
Multiplication and division are inverse operations.

Example 2: Use an inverse operation to check each answer.

$$\begin{array}{r} 139 \\ -47 \\ \hline 92 \end{array} \longrightarrow \begin{array}{r} 47 \\ +92 \\ \hline 139 \end{array}$$

Addition is used to
check subtraction.

$$14\overline{)3388} \xrightarrow{} \begin{array}{r} 242 \\ \longrightarrow 242 \\ \times 14 \\ \hline 3388 \end{array}$$

Multiplication is used
to check division.

Example 3: Simplify each phrase.

a. $\underbrace{t + 7 - 7}$
t

Subtracting
7 undoes
adding 7.

b. $\underbrace{n - 8 + 8}$
n

Adding 8
undoes subtract-
ing 8.

c. $\dfrac{3x}{3}$
x

Dividing by 3
undoes multi-
plying by 3.

d. $\dfrac{r}{4} \times 4$
r

Multiplying
by 4 undoes
dividing by 4.

■ Exercises

Assignment Guide 2.1
Oral: 1–10
Written: Min. 1–26
       Reg. 1–30
       Max. 1–36

A What is the inverse of each of the following?

1. adding 1   Subt. 1   **2.** subtracting 1   Add. 1

3. multiplying by 10   Div. by 10   **4.** dividing by 1000   Mult. by 1000

5. subtracting 10   Add. 10   **6.** multiplying by 45   Div. by 45

7. adding 7   Subt. 7   **8.** dividing by 3   Mult. by 3

9. subtracting 16   Add. 16   **10.** multiplying by 16   Div. by 16

B Find each answer. Then use an inverse operation to check.

11. $\begin{array}{r} 78 \\ -26 \end{array}$ 52   **12.** $25\overline{)625}$ 25   **13.** $4\overline{)76}$ 19   **14.** $\begin{array}{r} 65 \\ -32 \end{array}$ 33

15. $15\overline{)930}$ 62   **16.** $\begin{array}{r} 195 \\ -76 \end{array}$ 119   **17.** $\begin{array}{r} 352 \\ -48 \end{array}$ 304   **18.** $12\overline{)312}$ 26

Simplify each phrase.

19. $19 + 5 - 5$ 19   **20.** $27 - 3 + 3$ 27   **21.** $n + 7 - 7$ n

22. $\frac{12 \times 9}{12}$ 9   **23.** $\frac{15}{4} \times 4$ 15   **24.** $\frac{8x}{8}$ x

Which operation by what number would give the variable by itself?

Example: $a - 8$ *Answer:* Adding 8, because $a - 8 + 8 = a$

25. $n + 25$ Subt. 25   **26.** $t - 4$ Add. 4   **27.** $5m$ Div. by 5

28. $\frac{x}{7}$ Mult. by 7   **29.** $23y$ Div. by 23   **30.** $\frac{a}{4}$ Mult. by 4

C Simplify each phrase.

31. $4n - 6 + 6$ $4n$ **32.** $\frac{2t \times 3}{3}$ $2t$ **33.** $\frac{(w - 3)}{5} \times 5$ $w - 3$

34. $\frac{r + 6}{8} \times 8$ $r + 6$ **35.** $(x + 9) - 2 + 2$ $x + 9$ **36.** $\frac{t}{5} + 4 - 4$ $\frac{t}{5}$

Equations With Addition or Subtraction

In Chapter 1, you saw that it helps to think of a balance beam when solving some equations. It can also help to think of inverse operations. Remember that we have to get the variable by itself on one side of the equation.

Example 1: Solve $n + 3 = 5$.

Suggested Class Time

Course	Min.	Reg.	Max.
Days	1	1	1

$$n + 3 = 5$$

> Notice 3 is added to *n*.
> To undo this, subtract 3.

$$n + 3 - 3 = 5 - 3$$

To keep the balance, subtract 3 from each side.

$$n = 2$$

Check: $\quad n + 3 = 5$

$$2 + 3 = 5$$

$$5 = 5 \ \checkmark$$

The check is a required part of solving an equation.

Example 2: Solve $15 = a - 7$.

$$15 = a - 7$$

> Notice 7 is subtracted from *a*.
> To undo this, add 7.

$$15 + 7 = a - 7 + 7$$

Add 7 to each side.

$$22 = a$$

Check: $\quad 15 = a - 7$

$$15 = 22 - 7$$

$$15 = 15 \ \checkmark$$

▪ Exercises

Assignment Guide 2.2
Oral: 1–12
Written: Min. 13–39 odd
Reg. 13–47 odd
Max. 13–53 odd

A To solve each equation, what would you do on each side?

1. $s + 5 = 9$ $\quad -5$ **2.** $x - 10 = 34$ $\quad +10$ **3.** $13 = n + 7$ $\quad -7$

4. $8 = x + 8$ $\quad -8$ **5.** $n - 7 = 16$ $\quad +7$ **6.** $a + 14 = 23$ $\quad -14$

37

7. $n - 8 = 13$ $+8$ **8.** $y + 12 = 13$ -12 **9.** $a - 12 = 50$ $+12$

10. $y - 1 = 11$ $+1$ **11.** $27 = n + 17$ -17 **12.** $8 = x - 23$ $+23$

B Solve each equation. (Remember that checking is required.)

13. $x + 7 = 18$ 11   **14.** $n - 7 = 17$ 24   **15.** $x - 8 = 18$ 26

16. $8 = y + 8$ 0   **17.** $c - 4 = 2$ 6   **18.** $n - 12 = 0$ 12

19. $x + 13 = 27$ 14   **20.** $n - 21 = 11$ 32   **21.** $13 = a - 17$ 30

22. $14 = n + 11$ 3   **23.** $z - 19 = 14$ 33   **24.** $28 = x - 9$ 37

25. $n - 6 = 10$ 16   **26.** $t + 52 = 100$ 48   **27.** $49 = n + 23$ 26

28. $y - 6 = 6$ 12   **29.** $100 = n + 80$ 20   **30.** $x + 9 = 31$ 22

31. $x - 7 = 1$ 8   **32.** $r + 3 = 75$ 72   **33.** $12 = a + 10$ 2

34. $y - 8 = 5$ 13   **35.** $213 = x + 121$ 92   **36.** $x + 14 = 15$ 1

Use one of the given formulas to solve each problem.

Example: Find the "scratch score" for a handicap of 23 and a final score of 138. (See the formula below.)

scratch score   final score

$$s + h = f$$

handicap

$$s + 23 = 138$$
$$s + 23 - 23 = 138 - 23$$
$$s = 115 \leftarrow \text{Check as required.}$$

The scratch score is **115.**

37. Nancy's handicap is 58. Her scratch score was 133. What was her final score? 191

38. Peg's final score was 147. Her handicap is 42. What was her scratch score? 105

39. Joe's final score was 221. His handicap is 39. What was his scratch score? 182

H. Armstrong Roberts

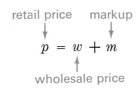

retail price   markup

$$p = w + m$$

wholesale price

sale price   discount

$$s = p - d$$

regular price

40. Find w if $p = 14$ and $m = 7$. 7 **41.** Find p if $s = 128$ and $d = 40$. 168

42. Find w if $p = 35$ and $m = 15$. 20 **43.** Find p if $s = 301$ and $d = 51$. 352

44. If a storekeeper added \$42 to the wholesale price of an item and charged \$78 for it, what was the wholesale price? \$36

45. If an appliance that sells at wholesale for \$90 has an \$87 markup, what is the retail price? \$177

46. What is the regular price of the bikes? \$67

47. What is the regular price of the dresses? \$23

C Solve for x.

Example:

$$x - a = b$$
$$x - a + a = b + a$$
$$x = b + a$$

Check:

$$x - a = b$$
$$b + a - a = b$$
$$b = b \checkmark$$

48. $1 = x + a$
$1 - a = x$

49. $x + 3 = d$
$x = d - 3$

50. $r = x - 2$
$r + 2 = x$

51. $7 = x - p$
$p + 7 = x$

52. $x - n = a$
$x = a + n$

53. $x - r + 5 = 7$
$x = 2 + r$

39

2.3 Equations With Multiplication or Division

Inverse operations can also be used to solve an equation if the variable has been multiplied or divided by a number.

Example 1: Solve $35 = 7x$.

$$35 = 7x$$

> Notice x is multiplied by 7. To undo this, divide by 7.

$$\frac{35}{7} = \frac{7x}{7}$$

Divide each side by 7.

$$5 = x$$

Check: $35 = 7x$

$$35 = 7(5)$$

> Remember that we use ( ) because 7x means 7 times x, but 75 does not mean 7 times 5.

$$35 = 35 \checkmark$$

Example 2: Solve $\frac{n}{4} = 8$.

$$\frac{n}{4} = 8$$

> Notice n is divided by 4. To undo this, multiply by 4.

$$\frac{n}{4} \times 4 = 8 \times 4$$

Multiply each side by 4.

$$n = 32$$

Check: $\frac{n}{4} = 8$

$$\frac{32}{4} = 8$$

$$8 = 8 \checkmark$$

Suggested Class Time

Course	Min.	Reg.	Max.
Days	1	1	1

Assignment Guide 2.3
Oral: 1–12
Written: Min. 13–41 odd
        Reg. 13–47 odd
        Max. 13–45 odd;
           46–49

■ Exercises

A To solve each equation, what would you do on each side?

1. $3n = 12$ ÷3   **2.** $140 = 10n$ ÷10   **3.** $0 = 3n$ ÷3

4. $7n = 49$ $\div 7$　　**5.** $8 = \frac{n}{5}$ $\times 5$　　**6.** $36 = 12n$ $\div 12$

7. $\frac{n}{5} = 1$ $\times 5$　　**8.** $\frac{x}{2} = 13$ $\times 2$　　**9.** $\frac{y}{9} = 2$ $\times 9$

10. $\frac{a}{7} = 12$ $\times 7$　　**11.** $\frac{n}{11} = 6$ $\times 11$　　**12.** $\frac{c}{20} = 5$ $\times 20$

B　Solve each equation. (Remember that checking is required.)

13. $8y = 64$　8　　**14.** $8a = 32$　4　　**15.** $10n = 350$　35

16. $7x = 49$　7　　**17.** $100 = 20y$　5　　**18.** $5c = 75$　15

19. $15x = 60$　4　　**20.** $144 = 12n$　12　　**21.** $6y = 72$　12

22. $50a = 400$　8　　**23.** $105 = 35x$　3　　**24.** $6x = 42$　7

25. $10 = \frac{n}{1}$　10　　**26.** $10 = \frac{n}{5}$　50　　**27.** $11 = \frac{n}{10}$　110

28. $\frac{n}{4} = 15$　60　　**29.** $\frac{n}{15} = 0$　0　　**30.** $\frac{n}{8} = 12$　96

31. $\frac{x}{7} = 30$　210　　**32.** $\frac{y}{2} = 34$　68　　**33.** $\frac{a}{20} = 4$　80

34. $9 = \frac{x}{6}$　54　　**35.** $\frac{n}{3} = 17$　51　　**36.** $\frac{z}{9} = 11$　99

37. $9y = 81$　9　　**38.** $25n = 75$　3　　**39.** $30a = 150$　5

40. $7x = 56$　8　　**41.** $84 = 12y$　7　　**42.** $50z = 250$　5

43. $96 = 6t$　16　　**44.** $11b = 77$　7　　**45.** $15c = 900$　60

Use one of the given formulas to solve each problem.

46. Maria earns $32 a day at the rate of $4 an hour. How many hours does she work a day?　8 hours

47. Joe earns $3 an hour. How many hours must he work to earn $117?　39 hours

C　**48.** What is the earned run average of a pitcher who allowed 52 earned runs in 117 innings?　4

49. A pitcher has an earned run average of 3 for 42 innings. How many earned runs did the pitcher allow?　14 runs

total
wages
hourly
rate
hours
worked

$w = pt$

innings
pitched
earned
runs
allowed

$ie = 9r$

earned
run
average

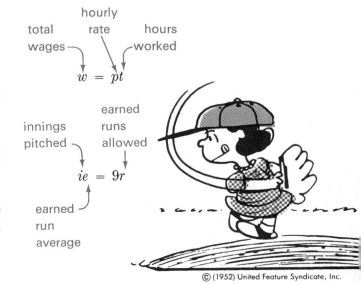

2.4　**Inequalities With One Operation**

Suggested Class Time			
Course	Min.	Reg.	Max.
Days	2	1	1

Like equations, inequalities can be solved by using inverse operations. Get the variable by itself on one side by doing the same operation on each side. (In this section, the replacement set is the whole numbers.) Always check at least one solution.

Example 1:　Solve $3x < 12$.

$$3x < 12$$

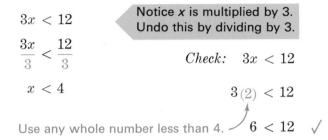
Notice x is multiplied by 3. Undo this by dividing by 3.

$$\frac{3x}{3} < \frac{12}{3}$$

$$x < 4$$

Use any whole number less than 4.

Check:　$3x < 12$

$$3(2) < 12$$

$$6 < 12 \quad \checkmark$$

A graph can help you "see" the solutions of an open sentence.

Example 2:　Graph $3x < 12$.

Step 1:　Solve the open sentence. (We solved this open sentence in Example 1. So $x < 4$; the solutions are 0, 1, 2, and 3.)

Step 2:　Make a number line. Graph the solutions.

Draw dots at 0, 1, 2, and 3.

Example 3:　Solve and graph $4 > n + 3$.

Step 1:　$$4 > n + 3$$

Notice 3 is added to n. Undo this by subtracting 3.

$$4 - 3 > n + 3 - 3$$

$$1 > n$$

The only whole number less than 1 is 0.

Check:　$4 > n + 3$

$$4 > 0 + 3$$

$$4 > 3 \quad \checkmark$$

Step 2:　Draw a dot at 0.

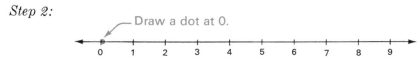

Example 4: Solve and graph $x - 6 > 10$.

Step 1: $x - 6 > 10$

$x - 6 + 6 > 10 + 6$

$x > 16$

> Notice 6 is subtracted from *x*.
> Undo this by adding 6.

Check: $x - 6 > 10$

$18 - 6 > 10$

Use any whole number greater than 16. ⟶

$12 > 10$ ✓

Step 2:

The dots and the ⟶ show that all whole numbers greater than 16 are in the graph.

■ **Exercises**

Assignment Guide 2.4
Oral: 1–14
Written:
Min. (day 1) 15–24
      (day 2) 25–35
Reg. 15–39 odd
Max. 15–39 odd; 40–42

A̲ To solve each inequality, what would you do on each side?

1. $n + 4 < 13$ -4 **2.** $n - 2 > 9$ $+2$ **3.** $n - 8 > 5$ $+8$

4. $3 > \frac{n}{6}$ $\times 6$ **5.** $7n > 35$ $\div 7$ **6.** $\frac{n}{3} < 11$ $\times 3$

Tell how you would graph each set on a number line.

7. $\{4, 5, 6\}$ Dots at 4, 5, 6   **8.** whole numbers greater than 8

Dots at 9, 10, 11, $\cdots$; shade arrow on right

9. $\{3\}$ Dot at 3   **10.** whole numbers less than 6

Dots at 0, 1, 2, 3, 4, 5

11. $\{$ $\}$ No dots   **12.** whole numbers greater than 4

Dots at 5, 6, 7, $\cdots$; shade arrow on right

13. $\{0, 1, 2, 3, 4, 5\}$ **14.** all whole numbers

Dots at 0, 1, 2, 3, 4, 5   Dots at 0, 1, 2, $\cdots$; shade arrow on right

B̲ Solve and graph. (Remember that checking is required.)

15. $n - 8 < 18$

$n < 26$

16. $3 > n - 8$

$11 > n$

17. $7 > n - 3$

$10 > n$

18. $n - 12 < 9$

$n < 21$

19. $n + 5 < 5$

$n < 0$

20. $n - 6 < 0$

$n < 6$

43

21. $\frac{n}{10} < 5$ $n < 50$ **22.** $\frac{n}{2} > 8$ $n > 16$ **23.** $n - 2 > 2$ $n > 4$

24. $\frac{n}{7} > 20$ $n > 140$ **25.** $\frac{n}{4} < 10$ $n < 40$ **26.** $n - 21 < 9$ $n < 30$

27. $\frac{n}{12} < 1$ $n < 12$ **28.** $\frac{n}{5} < 8$ $n < 40$ **29.** $n - 10 < 156$ $n < 166$

30. $\frac{n}{7} > 0$ $n > 0$ **31.** $n + 3 > 4$ $n > 1$ **32.** $5 < \frac{n}{6}$ $30 < n$

33. $13 < n - 12$ **34.** $4n > 12$ $n > 3$ **35.** $19n > 19$ $n > 1$
$25 < n$

36. $n + 8 < 12$ $n < 4$ **37.** $11n < 44$ $n < 4$ **38.** $108 < 6n$ $18 < n$

The temperature to which water can be heated in an open kettle depends on altitude. The formula below is based on the temperature at which water turns to vapor (boils).

39. How hot could you heat water in an open kettle in each city? (Approximate altitude is given.)

    a. Roanoke, Va.; 279 m
    Less than 99 °C
    b. Grand Junction, Colo.; 1395 m
    Less than 95 °C
    c. San Angelo, Tex.; 558 m
    Less than 98 °C

40. How hot could you heat water in an open kettle at 6138 meters on Mount McKinley in Alaska?
Less than 78 °C

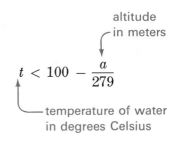

$$t < 100 - \frac{a}{279}$$

altitude in meters — temperature of water in degrees Celsius

|C| The formulas shown here describe what happens to rainfall in a desert.

41. Suppose an afternoon shower in the desert delivers 8 532 000 kilograms of water. According to the formula, about how much of this evaporates? About how much runs off?
More than 8 276 040 kg; less than 255 960 kg

42. About how many kilograms of rain must fall in the desert to allow 9 700 000 kilograms of water to evaporate? Less than 10 000 000 kg

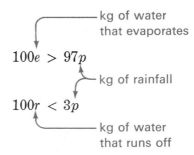

kg of water that evaporates

$$100e > 97p$$

kg of rainfall

$$100r < 3p$$

kg of water that runs off

This section is a review of solving and graphing open sentences. The replacement set is the whole numbers. Remember that checking is required.

Example: Solve and graph.

a. $x + 5 < 9$ **b.** $3x < 12$ **c.** $2 > \dfrac{x}{2}$

$x + 5 - 5 < 9 - 5$ $\dfrac{3x}{3} < \dfrac{12}{3}$ $2 \times 2 > \dfrac{x}{2} \times 2$

$x < 4$ $x < 4$ $4 > x$

Check: Replace each *x* with any whole number less than 4.

$x + 5 < 9$ $3x < 12$ $2 > \dfrac{x}{2}$

$1 + 5 < 9$ $3(3) < 12$ $2 > \dfrac{2}{2}$

$6 < 9$ ✓ $9 < 12$ ✓ $2 > 1$ ✓

For each open sentence, the solutions are 0, 1, 2, and 3. The graph of each open sentence is the same.

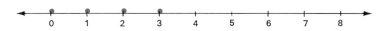

Assignment Guide 2.5
Oral: 1–4
Written:
Min. 5–19 odd; Quiz, p. 46
Reg. 5–27 odd; Quiz, p. 46
Max. 21–41 odd; Quiz, p. 46

■ Exercises

A Match each open sentence with its graph.

1. $n > 5$ b   **2.** $n = 5$ a   **3.** $5 > n$ c   **4.** $5 < n$ b

a.

b.

c.

45

B Solve and graph.

5. $x - 4 = 12$ ₁₆   **6.** $x - 5 > 10$ $x > 15$ **7.** $\frac{x}{2} = 15$ ₃₀

8. $x - 8 = 17$ ₂₅   **9.** $\frac{x}{3} > 5$ $x > 15$ **10.** $63 = 9x$ ₇

11. $\frac{x}{8} = 0$ ₀   **12.** $14 < 7x$ $2 < x$ **13.** $12x = 48$ ₄

14. $x - 11 = 1$ ₁₂   **15.** $9x < 9$ $x < 1$ **16.** $\frac{x}{10} = 7$ ₇₀

17. $\frac{x}{4} < 10$ $x < 40$ **18.** $\frac{x}{4} = 5$ ₂₀   **19.** $2x > 12$ $x > 6$

20. $x + 8 < 12$ $x < 4$ **21.** $7x = 21$ ₃   **22.** $x + 7 < 8$ $x < 1$

23. $\frac{x}{4} < 12$ $x < 48$ **24.** $x + 3 = 8$ ₅   **25.** $x + 7 > 8$ $x > 1$

26. $x - 5 > 1$ $x > 6$ **27.** $15x = 15$ ₁   **28.** $\frac{x}{1} > 10$ $x > 10$

number of millimeters,
milliliters, or milligrams

$$n = \frac{m}{1000}$$

number of meters,
liters, or grams

$$n = 1000k$$

number of kilometers,
kiloliters, or kilograms

C Complete. Use the given formulas.

29. 7 km $=$ ____ m   ₇₀₀₀   **30.** 4000 m $=$ ____ km   ₄

31. 7000 mm $=$ ____ m   ₇   **32.** 147 kg $=$ ____ g   147 000

33. $22\,000$ L $=$ ____ kL   ₂₂   **34.** $24\,000$ m $=$ ____ km   ₂₄

35. $13\,000$ mL $=$ ____ L   ₁₃   **36.** 91 m $=$ ____ mm   91 000

37. 135 g $=$ ____ mg   **38.** $320\,000$ g $=$ ____ kg   320

135 000

39. $17\,000$ km $=$ ____ m   **40.** 3000 kL $=$ ____ L   3 000 000

17 000 000

41. 7 L $=$ ____ mL   ₇₀₀₀   **42.** $20\,000$ mg $=$ ____ g   ₂₀

Quick Quiz
Sections 2.1 to 2.5

1. Subtraction and ____ are inverse operations.   Addition

2. Multiplication and ____ are inverse operations.   Division

Solve and graph.

3. $a - 12 = 15$ ₂₇   **4.** $714 = 7n$ ₁₀₂   **5.** $x + 8 = 10$ ₂

6. $n + 3 < 17$ $n < 14$ **7.** $12x > 24$ $x > 2$ **8.** $a - 6 < 4$

$a < 10$

9. $\frac{x}{5} = 10$ ₅₀   **10.** $8 > \frac{n}{4}$ $32 > n$

Equations With Two Operations

2.6

You have solved equations by doing the same operation on both sides. But to solve some equations, you must do more than one operation on both sides. First, see what operations have been done to the variable. To solve, undo these operations **in the reverse order.**

Example 1: What operations have been done to the variables?

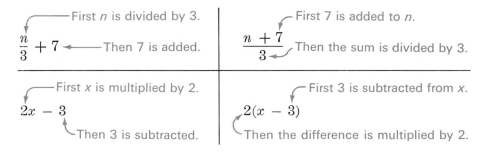

First n is divided by 3.

$\dfrac{n}{3} + 7$ ← Then 7 is added.

First 7 is added to n.

$\dfrac{n+7}{3}$ Then the sum is divided by 3.

First x is multiplied by 2.

$2x - 3$ Then 3 is subtracted.

First 3 is subtracted from x.

$2(x - 3)$ Then the difference is multiplied by 2.

Example 2: Solve $2x - 3 = 17$.

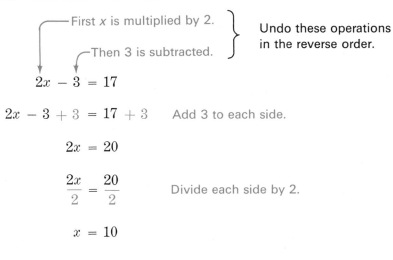

First x is multiplied by 2.

Then 3 is subtracted.

Undo these operations in the reverse order.

$$2x - 3 = 17$$

$$2x - 3 + 3 = 17 + 3 \qquad \text{Add 3 to each side.}$$

$$2x = 20$$

$$\dfrac{2x}{2} = \dfrac{20}{2} \qquad \text{Divide each side by 2.}$$

$$x = 10$$

Check:
$$2x - 3 = 17$$
$$2(10) - 3 = 17 \qquad \text{Multiply first.}$$
$$20 - 3 = 17 \qquad \text{Then subtract.}$$
$$17 = 17 \checkmark$$

In checking, do the operations in the usual order.

Example 3 : Solve $\frac{n+7}{3} = 12$.

$$\frac{n+7}{3} = 12$$

First 7 is added to n.
Then the sum is divided by 3. } Undo these operations in the reverse order.

$$\frac{n+7}{3} \times 3 = 12 \times 3 \quad \text{Multiply each side by 3.}$$

$$n + 7 = 36$$

$$n + 7 - 7 = 36 - 7 \quad \text{Subtract 7 from each side.}$$

$$n = 29$$

Check: $\dfrac{n+7}{3} = 12$

$$\frac{29+7}{3} = 12 \quad \text{Add first.}$$

$$\frac{36}{3} = 12 \quad \text{Then divide.}$$

$$12 = 12 \quad \checkmark$$

Assignment Guide 2.6
Oral: 1–12
Written:
Min. (day 1) 13–31 odd
   (day 2) 14–32 even
Reg. 13–35 odd
Max. 13–51 odd

1. a. × 3, then − 7
  b. + 7, then ÷ 3
3. a. ÷ 2, then + 10
  b. − 10, then × 2
5. a. + 10, then ÷ 5
  b. × 5, then − 10
7. a. ÷ 4, then + 7
  b. − 7, then × 4
9. a. × 9, then − 17
  b. + 17, then ÷ 9
11. a. + 7, then ÷ 3
  b. × 3, then − 7

■ Exercises

A Tell **(a)** what operations have been done to each variable and **(b)** the two steps you would use to solve each equation.

1–12. Odd answers at right above.

2. a. × 4, then + 9
  b. − 9, then ÷ 4
4. a. − 5, then ÷ 7
  b. × 7, then + 5
6. a. ÷ 8, then − 11
  b. + 11, then × 8
8. a. − 18, then ÷ 6
  b. × 6, then + 18
10. a. × 10, then + 3
  b. − 3, then ÷ 10
12. a. ÷ 5, then − 14
  b. + 14, then × 5

1. $3x - 7 = 8$

2. $4x + 9 = 29$

3. $\frac{n}{2} + 10 = 36$

4. $\frac{n-5}{7} = 4$

5. $12 = \frac{a+10}{5}$

6. $\frac{a}{8} - 11 = 21$

7. $47 = \frac{x}{4} + 7$

8. $5 = \frac{x-18}{6}$

9. $9y - 17 = 19$

10. $83 = 10y + 3$

11. $\frac{n+7}{3} = 11$

12. $\frac{n}{5} - 14 = 6$

B Solve.

13. $6x - 3 = 39$ 7

14. $7(x + 13) = 91$ 0

15. $\frac{x}{3} + 9 = 45$ 108

16. $\frac{x-8}{3} = 11$ 41

17. $\frac{x+1}{9} = 9$ 80

18. $\frac{x}{4} - 14 = 6$ 80

19. $\frac{x}{10} + 17 = 21$ 40

20. $\frac{x-2}{4} = 6$ 26

21. $8x - 9 = 7$ 2

22. $77 = 12x + 5$ 6

23. $\frac{x+25}{4} = 7$ 3

24. $\frac{x}{9} - 3 = 17$ 180

25. $3(x - 2) = 18$ 8

26. $8x + 4 = 76$ 9

27. $\frac{x}{6} + 5 = 10$ 30

28. $\frac{x}{7} - 5 = 11$ 112

29. $28 = 11x - 5$ 3

30. $\frac{x-1}{4} = 5$ 21

31. $\frac{x}{8} + 1 = 4$ 24

32. $4x - 6 = 10$ 4

33. $13x + 3 = 42$ 3

34. $52x - 104 = 364$ 9

This formula can be used when all objects in a container weigh the same amount.

total weight ⌐ ⌐ weight of each object

$$w = pn + c$$

number of objects ⌐ ⌐ weight of container

35. A box that weighs 790 g is filled with pears weighing 180 g each. The full box weighs 7990 g. How many pears are in it? 40

36. Machine parts that weigh 3 kg each are to be packed in a box that weighs 35 kg empty. If the packed box cannot weigh more than 347 kg, how many machine parts can be put in it? 104

C **37.** A spool wound with wire weighs 386 kg. If the spool weighs 1 kg when empty and the wire weighs 35 g per meter, how many meters of wire are on the spool? 11 m

Solve. (Use the same methods as for two-step equations.)

38. $8x - 4 < 12$ $x < 2$

39. $4x + 3 < 15$ $x < 3$

40. $5x + 4 < 29$ $x < 5$

41. $15x - 75 > 0$ $x > 5$

42. $121 > 11x + 11$ $10 > x$

43. $10x - 90 > 160$ $x > 25$

44. $\frac{x}{8} - 5 > 4$ $x > 72$

45. $12 > \frac{x}{6} + 3$ $54 > x$

46. $\frac{x}{16} + 4 < 4$ $x < 0$

47. $\frac{x}{16} - 4 > 4$ $x > 128$

48. $\frac{x+5}{8} < 5$ $x < 35$

49. $\frac{x-13}{3} < 2$ $x < 19$

50. $5 < \frac{x-9}{4}$ $29 < x$

51. $\frac{x+12}{7} > 2$ $x > 2$

U.S. Units of Measure

In the United States, the metric system of measurement is now more widely used than it has been in the past. But an older system, now often called the **U.S. system,** is still in use. Some units of this system are shown in the chart below.

To measure	you can use	Common equivalents
Length	inches (in.), feet (ft), yards (yd), miles (mi)	1 ft = 12 in. 1 yd = 3 ft 1 mi = 5280 ft
Weight	ounces (oz) pounds (lb) tons	1 lb = 16 oz 1 ton = 2000 lb
Capacity	cups (c), pints (pt), quarts (qt), gallons (gal.)	1 pt = 2 c 1 qt = 2 pt 1 gal. = 4 qt

To convert from larger units to smaller, multiply.

To convert from smaller units to larger, divide.

Examples:

12 yd = _____ ft

Each yard contains 3 feet.

So multiply 12 by 3.

12 yd = _36_ ft

38 pt = _____ qt

There are 2 pints in each quart.

So divide 38 by 2.

38 pt = _19_ qt

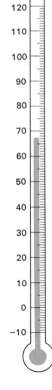

The degree Fahrenheit (°F) is the unit of temperature in the U.S. system.

- Water boils at 212 °F.

- Normal body temperature is between 98 °F and 99 °F.

- Comfortable room temperature is 68 °F.

- Water freezes at 32 °F.

Exercises

Assignment Guide 2.7
Oral: 1–8
Written: Min. 9–37 odd
Reg. 9–47 odd
Max. 9–55 odd

A **1.** How would you find how many feet are in 3 miles?
Multiply 3 by 5280.

2. How would you find how many pounds are in 5 tons?
Multiply 5 by 2000.

3. How would you find how many pints are in 8 cups?
Divide 8 by 2.

4. How would you find how many gallons are in 24 quarts?
Divide 24 by 4.

5. To convert from a larger to a smaller unit, (*divide, multiply*).

6. To convert from a smaller to a larger unit, (*divide, multiply*).

7. On the Fahrenheit scale, water boils at (*32, 100, 212*) degrees.

8. A feverish person's temperature could be (*37 °F, 102 °F, 212 °F*).

B Complete.

9. 6 pt = ____ c   12

10. 8 qt = ____ pt   16

11. 7 gal. = ____ qt   28

12. 3 tons = ____ lb   6000

13. 15 ft = ____ in.   180

14. 32 lb = ____ oz   512

15. 27 yd = ____ ft   81

16. 33 ft = ____ in.   396

17. 6 mi = ____ ft   31 680

18. 64 lb = ____ oz   1024

19. 4 gal. = ____ qt   16

20. 320 oz = ____ lb   20

21. 108 ft = ____ yd   36

22. 156 in. = ____ ft   13

23. 360 ft = ____ yd   120

24. 6 pt = ____ qt   3

25. 64 oz = ____ lb   4

26. 15,840 ft = ____ mi   3

27. 180 in. = ____ ft   15

28. 82 c = ____ pt   41

29. 8000 lb = ____ tons   4

30. 52 qt = ____ gal.   13

31. 76 qt = ____ gal.   19

32. 10 yd = ____ ft   30

33. 30 yd = ____ ft   90

34. 6 qt = ____ pt   12

35. 336 c = ＿＿ gal. 21

36. 3 gal. = ＿＿ c 48

37. 5 qt = ＿＿ c 20

38. 4 yd = ＿＿ in. 144

39. 72 pt = ＿＿ gal. 9

40. 108 in. = ＿＿ yd 3

41. 284 c = ＿＿ qt 71

42. 2 mi = ＿＿ yd 3520

43. The cheetah is the fastest land animal over short distances. A cheetah can run 600 yards in about 20 seconds. How fast is this in yards per second? In feet per second? 30 yd per sec; 90 ft per sec

Use this formula to convert the given temperatures.

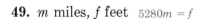

degrees Celsius

$$F = \frac{9C}{5} + 32$$

degrees Fahrenheit

44. 25 °C = ＿＿°F 77

45. 70 °C = ＿＿°F 158

46. 0 °C = ＿＿°F 32

47. 100 °C = ＿＿°F 212

48. Iron melts at 1535 °C. What is the melting point of iron in degrees Fahrenheit? (Use the formula above.) 2795 °F

C For each pair of measures, write a formula to show how they are related. Check your formula by substituting values.

Example: i inches, f feet

Answer: $i = 12f$ (or $f = \frac{i}{12}$)

Check:

f	1	2	3
i	12	24	36

"Did I say we had to plant them 4 feet deep? I meant 4 inches."

49. m miles, f feet $5280m = f$

50. t tons, p pounds $2000t = p$

51. p pints, g gallons $p = 8g$

52. g gallons, q quarts $4g = q$

53. f feet, y yards $f = 3y$

54. n ounces, p pounds $n = 16p$

55. c cups, q quarts $c = 4q$

56. p pints, c cups $2p = c$

Area and Volume

2.8

 The **area** of a figure is the amount of surface it covers.

Area is measured in *square units*.

1 cm² 1 cm
1 cm

1 square centimeter or 1 cm²

Suggested Class Time

Course	Min.	Reg.	Max.
Days	1	1	1

Example 1: Find the area of the rectangle.

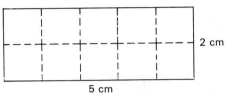

2 cm

5 cm

The rectangle covers the same amount of surface as 10 squares of 1 cm² each. So its area is 10 cm².

Length and width must be in the same units.

5   ×   2   =   10
↓   ↓   ↓
cm   cm   cm²

length × width = area

For a rectangle, $A = lw$.

The **volume** of a solid is the amount of space it occupies.

Volume is measured in *cubic units*.

1 cm 1 cm³
1 cm 1 cm

1 cubic centimeter or 1 cm³

Example 2: Find the volume of the solid. (The faces are rectangles.)

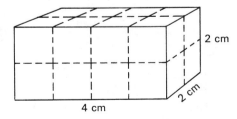

2 cm

4 cm

2 cm

The solid occupies the same amount of space as 16 cubes of 1 cm³ each. So its volume is 16 cm³.

Length, width, and height must be in the same units.

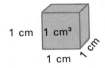

4   ×   2   ×   2   =   16
↓   ↓   ↓   ↓
cm   cm   cm   cm³

length × width × height = volume

For a rectangular solid, $V = lwh$.

■ **Exercises**

Assignment Guide 2.8
Oral: 1–16
Written:
Min. 17–39 odd
Reg. 17–31 odd; 33–39
Max. 17–31 odd; 33–44

A What unit of area has all sides of the given length?

1. 1 cm 1 cm²   **2.** 1 in. 1 sq in.   **3.** 1 yd 1 sq yd   **4.** 1 m 1 m²

What unit of volume has all edges of the given length?

5. 1 cm 1 cm³   **6.** 1 in. 1 cu in.   **7.** 1 ft 1 cu ft   **8.** 1 km
1 km³

What is the length of each side of the given unit of area?

9. 1 sq ft 1 ft   **10.** 1 km² 1 km   **11.** 1 sq mi 1 mi   **12.** 1 mm²
1 mm

What is the length of each edge of the given unit of volume?

13. 1 cu yd 1 yd   **14.** 1 mm³ 1 mm   **15.** 1 cu in. 1 in.   **16.** 1 m³ 1 m

B Find each area or volume.

RECTANGLES

	area	length	width
17. 21 sq in.	**17.**	7 in.	3 in.
18. 54 m²	**18.**	9 m	6 m
19. 48 sq yd	**19.**	12 yd	4 yd
20. 99 km²	**20.**	11 km	9 km
21. 273 sq ft	**21.**	21 ft	13 ft
22. 105 mm²	**22.**	15 mm	7 mm

RECTANGULAR SOLIDS

	volume	length	width	height
23.	120 m³	8 m	5 m	3 m
24.	594 cu ft	11 ft	6 ft	9 ft
25.	416 mm³	13 mm	8 mm	4 mm
26.	4080 cu in.	24 in.	17 in.	10 in.
27.	81 km³	9 km	1 km	9 km
28.	432 cu yd	8 yd	3 yd	18 yd

Find each width or height.

Examples:

area: 27 cm²
length: 9 cm $A = lw$
width: ? cm

$$27 = 9w$$
$$3 = w$$

width: 3 cm

volume: 30 cu in.
length: 5 in.
width: 2 in. $V = lwh$
height: ? in.

$$30 = (5 \times 2)h$$
$$3 = h$$

height: 3 in.

	area	length	width		volume	length	width	height
29.	65 sq yd	13 yd	5 yd	**31.**	90 mm³	6 mm	3 mm	5 mm
30.	48 m²	12 m	4 m	**32.**	140 cu ft	7 ft	5 ft	4 ft

Find the area. Use one of the given formulas.

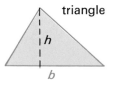

parallelogram   triangle

33. parallelogram; $b = 5$ cm, $h = 8$ cm   40 cm²

34. triangle; $b = 43$ m, $h = 24$ m   516 m²

35. trapezoid; $a = 3$ in., $b = 7$ in., $h = 9$ in.
                                45 sq in.

36. triangle; $h = 22$ mi, $b = 13$ mi   143 sq mi

$$A = bh \qquad A = bh \div 2$$

Find the volume. Use one of the given formulas.

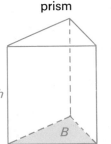
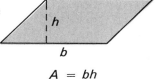

prism   trapezoid

37. prism; $B = 7$ cm², $h = 11$ cm   77 cm³

38. pyramid; $B = 21$ m², $h = 8$ m   56 m³

39. prism; $B = 16$ sq yd, $h = 5$ yd   80 cu yd

$$A = h(a + b) \div 2$$

C **40.** pyramid with triangular base; $h = 11$ in., h of base $= 4$ in., b of base $= 3$ in.   22 cu in.

$$V = \text{area of base} \times h$$
$$= Bh$$

Complete.

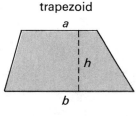

pyramid

41. For a rectangle, if $w = 2$ cm and $l = 30$ mm, then $A = $ ____ cm² or $A = $ ____ mm².   6; 600

42. For a rectangular solid, if $l = 2$ m, $w = 100$ cm, and $h = 3000$ mm, then $V = $ ____ m³ or $V = $ ____ cm³.
                                    6; 6 000 000

$$V = \text{area of base} \times h \div 3$$
$$= Bh \div 3$$

Solve. (1 L $= 1000$ cm³)

43. There are about 8543 cubic kilometers of usable fresh water on the earth. How many liters of fresh water is this?
                      8 543 000 000 000 000 L

44. There are about 29 200 cubic kilometers of fresh water in ice caps and glaciers. How many liters is this?   29 200 000 000 000 000 L

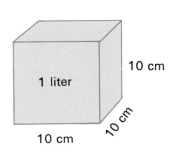

1 liter   10 cm   10 cm   10 cm

More Translating Into Symbols

2.9

Suggested Class Time

Course	Min.	Reg.	Max.
Days	1	1	1

Some English sentences can be translated directly into symbols.

Example 1: Translate into symbols.

Three plus twice a number n is fifteen.

$$3 + 2n = 15$$

If the variable is not given in the problem, you must start by choosing a variable and saying what it represents.

© Photo Graphics/Kreutzig

Example 2: Translate into symbols.

A 48-inch board is cut into two pieces.

One piece is 8 inches longer than the other.

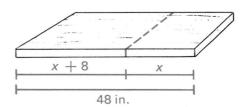

Let x = length of shorter piece.

Then $x + 8$ = length of longer piece.

$x + (x + 8) = 48$ ◀ The sum of the lengths is 48.

Example 3: Translate into symbols.

Bob's age is 6 more than twice Jim's age. Bob is 42.

Let a = Jim's age.

Then $2a + 6$ = Bob's age.

$2a + 6 = 42$ ◀ Bob's age is 42.

■ Exercises

Assignment Guide 2.9
Oral: 1–4
Written: Min. 5–12
Reg. 5–17
Max. 5–24

A̲ Tell how you would represent each quantity.

1. One number is five times a second number.

    a. second number n **b.** first number $5n$

2. One carton weighs 50 pounds less than a second carton.

    a. weight of second carton w **b.** weight of first carton $w - 50$

3. Arlene is 3 years older than her brother Paul.

    a. Paul's age P **b.** Arlene's age $P + 3$

4. One number is 2 less than twice a second number.

    a. second number n **b.** first number $2n - 2$

B̲ Translate into symbols.

5. Twenty-one is six more than a number.   Let $n =$ the number; $21 = n + 6$

6. 15 is subtracted from twice a number. The result is 11.   Let $a =$ the number; $2a - 15 = 11$

7. Twelve is twice Mario's age divided by 3.
Let $m =$ Mario's age;
$12 = \dfrac{2m}{3}$

8. The perimeter of a rectangle is 30 inches. The length is twice the width.
Let $x =$ width, $2x =$ length;
$2x + 2(2x) = 30$

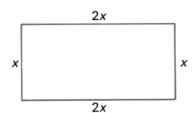

9. One shirt costs two dollars more than a second shirt. The total cost of the two shirts is twenty-four dollars.
Let $s =$ cost of 2nd shirt, $s + 2 =$ cost of 1st shirt; $s + (s + 2) = 24$

10. Jan has saved \$235. This is \$15 less than the amount she needs for her vacation.   Let $v =$ amt. needed; $235 = v - 15$

11. One number is 3 times a second number. The sum of the two numbers is 20.   Let $n =$ 2nd number, $3n =$ 1st number; $3n + n = 20$

12. Ann's father's age is 6 more than twice Ann's age. He is 51.
Let a = Ann's age, $2a + 6$ = father's age; $2a + 6 = 51$

13. An adult ticket costs $1 more than a student ticket. The cost of 2 adult and 3 student tickets is $12.
Let s = cost of student ticket, $s + 1$ = cost of adult ticket; $2(s + 1) + 3s = 12$

14. The difference between two numbers is 3. Their sum is 15.
Let n = one number, $n + 3$ = other number; $n + (n + 3) = 15$

15. Stuart and Evie played 20 games of rummy. Evie won 2 more games than Stuart did. Let s = Stuart's wins, $s + 2$ = Evie's wins; $s + (s + 2) = 20$

16. 52 students were placed in two classes. There were 4 more students in Ms. Krol's class than in Mr. Luster's class.
Let r = no. in Mr. L's class, $r + 4$ = no. in Ms. K's class; $r + (r + 4) = 52$

17. The Detroit Pistons beat the Chicago Bulls by 20 points. Their combined score was 210 points.
Let b = Bulls' score, $b + 20$ = Pistons' score; $b + (b + 20) = 210$

Courtesy Chicago Bulls

C Translate these sentences into inequalities.

Example: Twice a number is greater than 10.

Let n = number.

$$2n > 10$$

18. 45 is less than 3 times a number.
Let n = the number; $45 < 3n$

19. Rich is older than Karen. Karen is 27.
Let r = Rich's age; $r > 27$

20. A number divided by 3 is less than 15.
Let t = the number; $\frac{t}{3} < 15$

21. The sum of 11 and a number is greater than 36.
Let a = the number; $11 + a > 36$

22. $5.00 is more than what Diane wants to spend.
Let d = no. dollars Diane wants to spend; $5 > d$

23. Aretha scored more points in the game than Cora. Cora scored 18 points.
Let a = Aretha's score; $a > 18$

24. Mark spent less than $6.00 on the gift.
Let m = no. dollars Mark spent; $m < 6$

Terms and Symbols Review

Match each item with the best description.

Suggested Class Time

Course	Min.	Reg.	Max.
Days	1	1	1

1. addition c
2. subtraction e
3. multiplication a
4. division h
5. graph of $x < 3$ f
6. ounces and tons d
7. degrees Fahrenheit b
8. cups and gallons i
9. feet and yards g

a. inverse of division

b. units of temperature

c. inverse of subtraction

d. units of weight

e. inverse of addition

f. graph of $\{0, 1, 2\}$

g. units of length

h. inverse of multiplication

i. units of capacity

Assignment Guide Rev.
Oral: Terms & Symbols 1–9
Written: 1–49 odd

Chapter 2 Review

Find each answer.   Use an inverse operation to check.   2.1

1. $\begin{array}{r} 72 \\ -13 \end{array}$ 59
2. $\begin{array}{r} 195 \\ -23 \end{array}$ 172
3. $215 \div 5$ 43
4. $183 \div 3$ 61

Simplify each phrase.

5. $27 + 4 - 4$ 27
6. $9 \times 7 \div 7$ 9
7. $\frac{3}{2} \times 2$ 3
8. $14 - 5 + 5$ 14

Solve.

9. $x + 7 = 15$ 8
10. $2 = n - 5$ 7   2.2
11. $y - 32 = 17$ 49
12. $x - 11 = 0$ 11
13. $7n = 14$ 2
14. $\frac{x}{8} = 10$ 80   2.3
15. $84 = 12x$ 7
16. $31 = \frac{n}{3}$ 93

2.4 Solve.

17. $n + 11 < 16$ $n < 5$ **18.** $x + 7 > 10$ $x > 3$

19. $3 > y - 7$ $10 > y$ **20.** $31 < n - 8$ $39 < n$

21. $\frac{x}{7} > 1$ $x > 7$ **22.** $5 < \frac{n}{6}$ $30 < n$

23. $8x > 24$ $x > 3$ **24.** $120 < 10y$ $12 < y$

2.5 Solve and graph.

25. $n - 7 = 2$ 9 **26.** $\frac{y}{6} = 3$ 18

27. $5x = 20$ 4 **28.** $3 = y + 3$ 0

29. $\frac{n}{4} < 1$ $n < 4$ **30.** $12 < 4y$ $3 < y$

31. $x - 2 > 3$ $x > 5$ **32.** $5 > n - 14$ $19 > n$

2.6 Solve.

33. $3x - 4 = 8$ 4 **34.** $21 = 8x + 5$ 2

35. $\frac{n}{7} + 3 = 5$ 14 **36.** $7 = \frac{n + 8}{2}$ 6

37. $\frac{x - 6}{9} = 9$ 87 **38.** $\frac{a}{4} - 3 = 7$ 40

2.7 Complete.

39. 13 ft = <u>156</u> in.   **40.** 6 lb = <u>96</u> oz   **41.** 5 qt = <u>10</u> pt

42. 72 in. = <u>6</u> ft   **43.** 96 oz = <u>6</u> lb   **44.** 24 qt = <u>6</u> gal.

2.8 Find each area or volume.

	RECTANGLES				RECTANGULAR SOLIDS			
	area	length	width		volume	length	width	height
45.	91 km²	13 km	7 km	**47.**	1080 cu in.	9 in.	6 in.	20 in.
46.	540 sq ft	27 ft	20 ft	**48.**	420 cm³	12 cm	7 cm	5 cm

2.9 Translate into symbols.

49. Thirty-five is seven more than a number.
Let n = the number;
$35 = n + 7$

50. The profit is \$100. This is \$6 less than twice the cost.
Let c = cost; $100 = 2c - 6$

Assignment Guide Test
Written: 1–23

Solve.

1. $x + 7 = 19$ 12

2. $12 = y - 8$ 20

3. $9n = 72$ 8

4. $96 = \frac{x}{6}$ 576

5. $4n - 5 = 19$ 6

6. $72 = 7y + 2$ 10

7. $\frac{x}{8} + 7 = 10$ 24

8. $\frac{n-6}{3} = 10$ 36

9. $3x < 39$ $x < 13$

10. $\frac{n}{7} > 2$ $n > 14$

11. $n - 8 > 2$ $n > 10$

12. $6 < y + 5$ $1 < y$

Solve and graph.

13. $\frac{x}{2} = 6$ 12

14. $n + 8 = 13$ 5

15. $y + 3 < 7$ $y < 4$

16. $6n > 12$ $n > 2$

Complete.

17. 240 in. = _____ ft 20

18. 7 qt = _____ pt 14

19. 9 lb = _____ oz 144

20. 24 ft = _____ yd 8

RATE YOURSELF

	Number Correct	
22–23		Superior
20–21		Excellent
17–19		Good
12–16		Fair
0–11		Poor

21. A rectangle with length 15 centimeters and width 4 centimeters has area _____. 60 cm^2

22. A rectangular solid with length 7 inches, width 3 inches, and height 10 inches has volume _____. 210 cu in.

Translate into symbols.

23. Carolyn Andrews has 3 more strikes than twice the number her daughter Angie has. Carolyn has 7 strikes.
Let a = Angie's strikes,
$2a + 3$ = Carolyn's strikes; $2a + 3 = 7$

" I LIKE THE WAY THEY SPOT THE PINS HERE! "

UNIVERSAL PRODUCT CODE

Most packages in a food store are now marked with a pattern of bars and spaces like the one shown here. The bars are of three different widths. They are separated by spaces of three widths.

0 1 2345 67890

Part of the pattern stands for the manufacturer's code number. ——

Part of the pattern stands for the code number of the product.

These patterns can be "read" by a scanner connected to a computer. The computer has a matching pattern stored in it, along with the price of the item in the package.

Courtesy NCR Corporation

The check-out system works like this:

1. The shopper brings the packages to the check-out clerk.

2. The clerk runs the pattern on each package past an electronic scanner.

3. The scanner reads the pattern.

4. The computer looks up the pattern in its memory to find today's price on the item.

5. The computer prints the price on the cash-register tape. It also prints the name of the item.

6. The computer totals the bill and adds the tax.

7. The shopper pays the bill!

Getting Ready for Chapter 3

3

Answer each question.

1. What are the first 10 odd numbers? 1, 3, 5, 7, 9, 11, 13, 15, 17, 19

2. What are the first 10 even numbers greater than 0?
2, 4, 6, 8, 10, 12, 14, 16, 18, 20

Compute.

1.2

3. $5 + 6 + 8$ 19

4. $12 + (8 + 9)$ 29

5. $17 - (8 - 3)$ 12

6. $(12 - 9) - 2$ 1

Assignment Guide GR 3
Written: Min. 1–24
Reg. 1–24

7. $(3 \times 4) \times 3$ 36

8. $10 \times (2 \times 4)$ 80

9. $16 \div 2 \div 2$ 4

10. $12 \div (9 \div 3)$ 4

11. $1 + 7 \times 3$ 22

12. $8 \times 3 + 4$ 28

13. $(1 + 7) \times 3$ 24

14. $8 \times (3 + 4)$ 56

15. $(7 \times 2) + (7 \times 4)$ 42

16. $(2 \times 5) + (3 \times 5)$ 25

Solve.

17. $x + 8 = 20$ 12

18. $22 = n + 16$ 6

2.2

19. $y - 6 = 6$ 12

20. $6 = z - 13$ 19

21. $63 = 9r$ 7

22. $7y = 56$ 8

2.3

Solve.

1.9

23. A rectangle has a length of 8 inches and a width of 6 inches. What is its perimeter? $(p = 2l + 2w)$ 28 in.

24. A car is going 55 mph. How long will it take the car to go 165 miles? $(d = rt)$ 3 hr

IMPORTANT PROPERTIES

Courtesy American Trucking Association

A good driver follows the "rules of the road." Using the rules is an important part of a safe trip.

Some "rules of the road" in mathematics are called *properties*. Others are important facts about whole numbers. In this chapter you will use these rules to solve equations and to learn more about whole numbers.

Commutative Properties

Walk 5 blocks E and 2 N.   *Walk 2 blocks N and 5 E.*

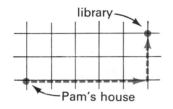

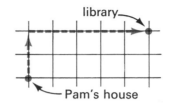

The order in which Pam walks from her house to the library does not change the result. She gets to the library either way.

Changing the order of some activities changes the result.

Go out and close the door.   *Close the door and go out.*

In mathematics an operation is **commutative** if you can change the order and still get the same result.

You can change the order of the numbers for some operations but not for others. For example, *addition is commutative.*

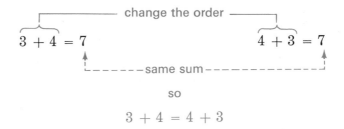

so

$$3 + 4 = 4 + 3$$

Commutative Property of Addition

Any two numbers *a* and *b* can be added in either order without changing the sum. So

$a + b = b + a$.   *Example:* $2 + 7 = 7 + 2$

Example 1:   Is multiplication commutative?

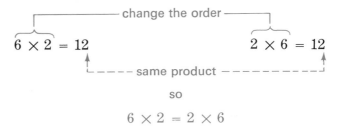

so

$$6 \times 2 = 2 \times 6$$

Yes, *multiplication is commutative.*

Commutative Property of Multiplication

Any two numbers *a* and *b* can be multiplied in either order without changing the product. So

$a \times b = b \times a$.   *Example:* $8 \times 3 = 3 \times 8$

Example 2:   Are subtraction and division commutative?

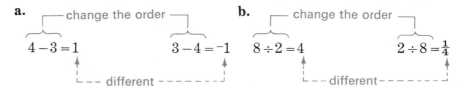

No, *subtraction and division are not commutative.*

Example 3: Sometimes changing the order of the factors makes the computation easier.

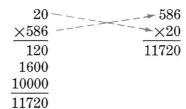

$$\begin{array}{r} 20 \\ \times 586 \\ \hline 120 \\ 1600 \\ 10000 \\ \hline 11720 \end{array} \qquad \begin{array}{r} 586 \\ \times 20 \\ \hline 11720 \end{array}$$

Example 4: For each equation, use the commutative property to write a new equation.

a. $5 + x = 7$

$x + 5 = 7$

b. $d \times 3 = 12$

$3d = 12$

▪ Exercises

Ⓐ Tell if you can change the order of the following activities without changing the result.

1. putting on your hat; putting on your coat   Yes

2. washing a car; waxing a car   No

3. taking the phone off the hook; dialing your number   No

4. salting your soup; peppering your soup   Yes

5. filling a swimming pool; diving in   No

6. addressing an envelope; putting a stamp on an envelope   Yes

Assignment Guide 3.1
Oral: 1–6
Written:
Min. 7–29 odd
Reg. 7–29 odd; 30–33
Max. 7–29 odd; 30–35

Ⓑ Compute. Whenever possible, use the commutative property to make the computation easier.

7. $\begin{array}{r} 20 \\ \times 425 \end{array}$ 8500

8. $\begin{array}{r} 300 \\ \times 625 \end{array}$ 187,500

9. $\begin{array}{r} 428 \\ \times 30 \end{array}$ 12,840

10. $\begin{array}{r} 200 \\ \times 856 \end{array}$ 171,200

11. $\begin{array}{r} 142 \\ \times 72 \end{array}$ 10,224

12. $\begin{array}{r} 83 \\ \times 524 \end{array}$ 43,492

13. $\begin{array}{r} 40 \\ \times 6295 \end{array}$ 251,800

14. $\begin{array}{r} 300 \\ \times 6675 \end{array}$ 2,002,500

For each equation, use the commutative properties to write a new equation. (See Example 4.) Then solve.

15. $5 + x = 9$
$x + 5 = 9; \ 4$

16. $4 + y = 10$
$y + 4 = 10; \ 6$

17. $14 = 8 + z$
$14 = z + 8; \ 6$

18. $m \times 3 = 15$
$3m = 15; \ 5$

19. $49 = t \times 7$
$49 = 7t; \ 7$

20. $r \times 6 = 42$
$6r = 42; \ 7$

21. $14 = 6 + t$
$14 = t + 6; \ 8$

22. $k \times 9 = 72$
$9k = 72; \ 8$

23. $11 + m = 69$
$m + 11 = 69; \ 58$

24. $96 = z \times 8$
$96 = 8z; \ 12$

25. $13 + n = 81$
$n + 13 = 81; \ 68$

26. $y \times 7 = 245$
$7y = 245; \ 35$

27. $18 + c = 96$
$c + 18 = 96; \ 78$

28. $r \times 11 = 242$
$11r = 242; \ 22$

29. $91 = 17 + d$
$91 = d + 17; \ 74$

Use the formulas below to solve the following problems.

30. It took Barb 3 hours to ride her bike 18 miles. What was her rate of speed? 6 mph

31. A train traveled 345 miles in 5 hours. How fast was the train going? 69 mph

32. The retail price of a record album is $7. If the wholesale price is $5, how much is the markup? $2

33. The retail price of a tennis racket is $27, and the wholesale price is $21. How much is the markup? $6

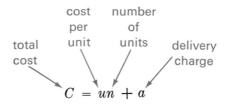

C **34.** A fence installer received an order of 54 fence posts. The total cost of the order was $123, and the delivery charge was $15. What was the cost of each fence post? $2

35. The total cost of an order for 13 shrubs was $77. If the cost of each shrub was $5, what was the delivery charge? $12

Associative Properties

3.2

You often have to find the sum of three numbers, such as

$$3 + 5 + 7$$

Should you begin by adding 3 and 5? Or 5 and 7? Or does it matter?

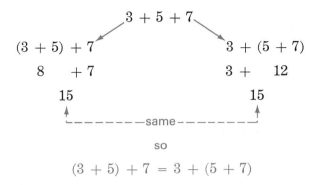

so

$$(3 + 5) + 7 = 3 + (5 + 7)$$

An operation is **associative** if you can group in different ways as above without changing the result.

Associative Property of Addition

Any three numbers *a*, *b*, and *c* can be added by grouping the first two or the last two numbers without changing the sum. So

$(a + b) + c = a + (b + c)$.   *Example:*
$$(1 + 3) + 6 = 1 + (3 + 6)$$

Multiplication is also associative.

$$6 \times 8 \times 5$$

$(6 \times 8) \times 5$ $6 \times (8 \times 5)$

$48 \quad \times 5$ $6 \times \quad 40$

240 240

same

so

$$(6 \times 8) \times 5 = 6 \times (8 \times 5)$$

Associative Property of Multiplication

Any three numbers *a*, *b*, and *c* can be multiplied by grouping the first two or the last two numbers without changing the product. So

$(a \times b) \times c = a \times (b \times c)$.

Example:
$(3 \times 5) \times 4 = 3 \times (5 \times 4)$

Example 1: Tell which method of grouping makes the computation easier.

$$28 + 96 + 4$$

$(28 + 96) + 4$	$28 + (96 + 4)$
$124 \quad + 4$	$28 + \quad 100$
128	128

$28 + (96 + 4)$ enables most people to do the addition mentally.

Example 2: Sometimes the commutative and associative properties are both used to make the computation easier.

Long way		*Short way*
$25 \times 68 \times 4$		$25 \times 68 \times 4$
$(25 \times 68) \times 4$	Associative property	
$(68 \times 25) \times 4$	Commutative property	
$68 \times (25 \times 4)$	Associative property	
68×100		68×100
6800		6800

Example 3: Sometimes the commutative and the associative properties are used in solving equations.

a. $(x + 5) + 6 = 39$

$x + (5 + 6) = 39$ Associative property

$x + 11 = 39$ Add.

$x + 11 - 11 = 39 - 11$ Inverse operation

$x = 28$ Check as required.

b. $54 = (2t)3$

$54 = 3(2t)$ Commutative property

$54 = (3 \times 2)t$ Associative property

$54 = 6t$ Multiply.

$\dfrac{54}{6} = \dfrac{6t}{6}$ Inverse operation

$9 = t$

■ Exercises

A Study the examples. Tell if subtraction and division are associative.

1.

$9 - 5 - 2$

$(9 - 5) - 2$ $9 - (5 - 2)$

$4 \quad - 2$ $9 - \quad 3$

$2 \leftarrow --\text{different}--\rightarrow 6$ No

2.

$24 \div 6 \div 2$

$(24 \div 6) \div 2$ $24 \div (6 \div 2)$

$4 \quad \div 2$ $24 \div \quad 3$

$2 \leftarrow --\text{different}--\rightarrow 8$ No

Tell how you would group the addends or the factors to make the computation easy.

3. $(30 + 60) + 18$ **4.** $72 + (91 + 9)$ **5.** $(54 + 6) + 27$

6. $(5 \times 2) \times 9$ **7.** $12 \times (4 \times 5)$ **8.** $(25 \times 4) \times 16$

9. $(16 + 84) + 99$ **10.** $33 \times (25 \times 8)$ **11.** $(4 \times 250) \times 172$

Assignment Guide 3.2
Oral: 1–11
Written:
Min. 13–37 odd
Reg. 13–37 odd; 39–42
Max. 13–37 odd; 39–44

B Compute. Use the properties to make the computation as easy as possible.

12. $6 + 4 + 9$ ₁₉

13. $5 \times 40 \times 6$ ₁₂₀₀

14. $19 + 13 + 17$ ₄₉

15. $9 \times 4 \times 25$ ₉₀₀

16. $20 \times 83 \times 50$ 83,000

17. $63 + 59 + 37$ ₁₅₉

18. $68 + 89 + 11$ ₁₆₈

19. $943 + 68 + 57$ 1068

20. $8 \times 25 \times 6$ ₁₂₀₀

21. $8 \times 250 \times 17$ 34,000

22. $4 \times 63 \times 25$ 6300

23. $83 + 69 + 31$ ₁₈₃

24. $16 + 24 + 48$ ₈₈

25. $72 + 83 + 17$ ₁₇₂

26. $50 \times 19 \times 20$ ₁₉,₀₀₀

Solve. (See Example 3.)

27. $(n + 3) + 7 = 20$ 10

28. $12 + (5 + p) = 34$ 17

29. $(4 + q) + 3 = 21$ 14

30. $40 = 6 + (r + 14)$ 20

31. $(2s + 1) + 3 = 16$ 6

32. $(8 + 3t) + 1 = 27$ 6

33. $48 = (2u)4$ 6

34. $36 = (6v)3$ 2

35. $(5w)2 = 120$ 12

36. $(15x)2 = 90$ 3

37. $12 = 2(y \times 3)$ 2

38. $(z \times 4)5 = 80$ 4

Use the formulas below to find the missing values.

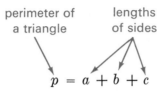

perimeter of a triangle   lengths of sides

$$p = a + b + c$$

volume of a box   length   width   height

$$v = lwh$$

39. The perimeter of a triangle is 16 in. If $a = 4$ in. and $c = 7$ in., find b.   5 in.

40. The perimeter of a triangle is 43 cm. If $a = 16$ cm and $c = 12$ cm, find b.   15 cm

41. The volume of a box is 36 cu ft. If $w = 3$ ft and $h = 2$ ft, find l.   6 ft

42. The volume of a box is 480 m³. If $l = 8$ m and $h = 12$ m, find w.   5 m

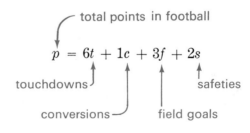

total points in football

$$p = 6t + 1c + 3f + 2s$$

touchdowns   conversions   field goals   safeties

$\boxed{C}$ **43.** Suppose $p = 47$, $t = 5$, $f = 3$, and $s = 2$. Find c.   4

44. Suppose $p = 36$, $t = 4$, $c = 4$, and $s = 1$. Find f.   2

Camerique

Zero and One

3.3

You already know that 0 and 1 have special properties. For example, what happens when you add 0 to a number?

$$8 + 0 = 8 \qquad 0 + 275 = 275 \qquad y + 0 = y$$

$$0 + t = t \qquad\qquad 0 + 0 = 0$$

Identity Property of Addition

0 is the *identity number for addition*. The sum of 0 and any number *n* is that number. So

$0 + n = n$ and $n + 0 = n$.   *Example:* $0 + 4 = 4$
                                            $4 + 0 = 4$

What about multiplying by 1?

$$1 \times 5 = 5 \qquad 6 \times 1 = 6 \qquad 1 \times w = w$$

$$r \times 1 = r \qquad\qquad 1 \times 1 = 1$$

Identity Property of Multiplication

1 is the *identity number for multiplication*. The product of 1 and any number *n* is that number. So

$1 \times n = n$ and $n \times 1 = n$.   *Example:* $1 \times 7 = 7$
                                            $7 \times 1 = 7$

© (1967) United Feature Syndicate, Inc.

Can you multiply by 0?

73

$$3 \times 0 = 0 \qquad 0 \times 37 = 0 \qquad a \times 0 = 0$$

$$0 \times t = 0 \qquad\qquad 0 \times 0 = 0$$

Multiplication Property of 0

The product of 0 and any number n is 0. So

$0 \times n = 0$ and $n \times 0 = 0.$ *Example:* $0 \times 2 = 0$
$2 \times 0 = 0$

What happens when you divide a number by itself?

$$4 \div 4 = 1 \qquad 24 \div 24 = 1 \qquad 142 \div 142 = 1$$

But what about $0 \div 0$?

$0 \div 0 = ?$ $\longrightarrow$ $0\overline{)0}^{\,?}$ *Check:* $\begin{array}{r} ? \\ \times 0 \\ \hline 0 \end{array}$ ◀ Every number works. So there is no answer for $0 \div 0$.

Any number except 0 divided by itself is 1. That is, for any nonzero number n,

$n \div n = 1.$ *Example:* $6 \div 6 = 1$

0 cannot be divided by itself, but 0 can be divided by other numbers.

$0 \div 5 = 0$ $\longrightarrow$ $5\overline{)0}^{\,0}$ *Check:* $\begin{array}{r} 0 \\ \times 5 \\ \hline 0 \end{array}$ ◀ It checks.

0 divided by any number except 0 is 0. That is, for any nonzero number n,

$0 \div n = 0.$ *Example:* $0 \div 16 = 0$

Dividing any number by 0 is meaningless.

$3 \div 0 = ?$ $\longrightarrow$ $0\overline{)3}^{\,?}$ *Check:* $\begin{array}{r} ? \\ \times 0 \\ \hline 3 \end{array}$ ◀ No number works. So there is no answer for $3 \div 0$.

Never divide by zero.

Exercises

Assignment Guide 3.3
Oral: 1–9
Written: Min. 10–30
           Reg. 10–30
           Max. 10–36

A Find the value of each phrase.

1. 4×1 4   **2.** 1×16 16   **3.** $42 + 0$ 42

4. $0 + 172$ 172   **5.** 19×0 0   **6.** 0×16 0

7. $0 \div 16$ 0   **8.** $0 \div 8$ 0   **9.** $3 \div 3$ 1

B Use the properties of 0 and 1 to solve each equation.

10. $1 \times 16 = m$ 16   **11.** $0 \div y = 0$ Any number   **12.** $184 + 0 = d$ 184

13. $37 \times 0 = k$ 0   **14.** $36 \div 36 = c$ 1   **15.** $k \times 32 = 32$ 1

16. $14 \div r = 1$ 14   **17.** $84 \times x = 0$ 0   **18.** $0 \times 189 = p$ 0

19. $79 \times 1 = r$ 79   **20.** $596 + m = 596$ 0   **21.** $h \times 0 = 0$ Any number

22. $t \div 4 = 0$ 0   **23.** $1 \times t = 89$ 89   **24.** $196 \times c = 196$ 1

25. $f + 0 = 296$ 296   **26.** $26 \div a = 1$ 26   **27.** $b \div 8 = 0$ 0

28. $g \div 31 = 1$ 31   **29.** $0 + n = 197$ 197   **30.** $s \times 597 = 0$ 0

C Find the value of each phrase without doing any written computation.

31. $32 + (9 - 9)$ 32   **32.** $(19 - 18) \times 56$ 56   **33.** $182 - (0 \div 4)$ 182

34. $385 \times (284 - 283)$ **35.** $(14 \div 14) \times 163$ 163   **36.** $24 \div [8 - (4 + 3)]$ 24
                       385

Suppose you buy 5 tapes and 4 records at the sale price. You can figure the cost in either of these two ways.

$$3 \times (5 + 4) \qquad (3 \times 5) + (3 \times 4)$$
$$3 \times 9 \qquad\qquad 15 \; + \; 12$$
$$27 \qquad\qquad\qquad 27$$

————same————

so

$$3(5 + 4) = (3 \times 5) + (3 \times 4)$$

This relationship is useful in solving problems. It is called the *distributive property of multiplication over addition.*

Distributive Property

For any numbers *a*, *b*, and *c*,

$$a(b + c) = ab + ac$$

and

$$ab + ac = a(b + c).$$

The commutative property allows us to state the distributive property as $ba + ca = (b + c)a$. This pattern is helpful in solving equations.

Example 1: Solve $7x + 9x = 64$.

$7x + 9x = 64$

$(7 + 9)x = 64$ Distributive property

$16x = 64$

$\dfrac{16x}{16} = \dfrac{64}{16}$ Inverse operation

$x = 4$

Check: $7x + 9x = 64$

$(7 \times 4) + (9 \times 4) = 64$

$28 + 36 = 64$

$64 = 64$ ✓

Example 2: Solve $21 = 2x + x$.

$21 = 2x + x$

$21 = 2x + 1x$ 1 is identity number for multiplication.

$21 = (2 + 1)x$ Distributive property

$21 = 3x$

$\dfrac{21}{3} = \dfrac{3x}{3}$ Inverse operation

$7 = x$

Check:

$21 = 2x + x$

$21 = (2 \times 7) + 7$

$21 = 14 + 7$

$21 = 21$ ✓

■ Exercises

Assignment Guide 3.4
Oral: 1–10
Written:
Min. 11–27 odd; Quiz, p. 79
Reg. 11–31 odd; Quiz, p. 79
Max. 11–37 odd; Quiz, p. 79

A Tell what number or variable should replace each ?.

1. $3(2 + 6) = (3 \times ?) + (3 \times 6)$ 2

2. $4(? + 8) = (4 \times 7) + (4 \times 8)$ 7

3. $(9 \times 6) + (9 \times 5) = 9(6 + ?)$ 5

4. $(8 \times 3) + (? \times 2) = 8(3 + 2)$ 8

5. $x + x = 1x + 1x = (? + 1)x$ 1

6. $4r + r = (4 + ?)r$ 1

7. $5x + 6x = (5 + 6)?$ x **8.** $8y + 16y = (? + 16)y$ 8

9. $10c + 3c = (10 + ?)c$ 3 **10.** $25d + 7d = (25 + 7)?$ d

Ⓑ Compute in two ways: **(a)** Add; then multiply.

                                  (b) Use the distributive property.

Example: **a.** $6(5 + 3)$ **b.** $6(5 + 3)$

                     $6(8)$ $(6 \times 5) + (6 \times 3)$

                      48 $30 \quad + \quad 18$

                                               48

11. $6(8 + 9)$ 102 **12.** $5(9 + 6)$ 75 **13.** $14(3 + 10)$ 182

14. $8(17 + 13)$ 240 **15.** $12(4 + 10)$ 168 **16.** $9(20 + 8)$ 252

Solve. (See Example 2.)

17. $7t + 2t = 72$ 8 **18.** $6c + 14c = 180$ 9

19. $198 = g + 8g$ 22 **20.** $300 = 57m + 43m$ 3

21. $16y + 34y = 2500$ 50 **22.** $2000 = 19n + n$ 100

23. $348 = 12a + 46a$ 6 **24.** $b + b = 420$ 210

Solve.

Example: $10x - 4x = 36$ *Check:* $10x - 4x = 36$

                 $(10 - 4)x = 36$ $(10 \times 6) - (4 \times 6) = 36$

                         $6x = 36$ $60 - 24 = 36$

                         $\dfrac{6x}{6} = \dfrac{36}{6}$ $36 = 36$ ✓

                           $x = 6$

25. $9a - 6a = 21$ 7 **26.** $12b - 7b = 25$ 5

27. $10c - c = 18$ 2 **28.** $30 = 25d - 10d$ 2

29. $18 = 20f - 11f$ 2 **30.** $17g - 7g = 100$ 10

31. $88 = 38h - 16h$ 4 **32.** $240 = 25j - j$ 10

C Solve.

Example:

$$5x + 3 + 2x + 6 = 23 \qquad \textit{Check:} \quad 5x + 3 + 2x + 6 = 23$$
$$(5x + 2x) + (3 + 6) = 23 \qquad (5 \times 2) + 3 + (2 \times 2) + 6 = 23$$
$$(5 + 2)x + 9 = 23 \qquad 10 + 3 + 4 + 6 = 23$$
$$7x + 9 - 9 = 23 - 9 \qquad (10 + 3) + (4 + 6) = 23$$
$$7x = 14 \qquad 13 + 10 = 23$$
$$\frac{7x}{7} = \frac{14}{7} \qquad 23 = 23 \checkmark$$
$$x = 2$$

33. $3a + 7 + 6a + 4 = 92$ ₉   **34.** $9b + 12 + 6b + 8 = 65$ ₃

35. $11c + 4 + 2c + 16 = 85$ ₅   **36.** $14d + 18 + 11d + 30 = 148$ ₄

37. $14x + 10 + x + 24 = 94$ ₄   **38.** $y + 23 + 7y + 14 = 237$ ₂₅

Quick Quiz Sections 3.1 to 3.4

Match each example with the property it illustrates.

1. $(3 \times 6) \times 4 = 3 \times (6 \times 4)$ c   **a.** commutative property of $\times$

2. $2 \times 5 = 5 \times 2$ a   **b.** distributive property

3. $9(8 + 7) = (9 \times 8) + (9 \times 7)$ b   **c.** associative property of $\times$

Solve.

4. $3 + a = 12$ 9   **5.** $30 = (m + 5) + 15$ 10

6. $36 = (6x)3$ 2   **7.** $22 \times 1 = y$ 22

8. $0 \times 25 = n$ 0   **9.** $32 + 0 = b$ 32

10. $18 \div 18 = f$ 1   **11.** $0 \div 17 = s$ 0

12. $5c + c = 60$ 10   **13.** $12h - 8h = 28$ 7

Factors and Divisibility

Camp Hiawatha's director has to buy tennis rackets for 48 girls. Each racket is to be shared by the same number of girls.

If the director buys 48 rackets, each girl gets a racket. If she buys 24 rackets, 2 girls share a racket. If she buys 16 rackets, 3 girls share a racket.

C. E. Pefley

48, 24, and 16 are *factors* of 48.

Suggested Class Time

Course	Min.	Reg.	Max.
Days	1	1	1

$$48 \times 1 = 48 \qquad 24 \times 2 = 48 \qquad 16 \times 3 = 48$$

factors of 48

| If two or more numbers are multiplied, each is a **factor** of the product.

Example 1: The director bought 12 rackets. Is 12 a factor of 48?

Yes, because $12 \times 4 = 48$.

Example 2: Find all the factors of 24.

$$
\begin{aligned}
24 &= 1 \times 24 \\
&= 2 \times 12 \\
&= 3 \times 8 \\
&= 4 \times 6
\end{aligned}
$$

factors of 24

| Listing all the ways to express a number as a product gives you all the factors of that number.

An easy way to check whether one whole number is a factor of another is by dividing. A number is *divisible* by each of its factors. That is, the quotient should be a whole number, and the remainder should be 0.

Example 3: Is 8 a factor of 96?

$96 \div 8 = 12$ 96 is divisible by 8.

So 8 is a factor of 96.

Example 4: Is 7 a factor of 96?

$96 \div 7 = 13 \text{ R}5$ 96 is not divisible by 7.

So 7 is not a factor of 96.

Assignment Guide 3.5
Oral: 1–14
Written: Min. 15–37 odd
        Reg. 15–43 odd
        Max. 15–49 odd

■ Exercises

A Find the factors of each number.

1–10. Answers at right below.

1. 6	**2.** 12	**3.** 8	**4.** 15	**5.** 21
6. 10	**7.** 18	**8.** 16	**9.** 20	**10.** 14

11. Is 7 a factor of 63? Yes

12. Is 9 a factor of 54? Yes

13. Is 6 a factor of 25? No

14. Is 11 a factor of 11? Yes

1. 1, 2, 3, 6
2. 1, 2, 3, 4, 6, 12
3. 1, 2, 4, 8
4. 1, 3, 5, 15
5. 1, 3, 7, 21
6. 1, 2, 5, 10
7. 1, 2, 3, 6, 9, 18
8. 1, 2, 4, 8, 16
9. 1, 2, 4, 5, 10, 20
10. 1, 2, 7, 14

B Divide to find whether 3 is a factor of each number.

15. 38 No   **16.** 117 Yes   **17.** 51 Yes   **18.** 144 Yes   **19.** 82 No

Divide to find whether 8 is a factor of each number.

20. 105 No   **21.** 216 Yes   **22.** 172 No   **23.** 87 No   **24.** 144 Yes

Express each number as the product of two factors other than 1.

25–34. Other answers possible.

Examples: $35 = 5 \times 7$ $20 = 2 \times 10 \text{ or } 4 \times 5$

25. 12 2×6 **26.** 16 8×2 **27.** 36 3×12 **28.** 32 4×8 **29.** 28 4×7

30. 45 5×9 **31.** 30 5×6 **32.** 70 7×10 **33.** 48 4×12 **34.** 26 2×13

Find all the factors you can for each number.

35. 26
1, 2, 13, 26

36. 27
1, 3, 9, 27

37. 33
1, 3, 11, 33

38. 35
1, 5, 7, 35

39. 32
1, 2, 4, 8, 16, 32

40. 28
1, 2, 4, 7, 14, 28

41. 25 1, 5, 25   **42.** 9 1, 3, 9   **43.** 13 1, 13   **44.** 17 1, 17

81

45. Write 18 as the product of three factors. Use factors other than 1.

$2 \times 3 \times 3$

46. Write 56 as the product of four factors. Use factors other than 1.

$2 \times 2 \times 2 \times 7$

47. Write 72 as the product of five factors. Use factors other than 1.

$2 \times 2 \times 2 \times 3 \times 3$

48. Write 37 as the product of two factors. 1×37

49. A number is a perfect number if the sum of its factors (other than the number itself) is that number.

Example : $\underbrace{1 + 2 + 3}_{\text{factors of 6}} = 6$, so 6 is a perfect number.

There is another perfect number under fifty. Try to find it.

$1 + 2 + 4 + 7 + 14 = 28$

50. 496 is a perfect number. Find its factors and prove that it is perfect.

$1 + 2 + 4 + 8 + 16 + 31 + 62 + 124 + 248 = 496$

Operation Decode

A spy intercepted this message: 426   7039   9240   91267.

The code below had previously been intercepted. It was known that the letter O is 3 and the letter A is 2. Find the number for each letter. Then decode the message given above.

CODE:

$$
\begin{array}{r}
\text{LOT} \\
\times \text{ALL} \\
\hline
\text{LOT} \\
\text{LOT} \\
\text{ANT} \\
\hline
\text{ASCOT}
\end{array}
\qquad
\begin{array}{r}
\text{ANT} \\
+ \text{LOT} \\
\hline
\text{OPT}
\end{array}
$$

CAN STOP PACT PLANS

3.6

Since a number is divisible by each of its factors, some rules for divisibility can help you find the factors of a number.

 A number is divisible by 2 if its last digit is even.

Example 1: Which of these numbers are divisible by 2?

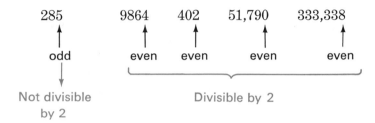

 A number is divisible by 3 if its digit sum is 3, 6, or 9.

Example 2: Which of these numbers are divisible by 3?

| 285 | 9864 | 402 | 51,790 | 333,338 |

Number	Add the digits.	If needed add again.
285	$2+8+5=15$	$1+5=6$
9864	$9+8+6+4=27$	$2+7=9$
402	$4+0+2=6$	
51,790	$5+1+7+9+0=22$	$2+2=4$
333,338	$3+3+3+3+3+8=23$	$2+3=5$

Digit sum

Divisible by 3

Not divisible by 3

 A number is divisible by 5 if its last digit is 0 or 5.
A number is divisible by 10 if its last digit is 0.

Example 3: Which of these numbers are divisible by 5? By 10?

Assignment Guide 3.6
Oral: 1–10
Written:
Min. 11–20
Reg. 11–18; 19–23 odd
Max. 11–23 odd; 24–29

285   9864   402   51,790   333,338

285 and 51,790 are divisible by 5.
51,790 is divisible by 10.

■ Exercises

[A] Which of these numbers are divisible by 2? By 3? By 5? By 10?

1. 84 _{2, 3} **2.** 205 ₅ **3.** 52 ₂ **4.** 2310 _{2, 3, 5, 10} **5.** 135 _{3, 5}

6. 77 None **7.** 110 _{2, 5, 10} **8.** 291 ₃ **9.** 450 _{2, 3, 5, 10} **10.** 111,111 ₃

[B] Which of these numbers are divisible by 2? By 3? By 5? By 10?
Use the rules for divisibility to help you.

11. 1560 _{2, 3, 5, 10} **12.** 5691 ₃ **13.** 2382 _{2, 3} **14.** 42,655 ₅

15. 12,345 _{3, 5} **16.** 711,026 ₂ **17.** 880,800 _{2, 3, 5, 10} **18.** 2,081,491 None

Find all the factors you can for each number.

19. 55 _{1, 5, 11, 55} **20.** 39 _{1, 3, 13, 39} **21.** 30 _{1, 2, 3, 5, 6, 10, 15, 30} **22.** 19 _{1, 19} **23.** 70 _{1, 2, 5, 7, 10, 14, 35, 70}

[C] To be divisible by 6, a number must be divisible by 2 and by 3.
Which of these numbers are divisible by 6?

24. 32,212 No **25.** 2916 Yes **26.** 22,440 Yes

27. 48,964 No **28.** 54,162 Yes **29.** 36,639 No

A Shorter Shortcut

When testing if a number is divisible by 3, you don't have to add all the digits. You can throw out all the 3's, 6's, and 9's. Now, a digit sum of 0 will also mean the number is divisible by 3.

Number	Throw out 3, 6, and 9.	Add digits.	If needed, add again.	
9864	9̶8̶6̶4̶	$8 + 4 = 12$	$1 + 2 = 3$ ◀—	Divisible by 3
333,338	3̶3̶3̶,3̶3̶8̶ ◀——————			Not divisible by 3
396	3̶9̶6̶ ◀———————			Divisible by 3

Primes and Composites

On TV, prime time is important because the biggest audience is tuned in. In mathematics, *prime numbers* are important because, among other things, they can be a big help when working with fractions.

The first ten prime numbers are

2, 3, 5, 7, 11, 13, 17, 19, 23, 29.

A whole number greater than 1 that has only 1 and itself as factors is a **prime number**.

The table below shows the ways to express each number from 2 to 9 as a product of its factors.

2	3	4	5	6	7	8	9
1×2	1×3	1×4	1×5	1×6	1×7	1×8	1×9
		2×2		2×3		2×4	3×3
						$2 \times 2 \times 2$	

Notice that each of the numbers 2, 3, 5, and 7 can be expressed as a product only one way—1 times the number. The numbers 2, 3, 5, and 7 are prime numbers. The numbers 4, 6, 8, and 9 are *composite numbers*.

A whole number greater than 1 that has at least one other factor besides itself and 1 is a **composite number**.

Example 1: Show that 24 can be written as a product of primes.

$$24 = 6 \times 4 \qquad\qquad 24 = 8 \times 3 \qquad\qquad 24 = 12 \times 2$$
$$= (2 \times 3) \times (2 \times 2) \qquad = (2 \times 2 \times 2) \times 3 \qquad = (3 \times 2 \times 2) \times 2$$
$$= 2 \times 3 \times 2 \times 2 \qquad\quad = 2 \times 2 \times 2 \times 3 \qquad\quad = 3 \times 2 \times 2 \times 2$$

Notice that each way yields the same prime factors.

Every composite number can be expressed as a product of prime numbers in only one way. This product of prime numbers is the **prime factorization** of the composite number.

Factor trees aid in finding the prime factorization of a number.

Example 2: Find the prime factorization of 210.

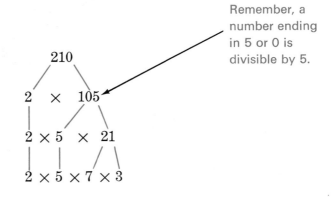

Remember, a number ending in 5 or 0 is divisible by 5.

So $210 = 2 \times 5 \times 7 \times 3$.

Example 3: Find the prime factorization of 396.

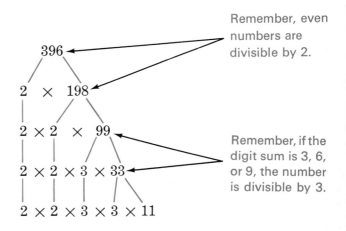

Remember, even numbers are divisible by 2.

Remember, if the digit sum is 3, 6, or 9, the number is divisible by 3.

So $396 = 2 \times 2 \times 3 \times 3 \times 11$.

Exercises

Assignment Guide 3.7
Oral: 1–7
Written:
Min. 8–27
Reg. 8–19; 21–37 odd
Max. 9–37 odd; 38–42

[A] Use the chart below to tell whether each number is prime or composite.

1. 10 C   **2.** 11 P   **3.** 12 C   **4.** 13 P   **5.** 14 C   **6.** 15 C   **7.** 16 C

10	11	12	13	14	15	16
1×10	1×11	1×12	1×13	1×14	1×15	1×16
2×5		2×6		2×7	3×5	2×8
		3×4				4×4
		$2 \times 2 \times 3$				$2 \times 2 \times 4$
						$2 \times 2 \times 2 \times 2$

[B] Tell whether each number is prime or composite.

8. 33 C   **9.** 17 P   **10.** 52 C   **11.** 30 C   **12.** 23 P   **13.** 19 P

14. 40 C   **15.** 45 C   **16.** 51 C   **17.** 49 C   **18.** 29 P   **19.** 77 C

Give the prime factorization of each number.
20–37. Answers at right.

20. 18	**21.** 26	**22.** 20	**23.** 22	**24.** 25	**25.** 35
26. 34	**27.** 27	**28.** 48	**29.** 36	**30.** 39	**31.** 49
32. 40	**33.** 144	**34.** 98	**35.** 225	**36.** 126	**37.** 585

20. $2 \times 3 \times 3$
21. 2×13
22. $2 \times 2 \times 5$
23. 2×11
24. 5×5
25. 5×7
26. 2×17
27. $3 \times 3 \times 3$
28. $2 \times 2 \times 2 \times 2 \times 3$
29. $2 \times 2 \times 3 \times 3$
30. 3×13
31. 7×7
32. $2 \times 2 \times 2 \times 5$
33. $2 \times 2 \times 2 \times 2 \times 3 \times 3$
34. $2 \times 7 \times 7$
35. $3 \times 3 \times 5 \times 5$
36. $2 \times 3 \times 3 \times 7$
37. $3 \times 3 \times 5 \times 13$

[C] Here's a way to find all the primes less than 100.

38. Write a list of all whole numbers from 2 to 100.

39. The first prime is 2. So cross off every second number after 2. That is, cross off 4, 6, 8, and so on (because they contain 2 as a factor).

40. The next prime is 3. So cross off every third number after 3. That is, cross off 6, 9, 12, and so on. (Why?) Because they contain 3 as a factor

41. The next prime is 5. So cross off every fifth number after 5.

42. What's the next prime? What numbers do you cross off now?
7   Every seventh number after 7

All numbers left not crossed off are prime numbers.

PRIMES: 2, 3, 5, 7, 11, 13, 17, 19, 23, 29, 31, 37, 41, 43, 47, 53, 59, 61, 67, 71, 73, 79, 83, 89, 97

3.8 Exponents and Powers

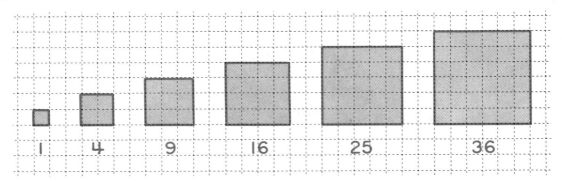

1, 4, 9, 16, 25, and 36 are **square numbers.** Each can be written as the product of two equal factors or as a power.

Number	Equal factors	Power
1	1×1	1^2
4	2×2	2^2
9	3×3	3^2

Number	Equal factors	Power
16	4×4	4^2
25	5×5	5^2
36	6×6	6^2

$2 = 2^1$ *two to the first power*

$2 \times 2 = 2^2$ *two squared* or *two to the second power*

$2 \times 2 \times 2 = 2^3$ *two cubed* or *two to the third power*

$2 \times 2 \times 2 \times 2 = 2^4$ *two to the fourth power*

$2 \times 2 \times 2 \times 2 \times 2 = 2^5$ *two to the fifth power*

Base — (The number used as a factor) 2^4 Exponent — (Number of times the base is a factor)

Example 1:   Write $n \times n \times n \times n \times n$ using exponents.

Since n is a factor 5 times, $n \times n \times n \times n \times n = n^5$.

Example 2: Express 3^4 as a product of factors. Then find the value of 3^4.

$$3^4 = 3 \times 3 \times 3 \times 3 = 81$$

Example 3: Find the cube of 4.

$$4^3 = 4 \times 4 \times 4 = 64$$

Example 4: Find the prime factorization of 72. Write the answer using exponents.

$$72 = 8 \times 9$$
$$= (2 \times 2 \times 2) \times (3 \times 3)$$
$$= 2^3 \times 3^2$$

Example 5: Express the prime factorization of 300 using exponents.

$$300 = 3 \times 100$$
$$= 3 \times (10 \times 10)$$
$$= 3 \times (5 \times 2) \times (5 \times 2)$$
$$= 3 \times (5 \times 5) \times (2 \times 2) \quad \text{Like factors have been grouped.}$$
$$= 3^1 \times 5^2 \times 2^2$$

If the exponent is 1, it does not have to be written.

$$= 2^2 \times 3 \times 5^2 \quad \text{Factors have been arranged from least to greatest.}$$

■ **Exercises**

Assignment Guide 3.8
Oral: 1–16
Written: Min. 17–35 odd
Reg. 17–39 odd
Max. 17–39 odd;
40–44

Ⓐ Tell how to read each expression. Then name the base and the exponent. 1–5. Answers at right.

1. 6^1 **2.** 10^4 **3.** 4^{10} **4.** x^5 **5.** 11^2

1. Six to the first power; base 6; exp. 1
2. Ten to the fourth power; base 10; exp. 4
3. Four to the tenth power; base 4; exp. 10
4. x to the fifth power; base x; exp. 5
5. Eleven squared or eleven to the second power; base 11; exp. 2

Express the following using exponents.

6. $1 \times 1 \times 1 \times 1 \times 1 \times 1$ 1^6 **7.** $x \times x \times x \times x \times x \times x \times x \times x$ x^8

8. $z \times z \times z \times z$ z^4 **9.** $5 \times 5 \times 5 \times 5 \times 5$ 5^5

Find the square of each number.

10. 7 $_{49}$ **11.** 8 $_{64}$ **12.** 9 $_{81}$ **13.** 10 $_{100}$ **14.** 12 $_{144}$

89

15. Does 2^3 equal 3^2? No

16. Does 3×4 equal 4^3? No

B Find the cube of each number.

17. 2 8 **18.** 3 27 **19.** 1 1 **20.** 5 125 **21.** 6 216 **22.** 8 512

Find the value of each expression.

23. 2^4 16 **24.** 2^5 32 **25.** 2^1 2 **26.** 1^8 1 **27.** 10^6 1,000,000

28. five to the fourth power 625

Express the prime factorization of each number using exponents. List the factors from least to greatest.

29. 54 2×3^3 **30.** 75 3×5^2 **31.** 88 $2^3 \times 11$ **32.** 196 $2^2 \times 7^2$ **33.** 288 $2^5 \times 3^2$

34. 720 $2^4 \times 3^2 \times 5$ **35.** 1250 2×5^4 **36.** 1053 $3^4 \times 13$ **37.** 1400 $2^3 \times 5^2 \times 7$ **38.** 1575 $3^2 \times 5^2 \times 7$

39. Does $2^2 + 3^2 = (2 + 3)^2$? No

C Compute the squares of these numbers.

40. 11 121 **41.** 111 12,321 **42.** 1111 1,234,321 **43.** 11,111 123,454,321

44. Predict the square of 111,111. 12,345,654,321

Complete these statements.

45. $1^3 + 2^3 = (1 + \underline{\quad})^2$ 2

46. $1^3 + 2^3 + 3^3 = (1 + 2 + \underline{\quad})^2$ 3

47. $1^3 + 2^3 + 3^3 + 4^3 = (\underline{\quad} + \underline{\quad} + \underline{\quad} + \underline{\quad})^2$ 1; 2; 3; 4

Find each exponent. Recall that $2^5 = 32$ and $2^6 = 64$.

48. $2^2 \times 2^3 = 2^?$ 5

49. $(2^3)^2 = 8^2 = 2^?$ 6

50. $(2^2)^3 = 4^3 = 2^?$ 6

Greatest Common Factor

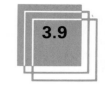

3.9

When you are simplifying fractions, you often need to find the *greatest common factor (GCF)* of the numerator and the denominator.

 The **GCF** of two or more numbers is the greatest number that is a factor of each number.

Prime factorization can help you find the GCF of two or more numbers.

Example 1: Find the GCF of 36 and 24.

$36 = 6 \times 6 = 3 \times 2 \times 3 \times 2 = 2^2 \times 3^2$

$24 = 3 \times 8 = 3 \times 2 \times 2 \times 2 = 2^3 \times 3$

—— 3 is a common factor once.
—— 2 is a common factor twice.

$2^2 \times 3 = 12$ ◀ GCF

To find the GCF of two or more numbers, find the smallest power of each *common* prime factor and multiply these powers.

Example 2: Find the GCF of 16 and 40.

$16 = 2 \times 8 = 2 \times 2 \times 2 \times 2 = 2^4$

$40 = 10 \times 4 = 2 \times 5 \times 2 \times 2 = 2^3 \times 5$

$2^3 = 8$ ◀ GCF

Example 3: Find the GCF of 49 and 30.

$49 = 7 \times 7$

$30 = 5 \times 6 = 5 \times 3 \times 2$

There are no common prime factors. Since 1 is a factor of every number, 1 is the GCF.

Example 4 : Find the GCF of 45, 75, and 120.

$$45 = 5 \times 9 = 5 \times 3 \times 3 \qquad\qquad = \quad 3^2 \times 5$$

$$75 = 3 \times 25 = 3 \times 5 \times 5 \qquad\qquad = \quad 3 \times 5^2$$

$$120 = 10 \times 12 = 2 \times 5 \times 3 \times 2 \times 2 = 2^3 \times 3 \times 5$$

$$3 \times 5 = 15 \quad \blacktriangleleft \text{GCF}$$

■ Exercises

A What is the GCF of each pair of numbers?

Assignment Guide 3.9
Oral: 1–9
Written: Min. 10–20
        Reg. 10–24
        Max. 10–27

1. $3 = 3$
$12 = 2^2 \times 3$ 3

2. $6 = 2 \times 3$
$18 = 2 \times 3^2$ 6

3. $3 = 3$
$7 = 7$ 1

4. $4 = 2^2$
$10 = 2 \times 5$ 2

5. $12 = 2^2 \times 3$
$18 = 2 \times 3^2$ 6

6. $66 = 2 \times 3 \times 11$
$77 = 7 \times 11$ 11

7. $27 = 3^3$
$39 = 3 \times 13$ 3

8. $9 = 3^2$
$16 = 2^4$ 1

9. $28 = 2^2 \times 7$
$52 = 2^2 \times 13$ 4

B Find the GCF of each set of numbers.

10. 30 and 50 10
11. 36 and 45 9
12. 34 and 85 17

13. 24 and 66 6
14. 3 and 19 1
15. 42 and 116 2

16. 38 and 57 19
17. 100 and 625 25
18. 198 and 396 198

19. 4, 8, and 24 4
20. 27, 54, and 108 27
21. 90 and 126 18

22. 50, 78, and 112 2
23. 16, 96, and 108 4
24. 33, 42, and 90 3

C **25.** 400, 696, and 1960 8
26. 128, 256, and 640 128

27. When is the GCF of two numbers equal to the lesser of the two numbers? When one number is a factor of the other

Least Common Multiple

3.10

Since $2 \times 3 = 6$, we say 2 and 3 are factors of 6. We also say 6 is a **multiple** of 2 and 3.

$$2 \times 3 = 6$$

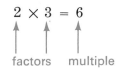

factors   multiple

	×1	×2	×3	×4	×5	×6	×7	×8	×9	×10 ···
Multiples of 2	2	4	6	8	10	12	14	16	18	20 ···
Multiples of 3	3	6	9	12	15	18	21	24	27	30 ···

Notice that 6, 12, and 18 are *common multiples* of 2 and 3. Later, in working with fractions, it will help to find the *least common multiple* (LCM). The LCM of 2 and 3 is 6.

> The LCM of two or more numbers is the least nonzero number that has each given number as a factor.

Example 1: Find the LCM of 36 and 24.

$$36 = 2 \times 2 \times 3 \times 3 = 2^2 \times 3^2$$
$$24 = 2 \times 2 \times 2 \times 3 = 2^3 \times 3$$

3 must be included twice.
2 must be included three times.

$$2^3 \times 3^2 = 72 \quad \blacktriangleleft LCM$$

> To find the LCM of two or more numbers, find the largest power of each prime factor and multiply these powers.

93

Example 2: Find the LCM of 15 and 45.

$$15 = 5 \times 3 \qquad = \boxed{3} \times \boxed{5}$$
$$45 = 5 \times 3 \times 3 = \boxed{3^2} \times \boxed{5}$$

$$3^2 \times 5 = 45 \quad \blacktriangleleft \text{LCM}$$

Example 3: Find the LCM of 15 and 8.

$$15 = 5 \times 3 \qquad = \qquad \boxed{3 \times 5}$$
$$8 = 2 \times 2 \times 2 = \boxed{2^3}$$

$$2^3 \times 3 \times 5 = 120 \quad \blacktriangleleft \text{LCM}$$

Example 4: Find the LCM of 18, 27, and 30.

Assignment Guide 3.10
Oral: 1–9
Written: Min. 10–18; 21
       Reg. 10–24
       Max. 11–31 odd; 32

$$18 = 3 \times 3 \times 2 = \boxed{2} \times \boxed{3^2}$$
$$27 = 3 \times 3 \times 3 = \qquad \boxed{3^3}$$
$$30 = 3 \times 2 \times 5 = \boxed{2} \times \boxed{3} \times \boxed{5}$$

$$2 \times 3^3 \times 5 = 270 \quad \blacktriangleleft \text{LCM}$$

▪ Exercises

A Find the LCM of each pair of numbers.

1. $4 = \boxed{2^2}$
   $6 = \boxed{2} \times \boxed{3}$ 12

2. $7 = \boxed{7}$
   $21 = \boxed{3} \times \boxed{7}$ 21

3. $4 = \boxed{2^2}$
   $15 = \boxed{3} \times \boxed{5}$ 60

4. $6 = \boxed{2} \times \boxed{3}$
   $48 = \boxed{2^4} \times \boxed{3}$ 48

5. $18 = \boxed{2} \times \boxed{3^2}$
   $24 = \boxed{2^3} \times \boxed{3}$ 72

6. $20 = \boxed{2^2} \times \boxed{5}$
   $35 = \boxed{5} \times \boxed{7}$ 140

7. $8 = \boxed{2^3}$
   $32 = \boxed{2^5}$ 32

8. $20 = \boxed{2^2} \times \boxed{5}$
   $40 = \boxed{2^3} \times \boxed{5}$ 40

9. $3 = \boxed{3}$
   $10 = \boxed{2} \times \boxed{5}$ 30

B Find the LCM of each set of numbers.

10. 9 and 36   36

11. 5 and 7   35

12. 35 and 12   420

13. 16 and 80   80

14. 18 and 32   288

15. 25 and 49   1225

94

16. 18 and 45 90   **17.** 36 and 72 72   **18.** 7, 21, and 84 84

19. 30 and 105 210   **20.** 39 and 26 78   **21.** 3, 4, and 6 12

22. 11, 33, and 44 132   **23.** 15, 75, and 50 150   **24.** 3, 5, and 7 105

C **25.** When is the LCM of a set of numbers equal to the greatest number in the set? When each number is a factor of the greatest number

Find the LCM of each set of numbers. You can leave the answer written as a product of powers.

26. 20, 90, and 36   **27.** 30, 40, 48, and 60   **28.** 144, 24, 18, and 72 $2^4 \times 3^2$ or 144
$2^2 \times 3^2 \times 5$ or 180 $2^4 \times 3 \times 5$ or 240

29. 66, 96, and 54   **30.** 28, 68, 88, and 110   **31.** 38, 42, 57, and 95 $2 \times 3 \times 5 \times 7 \times 19$
$2^5 \times 3^3 \times 11$ or 9504 $2^3 \times 5 \times 7 \times 11 \times 17$ or 52,360   or 3990

32. When is the LCM of two numbers the product of the numbers?
When the numbers have no common prime factors

LCM's Around You

1. Cartons 24 inches tall are being stacked next to cartons 36 inches tall. What is the shortest height at which the stacks will be the same height? 72 in.

2. The 17-year cicada is an insect that spends its preadult life underground. It appears aboveground as an adult only once every 17 years. Another breed of cicada appears every 13 years. If both breeds appear this year, how many years will pass before they again appear in the same year? 221 years

3. Susan, George, and Dick have part-time jobs after school. Susan works every other day, George works every third day, and Dick works every fourth day. If all three of them start work on the same day, in how many working days will they again all be working on the same day? 12 days

4. Some people think they can tell what kind of day they are going to have by checking their biorhythm cycles. There are three cycles. One is a 23-day physical cycle, another is a 28-day emotional cycle, and the third is a 33-day intellectual cycle. If all three cycles start on the day a person is born, how many days will it take before all three cycles again start on the same day? 21,252 days

© Alvin E. Staffan
from National Audubon Society

Terms and Symbols Review

Complete each sentence. Choose from these words.

Suggested Class Time

Course	Min.	Reg.	Max.
Days	2	1	1

associative   *commutative*   *distributive*   *identity*

1. Zero is the ____ number for addition. Identity

2. $7 \times 3 = 3 \times 7$ illustrates that multiplication is ____. Commutative

3. $(7 + 5) + 9 = 7 + (5 + 9)$ illustrates that addition is <u>Associative</u>.

4. $(9 \times 6) + (9 \times 5) = 9(6 + 5)$ illustrates the ____ property of multiplication over addition. Distributive

Choose the best term.

5. 2 is (<u>a factor of</u>, *divisible by*, *a multiple of*) 10.

6. (3×4, $3 \times 3 \times 2$, <u>$3 \times 2 \times 2$</u>) is the prime factorization of 12.

7. (<u>13</u>, *14*, *15*) is a prime number.

8. In the expression 3^5, 3 is the (<u>base</u>, *exponent*).

9. 6^2 is read (*two to the sixth power*, <u>six to the second power</u>).

10. 8 is the (<u>LCM</u>, *GCF*) of 2 and 8.

11. 2 is the (*LCM*, <u>GCF</u>) of 2 and 8.

Assignment Guide Rev.
Oral: Terms & Symbols 1–11
Written:
Min. (day 1) 1–36
    (day 2) 37–65
Reg. 1–63 odd; 64
Max. 1–63 odd; 64

Chapter 3 Review

3.1   For each equation, use the commutative property to write a new equation. Then solve.

1. $5 + x = 11$ $x + 5 = 11$; 6   **2.** $8 + y = 10$ $y + 8 = 10$; 2

3. $z \times 6 = 96$ $6z = 96$; 16   **4.** $r \times 5 = 85$ $5r = 85$; 17

Compute. Use the properties to make the computation easy. 3.2

5. $16 + 14 + 39$ 69

6. $29 + 83 + 17$ 129

7. $6 \times 5 \times 7$ 210

8. $69 \times 25 \times 4$ 6900

Solve.

9. $(a + 5) + 7 = 25$ 13

10. $78 = (3x)2$ 13

11. $1 \times 16 = x$ 16

12. $16 \div 16 = r$ 1 3.3

13. $0 \times 48 = y$ 0

14. $8 + 0 = s$ 8

15. $0 \div 96 = r$ 0

16. $32 \times 1 = t$ 32

17. $c = 7(19 + 21)$ 280

18. $q = (9 \times 16) + (9 \times 34)$ 450 3.4

19. $7r + 2r = 99$ 11

20. $10y - y = 18$ 2

21. $16n + 14n = 300$ 10

22. $19s - 7s = 48$ 4

Find all the factors you can for each number. 3.5

23. 34 1, 2, 17, 34

24. 4 1, 2, 4

25. 30 1, 2, 3, 5, 6, 10, 15, 30

26. 19 1, 19

Divide to find whether 7 is a factor of each number.

27. 54 No

28. 98 Yes

29. 105 Yes

30. 121 No

Which of these numbers are divisible by 2? By 3? By 5? By 10? 3.6

31. 870 2, 3, 5, 10

32. 3025 5

33. 192 2, 3

34. 61,215 3, 5

35. 7312 2

36. 45,100 2, 5, 10

Tell whether each number is prime or composite. 3.7

37. 23 P

38. 51 C

39. 17 P

40. 39 C

Find the prime factorization of each number.

41. 46 2×23

42. 56 $2 \times 2 \times 2 \times 7$

43. 81 $3 \times 3 \times 3 \times 3$

44. 65 5×13

Express the following using exponents.

45. $5 \times 5 \times 5 \times 5 \times 5 \times 5$ 5^6 **46.** $y \times y \times y$ y^3

47. $9 \times 9 \times 9 \times 9 \times 2 \times 2$ **48.** the prime factorization of 72
$9^4 \times 2^2$ $2^3 \times 3^2$

Find the value of each expression.

49. the cube of 9 729   **50.** the square of 13 169   **51.** 3^1 3   **52.** 1^7 1

Find the GCF of each set of numbers.

53. 63 and 84 21   **54.** 32 and 51 1   **55.** 22, 66, and 33 11

56. 29 and 75 1   **57.** 100, 50, and 6 2   **58.** 68 and 85 17

59. When is the GCF of two numbers equal to 1?
When the numbers have no common prime factors

Find the LCM of each set of numbers.

60. 23 and 92 92   **61.** 64 and 96 192   **62.** 35 and 9 315

63. 75 and 45 225   **64.** 6, 50, and 100 300   **65.** 68 and 85 340

Match each example with the property it illustrates.

1. $14 + (6 + 9) = (14 + 6) + 9$ c   **a.** commutative property of $+$

2. $126 + 621 = 621 + 126$ a   **b.** distributive property

3. $(9 \times 7) + (9 \times 4) = 9(7 + 4)$ b   **c.** associative property of $+$

Assignment Guide Test
Written: 1–32

Solve.

4. $295 \times 1 = v$ 295   **5.** $1 \times 85 = x$ 85   **6.** $76 \times 0 = t$ 0

7. $85 + 0 = k$ 85   **8.** $0 \div 96 = c$ 0   **9.** $26 \div 26 = b$ 1

10. $(36 + 14) + 39 = r$ 89   **11.** $4(5 \times 9) = s$ 180

12. $(5x)3 = 90$ 6   **13.** $6r + 2r = 96$ 12

14. $16m + m = 34$ 2   **15.** $16n - 11n = 50$ 10

Find all the factors you can for each number.

16. 11   1, 11   **17.** 20   1, 2, 4, 5, 10, 20   **18.** 22   1, 2, 11, 22

19. Is 620 divisible by 2? By 3? By 5? By 10?   Yes; No; Yes; Yes

Tell whether each number is prime or composite.

20. 39   C   **21.** 19   P   **22.** 29   P

Write the prime factorization of each number using exponents.

23. 60 $2^2 \times 3 \times 5$ **24.** 54 2×3^3 **25.** 72 $2^3 \times 3^2$

Find the value of each expression.

26. two to the fourth power   16   **27.** the square of 15   225   **28.** 6^1 6

Find the GCF of each pair of numbers.

29. 8 and 15   1   **30.** 24 and 36   12

Find the LCM of each set of numbers.

31. 28 and 40   280   **32.** 6, 9, and 18   18

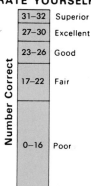

RATE YOURSELF

Number Correct	
31–32	Superior
27–30	Excellent
23–26	Good
17–22	Fair
0–16	Poor

MATH IN
LANDSCAPING

Courtesy Illinois Bell Telephone

A tree mover knows it is important to keep as much of the root system as possible when transplanting a tree. However, a large root ball adds weight and expense.

To compute the weight of a balled tree, use the following formula.

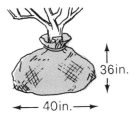

weight (lb)   height of ball (in.)

$$W = (d^2 \times h) \div 20$$

diameter of ball (in.)

You would proceed as follows to compute the weight of a balled tree where the diameter of the ball is $3\frac{1}{3}$ feet (40 inches) and the height of the ball is 3 feet (36 inches).

36 in.

40 in.

$$W = (d^2 \times h) \div 20$$
$$= (40^2 \times 36) \div 20$$
$$= 2880$$

The weight is 2880 pounds.

Compute the weight of each balled tree indicated in the table.

Diameter of ball	Height of ball	Weight of balled tree
20 in.	18 in.	——— 360 lb
60 in.	48 in.	——— 8640 lb
3 ft	$2\frac{1}{2}$ ft	——— 1944 lb

TRY A NEW TWIST

Before doing the activities on this page, you will need to do the following.

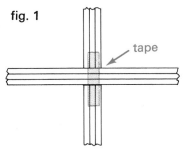
fig. 1

tape

1. Take a sheet or two of notebook paper and cut along every third line from the bottom until you have 13 strips of paper. Each strip will have 2 lines and 3 spaces on it.

2. Use 10 of the strips to make 5 crosses like the one in fig. 1.

fig. 2

Activity 1

A. Take one of the leftover strips and connect the ends to make a ring. (See fig. 2.) *Bisect* the ring by cutting between the lines on the ring. (See fig. 2.) What happens?
 You get 2 separate rings.

B. Take another of the leftover strips and give it a twist as in fig. 3. Then connect the ends to make a ring with a twist in it. Bisect the ring. What happens? You get a larger twisted ring.

fig. 3
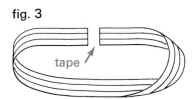
tape

C. Make another ring with a twist in it. *Trisect* the ring by cutting along the lines on the ring. (See fig. 4.) What happens?
 You get 2 linked twisted rings, one larger than the other.

fig. 4
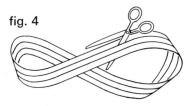

Activity 2

A. Take one of the crosses and make a ring without a twist with each strip. (See fig. 5. You will have two connected rings.) Bisect each ring. What happens? You get a square.

fig. 5
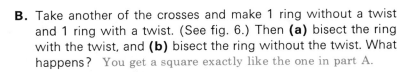

B. Take another of the crosses and make 1 ring without a twist and 1 ring with a twist. (See fig. 6.) Then **(a)** bisect the ring with the twist, and **(b)** bisect the ring without the twist. What happens? You get a square exactly like the one in part A.

C. Repeat part **B,** but do **(b)** first; then do **(a)**. Are activities **(a)** and **(b)** commutative? Yes (You get the same result as in part B.)

D. Make another figure like the one in fig. 6. Then **(c)** trisect the ring with the twist, and **(b)** bisect the ring without the twist. What happens? You get a square linked with a twisted ring.

fig. 6
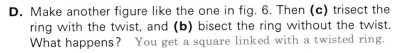
twist

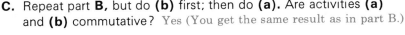
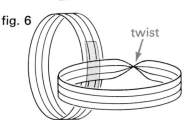

E. Repeat part **D,** but do **(b)** first, then do **(c)**. Are activities **(b)** and **(c)** commutative? No (You don't get the same result as in part D; you get a square and a separate strip.)

101

Terms and Symbols Review: Chapters 1–3

Ch. 1 Which term or symbol in parentheses is the best choice?

1. The (*liter*, *meter*, *gram*) is a metric unit of capacity.

2. The degree Celsius is the metric unit of (*angle measure*, *length*, *temperature*).

3. The prefix (*kilo-*, *centi-*, *milli-*) means "thousand."

4. The symbol (*m*, *mm*, *mg*) stands for a metric unit of weight.

5. The symbol ($<$, $>$, $=$) is read "is greater than."

6. To solve an open sentence means to find the (*replacement set*, *variable*, *solution set*).

7. A formula is a rule written as (*an inequality*, *an equation*, *a mathematical sentence*).

Ch. 2 What term best completes each statement?

8. Addition and _____ are inverse operations. Subtraction

9. If the replacement set is the whole numbers, the graph of $x < 5$ contains _____ points. 5

10. Pounds and ounces are units for measuring _____. Weight

11. The degree Fahrenheit is a unit for measuring _____. Temperature

12. Pints and quarts are units for measuring _____. Capacity

13. Inches and miles are units for measuring _____. Length

Ch. 3 Which lettered choice best matches each numbered item?

14. Associative property of $\times$ c

15. Commutative property of $\times$ g

16. Distributive property   a

17. A factor of 16   h

18. The GCF of 5 and 10   e

19. The prime factorization of 700   d

20. The exponent in the expression 2^{10} f

a. $3k + 7k = (3 + 7)k$

b. $4 \times 25 \times 7$

c. $3(5x) = (3 \times 5)x$

d. $2^2 \times 5^2 \times 7$

e. 5

f. 10

g. $b \times 5 = 5b$

h. 2

1. Your pencil is (_more_, _less_) than 1 centimeter long.

2. You are (_more_, _less_) than 1 meter tall.

Ch. 1

Find each value.

3. $6 + 8 \div 2$ 10

4. $3 + (2 \times 3) \times 2$ 15

5. $(n + 3) \times 6$ if n is replaced with 2   30

6. $4 + 7x$ if x is replaced with 3   25

Translate into symbols.

7. seven minus twice x $7 - 2x$

8. Divide a number n by ten. $\frac{n}{10}$ or $n \div 10$

9. Nine divided into a number b is less than seventy. $b \div 9 < 70$ or $\frac{b}{9} < 70$

10. The product of five and a number p is sixty. $5p = 60$

Classify as _True_, _False_, or _Open_.

11. $48 \div 12 = 4$ T

12. $9n < 23$ O

13. $21 \div 7 > 2$ T

Solve. Use $\{1, 2, 3, 4\}$ as the replacement set.

14. $2x + 1 > 9$ $\varnothing$

15. $7n - 5 < 10$ 1, 2

16. $6 < 2n - 1$ 4

17. $a + 5 = 7$ 2

18. $13 = n + 9$ 4

19. $x + 21 = 35$ $\varnothing$

20. Use the formula $m = c \div 100$ to find how many meters equals 31 300 centimeters.   313 m

Simplify.

Ch. 2

21. $13 - 7 + 7$ 13

22. $17 \times 5 \div 5$ 17

23. $42 + 8 - 8$ 42

Solve.

24. $x + 7 = 38$ 31

25. $4 = n - 18$ 22

26. $\frac{r}{4} = 8$ 32

27. $\frac{r}{6} = 15$ 90

28. $5a = 315$ 63

29. $52 = 4z$ 13

30. $6 = n - 3$ 9

31. $2x + 5 = 13$ 4

32. $5 = \frac{n + 4}{3}$ 11

Solve and graph.

33. $9 < y + 4$ $5 < y$ **34.** $7n < 35$ $n < 5$ **35.** $\frac{r}{2} < 1$ $r < 2$

Complete.

36. 6 ft = ____ in. 72 **37.** 48 oz = ____ lb 3 **38.** 8 qt = ____ gal. 2

39. Find the area of a rectangle with length 21 cm and width 17 cm.
357 cm²

40. Find the volume of a rectangular solid with length 7 ft, width 3 ft, and height 16 ft. 336 cu ft

41. Translate into symbols: The sum of a number and twice that same number is twenty-one. Let n = the number; $n + 2n = 21$

Ch. 3   Solve.

42. $6 + a = 25$ 19 **43.** $b \times 4 = 36$ 9 **44.** $29 = (c + 10) + 15$ 4

45. $(10d)8 = 160$ 2 **46.** $1 \times 25 = e$ 25 **47.** $f = 0 + 19$ 19

48. $g = 0 \div 21$ 0 **49.** $h = 31 \div 31$ 1 **50.** $17 \times 0 = j$ 0

51. $12k + 6k = 54$ 3 **52.** $5m + m = 42$ 7 **53.** $18n - 10n = 96$ 12

54. Find all the factors you can for 36. 1, 2, 3, 4, 6, 9, 12, 18, 36

55. Is 450 divisible by 2? By 3? By 5? By 10?
Yes   Yes   Yes   Yes

56. Tell whether each number is prime or composite.

   a. 30 C   **b.** 17 P   **c.** 29 P

57. Write the prime factorization of 72 using exponents. $2^3 \times 3^2$

58. Find the value of each expression.

   a. 5^1 5   **b.** the cube of 3 27   **c.** two to the fourth power 16

59. Find the GCF of 24 and 36. 12

60. Find the LCM of 5, 6, and 10. 30

Getting Ready for Chapter 4

Assignment Guide GR 4
Written: Min. 1–28

Find each remainder.

1. $6\overline{)13}$ 1

2. $32 \div 5$ 2

3. $52 \div 16$ 4

Find the prime factorization of each number.   3.7

4. 8 2^3

5. 9 3^2

6. 10 2×5

7. 14 2×7

8. 16 2^4

9. 20 $2^2 \times 5$

10. 24 $2^3 \times 3$

11. 25 5^2

Find the GCF of each pair of numbers.   3.9

12. $12 = 2^2 \times 3$

$18 = 2 \times 3^2$ 6

13. $15 = 3 \times 5$

$30 = 2 \times 3 \times 5$ 15

14. 6 and 9   3

15. 5 and 10   5

16. 3 and 7   1

17. 12 and 15   3

18. 21 and 28   7

19. 16 and 24   8

20. When is the GCF of two numbers equal to 1?   When the numbers have no common prime factors

Find the LCM of each pair of numbers.   3.10

21. $6 = 3 \times 2$

$8 = 2^3$ 24

22. $5 = 5$

$9 = 3^2$ 45

23. 3 and 4   12

24. 12 and 18   36

25. 6 and 10   30

26. 8 and 24   24

27. 4 and 5   20

28. 7 and 35   35

4

Arthur Lavine from De Wys

4 FRACTIONS AND MIXED NUMBERS

Many different kinds of workers are in the building trades. There are carpenters, plasterers, tile setters, electricians, plumbers. . . . The list goes on and on. When reading building plans and when making measurements, these workers often use fractions and mixed numbers.

Everyone uses fractions and mixed numbers at one time or another. In this chapter you will learn how and when to use them.

Meaning of Fractions

Fractions are used to indicate amounts.

$\frac{5}{8}$ of the pie   and $\frac{3}{2}$ quarts of milk   are gone.

Fractions are also used to indicate division. For this reason, *0 is never a denominator.*

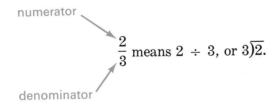

numerator

denominator

$\frac{2}{3}$ means $2 \div 3$, or $3\overline{)2}$.

Example 1: Express $7 \div 4$, $3\overline{)1}$, and $6 \div 1$ as fractions.

$$7 \div 4 = \frac{7}{4}$$

$$3\overline{)1} = \frac{1}{3}$$

$$6 \div 1 = \frac{6}{1}$$

Any whole number *n* divided by 1 equals itself. So

$\frac{n}{1} = n \div 1 = n.$ *Example:* $\frac{3}{1} = 3 \div 1 = 3$

Example 2: Express 2, 5, and 9 as fractions.

$$2 = \frac{2}{1} \qquad\qquad 5 = \frac{5}{1} \qquad\qquad 9 = \frac{9}{1}$$

Fractions that express the same amount are **equivalent**. In the diagram, $\frac{1}{2}$, $\frac{2}{4}$, and $\frac{4}{8}$ are equivalent.

Example 3: Use the rulers at right to find fractions equivalent to $\frac{1}{4}$, $\frac{6}{8}$, 1, $\frac{5}{4}$, and $\frac{6}{4}$.

$$\frac{1}{4} = \frac{2}{8} \qquad \frac{6}{8} = \frac{3}{4}$$

$$1 = \frac{2}{2} = \frac{4}{4} = \frac{8}{8}$$

$$\frac{5}{4} = \frac{10}{8} \qquad \frac{6}{4} = \frac{3}{2} = \frac{12}{8}$$

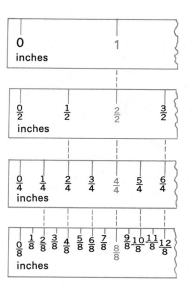

The diagram below shows how to add two fractions when their denominators are the same number.

$$\frac{3}{8} + \frac{4}{8} = \frac{3+4}{8} = \frac{7}{8} \quad\longleftarrow \text{sum of numerators}$$
$$\quad\longleftarrow \text{the common denominator}$$

The sum of any two fractions with a common denominator is equal to the sum of their numerators over the common denominator. So

$$\frac{a}{c} + \frac{b}{c} = \frac{a+b}{c}. \qquad \text{Example:} \quad \frac{2}{7} + \frac{3}{7} = \frac{2+3}{7} = \frac{5}{7}$$

Example 4 : Add $\frac{3}{5}$ and $\frac{4}{5}$.

$$\frac{3}{5} + \frac{4}{5} = \frac{3+4}{5} = \frac{7}{5}$$

Assignment Guide 4.1
Oral: 1–10
Written: Min. 11–34
         Reg. 11–36
         Max. 17–45

■ Exercises

Ⓐ **1.** $\frac{2}{3}$ means ($2 \div 3$, $2 + 3$, $3 \div 2$).   <u>2 ÷ 3</u>

2. Since fractions are used to indicate division, 0 can never be a (*numerator*, <u>*denominator*</u>, *quotient*).

Express as fractions.

3. $1 \div 4$ $\frac{1}{4}$ **4.** $4 \div 3$ $\frac{4}{3}$ **5.** $6\overline{)5}$ $\frac{5}{6}$ **6.** $2\overline{)11}$ $\frac{11}{2}$

7. 3 $\frac{3}{1}$ **8.** 20 $\frac{20}{1}$ **9.** 6 $\frac{6}{1}$ **10.** 1 $\frac{1}{1}$

Ⓑ Use the rulers to find equivalent fractions.

11. $\frac{1}{5} = \frac{\text{▨}}{10}$ ^{2} **12.** $\frac{18}{10} = \frac{\text{▨}}{5}$ ^{9}

13. $\frac{8}{10} = \frac{\text{▨}}{5}$ ^{4} **14.** $\frac{3}{2} = \frac{\text{▨}}{10}$ ^{15}

15. $\frac{1}{2} = \frac{\text{▨}}{10}$ ^{5} **16.** $\frac{4}{2} = \frac{\text{▨}}{5} = \frac{\text{▨}}{10}$ ${}^{10}\;{}^{20}$

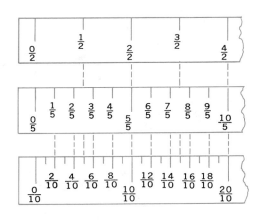

Use the rulers to find equivalent fractions.

17. $\frac{5}{6} = \frac{\text{▨}}{12}$ ^{10} **18.** $\frac{18}{12} = \frac{\text{▨}}{6}$ ^{9}

19. $\frac{4}{6} = \frac{\text{▨}}{3} = \frac{\text{▨}}{12}$ ${}^{2}\;{}^{8}$ **20.** $\frac{1}{3} = \frac{\text{▨}}{6} = \frac{\text{▨}}{12}$ ${}^{2}\;{}^{4}$

21. $\frac{14}{12} = \frac{\text{▨}}{6}$ ^{7} **22.** $\frac{4}{3} = \frac{\text{▨}}{6} = \frac{\text{▨}}{12}$ ${}^{8}\;{}^{16}$

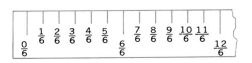

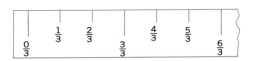

109

Add.

23. $\frac{1}{2} + \frac{4}{2}$ $\frac{5}{2}$ **24.** $\frac{2}{3} + \frac{3}{3}$ $\frac{5}{3}$ **25.** $\frac{2}{5} + \frac{2}{5}$ $\frac{4}{5}$ **26.** $\frac{3}{10} + \frac{6}{10}$ $\frac{9}{10}$

27. $\frac{5}{6} + \frac{2}{6}$ $\frac{7}{6}$ **28.** $\frac{4}{8} + \frac{3}{8}$ $\frac{7}{8}$ **29.** $\frac{7}{7} + \frac{2}{7}$ $\frac{9}{7}$ **30.** $\frac{6}{4} + \frac{3}{4}$ $\frac{9}{4}$

31. $\frac{1}{9} + \frac{9}{9}$ $\frac{10}{9}$ **32.** $\frac{2}{5} + \frac{3}{5}$ $\frac{5}{5}$ or 1 **33.** $\frac{4}{3} + \frac{4}{3}$ $\frac{8}{3}$ **34.** $\frac{5}{11} + \frac{2}{11}$ $\frac{7}{11}$

35. What whole number is equivalent to this sum: $\frac{8}{8} + \frac{8}{8} + \frac{8}{8}$?   3

36. For what number n is $\frac{n}{1} = \frac{n}{n}$?   1

C   Add.

Example: $\dfrac{5}{8} + \dfrac{3}{8} + \dfrac{7}{8} = \dfrac{5 + 3 + 7}{8} = \dfrac{15}{8}$

37. $\frac{2}{3} + \frac{4}{3} + \frac{2}{3}$ $\frac{8}{3}$ **38.** $\frac{4}{5} + \frac{2}{5} + \frac{3}{5}$ $\frac{9}{5}$ **39.** $\frac{1}{10} + \frac{7}{10} + \frac{5}{10}$ $\frac{13}{10}$

40. $\frac{5}{6} + \frac{1}{6} + \frac{5}{6}$ $\frac{11}{6}$ **41.** $\frac{3}{2} + \frac{1}{2} + \frac{5}{2}$ $\frac{9}{2}$ **42.** $\frac{7}{4} + \frac{3}{4} + \frac{3}{4}$ $\frac{13}{4}$

Example: $\dfrac{1}{a} + \dfrac{3}{a} = \dfrac{1 + 3}{a} = \dfrac{4}{a}$

43. $\frac{2}{x} + \frac{5}{x}$ $\frac{7}{x}$ **44.** $\frac{7}{y} + \frac{8}{y}$ $\frac{15}{y}$ **45.** $\frac{6}{z} + \frac{3}{z}$ $\frac{9}{z}$

In Other Words

The word *fraction* comes from the Latin word meaning "broken." The words for fraction in other languages also come from words meaning "broken." Some are given below. Pronunciation symbols are taken from Webster's *New Collegiate Dictionary*, eighth edition.

Language	Word	Pronunciation
French	fraction	frak-'syən
German	der bruch	da(ə)r-brək
Polish	ułamki	ü-wäm-kē
Spanish	fracción	fräk-sē-'ōn
Swedish	bråk	brōk

Multiplying Fractions

4.2

$\frac{4}{5}$ of Jill's backyard is covered with grass. She wants to dig up $\frac{2}{3}$ of the grass to plant a garden. How much of the whole yard will the garden cover?

The first rectangle shows $\frac{4}{5}$ of the yard covered with grass.

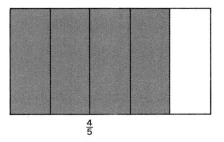

$\frac{4}{5}$

The second rectangle shows $\frac{2}{3}$ of the grass covered by the garden.

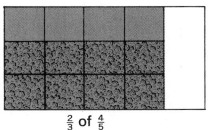

$\frac{2}{3}$ of $\frac{4}{5}$

The third rectangle shows the yard separated into 15 equal parts. The garden will be 8 of the parts. So the garden will cover $\frac{8}{15}$ of the whole yard.

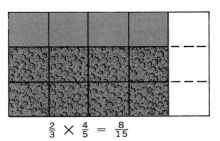

$\frac{2}{3} \times \frac{4}{5} = \frac{8}{15}$

Another way to find the answer is to multiply $\frac{2}{3}$ times $\frac{4}{5}$.

$$\frac{2}{3} \times \frac{4}{5} =$$

Multiply numerators.

$$\frac{2}{3} \times \frac{4}{5} = \frac{2 \times 4}{} = \frac{8}{-}$$

Multiply denominators.

$$\frac{2}{3} \times \frac{4}{5} = \frac{2 \times 4}{3 \times 5} = \frac{8}{15}$$

> The product of any two fractions is equal to the product of their numerators over the product of their denominators. So
>
> $\frac{a}{b} \times \frac{c}{d} = \frac{ac}{bd}$. *Example:* $\frac{2}{3} \times \frac{1}{5} = \frac{2 \times 1}{3 \times 5} = \frac{2}{15}$

Example 1: Multiply $\frac{4}{9}$ by $\frac{2}{5}$.

$$\frac{4}{9} \times \frac{2}{5} = \frac{8}{45}$$

Assignment Guide 4.2
Oral: 1–9
Written: Min. 10–24
   Reg. 11–33 odd
   Max. 11–29 odd;
      31–40

Example 2: Multiply $\frac{1}{3}$ by 2.

$$\frac{1}{3} \times \frac{2}{1} = \frac{2}{3}$$ Express 2 as a fraction.

▮ Exercises

Ⓐ Multiply.

1. $\frac{1}{2} \times \frac{1}{5}$ $\frac{1}{10}$

2. $\frac{5}{12} \times \frac{1}{2}$ $\frac{5}{24}$

3. $\frac{1}{2} \times \frac{7}{8}$ $\frac{7}{16}$

4. $3 \times \frac{1}{4}$ $\frac{3}{4}$

5. $\frac{1}{10} \times \frac{1}{3}$ $\frac{1}{30}$

6. $\frac{1}{12} \times \frac{1}{3}$ $\frac{1}{36}$

7. $\frac{3}{5} \times \frac{2}{5}$ $\frac{6}{25}$

8. $\frac{1}{3} \times \frac{1}{4}$ $\frac{1}{12}$

9. $\frac{1}{3} \times \frac{1}{9}$ $\frac{1}{27}$

Ⓑ Multiply.

10. $\frac{2}{7} \times \frac{2}{5}$ $\frac{4}{35}$

11. $\frac{1}{4} \times \frac{7}{9}$ $\frac{7}{36}$

12. $\frac{1}{6} \times \frac{7}{10}$ $\frac{7}{60}$

13. $\frac{1}{3} \times \frac{5}{8}$ $\frac{5}{24}$

14. $\frac{3}{8} \times \frac{3}{4}$ $\frac{9}{32}$

15. $\frac{3}{5} \times \frac{1}{8}$ $\frac{3}{40}$

16. $\frac{1}{7} \times \frac{3}{8}$ $\frac{3}{56}$

17. $\frac{1}{2} \times \frac{11}{12}$ $\frac{11}{24}$

18. $\frac{4}{5} \times \frac{1}{3}$ $\frac{4}{15}$

19. $\frac{1}{6} \times 5$ $\frac{5}{6}$

20. $3 \times \frac{2}{7}$ $\frac{6}{7}$

21. $\frac{9}{10} \times \frac{3}{4}$ $\frac{27}{40}$

22. $\frac{1}{5} \times \frac{2}{9}$ $\frac{2}{45}$

23. $\frac{1}{4} \times \frac{3}{5}$ $\frac{3}{20}$

24. $\frac{3}{10} \times 3$ $\frac{9}{10}$

25. $2 \times \frac{5}{5}$ $\frac{10}{5}$ or 2

26. $\frac{4}{7} \times \frac{4}{7}$ $\frac{16}{49}$

27. $8 \times \frac{3}{3}$ $\frac{24}{3}$ or 8

28. $\frac{2}{9} \times \frac{2}{5}$ $\frac{4}{45}$

29. $6 \times \frac{2}{11}$ $\frac{12}{11}$

30. $2 \times \frac{2}{3}$ $\frac{4}{3}$

31. How much is $\frac{1}{4}$ of 3 yd? $\frac{3}{4}$ yd

32. How much is $\frac{2}{3}$ of $\frac{4}{5}$ gallon? $\frac{8}{15}$ gal.

33. A piece of rope is $\frac{5}{8}$ yd long. How long is $\frac{1}{2}$ of the rope? $\frac{5}{16}$ yd

34. It takes 2 gallons of paint to cover a fence. How much paint would it take to cover only $\frac{2}{5}$ of the fence? $\frac{4}{5}$ gal.

Ⓒ Compute.

35. $\frac{a}{2} \times \frac{3}{5}$ $\frac{3a}{10}$

36. $\frac{a}{2} \times \frac{c}{5}$ $\frac{ac}{10}$

37. $a \times \frac{1}{5}$ $\frac{a}{5}$

38. $\left(\frac{3}{4}\right)^2$ $\frac{9}{16}$

39. $\left(\frac{1}{2}\right)^3$ $\frac{1}{8}$

40. $\left(\frac{2}{3}\right)^4$ $\frac{16}{81}$

Suggested Class Time

Course	Min.	Reg.	Max.
Days	1	1	1

"$\frac{3}{6}$ of the doctors questioned preferred Hope Mouthwash." It would also be correct to say that $\frac{1}{2}$ of the doctors preferred Hope Mouthwash.

$$\frac{3}{6} = \frac{3 \div 3}{6 \div 3} = \frac{1}{2}$$

Since $\frac{3}{6}$ can be *simplified* to $\frac{1}{2}$, $\frac{3}{6}$ and $\frac{1}{2}$ are equivalent.

$\frac{1}{2}$ is a fraction *in lowest terms*.

 A fraction is **in lowest terms** if its numerator and denominator have no common whole-number factor other than 1.   *Example:* $\frac{4}{7}$

Example 1: Express $\frac{8}{36}$ in lowest terms.

Step 1: Find the GCF of the numerator and denominator.

$$8 = 2^3$$
$$36 = 2^2 \times 3^2$$
$$2^2 = 4 \quad \blacktriangleleft \text{ GCF}$$

Step 2: Divide the numerator and denominator by the GCF.

$$\frac{8}{36} = \frac{8 \div 4}{36 \div 4} = \frac{2}{9}$$

Example 2: Express $\frac{10}{25}$ in lowest terms.

Step 1: The GCF of 10 and 25 is 5.

Step 2:   *Long way*   *Short way*

$$\frac{10}{25} = \frac{10 \div 5}{25 \div 5} = \frac{2}{5} \qquad \frac{\overset{2}{\cancel{10}}}{\underset{5}{\cancel{25}}} = \frac{2}{5}$$

113

Example 3: Multiply $\frac{5}{3}$ by $\frac{3}{10}$.

You can simplify before you multiply.

Assignment Guide 4.3
Oral: 1–6
Written: Min. 7–39 odd
      Reg. 7–45 odd
      Max. 7–43 odd;
         44–49

$$\frac{5}{3} \times \frac{3}{10} = \frac{\overset{1}{15}}{\underset{2}{30}} = \frac{1}{2} \quad \text{or} \quad \frac{\overset{1}{5}}{\underset{1}{3}} \times \frac{\overset{1}{3}}{\underset{2}{10}} = \frac{1}{2}$$

Divide by 15, the GCF.

Let's agree to *always* express a fraction in lowest terms.

◾ Exercises

Ⓐ Find the GCF of the numerator and denominator. (The numerators and denominators are factored into primes.)

1. $\frac{3}{12} = \frac{3}{2^2 \times 3}$ 3   **2.** $\frac{4}{8} = \frac{2^2}{2^3}$ 4   **3.** $\frac{10}{15} = \frac{2 \times 5}{3 \times 5}$ 5

4. $\frac{6}{10} = \frac{2 \times 3}{2 \times 5}$ 2   **5.** $\frac{14}{18} = \frac{2 \times 7}{2 \times 3^2}$ 2   **6.** $\frac{12}{30} = \frac{2^2 \times 3}{2 \times 3 \times 5}$ 6

Ⓑ Express each fraction in lowest terms.

7. $\frac{3}{12}$ $\frac{1}{4}$ **8.** $\frac{4}{8}$ $\frac{1}{2}$ **9.** $\frac{10}{15}$ $\frac{2}{3}$ **10.** $\frac{6}{10}$ $\frac{3}{5}$ **11.** $\frac{14}{18}$ $\frac{7}{9}$

12. $\frac{12}{30}$ $\frac{2}{5}$ **13.** $\frac{6}{9}$ $\frac{2}{3}$ **14.** $\frac{4}{6}$ $\frac{2}{3}$ **15.** $\frac{4}{16}$ $\frac{1}{4}$ **16.** $\frac{7}{21}$ $\frac{1}{3}$

17. $\frac{5}{20}$ $\frac{1}{4}$ **18.** $\frac{2}{8}$ $\frac{1}{4}$ **19.** $\frac{6}{12}$ $\frac{1}{2}$ **20.** $\frac{4}{12}$ $\frac{1}{3}$ **21.** $\frac{9}{15}$ $\frac{3}{5}$

22. $\frac{9}{12}$ $\frac{3}{4}$ **23.** $\frac{15}{20}$ $\frac{3}{4}$ **24.** $\frac{6}{8}$ $\frac{3}{4}$ **25.** $\frac{8}{10}$ $\frac{4}{5}$ **26.** $\frac{7}{35}$ $\frac{1}{5}$

27. $\frac{12}{20}$ $\frac{3}{5}$ **28.** $\frac{2}{16}$ $\frac{1}{8}$ **29.** $\frac{6}{16}$ $\frac{3}{8}$ **30.** $\frac{5}{15}$ $\frac{1}{3}$ **31.** $\frac{12}{18}$ $\frac{2}{3}$

Multiply. (Remember to express each answer in lowest terms.)

32. $\frac{4}{3} \times \frac{1}{2}$ $\frac{2}{3}$ **33.** $2 \times \frac{1}{8}$ $\frac{1}{4}$ **34.** $\frac{4}{3} \times \frac{3}{8}$ $\frac{1}{2}$ **35.** $\frac{1}{3} \times \frac{3}{5}$ $\frac{1}{5}$

36. $\frac{5}{4} \times \frac{2}{3}$ $\frac{5}{6}$ **37.** $\frac{5}{6} \times \frac{2}{5}$ $\frac{1}{3}$ **38.** $\frac{3}{2} \times \frac{4}{7}$ $\frac{6}{7}$ **39.** $\frac{3}{2} \times \frac{2}{9}$ $\frac{1}{3}$

40. $3 \times \frac{4}{15}$ $\frac{4}{5}$ **41.** $\frac{4}{5} \times \frac{5}{12}$ $\frac{1}{3}$ **42.** $\frac{1}{6} \times \frac{3}{4}$ $\frac{1}{8}$ **43.** $\frac{8}{9} \times \frac{1}{4}$ $\frac{2}{9}$

44. Gene travels a total of $\frac{4}{5}$ mile in a round trip from his home to school and back. How far is a one-way trip ($\frac{1}{2}$ of the trip)? $\frac{2}{5}$ mi

45. A recipe calls for $\frac{2}{3}$ cup milk. How much milk do you need for $\frac{1}{2}$ the recipe? $\frac{1}{3}$ cup

C Express each fraction in lowest terms.

Example: $\dfrac{3^2 \times 5}{2 \times 3} = \dfrac{3 \times \overset{1}{\cancel{3}} \times 5}{2 \times \underset{1}{\cancel{3}}} = \dfrac{15}{2}$

46. $\dfrac{2^3 \times 3 \times 5^2}{3^3 \times 5^3}$ $\frac{8}{45}$

47. $\dfrac{5^2 \times 7^3}{3^2 \times 5^3 \times 7}$ $\frac{49}{45}$

48. $\dfrac{3a^2}{15a}$ $\frac{a}{5}$

49. $\dfrac{10bc^3}{5b^3c^2}$ $\frac{2c}{b^2}$

Another Way

Another way to simplify fractions by factoring the numerators and denominators follows:

Example 1: $\dfrac{8}{12} = \dfrac{2 \times 2 \times 2}{2 \times 2 \times 3}$

$= \dfrac{2 \times 2}{2 \times 2} \times \dfrac{2}{3}$

$= 1 \times \dfrac{2}{3}$

$= \dfrac{2}{3}$

Example 2: $\dfrac{15}{18} = \dfrac{3 \times 5}{2 \times 3 \times 3}$

$= \dfrac{3}{3} \times \dfrac{5}{2 \times 3}$

$= 1 \times \dfrac{5}{6}$

$= \dfrac{5}{6}$

Express each fraction in lowest terms.

1. $\frac{4}{6}$ $\frac{2}{3}$ 　　**2.** $\frac{10}{15}$ $\frac{2}{3}$ 　　**3.** $\frac{2}{12}$ $\frac{1}{6}$ 　　**4.** $\frac{7}{28}$ $\frac{1}{4}$

5. $\frac{12}{20}$ $\frac{3}{5}$ 　　**6.** $\frac{6}{16}$ $\frac{3}{8}$ 　　**7.** $\frac{9}{21}$ $\frac{3}{7}$ 　　**8.** $\frac{18}{36}$ $\frac{1}{2}$

9. $\frac{25}{75}$ $\frac{1}{3}$ 　　**10.** $\frac{35}{45}$ $\frac{7}{9}$ 　　**11.** $\frac{24}{40}$ $\frac{3}{5}$ 　　**12.** $\frac{55}{99}$ $\frac{5}{9}$

Mixed Numbers

Suggested Class Time

Course	Min.	Reg.	Max.
Days	1	1	1

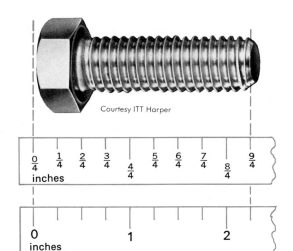

Courtesy ITT Harper

The length of the bolt can be given as either $\frac{9}{4}$ or $2\frac{1}{4}$ inches.

$2\frac{1}{4}$ stands for the sum of a whole number and a fraction.

$$2\frac{1}{4} = 2 + \frac{1}{4}$$

$$= (2 \times 1) + \frac{1}{4}$$

$$= \left(\frac{2}{1} \times \frac{4}{4}\right) + \frac{1}{4}$$

$$= \frac{8}{4} + \frac{1}{4}$$

$$= \frac{9}{4}$$

Equivalent expressions

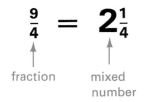

$$\frac{9}{4} \quad = \quad 2\frac{1}{4}$$

fraction   mixed number

$2\frac{1}{4}$ is read "two and one fourth."

Example 1: Express $5\frac{3}{8}$ as a fraction.

Long way

$$5\frac{3}{8} = 5 + \frac{3}{8}$$

$$= \left(\frac{5}{1} \times \frac{8}{8}\right) + \frac{3}{8}$$

$$= \frac{40}{8} + \frac{3}{8}$$

$$= \frac{43}{8}$$

Short way

$$5\frac{3}{8} = \frac{40 + 3}{8} = \frac{43}{8}$$

$$5 \times 8 = 40$$

Since a fraction indicates division, you divide the numerator by the denominator to find the equivalent mixed number.

Example 2: Express $\frac{32}{5}$ as a mixed number.

$$\frac{32}{5} = 32 \div 5 \quad\longrightarrow\quad \begin{array}{r} 6 \text{ R}2 = 6\frac{2}{5} \\ 5\overline{)32} \\ \underline{30} \\ 2 \end{array} \qquad \text{So } \frac{32}{5} = 6\frac{2}{5}.$$

Example 3: Multiply $\frac{9}{4}$ by $\frac{2}{3}$. Express the answer as a mixed number in lowest terms (fraction in lowest terms and less than 1).

$$\overset{3}{\cancel{9}} \times \overset{1}{\cancel{2}} = \frac{3}{2} = 1\frac{1}{2}$$
$$\underset{2}{\cancel{4}} \quad \underset{1}{\cancel{3}}$$

Let's agree to *always* change a fraction to a mixed number in lowest terms whenever possible.

Assignment Guide 4.4
Oral: 1–8
Written: Min. 9–33 odd
Reg. 9–39 odd
Max. 9–51 odd

■ Exercises

Ⓐ Express each of the following as the sum of a whole number and a fraction.

1. $2\frac{1}{3}$ $2 + \frac{1}{3}$ **2.** $7\frac{3}{8}$ $7 + \frac{3}{8}$ **3.** $21\frac{5}{6}$ $21 + \frac{5}{6}$ **4.** $12\frac{9}{10}$ $12 + \frac{9}{10}$

Show how you would divide to express each of the following as a mixed number.

Example: $\dfrac{3}{2} = 2\overline{)3}$

5. $\frac{5}{4}$ $4\overline{)5}$ **6.** $\frac{8}{3}$ $3\overline{)8}$ **7.** $\frac{14}{5}$ $5\overline{)14}$ **8.** $\frac{27}{10}$ $10\overline{)27}$

Ⓑ Express each mixed number as a fraction.

9. $2\frac{1}{3}$ $\frac{7}{3}$ **10.** $4\frac{1}{6}$ $\frac{25}{6}$ **11.** $1\frac{1}{5}$ $\frac{6}{5}$ **12.** $1\frac{1}{4}$ $\frac{5}{4}$ **13.** $2\frac{1}{2}$ $\frac{5}{2}$

14. $3\frac{7}{10}$ $\frac{37}{10}$ **15.** $5\frac{4}{5}$ $\frac{29}{5}$ **16.** $7\frac{1}{2}$ $\frac{15}{2}$ **17.** $4\frac{2}{3}$ $\frac{14}{3}$ **18.** $8\frac{3}{4}$ $\frac{35}{4}$

Express each fraction as a mixed number.

19. $\frac{5}{2}$ $2\frac{1}{2}$ **20.** $\frac{7}{6}$ $1\frac{1}{6}$ **21.** $\frac{5}{3}$ $1\frac{2}{3}$ **22.** $\frac{5}{4}$ $1\frac{1}{4}$ **23.** $\frac{7}{5}$ $1\frac{2}{5}$

24. $\frac{11}{3}$ $3\frac{2}{3}$ **25.** $\frac{16}{5}$ $3\frac{1}{5}$ **26.** $\frac{28}{3}$ $9\frac{1}{3}$ **27.** $\frac{31}{4}$ $7\frac{3}{4}$ **28.** $\frac{43}{8}$ $5\frac{3}{8}$

Multiply.

29. $\frac{1}{2} \times \frac{12}{5}$ $1\frac{1}{5}$ **30.** $\frac{4}{3} \times \frac{6}{5}$ $1\frac{3}{5}$ **31.** $10 \times \frac{1}{3}$ $3\frac{1}{3}$

32. $\frac{5}{7} \times \frac{7}{2}$ $2\frac{1}{2}$ **33.** $\frac{3}{5} \times \frac{15}{8}$ $1\frac{1}{8}$ **34.** $\frac{8}{9} \times 6$ $5\frac{1}{3}$

35. $5 \times \frac{7}{10}$ $3\frac{1}{2}$ **36.** $\frac{5}{3} \times \frac{11}{10}$ $1\frac{5}{6}$ **37.** $\frac{25}{12} \times \frac{3}{5}$ $1\frac{1}{4}$

38. The table shows the average amount of certain foods that an American eats in one day. Find the amounts per week. Express each answer in lowest terms.

	Daily average per person	Weekly average per person
Flour	$\frac{1}{3}$ pound	$2\frac{1}{3}$ lb
Meat	$\frac{1}{2}$ pound	$3\frac{1}{2}$ lb
Milk	$\frac{7}{10}$ pint	$4\frac{9}{10}$ pt
Sugar	$\frac{2}{7}$ pound	2 lb

39. On the average, each American disposes of $\frac{7}{2}$ pounds of trash a day. How much is this per week? Per year (365 days)? Express each answer in lowest terms. $24\frac{1}{2}$ lb; $1277\frac{1}{2}$ lb

C Multiply.

Example: $\dfrac{1}{2} \times 4 \times \dfrac{2}{3} = \dfrac{1}{\overset{}{\underset{1}{2}}} \times \dfrac{4}{1} \times \dfrac{\overset{1}{2}}{3} = \dfrac{4}{3} = 1\dfrac{1}{3}$

40. $\frac{3}{8} \times 3 \times \frac{2}{3}$ $\frac{3}{4}$ **41.** $12 \times \frac{3}{4} \times \frac{1}{6}$ $1\frac{1}{2}$ **42.** $\frac{4}{3} \times \frac{5}{4} \times \frac{2}{3}$ $1\frac{1}{9}$

43. $\frac{1}{2} \times \frac{3}{4} \times \frac{5}{6}$ $\frac{5}{16}$ **44.** $\frac{3}{4} \times \frac{3}{2} \times \frac{4}{5}$ $\frac{9}{10}$ **45.** $10 \times \frac{3}{5} \times \frac{1}{4}$ $1\frac{1}{2}$

Solve.

46. $2u = 5$ $2\frac{1}{2}$ **47.** $3v = 10$ $3\frac{1}{3}$ **48.** $7w = 30$ $4\frac{2}{7}$

49. $4x = 18$ $4\frac{1}{2}$ **50.** $12y = 40$ $3\frac{1}{3}$ **51.** $10z = 56$ $5\frac{3}{5}$

Multiplying Mixed Numbers

4.5

Terry wants to know how long $\frac{1}{2}$ of the wire is.

$4\frac{5}{8}$
← inches

Example 1: Find $\frac{1}{2}$ of $4\frac{5}{8}$ inches.

Step 1: Express the mixed number as a fraction.

$$4\frac{5}{8} = \frac{32 + 5}{8} = \frac{37}{8}$$

Step 2: Multiply. $\frac{1}{2} \times \frac{37}{8} = \frac{37}{16}$

Step 3: Express the answer in lowest terms.

$$
\begin{array}{r}
2\frac{5}{16} \\
16)\overline{37} \\
32 \\
\hline
5
\end{array}
\qquad
\frac{37}{16} = 2\frac{5}{16}
$$

$\frac{1}{2}$ of $4\frac{5}{8}$ inches is $2\frac{5}{16}$ inches.

Example 2: Multiply $3\frac{1}{3} \times 1\frac{1}{2}$.

$$3\frac{1}{3} \times 1\frac{1}{2} = \frac{\overset{5}{\cancel{10}}}{\underset{1}{\cancel{3}}} \times \frac{\overset{1}{\cancel{3}}}{\underset{1}{\cancel{2}}}$$

$$= \frac{5}{1} \text{ or } 5$$

119

Example 3: How many feet are there in $2\frac{5}{6}$ yards?

Each yard contains 3 ft, so multiply $2\frac{5}{6}$ by 3.

Assignment Guide 4.5
Oral: 1–12
Written:
Min. 13–25 odd; 35–39 odd;
    Quiz, p. 121
Reg. 13–39 odd; Quiz,
    p. 121
Max. 13–45 odd; Quiz,
    p. 121

$$2\frac{5}{6} \times 3 = \frac{17}{\underset{2}{\cancel{6}}} \times \frac{\overset{1}{\cancel{3}}}{1}$$

$$= \frac{17}{2} \text{ or } 8\frac{1}{2}$$

So $2\frac{5}{6}$ yd $= 8\frac{1}{2}$ ft.

■ Exercises

$\boxed{A}$ What fraction would you use in place of each whole or mixed number?

1. $3 \times 4\frac{1}{2}$ $\frac{3}{1}; \frac{9}{2}$ **2.** $1\frac{1}{2} \times 1\frac{1}{3}$ $\frac{3}{2}; \frac{4}{3}$ **3.** $\frac{3}{5} \times 4\frac{1}{6}$ $\frac{25}{6}$

4. $2\frac{1}{3} \times 2\frac{1}{4}$ $\frac{7}{3}; \frac{9}{4}$ **5.** $3\frac{1}{3} \times \frac{1}{5}$ $\frac{10}{3}$ **6.** $2\frac{2}{9} \times 1\frac{1}{10}$ $\frac{20}{9}; \frac{11}{10}$

7. $8 \times 1\frac{1}{8}$ $\frac{8}{1}; \frac{9}{8}$ **8.** $5\frac{1}{4} \times 5\frac{1}{7}$ $\frac{21}{4}; \frac{36}{7}$ **9.** $1\frac{3}{7} \times 2\frac{4}{5}$ $\frac{10}{7}; \frac{14}{5}$

What two numbers would you multiply to complete each of the following?

10. $3\frac{1}{2}$ yd = ____ ft   **11.** $6\frac{2}{3}$ ft = ____ in.   **12.** $2\frac{3}{4}$ lb = ____ oz

    1 yd = 3 ft   1 ft = 12 in.   1 lb = 16 oz

          $3\frac{1}{2} \times 3$ $6\frac{2}{3} \times 12$ $2\frac{3}{4} \times 16$

$\boxed{B}$ Multiply.

13. $3 \times \frac{1}{3}$ 1   **14.** $\frac{2}{5} \times 4$ $1\frac{3}{5}$ **15.** $2\frac{1}{2} \times \frac{2}{3}$ $1\frac{2}{3}$

16. $6 \times 2\frac{2}{9}$ $13\frac{1}{3}$ **17.** $1\frac{1}{2} \times \frac{1}{2}$ $\frac{3}{4}$ **18.** $\frac{4}{5} \times 6\frac{1}{4}$ 5

19. $3\frac{3}{4} \times 2$ $7\frac{1}{2}$ **20.** $\frac{2}{3} \times 5\frac{5}{8}$ $3\frac{3}{4}$ **21.** $2\frac{1}{2} \times 3\frac{1}{5}$ 8

22. $\frac{3}{7} \times 4\frac{2}{3}$ 2   **23.** $1\frac{1}{4} \times 1\frac{1}{4}$ $1\frac{9}{16}$ **24.** $5 \times 2\frac{1}{10}$ $10\frac{1}{2}$

25. $3\frac{1}{2} \times 2\frac{2}{3}$ $9\frac{1}{3}$ **26.** $2\frac{5}{8} \times 10\frac{2}{3}$ 28   **27.** $1\frac{2}{3} \times 2\frac{2}{5}$ 4

28. $3\frac{3}{5} \times 3\frac{3}{4}$ $13\frac{1}{2}$ **29.** $8\frac{1}{4} \times 7\frac{1}{3}$ $60\frac{1}{2}$ **30.** $\frac{3}{4} \times 5\frac{1}{3}$ 4

31. $5\frac{1}{3} \times 3\frac{3}{8}$ 18   **32.** $7\frac{1}{5} \times 4\frac{4}{9}$ 32   **33.** $4 \times 3\frac{1}{5}$ $12\frac{4}{5}$

Complete. Refer to the table on page 50 for a list of equivalent measures.

34. $3\frac{1}{2}$ yd = _____ ft $10\frac{1}{2}$

35. $6\frac{2}{3}$ ft = _____ in. 80

36. $2\frac{3}{4}$ lb = _____ oz 44

37. $4\frac{5}{8}$ pt = _____ c $9\frac{1}{4}$

38. $5\frac{1}{3}$ gal. = _____ qt $21\frac{1}{3}$

39. $1\frac{3}{8}$ qt = _____ pt $2\frac{3}{4}$

C The formula for finding the area of a rectangle is $A = l \times w$. Find the area of each rectangle whose length and width is given below.

40. $l = 9\frac{3}{4}$ ft, $w = 5\frac{1}{3}$ ft 52 sq ft

41. $l = 3\frac{1}{2}$ mi, $w = \frac{4}{5}$ mi $2\frac{4}{5}$ sq mi

42. $l = 8\frac{2}{3}$ yd, $w = 6$ yd 52 sq yd

43. $l = 6\frac{2}{3}$ in., $w = 5\frac{5}{8}$ in. $37\frac{1}{2}$ sq in.

44. $l = 4\frac{1}{2}$ ft, $w = 1\frac{1}{6}$ yd $15\frac{3}{4}$ sq ft or $1\frac{3}{4}$ sq yd

45. $l = 2\frac{2}{3}$ ft, $w = 1\frac{5}{16}$ in. 42 sq in. or $\frac{7}{24}$ sq ft

Quick Quiz
Sections 4.1 to 4.5

Express each of the following as a fraction.

1. $3 \div 5$ $\frac{3}{5}$

2. $7\overline{)4}$ $\frac{4}{7}$

3. $1\frac{2}{3}$ $\frac{5}{3}$

4. For $\frac{5}{8}$, 8 is the (numerator, _denominator_).

5. Express $\frac{7}{2}$ as a mixed number. $3\frac{1}{2}$

Add.

6. $\frac{1}{5} + \frac{2}{5}$ $\frac{3}{5}$

7. $\frac{5}{11} + \frac{3}{11}$ $\frac{8}{11}$

8. $\frac{7}{15} + \frac{7}{15}$ $\frac{14}{15}$

Multiply.

9. $\frac{3}{5} \times \frac{1}{7}$ $\frac{3}{35}$

10. $\frac{3}{4} \times \frac{2}{9}$ $\frac{1}{6}$

11. $\frac{18}{25} \times 5$ $3\frac{3}{5}$

12. $3\frac{1}{8} \times 1\frac{3}{5}$ 5

13. $12\frac{1}{2} \times 6$ 75

14. $7\frac{1}{9} \times \frac{3}{8}$ $2\frac{2}{3}$

121

USING RECIPES

John wants to make 12 servings of spaghetti sauce. But his recipe is for only 8 servings. So John thinks:

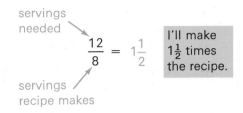

servings needed

$$\frac{12}{8} = 1\frac{1}{2}$$

servings recipe makes

I'll make $1\frac{1}{2}$ times the recipe.

Spaghetti Sauce
$1\frac{1}{3}$ lb ground beef
24 oz tomato sauce
$\frac{2}{3}$ c water
1 tsp salt
$\frac{1}{2}$ tsp oregano
$\frac{1}{4}$ tsp pepper
$\frac{1}{8}$ tsp garlic powder
$\frac{3}{4}$ c chopped onion

Since he needs to make $1\frac{1}{2}$ times the recipe, he will use $1\frac{1}{2}$ times the amount of each ingredient. For example, find how much ground beef he should use.

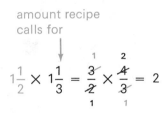

amount recipe calls for

$$1\frac{1}{2} \times 1\frac{1}{3} = \frac{\overset{1}{3}}{\underset{1}{2}} \times \frac{\overset{2}{4}}{\underset{1}{3}} = 2$$

He will use 2 lb ground beef.

36 oz, 1 c, $1\frac{1}{2}$ tsp, $\frac{3}{4}$ tsp, $\frac{3}{8}$ tsp, $\frac{3}{16}$ tsp, $1\frac{1}{8}$ c

1. Find how much of each remaining ingredient he should use.

2. Abby wants to make 30 servings from the same recipe. By what number should she multiply the amount of each ingredient? $3\frac{3}{4}$

3. Joe is going to make 4 servings from the recipe. By what number should he multiply the amounts? Find how much of each ingredient he should use.

$\frac{1}{2}$; $\frac{2}{3}$ lb, 12 oz, $\frac{1}{3}$ c, $\frac{1}{2}$ tsp, $\frac{1}{4}$ tsp, $\frac{1}{8}$ tsp, $\frac{1}{16}$ tsp, $\frac{3}{8}$ c

Dividing Fractions and Mixed Numbers

4.6

Divide $\frac{3}{4}$ yard of rope into $\frac{3}{8}$-yard pieces. How many pieces do you get? The diagram shows that $\frac{3}{4} \div \frac{3}{8} = 2$.

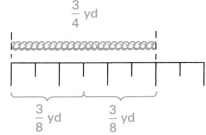

To find quotients, you can invert the divisor and multiply.

Example 1: Divide $\frac{3}{4}$ by $\frac{3}{8}$.

$$\frac{3}{4} \div \frac{3}{8} = \frac{3}{4} \times \frac{8}{3} \qquad \text{Invert divisor and multiply.}$$

$$= \frac{\overset{1}{\cancel{3}}}{\underset{1}{4}} \times \frac{8}{\underset{1}{\cancel{3}}}^{2}$$

$$= \frac{2}{1} \text{ or } 2 \qquad \text{Notice that this is the same answer you got from the diagram.}$$

> To find the quotient of any two fractions, invert the divisor, then multiply the fractions. So, where c is not zero,
>
> $$\frac{a}{b} \div \frac{c}{d} = \frac{a}{b} \times \frac{d}{c}. \qquad \textit{Example:} \quad \frac{1}{3} \div \frac{2}{5} = \frac{1}{3} \times \frac{5}{2} = \frac{5}{6}$$

Example 2: Divide $5\frac{1}{2}$ by $\frac{3}{4}$.

$$5\frac{1}{2} \div \frac{3}{4} = \frac{11}{2} \div \frac{3}{4}$$

$$= \frac{11}{\underset{1}{\cancel{2}}} \times \frac{\cancel{4}}{3}^{2}$$

$$= \frac{22}{3} \text{ or } 7\frac{1}{3}$$

123

Example 3: How many yards are there in $8\frac{1}{2}$ feet?

There are 3 ft in each yard, so divide $8\frac{1}{2}$ by 3.

$$8\frac{1}{2} \div 3 = \frac{17}{2} \div \frac{3}{1}$$

$$= \frac{17}{2} \times \frac{1}{3}$$

$$= \frac{17}{6} \text{ or } 2\frac{5}{6}$$

Assignment Guide 4.6
Oral: 1–6
Written: Min. 7–35 odd
     Reg. 7–39 odd
     Max. 7–45 odd

So $8\frac{1}{2}$ ft $= 2\frac{5}{6}$ yd.

■ Exercises

A Complete.

1. $\frac{1}{5} \div \frac{1}{2} = \frac{1}{5} \times$ ____ $\frac{2}{1}$

2. $\frac{1}{3} \div \frac{3}{4} = \frac{1}{3} \times$ ____ $\frac{4}{3}$

3. $2\frac{1}{2} \div 6 = \frac{5}{2} \times$ ____ $\frac{1}{6}$

4. $1\frac{3}{8} \div 1\frac{1}{2} = \frac{11}{8} \times$ ____ $\frac{2}{3}$

5. To find the number of yards in $7\frac{1}{2}$ ft, divide ____ by ____. $7\frac{1}{2}; 3$

6. To find the number of feet in 56 in., divide ____ by ____. $56; 12$

B Divide.

7. $\frac{1}{5} \div \frac{1}{2}$ $\frac{2}{5}$

8. $\frac{1}{3} \div 3$ $\frac{1}{9}$

9. $3 \div \frac{1}{3}$ 9

10. $\frac{3}{2} \div \frac{1}{2}$ 3

11. $\frac{1}{6} \div 2$ $\frac{1}{12}$

12. $\frac{1}{3} \div \frac{1}{4}$ $1\frac{1}{3}$

13. $\frac{2}{3} \div \frac{5}{6}$ $\frac{4}{5}$

14. $5 \div 1\frac{2}{3}$ 3

15. $3\frac{1}{3} \div 2\frac{1}{2}$ $1\frac{1}{3}$

16. $\frac{3}{4} \div 3$ $\frac{1}{4}$

17. $1\frac{1}{5} \div 3$ $\frac{2}{5}$

18. $3\frac{3}{4} \div \frac{5}{12}$ 9

19. $3\frac{1}{2} \div 4\frac{1}{5}$ $\frac{5}{6}$

20. $\frac{4}{5} \div \frac{2}{3}$ $1\frac{1}{5}$

21. $\frac{7}{10} \div 2\frac{4}{5}$ $\frac{1}{4}$

22. $4\frac{1}{2} \div 2\frac{2}{3}$ $1\frac{11}{16}$

23. $4\frac{1}{3} \div \frac{1}{9}$ 39

24. $2\frac{5}{8} \div 7$ $\frac{3}{8}$

25. $6 \div \frac{3}{5}$ 10

26. $5\frac{1}{3} \div 1\frac{3}{5}$ $3\frac{1}{3}$

27. $1\frac{1}{4} \div 1\frac{7}{8}$ $\frac{2}{3}$

28. $\frac{5}{8} \div 2\frac{1}{12}$ $\frac{3}{10}$

29. $10 \div 4\frac{1}{6}$ $2\frac{2}{5}$

30. $2\frac{2}{9} \div \frac{5}{6}$ $2\frac{2}{3}$

Complete. Refer to the table on page 50 for a list of equivalent measures.

31. $7\frac{1}{2}$ ft = ____ yd $2\frac{1}{2}$

32. 56 in. = ____ ft $4\frac{2}{3}$

33. $11\frac{1}{5}$ oz = ____ lb $\frac{7}{10}$

34. $13\frac{3}{4}$ c = ____ pt $6\frac{7}{8}$

35. $20\frac{1}{2}$ qt = ____ gal. $5\frac{1}{8}$

36. 1750 ft = ____ mi $\frac{175}{528}$

37. $8\frac{3}{4}$ in. of rain fell in 5 months. What is the average monthly rainfall? $1\frac{3}{4}$ in.

38. Mr. Lauraitis has to find the number of panels he needs for a wall. Each panel is $1\frac{1}{3}$ feet wide. How many panels does he need for a 20-foot wall? 15 panels

39. During a business trip, Mr. Levin traveled 125 miles in $2\frac{1}{2}$ hours. What was his average speed? 50 mph

40. Each character typed by a pica typewriter takes $\frac{1}{10}$ inch. A character typed by an elite typewriter takes $\frac{1}{12}$ inch. How many characters are in a $7\frac{1}{2}$-inch line of pica type? Of elite type? 75; 90

C Solve.

Example: $3x = 4\frac{1}{2}$

$$\frac{3x}{3} = \frac{4\frac{1}{2}}{3}$$

$$x = 4\frac{1}{2} \div 3$$

$$x = \frac{\overset{3}{\cancel{9}}}{2} \times \frac{1}{\underset{1}{\cancel{3}}}$$

$$x = \frac{3}{2} \text{ or } 1\frac{1}{2}$$

Check: $3x = 4\frac{1}{2}$

$$3 \times 1\frac{1}{2} = 4\frac{1}{2}$$

$$3 \times \frac{3}{2} = 4\frac{1}{2}$$

$$\frac{9}{2} = 4\frac{1}{2}$$

$$4\frac{1}{2} = 4\frac{1}{2}$$

41. $5a = 3\frac{1}{3}$ $\frac{2}{3}$

42. $9b = 6\frac{3}{4}$ $\frac{3}{4}$

43. $\frac{3}{7}c = 12$ 28

44. $\frac{9}{16}d = 2\frac{7}{10}$ $4\frac{4}{5}$

45. $2\frac{1}{8}e = 34$ 16

46. $3\frac{5}{6}f = 5\frac{1}{9}$ $1\frac{1}{3}$

Adding and Subtracting Like Fractions

A pizza was cut into 8 pieces. Jack and Pete ate 7 pieces, or $\frac{7}{8}$ of the pizza. If Jack ate $\frac{3}{8}$ of the pizza, what part of the pizza did Pete eat? To find the answer, subtract $\frac{3}{8}$ from $\frac{7}{8}$.

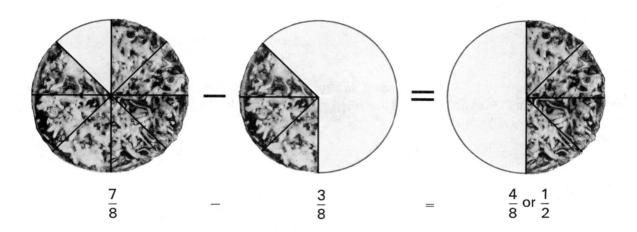

$$\frac{7}{8} \qquad - \qquad \frac{3}{8} \qquad = \qquad \frac{4}{8} \text{ or } \frac{1}{2}$$

Horizontal method:

$$\frac{7}{8} - \frac{3}{8} = \frac{7-3}{8}$$

$$= \frac{\overset{1}{4}}{\underset{2}{8}}$$

$$= \frac{1}{2}$$

Subtract numerators. Then simplify.

Vertical method:

$$\begin{array}{r} \frac{7}{8} \\ - \frac{3}{8} \\ \hline \frac{\overset{1}{4}}{\underset{2}{8}} = \frac{1}{2} \end{array}$$

Pete ate $\frac{1}{2}$ of the pizza.

The difference of any two like fractions (fractions with a common denominator) is equal to the difference of their numerators over the common denominator. So

$$\frac{a}{c} - \frac{b}{c} = \frac{a-b}{c}.$$ *Example:* $\frac{3}{5} - \frac{2}{5} = \frac{3-2}{5} = \frac{1}{5}$

Example 1: Add $3\frac{3}{7}$ and $1\frac{6}{7}$.

Add numerators.
Add whole numbers.
Then simplify.

$$3\frac{3}{7}$$
$$+\,1\frac{6}{7}$$
$$4\frac{9}{7} = 4 + 1\frac{2}{7} = 4 + 1 + \frac{2}{7} = 5\frac{2}{7}$$

Think: $\frac{9}{7} = 1\frac{2}{7}$

Example 2: Add $4\frac{3}{4}$ and $\frac{3}{4}$.

$$4\frac{3}{4}$$
$$+\,\frac{3}{4}$$
$$4\frac{6}{4} = 4 + 1\frac{1}{2} = 5\frac{1}{2}$$

Think: $\dfrac{\overset{3}{\cancel{6}}}{\underset{2}{\cancel{4}}} = 1\frac{1}{2}$

Example 3: Subtract $1\frac{5}{8}$ from $8\frac{3}{8}$.

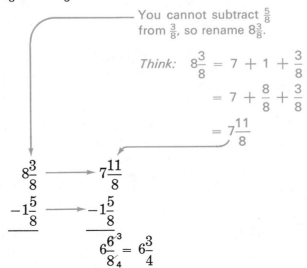

You cannot subtract $\frac{5}{8}$ from $\frac{3}{8}$, so rename $8\frac{3}{8}$.

Think:
$$8\frac{3}{8} = 7 + 1 + \frac{3}{8}$$
$$= 7 + \frac{8}{8} + \frac{3}{8}$$
$$= 7\frac{11}{8}$$

$$8\frac{3}{8} \longrightarrow 7\frac{11}{8}$$

Subtract numerators.
Subtract whole numbers.
Then simplify.

$$-1\frac{5}{8} \longrightarrow -1\frac{5}{8}$$
$$6\frac{\overset{3}{\cancel{6}}}{\underset{4}{\cancel{8}}} = 6\frac{3}{4}$$

127

Exercises

Assignment Guide 4.7
Oral: 1–6
Written: Min. 7–37 odd
   Reg. 7–47 odd
   Max. 7–53 odd

A Express each mixed number in lowest terms.

1. $1\frac{5}{4} = 2\frac{\text{▨}1}{4}$ 2. $3\frac{11}{7} = 4\frac{\text{▨}4}{7}$ 3. $2\frac{7}{6} = 3\frac{\text{▨}1}{6}$

Complete each renaming.

4. $2\frac{1}{5} = 1\frac{\text{▨}6}{5}$ 5. $4\frac{1}{6} = 3\frac{\text{▨}7}{6}$ 6. $1\frac{1}{3} = \frac{\text{▨}4}{3}$

B Find each sum or difference.

7. $\begin{array}{r}\frac{3}{4}\\ +\frac{1}{4}\end{array}$ 1   8. $\begin{array}{r}\frac{2}{3}\\ -\frac{1}{3}\end{array}$ $\frac{1}{3}$ 9. $\begin{array}{r}\frac{7}{8}\\ -\frac{3}{8}\end{array}$ $\frac{1}{2}$ 10. $\begin{array}{r}1\frac{5}{6}\\ -\frac{1}{6}\end{array}$ $1\frac{2}{3}$ 11. $\begin{array}{r}2\frac{1}{3}\\ +\frac{1}{3}\end{array}$ $2\frac{2}{3}$

12. $\begin{array}{r}1\frac{1}{8}\\ +\frac{7}{8}\end{array}$ 2   13. $\begin{array}{r}1\frac{1}{3}\\ -\frac{2}{3}\end{array}$ $\frac{2}{3}$ 14. $\begin{array}{r}2\frac{5}{12}\\ +5\frac{5}{12}\end{array}$ $7\frac{5}{6}$ 15. $\begin{array}{r}2\frac{2}{3}\\ +1\frac{2}{3}\end{array}$ $4\frac{1}{3}$

16. $\begin{array}{r}10\frac{5}{8}\\ -3\frac{3}{8}\end{array}$ $7\frac{1}{4}$ 17. $\begin{array}{r}2\frac{1}{4}\\ -\frac{3}{4}\end{array}$ $1\frac{1}{2}$ 18. $\begin{array}{r}4\frac{4}{5}\\ +1\frac{3}{5}\end{array}$ $6\frac{2}{5}$ 19. $\begin{array}{r}1\frac{9}{10}\\ -1\frac{3}{10}\end{array}$ $\frac{3}{5}$

20. $\begin{array}{r}3\frac{2}{5}\\ -2\frac{3}{5}\end{array}$ $\frac{4}{5}$ 21. $\begin{array}{r}2\frac{5}{6}\\ +1\frac{5}{6}\end{array}$ $4\frac{2}{3}$ 22. $\begin{array}{r}4\frac{1}{6}\\ -1\frac{5}{6}\end{array}$ $2\frac{1}{3}$ 23. $\begin{array}{r}5\frac{1}{8}\\ -2\frac{7}{8}\end{array}$ $2\frac{1}{4}$

24. $6\frac{4}{7} + \frac{2}{7}$ $6\frac{6}{7}$ 25. $5\frac{2}{3} + 1\frac{2}{3}$ $7\frac{1}{3}$ 26. $4\frac{5}{9} - \frac{2}{9}$ $4\frac{1}{3}$ 27. $2\frac{3}{5} - 1\frac{4}{5}$ $\frac{4}{5}$

28. Sandy picked $5\frac{3}{4}$ quarts of strawberries in the morning and $2\frac{3}{4}$ quarts in the afternoon. How many quarts did she pick altogether? $8\frac{1}{2}$ qt

29. Alex has $6\frac{2}{3}$ yards of string. If he uses $2\frac{1}{3}$ yards to tie a package, how much string will he have left? $4\frac{1}{3}$ yd

Subtract.

Example 1: $1 \;-\; \dfrac{3}{5} = \dfrac{5}{5} - \dfrac{3}{5}$

          $= \dfrac{5-3}{5}$

          $= \dfrac{2}{5}$

Example 2: $5 \;-\; 1\dfrac{2}{3} = (4+1) \;-\; 1\dfrac{2}{3}$

           $= \left(4 + \dfrac{3}{3}\right) \;-\; 1\dfrac{2}{3}$

           $= 4\dfrac{3}{3} \;-\; 1\dfrac{2}{3}$

           $= 3\dfrac{1}{3}$

30. $1 - \frac{1}{4}$ $\frac{3}{4}$

31. $1 - \frac{5}{6}$ $\frac{1}{6}$

32. $1 - \frac{7}{12}$ $\frac{5}{12}$

33. $2 - \frac{1}{3}$ $1\frac{2}{3}$

34. $8 - \frac{4}{5}$ $7\frac{1}{5}$

35. $13 - \frac{5}{9}$ $12\frac{4}{9}$

36. $2 - 1\frac{1}{5}$ $\frac{4}{5}$

37. $6 - 3\frac{2}{7}$ $2\frac{5}{7}$

38. $10 - 4\frac{5}{8}$ $5\frac{3}{8}$

39. English is spoken by about $\frac{1}{12}$ of the world's population. What part of the population does not speak English? (*Note:* 1, or $\frac{12}{12}$, represents the whole population.) $\frac{11}{12}$

40. About $\frac{5}{7}$ of the earth's surface is covered with water. What part of the surface is land? $\frac{2}{7}$

41. How much oil should you add to $\frac{3}{4}$ quart to have 5 quarts? $4\frac{1}{4}$ qt

42. John has walked $2\frac{1}{3}$ miles of a 4-mile hike. How much farther does he have to walk? $1\frac{2}{3}$ mi

Solve.

43. $m + \frac{2}{5} = \frac{4}{5}$ $\frac{2}{5}$

44. $n + 3\frac{1}{3} = 5\frac{2}{3}$ $2\frac{1}{3}$

45. $p - \frac{7}{8} = \frac{5}{8}$ $1\frac{1}{2}$

46. $q - 5\frac{1}{5} = 1\frac{2}{5}$ $6\frac{3}{5}$

47. $r + 1\frac{3}{7} = 4\frac{1}{7}$ $2\frac{5}{7}$

48. $s + \frac{10}{13} = 1$ $\frac{3}{13}$

C Use the distributive property to multiply.

Example: $2\frac{2}{5} \times 3 = \left(2 + \frac{2}{5}\right)3$

$$= (2 \times 3) + \left(\frac{2}{5} \times 3\right)$$

$$= 6 + \frac{6}{5}$$

$$= 7\frac{1}{5}$$

49. $1\frac{5}{8} \times 2$ $3\frac{1}{4}$

50. $4\frac{3}{4} \times 7$ $33\frac{1}{4}$

51. $8\frac{5}{6} \times 3$ $26\frac{1}{2}$

52. $10\frac{2}{9} \times 6$ $61\frac{1}{3}$

53. $12\frac{5}{12} \times 10$ $124\frac{1}{6}$

54. $15\frac{11}{18} \times 3$ $46\frac{5}{6}$

4.8 **Adding and Subtracting Unlike Fractions**

Suggested Class Time

Course	Min.	Reg.	Max.
Days	1	1	1

In Section 4.7 you added and subtracted like fractions (fractions with a common denominator). Unlike fractions have different denominators. To add or subtract unlike fractions, you must first rename the fractions so they have a common denominator.

Example 1: Add $\frac{3}{8}$ and $\frac{5}{12}$.

Step 1: Find the *least common denominator* by finding the LCM of the denominators.

$$8 = 2^3$$
$$12 = 2^2 \times 3$$

$$2^3 \times 3 = 24 \quad \blacktriangleleft \text{ LCM}$$

Step 2: Express each fraction as an equivalent fraction with the least common denominator.

$$\frac{3}{8} = \frac{||||}{24} \qquad\qquad \frac{5}{12} = \frac{||||}{24}$$

$$8 \times 3 = 24, \text{ so} \qquad\qquad 12 \times 2 = 24, \text{ so}$$

$$\frac{3}{8} = \frac{3}{8} \times \frac{3}{3} = \frac{9}{24} \qquad\qquad \frac{5}{12} = \frac{5}{12} \times \frac{2}{2} = \frac{10}{24}$$

Step 3: Add.

$$
\begin{array}{ccc}
\frac{3}{8} & \rightarrow & \frac{9}{24} \\
+\frac{5}{12} & \rightarrow & +\frac{10}{24} \\
\hline
& & \frac{19}{24}
\end{array}
$$

Example 2: Add $\frac{2}{5}$ and $\frac{3}{10}$.

Since 10 is a multiple of 5,
10 is the least common denominator.

$$\frac{2}{5} \longrightarrow \frac{2}{5} \times \frac{2}{2} \longrightarrow \frac{4}{10}$$

$$+\frac{3}{10} \longrightarrow +\frac{3}{10}$$

$$\frac{7}{10}$$

Example 3: How far is it between exits?
Subtract $\frac{1}{4}$ from $\frac{2}{3}$.

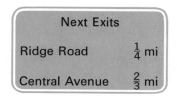

Next Exits

Ridge Road $\frac{1}{4}$ mi

Central Avenue $\frac{2}{3}$ mi

Since 3 and 4 have no common factors (except 1), 3×4,
or 12, is the least common denominator.

$$\frac{2}{3} \longrightarrow \frac{2}{3} \times \frac{4}{4} \longrightarrow \frac{8}{12}$$

$$-\frac{1}{4} \longrightarrow \frac{1}{4} \times \frac{3}{3} \longrightarrow -\frac{3}{12}$$

$$\frac{5}{12}$$

The distance between the exits is $\frac{5}{12}$ mile.

Assignment Guide 4.8
    Oral: 1–6
    Written: Min. 7–25 odd
        Reg. 7–31 odd
        Max. 7–37 odd

■ Exercises

A Complete each pair of equivalent fractions.

1. $\frac{1}{4} = \frac{\text{⫿}}{16}$ 4

2. $\frac{1}{5} = \frac{\text{⫿}}{15}$ 3

3. $\frac{1}{2} = \frac{\text{⫿}}{10}$ 5

4. $\frac{1}{3} = \frac{\text{⫿}}{12}$ 4

5. $\frac{3}{4} = \frac{\text{⫿}}{8}$ 6

6. $\frac{2}{3} = \frac{\text{⫿}}{6}$ 4

B For each pair of fractions, find equivalent fractions with the least common denominator.

7. $\frac{3}{8}, \frac{1}{16}$ $\frac{6}{16}, \frac{1}{16}$ 8. $\frac{1}{10}, \frac{2}{15}$ $\frac{3}{30}, \frac{4}{30}$ 9. $\frac{1}{5}, \frac{5}{6}$ $\frac{6}{30}, \frac{25}{30}$ 10. $\frac{1}{6}, \frac{2}{9}$ $\frac{3}{18}, \frac{4}{18}$

Find each sum or difference.

11. $\begin{array}{r}\frac{1}{2}\\[-2pt]+\frac{1}{4}\end{array}$ $\frac{3}{4}$ 12. $\begin{array}{r}\frac{2}{3}\\[-2pt]-\frac{1}{6}\end{array}$ $\frac{1}{2}$ 13. $\begin{array}{r}\frac{3}{8}\\[-2pt]-\frac{1}{4}\end{array}$ $\frac{1}{8}$ 14. $\begin{array}{r}\frac{1}{6}\\[-2pt]+\frac{1}{2}\end{array}$ $\frac{2}{3}$

15. $\begin{array}{r}\frac{1}{2}\\[-2pt]-\frac{1}{3}\end{array}$ $\frac{1}{6}$ 16. $\begin{array}{r}\frac{5}{6}\\[-2pt]-\frac{3}{8}\end{array}$ $\frac{11}{24}$ 17. $\begin{array}{r}\frac{1}{4}\\[-2pt]+\frac{2}{3}\end{array}$ $\frac{11}{12}$ 18. $\begin{array}{r}\frac{7}{8}\\[-2pt]-\frac{1}{12}\end{array}$ $\frac{19}{24}$

19. $\begin{array}{r}\frac{1}{3}\\[-2pt]+\frac{5}{8}\end{array}$ $\frac{23}{24}$ 20. $\begin{array}{r}\frac{1}{2}\\[-2pt]-\frac{2}{5}\end{array}$ $\frac{1}{10}$ 21. $\begin{array}{r}\frac{3}{4}\\[-2pt]-\frac{5}{12}\end{array}$ $\frac{1}{3}$ 22. $\begin{array}{r}\frac{1}{6}\\[-2pt]+\frac{4}{15}\end{array}$ $\frac{13}{30}$

23. $\begin{array}{r}\frac{2}{3}\\[-2pt]-\frac{1}{8}\end{array}$ $\frac{13}{24}$ 24. $\begin{array}{r}\frac{5}{24}\\[-2pt]+\frac{5}{12}\end{array}$ $\frac{5}{8}$ 25. $\begin{array}{r}\frac{9}{16}\\[-2pt]-\frac{1}{4}\end{array}$ $\frac{5}{16}$ 26. $\begin{array}{r}\frac{3}{20}\\[-2pt]+\frac{2}{5}\end{array}$ $\frac{11}{20}$

Solve.

27. $u + \frac{3}{4} = \frac{7}{8}$ $\frac{1}{8}$ 28. $v + \frac{5}{6} = \frac{8}{9}$ $\frac{1}{18}$ 29. $w - \frac{2}{7} = \frac{1}{4}$ $\frac{15}{28}$

30. $x - \frac{3}{10} = \frac{1}{2}$ $\frac{4}{5}$ 31. $y - \frac{3}{8} = \frac{5}{12}$ $\frac{19}{24}$ 32. $z + \frac{2}{9} = \frac{1}{2}$ $\frac{5}{18}$

C To arrange fractions in order, express the fractions as equivalent fractions with a common denominator. Then compare numerators.

Example: Which is the heaviest—$\frac{3}{4}$ oz, $\frac{2}{3}$ oz, or $\frac{5}{6}$ oz? The lightest?

12 is the LCM of 4, 3, and 6.

$$\frac{3}{4} = \frac{9}{12} \qquad \frac{2}{3} = \frac{8}{12} \qquad \frac{5}{6} = \frac{10}{12}$$

The order from least to greatest is $\frac{8}{12}, \frac{9}{12}, \frac{10}{12}$ or $\frac{2}{3}, \frac{3}{4}, \frac{5}{6}$.

The heaviest is $\frac{5}{6}$ oz and the lightest is $\frac{2}{3}$ oz.

Order each of the following sets from least to greatest.

33. $\frac{1}{2}, \frac{2}{5}, \frac{3}{10}$ $\frac{3}{10}, \frac{2}{5}, \frac{1}{2}$ 34. $\frac{3}{8}, \frac{1}{4}, \frac{5}{16}$ $\frac{1}{4}, \frac{5}{16}, \frac{3}{8}$ 35. $\frac{1}{6}, \frac{1}{2}, \frac{2}{3}$ $\frac{1}{6}, \frac{1}{2}, \frac{2}{3}$

36. $\frac{1}{4}, \frac{1}{5}, \frac{3}{10}$ $\frac{1}{5}, \frac{1}{4}, \frac{3}{10}$ 37. $\frac{1}{4}, \frac{1}{2}, \frac{1}{3}$ $\frac{1}{4}, \frac{1}{3}, \frac{1}{2}$ 38. $\frac{5}{9}, \frac{2}{3}, \frac{1}{2}$ $\frac{1}{2}, \frac{5}{9}, \frac{2}{3}$

Adding and Subtracting Mixed Numbers

4.9

A sewing pattern calls for $2\frac{7}{8}$ yards of fabric for a jacket and $1\frac{1}{4}$ yards of fabric for a skirt. How much fabric does Nancy need to make a matching jacket and skirt?

Example 1: Add $2\frac{7}{8}$ and $1\frac{1}{4}$.

The least common denominator of $\frac{7}{8}$ and $\frac{1}{4}$ is 8.

Suggested Class Time

Course	Min.	Reg.	Max.
Days	2	1	1

$$2\frac{7}{8} \longrightarrow 2\frac{7}{8}$$

$$+ 1\frac{1}{4} \longrightarrow + 1\frac{2}{8}$$

$$\overline{}\qquad\overline{}$$

$$3\frac{9}{8} = 3 + 1\frac{1}{8} = 4\frac{1}{8} \qquad \text{Nancy needs } 4\frac{1}{8} \text{ yards.}$$

Example 2: Subtract $2\frac{5}{6}$ from $5\frac{1}{4}$.

The least common denominator of $\frac{5}{6}$ and $\frac{1}{4}$ is 12.

You cannot subtract the numerators, so rename $5\frac{3}{12}$ as $4\frac{15}{12}$.

$$5\frac{1}{4} \longrightarrow 5\frac{3}{12} \longrightarrow 4\frac{15}{12}$$

$$- 2\frac{5}{6} \longrightarrow - 2\frac{10}{12} \longrightarrow - 2\frac{10}{12}$$

$$\overline{}\qquad\overline{}\qquad\overline{}$$

$$2\frac{5}{12}$$

Assignment Guide 4.9
Oral: 1–6
Written:
Min. (day 1) 7–16
      (day 2) 17–25
Reg. 7–29 odd
Max. 7–35 odd

▪ Exercises

A Express each mixed number in lowest terms.

1. $2\frac{5}{3} = 3\frac{\text{\tiny III}\,2}{3}$

2. $4\frac{3}{2} = 5\frac{\text{\tiny III}\,1}{2}$

3. $6\frac{7}{5} = 7\frac{\text{\tiny III}\,2}{5}$

Complete each renaming.

4. $1\frac{1}{4} = \frac{\text{\tiny III}\,5}{4}$

5. $2\frac{1}{5} = 1\frac{\text{\tiny III}\,6}{5}$

6. $5\frac{2}{3} = 4\frac{\text{\tiny III}\,5}{3}$

7. $9\frac{1}{2}$
$+ 2\frac{1}{4}$ $11\frac{3}{4}$

8. $8\frac{3}{5}$
$- 3\frac{1}{2}$ $5\frac{1}{10}$

9. $2\frac{1}{10}$
$- 1\frac{2}{5}$ $\frac{7}{10}$

10. $\frac{7}{10}$
$+ 10\frac{1}{2}$ $11\frac{1}{5}$

11. $7\frac{1}{8}$
$- 4\frac{3}{4}$ $2\frac{3}{8}$

12. $12\frac{3}{8}$
$+ 3\frac{5}{12}$ $15\frac{19}{24}$

13. $1\frac{1}{3}$
$- \frac{7}{12}$ $\frac{3}{4}$

14. $5\frac{1}{3}$
$+ 6\frac{5}{6}$ $12\frac{1}{6}$

15. $5\frac{3}{4}$
$- 2\frac{4}{5}$ $2\frac{19}{20}$

16. $14\frac{11}{12}$
$+ 8\frac{1}{4}$ $23\frac{1}{6}$

17. $9\frac{2}{3}$
$+ 7\frac{9}{10}$ $17\frac{17}{30}$

18. $6\frac{1}{6}$
$- 1\frac{4}{9}$ $4\frac{13}{18}$

19. $6\frac{2}{5}$
$+ 1\frac{1}{4}$ $7\frac{13}{20}$

20. $12\frac{1}{3}$
$+ 7\frac{5}{12}$ $19\frac{3}{4}$

21. $7\frac{1}{12}$
$- 3\frac{3}{8}$ $3\frac{17}{24}$

22. $4\frac{1}{10}$
$- 2\frac{3}{5}$ $1\frac{1}{2}$

23. Kay cut $2\frac{5}{8}$ yards of material from a piece $4\frac{1}{2}$ yards long. How much material did she have left? $1\frac{7}{8}$ yd

24. $10\frac{1}{2}$ in. of snow fell during the month of November and $14\frac{3}{4}$ in. fell during December. What was the total snowfall for both months? $25\frac{1}{4}$ in.

25. It took a mechanic $5\frac{2}{3}$ hours of work one day and $2\frac{1}{2}$ hours on the next day to fix a car. What was the total number of hours the mechanic worked on the car? $8\frac{1}{6}$ hr

C Add.

Example: $1\frac{2}{3} \rightarrow 1\frac{4}{6}$

$2\frac{1}{2} \rightarrow 2\frac{3}{6}$

$+ 1\frac{5}{6} \rightarrow + 1\frac{5}{6}$

$4\frac{12}{6} = 6$

Think: $4\frac{\overset{2}{\cancel{12}}}{\underset{1}{\cancel{6}}} = 4 + 2 = 6$

26. $4\frac{1}{2}$
$2\frac{1}{4}$
$+ 5\frac{1}{2}$ $12\frac{1}{4}$

27. $3\frac{1}{2}$
$2\frac{2}{3}$
$+ 1\frac{1}{6}$ $7\frac{1}{3}$

28. $\frac{5}{8}$
$2\frac{1}{4}$
$+ 3\frac{3}{8}$ $6\frac{1}{4}$

29. $1\frac{3}{4}$
$2\frac{1}{3}$
$+ 1\frac{5}{12}$ $5\frac{1}{2}$

Use the method shown below to multiply.

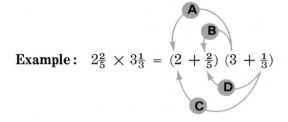

Example: $2\frac{2}{5} \times 3\frac{1}{3} = (2 + \frac{2}{5})(3 + \frac{1}{3})$

Multiply both parts of one mixed number by each part of the other.

Ⓐ   Ⓑ   Ⓒ   Ⓓ

$= 6 + \dfrac{6}{5} + \dfrac{2}{3} + \dfrac{2}{15}$ Then add the products.

$= 6 + \dfrac{18}{15} + \dfrac{10}{15} + \dfrac{2}{15}$

$= 6 + \dfrac{\overset{2}{\cancel{30}}}{\underset{1}{\cancel{15}}}$

$= 8$

30. $3\frac{1}{2} \times 2\frac{1}{4}$ $7\frac{7}{8}$

31. $4\frac{3}{5} \times 5\frac{1}{3}$ $24\frac{8}{15}$

32. $2\frac{3}{4} \times 2\frac{2}{5}$ $6\frac{3}{5}$

33. $6\frac{7}{8} \times 1\frac{1}{3}$ $9\frac{1}{6}$

34. $6\frac{2}{3} \times 2\frac{4}{5}$ $18\frac{2}{3}$

35. $8\frac{1}{2} \times 3\frac{2}{3}$ $31\frac{1}{6}$

Solving Problems With U.S. Units of Measure

A problem might require a whole-number answer, but the result of your computation is not a whole number. In such problems, the answer is usually the next larger or the next smaller whole number.

Suggested Class Time

Course	Min.	Reg.	Max.
Days	0	1	1

Example 1: Each chocolate bar weighs $2\frac{3}{4}$ ounces. How many bars would you buy to have the 10 ounces needed for the recipe?

$$10 \div 2\frac{3}{4} = \frac{10}{1} \div \frac{11}{4}$$

$$= \frac{10}{1} \times \frac{4}{11}$$

$$= \frac{40}{11} \text{ or } 3\frac{7}{11}$$

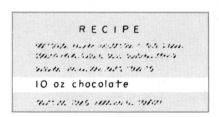

You can't buy $3\frac{7}{11}$ bars, and 3 bars would not be enough. So you would buy 4 bars.

Example 2: How many small boxes will fit on a 10-inch shelf?

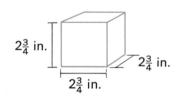

From Example 1, $10 \div 2\frac{3}{4} = 3\frac{7}{11}$.

You can't have $3\frac{7}{11}$ boxes, and 4 boxes would not fit. So you can fit only 3 boxes on the 10-inch shelf.

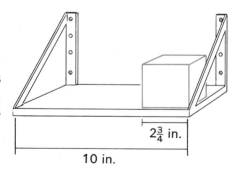

In the examples, the best answer is not the mixed number that resulted from the computation.

Exercises

Assignment Guide 4.10
Oral: Reg. & Max. 1–5
Written: Reg. 6–13
Max. 6–16

[A] The computation for each problem has a result that is not a whole number. Decide if the best answer would be

(a) the actual result,

(b) the next larger whole number, or

(c) the next smaller whole number.

1. Each wall panel is 4 feet wide. How many panels must you buy to panel a wall $18\frac{1}{2}$ feet wide? b

2. A 19-inch wire is cut in half. How long is each piece? a

3. Allen can make 8 posters in $2\frac{1}{2}$ hr. How many posters can he complete in 1 hr? c

Mary Elenz Tranter Photographics

4. You're serving dinner to 11 people. How much meat should you buy to serve each person $\frac{1}{2}$ pound of meat? a

5. How many $2\frac{1}{2}$-foot boards can be cut from a 12-foot board? c

[B] Find the number that best answers each question.

6. On Jane's part-time job, she works $4\frac{1}{2}$ hours a day. How many days must she work to put in 15 hours per week? 4 days

7. There are $2\frac{1}{4}$ cups of rice in a pound box. Chris uses $\frac{1}{2}$ cup each time he makes rice pudding. How many times can he make rice pudding from a pound box? 4 times

8. Each theater seat is $2\frac{1}{4}$ feet wide. How many seats can fit in a 15-foot row? 6 seats

9. Each can holds $1\frac{1}{2}$ quarts. How many cans are needed to hold 10 quarts of liquid? 7 cans

Connie and PC Peri

10. It takes $1\frac{1}{6}$ yd of tissue paper to make 1 kite. How many kites can be made with $4\frac{1}{3}$ yd? 3 kites

11. Fruit punch comes in 3-quart ($\frac{3}{4}$-gallon) bottles. How many bottles should you buy to have enough to fill a 2-gallon punch bowl? 3 bottles

12. The gas gauge on a car shows that $\frac{3}{8}$ of a tank of gas has been used since the tank was last filled. If the tank holds 20 gallons, how much gas was used? $7\frac{1}{2}$ gal.

13. A 28-inch piece of copper tubing is cut into 3 pieces of the same length. How long is each piece? $9\frac{1}{3}$ in.

C The formula for finding the area of a circle is $A = \pi r^2$, where r stands for the radius and π is approximately equal to $\frac{22}{7}$.

Example: $A = \pi r^2$

$$= \frac{22}{7} \times \left(3\frac{1}{2}\right)^2$$

$$= \frac{22}{7} \times \left(\frac{7}{2}\right)^2$$

$$= \frac{22}{7} \times \frac{7}{2} \times \frac{7}{2}$$

$$= \frac{77}{2} \text{ or } 38\frac{1}{2}$$

3½ in.

The area is $38\frac{1}{2}$ sq in.

Find the area of each circle. Use $\frac{22}{7}$ for π.

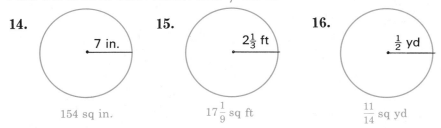

14. 7 in.

15. $2\frac{1}{3}$ ft

16. $\frac{1}{2}$ yd

154 sq in.

$17\frac{1}{9}$ sq ft

$\frac{11}{14}$ sq yd

Terms and Symbols Review

Choose the best term.

1. 3 is the (*denominator*, *numerator*) of $\frac{3}{4}$.

2. $\frac{8}{12}$ is equivalent to ($\frac{2}{3}$, $\frac{5}{6}$, $\frac{3}{4}$).

3. ($\frac{2}{3}$, $\frac{2}{4}$, $\frac{2}{6}$) is a fraction in lowest terms.

4. ($\frac{3}{4}$, $2\frac{2}{3}$, $\frac{5}{10}$) is a mixed number.

5. (2, 12, $\frac{1}{5}$) is the least common denominator of $\frac{1}{4}$ and $\frac{1}{6}$.

Assignment Guide Rev.
Oral: Terms & Symbols 1–5
Written:
Min. (day 1) 1–33
    (day 2) 34–60
Reg. 1–63 odd
Max. 1–63 odd

Chapter 4 Review

Express as a fraction.   4.1

1. $2 \div 5$ $\frac{2}{5}$ **2.** 4 $\frac{4}{1}$ **3.** $3\overline{)8}$ $\frac{8}{3}$ **4.** $5 \div 2$ $\frac{5}{2}$

Add.

5. $\frac{1}{5} + \frac{1}{5}$ $\frac{2}{5}$ **6.** $\frac{2}{7} + \frac{3}{7}$ $\frac{5}{7}$ **7.** $\frac{2}{9} + \frac{5}{9}$ $\frac{7}{9}$ **8.** $\frac{3}{8} + \frac{5}{8}$ 1

Multiply.   4.2

9. $\frac{3}{4} \times \frac{3}{4}$ $\frac{9}{16}$ **10.** $\frac{2}{3} \times \frac{4}{5}$ $\frac{8}{15}$ **11.** $\frac{5}{16} \times \frac{1}{2}$ $\frac{5}{32}$ **12.** $3 \times \frac{1}{4}$ $\frac{3}{4}$

Multiply. Express each answer in lowest terms.   4.3

13. $\frac{2}{3} \times \frac{3}{8}$ $\frac{1}{4}$ **14.** $\frac{1}{16} \times \frac{4}{5}$ $\frac{1}{20}$ **15.** $\frac{4}{3} \times \frac{3}{4}$ 1 **16.** $3 \times \frac{1}{6}$ $\frac{1}{2}$

Express each mixed number as a fraction.   4.4

17. $1\frac{2}{3}$ $\frac{5}{3}$ **18.** $2\frac{1}{2}$ $\frac{5}{2}$ **19.** $1\frac{3}{5}$ $\frac{8}{5}$ **20.** $3\frac{3}{4}$ $\frac{15}{4}$

Express each fraction as a mixed number.

21. $\frac{10}{3}$ $3\frac{1}{3}$ **22.** $\frac{9}{2}$ $4\frac{1}{2}$ **23.** $\frac{7}{4}$ $1\frac{3}{4}$ **24.** $\frac{11}{5}$ $2\frac{1}{5}$

Multiply.

25. $\frac{4}{5} \times \frac{11}{8}$ $1\frac{1}{10}$ **26.** $2 \times \frac{3}{4}$ $1\frac{1}{2}$ **27.** $\frac{8}{3} \times \frac{1}{6}$ $\frac{4}{9}$

28. $6 \times 1\frac{1}{2}$ 9 **29.** $1\frac{2}{3} \times \frac{3}{10}$ $\frac{1}{2}$ **30.** $2\frac{1}{2} \times 1\frac{1}{3}$ $3\frac{1}{3}$ 4.5

31. $2\frac{2}{5} \times 3\frac{1}{3}$ 8

32. $\frac{1}{3} \times 1\frac{4}{5}$ $\frac{3}{5}$

33. $1\frac{1}{4} \times 4\frac{3}{5}$ $5\frac{3}{4}$

4.6   Divide. Express each answer in lowest terms.

34. $\frac{5}{8} \div \frac{5}{12}$ $1\frac{1}{2}$

35. $\frac{1}{3} \div 5$ $\frac{1}{15}$

36. $\frac{1}{2} \div 1\frac{1}{2}$ $\frac{1}{3}$

37. $6 \div 1\frac{1}{8}$ $5\frac{1}{3}$

38. $1\frac{1}{2} \div 1\frac{1}{5}$ $1\frac{1}{4}$

39. $2\frac{1}{4} \div 6$ $\frac{3}{8}$

4.7   Express each mixed number in lowest terms.

40. $3\frac{5}{4} = 4\frac{1}{4}$

41. $2\frac{7}{5} = 3\frac{2}{5}$

42. $5\frac{11}{6} = 6\frac{5}{6}$

Complete each renaming.

43. $2\frac{2}{3} = 1\frac{5}{3}$

44. $6\frac{2}{5} = 5\frac{7}{5}$

45. $1 = \frac{8}{8}$

Find each sum or difference. Express each answer in lowest terms.

46. $1\frac{1}{2}$
$+ 2\frac{1}{2}$ 4

47. $2\frac{1}{3}$
$- 1\frac{2}{3}$ $\frac{2}{3}$

48. $4\frac{2}{5}$
$+ 1\frac{2}{5}$ $5\frac{4}{5}$

49. 5
$- 2\frac{5}{8}$ $2\frac{3}{8}$

4.8   Complete each pair of equivalent fractions.

50. $\frac{2}{3} = \frac{8}{12}$

51. $\frac{3}{4} = \frac{6}{8}$

52. $\frac{4}{5} = \frac{16}{20}$

Find each sum or difference. Express your answers in lowest terms.

53. $\frac{1}{3}$
$+ \frac{1}{2}$ $\frac{5}{6}$

54. $\frac{3}{4}$
$- \frac{1}{6}$ $\frac{7}{12}$

55. $\frac{1}{4}$
$+ \frac{5}{8}$ $\frac{7}{8}$

56. $\frac{3}{5}$
$- \frac{1}{2}$ $\frac{1}{10}$

Find each sum or difference. Express your answers in lowest terms.

4.9   **57.** $2\frac{3}{5}$
$+ 1\frac{3}{10}$ $3\frac{9}{10}$

58. $4\frac{1}{3}$
$- 3\frac{5}{6}$ $\frac{1}{2}$

59. $5\frac{3}{4}$
$+ 8\frac{2}{3}$ $14\frac{5}{12}$

60. $1\frac{1}{6}$
$- \frac{5}{8}$ $\frac{13}{24}$

4.10   Find the number that best answers each question.

61. Mr. Sosnowski's students need wire for an experiment. How many $2\frac{1}{2}$-foot pieces can he cut from a 32-foot piece? 12 pieces

62. Tomato juice comes in $5\frac{1}{3}$-ounce cans. How many cans should you buy if the recipe calls for 12 ounces? 3 cans

63. How many $\frac{3}{4}$-pound packages of bacon are needed to have at least 10 pounds of bacon? 14 packages

Assignment Guide Test
Written: Min. 1–32
Reg. 1–34
Max. 1–34

Express as a fraction.

1. 6 $\frac{6}{1}$

2. $4\frac{1}{2}$ $\frac{9}{2}$

3. $3 \div 2$ $\frac{3}{2}$

Express in lowest terms.

4. $\frac{5}{15}$ $\frac{1}{3}$

5. $\frac{5}{2}$ $2\frac{1}{2}$

6. $\frac{10}{6}$ $1\frac{2}{3}$

Compute.

7. $\frac{1}{5} \times \frac{2}{3}$ $\frac{2}{15}$

8. $\frac{2}{5} \times \frac{5}{6}$ $\frac{1}{3}$

9. $10 \times \frac{1}{4}$ $2\frac{1}{2}$

10. $1\frac{1}{2} \times 1\frac{1}{3}$ 2

11. $3 \times \frac{1}{7}$ $\frac{3}{7}$

12. $\frac{2}{3} \div \frac{1}{2}$ $1\frac{1}{3}$

13. $4\frac{1}{2} \div 3$ $1\frac{1}{2}$

14. $6 \div \frac{3}{8}$ 16

15. $8\frac{1}{3} \div 3\frac{1}{3}$ $2\frac{1}{2}$

Complete each pair of equivalent fractions.

16. $\frac{1}{2} = \frac{\text{IIII}}{12}$ 6

17. $\frac{2}{3} = \frac{\text{IIII}}{6}$ 4

18. $\frac{3}{4} = \frac{\text{IIII}}{8}$ 6

Express each mixed number in lowest terms.

19. $2\frac{4}{3} = 3\frac{\text{IIII}}{3}$ 1

20. $1\frac{7}{4} = 2\frac{\text{IIII}}{4}$ 3

21. $3\frac{11}{8} = 4\frac{\text{IIII}}{8}$ 3

Complete each renaming.

22. $2\frac{1}{4} = 1\frac{\text{IIII}}{4}$ 5

23. $6\frac{2}{5} = 5\frac{\text{IIII}}{5}$ 7

24. $5\frac{3}{10} = 4\frac{\text{IIII}}{10}$ 13

Find each sum or difference.

25.
$\begin{array}{r} \frac{1}{8} \\ + \frac{3}{8} \\ \hline \end{array}$ $\frac{1}{2}$

26.
$\begin{array}{r} 10 \\ - 8\frac{2}{3} \\ \hline \end{array}$ $1\frac{1}{3}$

27.
$\begin{array}{r} 2\frac{5}{6} \\ - 2\frac{1}{6} \\ \hline \end{array}$ $\frac{2}{3}$

28.
$\begin{array}{r} 6\frac{5}{8} \\ + 5\frac{5}{8} \\ \hline \end{array}$ $12\frac{1}{4}$

29.
$\begin{array}{r} \frac{2}{3} \\ - \frac{1}{2} \\ \hline \end{array}$ $\frac{1}{6}$

30.
$\begin{array}{r} 8\frac{1}{2} \\ - 7\frac{3}{4} \\ \hline \end{array}$ $\frac{3}{4}$

31.
$\begin{array}{r} 5\frac{1}{2} \\ + 3\frac{5}{6} \\ \hline \end{array}$ $9\frac{1}{3}$

32.
$\begin{array}{r} \frac{1}{3} \\ + \frac{1}{4} \\ \hline \end{array}$ $\frac{7}{12}$

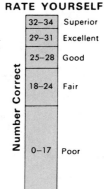

RATE YOURSELF

Number Correct	
32–34	Superior
29–31	Excellent
25–28	Good
18–24	Fair
0–17	Poor

Find the number that best answers each question.

33. How many $2\frac{1}{4}$-inch pieces of wire can be cut from a 10-inch piece?

4 pieces

34. How many $1\frac{1}{2}$-quart cans must you buy to have at least 8 quarts?

6 cans

MATH AND TYPING

Many people who work in offices must know how to type. Typing fast is important, but so is making as few errors as possible. That is why you must subtract for errors when finding your typing speed.

The formula below is used for a 20-minute typing test.

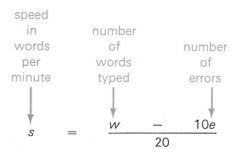

$$s = \frac{w - 10e}{20}$$

where s is the speed in words per minute, w is the number of words typed, and $10e$ is the number of errors.

Find the speed for each of these scores on a 20-minute test.

1. 670 words with 5 errors
31 words per minute

2. 720 words with 14 errors
29 words per minute

3. 1000 words with 10 errors
45 words per minute

4. 830 words with 7 errors
38 words per minute

142

Getting Ready for Chapter 5

Find each answer.

Assignment Guide GR 5
Written: Min. 1–30

1.   364
+148   512

2.   134
−94   40

3.   260
    42
+1486   1788

4.   36
×8   288

5. 425
×5   2125

6.   34
×25   850

7. 6)504   84

8. 8)1928   241

9. 672 ÷ 32   21

10. 34 + 186 + 7   227

11. 406 − 38   368

12. 16 × 42   672

Express each fraction in lowest terms.   4.3

13. $\frac{32}{100}$ $\frac{8}{25}$

14. $\frac{6}{10}$ $\frac{3}{5}$

15. $\frac{25}{1000}$ $\frac{1}{40}$

Find the value of each expression.   3.8

16. 10^3 1000

17. 10^2 100

18. 10^1 10

19. $\frac{1}{10^3}$ $\frac{1}{1000}$

20. $\frac{1}{10^2}$ $\frac{1}{100}$

21. $\frac{1}{10^1}$ $\frac{1}{10}$

Complete.   1.1

22. 1 kg = ____ g   1000

23. 1 L = ____ mL   1000

24. 1 m = ____ cm   100

25. 1 g = ____ mg   1000

26. 1 km = ____ m   1000

27. 1 cm = ____ mm   10

Write each mixed number as a fraction.   4.4

28. $3\frac{3}{8}$ $\frac{27}{8}$

29. $5\frac{7}{10}$ $\frac{57}{10}$

30. $6\frac{2}{3}$ $\frac{20}{3}$

5

5

DECIMALS AND ESTIMATING

In this chapter you will review the basic operations with decimals and learn how to solve equations involving decimals. You will also learn how to check answers by estimating them.

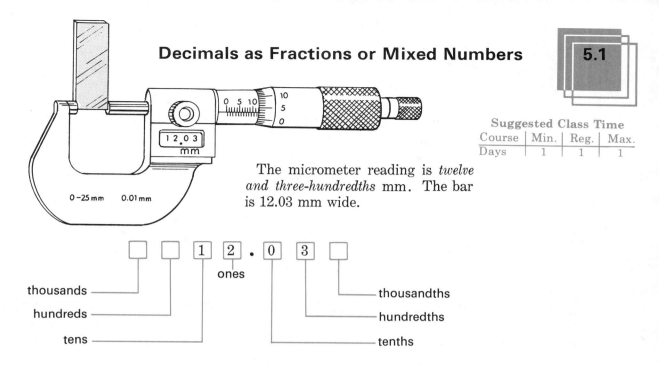

Decimals as Fractions or Mixed Numbers

Suggested Class Time

Course	Min.	Reg.	Max.
Days	1	1	1

The micrometer reading is *twelve and three-hundredths* mm. The bar is 12.03 mm wide.

thousands
hundreds
tens
ones
tenths
hundredths
thousandths

Example 1: Express 0.7, 12.03, and 123.456 as fractions or mixed numbers.

$$0.7 = \frac{7}{10} \qquad 12.03 = 12\frac{3}{100} \qquad 123.456 = 123\frac{456}{1000}$$

$$= 123\frac{57}{125}$$

Change to lowest terms whenever possible.

This 0 calls attention to the decimal point.

The number of digits here tells what the denominator should be.

The numbers 10, 100, 1000, and so on, are called *powers of ten*, since they can be written 10^1, 10^2, 10^3, and so on. A fraction whose denominator is a power of ten can easily be written as a decimal.

Example 2: Express $\frac{3}{10}$, $\frac{24}{100}$, and $2\frac{5}{1000}$ as decimals.

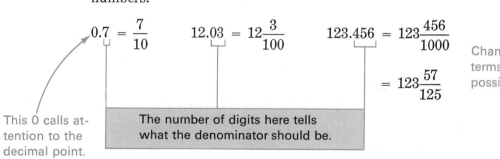

$$\frac{3}{10} = 0.3 \qquad \frac{24}{100} = 0.24 \qquad 2\frac{5}{1000} = 2.005$$

The denominator tells where the last digit of the numerator goes.

Use zeros here to put the 5 in the thousandths place.

145

Exercises

Assignment Guide 5.1
Oral: 1–12
Written: Min. 13–43 odd
       Reg. 13–47 odd
       Max. 13–51 odd

1–12. Answers at left.

A Tell how to read each decimal.

1. 0.1   **2.** 1.5   **3.** 7.9   **4.** 14.6

5. 0.12   **6.** 0.02   **7.** 6.55   **8.** 35.09

9. 0.123   **10.** 0.402   **11.** 8.063   **12.** 14.839

1. One tenth
2. One and five tenths
3. Seven and nine tenths
4. Fourteen and six tenths
5. Twelve hundredths
6. Two hundredths
7. Six and fifty-five hundredths
8. Thirty-five and nine hundredths
9. One hundred twenty-three thousandths
10. Four hundred two thousandths
11. Eight and sixty-three thousandths
12. Fourteen and eight hundred thirty-nine thousandths

B Write each decimal as a fraction or a mixed number.

13. 0.3 $\frac{3}{10}$ **14.** 0.8 $\frac{4}{5}$ **15.** 68.9 $68\frac{9}{10}$ **16.** 6.5 $6\frac{1}{2}$

17. 0.17 $\frac{17}{100}$ **18.** 0.36 $\frac{9}{25}$ **19.** 9.07 $9\frac{7}{100}$ **20.** 5.25 $5\frac{1}{4}$

21. 0.321 $\frac{321}{1000}$ **22.** 0.055 $\frac{11}{200}$ **23.** 18.009 $18\frac{9}{1000}$ **24.** 6.025 $6\frac{1}{40}$

25. 8.6 $8\frac{3}{5}$ **26.** 9.24 $9\frac{6}{25}$ **27.** 16.085 $16\frac{17}{200}$ **28.** 3.125 $3\frac{1}{8}$

Express each number as a decimal.

29. $\frac{5}{10}$ 0.5   **30.** $\frac{7}{10}$ 0.7   **31.** $3\frac{9}{10}$ 3.9   **32.** $17\frac{8}{10}$ 17.8

33. $\frac{16}{100}$ 0.16   **34.** $\frac{6}{100}$ 0.06   **35.** $4\frac{37}{100}$ 4.37   **36.** $43\frac{75}{100}$ 43.75

37. $\frac{225}{1000}$ 0.225   **38.** $\frac{25}{1000}$ 0.025   **39.** $6\frac{3}{1000}$ 6.003   **40.** $24\frac{502}{1000}$ 24.502

41. $6\frac{9}{10}$ 6.9   **42.** $6\frac{9}{100}$ 6.09   **43.** $6\frac{9}{1000}$ 6.009   **44.** $4\frac{75}{1000}$ 4.075

C Rewrite each fraction with a denominator that is a power of ten. Then rewrite as a decimal.

45. $\frac{2}{5}$ $\frac{4}{10}$; 0.4   **46.** $\frac{1}{2}$ $\frac{5}{10}$; 0.5   **47.** $\frac{9}{25}$ $\frac{36}{100}$; 0.36   **48.** $3\frac{7}{50}$ $3\frac{14}{100}$; 3.14

49. $7\frac{3}{20}$ $7\frac{15}{100}$; 7.15   **50.** $4\frac{21}{500}$ $4\frac{42}{1000}$; 4.042   **51.** $1\frac{121}{200}$ $1\frac{605}{1000}$; 1.605   **52.** $\frac{13}{250}$ $\frac{52}{1000}$; 0.052

Courtesy U.S. Mint

The Three-Cent Dollar

The Susan B. Anthony dollar is 1.043 inches in diameter, weighs 8.1 grams, and costs $0.03 to make.

Rounding Numbers

When speaking of the same sporting event, different people report the attendance in different ways.

A sportscaster _ _ _ _ _ _ 42,400 excited fans are enjoying . . .

An accountant _ _ _ _ _ 42,364 tickets sold . . .

A sports reporter _ _ _ _ 42,000 see X stomp Y . . .

Suggested Class Time			
Course	Min.	Reg.	Max.
Days	1	1	1

For many purposes, an exact number is not needed. Two of the persons reporting have *rounded* the number in attendance.

Example 1: Round 42,364 to the nearest thousand.

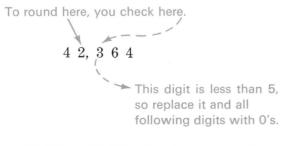

To round here, you check here.

4 2, 3 6 4

This digit is less than 5, so replace it and all following digits with 0's.

$42,364 \approx 42,000$ (to the nearest thousand)

This symbol means "is approximately equal to."

147

Example 2: Round 42,364 to the nearest hundred.

To round here, you check here.

4 2, 3 6 4 → This digit is 5 or greater, so
(1) replace it and all following digits with 0's.
(2) increase the hundreds digit by 1.

42,364 ≈ 42,400 (to the nearest hundred)

Example 3: Round as indicated.

number	to the nearest		
	one	tenth	hundredth
43.5762	44	43.6	43.58
1.6218	2	1.6	1.62
0.0421	0	0.0	0.04

Rounding can be used to **estimate** answers. An estimate serves as a check on whether a computed answer is reasonable.

Example 4: Estimate and then compute each answer. Compare the results.

$34827 + 3207$ 82×97

$35000 + 3000$ Round each number to any convenient place. 80×100

38000   ←——— estimates ———→   8000

$34827 + 3207 = 38034$ ←——computed answers——→ $82 \times 97 = 7954$

Assignment Guide 5.2
Oral: 1–20
Written: Min. 21–33 odd
      Reg. 21–33
      Max. 21–35

▓ Exercises

A Tell which digit you would check when rounding **(a)** to the nearest ten, **(b)** to the nearest hundred, and **(c)** to the nearest thousand.

    c b a   c b a   c b a   c b a
1. 5801   **2.** 546   **3.** 38,542   **4.** 645,123

    c b a   c b a   c b a   c b a
5. 3592.1   **6.** 32,546.78   **7.** 50,613.82   **8.** 1624.578

Tell which digit you would check when rounding **(a)** to the nearest one, **(b)** to the nearest tenth, **(c)** to the nearest hundredth, and **(d)** to the nearest thousandth.

      a b c d   a b c d   a b c d   a b c d

9. 6.0123   **10.** 0.2345   **11.** 0.9152   **12.** 8.0576

      a b c d   a b c d   a b c d   a b c d

13. 0.5724   **14.** 9.13428   **15.** 19.60572   **16.** 742.0536

Tell how you would estimate each answer.

17–20. Answers may vary.

17. 32×32 **18.** $989 - 285$ **19.** 89×11 **20.** $896 \div 32$

B Round as indicated.

number	to the nearest			
	one	tenth	hundredth	thousandth
21. 0.4532	0	0.5	0.45	0.453
22. 0.6051	1	0.6	0.61	0.605
23. 9.0826	9	9.1	9.08	9.083
24. 24.0580	24	24.1	24.06	24.058
25. 132.5158	133	132.5	132.52	132.516

number	to the nearest		
	ten	hundred	thousand
26. 1762	1760	1800	2000
27. 9835	9840	9800	10,000
28. 14.508	10	0	0
29. 672.54	670	700	1000
30. 80,521.3	80,520	80,500	81,000

(a) Estimate the value; **(b)** then compute the value.

31–33. a. Answers may vary.

31. 888×71 **32.** $638 - 183$ **33.** $135 + 27 + 212$
    b. 63,048   b. 455   b. 374

C Round 3.14159265358973 as indicated.

34. nearest hundred thousandth 3.14159   **35.** nearest millionth 3.141593

Adding and Subtracting Decimals

Suggested Class Time

Course	Min.	Reg.	Max.
Days	1	1	1

Brent Jones

By using the following rule, you can add or subtract with decimals just as you add or subtract whole numbers.

> Keep the decimal points aligned when adding or subtracting with decimals.

Example 1: A customer buys $6.75 worth of groceries and gives the clerk a $10 bill. How much change should the customer receive?

Align the decimal points.

These 0's do not change the value, but they are helpful in subtracting.

$$\begin{array}{r} \$10.00 \\ -6.75 \\ \hline \$\ 3.25 \end{array}$$

◀ total cost
◀ change

Example 2: Estimate and then compute the sum of 6, 0.41, 31.9, and 2.059.

Round each number to any convenient place.

Align.

These 0's do not change the value.

$$\begin{array}{r} 6 \\ 0 \\ 32 \\ +2 \\ \hline 40 \end{array}$$ estimate

$$\begin{array}{r} 6.000 \\ 0.410 \\ 31.900 \\ +2.059 \\ \hline 40.369 \end{array}$$ sum

■ Exercises

Assignment Guide 5.3
Oral: 1–5
Written: Min. 6–25
　　　　 Reg. 6–28
　　　　 Max. 6–32

A Answer the questions.

1. What rule must you use when adding or subtracting with decimals?
Align the decimal points.

2. How is adding with decimals like adding whole numbers?
The same except for decimal points

3. How is subtracting with decimals like subtracting whole numbers?
The same except for decimal points

4. Estimate $3.2 + 2.97 + 1.855 + 2.002$. $3 + 3 + 2 + 2 = 10$

5. Is 3.2 equal to 3.200? When might the 0's be helpful?
Yes; in addition or subtraction if other numbers have thousandths

B Add or subtract.

6. 3.25
　　 +4.3 7.55

7. 15.09
　　 +2.3 17.39

8. 42.3
　　 0.42
　 +1.093 43.813

9. 21.3
　　 0.94
　 +36 58.24

10. 1.45
　　 −1.05 0.40

11. 3.08
　　 −1.4 1.68

12. 13.5
　　 −0.25 13.25

13. 4.095
　　 −1.5 2.595

14. 3.425
　　 1.5
　 +0.93 5.855

15. 44.2
　　 9.9
　 +9 63.1

16. 25.5
　　 −5.35 20.15

17. 10.5
　　 −0.22 10.28

(a) Estimate the value; **(b)** then compute the value.

18–25. **a.** Answers may vary.

18. $3.4 - 2.45$ **b.** 0.95

19. $36.2 + 14.85 + 1.256$
b. 52.306

20. $9.6 - 3.125$ **b.** 6.475

21. $4.2 + 4.02 + 3.5$
b. 11.72

22. $0.7 + 7.7 + 7.77 + 7.777$
b. 23.947

23. $5 - 0.25$ **b.** 4.75

24. $3.6 + 5.256 + 8 + 9.25$
b. 26.106

25. $16 - 1.75$
b. 14.25

C **26.** Mechanics use the gauge shown to measure gaps.
The metal pieces are used one at a time or in com-
bination of two or more. Which of them could you
combine to measure a gap of the given width?
Other answers possible for **b**, **c**, and **d**.

a. 0.09 mm 0.05, 0.04　　**b.** 0.11 mm 0.06, 0.05

c. 0.17 mm 0.07, 0.06,　　**d.** 0.40 mm 0.20, 0.10, 0.06,
　　　　　　　　　0.04　　　　　　　　　　　　　　　 0.04

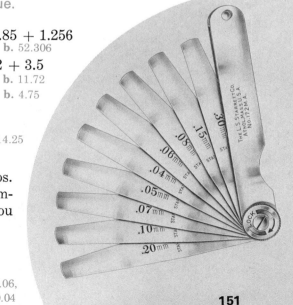

151

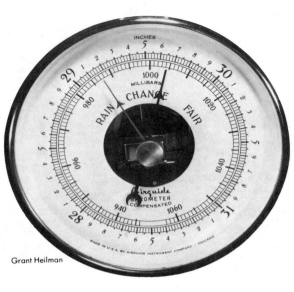

Grant Heilman

27. At 8 A.M. the barometer reading was 29.16. It rose steadily until 5 P.M., when the reading was 29.65. How much did the reading change?

0.49

28. For a three-minute phone call from Chicago to Atlanta, the charge is $1.18 if you "dial direct." An operator-assisted call costs $2.05. How much cheaper is the dial-direct call?

$0.87

Solve.

29. $x + 2.7 = 5.9$ 3.2

30. $8.36 = n + 4.61$

3.75

31. $5 = r + 0.2$ 4.8

32. $d - 1 = 3.7042$

4.7042

Rounding Pi

To describe a circle, you can state the circumference (C), the diameter (d), the radius (r), or the area (A). For every circle, of any size, $C \div d$ is the same number. This number cannot be named exactly as a fraction or as a decimal, so we say $C \div d = \pi$. (π is a Greek letter pronounced PĪ.) Computers have been used to find π to thousands of decimal places. Here are a few of them.

$$\pi = 3.14159265358973\cdots$$

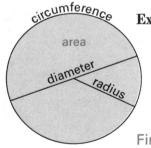

Example : Find the area of a circle with a radius of 6.

$$A = \pi r^2$$
$$= \pi \times 6^2$$
$$= \pi \times 36 \quad \text{So } 36\pi \text{ is the exact area.}$$

Find approximate values for this area by multiplying 36 by the decimal for π rounded to the place named.

1. the nearest one 108

2. the nearest tenth 111.6

3. the nearest hundredth 113.04

4. the nearest thousandth 113.112

The values you have found come closer and closer to the exact value of the area. But since π cannot be named exactly as a decimal, neither can the area.

152

Multiplying Decimals

Multiplying with decimals is like multiplying whole numbers. You must decide, however, where to place the decimal point.

Example 1: Find each product.

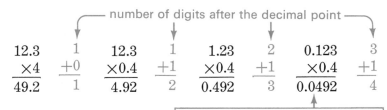

number of digits after the decimal point

$$
\begin{array}{cc}
12.3 & 1 \\
\underline{\times 4} & \underline{+0} \\
49.2 & 1
\end{array}
\qquad
\begin{array}{cc}
12.3 & 1 \\
\underline{\times 0.4} & \underline{+1} \\
4.92 & 2
\end{array}
\qquad
\begin{array}{cc}
1.23 & 2 \\
\underline{\times 0.4} & \underline{+1} \\
0.492 & 3
\end{array}
\qquad
\begin{array}{cc}
0.123 & 3 \\
\underline{\times 0.4} & \underline{+1} \\
0.0492 & 4
\end{array}
$$

Write in as many 0's as needed to properly place the decimal point.

Example 2: How can an estimate be used to decide where to put the decimal point in an answer?

estimate

$$
\begin{array}{cc}
12.3 & 12 \\
\underline{\times 4} & \underline{\times 4} \\
49.2 & 48
\end{array}
$$

estimate

$$
\begin{array}{cc}
24.326 & 24 \\
\underline{\times 11} & \underline{\times 10} \\
267{,}586 & 240
\end{array}
$$

Example 3: What shortcuts can be used to multiply by 10, 100, 1000, and so on?

$$10 \times 3.49 = 34.9$$

1 zero   1 digit

$$100 \times 3.49 = 349$$

2 zeros   2 digits

$$1000 \times 3.490 = 3490$$

3 zeros   3 digits

Count 0's.

Move this decimal point right that many places.

Copyright, Cartoons by JOHNS, 1978

JOHNS

"HE SURE MAKES A FUSS OVER ONE LITTLE DECIMAL POINT!"

Example 4:   2.4 kg = _____ g

Each kilogram contains 1000 grams.

So multiply 2.4 by 1000.

2.4 kg = 2400 g

■ Exercises

A Tell where the decimal point should be placed in each answer.

Assignment Guide 5.4
Oral: 1–14
Written: Min. 15–43 odd;
          Quiz, p. 156
     Reg. 15–47 odd;
          Quiz, p. 156
     Max. 15–57 odd;
          Quiz, p. 156

1. 56.7
  ×12
  6804

2. 5.67
  ×12
  6804

3. 0.567
  ×12
  6804

4. 0.0567
  ×12
  0.6804

5. 56.7
  ×1.2
  6804

6. 5.67
  ×0.12
  0.6804

7. 0.567
  ×1.2
  0.6804

8. 0.567
  ×0.12
  0.06804

Multiply.

9. 324
  ×0.01   3.24

10. 7.238
  ×100   723.8

11. 1000
  ×97   97,000

12. 0.1
  ×5.2   0.52

Complete.

13. To find how many meters in 75.6 kilometers, multiply by _____. 1000

14. To find how many centimeters in 3.2 meters, multiply by _____. 100

B For each product, **(a)** estimate the result; **(b)** then compute the result. 15–26. a. Answers may vary.

15. 75
  ×1.2   b. 90

16. 3.2
  ×7   b. 22.4

17. 0.21
  ×0.9   b. 0.189

18. 3.8
  ×0.5   b. 1.9

19. 0.421
  ×1.2   b. 0.5052

20. 5.18
  ×0.42   b. 2.1756

21. 30.9
  ×5.4   b. 166.86

22. 0.42
  ×0.25
  b. 0.105

23. 12.3
  ×2.4   b. 29.52

24. 42.1
  ×0.25   b. 10.525

25. 6.05
  ×0.02   b. 0.121

26. 0.0031
  ×6
  b. 0.0186

Multiply.

27. 4.012×3.1 12.4372 **28.** 6.2×0.25 1.55 **29.** 3.1×3.1 9.61

30. 6×19.5 117 **31.** 7.5×0.75 5.625 **32.** 0.3×0.16 0.048

33. 0.001×63.2 0.0632 **34.** 10×3.142 31.42 **35.** 0.079×0.01 0.00079

36. 0.0037×1000 3.7 **37.** 100×0.001 0.1 **38.** 0.01×0.001 0.00001

Complete.

39. $4.52 \text{ km} = \underline{4520} \text{ m}$ **40.** $0.023 \text{ km} = \underline{23} \text{ m}$

41. $1.9 \text{ m} = \underline{190} \text{ cm}$ **42.** $2.34 \text{ cm} = \underline{23.4} \text{ mm}$

43. $0.476 \text{ kg} = \underline{476} \text{ g}$ **44.** $37.2 \text{ g} = \underline{37,200} \text{ mg}$

45. The Morrows have found that it costs them $0.30 a mile to operate the family automobile. If they drive 675.3 miles on vacation, how much are their auto expenses? $202.59

46. At Marsh's Supermarket, tomatoes cost 43 cents a can. How much does a case (24 cans) cost? $10.32

47. Steel is manufactured in sheets of various thicknesses and stacked in piles for storage. How high is a stack of 50 sheets that are each 0.375 inches thick? 18.75 in.

A. Devaney, Inc.

C Solve.

48. $\frac{r}{5.2} = 4.1$ 21.32 **49.** $7 = \frac{p}{0.01}$ 0.07 **50.** $\frac{s}{6.25} = 1.9$ 11.875

Compute.

51. $(0.5)^2$ 0.25 **52.** $(2.01)^2$ 4.0401 **53.** $(0.2)^3$ 0.008 **54.** $(0.01)^4$ 0.00000001

55. $(3.4)(0.1)^2$ 0.034 **56.** $(7.24)10^2$ 724 **57.** $10(0.3)^2$ 0.9 **58.** $2^5(0.1)^5$ 0.00032

Quick Quiz
Sections 5.1 to 5.4

Write each decimal as a fraction or mixed number.

1. 0.9 $\frac{9}{10}$ **2.** 3.71 $3\frac{71}{100}$ **3.** 0.04 $\frac{1}{25}$ **4.** 7.25 $7\frac{1}{4}$

Write each fraction or mixed number as a decimal.

5. $\frac{7}{10}$ 0.7 **6.** $\frac{3}{100}$ 0.03 **7.** $3\frac{23}{100}$ 3.23 **8.** $4\frac{7}{1000}$ 4.007

Round **(a)** to the nearest ten and **(b)** to the nearest hundredth.

9. 7.051 **a.** 10 **b.** 7.05 **10.** 3.975 **a.** 0 **b.** 3.98 **11.** 206.4237 **a.** 210 **b.** 206.42 **12.** 723.5773 **a.** 720 **b.** 723.58

(a) Estimate the value; **(b)** then compute the value.

13–14. **a.** Answers may vary.

13. $75.3 + 15.94 + 9.312$ **b.** 100.552 **14.** 8.02×11.57 **b.** 92.7914

Math and Diving

H. Armstrong Roberts

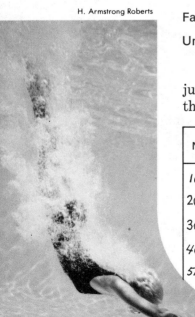

In school diving competitions, the judges give points as follows:

Failed: 0 Deficient: $2\frac{1}{2}$ to $4\frac{1}{2}$ Good: $6\frac{1}{2}$ to 8

Unsatisfactory: $\frac{1}{2}$ to 2 Satisfactory: 5 to 6 Very good: $8\frac{1}{2}$ to 10

The score for a dive is found by adding the points given by the judges and multiplying that sum by the "degree of difficulty." Find the total points earned by the diver whose scores are shown.

No.	Dive Name	Pos.	Judges 1	2	3	Total	Degree of Difficulty	Total for Dive
101	Forward Dive	L	8	$8\frac{1}{2}$	8	$24\frac{1}{2}$	1.4	34.3
202	Back Somersault	P	$7\frac{1}{2}$	$7\frac{1}{2}$	$7\frac{1}{2}$	$22\frac{1}{2}$	1.6	36
302	Reverse Somersault	L	7	$6\frac{1}{2}$	$7\frac{1}{2}$	21	1.7	35.7
401	Inward Dive	L	6	6	6	18	1.7	30.6
5112	Forward Dive, 1 Twist	P	5	6	5	16	2.1	33.6
?3	Forward $1\frac{1}{2}$ Somersault	T	8	$8\frac{1}{2}$	9	$25\frac{1}{2}$	1.6	40.8
							Total Points	211

Donald Dietz, Stock, Boston

Dividing Decimals by Whole Numbers

5.5

Suggested Class Time			
Course	Min.	Reg.	Max.
Days	1	1	1

Example 1 : Lee earned $6.75 in 3 hours. How much did Lee earn per hour?

Place decimal point directly above the decimal point in 6.75.

$$2.25$$
$$3\overline{)6.75}$$

Divide as you would whole numbers.

Lee earned $2.25 per hour.

Example 2 : Divide 2.3 by 8.

$$8\overline{)2.3}$$

$$0.2875$$
$$8\overline{)2.3000}$$

Continue including 0's until the remainder is 0 or the answer has as many digits as you'd like.

Example 3 : What shortcut can be used to divide by 10, 100, 1000, and so on?

$$23.49 \div 10 = 2.349$$

1 digit   1 zero

$$23.49 \div 100 = 0.2349$$

2 digits   2 zeros

$$0\,23.49 \div 1000 = 0.02349$$

3 digits   3 zeros

Count 0's.

Move this decimal point left that many places.

Example 4: $172.6 \text{ mL} = \underline{\quad} \text{ L}$

There are 1000 milliliters in each liter.

So divide 172.6 by 1000.

$172.6 \text{ mL} = \underline{0.1726} \text{ L}$

Example 5: Write as decimals: **a.** $\frac{3}{8}$ **b.** $5\frac{3}{8}$ **c.** $\frac{2}{3}$

a. $8\overline{)3.000} \quad \text{(0.375)}$ **b.** $5\frac{3}{8} = 5 + \frac{3}{8}$ OR $5\frac{3}{8} = \frac{43}{8}$

$$= 5 + 0.375$$

$$= 5.375 \qquad 8\overline{)43.000} \quad \text{(5.375)}$$

c. $3\overline{)2.000\cdots} \quad \text{(0.666}\cdots\text{)}$ ▶ Write $0.\overline{6}$ to show that the 6 repeats.

▪ Exercises

Assignment Guide 5.5
Oral: 1–8
Written: Min. 9–47 odd
     Reg. 9–51 odd
     Max. 9–61 odd

A Tell where the decimal point should be placed in each answer.

1. $8\overline{)9.6}$ (1.₍₎2)   **2.** $8\overline{)0.96}$ (0.₍₎12)   **3.** $8\overline{)0.096}$ (0.₍₎012)

4. $1234.5 \div 1000$ 1.2345   **5.** $0.123 \div 100$ 0.00123

Complete.

6. To find how many grams in 192 milligrams, divide by ____.   1000

7. To find how many meters in 36 centimeters, divide by ____.   100

8. The bar in $3.\overline{6}$ shows that the ____ repeats.   6

B Divide.

9. $7\overline{)8.61}$ 1.23   **10.** $8\overline{)99.2}$ 12.4   **11.** $6\overline{)0.21}$ 0.035   **12.** $5\overline{)6.3}$ 1.26

13. $3\overline{)3.069}$ 1.023   **14.** $2\overline{)9.006}$ 4.503   **15.** $6\overline{)0.0312}$ 0.0052   **16.** $8\overline{)338.4}$ 42.3

17. $16\overline{)6.72}$ 0.42   **18.** $12\overline{)15.6}$ 1.3   **19.** $43\overline{)53.75}$ 1.25   **20.** $55\overline{)0.165}$ 0.003

21. $28.26 \div 9$ _3.14_   **22.** $0.258 \div 6$ _0.043_   **23.** $45.6 \div 5$ _9.12_

24. $12.045 \div 3$ _4.015_   **25.** $103.02 \div 1000$ _0.10302_   **26.** $3.045 \div 7$ _0.435_

27. $45.6 \div 12$ _3.8_   **28.** $6.76 \div 100$ _0.0676_   **29.** $0.456 \div 10$ _0.0456_

Complete.

30. $1471 \text{ mL} = \underline{} \text{ L}$ _1.471_   **31.** $30 \text{ mL} = \underline{} \text{ L}$ _0.03_

32. $975 \text{ cm} = \underline{} \text{ m}$ _9.75_   **33.** $4356 \text{ m} = \underline{} \text{ km}$ _4.356_

34. $96 \text{ mg} = \underline{} \text{ g}$ _0.096_   **35.** $560 \text{ g} = \underline{} \text{ kg}$ _0.56_

Write as decimals.

36. $\frac{1}{8}$ _0.125_   **37.** $\frac{5}{8}$ _0.625_   **38.** $\frac{1}{16}$ _0.0625_   **39.** $1\frac{3}{16}$ _1.1875_

40. $2\frac{5}{16}$ _2.3125_   **41.** $\frac{3}{4}$ _0.75_   **42.** $4\frac{7}{8}$ _4.875_   **43.** $\frac{7}{16}$ _0.4375_

44. $\frac{1}{3}$ _0.$\overline{3}$_   **45.** $2\frac{2}{3}$ _2.$\overline{6}$_   **46.** $\frac{1}{9}$ _0.$\overline{1}$_   **47.** $\frac{4}{9}$ _0.$\overline{4}$_

48. If 15 fish weigh 10.5 kg, what is the average weight per fish? _0.7 kg_

49. The average annual rainfall in Mobile, Alabama, is 68.13 inches. What is the average monthly rainfall? _5.6775 in._

50. If a light plane uses 34.2 gallons of gasoline in 3 hours, how many gallons are used per hour? _11.4 gal._

[C] **51.** The greatest recorded distance bicycled in 24 hours is 515.8 miles. What is the average number of miles the bicyclist rode each hour? _21.4916 mi_

H. Armstrong Roberts

Write as decimals.

52. $\frac{5}{6}$ _0.8$\overline{3}$_   **53.** $\frac{91}{18}$ _5.0$\overline{5}$_   **54.** $\frac{78}{11}$ _7.$\overline{09}$_   **55.** $\frac{3}{11}$ _0.$\overline{27}$_

Solve. Write each solution as a decimal.

56. $16n = 5$ _0.3125_   **57.** $100x = 2.9$ _0.029_   **58.** $1 = 4x$ _0.25_

59. $7x = 2.1$ _0.3_   **60.** $7 = 4n$ _1.75_   **61.** $10y = 35$ _3.5_

Dividing by Decimals

Multiplying the numerator and the denominator of a fraction by the same number gives an equivalent fraction.

$$\frac{0.96}{1.2} = \frac{0.96}{1.2} \times \frac{10}{10} = \frac{9.6}{12}$$

But this is the same as $1.2\overline{)0.96}$

And this is the same as $12\overline{)9.6}$

So these two division problems have the same answer.

That is, if you move the decimal points in a division problem the same number of places, the answer is unchanged. You can use this idea to change division by a decimal to division by a whole number.

$1.2\overline{)0.96}$

$1.2\overline{)0.9\,6}$

Change so divisor is a whole number.

$1.2\overline{)0.9\,6}$ with quotient 0.8

Divide.

Example: Divide.

a. $2.4\overline{)76.8}$

b. $0.09\overline{)6.3}$

c. $0.34\overline{)2.7268}$

$2.4\overline{)76.8}$

$0.09\overline{)6.30}$

$0.34\overline{)2.72\,68}$

$2.4\overline{)76.8}$ with quotient 32

$0.09\overline{)6.30}$ with quotient 70

$0.34\overline{)2.72\,68}$ with quotient 8.02

Assignment Guide 5.6
Oral: 1–12
Written: Min. 13–41 odd
Reg. 13–57 odd
Max. 13–81 odd

▦ Exercises

[A] How would you change each division problem so the divisor is a whole number?

1. $0.2\overline{)8.4}$

2. $8.1\overline{)9.72}$

3. $0.56\overline{)14.00}$

4. $2.4\overline{)0.6}$

5. $3.4\overline{)0.0068}$

6. $0.87\overline{)23.49}$

7. $0.002\overline{)0.016}$

8. $0.014\overline{)0.084}$

9. $0.09\overline{)0.225}$

Where should the decimal point be placed in each answer?

10. $0.6\overline{)7.2}$ (answer: 1 2 ▲)

11. $0.18\overline{)1.116}$ (answer: 6 2 ▲)

12. $1.3\overline{)0.0338}$ (answer: 0 0 2 6 ▲)

B Divide.

13. $0.6\overline{)15.24}$ 25.4

14. $0.4\overline{)9.04}$ 22.6

15. $0.5\overline{)0.0125}$ 0.025

16. $0.08\overline{)4.984}$ 62.3

17. $0.003\overline{)0.01896}$ 6.32

18. $0.07\overline{)0.168}$ 2.4

19. $1.2\overline{)0.384}$ 0.32

20. $0.13\overline{)0.0169}$ 0.13

21. $2.5\overline{)0.9}$ 0.36

22. $0.014\overline{)0.0448}$ 3.2

23. $0.18\overline{)0.0756}$ 0.42

24. $1.8\overline{)4.68}$ 2.6

25. $2.2\overline{)7.92}$ 3.6

26. $3.4\overline{)0.136}$ 0.04

27. $0.14\overline{)9.1}$ 65

28. $2.94 \div 0.7$ 4.2

29. $1.62 \div 0.06$ 27

30. $0.0144 \div 0.12$ 0.12

31. $1.44 \div 1.2$ 1.2

32. $8.704 \div 3.4$ 2.56

33. $0.315 \div 0.015$ 21

34. $9.8 \div 0.1$ 98

35. $4.75 \div 0.01$ 475

36. $7.2 \div 0.01$ 720

37. $0.395 \div 0.001$ 395

38. $5.6 \div 0.001$ 5600

39. $0.38 \div 0.1$ 3.8

40. $632 \div 0.01$ 63,200

41. $76.41 \div 0.001$ 76,410

After a vacation trip, the Mortons wanted to know how much they had paid per gallon of gasoline at each stop. They had recorded only the number of gallons and the total cost. Complete the charts.

	gallons	total cost	paid per gallon		gallons	total cost	paid per gallon
42.	9.8	$10.29	$1.05	43.	8.0	$10.08	$1.26
44.	6.0	7.50	1.25	45.	8.5	10.37	1.22
46.	8.1	9.72	1.20	47.	3.5	3.85	1.10
48.	12.5	15.50	1.24	49.	8.6	9.89	1.15
50.	6.0	7.08	1.18	51.	10.0	11.10	1.11

C Solve.

52. $7.5r = 317.25$ ₄₂.₃

53. $4.19s = 1.0475$ ₀.₂₅

54. $0.3125d = 1$ ₃.₂

55. $0.75n = 3$ ₄

56. $50.92 = 6.365x$ ₈

57. $2.8384 = 0.887y$ ₃.₂

58. $3.5t + 6.8 = 7.675$ ₀.₂₅

59. $0.12v + 0.19 = 0.91$ ₆

60. $0.5a + 2.6 = 2.95$ ₀.₇

61. $0.08b + 3.09 = 4.1028$ ₁₂.₆₆

62. $1.19 = 1.2c - 0.25$ ₁.₂

63. $0.6d - 0.55 = 1.49$ ₃.₄

64. $3.2e - 0.9 = 0.7$ ₀.₅

65. $0.006f - 0.152 = 1$ ₁₉₂

66. $7.2g - 16.5 = 163.5$ ₂₅

67. $5 = 0.25x + 4.85$ ₀.₆

68. $1.3m - 22.5 = 11.3$ ₂₆

69. $0.12y + 2.5 = 3.256$ ₆.₃

70. $0.25x + 0.75x = 5.9$ ₅.₉

71. $1.34n + 0.06n = 4.2$ ₃

72. $8.2 = 1.09y + 0.91y$ ₄.₁

73. $18 = 3.45a + 1.55a$ ₃.₆

74. $6.24r - 0.74r = 2.75$ ₀.₅

75. $1.68 = 9.1m - 4.9m$ ₀.₄

Another way to decide where to put the decimal point in a quotient is by estimating.

Examples:

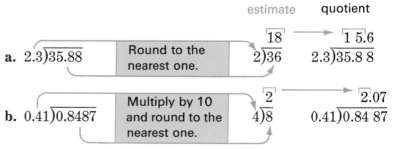

(a) Estimate the value; (b) then compute the value.

76–81. **a.** Answers may vary.

76. $5.7\overline{)17.784}$ **b.** ₃.₁₂

77. $0.21\overline{)4.998}$ **b.** ₂₃.₈

78. $0.075\overline{)0.48}$ **b.** ₆.₄

79. $3.9\overline{)5.538}$ **b.** ₁.₄₂

80. $0.00126 \div 6.3$ **b.** ₀.₀₀₀₂

81. $0.0003\overline{)0.168}$ **b.** ₅₆₀

UNIT PRICING

Ed Hoppe Photography

The 312-gram box of cereal costs $1.19.

The 198-gram box of cereal costs $0.85.

Which is the better buy?

Probably the best way to find out is to find how much one gram of cereal costs in each case. To do this, divide price by amount.

$$\frac{1.19}{312} \approx 0.0038$$

The cereal in the larger box costs $0.0038 or 0.38¢ a gram.

$$\frac{0.85}{198} \approx 0.0043$$

The cereal in the smaller box costs $0.0043 or 0.43¢ a gram.

So the larger box is the better buy.

The price of one gram of cereal is called a **unit price.** For another product, a different unit could be used. It might be a pound, an ounce, a kilogram, a quart, a liter, a piece, or 100 pieces, depending on the product. But the same unit should be used for products that are to be compared.

Of course, it is not easy for shoppers to figure unit prices for each product they buy in a store. So many stores label their shelves to show the unit prices of the products they sell.

Use unit prices to tell which is the better buy.

1. notebook paper: 200 sheets for $1.24 or 300 sheets for $1.84

2. two-ply facial tissue: 70 for 30¢ or 200 for 84¢

3. shampoo: 230 mL for $1.61 or 360 mL for $2.59

4. potato chips: $8\frac{1}{2}$ ounces for $1.11, 9 ounces for $1.19, or $13\frac{1}{2}$ ounces for $1.74

Solving Problems With Metric Units

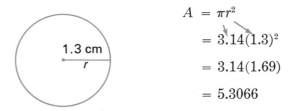

Example 1: Find the area of the circle. Use 3.14 for π. $(A = \pi r^2)$

1.3 cm
r

$$A = \pi r^2$$
$$= 3.14(1.3)^2$$
$$= 3.14(1.69)$$
$$= 5.3066$$

The area is 5.3066 square centimeters or 5.3066 cm².

To compute with metric measurements, you must express them in the same units.

Example 2: Add 8.9 cm, 37 mm, and 0.16 m.

Here are three ways to do this addition.

8.9 cm →	8.9 cm →	89 mm →	0.089 m
37 mm →	3.7 cm →	37 mm →	0.037 m
0.16 m →	+16.0 cm →	+160 mm →	+0.16 m
	28.6 cm	286 mm	0.286 m

Any one of these can be given as the answer.

Example 3: Find the area of a rectangle that is 13.2 centimeters wide and 2.4 meters long. $(A = lw)$

In meters	In centimeters
13.2 cm = (13.2 ÷ 100) m	2.4 m = (2.4 × 100) cm
= 0.132 m	= 240 cm

$A = lw$ ▶

$A = 2.4(0.132)$	$A = 240(13.2)$
$= 0.3168$	$= 3168$

The area is 0.3168 m² or 3168 cm².

Exercises

A Tell what number should replace each ? .

1. 15.6 cm   ? mm   156   **2.** 15.6 cm   15.6 cm
    88 mm   +88 mm   88 mm   + ? cm   8.8

3. 9.47 kg   ? g   9470   **4.** 9.47 kg   9.47 kg
    30 g   +30 g   30 g   + ? kg   0.03

B Compute.

5. 180 km − 31 007 m
148 993 m or 148.993 km

6. 12.06 cm − 88 mm   32.6 mm or 3.26 cm

7. 27.54 m + 3895 cm + 65.9 m
132.39 m or 13 239 cm

8. 3.4 km + 178 m + 5300 cm
3631 m or 363 100 cm or 3.631 km

9. There are 37.4 mL of orange juice in a bottle that held 236 mL of orange juice when bought. How much has been used?   198.6 mL

10. René drove 79.8 km. When he started, the odometer read 1395.4 km. What did it read at the end of the drive?   1475.2 km

11. The Kulik family has three suitcases packed for a trip to Europe. The suitcases weigh 17.8 kg, 13.7 kg, and 22.1 kg.

    a. What is the total weight of the suitcases?   53.6 kg

    b. The airline will allow the Kuliks 60 kg for the three suitcases. Are they over or under the weight limit? By how much?   Under, by 6.4 kg

Solve. Use 3.14 for π.

Ex. 12

12. Aluminum can lids are stamped from rectangular sheets 32 cm long and 24 cm wide. If each lid has a radius of 4 cm, how much of each sheet (in area) is used to make the lids? How much is wasted?
602.88 cm^2; 165.12 cm^2

Courtesy Nebraska Dept. of Economic Development

13. In a center-pivot irrigation system, a length of pipeline mounted on wheels is attached at one end to a source of water. Driven by electricity or water power, the pipeline rotates around the source, spreading water in a circle whose radius is the pipeline. If the pipeline is 90 m long, what is the area of the circle it irrigates?
25 434 m^2

14. A section of highway 6.1 meters wide and 1.75 kilometers long needs repaving. What is the area of this section? $10\,675\ m^2$

15. Gruener Park has a swimming pool that is 28.25 meters long. How many kilometers would a person swim in 20 lengths of the pool? 30 lengths? 45 lengths? $0.565\ km;\ 0.8475\ km;\ 1.27125\ km$

16. Jan's car gets an average of 6.8 kilometers per liter of gasoline. The tank holds 77.5 liters. About how far will the car go on one tank of gas? $527\ km$

17. If gasoline costs $0.30 a liter, how much does it cost to fill a tank that holds 77.5 liters? $23.25

Eddie Adams/De Wys, Inc.

Sven Simon—Katherine Young

Willi Ostgathe/De Wys, Inc.

[C] **18.** Some Olympic records for running and freestyle swimming are listed below. Using the formula $d = rt$, find each rate in meters per second to the nearest hundredth.

MEN'S RECORDS

distance	running		swimming	
	sec	rate	sec	rate
100 m	9.9	10.10	49.99	2.00
200 m	19.8	10.10	110.29	1.81
400 m	43.8	9.13	231.93	1.72
1500 m	214.9	6.98	902.40	1.66

WOMEN'S RECORDS

distance	running		swimming	
	sec	rate	sec	rate
100 m	11.0	9.09	55.65	1.80
200 m	22.37	8.94	119.26	1.68
400 m	49.29	8.12	249.89	1.60
800 m	114.94	6.96	517.14	1.55

Terms and Symbols Review

Choose the answer in ( ) that best completes each sentence.

Assignment Guide Rev.
Oral: Terms & Symbols 1–7
Written: 1–57 odd

1. The decimal for three and three tenths is (*0.33*, *3.3*, $3\frac{3}{10}$).

2. The 1 in (*3.412*, *3.142*, *3.421*) is in the thousandths place.

3. The symbol for "is approximately equal to" is ($=$, $\neq$, $\approx$).

4. 4.185 rounded to the nearest hundredth is (*4.2*, *4.18*, *4.19*).

5. When (*adding*, *multiplying*) with decimals, always keep the decimal points aligned.

6. When you multiply 3.1 by 0.05, there should be (*one*, *two*, *three*) places after the decimal point in the answer.

7. To (*compute*, *estimate*) a product, round both factors and then multiply.

Chapter 5 Review

Express each decimal as a fraction or mixed number. 5.1

1. 0.7 $\frac{7}{10}$
2. 0.5 $\frac{1}{2}$
3. 2.9 $2\frac{9}{10}$
4. 3.25 $3\frac{1}{4}$
5. 1.035 $1\frac{7}{200}$
6. 0.08 $\frac{2}{25}$
7. 5.42 $5\frac{21}{50}$
8. 3.6 $3\frac{3}{5}$

Express the following as decimals.

9. $\frac{5}{10}$ 0.5
10. $6\frac{8}{10}$ 6.8
11. $\frac{9}{100}$ 0.09
12. $4\frac{125}{1000}$ 4.125
13. $2\frac{16}{100}$ 2.16
14. $\frac{75}{1000}$ 0.075
15. $6\frac{6}{100}$ 6.06
16. $\frac{3}{1000}$ 0.003

Round as indicated. 5.2

	to the nearest			
number	ten	one	tenth	hundredth
17. 54.129	50	54	54.1	54.13
18. 7.650	10	8	7.7	7.65

(a) Estimate the value; **(b)** then compute the value.

19–21. **a.** Answers may vary.

19. 312×57
20. $416 + 273 + 550$
21. $526 - 288$

b. 17,784   **b.** 1239   **b.** 238

(a) Estimate the value; **(b)** then compute the value.

22–29. **a.** Answers may vary.

5.3 **22.** $68.2 + 25.4$ **b.** 93.6   **23.** $73.4 - 26.6$ **b.** 46.8

24. $3.1 + 2.42 + 0.196$ **b.** 5.716   **25.** $13.12 - 4.221$ **b.** 8.899

5.4 **26.** 6.8×26 **b.** 176.8   **27.** 42.3×2.1 **b.** 88.83

28. 0.04×3.02 **b.** 0.1208   **29.** 6.14×0.35 **b.** 2.149

Multiply.

30. 6.247×100 624.7   **31.** 5.3×1000 5300   **32.** 0.006×10 0.06

Complete.

33. $3.5 \text{ km} = \underline{\hspace{1cm}} \text{ m}$ 3500   **34.** $0.054 \text{ L} = \underline{\hspace{1cm}} \text{ mL}$ 54

5.5 Divide.

35. $21.24 \div 6$ 3.54   **36.** $3.72 \div 3$ 1.24   **37.** $0.336 \div 14$ 0.024

38. $86.4 \div 10$ 8.64   **39.** $4.32 \div 1000$ 0.00432   **40.** $1104.6 \div 100$
11.046

Complete.

41. $425 \text{ mm} = \underline{\hspace{1cm}} \text{ m}$ 0.425   **42.** $1954 \text{ g} = \underline{\hspace{1cm}} \text{ kg}$ 1.954

Write as decimals.

43. $\frac{7}{8}$ 0.875   **44.** $6\frac{2}{3}$ 6.$\overline{6}$ **45.** $\frac{5}{9}$ 0.$\overline{5}$ **46.** $2\frac{3}{5}$ 2.6

5.6 Divide.

47. $5.06 \div 0.2$ 25.3   **48.** $1.944 \div 0.6$ 3.24   **49.** $0.02496 \div 0.008$
3.12

50. $28.8 \div 1.2$ 24   **51.** $0.8 \div 0.25$ 3.2   **52.** $9 \div 0.36$ 25

5.7 Compute.

53. $416.04 \text{ m} + 2509 \text{ cm}$
441.13 m or 44 113 cm

54. $5042 \text{ g} - 2.075 \text{ kg}$
2.967 kg or 2967 g

55. $67.1 \text{ km} \times 2.3 \text{ m}$
154 330 m² or 0.154 33 km²

56. $350 \text{ m} + 1.1 \text{ km} + 5000 \text{ cm}$
1.5 km or 1500 m or 150 000 cm

57. A car averages 10.9 kilometers per liter of gasoline. At that rate, how many kilometers could the car travel on 30.2 liters? 329.18 km

Write each decimal as a fraction or mixed number. Write each fraction or mixed number as a decimal.

1. 0.9 $\frac{9}{10}$

2. 8.25 $8\frac{1}{4}$

3. 0.035 $\frac{7}{200}$

4. $\frac{19}{1000}$ 0.019

5. $\frac{3}{5}$ 0.6

6. $5\frac{3}{4}$ 5.75

Assignment Guide Test
Written: 1–30

Round as indicated.

number	to the nearest		
	hundred	one	tenth
7. 765.21	800	765	765.2
8. 425.902	400	426	425.9

(a) Estimate the value; **(b)** then compute the value.

9–14. **a.** Answers may vary.

9. $12 + 3.42 + 1.6$ **b.** 17.02

10. $6.124 - 3.5$ **b.** 2.624

11. 3.6×0.8 **b.** 2.88

12. 4.25×1.8 **b.** 7.65

13. 30.5×0.04 **b.** 1.22

14. 7.5×6 **b.** 45

Divide.

15. $40.8 \div 12$ 3.4

16. $0.72 \div 0.02$ 36

17. $3.5 \div 1.4$ 2.5

18. $1.125 \div 0.5$ 2.25

Complete.

19. 4.8 km = _____ m 4800

20. 1.6 cm = _____ m 0.016

21. 92 mm = _____ cm 9.2

22. 5.8 g = _____ mg 5800

Compute.

23. 675.42×100 67,542

24. 7.832×10 78.32

25. $8.55 \div 100$ 0.0855

26. 92.63 m − 45 mm
92.585 m or 92 585 mm

27. 4.2 kg + 6200 g
10.4 kg or 10 400 g

28. 3.6 cm × 2 mm
72 mm² or 0.72 cm²

29. 9.76 m + 395 cm + 14.12 m
27.83 m or 2783 cm

30. If the juice in a bottle that holds 3.78 liters is divided into four equal servings, how much is in each serving? 0.945 L

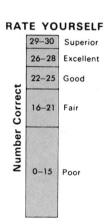

RATE YOURSELF

Number Correct	
29–30	Superior
26–28	Excellent
22–25	Good
16–21	Fair
0–15	Poor

TOLERANCES IN INDUSTRY

Courtesy ITT Harper

In industry, **tolerance** is the amount a measurement can vary from the designed measurement. For example, the length of a bolt might be given as follows:

$$3.6 \pm 0.1 \text{ cm}$$

read "plus or minus"

The tolerance is ± 0.1. This means that the bolt should be as near as possible to 3.6 cm long, but it will work if its length is anywhere between two limits.

$$3.6 - 0.1 \text{ cm} = 3.5 \text{ cm} \text{ to } 3.6 + 0.1 \text{ cm} = 3.7 \text{ cm}$$

lower limit   upper limit

(Another way to name a tolerance is by giving these upper and lower limits.)

Sometimes a measurement can be allowed to vary in one direction only. For example, if the bolt should be 3.6 cm long and it will not work if it is any shorter, the length might be given as

lower limit —

$$3.6 + 0.1 \text{ cm.}$$

$$= 3.7 \text{ cm} \longleftarrow \text{upper limit}$$

Example: A gasoline intake valve is designed to have a stem length of 7.945 ± 0.005 mm. What are the limits on its size?

$$7.945 - 0.005 \text{ mm} = 7.940 \text{ mm} \qquad 7.945 + 0.005 \text{ mm} = 7.950 \text{ mm}$$

lower limit   upper limit

Copy and complete the chart.

Designed measurement	Tolerance	Lower limit	Upper limit
63.204 cm	± 0.002 cm	63.202 cm	63.206 cm
0.050 mm	± 0.001 mm	0.049 mm	0.051 mm
30.0 cm	-0.2 cm	29.8 cm	30.0 cm
146.00 mm	$+0.05$ mm	146.00 mm	146.05 mm

Which lettered choice best matches each numbered item?

1. $\{0, 1, 2, 3, \cdots\}$ c   **a.** identity number for addition   1.8

2. $\{1, 2, 3, 4, \cdots\}$ d   **b.** commutative property of addition   1.8

3. $n + 2 = 2 + n$ b   **c.** set of whole numbers   3.1

4. $n + 0 = n$ a   **d.** set of whole numbers greater   3.3
than 0

Solve each equation.   2.2

5. $x + 7 = 16$ 9   6. $x + 9 = 14$ 5

7. $n - 7 = 6$ 13   8. $10 = y - 8$ 18

9. $28 = x + 16$ 12   10. $x - 14 = 50$ 64

Solve and graph each inequality.   2.4

11. $x + 4 < 9$ $x < 5$ 12. $y + 7 > 8$ $y > 1$

13. $y - 8 > 11$ $y > 19$ 14. $12 > y - 5$ $17 > y$

15. $38 < x - 7$ $45 < x$ 16. $y + 15 > 29$ $y > 14$

Suggested Class Time

Course	Min.	Reg.	Max.
Days	*	1	0

Assignment Guide GR 6
Written: Min. 1–10
Reg. 1–16

* Combine with Section 6.1.

ADDING AND SUBTRACTING INTEGERS

Opposites occur often in daily life. Coming down is the opposite of going up. A gain is the opposite of a loss. Moving backward is the opposite of moving forward. There are many other similar examples.

In algebra, these ideas are generalized and developed in terms of positive and negative numbers. In this chapter you will learn what positive and negative numbers are and begin to work with them.

Opposites of Whole Numbers

6.1

Notice how positive and negative numbers can be used to name some opposite activities.

Activity	Number	Opposite Activity	Number
earning $10	$^+10$	spending $10	$^-10$
gaining 8 yards	$^+8$	losing 8 yards	$^-8$
winning 6 points	$^+6$	losing 6 points	$^-6$
walking 2 blocks east	$^+2$	walking 2 blocks west	$^-2$

A "$-$" is always used when naming a negative number.

negative sixteen $^-16$

A "$+$" may (but need not) be used when naming a positive number.

positive sixteen $^+16$ or 16

On a number line, a number and its opposite are the same distance from 0 but in opposite directions. (0 is its own opposite.)

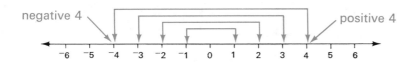

Example 1: How do you read $^-2$?

$^-2$ is read as "negative two."

Example 2: What is the opposite of $^-3$? Of 5?

173

> The whole numbers and their opposites make up the set of numbers called the **integers**.

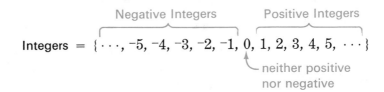

Negative Integers   Positive Integers

Integers = $\{\cdots, -5, -4, -3, -2, -1, 0, 1, 2, 3, 4, 5, \cdots\}$

— neither positive nor negative

■ Exercises

Assignment Guide 6.1
Oral: 1–10
Written: Min. 11–33 odd
      Reg. 11–34
      Max. 11–41

A Name the opposite of each number.

1. 2 ⁻2   **2.** +28 ⁻28   **3.** ⁻17 17   **4.** 438 ⁻438

5. ⁻2 2   **6.** ⁻28 28   **7.** 86 ⁻86   **8.** 0 0

9. Which integer is neither positive nor negative? 0

10. Which integer is its own opposite? 0

B Complete the table below.

	Activity	*Integer*	*Activity*	*Integer*
11.	down 3 fathoms	−3	up 3 fathoms	⁺3
12.	250 miles north	+250	250 mi south	−250
13.	five meters forward	+5	Five m backward	−5
14.	up 6 floors	+6	down 6 floors	⁻6
15.	100 feet above sea level	+100	100 ft below sea level	−100
16.	$1000 profit	⁺1000	$1000 loss	−1000
17.	8-yard loss	−8	8-yard gain	⁺8
18.	increase of 10°	⁺10	decrease of 10°	−10
19.	70 kilometers west	⁻70	70 kilometers east	+70
20.	8 seconds before blast-off	−8	8 seconds after blast-off	⁺8

The greater of two integers is farther to the right on the number line. Use the number line below to decide which integer in each pair is greater.

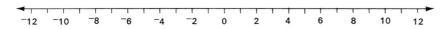

21. 0 or 10 _10_   **22.** 0 or ⁻10 _0_   **23.** ⁻10 or 10 _10_

24. ⁻12 or 4 _4_   **25.** ⁻12 or ⁻7 _⁻7_   **26.** ⁻8 or ⁻12 _⁻8_

For each exercise, arrange the numbers in order from least to greatest.

27. 5, ⁻3, 3, ⁻1
  _⁻3, ⁻1, 3, 5_

28. 2, ⁻2, 3, ⁻3
  _⁻3, ⁻2, 2, 3_

29. 0, ⁻10, ⁻20, 30, ⁻25
  _⁻25, ⁻20, ⁻10, 0, 30_

30. ⁻5, 10, ⁻15, ⁻20, 25
  _⁻20, ⁻15, ⁻5, 10, 25_

31. 3, ⁻5, 7, 0, 9, ⁻8
  _⁻8, ⁻5, 0, 3, 7, 9_

32. ⁻2, ⁻6, 1, 8, 0, ⁻3
  _⁻6, ⁻3, ⁻2, 0, 1, 8_

33. 3, ⁻3, 4, ⁻4, 5, ⁻5, 0
  _⁻5, ⁻4, ⁻3, 0, 3, 4, 5_

34. 21, ⁻12, 48, ⁻53, 78, ⁻91
  _⁻91, ⁻53, ⁻12, 21, 48, 78_

C **35.** Copy and complete the table.

Words	Symbol
the opposite of ⁻7	⁻(⁻7) or 7
The opposite of ⁻3	⁻(⁻3) or _3_
the opposite of ⁻5	_⁻(⁻5)_ or _5_
the opposite of ⁺5	⁻(⁺5) or ⁻5
The opposite of ⁺7	⁻(⁺7) or ⁻7

The expression ⁻x is read *the opposite of x.* Find ⁻x if

36. $x = {}^-8$ _8_   **37.** $x = 15$ _⁻15_   **38.** $x = 19 - 9 + 5$ _⁻15_

Find x if

39. $^-x = 9$ _⁻9_   **40.** $^-x = {}^-9$ _9_   **41.** $^-x = {}^-3$ _3_

Addition on a Number Line

You can show addition of whole numbers on a number line.

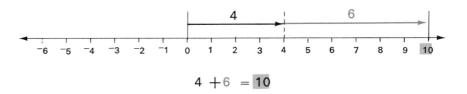

$$4 + 6 = \boxed{10}$$

You can use the same methods to find sums of integers.

Example 1: Show $^-4 + 6$ on a number line.

Step 1: The first addend is $^-4$, so start at 0 and draw an arrow 4 units to the left (negative direction).

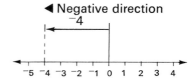

Step 2: The second addend is 6, so start at $^-4$ and draw an arrow 6 units to the right (positive direction).

Step 3: The sum is given at the head of the second arrow.

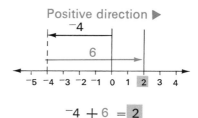

$$^-4 + 6 = \boxed{2}$$

Example 2: Show $4 + {}^-6$ on a number line.

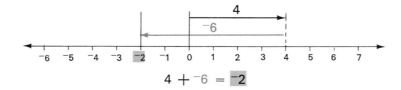

$$4 + {}^-6 = \boxed{^-2}$$

Example 3: Show $^-4 + {}^-6$ on a number line.

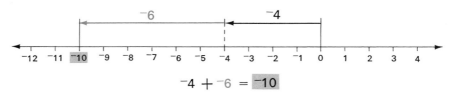

$$^-4 + {}^-6 = \boxed{^-10}$$

■Exercises

Assignment Guide 6.2
Oral: 1–4
Written: Min. 5–25
     Reg. 5–28
     Max. 5–37

A State an addition sentence for each drawing.

1.
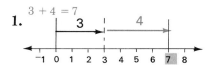
$3 + 4 = 7$

2.
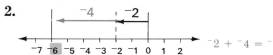
$^-2 + {}^-4 = {}^-6$

3.
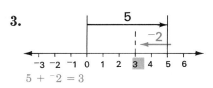
$5 + {}^-2 = 3$

4.
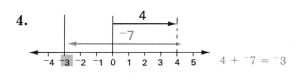
$4 + {}^-7 = {}^-3$

B Find each sum. Use a number line to help you.

5. $6 + 5$ 11   **6.** $^-3 + {}^-6$ $^-9$ **7.** $^-9 + 4$ $^-5$

8. $8 + {}^-7$ 1   **9.** $^-6 + {}^-3$ $^-9$ **10.** $2 + {}^-9$ $^-7$

11. $6 + {}^-1$ 5   **12.** $8 + {}^-8$ 0   **13.** $^-6 + 2$ $^-4$

14. $^-2 + 9$ 7   **15.** $5 + 5$ 10   **16.** $^-3 + 7$ 4

17. $3 + {}^-7$ $^-4$ **18.** $3 + 7$ 10   **19.** $^-6 + 6$ 0

20. $^-4 + {}^-4$ $^-8$ **21.** $5 + {}^-4$ 1   **22.** $^-7 + 3$ $^-4$

23. $^-1 + 7$ 6   **24.** $9 + {}^-5$ 4   **25.** $8 + {}^-3$ 5

C Use a number line to help you find each sum.

Example: $1 + 2 + 3$

$$1 + 2 + 3 = 6$$

26. $2 + 3 + 4$ 9   **27.** $6 + {}^-1 + {}^-3$ 2   **28.** $10 + {}^-8 + 5$ 7

29. $^-3 + 4 + {}^-6$ $^-5$ **30.** $7 + 7 + 3$ 17   **31.** $^-1 + 1 + 8$ 8

32. $^-2 + 3 + {}^-4$ $^-3$ **33.** $6 + {}^-7 + 1$ 0   **34.** $2 + {}^-3 + 2$ 1

35. $^-7 + {}^-5 + 4$ $^-8$ **36.** $^-2 + {}^-4 + {}^-3$ $^-9$ **37.** $^-6 + 5 + {}^-3$ $^-4$

Adding Integers

Now that we have opposites of whole numbers, we have an important new property of addition.

Inverse Property of Addition

Any number a and its opposite ^-a have a sum of 0. So

$$a + {}^-a = 0$$

$$^-a + a = 0$$

Example: $5 + {}^-5 = 0$

$$^-5 + 5 = 0$$

This new property and the idea of absolute value are helpful when adding integers.

Number	Its absolute value
$^+4$ or 4	4
0	0
5	5
$^-5$	5
$^-3$	3

The absolute value of a positive number or 0 is that number itself.

The absolute value of a negative number is its opposite.

Example 1: How do you add integers with the same sign?

both negative   both positive

$^-4 + {}^-3$ $^+4 + {}^+3$

Add the absolute values. $4 + 3$ $4 + 3$

The result has the same sign as the addends. $^-7$ $^+7$ or 7

Example 2 : How do you add integers with different signs?

If the numbers are
opposites, use the inverse
property of addition.

$$^+4 + {}^-4 = 0 \qquad {}^-7 + {}^+7 = 0$$

If the numbers are not
opposites,

Find the difference of
the absolute values.

The result has the same
sign as the addend with
the greater absolute value.

Example 3 : How do you add ⁻4, 6, and ⁻5?

Take your choice of which integers to add first.

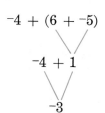

Assignment Guide 6.3
Oral: 1–12
Written:
Min. 13–45 odd
Reg. 13–45 odd; 46–50
Max. 13–45 odd; 46–50

■ Exercises

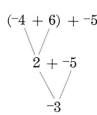 State the absolute value of each integer.

1. ⁺16 16   **2.** ⁻24 24   **3.** 325 325

4. ⁻96 96   **5.** 0 0   **6.** ⁻1978 1978

Tell whether the sum is positive, negative, or zero.

7. 18 + 48 Pos.   **8.** ⁻63 + ⁻49 Neg.   **9.** 18 + ⁻18 0

10. ⁻16 + 13 Neg.   **11.** 16 + ⁻34 Neg.   **12.** ⁻83 + 149 Pos.

179

Find each sum.

13. 16 + 12 28
14. ⁻17 + ⁻18 ⁻35
15. 14 + ⁻14 0

16. 32 + ⁻49 ⁻17
17. ⁻18 + ⁻39 ⁻57
18. ⁻47 + 21 ⁻26

19. 37 + 48 85
20. ⁻23 + ⁻36 ⁻59
21. 88 + ⁻72 16

22. ⁻17 + 12 ⁻5
23. 103 + ⁻111 ⁻8
24. ⁻15 + 18 3

25. ⁻619 + ⁻832 ⁻1451
26. 173 + ⁻846 ⁻673
27. 395 + ⁻395 0

28. 792 + ⁻628 164
29. ⁻485 + ⁻96 ⁻581
30. 278 + ⁻475 ⁻197

31. ⁻1692 + 1968 276
32. 1795 + ⁻492 1303
33. 672 + 896 1568

34. ⁻849 + ⁻782 ⁻1631
35. 6742 + ⁻4385 2357
36. ⁻6275 + 4675 ⁻1600

37. (2 + 4) + 3 9
38. (⁻2 + 4) + 6 8
39. (8 + ⁻5) + 3 6

40. 6 + (5 + ⁻7) 4
41. ⁻4 + (⁻3 + 2) ⁻5
42. ⁻5 + (7 + ⁻8) ⁻6

43. 2 + ⁻7 + ⁻4 ⁻9
44. ⁻2 + ⁻5 + ⁻7 ⁻14
45. ⁻6 + 5 + ⁻8 ⁻9

Copy and complete the table.

Words	Symbols	Sum
a temperature of 20° followed by a drop of 10°	20 + ⁻10	10
46. a profit of $3000 followed by a loss of $5000	3000 + ⁻5000	⁻2000
47. a loss of $500 followed by a loss of $200	⁻500 + ⁻200	⁻700
48. a deposit of $75 followed by a withdrawal of $20	75 + ⁻20	55
49. a deposit of $80 followed by a withdrawal of $100	80 + ⁻100	⁻20
50. a 20-yard gain followed by a 12-yard loss	20 + ⁻12	8

Subtracting Integers  6.4

Subtracting 2 from 6 gives the same answer as adding $^-2$ to 6.

subtraction   addition

$$6 - 2 = 4 \qquad\qquad 6 + {}^-2 = 4$$

opposites

It appears that subtracting a number is equivalent to adding its opposite. Let's try another example.

subtraction   addition

$$5 - 3 = 2 \qquad\qquad 5 + {}^-3 = 2$$

opposites

Again the pattern holds. Such examples suggest the following property.

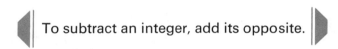

To subtract an integer, add its opposite.

Example 1: How do you subtract 6 from $^-1$?

Add its opposite.

$$^-1 - 6 = {}^-1 + {}^-6$$
$$= {}^-7$$

Example 2: How do you subtract $^-7$ from $^-2$?

Add its opposite.

$$^-2 - {}^-7 = {}^-2 + 7$$
$$= 5$$

■ Exercises

A Tell how to change each subtraction to an addition.

1. 6 − 7   6 + ⁻7

2. 8 − ⁻5   8 + 5

3. 9 − ⁻12   9 + 12

4. ⁻5 − 6   ⁻5 + ⁻6

5. ⁻4 − ⁻2   ⁻4 + 2

6. 19 − 15
19 + ⁻15

B Find each difference.

Assignment Guide 6.4
Oral: 1–6
Written:
Min. 7–27 odd; Quiz,
    p. 182
Reg. 7–27 odd; 28–31;
    Quiz, p. 182
Max. 7–27 odd; 28–35;
    Quiz, p. 182

7. 15 − 19   ⁻4

8. ⁻6 − 8   ⁻14

9. ⁻12 − 17   ⁻29

10. 11 − ⁻5   16

11. ⁻11 − 3   ⁻14

12. 4 − 10   ⁻6

13. ⁻8 − ⁻12   4

14. 26 − ⁻14   40

15. ⁻11 − ⁻33   22

16. ⁻6 − ⁻5   ⁻1

17. ⁻16 − ⁻4   ⁻12

18. ⁻8 − 32   ⁻40

19. ⁻18 − 16   ⁻34

20. ⁻12 − 12   ⁻24

21. ⁻38 − 54   ⁻92

22. ⁻518 − 303   ⁻821

23. 219 − ⁻118   337

24. 416 − ⁻303   719

25. 1776 − ⁻1865   3641

26. ⁻1069 − 433   ⁻1502

27. ⁻600 − ⁻439   ⁻161

C Find the value of each phrase.

28. (7 − 3) − 5   ⁻1

29. 7 − (3 − 5)   9

30. ⁻5 − (7 − 8)   ⁻4

31. (⁻5 − 7) − 8   ⁻20

32. (⁻4 − 3) − ⁻2   ⁻5

33. ⁻4 − (3 − ⁻2)   ⁻9

34. (⁻5 − ⁻6) − 7   ⁻6

35. ⁻5 − (⁻6 − 7)   8

Quick Quiz
Sections 6.1 to 6.4

Find each sum or difference.

1. 8 + ⁻9   ⁻1

2. ⁻4 + ⁻7   ⁻11

3. 12 + ⁻27   ⁻15

4. 12 + ⁻12   0

5. ⁻28 + 45   17

6. ⁻30 + 142   112

7. 17 − ⁻8   25

8. ⁻23 − 75   ⁻98

9. 16 − 19   ⁻3

10. ⁻14 − ⁻5   ⁻9

11. ⁻56 − ⁻56   0

12. 87 − ⁻15
102

Solving Addition Equations

6.5

Before, you solved addition equations by subtracting the same number from each side. You can still do that. But now you can also use a new way.

Example 1: Solve $x + 3 = 19$.

Old way

$x + 3 = 19$

$x + 3 - 3 = 19 - 3$ Inverse operation.

$x + 0 = 16$

$x = 16$

New way

$x + 3 = 19$

$x + 3 + {}^-3 = 19 + {}^-3$ Add opposite.

$x + 0 = 16$

$x = 16$

Check:

$x + 3 = 19$

$16 + 3 = 19$

$19 = 19$ ✓

Example 2: Solve $x + 3 = {}^-19$.

$x + 3 = {}^-19$

$x + 3 + {}^-3 = {}^-19 + {}^-3$ Add $^-3$ to each side.

$x + 0 = {}^-22$

$x = {}^-22$

Check: $x + 3 = {}^-19$

${}^-22 + 3 = {}^-19$ Replace x with $^-22$.

${}^-19 = {}^-19$ ✓

Example 3: Solve $6 = n + {}^-5$.

$6 = n + {}^-5$

$6 + 5 = n + {}^-5 + 5$ Add 5 to each side.

$11 = n + 0$

$11 = n$

Check: $6 = n + {}^-5$

$6 = 11 + {}^-5$ Replace n with 11.

$6 = 6$ ✓

183

■ Exercises

Assignment Guide 6.5
Oral: 1–6
Written: Min. 7–23 odd
Reg. 7–35 odd
Max. 7–35 odd;
37–39

A To solve each equation, what number would you add to each side?

1. $n + 7 = {}^-6$ ${}^-7$

2. $n + {}^-4 = 6$ 4

3. $14 = k + 9$ ${}^-9$

4. ${}^-6 = m + {}^-11$ 11

5. $x + 8 = 0$ ${}^-8$

6. $z + {}^-9 = 0$ 9

B Solve.

7. $n + 3 = 9$ 6

8. $m + 8 = {}^-16$ ${}^-24$

9. $8 = x + {}^-9$ 17

10. $p + {}^-9 = {}^-16$ ${}^-7$

11. $n + 16 = 9$ ${}^-7$

12. ${}^-6 = r + {}^-6$ 0

13. $k + {}^-7 = 16$ 23

14. $q + {}^-17 = {}^-9$ 8

15. ${}^-7 = x + 14$ ${}^-21$

16. $x + {}^-7 = 19$ 26

17. $m + 9 = {}^-32$ ${}^-41$

18. ${}^-72 = k + {}^-6$ ${}^-66$

19. $10 = x + {}^-1$ 11

20. $y + 7 = {}^-7$ ${}^-14$

21. $y + {}^-7 = 7$ 14

22. ${}^-16 = c + {}^-2$ ${}^-14$

23. $13 = a + {}^-5$ 18

24. $r + {}^-6 = {}^-12$ ${}^-6$

C Solve as shown in the example. Notice that the commutative property of addition is used.

Example:

$$\begin{aligned}
{}^-7 + n &= 10 \\
n + {}^-7 &= 10 \\
n + {}^-7 + 7 &= 10 + 7 \\
n + 0 &= 17 \\
n &= 17
\end{aligned}$$

Check:
$$\begin{aligned}
{}^-7 + n &= 10 \\
{}^-7 + 17 &= 10 \\
10 &= 10 \checkmark
\end{aligned}$$

25. $7 + x = 5$ ${}^-2$

26. ${}^-5 + x = 9$ 14

27. $9 + x = {}^-4$ ${}^-13$

28. ${}^-9 + x = 6$ 15

29. $6 = 7 + x$ ${}^-1$

30. $9 = {}^-7 + z$ 16

Solve as shown in the example. Notice that the associative property of addition is used.

Example: $(r + {}^-6) + {}^-3 = 7$

$$r + ({}^-6 + {}^-3) = 7 \qquad \textit{Check:} \quad (r + {}^-6) + {}^-3 = 7$$
$$r + {}^-9 = 7 \qquad\qquad (16 + {}^-6) + {}^-3 = 7$$
$$r + {}^-9 + 9 = 7 + 9 \qquad\qquad 10 + {}^-3 = 7$$
$$r + 0 = 16 \qquad\qquad 7 = 7 \checkmark$$
$$r = 16$$

31. $(m + {}^-2) + 3 = 5$ ⁴   **32.** $(x + 3) + {}^-1 = 5$ ³

33. $(r + {}^-2) + 1 = 7$ ⁸   **34.** $(y + {}^-5) + 2 = 6$ ⁹

35. $7 = (a + {}^-8) + 2$ ¹³   **36.** $10 = (t + {}^-3) + 2$ ¹¹

Solve each problem. First write an addition equation.

37. At dawn the temperature was $^-7°$. The temperature is $10°$ now. How much has the temperature changed? 17°

Hint: Solve $^-7 + n = 10$.

38. Last year Eve Buckley's blood pressure was 6 millimeters above normal. This year it is 2 millimeters below normal. How much has her blood pressure changed? ⁻8 mm

Hint: Solve $6 + n = {}^-2$.

39. A submarine is at the $^-240$-foot level (240 feet below sea level). By how many feet will it have to change its depth to be at the $^-170$-foot level? 70 ft

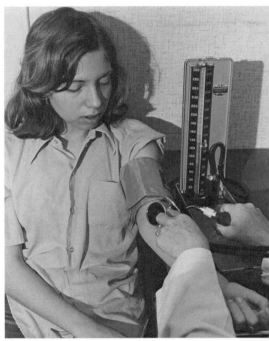

Photri

Solving Subtraction Equations

Before, you solved subtraction equations by adding the same number to each side. But in Section 6.4, you learned that

$$7 - {}^-2 \text{ is equivalent to } 7 + 2.$$

This idea can now be used in solving subtraction equations. Each subtraction equation below is first changed to an addition equation. Then the equation is solved by the method you used in the preceding section.

Example 1: Solve $x - {}^-5 = 14$.

$$x - {}^-5 = 14$$

$$x + 5 = 14 \qquad \text{Change } x - {}^-5 \text{ to } x + 5.$$

$$x + 5 + {}^-5 = 14 + {}^-5 \qquad \text{Add } {}^-5 \text{ to each side.}$$

$$x + 0 = 9$$

$$x = 9$$

Check: $x - {}^-5 = 14$

$$9 - {}^-5 = 14 \qquad \text{Replace } x \text{ with 9.}$$

$$9 + 5 = 14$$

$$14 = 14 \checkmark$$

Example 2: Solve ${}^-6 = x - 4$.

$${}^-6 = x - 4$$

$${}^-6 = x + {}^-4 \qquad \text{Change } x - 4 \text{ to } x + {}^-4.$$

$${}^-6 + 4 = x + {}^-4 + 4 \qquad \text{Add 4 to each side.}$$

$${}^-2 = x + 0$$

$${}^-2 = x$$

Check: ${}^-6 = x - 4$

$${}^-6 = {}^-2 - 4 \qquad \text{Replace } x \text{ with } {}^-2.$$

$${}^-6 = {}^-2 + {}^-4$$

$${}^-6 = {}^-6 \checkmark$$

Exercises

Assignment Guide 6.6
Oral: 1–6
Written: Min. 7–21 odd
Reg. 7–21
Max. 7–21 odd;
22–25

A For each equation

a. Change the indicated subtraction to addition.

b. Tell what number you would add to each side of the resulting equation.

1. $n - 7 = {}^-6$
  a. $n + {}^-7 = {}^-6$; **b.** 7

2. $n - {}^-4 = 6$
  a. $n + 4 = 6$; **b.** ${}^-4$

3. $14 = k - 7$
  a. $14 = k + {}^-7$; **b.** 7

4. $m - {}^-11 = {}^-6$
  a. $m + 11 = {}^-6$; **b.** ${}^-11$

5. $x - 8 = 0$
  a. $x + {}^-8 = 0$; **b.** 8

6. $0 = z - {}^-9$
  a. $0 = z + 9$; **b.** ${}^-9$

B Solve.

7. $x - 9 = 7$ 16

8. $t - 11 = {}^-6$ 5

9. $13 = x - {}^-8$ 5

10. $r - {}^-16 = {}^-9$ ${}^-25$

11. $k - 3 = 19$ 22

12. ${}^-27 = t - 13$ ${}^-14$

13. $x - {}^-27 = 15$ ${}^-12$

14. $s - {}^-17 = {}^-48$ ${}^-65$

15. $16 = m - 16$ 32

16. $b - 13 = {}^-49$ ${}^-36$

17. $c - {}^-9 = {}^-41$ ${}^-50$

18. $27 = d - {}^-93$ ${}^-66$

19. $t - 6 = 7$ 13

20. $r - {}^-7 = 14$ 7

21. ${}^-19 = s - 8$ ${}^-11$

C Solve as shown in the example.

Example: ${}^-7 - {}^-x = 10$

$$^-7 + x = 10$$

$$x + {}^-7 = 10$$

$$x + {}^-7 + 7 = 10 + 7$$

$$x + 0 = 17$$

$$x = 17$$

Check: ${}^-7 - {}^-x = 10$

$$^-7 - {}^-17 = 10$$

$$^-7 + 17 = 10$$

$$10 = 10 \checkmark$$

22. $5 - {}^-n = 14$ 9

23. $11 - {}^-n = {}^-16$ ${}^-27$

24. ${}^-11 - {}^-x = 12$ 23

25. ${}^-7 - {}^-a = {}^-5$ 2

187

You already know how to solve such equations as $x + 4 = {}^-3$ and $x - {}^-3 = 2$. Notice how inequalities similar to these can be solved in the same way.

Example 1: Solve $x + 4 < {}^-3$.

$$x + 4 < {}^-3$$

$$x + 4 + {}^-4 < {}^-3 + {}^-4 \quad \text{Add } {}^-4 \text{ to each side.}$$

$$x + 0 < {}^-7$$

$$x < {}^-7$$

Check: Try any integer less than $^-7$.

$$x + 4 < {}^-3$$

$${}^-8 + 4 < {}^-3 \quad \text{Replace } x \text{ with } {}^-8.$$

$${}^-4 < {}^-3 \checkmark$$

But with inequalities, it is usually a good idea to draw a graph to help "see" the solutions.

Example 2: Graph $x + 4 < {}^-3$. (We solved this inequality in Example 1.)

Draw a number line and use dots and an arrowhead to show all integers less than $^-7$.

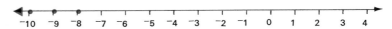

Example 3: Solve and graph $x - {}^-3 > 2$.

$$x - {}^-3 > 2$$

$$x + 3 > 2 \quad \text{Change } x - {}^-3 \text{ to } x + 3.$$

$$x + 3 + {}^-3 > 2 + {}^-3 \quad \text{Add } {}^-3 \text{ to each side.}$$

$$x + 0 > {}^-1$$

$$x > {}^-1$$

Check: Try any integer greater than $^-1$.

$$x - {}^-3 > 2$$

$$0 - {}^-3 > 2 \quad \text{Replace } x \text{ with } 0.$$

$$0 + 3 > 2$$

$$3 > 2 \checkmark$$

Graph: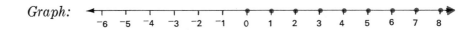

■ Exercises

Assignment Guide 6.7
Oral: Reg. & Max. 1–6
Written: Reg. 7–29 odd
Max. 7–39 odd

A To solve each inequality, what number would you add to each side?

1. $x + {}^-5 > 2$ 5   2. $y + 6 < {}^-4$ ⁻6   3. $m + {}^-7 > {}^-2$ 7

For each inequality.

a. Change the indicated subtraction to addition.

b. Tell what number you would add to each side of the resulting inequality.

4. $n - {}^-8 < 2$
   a. $n + 8 < 2$; b. ⁻8

5. $t - 6 > {}^-9$
   a. $t + {}^-6 > {}^-9$; b. 6

6. $k - {}^-19 < {}^-64$
   a. $k + 19 < {}^-64$; b. ⁻19

B Solve and graph each inequality.

7. $x + 5 > 4$
   $x > {}^-1$

8. $n + 15 < {}^-6$
   $n < {}^-21$

9. $a + {}^-7 > 6$
   $a > 13$

10. $t + {}^-8 < {}^-6$
    $t < 2$

11. $z + 7 > 9$
    $z > 2$

12. $m + 13 < {}^-19$
    $m < {}^-32$

13. $b + {}^-8 > 14$
    $b > 22$

14. $u + {}^-15 < {}^-17$
    $u < {}^-2$

15. $n + 8 < 6$
    $n < {}^-2$

16. $k + 26 > {}^-7$
    $k > {}^-33$

17. $c + {}^-9 < 3$
    $c < 12$

18. $w + {}^-11 > {}^-19$
    $w > {}^-8$

19. $k - 5 < 3$
    $k < 8$

20. $a - 4 > {}^-6$
    $a > {}^-2$

21. $t - {}^-5 < 2$
    $t < {}^-3$

22. $v - {}^-8 > {}^-3$
    $v > {}^-11$

23. $j - 8 < 12$
    $j < 20$

24. $b - 4 > {}^-3$
    $b > 1$

25. $r - {}^-11 < 13$
    $r < 2$

26. $w - {}^-14 > {}^-19$
    $w > {}^-33$

27. $m - 6 > 2$
    $m > 8$

28. $c - 5 < {}^-9$
    $c < {}^-4$

29. $s - {}^-7 > 19$
    $s > 12$

30. $y - {}^-23 < {}^-19$
    $y < {}^-42$

C 31. $6 < a + {}^-7$
    $13 < a$

32. $^-7 + a > 6$
    $a > 13$

33. $^-8 < y + 2$
    $^-10 < y$

34. $3 + x < {}^-5$
    $x < {}^-8$

35. $^-1 > m + 4$
    $^-5 > m$

36. $^-3 > a + {}^-5$
    $2 > a$

37. $(a - 1) + {}^-2 < 10$
    $a < 13$

38. $(y - 5) + {}^-3 > {}^-8$
    $y > 0$

39. $(x - {}^-5) + {}^-5 < 8$
    $x < 8$

40. $(z - {}^-6) + 7 > {}^-5$
    $z > {}^-18$

189

6.8

Using Equations to Solve Problems

Suggested Class Time

Course	Min.	Reg.	Max.
Days	1	1	1

Here is a good problem-solving method:

- Read the problem carefully to get a general understanding.

- Read the problem as many more times as necessary to determine all the given facts.

- Represent any unknown facts with variables.

- Translate the word statement of the problem into an equation.

- Solve the equation.

- Check the solution against the conditions of the problem.

  Note: This can replace checking the solution in the equation. If you made a mistake in setting up the equation, the solution might check in it, but still be wrong for the problem.

- Answer the problem.

Example 1: Since noon, the temperature has changed $^-11$ °C. The temperature now is $^-9$ °C. What was the temperature at noon?

Let x = the temperature at noon.

Then $x + {}^-11 = {}^-9$

temperature   change   temperature
at noon   since noon   now

$$x + {}^-11 = {}^-9$$

$$x + {}^-11 + 11 = {}^-9 + 11$$

$$x + 0 = 2$$

$$x = 2$$

You can check this in the equation if you want to.

Check: To check against the conditions of the problem, ask yourself this question: Does a temperature of 2 °C followed by a $^-11$ °C change give a temperature of $^-9$ °C? ✓

So the temperature at noon was 2 °C.

Example 2: A mountain climber starts from an elevation of ⁻282 feet (282 feet below sea level) and climbs to an elevation of 2000 feet (above sea level). What is the change in elevation?

Let n = the change in elevation.

Then $\underset{\text{starting elevation}}{\overset{}{^-282}} + \underset{\text{change}}{n} = \underset{\text{ending elevation}}{2000}$

$$^-282 + n = 2000$$

$$n + {}^-282 = 2000$$

$$n + {}^-282 + 282 = 2000 + 282$$

$$n + 0 = 2282$$

$$n = 2282$$

Check: Does a climb from 282 feet below sea level to 2000 feet above sea level give a change of 2282 feet? ✓

So the change in elevation is 2282 feet.

A. Devaney, Inc.

◾ Exercises

Assignment Guide 6.8
Oral: 1–6
Written: Min. 7–12
    Reg. 7–16
    Max. 7–18

A Match each problem in **1–6** with an equation in **a–f.**

a. $150 + n = 100$ **b.** $^-100 + n = 150$ **c.** $n + {}^-30 = 15$

d. $150 + n = {}^-100$ **e.** $^-150 + n = {}^-100$ **f.** $x - 2 = {}^-25$

1. The sum of a number and ⁻30 is 15. What is the number? ᶜ

2. When 2 is subtracted from a number, the difference is ⁻25. What is the number? ᶠ

3. A checking account had a balance of ⁻100 dollars. (It was overdrawn.) After a deposit was made, the account had a balance of 150 dollars. How much money was deposited? ᵇ

4. A submarine is at the ⁻150-foot level. How many feet will it have to rise to be at the ⁻100-foot level? ᵉ

5. In a card game, Ceil made 150 points on the first hand. After the second hand, her total score was 100 points. What was her score on the second hand? a

6. A cable car goes from an elevation of 150 feet to an elevation of ⁻100 feet. What is the change in elevation? d

B Solve each problem by using an equation.

7. The sum of a number and ⁻10 is ⁻30. What is the number? ⁻20

8. When 12 is subtracted from a number, the difference is ⁻18. What is the number? ⁻6

9. In May the balance on a charge account was ⁻78 dollars. In June the balance was ⁻95 dollars. What was the change in the balance?
⁻$17

10. The temperature at 8 A.M. was ⁻8 °C. By noon it had changed to 7 °C. What was the change in temperature? 15 °C

11. A sky diver jumped out of a plane at an elevation of 4500 feet. The sky diver landed in a valley where the elevation was ⁻121 feet. What was the change in elevation? ⁻4621 ft

12. A checking account had a balance of $250. A month later the balance was $135. What was the change in the balance? ⁻$115

13. The elevation of the Dead Sea is ⁻1296 feet. The highest point in the world is Mount Everest. The elevation of Mount Everest is 29,028 feet. What is the change in elevation from the Dead Sea to Mount Everest? 30,324 ft

14. Mr. Ortíz's savings account had a balance of $1500. Four months later the balance was $650. What was the change in the balance?
⁻$850

15. The regular price of a stereo was $499. The sale price is $439. What was the change in price? ⁻$60

16. The temperature has changed ⁺6 °C since 7 A.M. The temperature is now ⁻2 °C. What was the temperature at 7 A.M.? ⁻8 °C

C **17.** If you add 6 to a number and then subtract ⁻8 from the result, you get 13. What is the number? ⁻1

18. The temperature changed ⁻2 °C. Then it changed ⁺5 °C. The resulting temperature was 20 °C. What was the starting temperature?
17 °C

WEATHER REPORTS

Two terms that you frequently hear in a weather report are *windchill* and *temperature-humidity index*.

The chart below shows the chilling effect of wind (windchill). For example, when there is a reported temperature of 50 °F and a wind of 20 mph, the windchill is 32 °F. (Your body loses heat as fast as on a calm day at 32 °F.)

WINDCHILL CHART (in °F)

Wind (mph)	Reported Temperature					
	50	40	30	20	10	0
5	48	37	27	16	6	⁻5
10	40	28	16	4	⁻9	⁻24
15	36	22	9	⁻5	⁻18	⁻32
20	32	18	4	⁻10	⁻25	⁻39
25	30	16	0	⁻15	⁻29	⁻44
30	28	13	⁻2	⁻18	⁻33	⁻48
35	27	11	⁻4	⁻20	⁻35	⁻51
40	26	10	⁻6	⁻21	⁻37	⁻53

Chicago Tribune

What is the windchill when

1. the reported temperature is 20 °F and the wind is 10 mph? 4 °F

2. the reported temperature is 0 °F and the wind is 15 mph? ⁻32 °F

The temperature-humidity index (THI) is based on the air temperature (t) and the temperature (w) of a wet-bulb thermometer. A wet-bulb thermometer has a moistened cloth on its bulb, and its reading depends on both air temperature and humidity. The temperature (w) represents the lowest temperature to which the skin can be cooled by evaporation of perspiration. The following formula can be used to find the THI.

$$\text{THI} = 0.4(t + w) + 15 \qquad \text{(Temperatures are Fahrenheit.)}$$

People begin to feel discomfort when the THI is 70 or above. When the THI reaches 80, there is danger of heat exhaustion.

Chicago Tribune

3. Find the THI when $t = 80°$ and $w = 60°$.

4. Find the THI when $t = 65°$ and $w = 50°$.

71   61

Equipment ▷ An ordinary deck of 52 playing cards

Black cards (clubs and spades) stand for positive numbers; red cards (hearts and diamonds) stand for negative numbers as follows:

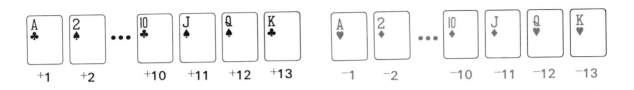

Setup ▷ Two to four players take seats around a table. One of them deals four cards to each player. The remaining cards become a draw pile, placed facedown on the table. The dealer puts the top two cards from the draw pile into the field of play by turning them faceup on the table.

Play ▷ START AND ORDER OF PLAY: The first player to the left of the dealer starts, and play proceeds around the table to the left.

(VARIATION 1)

OBJECT: The object is to use *one* card in your hand to pick up *one* or *two* cards from the field of play. A pickup can be made only when a card in your hand and the card(s) in the field of play have a sum of 0. *Examples:*

Ed Hoppe Photography

| 7♥ picks up | 7♣ | because $^-7 + {}^+7 = 0$ |

| K♠ picks up | K♦ | because $^+13 + {}^-13 = 0$ |

| 10♦ picks up | 7♣ and 3♠ | because $^-10 + ({}^+7 + {}^+3) = 0$ |

| Q♣ picks up | J♥ and A♦ | because $^+12 + ({}^-11 + {}^-1) = 0$ |

NOTE: The two cards picked up must be the *same* color. (See also Variation 2.)

194

POINT PILE: The card played and those it picks up are placed in the player's point pile (to be scored at the end of the game).

WHEN IT IS YOUR TURN:

If you can make at least one pickup:

a. Make *all* possible pickups in succession.

b. Then draw a card from the draw pile.

c. Your turn ends.

If you cannot make a pickup:

a. Discard a card into the field of play.

b. Then draw a card from the draw pile.

c. Your turn ends.

EXHAUSTING THE FIELD: If there are no cards left in the field of play (because of pickups), play your turn as at the right above.

EXHAUSTING THE DRAW PILE: If there are no cards left in the draw pile, play continues as before, except that no more cards are drawn as in **b**.

END OF GAME: The game ends when the draw pile has been exhausted and any one player has no cards left to play.

A misplay occurs when a player discards a card that could have been used to make a pickup. Any other player can challenge a misplay by saying "Sum 0." If the challenge is correct, the misplayed card and those it could pick up are added to the challenger's point pile. If the challenge is in error (no misplay has occurred), the challenger loses his or her next turn, and the cards involved stay in play. A challenge *must* be made *before* the next player has started play. ◁ **Challenging**

Any picture card (jack, queen, or king) counts 2 points. Any other card counts 1 point. Your score is the total points in your point pile minus any points left in your hand at the end of the game. High score wins. ◁ **Scoring**

Play is the same as in Variation 1, except that two cards to be picked up may be the same color (as in Variation 1) or different colors. *Examples:* ◁ VARIATION 2

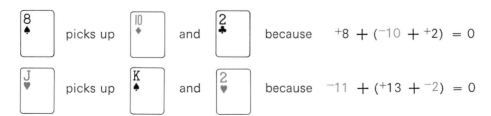

8♠   picks up   10♦   and   2♣   because $^{+}8 + (^{-}10 + {}^{+}2) = 0$

J♥   picks up   K♠   and   2♥   because $^{-}11 + (^{+}13 + {}^{-}2) = 0$

Terms and Symbols Review

Match each item with the best description.

1. 9 and $^-9$ d

a. $x + 9$

2. $\{1, 2, 3, 4, \cdots\}$ c

b. set of negative integers

Assignment Guide Rev.

Oral: Terms & Symbols 1–6
Written:
Min. (day 1) 1–20
  (day 2) 21–32; 39–40
Reg. 1–39 odd
Max. 1–39 odd

3. 10 e

c. set of positive integers

4. 9 f

d. opposites

5. $\{^-1, ^-2, ^-3, ^-4, \cdots\}$ b

e. absolute value of $^-10$

6. $x - {}^-9$ a

f. absolute value of 9

Chapter 6 Review

6.1   Name the opposite of each integer.

1. 6 $^-6$

2. $^-7$ 7

3. 0 0

4. $^+9$ $^-9$

6.2   Find each sum.

5. $6 + {}^-3$ 3

6. $4 + 7$ 11

7. $^-8 + 6$ $^-2$

8. $^-7 + {}^-5$ $^-12$

6.3   **9.** $37 + 19$ 56

10. $16 + {}^-23$ $^-7$

11. $^-18 + 37$ 19

12. $^-15 + {}^-39$ $^-54$

13. $100 + {}^-100$ 0

14. $^-75 + 95$ 20

6.4   Find each difference.

15. $^-3 - 8$ $^-11$

16. $^-6 - {}^-8$ 2

17. $37 - 84$ $^-47$

18. $^-18 - 37$ $^-55$

19. $^-76 - 38$ $^-114$

20. $39 - {}^-16$ 55

Solve. 6.5

21. $n + 7 = 2$ $^-5$ **22.** $s + {}^-6 = 4$ 10

23. $^-7 = x + {}^-2$ $^-5$ **24.** $w + {}^-5 = 12$ 17

25. $m + {}^-41 = {}^-12$ 29 **26.** $17 = a + {}^-20$ 37

27. $x - 5 = 14$ 19 **28.** $y - {}^-2 = 6$ 4 6.6

29. $16 = y - {}^-7$ 9 **30.** $t - {}^-6 = 14$ 8

31. $r - 12 = 28$ 40 **32.** $29 = s - 50$ 79

Solve and graph. 6.7

33. $y + 17 < 10$ $y < {}^-7$ **34.** $x + {}^-6 > 5$ $x > 11$

35. $t + {}^-5 > 5$ $t > 10$ **36.** $m - 7 < 20$ $m < 27$

37. $x - 14 < 21$ $x < 35$ **38.** $v - {}^-6 > {}^-10$ $v > {}^-16$

Solve each problem. 6.8

39. Since 4 P.M., the temperature has changed $^-7$ °C. The temperature now is 4 °C. What was the temperature at 4 P.M.? 11 °C

40. Last month the balance in a charge account was $^-38$ dollars. This month the balance is $^-57$ dollars. What was the change in balance?

$^-\$19$

Chapter 6 Test

Assignment Guide Test
Written: Min. 1–16; 21
      Reg. 1–21
      Max. 1–21

Find each sum.

1. $8 + {}^-6$ 2

2. ${}^-7 + 8$ 1

3. ${}^-16 + {}^-23$ ${}^-39$

4. $18 + {}^-26$ ${}^-8$

5. ${}^-48 + {}^-23$ ${}^-71$

6. ${}^-27 + {}^-49$ ${}^-76$

Find each difference.

7. $16 - 42$ ${}^-26$

8. ${}^-18 - 16$ ${}^-34$

9. $92 - {}^-16$ 108

10. ${}^-84 - {}^-48$ ${}^-36$

11. ${}^-48 - {}^-84$ 36

12. ${}^-36 - 52$ ${}^-88$

Solve.

13. $x + {}^-4 = 17$ 21

14. $y + {}^-7 = {}^-13$ ${}^-6$

15. $x - 9 = {}^-14$ ${}^-5$

16. $z - {}^-4 = 15$ 11

Solve and graph.

17. $x - 4 < {}^-7$ $x < {}^-3$

18. $x + {}^-3 > 2$ $x > 5$

19. $n + {}^-7 < 6$ $n < 13$

20. $x - {}^-4 > 5$ $x > 1$

Solve this problem.

21. In going from 1750 feet elevation to ${}^-175$ feet elevation, what is the change in elevation? ${}^-1925$ ft

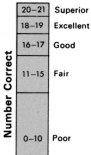

RATE YOURSELF

Number Correct

20–21	Superior
18–19	Excellent
16–17	Good
11–15	Fair
0–10	Poor

Which lettered choice best matches each numbered item?

1. $3 \times 5 = 5 \times 3$ c

2. $(2 \times 3) \times 4 = 2 \times (3 \times 4)$ d

3. $\frac{n}{6}$ b

4. multiplying by 6   a

a. inverse of dividing by 6   3.1

b. $n \div 6$ 3.2

c. commutative property of   4.1
multiplication

d. associative property of   2.1
multiplication

Compute as indicated.

5. $\frac{12}{2}$ 6

6. $\frac{15}{3}$ 5   4.1

7. 0×34 0

8. $0 \div 41$ 0   3.3

Solve each equation or inequality.

9. $4x = 20$ 5

10. $2m = 14$ 7   2.3

11. $\frac{x}{6} = 7$ 42

12. $\frac{a}{5} = 20$ 100

13. $2m + 7 = 9$ 1

14. $3y - 28 = 20$ 16   2.7

15. $\frac{n}{6} + 3 = 9$ 36

16. $\frac{n}{4} - 7 = 6$ 52

17. $\frac{n}{4} < 16$ $n < 64$

18. $\frac{z}{6} > 5$ $z > 30$ 2.4

19. $7m > 35$ $m > 5$

20. $8w > 32$ $w > 4$

Suggested Class Time			
Course	Min.	Reg.	Max.
Days	1	1	0

Assignment Guide GR 7
Written: Min. 1–16
Reg. 1–20

© 1967 United Feature Syndicate, Inc.

7 MULTIPLYING AND DIVIDING INTEGERS

In Chapter 6 you added and subtracted integers. Now you will extend your skills to include multiplying and dividing integers. You will also continue to use integers to solve problems.

Multiplying a Positive and a Negative Integer

You already know how to multiply positive integers. That's just like multiplying whole numbers.

But how can you find a product like $3 \times {}^-4$?

Suggested Class Time

Course	Min.	Reg.	Max.
Days	1	1	1

Think of multiplication as repeated addition. Thus, $3 \times {}^-4$ can be shown on a number line as follows.

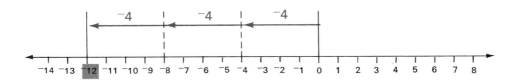

$$3 \times {}^-4 = {}^-12$$

How can you find a product like $^-4 \times 3$?

Since you can change the order of the factors without changing the product,

$$3 \times {}^-4 = {}^-4 \times 3.$$

You already know $3 \times {}^-4 = {}^-12$, so $^-4 \times 3 = {}^-12$ also.

The examples above suggest the following rule.

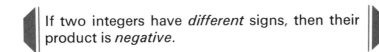

If two integers have *different* signs, then their product is *negative*.

Example 1 :   Multiply 8 by $^-9$.

$$8 \times {}^-9 = {}^-(8 \times 9)$$
$$= {}^-72$$

Example 2 :   Multiply -14 by 6.

$$^-14 \times 6 = {}^-(14 \times 6)$$
$$= {}^-84$$

In Chapter 3 you learned that the product of 0 and any number n is 0. This property is true when n is an integer.

Example 3 : $\quad 0 \times {}^-5 = 0 \qquad\qquad {}^-8 \times 0 = 0$

■ Exercises

Assignment Guide 7.1
Oral: 1–9
Written: Min. 10–30
    Reg. 10–33
    Max. 10–41

A Tell whether the product is positive, negative, or zero.

1. 3×4 Pos.
2. ${}^-3 \times 4$ Neg.
3. $3 \times {}^-4$ Neg.

4. $6 \times {}^-5$ Neg.
5. $5 \times {}^-7$ Neg.
6. ${}^-8 \times 0$ Zero

7. ${}^-42 \times 79$ Neg.
8. 8×79 Pos.
9. ${}^-85 \times 69$ Neg.

B Find each product.

10. 7×3 21
11. $3 \times {}^-6$ ${}^-18$
12. ${}^-6 \times 4$ ${}^-24$

13. ${}^-3 \times 7$ ${}^-21$
14. 9×14 126
15. $5 \times {}^-8$ ${}^-40$

16. $7 \times {}^-3$ ${}^-21$
17. ${}^-5 \times 8$ ${}^-40$
18. 8×17 136

19. $8 \times {}^-10$ ${}^-80$
20. ${}^-9 \times 7$ ${}^-63$
21. $0 \times {}^-10$ 0

22. $9 \times {}^-7$ ${}^-63$
23. ${}^-13 \times 12$ ${}^-156$
24. ${}^-16 \times 22$ ${}^-352$

25. $84 \times {}^-3$ ${}^-252$
26. $11 \times {}^-11$ ${}^-121$
27. ${}^-76 \times 6$ ${}^-456$

28. $38 \times {}^-19$ ${}^-722$
29. ${}^-42 \times 17$ ${}^-714$
30. ${}^-11 \times 0$ 0

31. $8 \times {}^-119$ ${}^-952$
32. ${}^-476 \times 12$ ${}^-5712$
33. $692 \times {}^-48$ ${}^-33{,}216$

C Compute as indicated.

34. $8({}^-7) + 8(6)$ ${}^-8$
35. $8({}^-7 + 6)$ ${}^-8$

36. $9({}^-7) + 9({}^-8)$ ${}^-135$
37. $9({}^-7 + {}^-8)$ ${}^-135$

38. $12(8 + {}^-13)$ ${}^-60$
39. $6(18 + {}^-24)$ ${}^-36$

40. ${}^-18(24 + 37)$ ${}^-1098$
41. $19(12 + {}^-19)$ ${}^-133$

Multiplying Two Negative Integers

To learn how to find the product of two negative integers, consider the following pattern.

These factors
are decreasing
by 1.

These products
are increasing
by 6.

$$3 \times {}^-6 = {}^-18$$
$$+6$$
$$2 \times {}^-6 = {}^-12$$
$$+6$$
$$1 \times {}^-6 = {}^-6$$
$$+6$$
$$0 \times {}^-6 = 0$$
$$^-1 \times {}^-6 = ?$$
$$^-2 \times {}^-6 = ?$$

For the pattern to continue, you have the following.

$$^-1 \times {}^-6 = 6$$

$$^-2 \times {}^-6 = 12$$

Many other examples suggest this conclusion.

 The product of two negative integers is positive.

Example 1: Multiply $^-5$ by $^-75$.

$$^-5 \times {}^-75 = 5 \times 75$$

$$= 375$$

Example 2: How do you multiply $^-3$, 4, and $^-6$?

Take your choice of which integers to multiply first.

$$(^-3 \times 4) \times {}^-6 \qquad \text{or} \qquad ^-3 \times (4 \times {}^-6)$$

Then proceed as follows to find the product.

$$(^-3 \times 4) \times {}^-6 = {}^-12 \times {}^-6 \qquad ^-3 \times (4 \times {}^-6) = {}^-3 \times {}^-24$$

$$= 72 \qquad\qquad\qquad = 72$$

■ Exercises

A Tell whether each product is positive or negative.

1. 7×6 Pos.

2. $18 \times {}^-6$ Neg.

3. $^-16 \times 18$ Neg.

4. $^-48 \times {}^-27$ Pos.

5. $^-76 \times 7$ Neg.

6. $^-83 \times {}^-72$ Pos.

B Find each product.

Assignment Guide 7.2
Oral: 1–6
Written: Min. 7–21
　　　Reg. 7–33 odd
　　　Max. 7–25 odd;
　　　　　26–35

7. $^-7 \times {}^-6$ 42

8. $^-9 \times {}^-10$ 90

9. $^-8 \times {}^-4$ 32

10. $^-12 \times {}^-13$ 156

11. $^-15 \times {}^-17$ 255

12. $^-11 \times {}^-16$ 176

13. $^-19 \times {}^-20$ 380

14. $^-23 \times {}^-23$ 529

15. $^-18 \times {}^-18$ 324

16. $^-4 \times {}^-5 \times {}^-6$ $^-120$

17. $11 \times {}^-4 \times {}^-5$ 220

18. $^-8 \times 6 \times {}^-2$ 96

19. $8 \times 7 \times {}^-6$ $^-336$

20. $^-14 \times {}^-4 \times {}^-8$ $^-448$

21. $1 \times {}^-8 \times {}^-19$ 152

22. $^-25 \times {}^-25 \times 25$ 15,625

23. $^-72 \times {}^-73 \times 43$ 226,008

24. $48 \times {}^-99 \times {}^-101$ 479,952

25. $18 \times {}^-19 \times {}^-21$ 7182

C **26.** $7 \times 6 \times 3$ 126

27. $8 \times {}^-7 \times 5$ $^-280$

28. $^-7 \times {}^-4 \times 2$ 56

29. $^-6 \times {}^-7 \times {}^-8$ $^-336$

30. $^-7 \times 4 \times {}^-9$ 252

31. $^-8 \times 7 \times {}^-17 \times {}^-5$ $^-4760$

32. $^-17 \times {}^-4 \times {}^-8 \times {}^-3$ 1632

33. $^-8 \times {}^-17 \times {}^-13 \times 3$ $^-5304$

Use your answers to Exercises 26–33 to decide if the following statements are true or false.

34. If there is an *even number of negative factors* and no other factor is 0, then the product is positive. T

35. If there is an *odd number of negative factors* and no other factor is 0, then the product is negative. T

Dividing Integers

7.3

Multiplication and division are inverse operations. You can use this idea to discover how to divide integers.

both positive

If $3 \times 4 = 12$,   then $12 \div 4 = 3$.

positive quotients

If $3 \times {}^-4 = {}^-12$,   then ${}^-12 \div {}^-4 = 3$.

both negative

 If two integers have the *same* sign, then their quotient is *positive*.

Example 1:   Divide ${}^-18$ by ${}^-2$.

same sign

$${}^-18 \div {}^-2 = 18 \div 2$$
$$= 9 \qquad \textit{positive quotient}$$

What if the signs are different?

different signs

If ${}^-3 \times 4 = {}^-12$,   then ${}^-12 \div 4 = {}^-3$.

negative quotients

If ${}^-3 \times {}^-4 = 12$,   then $12 \div {}^-4 = {}^-3$.

different signs

 If two integers have *different* signs, then their quotient is *negative*.

Example 2:   Divide 28 by ${}^-4$.

different signs

$$28 \div {}^-4 = {}^-(28 \div 4)$$
$$= {}^-7 \qquad \textit{negative quotient}$$

Example 3: Find the quotient $\frac{-84}{7}$.

$$\frac{-84}{7} = \overbrace{-84 \div 7}^{\text{different signs}} = -(84 \div 7)$$

$$= -12 \qquad \text{negative quotient}$$

■ Exercises

Assignment Guide 7.3
Oral: 1–9
Written: Min. 11–37 odd
Reg. 11–43 odd
Max. 11–43 odd;
44–52

Ⓐ Tell whether the quotient is positive or negative.

1. $8 \div 2$ Pos.
2. $\frac{18}{-6}$ Neg.
3. $-24 \div 8$ Neg.
4. $\frac{-36}{4}$ Neg.
5. $84 \div -12$ Neg.
6. $\frac{-42}{-7}$ Pos.
7. $-48 \div -16$ Pos.
8. $\frac{96}{8}$ Pos.
9. $78 \div -3$ Neg.

Ⓑ Find each quotient.

10. $48 \div 16$ 3
11. $16 \div -4$ -4
12. $-21 \div 3$ -7
13. $-27 \div -3$ 9
14. $81 \div -9$ -9
15. $30 \div -5$ -6
16. $-18 \div 6$ -3
17. $72 \div -8$ -9
18. $-30 \div -6$ 5
19. $-121 \div 11$ -11
20. $96 \div 16$ 6
21. $91 \div 13$ 7
22. $-100 \div 5$ -20
23. $91 \div -7$ -13
24. $-70 \div 5$ -14
25. $\frac{-9}{3}$ -3
26. $\frac{20}{-5}$ -4
27. $\frac{-15}{-3}$ 5
28. $\frac{78}{13}$ 6
29. $\frac{-75}{5}$ -15
30. $\frac{225}{-25}$ -9
31. $\frac{-144}{-16}$ 9
32. $\frac{-288}{9}$ -32
33. $\frac{324}{-18}$ -18

Find each value. (Remember the order of operations, pages 6–7.)

34. $9 + -42 \div 3$ -5
35. $-6 \times 14 \div -2$ 42
36. $-81 \div 9 + -16$ -25
37. $-84 \div -7 \times 6$ 72
38. $16 + -9 \times 4 \div 2$ -2
39. $-6 \times 12 + 3 \div -5$ -29
40. $-20 + 12 \div -3 \times 6$ -44
41. $16 \times -3 \div 4 + -8$ -20
42. $10 \times -5 \div 2 - -2$ -23
43. $-50 + 36 \times -2 \div -2$ -14

Study the following statements and examples before you do Exercises 44–52.

0 cannot be divided by itself, but 0 can be divided by any other number.

Dividing by 0 is meaningless.

Examples : $0 \div {}^-5 = 0$ ${}^-5 \div 0 = ?$

Check: 0
          $\times\ {}^-5$
          $\overline{\hphantom{xx}0}$

Check: ? ◄── No number works.
          $\times\ 0$ So there is no
          $\overline{\hphantom{xx}5}$ answer for ${}^-5 \div 0$.

Find each quotient or product, if possible. Write *meaningless* if division by 0 is involved.

44. $0 \div {}^-8$ 0

45. $\frac{{}^-8}{0}$ Meaningless

46. $0 \div 0$ Meaningless

47. $0 \times {}^-8$ 0

48. ${}^-6 \div 0$ Meaningless

49. 0×0 0

50. ${}^-8 \times 0$ 0

51. $\frac{0}{{}^-5}$ 0

52. $\frac{0}{0}$ Meaningless

Do You Speak Mathematics?

Sometimes words in other languages are very similar to English words with the same meaning. Can you guess the English words which have the same meaning as these?

Spanish :	**French :**	**German :**	
número positivo	*nombre positif*	*positive zahl*	positive number
cero	*zéro*	*null*	zero
número negativo	*nombre négatif*	*negative zahl*	negative number

If you speak another language, can you name foreign words from mathematics which are similar to English words?

7.4 Solving Multiplication Equations

You already know how to solve equations like $3x = 12$.

$$3x = 12$$

$$\frac{3x}{3} = \frac{12}{3} \qquad \text{Divide each side by 3.}$$

$$x = 4$$

Check:

$$3x = 12$$

$$3(4) = 12$$

$$12 = 12 \quad \checkmark$$

The same method is used to solve equations involving integers.

Example 1: Solve $3n = {}^-12$.

$$3n = {}^-12$$

$$\frac{3n}{3} = \frac{{}^-12}{3} \qquad \text{Divide each side by 3.}$$

$$n = {}^-4$$

Check: $\quad 3n = {}^-12$

$$3({}^-4) = {}^-12 \qquad \text{Replace } n \text{ with } {}^-4.$$

$$^-12 = {}^-12 \quad \checkmark$$

Example 2: Solve $15 = {}^-5z$.

$$15 = {}^-5z$$

$$\frac{15}{{}^-5} = \frac{{}^-5z}{{}^-5} \qquad \text{Divide each side by } {}^-5.$$

$$^-3 = z$$

Check: $\quad 15 = {}^-5z$

$$15 = {}^-5({}^-3) \qquad \text{Replace } z \text{ with } {}^-3.$$

$$15 = 15 \quad \checkmark$$

Exercises

Assignment Guide 7.4
Oral: 1–12
Written:
Min. 13–29 odd; Quiz, p. 210
Reg. 13–33 odd; Quiz, p. 210
Max. 13–39 odd; Quiz, p. 210

A To solve each equation, what would you do to each side ?

1. $7x = 42$ $\div 7$

2. $8y = {}^-48$ $\div 8$

3. $27 = {}^-9x$ $\div {}^-9$

4. $^-18z = {}^-90$ $\div {}^-18$

5. $12x = 0$ $\div 12$

6. $^-70 = 14b$ $\div 14$

Find each quotient.

7. $\frac{16}{8}$ 2

8. $\frac{^-16}{8}$ $^-2$

9. $\frac{16}{^-8}$ $^-2$

10. $\frac{^-24}{^-6}$ 4

11. $\frac{35}{^-7}$ $^-5$

12. $\frac{^-42}{^-6}$ 7

B Solve each equation.

13. $9x = 54$ 6

14. $8y = {}^-40$ $^-5$

15. $36 = {}^-9t$ $^-4$

16. $^-7n = {}^-21$ 3

17. $6x = {}^-96$ $^-16$

18. $72 = 12x$ 6

19. $^-8t = 96$ $^-12$

20. $^-9k = {}^-117$ 13

21. $^-168 = 12n$ $^-14$

22. $24z = 192$ 8

23. $^-14s = 252$ $^-18$

24. $^-512 = {}^-32p$ 16

25. $27n = {}^-243$ $^-9$

26. $^-18t = 126$ $^-7$

27. $^-138 = {}^-23n$ 6

28. $^-17t = 153$ $^-9$

29. $^-16t = {}^-192$ 12

30. $^-1056 = 48n$ $^-22$

Solve each problem.

31. A submarine left the surface of the water at a rate of $^-2$ feet per second. At that rate, how long would it take the submarine to reach the $^-100$-foot level? 50 sec

32. The stock market changed $^-18$ points in 3 days. What was the average change each day? $^-6$ points

33. The Mills Company profit-and-loss statement showed a change of $^-\$1200$ in 3 weeks. What was the average change each week? $^-\$400$

Harold M. Lambert

34. On four running plays, a back for the Bears' football team made
$^-16$ yards net yardage. What was the average per run? $^-4$ yd

C Solve each equation.

Example:
$$^-7x - 3x = 50$$
$$(^-7 - 3)x = 50$$
$$-10x = 50$$
$$\frac{-10x}{-10} = \frac{50}{-10}$$
$$x = ^-5$$

Check:
$$^-7x - 3x = 50$$
$$^-7(^-5) - 3(^-5) = 50$$
$$35 - ^-15 = 50$$
$$35 + 15 = 50$$
$$50 = 50 \checkmark$$

35. $7z - 2z = ^-35$ $^-7$

36. $3n - 5n = 42$ $^-21$

37. $^-5k - 2k = ^-49$ 7

38. $7x + 2x = ^-54$ $^-6$

39. $^-7x + 4x = 36$ $^-12$

40. $^-2x + ^-3x = ^-25$ 5

Quick Quiz
Sections 7.1 to 7.4

Find each product.

1. $8 \times ^-7$ $^-56$

2. $^-6 \times 9$ $^-54$

3. $^-7 \times ^-6$ 42

4. $^-10 \times 5$ $^-50$

5. $15 \times ^-18$ $^-270$

6. $^-26 \times 14$ $^-364$

7. $4 \times ^-6 \times ^-2$ 48

8. $^-3 \times ^-4 \times ^-5$ $^-60$

Find each quotient.

9. $^-18 \div 2$ $^-9$

10. $^-25 \div ^-5$ 5

11. $56 \div ^-8$ $^-7$

Solve each equation.

12. $8m = ^-64$ $^-8$

13. $56 = ^-7x$ $^-8$

14. $^-12x = ^-48$ 4

Solving Division Equations

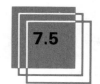

You already know how to solve equations like $\frac{n}{7} = 2$.

$$\frac{n}{7} = 2$$

$$\frac{n}{7} \times 7 = 2 \times 7 \quad \text{Multiply each side by 7.}$$

$$n = 14$$

Check:

$$\frac{n}{7} = 2$$

$$\frac{14}{7} = 2$$

$$2 = 2 \quad \checkmark$$

The same method is used to solve equations involving integers.

Example 1: Solve $\frac{k}{3} = {}^-8$.

$$\frac{k}{3} = {}^-8$$

$$\frac{k}{3} \times 3 = {}^-8 \times 3 \quad \text{Multiply each side by 3.}$$

$$k = {}^-24$$

Check:

$$\frac{k}{3} = {}^-8$$

$$\frac{{}^-24}{3} = {}^-8 \quad \text{Replace } k \text{ with } {}^-24.$$

$${}^-8 = {}^-8 \quad \checkmark$$

Example 2: Solve $15 = \frac{m}{{}^-2}$.

$$15 = \frac{m}{{}^-2}$$

$$15 \times {}^-2 = \frac{m}{{}^-2} \times {}^-2 \quad \text{Multiply each side by } {}^-2.$$

$${}^-30 = m$$

$$Check: \quad 15 = \frac{m}{^-2}$$

$$15 = \frac{^-30}{^-2} \qquad \text{Replace } m \text{ with } ^-30.$$

$$15 = 15 \checkmark$$

■ Exercises

A To solve each equation, what would you do to each side?

Assignment Guide 7.5
Oral: 1–12
Written:
Min. 13–29 odd; 31–32
Reg. 13–32
Max. 13–41

1. $\frac{m}{3} = ^-5$ $\times 3$ **2.** $\frac{x}{^-2} = 3$ $\times ^-2$ **3.** $4 = \frac{s}{^-5}$ $\times ^-5$

4. $6 = \frac{x}{^-4}$ $\times ^-4$ **5.** $\frac{d}{^-6} = ^-8$ $\times ^-6$ **6.** $\frac{d}{5} = ^-7$ $\times 5$

Find each product.

7. $8 \times ^-7$ $^-56$ **8.** $^-8 \times ^-7$ 56 **9.** $^-8 \times 7$ $^-56$

10. $^-4 \times 9$ $^-36$ **11.** $^-5 \times 20$ $^-100$ **12.** $^-8 \times ^-11$ 88

B Solve each equation.

13. $\frac{n}{3} = 9$ 27 **14.** $\frac{m}{2} = ^-8$ $^-16$ **15.** $5 = \frac{k}{^-3}$ $^-15$

16. $\frac{t}{^-2} = ^-9$ 18 **17.** $\frac{a}{6} = 12$ 72 **18.** $^-15 = \frac{a}{5}$ $^-75$

19. $\frac{d}{^-6} = 13$ $^-78$ **20.** $\frac{c}{^-7} = ^-21$ 147 **21.** $^-2 = \frac{x}{11}$ $^-22$

22. $\frac{n}{4} = 4$ 16 **23.** $\frac{x}{18} = ^-1$ $^-18$ **24.** $^-12 = \frac{x}{^-3}$ 36

25. $\frac{y}{82} = 6$ 492 **26.** $\frac{n}{101} = ^-4$ $^-404$ **27.** $^-16 = \frac{x}{12}$ $^-192$

28. $\frac{n}{^-17} = ^-5$ 85 **29.** $\frac{p}{^-13} = 6$ $^-78$ **30.** $^-13 = \frac{a}{14}$ $^-182$

Solve each problem.

31. A number is divided by 3. The result is $^-14$. What is the number?

$^-42$

32. In a certain experiment, the temperature of a solution is lowered in 5 stages from $0\,°C$ to $^-90\,°C$. If the temperature is lowered the same amount in each stage, what is the temperature after the first stage? $^-18\,°C$

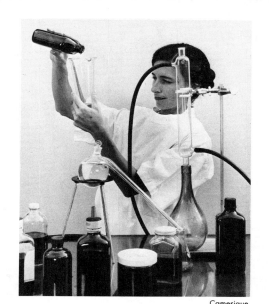

Camerique

C Solve each equation.

Example: $\dfrac{-10}{n} = 5$

$\dfrac{-10}{n} \times n = 5 \times n$ Multiply each side by n.

$-10 = 5n$

$\dfrac{-10}{5} = \dfrac{5n}{5}$ Divide each side by 5.

$-2 = n$

Check: $\dfrac{-10}{n} = 5$

$\dfrac{-10}{-2} = 5$ Replace n with $^-2$.

$5 = 5$ ✓

33. $\dfrac{12}{n} = 6$ 2

34. $\dfrac{^-18}{n} = 6$ $^-3$

35. $\dfrac{24}{n} = -8$ $^-3$

36. $\dfrac{^-27}{n} = -3$ 9

37. $\dfrac{36}{n} = 9$ 4

38. $\dfrac{42}{n} = -6$ $^-7$

39. $\dfrac{^-18}{n} = 9$ $^-2$

40. $\dfrac{^-56}{n} = -4$ 14

41. $\dfrac{63}{n} = -9$ $^-7$

7.6 Solving Division Inequalities

Suggested Class Time			
Course	Min.	Reg.	Max.
Days	0	1	1

If each side of a true inequality is multiplied by a *positive* integer, the resulting inequality has the same inequality symbol.

$$^-3 > ^-4$$ same symbol

$$^-3 \times 5 > ^-4 \times 5$$

$$^-15 > ^-20$$

$$6 < 10$$

$$6 \times 5 < 10 \times 5$$

$$30 < 50$$

$$^-5 < 2$$

$$^-5 \times 5 < 2 \times 5$$

$$^-25 < 10$$

Notice what happens when each side of an inequality is multiplied by a negative integer.

$$^-3 > ^-4$$

$$^-3 \times ^-5 < ^-4 \times ^-5$$ Multiplying by $^-5$ changes the inequality symbol.

$$15 < 20$$

$$^-5 < 2$$

$$^-5 \times ^-5 > 2 \times ^-5$$

$$25 > ^-10$$

Multiplying each side of an inequality by a negative integer changes $<$ to $>$, and vice versa.

You can use multiplication as follows to solve inequalities. We will also draw graphs to help "see" the solutions.

Example 1: Solve and graph $\frac{n}{4} < ^-6$.

$$\frac{n}{4} < ^-6$$

$$\frac{n}{4} \times 4 < ^-6 \times 4$$ Multiply each side by 4.
Keep the same inequality symbol.

$$n < ^-24$$

Check: Try any integer less than $^-24$ in the original inequality.

$$\frac{n}{4} < ^-6$$

$$\frac{^-28}{4} < ^-6$$ Replace *n* with $^-28$.

$$^-7 < ^-6 \quad \checkmark$$

Graph: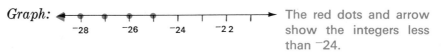

The red dots and arrow show the integers less than $^-24$.

214

Example 2: Solve and graph $4 > \frac{n}{-3}$.

$$4 > \frac{n}{-3}$$

$$4 \times {}^-3 < \frac{n}{-3} \times {}^-3 \qquad \text{Multiply each side by } {}^-3.$$
$$\text{Change the inequality symbol.}$$

$${}^-12 < n$$

Check: Try any integer greater than $^-12$ in the original inequality.

$$4 > \frac{n}{-3}$$

$$4 > \frac{^-9}{-3} \qquad \text{Replace } n \text{ with } {}^-9.$$

$$4 > 3 \; \checkmark$$

Graph:

Assignment Guide 7.6
Oral: Reg. & Max. 1–6
Written: Reg. 7–25
Max. 7–25; 35–39

■ Exercises

A Tell whether the inequality symbol will change when each side is multiplied by the number given.

1. $^-5 < 8$ 7   No   **2.** $10 > 7$ -3 Yes

3. $^-10 > ^-15$ 4   No   **4.** $^-8 < 2$ -4 Yes

5. $\frac{x}{-4} < 7$ -4 Yes   **6.** $\frac{x}{7} < ^-5$ 7   No

B Multiply each side of the given inequality by the number indicated, and write the resulting inequality.

7. $6 < 4$ 3 $18 > 12$ **8.** $10 > 7$ -4 $^-40 < ^-28$

9. $8 > ^-2$ -7 $^-56 < 14$ **10.** $^-11 < 10$ -2 $22 > ^-20$

11. $^-6 < 0$ 5 $^-30 < 0$ **12.** $5 > 3$ -3 $^-15 < ^-9$

215

13. $\frac{x}{4} < {}^-8$ 4 $x < {}^-32$ **14.** $\frac{x}{{}^-6} > {}^-7$ ${}^-6$ $x < 42$

15. $\frac{x}{{}^-7} < 10$ ${}^-7$ $x > {}^-70$ **16.** $\frac{x}{9} > 9$ 9 $x > 81$

Solve and graph each inequality.

17. $\frac{x}{4} < {}^-9$ $x < {}^-36$ **18.** $\frac{m}{{}^-4} > 8$ $m < {}^-32$ **19.** $8 < \frac{k}{6}$
$48 < k$

20. $\frac{x}{{}^-9} > {}^-2$ $x < 18$ **21.** $\frac{x}{3} < {}^-2$ $x < {}^-6$ **22.** $8 > \frac{n}{{}^-9}$
${}^-72 < n$

23. $\frac{t}{11} < 12$ $t < 132$ **24.** $\frac{x}{5} > {}^-9$ $x > {}^-45$ **25.** $7 < \frac{n}{{}^-8}$
${}^-56 > n$

26. $\frac{m}{5} > 7$ $m > 35$ **27.** $\frac{x}{{}^-6} < {}^-4$ $x > 24$ **28.** $7 > \frac{t}{{}^-16}$
${}^-112 < t$

29. $\frac{a}{{}^-15} > {}^-4$ $a < 60$ **30.** $\frac{n}{18} > {}^-9$ $n > {}^-162$ **31.** $16 < \frac{d}{{}^-18}$
${}^-288 > d$

32. $\frac{b}{{}^-13} < {}^-13$ $b > 169$ **33.** $\frac{c}{35} > {}^-7$ $c > {}^-245$ **34.** ${}^-32 < \frac{f}{{}^-15}$
$480 > f$

C Should $>$, $<$, or $=$ replace each ▓ to make each sentence true?

35. ${}^-6 < 2$

${}^-6 \times 0$ ▓ 2×0
$=$

36. $4 > {}^-3$

4×0 ▓ ${}^-3 \times 0$
$=$

37. $8 > 7$

8×0 ▓ 7×0
$=$

38. ${}^-5 < {}^-3$

${}^-5 \times 0$ ▓ ${}^-3 \times 0$
$=$

39. What is the effect of multiplying each side of a true inequality by 0?   The true equation $0 = 0$ results.

Solving Multiplication Inequalities

If each side of a true inequality is divided by a *positive* integer, the resulting inequality has the same inequality symbol.

$$6 < 10 \qquad\qquad 4 > {}^-4 \qquad\qquad {}^-8 > {}^-12$$

$$\frac{6}{2} < \frac{10}{2} \qquad\qquad \frac{4}{2} > \frac{{}^-4}{2} \qquad\qquad \frac{{}^-8}{2} > \frac{{}^-12}{2}$$

$$3 < 5 \qquad\qquad 2 > {}^-2 \qquad\qquad {}^-4 > {}^-6$$

Notice what happens when each side of an inequality is divided by a *negative* integer.

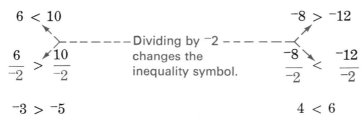

Dividing by $^-2$ changes the inequality symbol.

$$6 < 10 \qquad\qquad\qquad\qquad\qquad {}^-8 > {}^-12$$

$$\frac{6}{{}^-2} > \frac{10}{{}^-2} \qquad\qquad\qquad\qquad \frac{{}^-8}{{}^-2} < \frac{{}^-12}{{}^-2}$$

$${}^-3 > {}^-5 \qquad\qquad\qquad\qquad\qquad 4 < 6$$

> Dividing each side of an inequality by a negative integer changes $>$ to $<$, and vice versa.

Example 1: Solve and graph $3n < {}^-12$.

$$3n < {}^-12$$

$$\frac{3n}{3} < \frac{{}^-12}{3} \qquad \text{Divide each side by 3.}$$
Keep the same inequality symbol.

$$n < {}^-4$$

Check: Try any integer less than $^-4$ in the original inequality.

$$3n < {}^-12$$

$$3\,({}^-5) < {}^-12 \qquad \text{Replace } n \text{ with } {}^-5.$$

$$^-15 < {}^-12 \ \checkmark$$

Graph: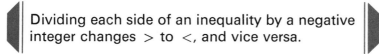

Example 2: Solve and graph $20 > {}^-4n$.

$$20 > {}^-4n$$

$$\frac{20}{{}^-4} < \frac{{}^-4n}{{}^-4}$$ Divide each side by $^-4$.
Change the inequality symbol.

$$^-5 < n$$

Check: Try any integer greater than $^-5$ in the original inequality.

$$20 > {}^-4n$$

$$20 > {}^-4({}^-4)$$ Replace n with $^-4$.

$$20 > 16 \checkmark$$

Graph:

■ Exercises

Assignment Guide 7.7
Oral: Reg. & Max. 1–6
Written:
Reg. 7–25; Quiz, p. 219
Max. 7–25; 35–41;
    Quiz, p. 219

A Tell whether the inequality symbol will change when each side is divided by the given number.

1. $6 < 8$ 2   No   **2.** $14 > 10$ -2 Yes

3. $^-8 > {}^-12$ -4 Yes   **4.** $^-12 < {}^-6$ 6   No

5. $^-4x > 8$ 4   No   **6.** $3x < {}^-9$ 3   Yes

B Divide each side of the given inequality by the number indicated, and write the resulting inequality.

7. $8 > 4$ 2 $4 > 2$ **8.** $15 < 25$ $^-5$ $^-3 > {}^-5$

9. $36 < 64$ -4 $^-9 > {}^-16$ **10.** $12 > {}^-4$ $^-4$ $^-3 < 1$

11. $^-14 > {}^-16$ 2 $^-7 > {}^-8$ **12.** $^-18 < {}^-12$ $^-6$ $3 > 2$

13. $3x > 15$ 3 $x > 5$ **14.** $^-5x < 25$ $^-5$ $x > {}^-5$

15. $^-6x < 24$ $^-6$ $x > {}^-4$ **16.** $10x > {}^-10$ 10 $x > {}^-1$

Solve and graph each inequality.

17. $6x < 48$ $\quad x < 8$

18. $7x > {}^-42$ $\quad x > {}^-6$

19. $81 > {}^-9x$ $\quad {}^-9 < x$

20. ${}^-3x < 6$ $\quad x > {}^-2$

21. $8x > 16$ $\quad x > 2$

22. ${}^-15 < 5x$ $\quad {}^-3 < x$

23. ${}^-10x > {}^-100$ $\quad x < 10$

24. ${}^-2x < 12$ $\quad x > {}^-6$

25. ${}^-64 > 4x$ $\quad {}^-16 > x$

26. $9x > {}^-108$ $\quad x > {}^-12$

27. ${}^-6x < 36$ $\quad x > {}^-6$

28. ${}^-121 > {}^-11x$ $\quad 11 < x$

29. $16x > 256$ $\quad x > 16$

30. ${}^-2x > {}^-24$ $\quad x < 12$

31. $196 > {}^-4x$ $\quad {}^-49 < x$

32. ${}^-8x < 24$ $\quad x > {}^-3$

33. ${}^-24x < 72$ $\quad x > {}^-3$

34. ${}^-52 > 13x$ $\quad {}^-4 > x$

C **35.** $2x + 3x > 15$ $\quad x > 3$

36. $7x - 2x < 25$ $\quad x < 5$

37. $3(4x) < 72$ $\quad x < 6$

38. $\frac{8x}{2} < 60$ $\quad x < 15$

39. ${}^-5x + 2x < 9$ $\quad x > {}^-3$

40. $5x - 8x > 36$ $\quad x < {}^-12$

41. ${}^-3(2x) < 54$ $\quad x > {}^-9$

42. $\frac{9x}{3} > {}^-54$ $\quad x > {}^-18$

43. $4x - 7x < {}^-54$ $\quad x > 18$

44. ${}^-3(2x) > {}^-36$ $\quad x < 6$

45. $8x - 5x < {}^-39$ $\quad x < {}^-13$

46. $15x - 36x > {}^-84$ $\quad x < 4$

Quick Quiz
Sections 7.5 to 7.7

Solve each equation.

1. $\frac{n}{5} = {}^-6$ $\quad {}^-30$

2. $\frac{n}{{}^-5} = {}^-10$ $\quad 50$

3. ${}^-6 = \frac{w}{4}$ $\quad {}^-24$

4. $\frac{n}{4} = 7$ $\quad 28$

5. ${}^-12 = \frac{a}{{}^-5}$ $\quad 60$

6. $15 = \frac{c}{{}^-4}$ $\quad {}^-60$

Solve and graph each inequality.

7. $\frac{n}{3} < {}^-2$ $\quad n < {}^-6$

8. $1 > \frac{a}{{}^-4}$ $\quad {}^-4 < a$

9. $\frac{x}{{}^-8} < {}^-2$ $\quad x > 16$

10. ${}^-10 < 5x$ $\quad {}^-2 < x$

11. ${}^-9 > {}^-3x$ $\quad 3 < x$

12. $12\,t > 36$ $\quad t > 3$

219

7.8 **Equations With Two Operations**

Earlier you have solved equations with two operations involving whole numbers. Now you will solve such equations involving integers.

Example 1: Solve $3n + {}^-7 = {}^-19$.

$$3n + {}^-7 = {}^-19$$

$$3n + {}^-7 + 7 = {}^-19 + 7 \qquad \text{Add 7 to each side.}$$

$$3n + 0 = {}^-12$$

$$3n = {}^-12$$

$$\frac{3n}{3} = \frac{{}^-12}{3} \qquad \text{Divide each side by 3.}$$

$$n = {}^-4$$

Check: $\quad 3n + {}^-7 = {}^-19$

$$3({}^-4) + {}^-7 = {}^-19 \qquad \text{Replace } n \text{ with } {}^-4.$$

$$^-12 + {}^-7 = {}^-19$$

$$^-19 = {}^-19 \quad \checkmark$$

Example 2: Solve ${}^-3 = \frac{n}{{}^-6} + 9$.

$$^-3 = \frac{n}{{}^-6} + 9$$

$$^-3 + {}^-9 = \frac{n}{{}^-6} + 9 + {}^-9 \qquad \textit{Check:} \quad {}^-3 = \frac{n}{{}^-6} + 9$$

$$^-12 = \frac{n}{{}^-6} + 0 \qquad\qquad\qquad\quad {}^-3 = \frac{72}{{}^-6} + 9$$

$$^-12 = \frac{n}{{}^-6} \qquad\qquad\qquad\qquad {}^-3 = {}^-12 + 9$$

$$^-12 \times {}^-6 = \frac{n}{{}^-6} \times {}^-6 \qquad\qquad {}^-3 = {}^-3 \quad \checkmark$$

$$72 = n$$

Example 3: Solve $\frac{k-6}{3} = {}^-12$.

$$\frac{k-6}{3} = {}^-12$$

$$\frac{k-6}{3} \times 3 = {}^-12 \times 3$$

$$k - 6 = {}^-36$$

$$k + {}^-6 = {}^-36$$

$$k + {}^-6 + 6 = {}^-36 + 6$$

$$k + 0 = {}^-30$$

$$k = {}^-30$$

Check:
$$\frac{k-6}{3} = {}^-12$$

$$\frac{{}^-30 - 6}{3} = {}^-12$$

$$\frac{{}^-36}{3} = {}^-12$$

$${}^-12 = {}^-12 \checkmark$$

Assignment Guide 7.8
Oral: Reg. & Max. 1–6
Written: Reg. 7–23 odd
Max. 7–23 odd;
25–30

■ Exercises

A What would you do to each side to solve each equation?

1. $2n + {}^-7 = 7$ $+7$, then $\div 2$ **2.** $\frac{m}{6} + {}^-7 = 2$ $+7$, then $\times 6$

3. $\frac{k-9}{^-4} = 6$ $\times {}^-4$, then $+9$ **4.** ${}^-2k + 7 = 9$ $+ {}^-7$, then $\div {}^-2$

5. $\frac{x}{^-7} + 5 = {}^-2$ $+ {}^-5$, then $\times {}^-7$ **6.** $3t + {}^-9 = {}^-18$ $+9$, then $\div 3$

B Solve each equation.

7. $2k + {}^-5 = {}^-9$ ${}^-2$ **8.** $\frac{m}{8} + {}^-5 = 6$ 88 **9.** $6 = \frac{k-5}{4}$ 29

10. $\frac{k}{^-6} + 8 = 4$ 24 **11.** $5n - 7 = 18$ 5 **12.** $9 = \frac{n + {}^-7}{6}$ 61

13. $\frac{m+5}{^-4} = 16$ ${}^-69$ **14.** $\frac{m}{8} - 6 = {}^-14$ ${}^-64$ **15.** ${}^-27 = {}^-6x + {}^-9$ 3

16. ${}^-4t + 8 = 40$ ${}^-8$ **17.** $\frac{x + {}^-5}{3} = 7$ 26 **18.** $10 = \frac{r}{^-9} - 5$ ${}^-135$

19. $\frac{t}{5} + {}^-7 = {}^-14$ ${}^-35$ **20.** $8m + {}^-7 = 41$ 6 **21.** $5 = \frac{x-8}{^-16}$ ${}^-72$

22. $\frac{x+9}{4} = {}^-5$ ${}^-29$ **23.** $\frac{m}{^-11} - 7 = {}^-9$ 22 **24.** $33 = {}^-7t + {}^-9$ ${}^-6$

C **25.** $7 + 2x = {}^-5$ ${}^-6$ **26.** ${}^-7 + 3x = {}^-10$ ${}^-1$

27. $5 + {}^-4x = 13$ ${}^-2$ **28.** $3 + {}^-5x = {}^-17$ 4

29. $2n + (3 + {}^-2) = 7$ 3 **30.** $(3m + 3) + {}^-7 = 14$ 6

Solving Problems

Problems about *rates of change* and *averages* can often be solved by using multiplication and division of negative integers. Such problems also involve the following two formulas.

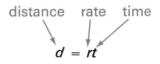

distance   rate   time

$$d = rt$$

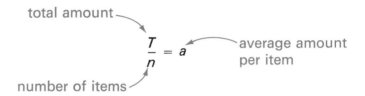

total amount

$$\frac{T}{n} = a$$

average amount per item

number of items

De Wys, Inc.

Example 1: A hot-air balloon changes its altitude $^-2000$ feet in 40 minutes. What is the rate of change in altitude?

Let r = rate of change in altitude.

Then $^-2000 = r(40)$ ◀ $d = rt$

$^-2000 = 40r$

$$\frac{^-2000}{40} = \frac{40r}{40}$$

$^-50 = r$

Note: Since the distance is in feet and the time is in minutes, the rate has been found in *feet per minute*.

Check: At $^-50$ ft/min for 40 min, will the balloon change its altitude $^-2000$ feet? ✓

So the rate of change in altitude is $^-50$ feet per minute.

Example 2: A chain of restaurants had an average profit-and-loss balance of $^-4100$ dollars per restaurant for a total of 8 restaurants. What was the total balance for all the restaurants?

Let T = total balance.

Then $\dfrac{T}{8} = {}^-4100.$ ◀ $\dfrac{T}{n} = a$

$\dfrac{T}{8} \times 8 = {}^-4100 \times 8$ *Check:* Does a total balance of $^-32{,}800$ dollars for 8 restaurants give an average balance of $^-4100$ dollars per restaurant? ✓

$T = {}^-32{,}800$

The total balance was $^-32{,}800$ dollars. (Another way to say this is that the chain of restaurants lost \$32,800.)

Assignment Guide 7.9
Oral: Reg. & Max. 1–2
Written: Reg. 3–12
Max. 3–14

■ Exercises

A **1.** What does each letter in the formula $d = rt$ stand for?
$d =$ distance, $r =$ rate, $t =$ time

2. What does each letter in the formula $\dfrac{T}{n} = a$ stand for?
$T =$ total amount, $n =$ number of items, $a =$ average amount per item

B Solve each problem.

3. A submarine descends from the surface (0 feet) to $^-55$ feet in 5 minutes. What is the rate of change? $^-11$ ft/min

4. An airplane changes its altitude $^-18{,}000$ feet in 15 minutes. What is the rate of change in altitude? $^-1200$ ft/min

5. In a certain city, the average change in population has been $^-143$ people per year. What has been the population change during the last 5 years? $^-715$ people

6. A company showed an average profit-and-loss balance of $^-345$ dollars per month for 12 months. What was the total balance for 12 months? $^-\$4140$

7. Until recently, the city of Venice, Italy, was changing its elevation an average of $^-5$ millimeters per year. At that rate, what was the change during 25 years? $^-125$ mm

8. The temperature changed $^-21$ degrees in 7 hours. What was the average change per hour? $^-3°/$h

223

9. A helicopter changed altitude $^-840$ meters in 7 minutes. What was the average change per minute? $^-120$ m

10. An insurance company had 152 customers in a region which suffered a flood. The company recorded the average amount it paid out to each customer as $^-8200$ dollars. How would they record the total amount paid out? $^-\$1{,}246{,}400$

11. A miner descended from the surface (0 feet) to $^-128$ feet in 16 minutes. What was the rate of change? $^-8$ ft/min

12. In a 7-day period, an airline reported an average change in income of $^-150{,}000$ dollars per day because of a strike. What was the total change in income? $^-\$1{,}050{,}000$

C 13. A family reported the following monthly budget balances: January, 17 dollars; February, $^-3$ dollars; March, 8 dollars; April, $^-2$ dollars. What was the average monthly budget balance for the four months? $\$5$

14. A business showed the following profit-and-loss balances: 7350 dollars for the first quarter, $^-850$ dollars for the second quarter, $^-1450$ dollars for the third quarter, and 6150 dollars for the fourth quarter. What was the average balance per quarter? $\$2800$

Courtesy General Electric Co.,
Circuit Protective Devices Dept.

WATTS THE LIMIT?

Your house or apartment has a circuit-breaker box like the one at the left. Each circuit breaker, which is a switch, is there to protect part of the electrical wiring in the building from catching on fire.

CONSUMER CORNER

Here's how it works. Suppose your living room has a 120-volt line (you can tell this by looking in the circuit-breaker box) and a 15-ampere circuit breaker. How many 100-watt light bulbs could you operate on that line? Watts, volts, and amperes are related by this formula:

watts   volts   amperes

$$P = EI$$
$$P = 120 \times 15$$
$$P = 1800$$

So a 120-volt, 15-ampere circuit could handle 1800 watts and you could operate 18 light bulbs, each rated at 100 watts.

Appliances have watt ratings printed on them too. Could you operate the following on a 120-volt, 20-ampere line?

Blender	450 watts	
Refrigerator	300 watts	
Dishwasher	740 watts	
Toaster	750 watts	
Light bulbs	400 watts	
total	2640 watts	

$$P = EI$$
$$2640 = 120\,I$$
$$\frac{2640}{120} = \frac{120\,I}{120}$$
$$22 = I$$

This is greater than the 20-ampere circuit rating. So you could not use all the appliances and bulbs. The circuit breaker would stop the flow of electricity.

1. Find if you can operate the following on a 120-volt, 20-ampere line: iron, 1000 watts; hair dryer, 740 watts; refrigerator, 300 watts; microwave oven, 470 watts; light bulbs, 610 watts. No

2. Find if you can operate the following on a 240-volt, 30-ampere line: air conditioner, 2400 watts; water heater, 4080 watts. Yes

Terms and Symbols Review

Give the letter of the best ending for each sentence.

1. Multiplying each side of $\frac{x}{3} > {}^-7$ by 3   a

2. Dividing each side of ${}^-3x < {}^-9$ by ${}^-3$ b

3. The product of two negative integers is   c

4. The product of one positive and one negative integer is   d

5. The quotient of two negative integers is   c

6. The quotient of one positive and one negative integer is   d

a. does not change the inequality symbol.

b. changes the inequality symbol.

c. positive.

d. negative.

Assignment Guide Rev.
Oral:
Min. Terms & Symbols 3–6
Reg. Terms & Symbols 1–6
Max. Terms & Symbols 1–6
Written: Min. 1–26
 Reg. 1–39 odd
 Max. 1–39 odd

Chapter 7 Review

7.1   Find each product.

1. 7×9 63

2. $4 \times {}^-7$ ${}^-28$

3. ${}^-8 \times 6$ ${}^-48$

4. ${}^-11 \times 7$ ${}^-77$

5. $11 \times {}^-13$ ${}^-143$

6. ${}^-26 \times 17$ ${}^-442$

7.2   7. ${}^-8 \times {}^-3$ 24

8. ${}^-10 \times {}^-10$ 100

9. ${}^-13 \times {}^-14$ 182

10. ${}^-18 \times {}^-16$ 288

7.3   Find each quotient.

11. $8 \div {}^-2$ ${}^-4$

12. ${}^-16 \div 8$ ${}^-2$

13. ${}^-24 \div {}^-6$ 4

14. $48 \div 4$ 12

15. $\frac{69}{-13}$ ${}^-5$

16. $\frac{-72}{4}$ ${}^-18$

17. $\frac{-96}{-6}$ 16

18. $\frac{144}{-9}$ ${}^-16$

Solve each equation.

19. $8x = 72$ 9

20. $^-48 = 6y$ $^-8$

21. $^-7x = 84$ $^-12$

22. $^-5m = ^-35$ 7

23. $\frac{n}{3} = 6$ 18

24. $\frac{n}{2} = ^-7$ $^-14$

25. $\frac{m}{^-4} = 7$ $^-28$

26. $^-12 = \frac{k}{^-8}$ 96

Solve and graph each inequality.

27. $\frac{x}{4} < ^-6$ $x < ^-24$

28. $\frac{t}{6} > 8$ $t > 48$

29. $8 < \frac{m}{^-3}$ $^-24 > m$

30. $\frac{y}{^-2} < ^-9$ $y > 18$

31. $6x > 54$ $x > 9$

32. $^-35 > 7t$ $^-5 > t$

33. $84 > ^-7x$ $^-12 < x$

34. $^-108 < ^-9w$ $12 > w$

Solve each equation.

35. $3x + ^-5 = 10$ 5

36. $^-8 = ^-5x - 3$ 1

37. $5 = \frac{x + ^-8}{^-2}$ $^-2$

38. $\frac{x}{5} + 3 = 7$ 20

Solve each problem.

39. An airplane changes its altitude $^-20{,}000$ feet in 10 minutes. What is the rate of change in altitude? $^-2000$ ft/min

40. According to the United States Chamber of Commerce, the buying power of the average American family changed $^-612$ dollars in a recent year. If this continued, what would the total change be over 3 years? $^-\$1836$

Chapter 7 Test

Assignment Guide Test
Written: Min. 1–14
    Reg. 1–25
    Max. 1–25

Find each product or quotient.

1. $3 \times {}^-3$ ⁻9

2. ${}^-8 \times {}^-5$ 40

3. ${}^-19 \times {}^-21$ 399

4. ${}^-24 \times 32$ ⁻768

5. ${}^-120 \div 8$ ⁻15

6. ${}^-196 \div {}^-14$ 14

7. $\frac{{}^-64}{16}$ ⁻4

8. $\frac{360}{{}^-45}$ ⁻8

Solve each equation.

9. ${}^-5c = 45$ ⁻9

10. ${}^-16 = 4x$ ⁻4

11. ${}^-72 = {}^-8w$ 9

12. $\frac{a}{{}^-9} = {}^-18$ 162

13. $\frac{k}{3} = {}^-7$ ⁻21

14. ${}^-12 = \frac{m}{{}^-5}$ 60

Solve and graph each inequality.

15. $\frac{r}{4} < {}^-8$ $r < {}^-32$

16. $15 < \frac{w}{{}^-6}$ ⁻90 > w

17. ${}^-10 < \frac{c}{{}^-2}$ 20 > c

18. $7m > {}^-28$ $m > {}^-4$

19. ${}^-50 > {}^-10x$ $5 < x$

20. ${}^-9r > 45$ $r < {}^-5$

Solve each equation.

21. $2x + 5 = {}^-15$ ⁻10

23. ${}^-14 = {}^-3x - 2$ 4

22. $\frac{x}{4} + {}^-1 = 7$ 32

24. $\frac{y + {}^-3}{2} = 10$ 23

25. A union figured that because of inflation, the purchasing power of each member changed an average of ⁻20 dollars a month for the last 12 months. What was the total change in the 12 months?
⁻$240

RATE YOURSELF

24–25	Superior
21–23	Excellent
18–20	Good
13–17	Fair
0–12	Poor

Number Correct

POWER LINES AND PIPELINES

Metal expands and contracts with changes in temperature. When power lines are strung during warm weather, a certain amount of slack must be left. Otherwise, the wires might contract and break in colder weather.

A person who strings copper wire can use the following formula to compute the change in length of a copper wire due to temperature changes.

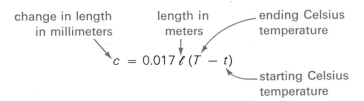

change in length in millimeters — length in meters — ending Celsius temperature — starting Celsius temperature

$$c = 0.017\, \ell\, (T - t)$$

A pipefitter who lays brass pipe can use the following formula to compute the change in length of brass pipe because of temperature changes.

change in length in inches — length in feet — ending Fahrenheit temperature — starting Fahrenheit temperature

$$c = 0.0001248\, \ell\, (T - t)$$

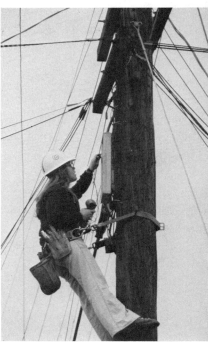

© Yoram Kahana Photo

Use the formulas above to solve these problems.

1. When the temperature changes from ⁻10 °C to 14 °C, what is the change in length of a copper wire that is 15 meters long? 6.12 mm

2. When the temperature changes from 150 °F to 40 °F, what is the change in the length of a 300-foot brass pipe? ⁻4.1184 in.

ssignment Guide Rev.
'ral: Terms & Symbols 1–19

Which term or symbol in parentheses is the best choice?

Ch. 1

1. The (*liter, meter, gram*) is a metric unit of weight.

2. The prefix (*kilo-, centi-, milli-*) means "hundredth."

3. The symbol ($<$, $>$, $=$) is read "is less than."

Ch. 2

4. The pound is a unit for measuring (*weight, capacity, length*).

5. The inverse operation of addition is (*multiplication, subtraction*).

6. If the replacement set is the whole numbers, the graph of $x < 2$ contains (*0, 1, 2*) points.

Ch. 3

7. The (*commutative, associative*) property of multiplication is illustrated by the equation $3a = a \times 3$.

8. The number 7 is (*prime, composite*).

9. The exponent in the expression 3^2 is (*3, 2*).

Ch. 4

10. 5 is the (*numerator, denominator*) of $\frac{5}{8}$.

11. $\frac{9}{12}$ is equivalent to ($\frac{2}{3}$, $\frac{3}{4}$, $\frac{5}{6}$).

12. The least common denominator of $\frac{1}{6}$ and $\frac{1}{8}$ is (*2, 24, $\frac{1}{7}$*).

Ch. 5

13. The decimal for two and two tenths is (*0.22, 2.2, $2\frac{2}{10}$*).

14. The 3 in (*1.234, 4.123, 4.321*) is in the hundredths place.

15. When you multiply 1.8 by 0.3, there should be (*one, two, three*) places after the decimal point in the product.

Ch. 6

16. The absolute value of $^-8$ is (*8, $^-8$, 0*).

17. $x - {^-3}$ is equivalent to ($x - 3$, $x + 3$, $3 - x$).

Ch. 7

18. The product of two negative integers is (*positive, negative*).

19. The quotient of one positive and one negative integer is (*positive, negative*).

Find each value.

1. $10 + 4 \div 2$ 12

2. $(7 + 3) \times (4 - 2)$ 20

3. $(n + 4) \times 5$ if n is replaced with 2   30

4. $3 + 6x$ if x is replaced with 3   21

Assignment Guide Rev.
Written:
Min. (day 1) 1–29
   (day 2) 30–61
   (day 3) 64–92; 97–107
Reg. & Max.
   (day 1) 1–63 odd
   (day 2) 65–113 odd

Translate into symbols.

5. four plus twice y $4 + 2y$

6. a number n divided by three $\frac{n}{3}$ or $n \div 3$

7. The product of six and a number z is thirty. $6z = 30$

8. The quotient of a number s divided by two is less than ten. $\frac{s}{2} < 10$

Classify as *True*, *False*, or *Open*.

9. $3x + 2 = 13$ O

10. $12 - 3 < 9$ F

11. $8 > 4$ T

Solve. Use {1, 2, 3, 4, 5} as the replacement set.

12. $x + 4 = 7$ 3

13. $12 = a + 8$ 1, 2, 3

14. $m + 13 = 22$ $\varnothing$

Simplify.

15. $13 \times 6 \div 6$ 13

16. $11 - 8 + 8$ 11

17. $34 + 7 - 7$ 34

Solve.

18. $m + 8 = 14$ 6

19. $16 = y - 5$ 21

20. $42 = 6n$ 7

21. $\frac{x}{4} < 13$ 52

22. $t - 4 > 5$ 9

23. $5a + 4 = 24$ 4

24. $12 = \frac{y}{2} + 8$ 8

25. $\frac{t - 6}{5} = 4$ 26

26. $16 = 3t + 1$ 5

Solve and graph.

27. $7 = x + 4$ $3 < x$

28. $4n < 28$ $n < 7$

29. $21 > t + 19$ $2 > t$

Complete.

30. 4 ft = _____ in. *48*   **31.** 64 oz = _____ lb *4*   **32.** 8 qt = _____ gal. *2*

33. Find the area of a rectangle with length 29 meters and width 18 meters. *522 m²*

34. Find the volume of a rectangular solid with length 12 inches, width 9 inches, and height 8 inches. *864 in.³*

Translate into symbols.

35. One number is four times another number. The sum of the two numbers is thirty. *Let a = second no., $4a$ = first no.; $a + 4a = 30$.*

Ch. 3   Using a property of numbers, solve.

36. $25 \times 1 = a$ *25*   **37.** $0 \times 17 = b$ *0*   **38.** $12 + 0 = c$ *12*

39. $0 \div 8 = d$ *0*   **40.** $5 \div 5 = e$ *1*   **41.** $5(4f) = 40$ *2*

42. $5 + g = 13$ *8*   **43.** $10h + h = 66$ *6*   **44.** $25j - 12j = 39$ *3*

45. Find all the factors of 42. *1, 2, 3, 6, 7, 14, 21, 42*

46. Is 310 divisible by 2? By 3? By 5? By 10? *Yes; No; Yes; Yes*

47. Write the prime factorization of 40. *$2^3 \times 5$*

48. Find the GCF of 30 and 12. *6*

49. Find the LCM of 8 and 12. *24*

Ch. 4   Compute. Express each answer in lowest terms.

50. $\frac{1}{3} \times \frac{2}{5}$ *$\frac{2}{15}$*   **51.** $8 \times \frac{1}{4}$ *2*   **52.** $1\frac{2}{3} \times 2\frac{1}{2}$ *$4\frac{1}{6}$*

53. $\frac{3}{7} \div \frac{1}{3}$ *$1\frac{2}{7}$*   **54.** $3\frac{1}{3} \div 5$ *$\frac{2}{3}$*   **55.** $6\frac{1}{4} \div 1\frac{7}{8}$ *$3\frac{1}{3}$*

56. $\begin{array}{r} \frac{2}{7} \\ + \frac{3}{7} \\ \hline \frac{5}{7} \end{array}$ **57.** $\begin{array}{r} 5\frac{3}{8} \\ + 7\frac{5}{8} \\ \hline 13 \end{array}$ **58.** $\begin{array}{r} 3\frac{1}{3} \\ + 5\frac{1}{4} \\ \hline 8\frac{7}{12} \end{array}$

59.
$$5\frac{3}{4}$$
$$-\,1\frac{1}{4}$$
$$4\frac{1}{2}$$

60.
$$\frac{2}{5}$$
$$-\,\frac{1}{3}$$
$$\frac{1}{15}$$

61.
$$9\frac{1}{2}$$
$$-\,7\frac{2}{3}$$
$$1\frac{5}{6}$$

Answer each question.

62. How many $1\frac{1}{2}$-foot boards can be cut from a 6-foot board? 4 boards

63. If 1 can of juice holds $8\frac{1}{2}$ ounces, how many ounces are in 4 cans of the juice? 34 ounces

Round as indicated.

	to the nearest		
number	hundred	one	tenth
64. 128.38	100	128	128.4
65. 763.248	800	763	763.2

(a) Estimate each answer; **(b)** then compute each answer.

66–71. **a.** Answers may vary.

66. $19 + 2.8 + 5.62$ **b.** 27.42

67. $3.188 - 2.5$ **b.** 0.688

68. 5.4×0.6 **b.** 3.24

69. 7.4×3.58 **b.** 26.492

70. 0.09×78.3 **b.** 7.047

71. $19.5 \div 6$ **b.** 117

Divide.

72. $57.6 \div 18$ 3.2

73. $0.78 \div 0.04$ 19.5

74. $6.8 \div 1.7$ 4

75. $2.484 \div 0.04$ 62.1

Complete.

76. 2.9 km = <u>2900</u> m

77. 8.4 cm = <u>0.084</u> m

78. 47 mm = <u>4.7</u> cm

79. 8.9 g = <u>8900</u> mg

Compute.

80. 138.46×100
13,846

81.
$$4.63 \text{ m}$$
$$186 \text{ cm}$$
$$+\,1.38 \text{ m}$$
7.87 m or
787 cm

82.
$$5.2 \text{ cm}$$
$$\times\,3 \text{ mm}$$
1.56 cm^2 or
156 mm^2

233

Find each sum or difference.

83. $^-27 + ^-18$ $^-45$ **84.** $^-46 + 38$ $^-8$ **85.** $50 + ^-12$ 38

86. $^-14 - 17$ $^-31$ **87.** $25 - ^-26$ 51 **88.** $^-19 - ^-13$ $^-6$

Solve.

89. $x + 12 = ^-6$ $^-18$ **90.** $^-22 = y + ^-10$ $^-12$

91. $y - ^-29 = 17$ $^-12$ **92.** $a - 5 = ^-32$ $^-27$

Solve and graph.

93. $a - 9 < ^-6$ $a < 3$ **94.** $x + ^-6 > 3$ $x > 9$

95. $m + ^-19 < ^-16$ $m < 3$ **96.** $d - ^-3 > 2$ $d > ^-1$

97. Before a deposit was made, a checking account had a balance of $^-16$ dollars. After the deposit was made, the balance was 34 dollars. How much money was deposited? $50

Find each product or quotient.

98. $18 \times ^-5$ $^-90$ **99.** $^-7 \times ^-14$ 98 **100.** $^-28 \times 12$ $^-336$

101. $^-48 \div 8$ $^-6$ **102.** $95 \div ^-5$ $^-19$ **103.** $^-84 \div ^-12$ 7

Solve.

104. $3k = ^-21$ $^-7$ **105.** $^-18x = ^-90$ 5

106. $\frac{x}{^-6} = ^-7$ 42 **107.** $\frac{t}{4} = ^-6$ $^-24$

108. $6x + ^-2 = ^-14$ $^-2$ **109.** $1 = \frac{x}{5} - ^-3$ $^-10$

Solve and graph.

110. $^-8y > ^-40$ $y < 5$ **111.** $^-55 < 11t$ $^-5 < t$

112. $\frac{m}{4} < ^-8$ $m < ^-32$ **113.** $^-14 > \frac{s}{^-2}$ $28 < s$

114. An airplane changes its altitude $^-12,000$ feet in 10 minutes. What is the rate of change in altitude? $^-1200$ ft/min

Suggested Class Time

Course	Min.	Reg.	Max.
Days	1	*	0

Compute.

1. $5 + 2(\frac{12}{3})$ 13

2. $15 \div (21 - 18)$ 5

3. $(38 - 15) \times 2$ 46

4. $(5 + 4) \times (17 - 8)$ 81

Find the value of each phrase.

5. $8y - 11$ if $y = 4$ 21

6. $7(\frac{x}{8}) + 16$ if $x = 56$ 65

7. $(5a \div 2) + 7$ if $a = 6$ 22

8. $\frac{n+5}{3} - 1$ if $n = 7$ 3

1.2

Assignment Guide GR 8
Written: Min. 1–23
            Reg. 1–23 odd

1.3

Compute.

9. $^-3 + 7$ 4

10. $^-8 + ^-9$ $^-17$

11. $(2 + ^-5) + 7$ 4

12. $^-10 - 4$ $^-14$

13. $8 - ^-7$ 15

14. $^-8 - ^-12$ 4

15. $^-10 \times ^-5$ 50

16. $^-4 \times 5$ $^-20$

17. $8 \times ^-3 \times ^-2$ 48

18. $18 \div ^-3$ $^-6$

19. $^-20 \div ^-5$ 4

20. $\frac{15}{^-5}$ $^-3$

6.3

6.4

7.2

7.3

Solve these problems.

21. The Wildcats made 23 field goals and 14 free throws. What was their score? 60 points

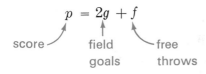

$$p = 2g + f$$

score — field goals — free throws

1.9

22. The Cardinals scored 71 points in a game. They made 29 field goals. How many free throws did they make? 13

23. The base of a triangle is 18 cm long. The altitude is 5 cm long. Find the area of the triangle.

45 cm²

* Combine with Section 8.1.

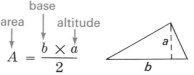

base — altitude — area

$$A = \frac{b \times a}{2}$$

Wide World

2.8

235

8
GRAPHING

Reprinted courtesy of the Chicago Tribune

Graphs are used for many things in math and in everyday life. In this chapter you will draw graphs like those above. You will also see how graphs are used in other ways.

Mary Elenz Tranter Photographics

Suggested Class Time			
Course	Min.	Reg.	Max.
Days	1	1	1

In a math game, Ann drew a rule card. She will apply that rule to any number you give her.

If your number is 2, Ann's number is $2 + 3$ or 5. If your number is 4, what is Ann's number? If your number is x, what is Ann's number?

The rule could also be given as an equation.

$$a = x + 3$$

Ann's number ⤺ ⤻ Your number

Example 1: Use Ann's rule to complete the table.

Your number (x)	0	1	2	3	4	5
Ann's number (a)	3	4	5	6	7	8

$a = x + 3$ $a = x + 3$ Replace x with
$\ \ = 0 + 3$ $\ \ = 1 + 3$ each number.
$\ \ = 3$ $\ \ = 4$ Solve for a.

You can list these pairs of numbers in another way. In each pair, list your number first and Ann's number second.

$$(0, 3),\ (1, 4),\ (2, 5),\ (3, 6),\ (4, 7),\ (5, 8)$$

Since we have specified an order, these are called **ordered pairs** of numbers.

Example 2: Write the rule as an equation.
Use the rule to complete the table.

Rule: To find the second number,
multiply the first number by 2. Then add 3.

Let x be the first
number and y be
the second number.

$$y = 2x + 3$$

x	0	1	2	3	4	5	6	7	8
y	3	5	7	9	11	13	15	17	19

$$y = 2x + 3$$
$$= 2(0) + 3$$
$$= 0 + 3$$
$$= 3$$

$$y = 2x + 3$$
$$= 2(1) + 3$$
$$= 2 + 3$$
$$= 5$$

Replace x with
each number.
Solve for y.

■ Exercises

A State each rule as an equation. Let x be the first number. To find
the second number y:

Assignment Guide 8.1
Oral: 1–11
Written: Min. 12–18
Reg. 12–18
Max. 12–20

1. Add 7 to the first number.
$y = x + 7$

2. Divide the first number by 2.
$y = \dfrac{x}{2}$

3. Multiply the first number
by 8. $y = 8x$

4. Subtract 2 from the first number. $y = x - 2$

5. Multiply the first number
by 3. Then subtract 2.
$y = 3x - 2$

6. Multiply the first number by
4. Then add 1. $y = 4x + 1$

7. Divide the first number by 3. Then add 2. $y = \dfrac{x}{3} + 2$

Interchange the numbers in each ordered pair. Then tell what the
new ordered pair means.

Example: The date 2–12 means February 12th.

The date 12–2 means December 2nd.

8. The date 5–10 means May 10th.
The date 10–5 means October 5.

9. Section 8.1 means chapter 8, section 1.
Section 1.8 means Chapter 1, section 8.

10. A count of 1–2 in baseball means 1 ball, 2 strikes.
A count of 2–1 in baseball means 2 balls, 1 strike.

11. A volleyball score of 11–6 means the serving team has 11,
the other team has 6. A volleyball score of 6–11 means the serving
team has 6, the other team has 11.

Use the rule to complete the table.

12. $y = x - 2$

x	5	6	7	8	9	10	11
y	3	4	5	6	7	8	9

13. $y = 4x - 3$

x	1	2	3	4	5	6	7
y	1	5	9	13	17	21	25

14. $y = \frac{x}{2} + 5$

x	2	4	6	8	10	12	14
y	6	7	8	9	10	11	12

15. $y = 7x$

x	0	1	2	3	4	5	6
y	0	7	14	21	28	35	42

Use the rule to complete the ordered pairs.
The values of x are given first.

16. $y = 3x + 2$

(2, 8), (3, 11), (4, 14), (5, 17), (6, 20), (7, 23)

17. $y = 10x$

(3, 30), (5, 50), (7, 70), (9, 90), (11, 110), (13, 130)

18. $y = x + 6$

(3, 9), (4, 10), (5, 11), (6, 12), (7, 13), (8, 14)

Discover the rule for each table.

19.

length of side (s)	1	2	3	4	5	6	
perimeter (p)	4	8	12	16	20	24	$p = 4s$

20.

millimeters (m)	10	20	30	40	50	60	70	
centimeters (c)	1	2	3	4	5	6	7	$c = \frac{m}{10}$

Graphing Ordered Pairs

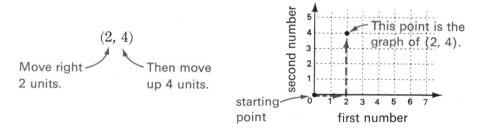

Suppose this is your ticket stub.

To find your seating location, you would go to row D, then to seat 5. The letter D tells you how far to go in one direction. The number 5 tells you how far to go in another direction.

An *ordered pair* of numbers like (2, 4) can be graphed in the same way. You can use graph paper as shown below.

(2, 4)

Move right 2 units. Then move up 4 units.

second number

This point is the graph of (2, 4).

starting point

first number

The dashed arrows show the moves. Do not draw them as part of the graph. Just draw a dot at the ending point.

Example 1: Graph the ordered pairs (3, 0) and (0, 3).

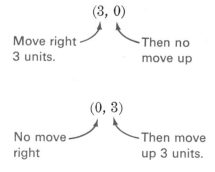

(3, 0)

Move right 3 units. Then no move up

(0, 3)

No move right Then move up 3 units.

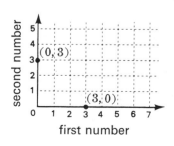

Example 2: Graph the ordered pairs.

x (first number)	0	1	2	3	4	5	6
y (second number)	3	2	6	5	4	0	1

If it helps, list the ordered pairs as follows.

(0, 3), (1, 2), (2, 6), (3, 5), (4, 4), (5, 0), (6, 1)

On a piece of graph paper, draw and label two number scales as shown at the right. Then graph each ordered pair as shown in Example 1.

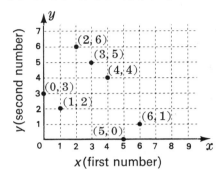

Exercises

Ⓐ Tell the moves you would make to graph each ordered pair.

1. (3, 4)
3 rt., 4 up

2. (5, 8)
5 rt., 8 up

3. (0, 5)
0 rt., 5 up

4. (3, 3)
3 rt., 3 up

5. (6, 2)
6 rt., 2 up

6. (1, 0)
1 rt., 0 up

7. (10, 7)
10 rt., 7 up

8. (2, 9)
2 rt., 9 up

Name the ordered pair for each point.

9. A (0, 4)

10. B (3, 8)

11. C (8, 3)

12. D (5, 0)

13. E (9, 9)

14. F (10, 6)

15. G (7, 7)

16. H (3, 5)

17. I (5, 3)

18. O (0, 0)

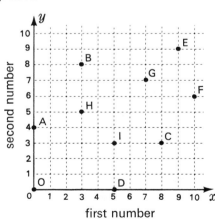

Assignment Guide 8.2
Oral: 1–18
Written: Min. 19–27 odd
Reg. 19–29 odd
Max. 19–29

B Graph each set of ordered pairs, using a different pair of number scales for each set.

19.

x	1	2	3	4	5	6
y	4	5	6	7	8	9

20.

x	0	2	4	6	8	10
y	4	3	2	3	4	5

21.

x	0	1	2	3	4	55
y	4	4	4	4	4	4

22.

x	0	1	2	3	4	5
y	0	1	2	3	4	5

23. (0, 5), (1, 4), (2, 3), (3, 2), (4, 1), (5, 0)

24. (3, 0), (3, 1), (3, 2), (3, 3), (3, 4), (3, 5)

25. (1, 2), (2, 3), (3, 4), (3, 5), (4, 6), (5, 7)

26. (1, 1), (2, 4), (3, 1), (4, 4), (5, 1), (6, 4)

C Graph the set of ordered pairs, using a different pair of number scales for each set. Then join the points by line segments in the order listed.

27. (2, 0), (1, 2), (2, 1), (3, 2), (5, 3), (8, 3),

(10, 2), (9, 4), (9, 5), (10, 6), (11, 6), (12, 5),

(15, 4), (12, 4), (11, 3), (12, 2), (12, 1), (11, 0)

28. (3, 0), (2, 2), (5, 2), (5, 8), (8, 3), (6, 2), (11, 2),

(11, 11), (16, 3), (12, 2), (18, 2), (22, 4), (21, 0)

29. Make up your own list of ordered pairs for a picture. Let a friend draw the picture.

Integers and the Coordinate System

8.3

In Chapter 6, we graphed integers on a number line. If we use two number lines, called **axes,** we can graph ordered pairs of integers.

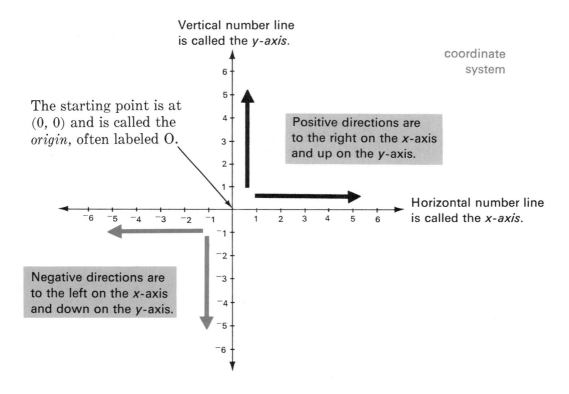

Vertical number line is called the *y-axis*.

coordinate system

The starting point is at (0, 0) and is called the *origin*, often labeled O.

Positive directions are to the right on the *x*-axis and up on the *y*-axis.

Horizontal number line is called the *x-axis*.

Negative directions are to the left on the *x*-axis and down on the *y*-axis.

Example 1: Graph (⁻2, 5) and (5, ⁻2).

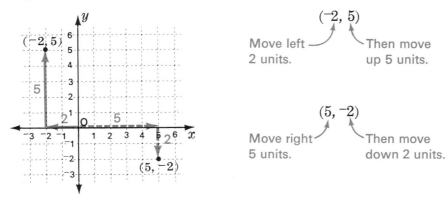

(⁻2, 5)

Move left 2 units. — Then move up 5 units.

(5, ⁻2)

Move right 5 units. — Then move down 2 units.

Notice that (⁻2, 5) and (5, ⁻2) name different points.

243

The numbers of an ordered pair are called **coordinates.**

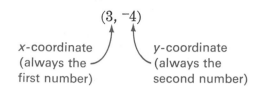

$(3, {}^-4)$

x-coordinate
(always the
first number)

y-coordinate
(always the
second number)

Example 2:   Name the coordinates of each point shown on the graph.

Point	*Coordinates*
A	$(3, 4)$
B	$({}^-3, 4)$
C	$({}^-3, {}^-4)$
D	$(3, {}^-4)$
E	$(0, 3)$
F	$(4, 0)$
G	$(0, {}^-3)$
H	$({}^-4, 0)$
O	$(0, 0)$

■ Exercises

A   **1.** The positive direction on the *x*-axis is to the _____.   Right

2. The negative direction on the *y*-axis is _____.   Down

3. The coordinates of the origin are _____.   (0, 0)

4. For $(3, 6)$, the *x*-coordinate is _____.   3

Tell the moves you would make to graph each ordered pair.

5. $(1, {}^-2)$
    1 rt., 2 dn.

6. $({}^-3, {}^-6)$
    3 lt., 6 dn.

7. $(1, 4)$
    1 rt., 4 up

8. $(0, 8)$
    0 rt., 8 up

9. $({}^-3, 8)$
    3 lt., 8 up

10. $(10, {}^-7)$
    10 rt., 7 dn.

11. $({}^-18, {}^-25)$
    18 lt., 25 dn.

12. $(0, 0)$
    0 rt., 0 up

Name the coordinates of
each point.

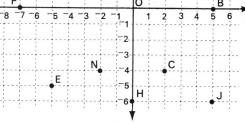

13. A (2, 1) **14.** E (⁻5, ⁻5) **15.** M (⁻3, 4)

16. F (⁻7, 0) **17.** B (5, 0) **18.** J (5, ⁻6)

19. N (⁻2, ⁻4) **20.** G (0, 4) **21.** C (2, ⁻4)

22. H (0, ⁻6) **23.** D (⁻2, 2) **24.** I (4, 5)

B On graph paper, draw a pair of axes. Then graph the points given
below. Label each point with its letter.

25. K(5, 6) **26.** O (0, 0) **27.** R(–5, –4)

28. U(–8, 2) **29.** L(–7, –3) **30.** P(–5, 4)

31. S(5, –4) **32.** V(–6, 0) **33.** M(6, 0)

34. Q(5, 4) **35.** T(2, 1) **36.** W(5, –2)

C Use the rule to complete the table. Then graph each set of ordered
pairs on its own pair of axes.

37. $y = 6x$

x-coordinate	–3	–2	–1	0	1	2	3	4
y-coordinate	–18	⁻12	⁻6	0	6	12	18	24

38. $y = 2x - 3$

x-coordinate	–3	–2	–1	0	1	2	3	4
y-coordinate	⁻9	⁻7	⁻5	⁻3	⁻1	1	3	5

39. $y = {}^{-}4x$

x-coordinate	–3	–2	–1	0	1	2	3	4
y-coordinate	12	8	4	0	⁻4	⁻8	⁻12	⁻16

40. $y = {}^{-}3x + 8$

x-coordinate	–4	–2	0	2	4	6	8	10
y-coordinate	20	14	8	2	⁻4	⁻10	⁻16	⁻22

8.4 Drawing Line Graphs

A pair of axes can be used to graph many things. For example, Elizabeth kept the following record of a bicycle trip.

hour of the trip	0	1	2	3	4	5	6
number of miles traveled in the hour	0	2	5	1	3	4	2

Shawn Walker/Taurus Ph

Suggested Class Time

Course	Min.	Reg.	Max.
Days	1	1	1

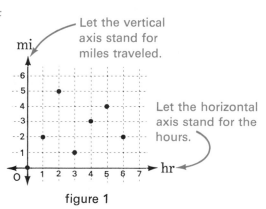

Let the vertical axis stand for miles traveled.

Let the horizontal axis stand for the hours.

figure 1

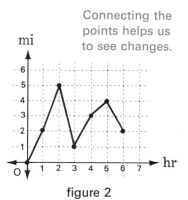

Connecting the points helps us to see changes.

figure 2

The graph in figure 2 is called a *line graph*.

Example 1: Draw a line graph for the table below.

meters	0	1	2	3	4	5	6	7
centimeters	0	100	200	300	400	500	600	700

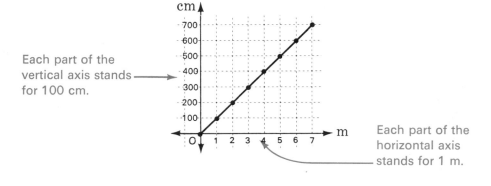

Each part of the vertical axis stands for 100 cm.

Each part of the horizontal axis stands for 1 m.

246

Example 2: Draw a line graph for each table.

a.

time (hr)	0	2	4	6	8	10	12
temp. (°C)	−6	−2	1	5	6	3	2

b.

x	0	0.1	0.2	0.3	0.5	0.7	0.9
y	0	10	20	30	50	70	90

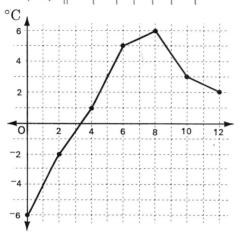

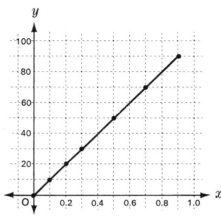

Assignment Guide 8.4
Oral: 1–4
Written: Min. 5–9
Reg. 5–15 odd
Max. 5–19 odd

Exercises

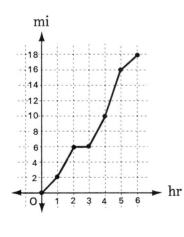

A **1.** The graph at left is called a _____ graph. Line

2. What does each part of the horizontal axis stand for? 1 hr

3. What does each part of the vertical axis stand for? 2 mi

4. Complete the table from the graph at left.

hours	0	1	2	3	4	5	6
miles	0	2	6	?	?	?	?
				6	10	16	18

B Draw a line graph for each table.

5.

x	0	1	2	3	4	5	6	7
y	0	5	7	6	9	3	1	1

247

6.

x	-3	-2	-1	0	1	2	3
y	9	4	1	0	1	4	9

7.

ft	0	1	2	3	4	5	6	7
in.	0	12	24	36	48	60	72	84

8.

min	0	60	120	180	240	300	360	420
hr	0	1	2	3	4	5	6	7

9.

cm	0	1	2	3	4	5	6	7
approx. in.	0	0.4	0.8	1.2	1.6	2.0	2.4	2.8

10.

km	0	1	2	3	4	5	6	7
approx. mi	0	0.6	1.2	1.8	2.4	3.0	3.6	4.2

11.

pounds bought	1	2	3	4	5	6	7
price per lb ($)	5	5	4	4	3	3	3

12.

weight of object on moon (lb)	0	5	10	15	20	25	30
weight of object on earth (lb)	0	30	60	90	120	150	180

13.

age of a car (yr)	0	1	2	3	4	5
change in value ($)	0	-900	-1200	-1600	-1800	-2000

14.

snowfall (in.)	0	2	4	6	8	10	12	14
equivalent rainfall (in.)	0	0.2	0.4	0.6	0.8	1.0	1.2	1.4

15.

time (hr)	0	1	2	3	4	5	6	7
temp. (°C)	-10	-7	-2	4	5	2	-1	-5

16.

price ($)	0	5	10	15	20	25	30	35
discount ($)	0	-1	-2	-3	-4	-5	-6	-7

The reported temperature on two different days may have been the same, but you felt colder on one day than you did on the other. This is partly because of the wind. For example, if the reported temperature is 30 °F and the wind speed is 10 mph, then it feels like a reported temperature of 16 °F on a calm day (no wind). 16 °F is called the *windchill*. Draw a line graph for each table below.

17. Windchill for a reported temperature of 30 °F.

wind speed (mph)	0	5	10	15	20	25	30	35	40	45
windchill (°F)	30	27	16	9	4	1	-2	-4	-5	-6

18. Windchill for a reported temperature of 0 °F.

wind speed (mph)	0	5	10	15	20	25	30	35	40	45
windchill (°F)	0	-5	-22	-31	-39	-44	-49	-52	-53	-54

19. Use the rule for changing Celsius temperatures to Fahrenheit temperatures to complete the table below. Then draw a line graph.

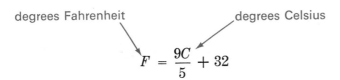

degrees Fahrenheit　　　　　degrees Celsius

$$F = \frac{9C}{5} + 32$$

Example: Change -25 °C to degrees Fahrenheit.

$$F = \frac{9C}{5} + 32$$

$$F = \frac{9(\overset{-5}{\cancel{-25}})}{\underset{1}{\cancel{5}}} + 32$$

$$F = -45 + 32$$

$$F = -13$$

°C	-25	-20	-15	-10	-5	0	5	10	15	20	25
°F	-13	-4	5	14	23	32	41	50	59	68	77

8.5 Functions

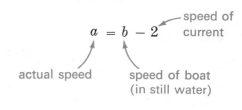

$$a = b - 2$$

actual speed — speed of boat (in still water) — speed of current

Suggested Class Time

Course	Min.	Reg.	Max.
Days	1	1	1

speed of boat (b)	4	5	6	7	8	9
actual speed (a)	2	3	4	5	6	7

The ordered pairs in the table can be written as

(4, 2), (5, 3), (6, 4), (7, 5), (8, 6), (9, 7).

Are any values of b (*first numbers*) ever repeated?

For every value of b, there is only one value of a. So, no two ordered pairs have the same first number. Such a set of ordered pairs is called a *function*.

> A **function** is a set of ordered pairs whose first numbers are all different.

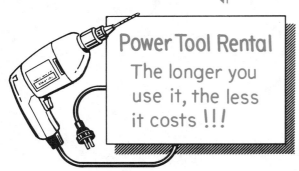

Power Tool Rental
The longer you use it, the less it costs !!!

For this number of dollars	2	4	5	6	7	7	8
You can use it for this number of hours	1	2	3	4	5	6	7

The ordered pairs in the table can be written as

(2, 1), (4, 2), (5, 3), (6, 4), (7, 5), (7, 6), (8, 7).

This set of ordered pairs is *not* a function. Why? Because the first numbers of the ordered pairs are not all different. The ordered pairs (7, 5) and (7, 6) have the *same* first number.

Example 1 :   Is (2, 3), (3, 4), (3, 5), (4, 6) a function?

(2, 3), (3, 4), (3, 5), (4, 6)

NO.   There are two ordered pairs with the same first
number.

Example 2 :   Is (4, 6), (5, 6), (6, 6), (7, 6) a function?

YES.   Every first number is different.

Let's look at the graph of the function.

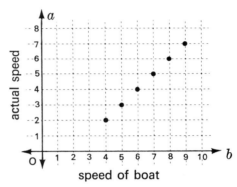

Every first number is
different. So the graph of
a function *never* has one
point directly above an-
other.

Example 3 :   Is the following the graph of a function?

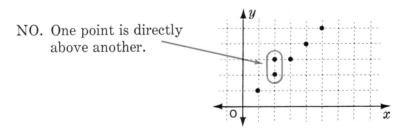

NO. One point is directly
above another.

Example 4 :   Is the following the graph of a function?

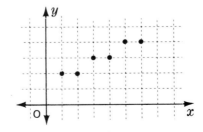

YES. No point is directly
above another.

■ Exercises

Assignment Guide 8.5
Oral: 1–6
Written:
Min. 7–17 odd; Quiz,
   p. 253
Reg. 7–18; Quiz, p. 253
Max. 7–22; Quiz, p. 253

A Is each set of ordered pairs a function? If not, tell why not.

1. (7, 7), (8, 6), (9, 5), (10, 4), (11, 3) Yes

2. (5, 0), (6, 1), (7, 2), (7, 3), (8, 4) No; two ordered pairs have the same first number.

3.
first number	2	4	6	8	10
second number	3	5	5	7	9

Yes

4.
first number	1	3	5	7	9
second number	⁻1	⁻9	⁻25	⁻49	⁻81

Yes

Is each graph the graph of a function? If not, tell why not.

5. 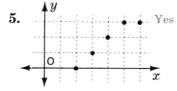 Yes

6. 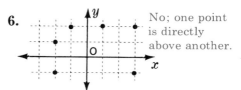 No; one point is directly above another.

B Tell whether each set of ordered pairs is a function.

7. (1, 6), (2, 7), (3, 8), (4, 9), (5, 10) Yes

8. (5, 7), (5, 8), (6, 9), (7, 10), (8, 11) No

9. (⁻3, ⁻2), (⁻2, ⁻1), (⁻3, 0), (⁻3, 1), (⁻4, 2) No

10.
first number	4	5	6	7	8
second number	2	2	2	2	2

Yes

11.
first number	1	2	3	4	5
second number	2	4	6	8	10

Yes

12.
first number	0	1	2	3	4
second number	0	⁻1	⁻2	⁻3	⁻4

Yes

Tell whether each graph is the graph of a function.

13. 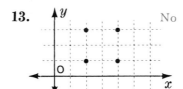 No

14. 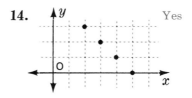 Yes

15. 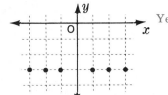 Yes

16. 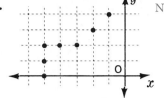 No

17. 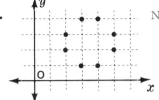 No

18. 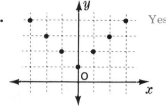 Yes

C Make a table of 6 ordered pairs for each rule.
Then tell whether each rule describes a function.   **19–22.** Tables may vary.

19. Multiply the first number by itself to get the second number. Yes

20. The first number is always 1. The second number can be any whole number. No

21. The first number can be any whole number. The second number is always 3. Yes

22. The second number is the same as the first number. Yes

Quick Quiz
Sections 8.1 to 8.5

1. Use the rule to complete the table.

$y = 3x + 1$

x	0	1	2	3	4	5	6
y	1	4	7	10	13	16	19

2. Name the coordinates of each point on the graph at the right.

   a. A   **b.** B   **c.** C   **d.** D

   (1, 2)   ($^-$3, 0)   (4, $^-$5)   ($^-$5, 4)

Ex. 2

3. Draw a line graph for the table.

x	0	1	2	3	4	5	6	7	8
y	-5	-2	0	3	5	4	1	-3	-6

4. Is the set of ordered pairs in Exercise 3 a function? Yes

253

Suggested Class Time

Course	Min.	Reg.	Max.
Days	1	1	1

Erich Bach/Photri

Jim heard the thunder 4 seconds after he saw the lightning. He wondered how far away the lightning was.

Sound travels about 1100 feet per second through air. So the following equation shows how *distance* and *time* are related.

distance (ft)   time (sec)

$$d = 1100\,t$$

Let's solve Jim's problem.

$$d = 1100t$$
$$= 1100\,(4) \qquad \text{Replace } t \text{ with 4.}$$
$$= 4400$$

The lightning was 4400 feet away.

Let's make a table and a graph for $d = 1100t$.

t	d
0	0
1	1100
2	2200
3	3300
4	4400
5	5500
6	6600

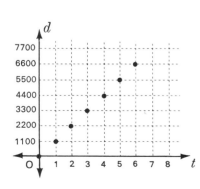

Are any values of t repeated in the table?

Suppose you try 3 again. Would d still be 3300?

Does the value of d depend on the value of t?

Is the graph the graph of a function?

Such a time-distance relationship is a function. Other functions from nature and everyday life are used in the exercises.

■ Exercises

Assignment Guide 8.6
Oral: 1–3
Written: Min. 4–11
           Reg. 4–13
           Max. 4–17

A Answer these questions.

1. Jim saw lightning strike a tree that was 5500 feet away. How long after that did he hear the noise? (See the table and graph on page 254.) 5 sec

2. Light travels about 186,000 miles per second. Give an equation that tells the distance d that light will travel in t seconds. $d = 186{,}000t$

3. How can you find the number of seconds it takes for light to travel from the sun to the earth?

93,000,000 miles

Earth

Sun

Solve the equation $93{,}000{,}000 = 186{,}000t$.

B Solve these problems.

Wind
34 mph

speed of wind
directly against
plane
↓
$$g = a - 34$$

ground speed
(speed over
ground)

airspeed
(speed through
the air)

4. If the plane's airspeed is 140 mph, what is its ground speed? 106 mph

5. To be on time, the plane must make a ground speed of 126 mph. At what airspeed should it fly? 160 mph

255

Wind
45 mph

Courtesy Boeing

speed of wind
directly behind
plane

$$g = a + 45$$

ground speed
(speed over
ground)

airspeed
(speed through
the air)

6. To be on time, a passenger jet must make a ground speed of 520 mph. At what airspeed should it fly?   475 mph

7. If the passenger jet's airspeed is 465 mph, what is its ground speed?   510 mph

Free-falling object

$$d = 16t^2$$

distance
(ft)

time
(sec)

8. Tom dropped a stone in the well. It hit bottom in 2 seconds. How deep was the well?   64 ft

9. A helicopter dropped a life raft. It hit the water in 10 seconds. How high was the helicopter?   1600 ft

d in.

w lb

Breaking strength of a certain kind of rope

$$w = 5000d(d + 1)$$

weight
(lb)

diameter of
rope (in.)

10. At what weight would a 1-inch rope break?   10,000 lb

11. At what weight would a 2-inch rope break?   30,000 lb

$$C = \frac{5(F - 32)}{9}$$

degrees Celsius $\quad$ degrees Fahrenheit

12. What is the temperature in degrees Celsius if the Fahrenheit temperature is $^-22°$? $\quad$ $^-30\ °C$

13. What is the temperature in degrees Fahrenheit if the Celsius temperature is $^-40°$? $\quad$ $^-40\ °F$

C **14.** To see n miles out to sea, you must be h feet above sea level, where $h = \frac{2n^2}{3}$. How tall should the lighthouse be if you are to see 9 miles out to sea? $\quad$ 54 ft

15. During a search at sea, a helicopter crew wanted to see at least 18 miles. They must be at least how high? $\quad$ 216 ft

16. A sonar set measures the time it takes for sound waves to reach an object and return. Sound travels through water about 4800 feet per second.

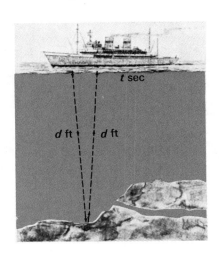

distance (ship to object in feet) $\qquad$ time in seconds for "round trip" of sound waves

$$d = \frac{4800t}{2}$$

or

$$d = 2400t$$

It took 3 seconds for the sound waves to reach the ocean floor and return. How deep is the ocean at that point? $\quad$ 7200 ft

17. A submarine was 4800 feet from the ship. How long did it take the sound waves to reach the submarine and return? $\quad$ 2 sec

8.7 Using Graphs to Enlarge and Reduce

A lab worker sometimes studies enlarged pictures of germs.

A construction worker or drafter often uses reduced drawings of buildings.

Example 1: Make a 1-to-2 enlargement of the square.

"1-to-2 enlargement" means that all measurements of the new square will be 2 times those of the original square.

Suggested Class Time			
Course	Min.	Reg.	Max.
Days	0	0	1

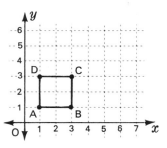

Step 1: For a 1-to-2 enlargement, multiply both numbers in each original ordered pair by 2.

Point	Original ordered pair	Point	New ordered pair
	A(1, 1)		A'(2, 2)
	B(3, 1)		B'(6, 2)
	C(3, 3)		C'(6, 6)
	D(1, 3)		D'(2, 6)

A' is read *A prime.* Using A' rather than some other letter makes it easy to see that point A' corresponds to point A.

Step 2: Graph the new ordered pairs. Draw the new square.

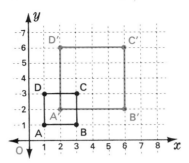

Example 2: Make a 1-to-3 reduction of the triangle.

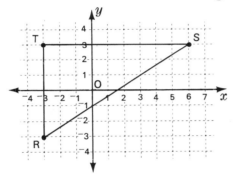

For a 1-to-3 reduction, divide both numbers in each original ordered pair by 3.

Original triangle	New triangle
R(⁻3, ⁻3)	R′(⁻1, ⁻1)
S(6, 3)	S′(2, 1)
T(⁻3, 3)	T′(⁻1, 1)

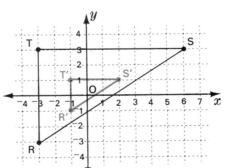

Assignment Guide 8.7
Oral: Max. 1–4
Written: Max. 5–10

▮ Exercises

Ⓐ What would you do with the numbers in each ordered pair to make each of the following ?

1. a 1-to-4 enlargement × 4

2. a 1-to-10 enlargement × 10

3. a 1-to-2 reduction ÷ 2

4. a 1-to-5 reduction ÷ 5

B Copy and graph the following.

5. a 1-to-3 enlargement of

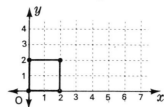

6. a 1-to-5 enlargement of

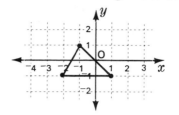

7. a 1-to-2 reduction of

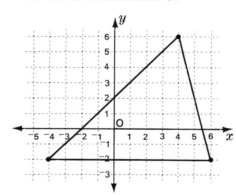

8. a 1-to-4 reduction of

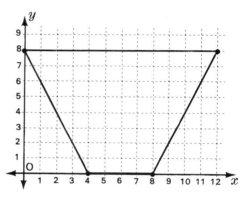

C Complete each set of ordered pairs. Graph all four triangles on the same pair of axes.

9.

Original ordered pair	Multiply first number by 4.	Multiply second number by 4.	Multiply both numbers by 4.
(1, 1)	(4, 1)	(1, 4)	(4, 4)
(3, 1)	(12, 1)	(3, 4)	(12, 4)
(2, 3)	(8, 3)	(2, 12)	(8, 12)

260

a. How does multiplying only the first numbers change the shape of a figure? Stretches figure horizontally

b. How does multiplying only the second numbers change the shape of a figure? Stretches figure vertically

c. How does multiplying both numbers change the shape of a figure?
Stretches figure horizontally and vertically

Complete each set of ordered pairs. Graph all four triangles on the same pair of axes.

10.

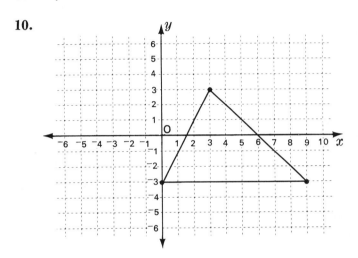

Original ordered pair	Divide first number by 3.	Divide second number by 3.	Divide both numbers by 3.
(0, ⁻3)	(0, ⁻3)	(0, ⁻1)	(0, ⁻1)
(9, ⁻3)	(_3_, ⁻3)	(9, _⁻1_)	(_3_, _⁻1_)
(3, 3)	(_1_, 3)	(3, _1_)	(_1_, _1_)

a. How does dividing only the first numbers change the shape of a figure? Shrinks figure horizontally

b. How does dividing only the second numbers change the shape of a figure? Shrinks figure vertically

c. How does dividing both numbers change the shape of a figure?
Shrinks figure horizontally and vertically

8.8 Sliding by Graphing

You can slide or move
a drawing by graphing.

Example 1: Slide the triangle 5 units to the right.

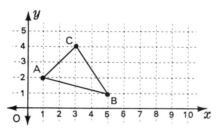

Suggested Class Time			
Course	Min.	Reg.	Max.
Days	0	0	1

Step 1: To slide a drawing 5 units to the right, add 5 to the
first number in each ordered pair.

Point	Original ordered pair		Point	New ordered pair
	A(1, 2)			A'(6, 2)
	B(5, 1)			B'(10, 1)
	C(3, 4)			C'(8, 4)

Step 2: Graph the new ordered pairs. Draw the new triangle.

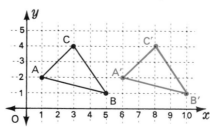

How would you slide a drawing *to the left* by graphing?

Example 2: Slide the figure 4 units down.

To slide a figure 4 units down, subtract 4 from the second number in each ordered pair.

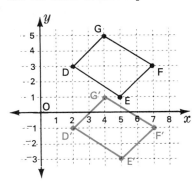

Original figure	New figure
D(2, 3)	D'(2, ⁻1)
E(5, 1)	E'(5, ⁻3)
F(7, 3)	F'(7, ⁻1)
G(4, 5)	G'(4, 1)

How would you slide a figure *up* by graphing?

Assignment Guide 8.8
Oral: Max. 1–6
Written: Max. 7–14

▪ **Exercises**

Ⓐ What would you do with the numbers in each ordered pair to make the following slides?

1. 6 units to the right
    Add 6 to 1st no.

2. 5 units down
    Sub. 5 from 2nd no.

3. 3 units to the left
    Sub. 3 from 1st no.

4. 7 units up
    Add 7 to 2nd no.

5. 2 units to the right and 5 units up
    Add 2 to 1st no. and add 5 to 2nd no.

6. 4 units down and 6 units to the left
    Sub. 6 from 1st no. and sub. 4 from 2nd no.

Ⓑ Copy and make the following slides by graphing.

7. 3 units to the right

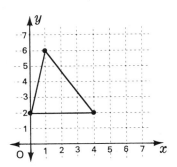

8. 5 units to the left

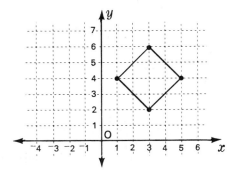

9. 4 units down

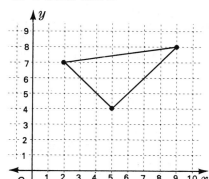

10. 6 units up

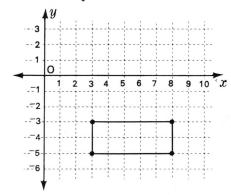

11. 4 units to the right
and 2 units down

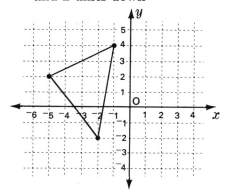

12. 5 units up and
3 units to the left

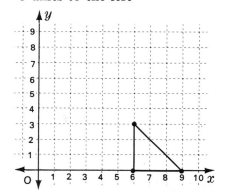

C Copy and graph the following.

13. a 1-to-3 enlargement,
then a slide 4 units
to the right

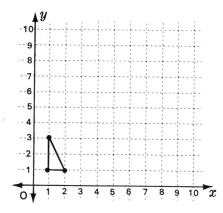

14. a slide 5 units down,
then a 1-to-2 reduction

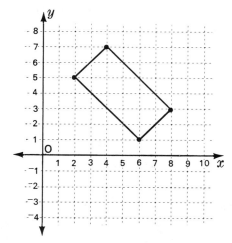

Terms and Symbols Review

Which term best completes each sentence?

a. x-axis   **f.** to the right

b. y-axis   **g.** up

c. origin   **h.** coordinates

d. ordered pair   **i.** $(5, 6), (7, 8), (9, 8)$

e. point   **j.** $(4, {}^-3), ({}^-4, 3), (4, 2)$

Assignment Guide Rev.
Oral: Terms & Symbols 1–7
Written: Min. 1–15
         Reg. 1–15
         Max. 1–19

1. Two numbers listed in a certain order are a(n) __d__.

2. When you draw a pair of axes, the horizontal number line is the __a__.

3. The point at $(0, 0)$ is the __c__.

4. The numbers 3 and 5 are the __h__ of the point at $(3, 5)$.

5. The graph of $(3, 5)$ is a(n) __e__.

6. The positive direction on the y-axis is __g__.

7. An example of a set of ordered pairs that is a function is __i__.

Chapter 8 Review

Use the rule to complete each table.   8.1

1. $y = 2x + 5$

x	0	1	2	3	4	5
y	5	7	9	11	13	15

2. $y = \frac{x}{3} - 1$

x	3	6	9	12	15	18
y	0	1	2	3	4	5

Graph each set of ordered pairs on a different pair of axes.

8.2　**3.** (1, 3), (2, 4), (3, 5), (4, 6), (4, 7)

4.

x	0	1	2	3	4	5
y	3	4	5	2	3	1

8.3

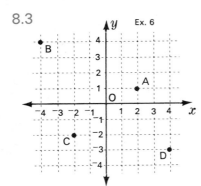

Ex. 6

5. What moves would you make to graph (5, ⁻6)?

5 rt., 6 dn.

6. Name the coordinates of each point on the graph at the right.

  a. A   **b.** B   **c.** C   **d.** D

   (2, 1)   (⁻4, 4)   (⁻2, ⁻2)   (4, ⁻3)

7. Draw a coordinate system on graph paper. Then graph the following points:

  W(0, 0)   X(⁻2, ⁻1)   Y(5, 5)   Z(1, ⁻2)

8.4　Draw a line graph for each table.

8.

x	0	2	4	6	8	10
y	−5	−4	−3	−2	−1	0

9.

yd	0	1	2	3	4	5	6
ft	0	3	6	9	12	15	18

8.5　Is each set of ordered pairs a function ?

10. (0, 2), (1, 2), (2, 4), (3, 4), (4, 5)　Yes

11. (3, 4), (3, 5), (4, 6), (5, 7), (6, 8)　No

Tell whether each graph is the graph of a function.

12. No

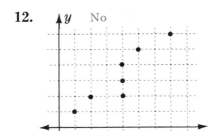

13. Yes

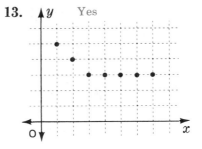

Solve each problem.   8.6

14. A plane's airspeed (*a*) is 135 mph, and the speed of the wind
directly against the plane is 34 mph. What is the plane's ground
speed (*g*)? $g = a - 34$ 101 mph

15. To be on time, a passenger jet must make a ground speed (*g*) of
515 mph. If the speed of the wind directly behind the plane is
45 mph, at what airspeed should the plane fly? $g = a + 45$ 470 mph

Copy and graph the following.   8.7

16. a 1-to-4 enlargement of

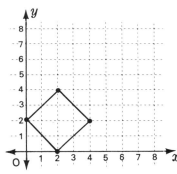

17. a 1-to-3 reduction of

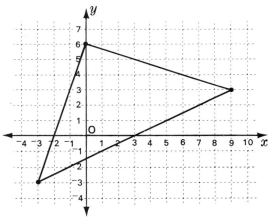

Copy and make the following slides by graphing.   8.8

18. 4 units up

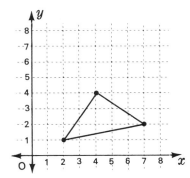

19. 5 units to the right

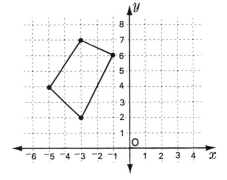

Chapter 8 Test

Assignment Guide Test
Written: Min. 1–12
    Reg. 1–12
    Max. 1–14

Use the rule to complete the ordered pairs. *x* is given first.

1. $y = 4x - 3$

x	2	3	4	5	6	7
y	5	9	13	17	21	25

2. $y = x + 6$

$(0, \underline{6})$, $(1, \underline{7})$, $(3, \underline{9})$, $(4, \underline{10})$

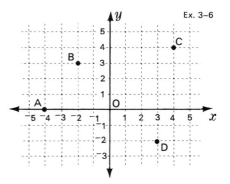

Ex. 3–6

Write the ordered pair for each point on the graph at the right.

3. A $(^-4, 0)$ **4.** B $(^-2, 3)$

5. C $(4, 4)$ **6.** D $(3, ^-2)$

Draw a line graph for each table.

7.

fluid ounces	0	1	2	3	4	5
tablespoons	0	2	4	6	8	10

8.

x	0	1	2	3	4	5
y	3	3	3	0	-1	-2

Answer these questions.

9. Is the graph for Exercises 3–6 the graph of a function? Yes

10. Is the set of ordered pairs $(2, 5)$, $(2, 6)$, $(2, 7)$, and $(2, 8)$ a function?

No

11. Is the set of ordered pairs in Exercise 8 a function? Yes

12. You notice the flash of an explosion. You hear the "boom" 9 seconds (t) later. How far (d) are you from the explosion? $d = 1100t$

9900 ft

Copy and graph the following.

13. a slide 4 units right

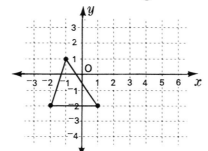

14. a 1-to-2 reduction

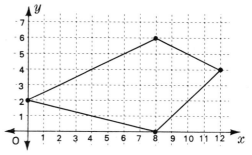

MISLEADING GRAPHS

Line graphs are sometimes used to show trends. But beware! The way information is put on a graph can change the appearance of a trend. At first glance, which graph below makes it look like the number of subscriptions has increased more and faster? Why?

Second graph; different units on the axes make the graph rise higher and more steeply.

SUBSCRIPTIONS, 1970–1980
SKATEBOARD MONTHLY

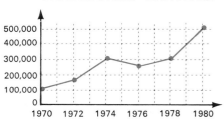

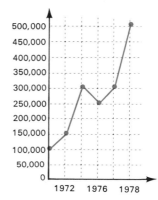

At first glance, which graph below makes it look as if profits had been going up each year? What really happened? *Second graph; profits went down each year.*

PROFIT RECORD FOR ZAPPO, INC.

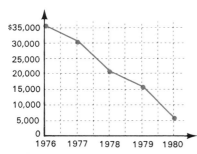

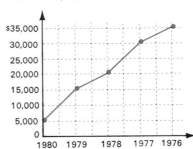

Which graph below makes it look like the price of stock has always been going up? How do the prices for 1970–1972 change the trend? *Second graph; they show the price went down some years.*

PRICE OF ROUND WHEEL CO. STOCK

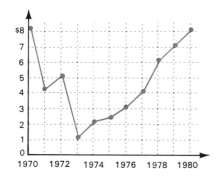

"MAGIC NUMBER 30" FORMULA

One of the first things a wallpaper hanger must do is estimate the amount of wallpaper needed for a room. One way to do this is to use the "Magic Number 30" formula. Most wallpapers come in rolls that contain 36 square feet of paper. That is, a roll of 18-inch-wide paper is 24 feet long (18 in. = $1\frac{1}{2}$ ft and $1\frac{1}{2}$ ft $\times$ 24 ft = 36 ft^2) and a roll of 27-inch-wide paper is 16 feet long (27 in. = $2\frac{1}{4}$ ft and $2\frac{1}{4}$ ft $\times$ 16 ft = 36 ft^2). Waste and allowances for matching patterns are taken care of by assuming that a roll will cover only 30 square feet of wall (instead of 36 ft^2). Also, $\frac{1}{2}$ roll of paper is subtracted for each normal-size door or window.

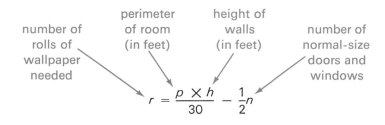

$$\underset{\substack{\text{number of} \\ \text{rolls of} \\ \text{wallpaper} \\ \text{needed}}}{} \quad r = \frac{\overset{\substack{\text{perimeter} \\ \text{of room} \\ \text{(in feet)}}}{p} \times \overset{\substack{\text{height of} \\ \text{walls} \\ \text{(in feet)}}}{h}}{30} - \frac{1}{2}\overset{\substack{\text{number of} \\ \text{normal-size} \\ \text{doors and} \\ \text{windows}}}{n}$$

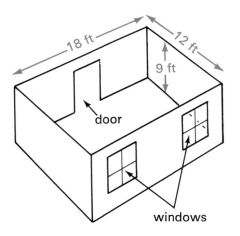

For the room shown at left:

$p = 2(18 \text{ ft} + 12 \text{ ft}) = 60 \text{ ft}$

$h = 9 \text{ ft}$

$n = 3$

$r = \dfrac{60 \times 9}{30} - \dfrac{1}{2}(3)$

$= 18 - 1\dfrac{1}{2}$

$= 16\dfrac{1}{2}$

So, it will take about 17 rolls to paper the room.

Sometimes a wall of a room has several large areas that are not to be covered. Then the amount of paper needed can be found by making a reduced drawing of the wall on graph paper. Vertical lines are drawn to show each strip of wallpaper. For the wall below, the paper being used is 18 inches (or $1\frac{1}{2}$ ft) wide. The number (r) of rolls needed is found by adding the number of feet in each strip, then dividing by 24 (24 ft in each roll).

$$r = \frac{5(9) + 3(2\frac{1}{2}) + 2(2)}{24}$$

$$= \frac{45 + 7\frac{1}{2} + 4}{24}$$

$$= \frac{56\frac{1}{2}}{24}$$

$$= 56\frac{1}{2} \div 24$$

$$= \frac{113}{2} \times \frac{1}{24}$$

$$= 2\frac{17}{48}$$

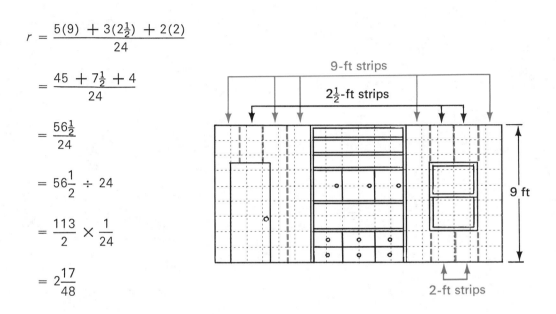

9-ft strips

$2\frac{1}{2}$-ft strips

2-ft strips

9 ft

So, it will take about 3 rolls plus 1 roll for waste and allowance for matching patterns, or 4 rolls, to paper the wall.

TREASURE HUNT

Players: Two (The instructions are the same for each player.)

Materials for each player: Graph paper, pencil

Prepare to play: Draw two graphs with units from ⁻10 to 10 on each axis. (See example below.) One is your *island* and the other is your *map*. Do not let the other player see your *island* after this (place your hand or a book in front of it).

Example of an island:

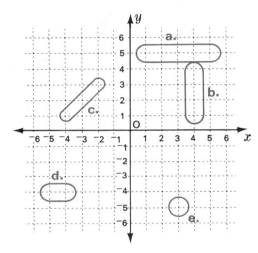

You will bury treasure chests on your *island*, and each contains a certain number of points.

Kind of treasure chest	Number of points
a. diamonds	5
b. emeralds	4
c. rubies	3
d. gold coins	2
e. silver coins	1

Bury one of each kind of treasure chest by circling horizontal, vertical, or diagonal rows of points on your *island*.

To play: Take turns "digging" for buried treasure by saying the coordinates of a point. The object is to find all the treasure chests on the other player's *island*. (A treasure chest is found when all its points have been named.)

When you dig, the other player must say "in" or "out" to tell you whether or not the point is inside or outside a treasure chest. Mark your "ins" (X) and "outs" (O) on your *map* so you can plan your next move.

Mark the other player's "ins" on your *island*. Do *not* tell the other player what *kind* of treasure chest is being dug. But if a point is the last one inside a chest, you must say "in and found."

The first player to find all the other player's buried treasure wins.

Getting Ready for Chapter 9

Assignment Guide GR 9
Written: Min. & Reg. 1–53 odd

Express as a fraction or mixed number in lowest terms.

1. $\frac{3}{6}$ $\quad \frac{1}{2}$ **2.** $\frac{16}{48}$ $\quad \frac{1}{3}$ **3.** $\frac{20}{80}$ $\quad \frac{1}{4}$ **4.** $\frac{25}{100}$ $\quad \frac{1}{4}$ $\quad$ 4.3

5. $\frac{178}{100}$ $\quad 1\frac{39}{50}$ **6.** $\frac{185}{100}$ $\quad 1\frac{17}{20}$ **7.** $\frac{142}{100}$ $\quad 1\frac{21}{50}$ **8.** $\frac{120}{100}$ $\quad 1\frac{1}{5}$ $\quad$ 4.4

Solve.

9. $4x = 60$ $\quad$ 15   **10.** $25n = 250$ $\quad$ 10 $\qquad$ 2.3

11. $4.20 = 12a$ $\quad$ 0.35   **12.** $8y = 76$ $\quad$ 9.5 $\qquad$ 5.5

13. $0.1x = 0.25$ $\quad$ 2.5   **14.** $1.5n = 6$ $\quad$ 4 $\qquad$ 5.6

Multiply 120 by each fraction or decimal.

15. $\frac{1}{4}$ $\quad$ 30   **16.** $\frac{1}{3}$ $\quad$ 40   **17.** $\frac{2}{3}$ $\quad$ 80   **18.** $\frac{3}{4}$ $\quad$ 90 $\quad$ 4.2

19. 0.3 $\quad$ 36   **20.** 0.34 $\quad$ 40.8   **21.** 0.6 $\quad$ 72   **22.** 0.68 $\quad$ 81.6 $\quad$ 5.4

Express as a fraction in lowest terms. $\qquad$ 4.4

23. $1\frac{3}{5}$ $\quad \frac{8}{5}$ **24.** $3\frac{7}{8}$ $\quad \frac{31}{8}$ **25.** $5\frac{1}{4}$ $\quad \frac{21}{4}$ **26.** $11\frac{1}{2}$ $\quad \frac{23}{2}$

Express as a fraction with a denominator of 100. $\qquad$ 5.1

27. 0.5 $\quad \frac{50}{100}$ **28.** 0.25 $\quad \frac{25}{100}$ **29.** 0.68 $\quad \frac{68}{100}$ **30.** 2.33 $\quad \frac{233}{100}$

31. 0.75 $\quad \frac{75}{100}$ **32.** 0.875 $\quad \frac{87.5}{100}$ **33.** 0.05 $\quad \frac{5}{100}$ **34.** 7 $\quad \frac{700}{100}$

Express as a decimal. $\qquad$ 5.5

35. $\frac{3}{5}$ $\quad$ 0.6   **36.** $\frac{1}{4}$ $\quad$ 0.25   **37.** $\frac{1}{2}$ $\quad$ 0.5   **38.** $\frac{1}{3}$ $\quad$ $0.\overline{3}$

39. $\frac{3}{10}$ $\quad$ 0.3   **40.** $\frac{11}{20}$ $\quad$ 0.55   **41.** $\frac{17}{50}$ $\quad$ 0.34   **42.** $\frac{2}{3}$ $\quad$ $0.\overline{6}$

43. $\frac{31}{100}$ $\quad$ 0.31   **44.** $\frac{38}{5}$ $\quad$ 7.6   **45.** $\frac{235}{100}$ $\quad$ 2.35   **46.** $\frac{19.5}{100}$ $\quad$ 0.195

Round to the nearest tenth. $\qquad$ 5.2

47. 0.32 $\quad$ 0.3   **48.** 0.45 $\quad$ 0.5   **49.** 0.76 $\quad$ 0.8   **50.** 0.64 $\quad$ 0.6

Round **(a)** to the nearest ten and **(b)** to the nearest hundred. $\qquad$ 5.2

51. 327 $\quad$ **a.** 330
$\qquad$ **b.** 300   **52.** 787 $\quad$ **a.** 790
$\qquad$ **b.** 800   **53.** 1243 $\quad$ **a.** 1240
$\qquad$ **b.** 1200   **54.** 974 $\quad$ **a.** 970
$\qquad$ **b.** 1000

9

RATIOS, PROPORTIONS, AND PER CENTS

9

Bricklayers use *mortar* to hold bricks together. One kind of mortar is made with 1 part lime and 3 parts sand. Each part can be a bucketful, a bagful, or a truckload. But the *ratio* of lime to sand must be 1 to 3.

In this chapter, you will learn about ratios and about equations, called proportions, that use ratios.

Courtesy Schwinn

Gear ratio 1:1.33

Scale: $\frac{1}{4}$

Suggested Class Time

Course	Min.	Reg.	Max.
Days	1	1	1

The jury foreman told news reporters that the jury voted for conviction by an 11-to-1 ratio on most of the charges.

A **ratio** compares two numbers by division. The ratio of a to b can be written

$$a \text{ to } b \quad \text{or} \quad a : b \quad \text{or} \quad \frac{a}{b}.$$

Example: Give each ratio in three ways.

a. colored tiles to total tiles: 2 to 5 or 2:5 or $\dfrac{2}{5}$

b. total tiles to colored tiles: 5 to 2 or 5:2 or $\dfrac{5}{2}$

c. colored tiles to white tiles: 2 to 3 or 2:3 or $\dfrac{2}{3}$

d. white tiles to total tiles: 3 to 5 or 3:5 or $\dfrac{3}{5}$

In mathematics, we usually write a ratio as a fraction.

■ Exercises

A Give each ratio as a fraction.

1. a. circles to stars $\frac{3}{5}$

   b. stars to circles $\frac{5}{3}$

Assignment Guide 9.1
Oral: 1–7
Written: Min. 8–22
      Reg. 8–22
      Max. 8–25

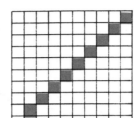

2. a. total squares to shaded squares $\frac{100}{9}$

   b. shaded squares to total squares $\frac{9}{100}$

3. a. wins to losses $\frac{13}{8}$

   b. losses to games played $\frac{8}{21}$

   c. wins to games played $\frac{13}{21}$

GAMES PLAYED
21
WINS   LOSSES
13   8

Choose the correct ratio for each of the following.

4. 15 squares to 11 circles

    $\frac{15}{26}$ $\frac{11}{15}$ $\boxed{\frac{15}{11}}$ $\frac{26}{15}$

5. 2400 boys to 100 girls

    $\frac{100}{2400}$ $\frac{2400}{2500}$ $\frac{100}{2500}$ $\boxed{\frac{2400}{100}}$

6. 27 pounds to 1 cubic foot

    $\frac{1}{27}$ $\boxed{\frac{27}{1}}$ $\frac{1}{28}$ $\frac{28}{1}$

7. 65 miles to 2 hours

    $\frac{2}{65}$ $\frac{67}{2}$ $\frac{2}{67}$ $\boxed{\frac{65}{2}}$

B Give each ratio in three ways.

8. shaded parts to unshaded parts
                          $\frac{5}{7}$; 5 : 7; 5 to 7

9. unshaded parts to total parts
                $\frac{7}{12}$; 7 : 12; 7 to 12

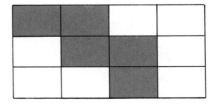

Express each ratio as a fraction.

10. Write the ratio of 27 pounds to 50 pounds. $\frac{27}{50}$

11. A rock that weighs 6 kg on earth would weigh only 1 kg on the moon. Write the ratio of the weight on moon to weight on earth. $\frac{1}{6}$

12. Most cars have 4 tires in use and carry 1 spare tire. Write the usual ratio of cars to tires. $\frac{1}{5}$

13. A pinch hitter was at bat 4 times and got 1 hit. What is the ratio of hits to times at bat? $\frac{1}{4}$

14. The girls' basketball team won 7 games and lost 3. What is the ratio of games won to games played? $\frac{7}{10}$

15. Donna received a 3 to 2 vote over Jackie for class president. Write the ratio of Jackie's votes to total votes. $\frac{2}{5}$

16. A recipe calls for 3 cups of milk and 1 cup of water. What is the ratio of water to milk? $\frac{1}{3}$

Decide what property of the figures each ratio compares.

$\dfrac{\triangle}{\square} \quad \dfrac{3}{4}$
$\dfrac{\pentagon}{\hexagon} \quad \dfrac{5}{6}$
$\dfrac{\hexagon}{\triangle} \quad \dfrac{6}{3}$

Use the same method to compare the figures below.

17. $\dfrac{\square}{\triangle} \quad \dfrac{4}{3}$

18. $\dfrac{\pentagon}{\square} \quad \dfrac{5}{4}$

19. $\dfrac{\square}{\pentagon} \quad \dfrac{4}{5}$

20. $\dfrac{\pentagon}{\triangle} \quad \dfrac{5}{3}$

21. $\dfrac{\hexagon}{\pentagon} \quad \dfrac{6}{5}$

22. $\dfrac{\triangle}{\pentagon} \quad \dfrac{3}{5}$

C Decide what property of the sets of points each ratio compares.

$\dfrac{\bullet\!-\!\bullet}{\triangle} \quad \dfrac{1}{3}$
$\dfrac{\triangle}{\boxtimes} \quad \dfrac{3}{6}$

Use the same method to compare the sets of points below.

23. $\dfrac{6}{3}$

24. $\dfrac{6}{10}$

25. $\dfrac{10}{15}$

277

GEAR RATIOS

Millions of people in the United States work in industrial production. Most of these workers are employed in factories. Semiskilled workers, such as assemblers and certain machine operators, may need only brief on-the-job training. Skilled workers, such as patternmakers and machinists, may have to complete a 3- or 4-year apprenticeship program. Many of these skilled factory workers must know about gear ratios.

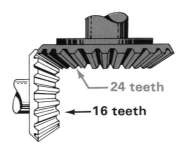

24 teeth

16 teeth

When power is applied to gear **A,** it causes gear **B** to revolve 3 times for every 2 times gear **A** revolves. So the gear ratio is 3 to 2. If power is applied to gear **B,** it causes gear **A** to revolve 2 times for every 3 times gear **B** revolves. So the gear ratio is 2 to 3. These ratios can be found by comparing the number of teeth on the two gears.

teeth on powered gear

$$\frac{24}{16} = \frac{3}{2} \qquad\qquad \frac{16}{24} = \frac{2}{3}$$

teeth on other gear

Find the gear ratio for each pair of gears below. (Power is applied to each gear shown in color.)

$\dfrac{12}{16} = \dfrac{3}{4}$ $\dfrac{12}{8} = \dfrac{3}{2}$ $\dfrac{12}{32} = \dfrac{3}{8}$

a.   **b.**   **c.**

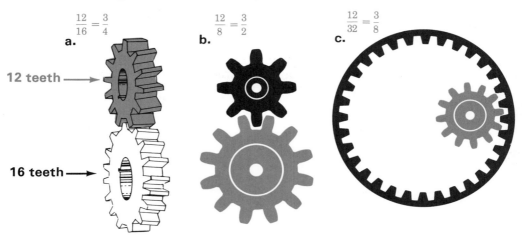

12 teeth →

16 teeth →

9.2

Three ways of comparing four ■ 's to eight △ 's are shown below.

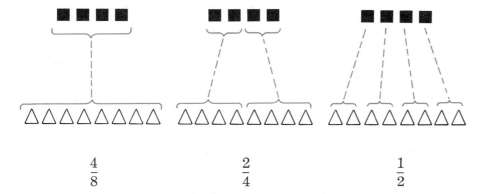

$$\frac{4}{8} \qquad\qquad \frac{2}{4} \qquad\qquad \frac{1}{2}$$

The ratios $\frac{4}{8}$, $\frac{2}{4}$, and $\frac{1}{2}$ are different ways of comparing the same sets. They are called **equivalent ratios**.

For the equivalent ratios $\frac{4}{8}$, $\frac{2}{4}$, and $\frac{1}{2}$, the ratio $\frac{1}{2}$ is in *lowest terms* because the fraction $\frac{1}{2}$ is in lowest terms. (The numerator and the denominator have no common whole-number factor other than 1.)

> A ratio can be changed to an equivalent ratio by multiplying the numerator and the denominator by the same number (but not zero).

Example 1: Find two ratios equivalent to $\frac{3}{5}$.

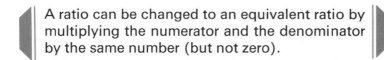

$$\frac{3}{5} = \frac{3 \times 2}{5 \times 2} = \frac{6}{10} \qquad\qquad \frac{3}{5} = \frac{3 \times 3}{5 \times 3} = \frac{9}{15}$$

> A ratio can be changed to an equivalent ratio by dividing the numerator and the denominator by the same number (but not zero).

Example 2: Change each ratio to lowest terms.

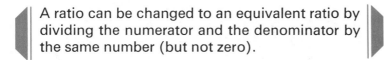

$$\frac{6}{10} = \frac{6 \div 2}{10 \div 2} = \frac{3}{5} \qquad\qquad \frac{24}{32} = \frac{24 \div 8}{32 \div 8} = \frac{3}{4}$$

GCF of 6 and 10 ⟋   GCF of 24 and 32 ⟋

■ Exercises

Assignment Guide 9.2
Oral: 1–8
Written:
Min. 9–41 odd
Reg. 9–25 odd; 27–41
Max. 9–59 odd

[A] Answer the following.

1. What is the ratio of shaded sections to unshaded sections in each circle? Are they equivalent ratios? $\frac{1}{3}, \frac{2}{6}, \frac{4}{12}$; yes

 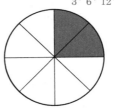 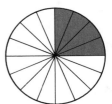

2. What is the ratio of ●'s to △'s in each comparison? Are they equivalent ratios? $\frac{4}{6}, \frac{2}{3}$; yes

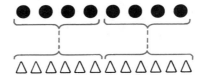 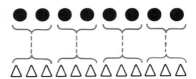

Tell what number should replace each ?.

3. $\frac{3}{5} = \frac{3 \times ?}{5 \times 20}$ 20

4. $\frac{4}{9} = \frac{4 \times 6}{? \times 6}$ 9

5. $\frac{5}{7} = \frac{? \times 2}{7 \times ?}$ 5, 2

6. $\frac{6}{18} = \frac{6 \div 6}{18 \div ?}$ 6

7. $\frac{48}{72} = \frac{48 \div ?}{72 \div 24}$ 24

8. $\frac{150}{250} = \frac{? \div 75}{? \div 75}$ 150, 250

[B] Find two equivalent ratios for each ratio below. 9–26. Answers may vary.

9. $\frac{1}{4}$ 10. $\frac{2}{5}$ 11. $\frac{6}{7}$ 12. $\frac{4}{7}$ 13. $\frac{10}{13}$ 14. $\frac{9}{11}$

15. $\frac{1}{5}$ 16. $\frac{7}{9}$ 17. $\frac{14}{17}$ 18. $\frac{15}{23}$ 19. $\frac{20}{31}$ 20. $\frac{30}{31}$

21. $\frac{5}{8}$ 22. $\frac{3}{4}$ 23. $\frac{5}{9}$ 24. $\frac{19}{21}$ 25. $\frac{7}{12}$ 26. $\frac{5}{7}$

Change each ratio to lowest terms.

27. $\frac{2}{6}$ $\frac{1}{3}$ 28. $\frac{8}{6}$ $\frac{4}{3}$ 29. $\frac{6}{12}$ $\frac{1}{2}$ 30. $\frac{18}{24}$ $\frac{3}{4}$ 31. $\frac{15}{35}$ $\frac{3}{7}$

32. $\frac{14}{28}$ $\frac{1}{2}$ 33. $\frac{18}{81}$ $\frac{2}{9}$ 34. $\frac{20}{50}$ $\frac{2}{5}$ 35. $\frac{20}{45}$ $\frac{4}{9}$ 36. $\frac{30}{100}$ $\frac{3}{10}$

37. $\frac{60}{24}$ $\frac{5}{2}$ 38. $\frac{8}{10}$ $\frac{4}{5}$ 39. $\frac{21}{9}$ $\frac{7}{3}$ 40. $\frac{150}{200}$ $\frac{3}{4}$ 41. $\frac{18}{54}$ $\frac{1}{3}$

C When a ratio compares two similar measurements (such as two distances or two capacities), both measurements should be in the same unit.

Example : Use a ratio to compare 2 feet to 6 inches.
First express both measurements in the same unit.

$$\frac{2 \text{ feet}}{6 \text{ inches}} \longrightarrow \frac{24 \text{ inches}}{6 \text{ inches}} \longrightarrow \frac{24}{6} = \frac{24 \div 6}{6 \div 6} = \frac{4}{1}$$

Write a ratio in lowest terms to compare the measurements.

42. 4 yards to 3 feet $\frac{4}{1}$

43. 3 hours to 5 seconds $\frac{2160}{6}$

44. 6 pints to 1 gallon $\frac{3}{4}$

45. 75 centimeters to 2 meters $\frac{3}{8}$

46. 2 pounds to 1 ton $\frac{1}{1000}$

47. 8 ounces to 3 pounds $\frac{1}{6}$

48. 40 minutes to 2 hours $\frac{1}{3}$

49. 450 grams to 2 kilograms $\frac{9}{40}$

50. 9 grams to 18 milligrams $\frac{500}{1}$

51. 5000 milligrams to 10 kilograms $\frac{1}{2000}$

52. 70 milliliters to 14 liters $\frac{1}{200}$

When a ratio compares the *number of units* in two measurements, the measurements need not be in the same unit. In fact, they need not even be similar measurements.

Example : Use a ratio to express "135 miles in 3 hours."

$$\frac{135 \text{ miles}}{3 \text{ hours}} \longrightarrow \frac{(135 \div 3) \text{ miles}}{(3 \div 3) \text{ hours}} \longrightarrow \frac{45 \text{ miles}}{1 \text{ hour}} \qquad \text{or 45 miles per hour}$$

Artstreet

Write a ratio in lowest terms to compare the number of units in the measurements.

53. 100 miles for every 5 gallons 20 mpg

54. $500 for 100 hours of work $5/h

55. 200 feet in 4 minutes 50 ft/min

56. 8 pounds lost in 4 weeks 2 lb/wk

57. 96¢ for 12 pencils 8c/pencil

58. 60 meters every 5 minutes 12 m/min

59. 80 kilometers for 8 liters 10 km/L

60. 10 °C drop every 5 hours 2 °C/h

CONSUMER CORNER

RATIOS IN ADVERTISING

In a nationwide survey, veterinarians preferred Ken-L Ration over any other canned dog food— and by 6 to 1 over the other leading canned food.

This ad compares two canned dog foods.

1. If 7 veterinarians (animal doctors) took part in the survey, how many preferred Ken-L Ration? How many preferred the other food? 6, 1

2. If 42 veterinarians took part in the survey, how many preferred Ken-L Ration? How many preferred the other food? 36, 6

3. Use the ad to find a comparison that would be described by the ratio $\frac{1}{7}$; by the ratio $\frac{6}{7}$. No. who prefer other food to total no. in survey; no. who prefer Ken-L Ration to total no. in survey

You'd probably never dream of writing a love letter to the company that built your car. Yet at Volvo, we get them all the time. Maybe because 9 out of 10 people who buy new Volvos are happy.

This ad compares certain automobile buyers.

1. If 10 people bought new Volvos, how many of them does this ad claim are happy? 9

2. If 10,000 people bought new Volvos, how many of them should be happy? 9000

3. Use the ad to find a comparison that would be described by the ratio $\frac{1}{10}$; by the ratio $\frac{9}{1}$. No. of unhappy buyers to total no. of buyers; no. of happy buyers to no. of unhappy buyers

In blindfold tests, 3 out of every 4 women chose piecrusts made with digestible all-vegetable Crisco as tasting flakier than those made with the leading part-vegetable shortening.

This ad compares piecrust made with Crisco to piecrust made with another shortening.

1. If 4 women took part in the tests, how many thought the Crisco piecrust tasted flakier? How many did not? 3, 1

2. If 20 women took part in the tests, how many thought the Crisco piecrust tasted flakier? How many did not? 15, 5

3. Use the ad to find a comparison that would be described by the ratio $\frac{3}{1}$; by the ratio $\frac{1}{4}$. No. who chose Crisco to no. who did not; no. who did not choose Crisco to total no. in test

In Section 9.2, you learned to find equivalent ratios. You probably wrote them in equations like these:

$$\frac{1}{4} = \frac{2}{8} \qquad \frac{2}{6} = \frac{1}{3} \qquad \frac{8}{10} = \frac{4}{5}$$

 A **proportion** is an equation that names two equivalent ratios.

 1 and 8 are called the **extremes.**
4 and 2 are called the **means.**

1×8 and 4×2 are called the **cross products.**

Example 1: Find the cross products in each proportion.

a. $\frac{2}{6} = \frac{1}{3}$ **b.** $\frac{8}{10} = \frac{4}{5}$ **c.** $\frac{2}{3} = \frac{6}{9}$

$$
\begin{array}{cc}
2 \times 3 & 6 \times 1 \\
\downarrow & \downarrow \\
6 & 6
\end{array}
\qquad
\begin{array}{cc}
8 \times 5 & 10 \times 4 \\
\downarrow & \downarrow \\
40 & 40
\end{array}
\qquad
\begin{array}{cc}
2 \times 9 & 3 \times 6 \\
\downarrow & \downarrow \\
18 & 18
\end{array}
$$

Notice that the cross products for each proportion are equal.

 In a proportion, the product of the extremes equals the product of the means.

Example 2: Use cross products to solve $\frac{2}{3} = \frac{34}{n}$.

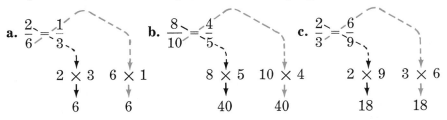

multiply
the extremes

$2n = 3 \times 34$

$2n = 102$

$\dfrac{2n}{2} = \dfrac{102}{2}$

$n = 51$

Check:

$$\frac{2}{3} = \frac{34}{n}$$

$$\frac{2}{3} = \frac{34}{51}$$

$2 \times 51 = 3 \times 34$ cross products

$102 = 102$ ✓

■ Exercises

Assignment Guide 9.3
Oral: 1–9
Written: Min. 11–37 odd
Reg. 11–41 odd
Max. 11–47 odd

A Use cross products to tell whether each sentence is true.

Examples:

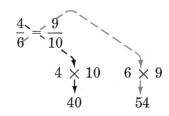

$$\frac{2}{3} = \frac{6}{9}$$

$2 \times 9 \quad\quad 3 \times 6$

$18 \quad\quad\quad 18$

True

$$\frac{4}{6} = \frac{9}{10}$$

$4 \times 10 \quad\quad 6 \times 9$

$40 \quad\quad\quad 54$

False

1. $\frac{21}{7} = \frac{3}{1}$ T

2. $\frac{5}{2} = \frac{10}{4}$ T

3. $\frac{6}{8} = \frac{2}{3}$ F

4. $\frac{7}{5} = \frac{9}{3}$ F

5. $\frac{6}{9} = \frac{4}{6}$ T

6. $\frac{4}{7} = \frac{8}{10}$ F

7. $\frac{10}{3} = \frac{50}{9}$ F

8. $\frac{10}{18} = \frac{5}{9}$ T

9. $\frac{5}{6} = \frac{10}{12}$ T

B Solve each proportion.

10. $\frac{3}{4} = \frac{n}{20}$ 15

11. $\frac{2}{3} = \frac{6}{n}$ 9

12. $\frac{6}{n} = \frac{3}{8}$ 16

13. $\frac{1}{2} = \frac{n}{24}$ 12

14. $\frac{45}{90} = \frac{n}{100}$ 50

15. $\frac{3}{4} = \frac{n}{40}$ 30

16. $\frac{8}{6} = \frac{32}{n}$ 24

17. $\frac{n}{8} = \frac{25}{40}$ 5

18. $\frac{24}{36} = \frac{n}{12}$ 8

19. $\frac{4}{5} = \frac{n}{15}$ 12

20. $\frac{3}{8} = \frac{n}{16}$ 6

21. $\frac{n}{5} = \frac{10}{25}$ 2

22. $\frac{4}{n} = \frac{3}{3}$ 4

23. $\frac{2}{3} = \frac{4}{n}$ 6

24. $\frac{n}{7} = \frac{9}{63}$ 1

25. $\frac{n}{4} = \frac{18}{8}$ 9

26. $\frac{6}{n} = \frac{60}{70}$ 7

27. $\frac{5}{12} = \frac{75}{n}$ 180

28. $\frac{0.2}{n} = \frac{1}{3}$ 0.6

29. $\frac{n}{1.4} = \frac{3}{1}$ 4.2

30. $\frac{2}{5} = \frac{n}{1.5}$ 0.6

31. $\frac{2.4}{32} = \frac{n}{10}$ 0.75

32. $\frac{n}{7} = \frac{9}{6.3}$ 10

33. $\frac{5}{n} = \frac{0.5}{1}$ 10

The four proportions below all have equal cross products. They are
equivalent proportions.

given
proportion

switch
means

switch
extremes

invert both
ratios

$$\frac{2}{5} = \frac{4}{10}$$

$$\frac{2}{4} = \frac{5}{10}$$

$$\frac{10}{5} = \frac{4}{2}$$

$$\frac{5}{2} = \frac{10}{4}$$

Write three proportions equivalent to the given proportion. Then find the cross products. *34–42. Only cross products are given.*

34. $\frac{3}{7} = \frac{9}{21}$ $63 = 63$

35. $\frac{12}{18} = \frac{2}{3}$ $36 = 36$

36. $\frac{4}{5} = \frac{16}{20}$ $80 = 80$

37. $\frac{1.2}{1.6} = \frac{3}{4}$ $4.8 = 4.8$

38. $\frac{5}{1} = \frac{3.5}{0.7}$ $3.5 = 3.5$

39. $\frac{2.6}{5.2} = \frac{7.8}{15.6}$ $40.56 = 40.56$

C **40.** $\frac{n}{3} = \frac{15}{9}$ $9n = 45$

41. $\frac{12}{n} = \frac{15}{2}$ $24 = 15n$

42. $\frac{3}{11} = \frac{13}{n}$ $3n = 143$

Solve.

43. $\frac{0.25}{0.75} = \frac{1}{n}$ 3

44. $\frac{4.45}{0.25} = \frac{n}{2.6}$ 46.28

45. $\frac{70}{0.35} = \frac{6.25}{n}$ 0.03125

46. $\frac{n}{6.22} = \frac{9.93}{18.66}$ 3.31

47. $\frac{0.95}{1.5} = \frac{n}{0.3}$ 0.19

48. $\frac{0.26}{7.8} = \frac{1.2}{n}$ 36

Postal Ratios

The United States Postal Service can refuse or charge extra for mail that is not a standard size. A standard-size envelope must fit the description below.

length

height

a. height: from $3\frac{1}{2}$ to $6\frac{1}{8}$ inches

b. length: from 5 to $11\frac{1}{2}$ inches

c. the ratio $\frac{\text{height}}{\text{length}}$: from $\frac{2}{5}$ to $\frac{10}{13}$

To be standard, how long may an envelope be if it is 4 inches high?

Hint: To find the longest and shortest possible lengths, solve $\frac{4}{x} = \frac{2}{5}$ and $\frac{4}{x} = \frac{10}{13}$.

Longest: 10 in.; shortest: $5\frac{1}{5}$ in.

285

Courtesy U.S. Postal Service

9.4 Using Proportions to Solve Problems

Example : There are 150 calories in 12 ounces of limeade. How many calories are there in 8 ounces?

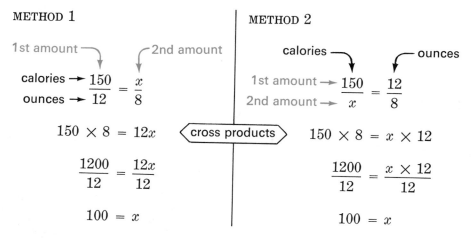

METHOD 1

1st amount ⟶   ⟵ 2nd amount

$$\text{calories} \rightarrow \frac{150}{12} = \frac{x}{8} \leftarrow \text{ounces}$$

$$150 \times 8 = 12x \quad \langle \text{cross products} \rangle$$

$$\frac{1200}{12} = \frac{12x}{12}$$

$$100 = x$$

METHOD 2

calories ⟶   ⟵ ounces

$$\text{1st amount} \rightarrow \frac{150}{x} = \frac{12}{8} \leftarrow \text{2nd amount}$$

$$150 \times 8 = x \times 12$$

$$\frac{1200}{12} = \frac{x \times 12}{12}$$

$$100 = x$$

Check: Is 100 calories in 8 ounces equivalent to 150 calories in 12 ounces? (Use cross products or reduce ratios to lowest terms.) ✓

So there are 100 calories in 8 ounces of limeade.

■ Exercises

A Find the cross products.

1. $\frac{1}{5} = \frac{3}{x}$ $x = 15$

2. $\frac{x}{7} = \frac{2}{3.5}$ $3.5x = 14$

3. $\frac{6}{x} = \frac{0.3}{2}$ $12 = 0.3x$

4. $\frac{x}{0.5} = \frac{1}{10}$ $10x = 0.5$

5. $\frac{1.8}{36} = \frac{1}{x}$ $1.8x = 36$

6. $\frac{2}{9} = \frac{x}{0.3}$ $0.6 = 9x$

B Use a proportion to solve each problem.

Assignment Guide 9.4
Oral: 1–6
Written:
Min. (day 1) 7–14
    (day 2) 15–17; Quiz,
    p. 289
Reg. 7–19 odd; Quiz,
    p. 289
Max. 7–27 odd; Quiz,
    p. 289

7. Out of 3514 voters in Hay County, 502 are chosen for jury duty. At this rate, how many more voters are needed to get 86 more jurors? 602 more voters

8. If a 3-pound roast requires 60 minutes to cook, how long should a 4-pound roast be cooked? 80 min

286

For some 1-inch diameter fluorescent lights, the ratio of watts to length in inches is $\frac{5}{6}$. Use this ratio and a proportion to solve.

9. How long is a 15-watt fluorescent light? 18 in.

10. Find the number of watts for a 36-inch fluorescent light. 30 watts

11. Find the number of watts for a 24-inch fluorescent light. 20 watts

12. How long is a 40-watt fluorescent light? 48 in.

Use a proportion to solve each problem.

13. At 60 mph a car travels 88 feet per second. How many feet per second does a car travel at 15 mph? 22 ft/sec

14. A car used 6 gallons of gasoline in 120 miles. At this rate, how much gasoline will the car use in 360 miles? 18 gal.

15. Mrs. Rackow won an election by a 5 to 2 margin. Her opponent got 2800 votes. How many votes did Mrs. Rackow get? 7000 votes

16. There are 180 calories in 3 ounces of veal. How many calories are there in 4 ounces? 240 cal

17. If a lawn mower uses a fuel mixture of 4 ounces of oil for each 0.5 gallon of gasoline, how much oil should be mixed with 5 gallons of gasoline? 40 oz

18. If 32 bags of cement are needed to make 5 cubic yards of concrete, how many cubic yards of concrete will 12 bags of cement make?
$1\frac{7}{8}$ cu yd

19. It costs the Mahans 36 cents a month to operate their electric frying pan, which uses 8 units of electricity a month. If their slow cooker uses 12 units a month, how much does it cost to operate? $0.54

20. The Georges have two solid-state TV sets. Their black-and-white set uses 6 units of electricity a month and costs 27 cents to operate. If their color set uses 28 units a month, how much does it cost to operate? $1.26

Courtesy Commonwealth Edison Co.

John Running/After Image

[C] **21.** A water tank in the shape of a cylinder is 18 feet deep and holds 1200 gallons of water. How many gallons are in the tank when it is filled to the 15-foot level? 1000 gal.

22. According to the United States Department of Agriculture, the best light for growing plants indoors uses 3 watts of fluorescent light for each watt of regular (incandescent) light. If a regular 75-watt bulb is used, how many 75-watt fluorescent lights should be used? If a regular 100-watt bulb is used, how many 75-watt fluorescent lights should be used? 3; 4

23. The ratio of weight to volume of a substance is called *density*. If the density of silver is 10.5 g/cm³, what is the weight of 15 cm³ of silver? What is the volume of 21 g of silver? 157.5 g; 2 cm³

Use a proportion to solve as in the example.

Example : In making plate glass, 18 kilograms of sand are used for every 7 kilograms of other ingredients. How many kilograms of sand are needed to make 125 kilograms of glass? (A diagram can help you set up the proportion.)

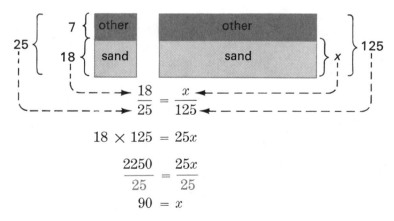

$$18 \times 125 = 25x$$

$$\frac{2250}{25} = \frac{25x}{25}$$

$$90 = x$$

Check: Is 90 kg out of 125 equivalent to 18 kg out of 25? ✓

So 90 kilograms of sand are needed.

24. To make violet food coloring, you mix 3 drops of red for every 5 drops of blue. How much of each color should you mix to make 16 drops of violet food coloring? 6 drops red; 10 drops blue

25. Brass is an alloy made by adding 1 kilogram of zinc for every 4 kilograms of copper. How much copper is needed to make 500 kilograms of brass? 400 kg

26. The alloy for 18-karat gold is made by adding 6 grams of gold for every 2 grams of other ingredients (silver and copper). How much gold is in an 18-karat bracelet that weighs 24 grams? 18 g

27. Bronze is an alloy made by adding 1 kilogram of tin for every 19 kilograms of copper. How much tin is needed to make 300 kilograms of bronze? 15 kg

28. To make the alloy for solid-silver tableware, you add 1 pound of copper for every 9 pounds of silver. How much silver is in a 50-piece service that weighs 8 pounds? $7\frac{1}{5}$ lb

Quick Quiz
Sections 9.1 to 9.4

1. Write the ratio 6 to 5 in two other forms. $6:5; \frac{6}{5}$

Write three equivalent ratios for each given ratio.

2–4. Answers may vary.

2. $\frac{4}{7}$

3. $\frac{6}{12}$

4. $\frac{30}{100}$

Solve.

5. $\frac{3}{4} = \frac{n}{16}$ 12

6. $\frac{2}{3} = \frac{8}{n}$ 12

7. $\frac{n}{8} = \frac{25}{40}$ 5

8. A syrup for use in freezing fruits can be made by mixing 6 cups of sugar with water to make 11 cups of syrup. If 72 cups of sugar are available, how many cups of syrup can be made? 132 c

9.5 Meaning of Per Cent

 A ratio that compares a number to 100 is a **per cent.** The symbol for per cent is %.

Example 1: Express each ratio as a per cent.

3 to 100	3:100	$\frac{3}{100}$
3 per 100	3 out of 100	

These are all equal to 3%.

Suggested Class Time			
Course	Min.	Reg.	Max.
Days	1	1	1

Any per cent can be changed to a fraction with a denominator of 100. But the fraction should then be reduced or simplified if possible. Or the fraction may be changed to a decimal.

Example 2: Change each per cent to a fraction or mixed number.

a. $35\% = \dfrac{35}{100}$

$= \dfrac{7}{20}$

b. $166\% = \dfrac{166}{100}$

$= \dfrac{83}{50}$

$= 1\dfrac{33}{50}$

c. $37\frac{1}{2}\% = \dfrac{37\frac{1}{2}}{100}$

$= \dfrac{37\frac{1}{2} \times 2}{100 \times 2}$

$= \dfrac{75}{200}$

$= \dfrac{3}{8}$

Example 3: Change each per cent to a decimal.

a. $35\% = \dfrac{35}{100}$

$= 0.35$

b. $166\% = \dfrac{166}{100}$

$= 1.66$

c. $37\frac{1}{2}\% = 37.5\%$

$= \dfrac{37.5}{100}$

$= 0.375$

Shortcut: $35\% = 0.35$ $166\% = 1.66$ $37.5\% = 0.375$

> To write a per cent as a decimal:

Move the decimal point two places to the left and drop the symbol %.

Exercises

Assignment Guide 9.5
Oral: 1–18
Written:
Min. 19–49 odd
Reg. 19–51 odd; 52–54
Max. 19–51 odd; 52–62

A Give each of the following as a per cent.

1. 50 out of 100 $\quad$ 50 %

2. 70 per 100 $\quad$ 70 %

3. $\frac{9}{100}$ $\quad$ 9 %

4. 45 to 100 $\quad$ 45 %

5. 59 out of 100 $\quad$ 59 %

6. 85 per 100 $\quad$ 85 %

7. $\frac{64}{100}$ $\quad$ 64 %

8. n out of 100 $\quad$ n %

9. $\frac{135}{100}$ $\quad$ 135 %

Change each per cent to a decimal.

10. 4% $\quad$ 0.04

11. 3.75% $\quad$ 0.0375

12. 5.5% $\quad$ 0.055

13. A per cent (*greater than, less than*) 100% can be changed to a number less than 1.

14. A per cent (*greater than, less than*) 100% can be changed to a number greater than 1.

What number should replace each *n*?

15. $68\% = \frac{n}{100}$ $\quad$ 68

16. $28\% = \frac{n}{100}$ $\quad$ 28

17. $135\% = \frac{n}{100}$ $\quad$ 135

18. $232\% = \frac{n}{100}$ $\quad$ 232

B Copy and complete each table.

	per cent	fraction	decimal		per cent	fraction	decimal
19.	21%	$\frac{21}{100}$	0.21	**20.**	7%	$\frac{7}{100}$	0.07
21.	61%	$\frac{61}{100}$	0.61	**22.**	49%	$\frac{49}{100}$	0.49
23.	70%	$\frac{7}{10}$	0.7	**24.**	30%	$\frac{3}{10}$	0.3
25.	50%	$\frac{1}{2}$	0.5	**26.**	20%	$\frac{1}{5}$	0.2
27.	35%	$\frac{7}{20}$	0.35	**28.**	75%	$\frac{3}{4}$	0.75
29.	$12\frac{1}{2}\%$	$\frac{1}{8}$	0.125	**30.**	$62\frac{1}{2}\%$	$\frac{5}{8}$	0.625
31.	6.3%	$\frac{63}{1000}$	0.063	**32.**	7.9%	$\frac{79}{1000}$	0.079

Copy and complete each table.

	per cent	fraction or mixed number	decimal		per cent	fraction or mixed number	decimal
33.	33.3%	$\frac{333}{1000}$	0.333	**34.**	71.7%	$\frac{717}{1000}$	0.717
35.	$8\frac{3}{4}\%$	$\frac{7}{80}$	0.0875	**36.**	$9\frac{1}{4}\%$	$\frac{37}{400}$	0.0925
37.	101%	$1\frac{1}{100}$	1.01	**38.**	143%	$1\frac{43}{100}$	1.43
39.	127%	$1\frac{27}{100}$	1.27	**40.**	125%	$1\frac{1}{4}$	1.25
41.	250%	$2\frac{1}{2}$	2.5	**42.**	342%	$3\frac{21}{50}$	3.42

Change each per cent to a fraction or a whole number.

43. 10% $\frac{1}{10}$ **44.** 40% $\frac{2}{5}$ **45.** 60% $\frac{3}{5}$ **46.** 100% 1

47. 400% 4 **48.** 600% 6 **49.** 1000% 10 **50.** 5000% 50

51. 6000% 60 **52.** $x\%$ $\frac{x}{100}$ **53.** $(a+3)\%$ $\frac{a+3}{100}$ **54.** $4n\%$ $\frac{7n}{100}$

[C] Change each per cent to a decimal.

55. 0.3% 0.003 **56.** 0.01% 0.0001 **57.** $\frac{1}{4}\%$ 0.0025 **58.** $\frac{3}{5}\%$ 0.006

Change each per cent to a fraction.

59. 0.02% $\frac{1}{5000}$ **60.** $\frac{1}{3}\%$ $\frac{1}{300}$ **61.** $\frac{1}{12}\%$ $\frac{1}{1200}$ **62.** 0.5% $\frac{1}{200}$

% % % % % % % % % % % % % % % % % % % %

The use of the per cent symbol developed slowly over many centuries. By the fifteenth century (the century in which Columbus came to America), the words *per cento*, from the Latin *per centum*, were used to mean "for a hundred." Then the words were abbreviated, and gradually the abbreviation changed in form.

15th century   modern

per cento > per c̊ or p c̊ > per ⸰/⸰ > ⸰/⸰ > %

RATIOS AT WORK

If water is to flow through a pipe, one end must be lower than the other. If a ramp is to raise a car from one level to another, one end must be higher than the other. In many construction trades, rate of rise or fall (called *grade*) is written as a ratio. Sometimes this ratio is expressed as a per cent.

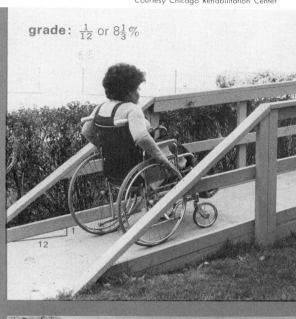

grade: $\frac{1}{12}$ or $8\frac{1}{3}$%

grade: $\frac{1}{200}$

Changing Numbers to Per Cents

Suggested Class Time

Course	Min.	Reg.	Max.
Days	1	1	1

A baseball player's batting average is written as a decimal. Lou Gehrig had a lifetime batting average of 0.340, while Babe Ruth's was 0.342.

Example 1: What per cent of his times at bat did each player hit safely?

a. Lou Gehrig **b.** Babe Ruth

$$0.340 = 0.34$$

$$= \frac{34}{100}$$

$$= 34\%$$

$$0.340 = 34\%$$

$$0.342 = \frac{34.2}{100}$$

$$= 34.2\%$$

$$0.342 = 34.2\%$$

To write a decimal as a per cent:	Move the decimal point two places to the right and write the symbol %.

Example 2: Change each fraction to a per cent.

a. $\frac{3}{4}$ **b.** $\frac{3}{8}$ **c.** $\frac{2}{3}$

Change the fraction to a decimal.

$$4)\overline{3.00} \quad 0.75$$

$$8)\overline{3.000} \quad 0.375$$

$$3)\overline{2.00} \quad 0.66\frac{2}{3}$$

Change the decimal to a per cent.

$$75\% \qquad 37.5\% \qquad 66\frac{2}{3}\%$$

This form is usually used rather than $66.\overline{6}\%$.

Example 3: Change $2\frac{3}{5}$ to a per cent.

Write $2\frac{3}{5}$ as a fraction.

$$2\frac{3}{5} = \frac{13}{5}$$

Change the fraction to a per cent as in Example 2.

$$5)\overline{13.00} \quad 2.60 \longrightarrow 260\%$$

■ Exercises

[A] Change each of the following to a per cent.

1. 0.28 28 % **2.** 7.21 721 % **3.** 4.6 460 % **4.** 0.5 50 %

5. 1 100 % **6.** 4 400 % **7.** $\frac{31}{100}$ 31 % **8.** $\frac{300}{100}$ 300 %

[B] **9.** 0.53 53 % **10.** 0.06 6 % **11.** 0.7 70 % **12.** 0.002 0.2 %

13. 1.12 112 % **14.** 2.5 250 % **15.** 4 400 % **16.** 23 2300 %

17. 0.125 12.5 % **18.** 0.075 7.5 % **19.** 1.375 137.5 % **20.** $2.33\frac{1}{3}$ $233\frac{1}{3}$ %

21. $\frac{3}{10}$ 30 % **22.** $\frac{1}{20}$ 5 % **23.** $\frac{1}{2}$ 50 % **24.** $\frac{3}{4}$ 75 %

25. $\frac{1}{5}$ 20 % **26.** $\frac{1}{6}$ $16\frac{2}{3}$ % **27.** $\frac{3}{8}$ 37.5 % **28.** $\frac{2}{5}$ 40 %

29. $\frac{1}{4}$ 25 % **30.** $\frac{1}{3}$ $33\frac{1}{3}$ % **31.** $\frac{3}{5}$ 60 % **32.** $\frac{5}{6}$ $83\frac{1}{3}$ %

33. $\frac{1}{8}$ 12.5 % **34.** $\frac{4}{5}$ 80 % **35.** $\frac{5}{8}$ 62.5 % **36.** $\frac{7}{10}$ 70 %

37. $\frac{7}{8}$ 87.5 % **38.** $\frac{9}{20}$ 45 % **39.** $\frac{4}{25}$ 16 % **40.** $\frac{7}{50}$ 14 %

41. $\frac{9}{10}$ 90 % **42.** $\frac{2}{25}$ 8 % **43.** $\frac{7}{20}$ 35 % **44.** $\frac{9}{25}$ 36 %

45. $1\frac{1}{3}$ $133\frac{1}{3}$ % **46.** $1\frac{3}{4}$ 175 % **47.** $1\frac{1}{2}$ 150 % **48.** $1\frac{1}{4}$ 125 %

49. $2\frac{5}{8}$ 262.5 % **50.** $1\frac{7}{8}$ 187.5 % **51.** $3\frac{5}{6}$ $383\frac{1}{3}$ % **52.** $3\frac{1}{2}$ 350 %

53. A 20% alcohol solution means there are 20 parts alcohol for 100 parts solution. How would you describe a solution which is 15 parts alcohol for 100 parts solution? 15 % solution

54. The interest for a new-car loan is stated as $8 per $100. What is the per cent of interest? 8 %

[C] Change each ratio to a per cent.

55. 3 to 2 150 % **56.** 6:5 120 % **57.** 4 to 3 $133\frac{1}{3}$ %

58. $\frac{3}{4}$ to $\frac{1}{2}$ 150 % **59.** $\frac{7}{8}$:$\frac{5}{8}$ 140 % **60.** $1\frac{1}{2}$ to $1\frac{1}{4}$ 120 %

61. 7.5 to 5.0 150 % **62.** 3.2:2.4 $133\frac{1}{3}$ % **63.** 3.25 to 2.5 130 %

The Three Kinds of Per Cent Problems

When a proportion involves per cent, one denominator is 100. In a problem, you might have to find any one of the other three numbers.

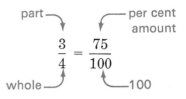

What per cent?

Example 1: 12 is what per cent of 30?

part — per cent amount — 100 — whole

$$\frac{12}{30} = \frac{p}{100}$$

$$p = 40$$

So 12 is 40% of 30.

Check:

$$\frac{12}{30} = \frac{p}{100}$$

$$\frac{12}{30} = \frac{40}{100}$$

$$12 \times 100 = 30 \times 40$$

$$1200 = 1200 \checkmark$$

Suggested Class Time			
Course	Min.	Reg.	Max.
Days	2	1	1

What part?

Example 2: What is 71% of 142?

part — per cent amount — 100 — whole

$$\frac{x}{142} = \frac{71}{100}$$

$$x = 100.82$$

So 71% of 142 is 100.82.

Check:

$$\frac{x}{142} = \frac{71}{100}$$

$$\frac{100.82}{142} = \frac{71}{100}$$

$$100.82 \times 100 = 142 \times 71$$

$$10082 = 10082 \checkmark$$

What whole?

Example 3: 7 is 25% of what?

part — per cent amount — 100 — whole

$$\frac{7}{n} = \frac{25}{100}$$

$$n = 28$$

So 7 is 25% of 28.

Check:

$$\frac{7}{n} = \frac{25}{100}$$

$$\frac{7}{28} = \frac{25}{100}$$

$$7 \times 100 = 28 \times 25$$

$$700 = 700 \checkmark$$

Exercises

Assignment Guide 9.7
Oral: 1–6
Written:
Min. (day 1) 7–27 odd
    (day 2) 8–28 even
Reg. 7–23 odd; 25–30
Max. 7–23 odd; 25–36

A Match each question with the correct proportion.

a. $\frac{75}{x} = \frac{60}{100}$ **b.** $\frac{x}{90} = \frac{45}{100}$ **c.** $\frac{x}{75} = \frac{60}{100}$

d. $\frac{45}{90} = \frac{x}{100}$ **e.** $\frac{60}{75} = \frac{x}{100}$ **f.** $\frac{90}{x} = \frac{45}{100}$

1. What is 60% of 75?   c   **2.** 60 is what per cent of 75?   e

3. 75 is 60% of what?   a   **4.** What is 45% of 90?   b

5. 45 is what per cent of 90?   d   **6.** 90 is 45% of what?   f

B Use proportions to solve.

7. 45 is what per cent of 75? 60% **8.** 80 is what per cent of 120? $66\frac{2}{3}\%$

9. 90 is what per cent of 150? 60% **10.** 66 is what per cent of 90? $73\frac{1}{3}\%$

11. What per cent of 80 is 24? 30% **12.** 8.5 out of 68 is what per cent?
12.5%

See Example 1.

13. What is 16% of 85? 13.6 **14.** What is 40% of 25? 10

15. What is 60% of 80? 48 **16.** What is $33\frac{1}{3}\%$ of 6? 2

17. 25% of 28 is what? 7 **18.** How much is 40% of 60? 24

See Example 2.

19. 60 is 75% of what? 80 **20.** 90 is 40% of what? 225

21. 18 is 45% of what? 40 **22.** 88 is 80% of what? 110

23. 30% of what is 48? 160 **24.** 50% is 19 out of what? 38

See Example 3.

C **25.** What is 100% of 28? 28 **26.** What is 125% of 28? 35

27. 92.4 is 28% of what? 330 **28.** 22 is what per cent of 50? 44%

29. 43% of 628 is what? 270.04 **30.** 48% of what is 300? 625

31. How much is 46% of 120?
55.2 **32.** 6 out of 25 is what per cent? 24%

33. 75% of what is 0.69? 0.92 **34.** 92% of 4000 is what? 3680

35. 62% of what is 38.44? 62 **36.** What per cent of 100 is 23? 23%

Solving Per Cent Problems

Per cent problems can be solved using almost the same method you use for other problems.

- Read the problem as many times as necessary to determine the given facts.

- Decide which of these questions is asked:
  What per cent?   What part?   What whole?

- Represent the unknown fact with a variable.

- Translate the problem into a proportion and solve.

- Check the solution against the conditions of the problem.

- Answer the problem.

Example 1: Wes made 9 out of 15 field-goal attempts. What per cent of his field-goal attempts did he make?

Question: 9 out of 15 is <u>what per cent</u>?

Let n = the per cent amount.

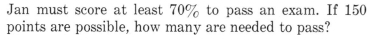

Proportion: $\dfrac{9}{15} = \dfrac{n}{100}$ *Solution:* $n = 60$

Check: Is 60% of 15 equal to 9? ✓

So Wes made 60% of his field-goal attempts.

Example 2: Jan must score at least 70% to pass an exam. If 150 points are possible, how many are needed to pass?

Question: <u>What part</u> out of 150 is 70%?

Let n = the part.

Proportion: $\dfrac{n}{150} = \dfrac{70}{100}$ *Solution:* $n = 105$

Check: Is 105 points out of 150 equivalent to 70 out of 100? ✓

So Jan must score at least 105 points to pass.

Russ Reed—Photo Trends

Example 3: At a sale, each item was reduced 20%. What was the regular price of a radio that was reduced $8?

Question: 8 out of <u>what whole</u> is 20%?

Let n = the whole.

Proportion: $\dfrac{8}{n} = \dfrac{20}{100}$ *Solution:* $n = 40$

Check: Is 20% of $40 equal to $8? ✓

So the regular price of the radio was $40.

▪ Exercises

A Decide what is asked in each problem. Express it as a question as in the examples.

1. At Lyle's restaurant, Iris received $28 in tips on customer bills of $200. What per cent did her customers tip? 28 out of 200 is what per cent?

2. A certain cereal is 12% protein. How many ounces of protein are in a 14-ounce package? What part out of 14 is 12%?

3. Salespeople at Thorn's make 3% commission. How much must a person sell to make $150 in commissions? 150 out of what whole is 3%?

Webb Photos

B Use a proportion to solve. (See Example 1 on page 298.)

4. Exercise 1 above. 14%

5. Rona answered 32 out of 40 test questions correctly. What per cent did she answer correctly? 80%

6. Ruth paid $640 in income tax on a gross income of $8000. What per cent of her gross income was the tax? 8%

7. The Crusade of Mercy has collected $21,000. Their goal is $28,000. What per cent of their goal have they reached? 75%

8. The body of a 140-pound person has 56 to 91 pounds of water in the tissues. At least what per cent of the person's weight is due to the water? At most what per cent? 40%; 65%

Assignment Guide 9.8
Oral: 1–3
Written:
Min. (day 1) 5–23 odd
       (day 2) 4–22 even
Reg. 5–29 odd
Max. 5–37 odd

9. In a contest, Wally scored 37 points out of a possible 40. Express his score as a per cent. 92.5%

10. There were 80 flights into the air terminal yesterday. Of these, 68 were jets. What per cent of the flights were jets? 85%

11. Elaine needs 720 points to win a prize. She has 630 points now. What per cent of the number of points needed does she have now?
87.5%

Use a proportion to solve. (See Example 2 on page 298.)

12. Exercise 2 on page 299. 1.68 oz

13. Joan can save $33\frac{1}{3}\%$ by buying some clothing at a sale. How much can she save on clothes that regularly sell for $120? $40

14. James borrowed $680 at 8.5% interest for one year. How much interest will he pay if he pays off the loan on time? $57.80

15. About 7.5% of men are color-blind. Out of every 2000 men, about how many are color-blind? 150 men

Collier Photographics

16. About 0.1% of women are color-blind. Out of every 2000 women, about how many are color-blind? 2 women

17. At Davis Realty Company, a broker gets a 3% commission on each sale. What is the commission for selling a $70,000 house?
$2100

18. The monthly carrying charge on many charge accounts is 1.5% of the unpaid balance. What is the carrying charge on a balance of $160? $2.40

19. For adults, the recommended daily allowance (RDA) of calcium is 1 gram. One cup of whole milk contains 28.8% of the RDA. How much calcium is in a cup of milk? 0.288 g

20. For teenagers, the RDA (see Exercise 19) of iron is 18 milligrams. One whole egg contains about 6.5% of the RDA. How much iron is in an egg? 1.17 mg

Use a proportion to solve. (See Example 3 on page 299.)

21. Exercise 3 on page 299. $5000

22. The profit on each item Helen sells is 5%. How much must she sell to make a profit of $50? $1000

23. The Badgers won $66\frac{2}{3}\%$ of their games. If they won 12 games, how many did they play? 18 games

24. At the age of 7, a girl is about 74% of her adult height. If a 7-year-old girl is 48 inches tall, how tall can she expect to be? Give your answer to the nearest inch. 65 in.

25. At the age of 10, a boy is about 78% of his adult height. If a 10-year-old boy is 56 inches tall, how tall can he expect to be? Give your answer to the nearest inch. 72 in.

26. One cup of pineapple juice supplies about 22.2 milligrams, or 37% of the RDA, of vitamin C. (See Exercise 19.) What is the RDA of vitamin C? 60 mg

C Solve each problem.

27. What is 220% of 30? 66

28. What is 0.1% of 20? 0.02

29. 150% of what is 72? 48

30. 40 is what per cent of 20? 200%

31. What is 0.01% of 153? 0.0153

32. 75 is what per cent of 25? 300%

33. 230 is what per cent of 100? 230%

34. 132 is what per cent of 100? 132%

35. 152% of what is 152? 100

36. 300% of what is 3? 1

De Wys, Inc.

37. The speedometer on a car may be as much as 5% off. If a speedometer reads 55 miles per hour, by how many miles per hour may it be wrong? What is the fastest the car might be going? The slowest?
2.75 mph; 57.75 mph; 52.25 mph

38. The largest mountain lion on record weighed 276 pounds. This is 184% of the weight of the average mountain lion. How much does the average mountain lion weigh? 150 lb

9.9

Estimating Per Cents

You have seen that per cent problems can be translated into proportions. But a problem that asks "What part?" can also be translated directly into an equation that is not a proportion.

Example 1: What is 71% of 142?

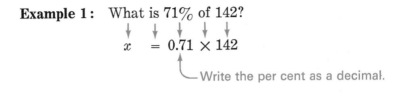

$$x = 0.71 \times 142$$

└─ Write the per cent as a decimal.

Now the answer to the question can easily be estimated.

Example 2: Estimate 71% of 142.

$$x = 0.71 \times 142$$

0.7×140 { Round the per cent to the nearest tenth.
Round the other number to any convenient place.

$7 \times 0.1 \times 140$ Rewrite 0.7 as 7×0.1.

7×14.0 Use the shortcut to multiply by 0.1.

98   Estimate

Notice how close the estimate is to the exact amount.

exact amount
$0.71 \times 142 = 100.82$

■ Exercises

A Express each per cent as a decimal.

Assignment Guide 9.9
Oral: Reg. & Max. 1–24
Written: Reg. 25–36
       Max. 25–40

1. 23% 0.23   **2.** 50% 0.5   **3.** 64.5% 0.645

4. $33\frac{1}{3}\%$ $0.33\frac{1}{3}$ or $0.\overline{3}$ **5.** 122% 1.22   **6.** 0.1% 0.001

7. 43% 0.43   **8.** 140% 1.4   **9.** 1.5% 0.015

How would you round to estimate each answer? 10–18. Typical answers

10. 0.92×239 0.9×240 **11.** 0.83×19 0.8×20 **12.** 0.48×78 0.5×80

13. 1.23×64 1.2×60 **14.** 5.66×22 5.7×20 **15.** $0.66\frac{2}{3} \times 46$ 0.7×50

16. 0.625×73 0.6×70 **17.** 0.68×93.6 0.7×90 **18.** 0.07×138 0.1×140

Express as a product in which one factor is 0.1.

19. 0.3 3×0.1 **20.** 0.9 9×0.1 **21.** 0.5 5×0.1

22. 1.2 12×0.1 **23.** 5.7 57×0.1 **24.** 11.6 116×0.1

B Copy and complete each table. 25–32. Estimates may vary.

	%	of	estimate	exact		%	of	estimate	exact
25.	37%	113		41.81	**26.**	62%	212		131.44
27.	19%	369		70.11	**28.**	8%	783		62.64
29.	27%	238		64.26	**30.**	41%	28		11.48
31.	73%	188		137.24	**32.**	94%	64		60.16

For each exercise listed below, estimate the answer. 33–36. Estimates may vary.

33. Exercise 2 on page 299   **34.** Exercise 13 on page 300

35. Exercise 14 on page 300   **36.** Exercise 19 on page 300

C The results of some recent elections are given below. The total vote and the per cent of those voting for each candidate is listed. Estimate how many people voted for each candidate. Express your answers in hundred thousands.

Jim Anderson/Woodfin Camp & Associates, Inc.

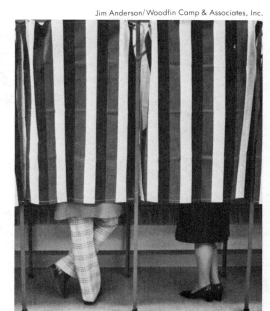

37. 523,527; Babbit 56%, Mecham 44%
       300,000   200,000
38. 530,695; Clinton 63%, Lowe 37%
       300,000   200,000
39. 6,621,313; Brown 61%, Younger 39%
       4,000,000   2,600,000
40. 800,535; Lanam 60%, Strickland 40%
       500,000   300,000

9.10

More Per Cent Problems

Suggested Class Time

Course	Min.	Reg.	Max.
Days	0	0	1

Often you must do some computing before writing a proportion.

Examples: Write a proportion for each problem below.

1. A shirt sells for $12.60 after it is reduced 30%. What is the regular price?

The regular price is the full amount.	This much is taken off.	The selling price is the amount left.

$$100\% \quad - \quad 30\% \quad = \quad 70\%$$

$12.60 out of what is 70%?

$$\frac{12.60}{p} = \frac{70}{100}$$

2. Food that cost $10 last month cost $10.90 this month. What was the per cent of increase (or per cent of *inflation*)?

cost this month	cost last month	increase in cost

$$\$10.90 \quad - \quad \$10.00 \quad = \quad \$0.90$$

$0.90 out of $10 is what per cent?

$$\frac{0.90}{10} = \frac{p}{100}$$

3. If 1 pound (16 ounces) of ground meat makes 12 ounces of cooked meat patties, what is the per cent of decrease?

raw weight	cooked weight	decrease in weight

$$16 \text{ oz} \quad - \quad 12 \text{ oz} \quad = \quad 4 \text{ oz}$$

4 out of 16 is what per cent?

$$\frac{4}{16} = \frac{p}{100}$$

304

A What operation must be done in each case before a proportion can be written?

1. If the price was $4 after it was reduced 20%, what was the regular price? Subtract 20% from 100%.

2. If $5546 was left after a 6% commission was taken out, what was the original amount? Subtract 6% from 100%.

3. If the price of gasoline rises from $1.25 to $1.50 a gallon, what is the per cent of increase? Subtract $1.25 from $1.50.

4. If the price of a shirt is reduced from $7 to $5.60, by what per cent is it reduced? Subtract $5.60 from $7.

B Write and solve a proportion for each problem.

5. Exercise 1 $5   6. Exercise 2 $5900   7. Exercise 3 20%   8. Exercise 4 20%

	per cent reduced	sale price	regular price		per cent reduced	sale price	regular price
9.	20%	$ 8.56	$10.70	10.	25%	$ 15.99	$21.32
11.	30%	$ 42.63	$60.90	12.	$33\frac{1}{3}$%	$ 63.60	$95.40
13.	45%	$137.50	$250	14.	42%	$348	$600
15.	15%	$ 6.80	$8	16.	50%	$ 6.50	$13

17. An actor's agent receives 10% commission. How much must the actor make to have $450 left after the commission is deducted? $500

18. The Bartons are selling their house. The real-estate agent's commission is 7%. The Bartons want to have $46,500 left after the commission is deducted. What should be the selling price? $50,000

19. Mark works for Stein's Department Store. He gets a 20% discount on everything he buys at Stein's. He has $16 to spend on a ski sweater. How expensive a sweater can he buy, if he buys the sweater at Stein's? $20

20. An increase from 10 to 15 is what per cent of increase? 50%

21. An increase from 8 to 10 is what per cent of increase? 25%

22. An increase from 3.2 to 3.6 is what per cent of increase? 12.5%

23. An increase from $2\frac{1}{2}$ to $3\frac{3}{4}$ is what per cent of increase? 50%

24. Mr. Larson's salary increased from $160 to $180. What was the per cent of increase? 12.5%

25. At N Enterprises, sales increased from $250,000 to $350,000. What was the per cent of increase? 40%

26. A decrease from 10 to 7 is what per cent of decrease? 30%

27. A decrease from 20 to 16 is what per cent of decrease? 20%

28. A decrease from $\frac{3}{4}$ to $\frac{1}{2}$ is what per cent of decrease? $33\frac{1}{3}$%

29. A decrease from 3.2 to 2.4 is what per cent of decrease? 25%

30. An item which regularly sells for $25 was purchased on sale for $17.50. What was the per cent of decrease? 30%

31. Mrs. Catalano sold 16 houses last year. This year she sold 14. What was the per cent of decrease in her number of sales? 12.5%

C. E. Pelley

C When a hole is dug, the dirt removed is looser and occupies more space than before its removal. Builders often use the rule that there is a 25% increase in the volume of excavated material. Use this rule to do the following problems.

32. For a basement, a contractor digs a hole 6 by 9 by 2 meters. What volume of dirt must he get rid of? 135 m³

33. A landscaper needs 20 cubic yards of loose dirt for a garden. About how large a hole must be dug to supply it? 16 cu yd

Terms and Symbols Review

Which example would you give for each item?

1. ratio of 2 to 5 ^{g}

2. 3 ratios equivalent to $\frac{3}{4}$ ^{d}

3. proportion ^{a}

4. per cent ^{f}

5. 3 ways to write a ratio ^{e}

6. cross products for $\frac{3}{4} = \frac{12}{16}$ ^{b}

7. means for $\frac{3}{4} = \frac{12}{16}$ ^{c}

a. $\frac{3}{4} = \frac{12}{16}$

b. $3 \times 16 = 4 \times 12$

c. 4 and 12

d. $\frac{6}{8}, \frac{9}{12}, \frac{12}{16}$

e. $\frac{1}{2}$, 1 to 2, 1:2

f. $16\frac{2}{3}\%$

g. 2:5

h. 3 and 16

Assignment Guide Rev.
Oral: Terms & Symbols 1–7
Written:
Min. (day 1) 1–18
    (day 2) 19–42
Reg. 1–43 odd
Max. 1–43 odd; 44

Chapter 9 Review

Write a ratio for each of the following.   9.1

1. 3 hits to 4 times at bat $\frac{3}{4}$

2. 3 votes to 2 votes $\frac{3}{2}$

3. 4 baskets to 9 attempts $\frac{4}{9}$

4. 7 baseballs to 10 bats $\frac{7}{10}$

Write two equivalent ratios for each ratio.   5–10. Answers may vary.   9.2

5. $\frac{1}{2}$ 6. $\frac{3}{4}$ 7. $\frac{10}{16}$

8. $\frac{5}{3}$ 9. $\frac{8}{6}$ 10. $\frac{3}{3}$

Solve each proportion.   9.3

11. $\frac{1}{4} = \frac{n}{20}$ 5

12. $\frac{2}{3} = \frac{6}{n}$ 9

13. $\frac{n}{8} = \frac{10}{16}$ 5

14. $\frac{8}{n} = \frac{16}{18}$ 9

15. $\frac{4}{5} = \frac{n}{10}$ 8

16. $\frac{n}{8} = \frac{14}{16}$ 7

Use a proportion to solve each problem.   9.4

17. There are 90 calories in 2 slices of bacon. How many calories are in 5 slices?   225 cal

18. If a 200-meter roll of wire weighs 480 kg, how much do 93 meters of the wire weigh? 223.2 kg

9.5   Copy and complete the tables below.

	per cent	fraction	decimal		per cent	fraction or mixed number	decimal
19.	72%	$\frac{18}{25}$	0.72	**20.**	2.8%	$\frac{7}{250}$	0.028
21.	$6\frac{1}{2}\%$	$\frac{13}{200}$	0.065	**22.**	121%	$1\frac{21}{100}$	1.21

9.6   Express as a per cent.

23. 0.47 47%   **24.** 1.03 103%   **25.** 0.426 42.6%

26. $\frac{3}{4}$ 75%   **27.** $\frac{3}{12}$ 25%   **28.** $\frac{7}{20}$ 35%

29. $\frac{3}{2}$ 150%   **30.** 1 100%   **31.** 2 200%

32. $\frac{5}{2}$ 250%   **33.** $3\frac{1}{4}$ 325%   **34.** $3\frac{1}{2}$ 350%

9.7   Solve each of the following.

35. 50% of 75 is what number? 37.5   **36.** 56% of 56 is what number? 31.36

37. 20% of what number is 9? 45   **38.** 6% of what number is 18? 300

39. 12 is what per cent of 16? 75%   **40.** 8 is what per cent of 10? 80%

9.8   Solve.

41. Jean bought a coat marked down 35% from the regular price of $60. How much did she save? $21

42. Mr. Bathke sold 16 cases of merchandise last week. This was 40% of his monthly quota. What was his monthly quota? 40 cases

9.9   **43.** Estimate 48% of 281.
          Answers may vary.

9.10   **44.** The price of the book was reduced 20%. What is the regular price? $13.50

SALE PRICE
$10.80

Chapter 9 Test

Change each ratio to lowest terms.

1. $\frac{30}{50}$ $\frac{3}{5}$

2. $\frac{36}{48}$ $\frac{3}{4}$

3. $\frac{16}{24}$ $\frac{2}{3}$

4. $\frac{27}{81}$ $\frac{1}{3}$

5. $\frac{21}{12}$ $\frac{7}{4}$

6. $\frac{18}{54}$ $\frac{1}{3}$

Assignment Guide Test
Written:
Min. 1–24; 26–27
Reg. 1–27
Max. 1–28

Solve each proportion.

7. $\frac{2}{3} = \frac{n}{24}$ 16

8. $\frac{5}{8} = \frac{15}{n}$ 24

9. $\frac{7}{8} = \frac{n}{16}$ 14

10. $\frac{5}{n} = \frac{20}{48}$ 12

11. $\frac{n}{6} = \frac{20}{24}$ 5

12. $\frac{3}{4} = \frac{18}{n}$ 24

Solve.

13. 6% of 200 is what number? 12

14. 2.5% of 40 is what number? 1

15. 12 is what per cent of 25? 48%

16. 9 is what per cent of 20? 45%

17. 25% of what number is 8? 32

18. 75% of what number is 90? 120

Complete the following tables.

fraction	decimal	per cent
19. $\frac{1}{5}$	0.2	20%
21. $\frac{9}{10}$	0.9	90%
23. $\frac{63}{100}$	0.63	63%

fraction or mixed number	decimal	per cent
20. $\frac{7}{8}$	0.875	87.5%
22. $\frac{3}{8}$	0.375	37.5%
24. $1\frac{1}{2}$	1.5	150%

RATE YOURSELF

Number Correct:
- 27–28 Superior
- 24–26 Excellent
- 21–23 Good
- 15–20 Fair
- 0–14 Poor

25. Estimate 52% of 679. Answers may vary.

Use a proportion to solve each problem.

26. At a fast walk, you use about 80 calories in 15 minutes. How long must you walk fast to use up the calories in a 360-calorie slice of pie? 67.5 min

27. An author received a check for $150. This was 5% of the sales of her book. What were the sales for the book? $3000

28. If a wrench sells for $4 after it is reduced 20%, what is the regular price? $5

H. Armstrong Roberts

309

SCRAMBLED CROSSWORD

Copy the pattern below on graph paper. Then unscramble each term and write it in the proper boxes.

ACROSS

2. EVAQUELINT
6. TROFY
7. HELOW
8. BRAVELIAS
9. THIGE
12. CUNEO
14. ABES
17. LAQUE
19. TREME
21. FOURLAM
23. ELUVA
24. IP
25. TSE
28. TRAMENOUR
30. ITGID
31. IXS
32. LIME
34. VEGATINE
35. RAGAVEE
38. NET
39. LYMBOS
41. THIXS
44. WEVELT
46. ANDTHUSHOT
48. MOULVE
49. ATRIO
50. DUNHERD

DOWN

1. RINGIO
2. PLAXEME
3. TUNI
4. WOT
5. SEDGERE
9. MEERSTEX
10. TRUMPERATEE
11. CARTOF
13. TUMTAMVOICE
15. LAHF
16. EMDRAINER
18. RORED
20. NEVE
22. TIXSY
26. USADIR
27. TIFFY
29. NOE
32. MHAT
33. THENGL
36. DADED
37. VEENEL
39. VOLES
40. TRILE
42. THENT
43. FOTO
45. PUC
47. ONT

Tell which figures are named by each of these words.

a.   b.   c.   d.

e.   f.   g.   h.

1. circles   c, h   **2.** rectangles   b, d, e, f

3. squares   b, e   **4.** triangles   a, g

Write two equivalent ratios for each ratio.   **5–13.** Answers may vary.   9.2

5. $\frac{1}{3}$ **6.** $\frac{3}{4}$ **7.** $\frac{2}{5}$

8. $\frac{5}{2}$ **9.** $\frac{9}{4}$ **10.** $\frac{3}{2}$

11. $\frac{12}{15}$ **12.** $\frac{24}{20}$ **13.** $\frac{18}{72}$

Solve each proportion.   9.3

14. $\frac{3}{4} = \frac{n}{20}$ 15   **15.** $\frac{n}{8} = \frac{1}{4}$ 2

16. $\frac{6}{9} = \frac{24}{n}$ 36   **17.** $\frac{3}{n} = \frac{9}{15}$ 5

Compute.

18. $8 \times 2\frac{3}{4}$ 22   **19.** $3\frac{1}{2} \times 16$ 56   4.5

20. 0.6×14 8.4   **21.** 12×3.5 42   5.4

10

Suggested Class Time

Course	Min.	Reg.	Max.
Days	1	0	0

Assignment Guide GR 10
Written: Min. 1–21

INDIRECT MEASUREMENT

Courtesy Robertshaw Controls Co.

Courtesy Sears, Roebuck & Co.

There's an old mathematical joke that goes something like this:

Problem: Give three ways a clock can be used to find the height of a tall building:

Answer:
1. Lower the clock by a tape measure from the roof to the ground.
2. Drop the clock off the roof, time the fall, and find the distance by using the formula $d = 16t^2$ for falling bodies.
3. On a sunny day, find the ratio of the clock's height to the length of its shadow. Measure the building's shadow and use a proportion to find the height.

The first method is a *direct measurement* because you are actually measuring the building itself. The other two methods are *indirect measurements* because you are really measuring something else. You'll learn how to make indirect measurements in this chapter.

Suggested Class Time

Course	Min.	Reg.	Max.
Days	1	1	1

H. Armstrong Roberts

When a photograph is enlarged, you expect it to look like the original. You wouldn't want the picture made 5 times as tall but only 2 times as wide. Everything would look tall and skinny in the enlargement. You want everything to keep the same shape.

In mathematics, when figures have the same shape, we say the figures are *similar*.

similar figures

figures that are not similar

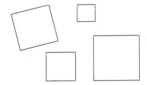

 Similar figures have exactly the same shape but may have different sizes.

Similar figures could be the same size. In that case, one figure is an exact copy of the other. If similar figures have different sizes, then one figure can be enlarged or reduced to make it an exact copy of the other.

These two triangles are similar. You could enlarge the first figure to make it an exact copy of the other.

These figures may not look similar at first. If you "turn" one of the triangles, it makes it easier to see that they have the same shape.

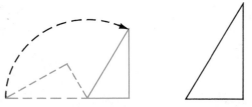

The two figures below are also similar. You could reduce the first figure to make it an exact copy of the other.

Again, the figures may not look similar at first. Turning either figure does not help. But you can "flip" one of them to make it easier to see that they are similar.

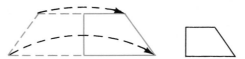

When we use triangles, the angles are usually labeled with letters. We name a triangle by using these letters. The letters can be named in any order. ($\triangle$ is the symbol for "triangle.")

Example 1: Give six names for the triangle shown.

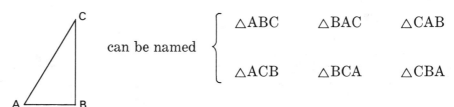

can be named
$$\begin{cases} \triangle ABC & \triangle BAC & \triangle CAB \\ \triangle ACB & \triangle BCA & \triangle CBA \end{cases}$$

Example 2: Tell which triangles are similar.

△ABC is similar to △RST because it could be reduced to be an exact copy. △DEF is not similar to either of the other triangles. It could never be enlarged or reduced so that it would be an exact copy of either of the other two triangles.

Assignment Guide 10.1
Oral: 1–4
Written: Min. 5–20
Reg. 5–20
Max. 5–28

■ Exercises

Ⓐ Choose the figure in each row that is similar to the colored figure.

1.
c

  a.   **b.**  **c.**   **d.**

2.
b

  a.   **b.**   **c.**   **d.**

3.
c

  a.   **b.** 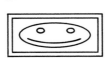 **c.**   **d.**

4.
b

  a.  **b.**   **c.**   **d.**

315

B Are the two figures similar? (*Hint:* Could you enlarge or reduce the first figure to make it an exact copy of the other?)

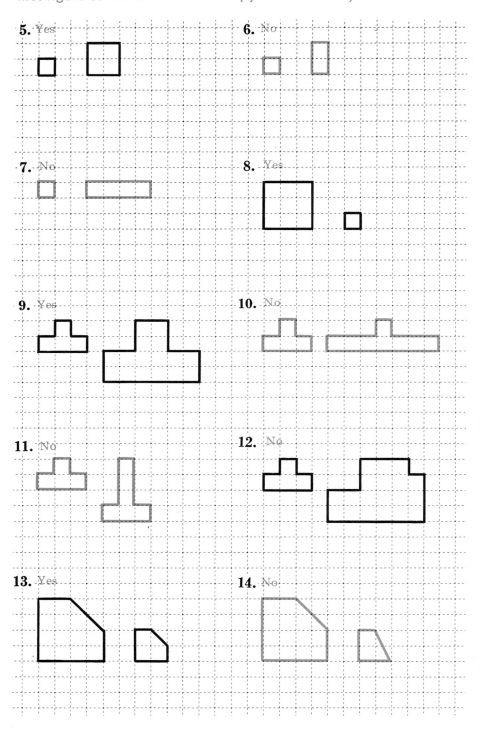

5. Yes

6. No

7. No

8. Yes

9. Yes

10. No

11. No

12. No

13. Yes

14. No

15. No

16. Yes

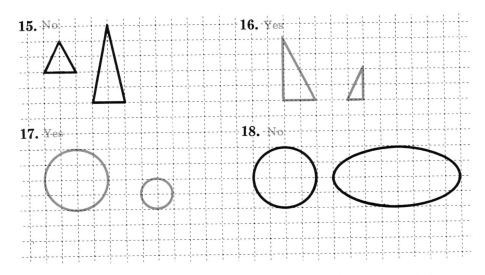

17. Yes

18. No

19. Using the figures below, name the triangles that are similar.
△ABC and △JKL; △DEF and △GTH

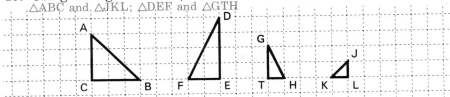

20. Give 5 other names for △DEF. △DFE, △EFD, △EDF, △FED, △FDE

C Answer each question.

21. Are all squares similar? Yes

22. Are all rectangles similar? No

23. Are all circles similar? Yes

24. Are all triangles similar? No

Use graph paper to do the following. Answers may vary.

25. Draw 2 rectangles that are similar.

26. Draw 2 rectangles that are not similar.

27. Draw 2 triangles that are similar.

28. Draw 2 triangles that are not similar.

10.2 Corresponding Angles and Sides

Enlarging or reducing a triangle changes the lengths of the sides, but the measures of the angles remain the same. The symbols $\dashv$, $\ne$, and $\not\equiv$ are used to show which angles have the same measure.

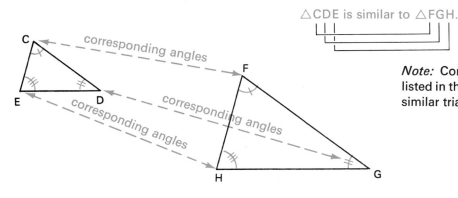

△CDE is similar to △FGH.

Note: Corresponding angles are listed in the same order when two similar triangles are named.

> In similar triangles, angles that have the same measure are **corresponding angles.**

Example 1: Tell which angles are corresponding angles.

△ABC is similar to △RTS.

Solution: ∠A and ∠R ⟵ ∠ is the symbol for "angle."

∠B and ∠T

∠C and ∠S ⟵ Notice that when two pairs of angles are marked, the third pair can be left unmarked.

Example 2: Tell which sides are corresponding sides.

△KLM is similar to △XZY.

Solution: There are three pairs of corresponding sides.

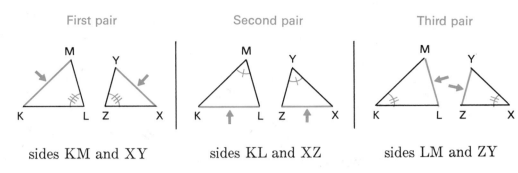

First pair	Second pair	Third pair
sides KM and XY	sides KL and XZ	sides LM and ZY

> In similar triangles, **corresponding sides** are the sides opposite corresponding angles.

Assignment Guide 10.2
Oral: 1–4
Written: Min. 5–13 odd
Reg. 5–14
Max. 5–13 odd;
15–18

Exercises

A Name the corresponding angles for each pair of similar triangles. (See Example 1.)

1.

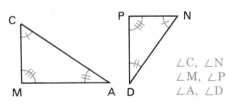

∠C, ∠N
∠M, ∠P
∠A, ∠D

2.

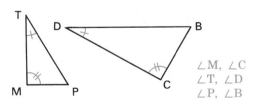

∠M, ∠C
∠T, ∠D
∠P, ∠B

Name the corresponding sides for each pair of similar triangles. (See Example 2.)

3.

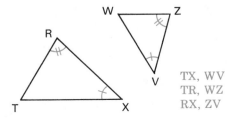

TX, WV
TR, WZ
RX, ZV

4.

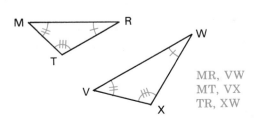

MR, VW
MT, VX
TR, XW

319

B Name the corresponding angles and sides for each pair of similar triangles.

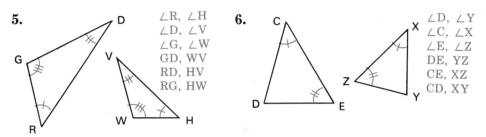

5.
∠R, ∠H
∠D, ∠V
∠G, ∠W
GD, WV
RD, HV
RG, HW

6.
∠D, ∠Y
∠C, ∠X
∠E, ∠Z
DE, YZ
CE, XZ
CD, XY

Corresponding angles of the similar triangles are listed. Name the corresponding sides.

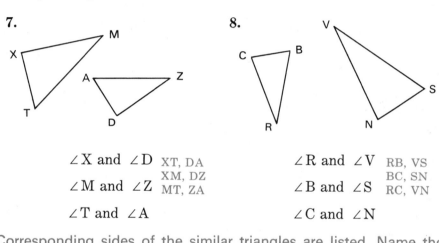

7.

∠X and ∠D   XT, DA
             XM, DZ
∠M and ∠Z   MT, ZA

∠T and ∠A

8.

∠R and ∠V   RB, VS
             BC, SN
∠B and ∠S   RC, VN

∠C and ∠N

Corresponding sides of the similar triangles are listed. Name the corresponding angles.

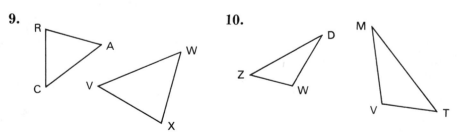

9.

sides AC and VW   ∠R, ∠X
                   ∠A, ∠V
sides CR and WX   ∠C, ∠W

sides RA and XV

10.

sides DW and MV   ∠Z, ∠T
                   ∠D, ∠M
sides ZW and TV   ∠W, ∠V

sides ZD and TM

Name the corresponding angles and the corresponding sides for each pair of similar triangles.

Example:

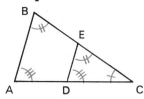

Hint: Think of sliding △DEC off △ABC.

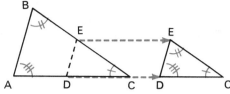

Solution:

Corresponding angles

∠A and ∠EDC ← Using three letters shows that we don't mean ∠EDA.

∠B and ∠DEC

∠C is the same for both triangles.

(But we could name it two ways to show what we mean: ∠ACB and ∠DCE.)

Corresponding sides

sides BC and EC

sides AC and DC

sides AB and DE

11.

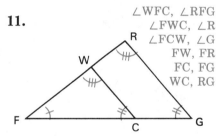

∠WFC, ∠RFG
∠FWC, ∠R
∠FCW, ∠G
FW, FR
FC, FG
WC, RG

12.

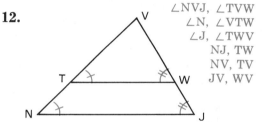

∠NVJ, ∠TVW
∠N, ∠VTW
∠J, ∠TWV
NJ, TW
NV, TV
JV, WV

13.

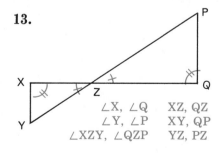

∠X, ∠Q   XZ, QZ
∠Y, ∠P   XY, QP
∠XZY, ∠QZP   YZ, PZ

14.

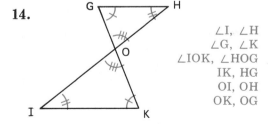

∠I, ∠H
∠G, ∠K
∠IOK, ∠HOG
IK, HG
OI, OH
OK, OG

Ⓒ Give all the pairs of corresponding angles and sides.
15–16. Answers at right.

15. △PQR is similar to △MTF.

16. △YWZ is similar to △PEG.

17. △DEF is similar to △KLO.
∠D, ∠K; ∠E, ∠L; ∠F, ∠O;
DE, KL; EF, LO; DF, KO

18. △TUV is similar to △ABC.
∠T, ∠A; ∠U, ∠B; ∠V, ∠C;
TU, AB; UV, BC; TV, AC

15. ∠P, ∠M; ∠Q, ∠T;
∠R, ∠F; PQ, MT;
PR, MF; QR, TF

16. ∠Y, ∠P; ∠W, ∠E;
∠Z, ∠G; YW, PE;
WZ, EG; YZ, PG

321

Similar Triangles

When a triangle is enlarged or reduced, the ratios of the lengths of corresponding sides are equal. Note that symbols like AB and DE stand for the lengths of the sides.

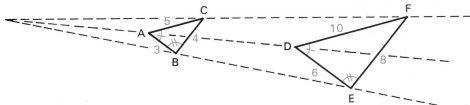

$$\frac{AB}{DE} = \frac{3}{6} \qquad \frac{BC}{EF} = \frac{4}{8} \qquad \frac{AC}{DF} = \frac{5}{10}$$

$$= \frac{1}{2} \qquad\qquad = \frac{1}{2} \qquad\qquad = \frac{1}{2}$$

Note: The numerator of each ratio is from △ABC and the denominator from △DEF.

Since the ratios of the lengths of corresponding sides are equal, the ratios can be expressed as proportions in many different ways.

$$\frac{AB}{DE} = \frac{BC}{EF} \qquad \frac{BC}{EF} = \frac{AC}{DF} \qquad \frac{AB}{DE} = \frac{AC}{DF}$$

$$\frac{3}{6} = \frac{4}{8} \qquad\qquad \frac{4}{8} = \frac{5}{10} \qquad\qquad \frac{3}{6} = \frac{5}{10}$$

We can also choose the numerator of each ratio from △DEF and the denominator from △ABC. In that case, we obtain the following proportions. Notice that these proportions are the same as those above with both sides inverted.

$$\frac{DE}{AB} = \frac{EF}{BC} \qquad \frac{EF}{BC} = \frac{DF}{AC} \qquad \frac{DE}{AB} = \frac{DF}{AC}$$

$$\frac{6}{3} = \frac{8}{4} \qquad\qquad \frac{8}{4} = \frac{10}{5} \qquad\qquad \frac{6}{3} = \frac{10}{5}$$

In similar triangles, corresponding sides are proportional.

Example 1: What letter should replace each question mark?

△RST is similar to △XYZ.

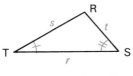
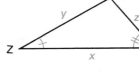

$$\frac{s}{y} = \frac{r}{?} \quad x$$

$$\frac{t}{z} = \frac{s}{?} \quad y$$

$$\frac{r}{x} = \frac{t}{?} \quad z$$

Example 2: Find the values of x and z.

△ABC is similar to △XYZ.

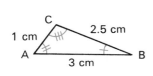
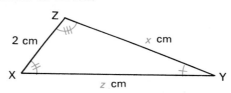

$$\frac{AC}{XZ} = \frac{AB}{XY}$$

$$\frac{1}{2} = \frac{3}{z}$$

$$z = 2 \times 3$$

$$z = 6$$

Check: Are the ratios 3 to 6 and 1 to 2 equivalent? ✓

$$\frac{AC}{XZ} = \frac{BC}{YZ}$$

$$\frac{1}{2} = \frac{2.5}{x}$$

$$x = 2 \times 2.5$$

$$x = 5$$

Check: Are the ratios 2.5 to 5 and 1 to 2 equivalent? ✓

■ Exercises

Ⓐ What letter should replace each question mark?

△MNQ is similar to △RST.

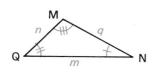
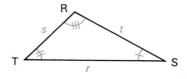

Assignment Guide 10.3
Oral: 1–12
Written:
Min. 13–19 odd; Quiz, p. 325
Reg. 13–19 odd; 20; Quiz, p. 325
Max. 13–21 odd; Quiz, p. 325

1. $\frac{n}{s} = \frac{q}{?}$ t

2. $\frac{n}{s} = \frac{m}{?}$ r

3. $\frac{s}{n} = \frac{t}{?}$ q

4. $\frac{r}{m} = \frac{?}{n}$ s

5. $\frac{q}{?} = \frac{m}{r}$ t

6. $\frac{?}{q} = \frac{s}{n}$ t

△ABC is similar to △AED.

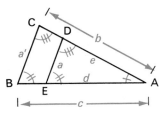

Note: a' is read a prime.

7. $\frac{e}{b} = \frac{d}{?}$ c

8. $\frac{a'}{?} = \frac{c}{d}$ a

9. $\frac{a}{a'} = \frac{?}{c}$ d

10. $\frac{b}{?} = \frac{c}{d}$ e

11. $\frac{?}{a'} = \frac{d}{c}$ a

12. $\frac{d}{c} = \frac{?}{b}$ e

B Find the values of *x* and *z*.

13. △ABC is similar to △DEF.

$x = 10,\ z = 8$

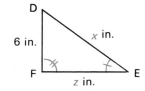

14. △GHI is similar to △JKL.

$x = 2.625,\ z = 1.875$

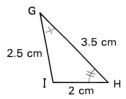

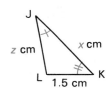

15. △MQN is similar to △PRT.

$x = 2\frac{1}{2},\ z = 3\frac{3}{4}$

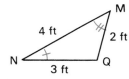

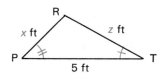

16. △STU is similar to △VWX.

$x = 2.625,\ z = 4.5$

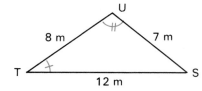

17. △YZA is similar to △BCD.

$x = 3,\ z = 2$

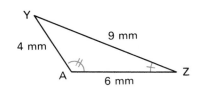

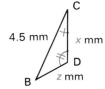

18. △TRE is
similar
to △TMN.

$x = 120, z = 160$

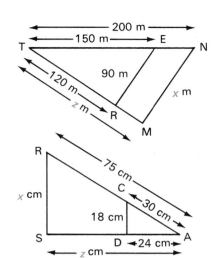

19. △RSA is
similar
to △CDA.

$x = 45, z = 60$

20. △AED is
similar
to △CEB.

$x = 2, z = 6$

C **21.** △COD is
similar
to △HOG.

$x = 10, z = 8$

Quick Quiz
Sections 10.1 to 10.3

Are the two figures similar?

1. No

2. Yes

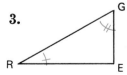

Name the corresponding angles and sides for each pair of similar
triangles.

3–4. Answers at right.

3.

4.

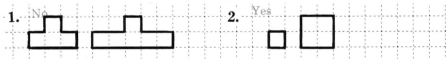

3. ∠R, ∠T; ∠G, ∠S;
∠E, ∠A; RE, TA;
EG, AS; RG, TS

4. ∠L, ∠A; ∠M, ∠B;
∠V, ∠C; VL, CA;
VM, CB; LM, AB

5. Find the values of x and z in Exercise 4. $x = 11.25, z = 12.75$

325

Measuring With Similar Triangles

10.4

Suggested Class Time

Course	Min.	Reg.	Max.
Days	1	1	1

Similar triangles can be used to make indirect measurements.

Example 1: How tall is the pole?

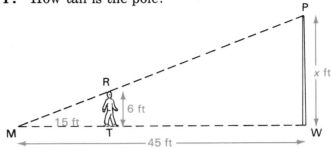

Step 1: △MRT is similar to △MPW.

Step 2: $\dfrac{MT}{MW} = \dfrac{15}{45}$ or $\dfrac{1}{3}$

Step 3: $\dfrac{MT}{MW} = \dfrac{RT}{PW}$ ⟹ $\dfrac{1}{3} = \dfrac{6}{x}$

$x = 3 \times 6$

$x = 18$

Check: Are the ratios 6 to 18 and 1 to 3 equivalent? ✓

So the pole is 18 feet high.

Example 2: How far is it from the post at A to the post at B?

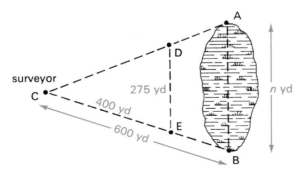

Step 1: Notice the two triangles that are similar.

△ABC is similar to △DEC.

326

Step 2: Write a proportion that includes the unknown distance.

$$\frac{CE}{CB} = \frac{DE}{AB} \qquad \text{or} \qquad \frac{400}{600} = \frac{275}{n}$$

Step 3: Solve the proportion.

$$\frac{400}{600} = \frac{275}{n}$$

$$400n = 600 \times 275$$

$$n = \frac{600 \times 275}{400}$$

$$n = 412\frac{1}{2}$$

Check: Are the ratios 275 to $412\frac{1}{2}$ and 400 to 600 equivalent? ✓

So the distance from A to B is $412\frac{1}{2}$ yards.

Assignment Guide 10.4
Oral: 1–12
Written: Min. 13–16
Reg. 13–18
Max. 13–20

■ Exercises

A **1.** What is true about the ratios of corresponding sides of similar triangles?   The ratios are equivalent.

What letter should replace each question mark?

△CDA is similar to △BEA.

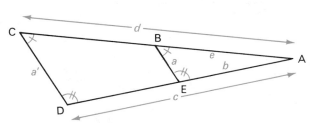

2. $\frac{e}{d} = \frac{b}{?}$ c **3.** $\frac{a}{a'} = \frac{e}{?}$ d **4.** $\frac{c}{b} = \frac{a'}{?}$ a

5. $\frac{d}{e} = \frac{?}{b}$ c **6.** $\frac{b}{?} = \frac{a}{a'}$ c **7.** $\frac{?}{a} = \frac{d}{e}$ a'

The ratio $\frac{e}{d}$ is $\frac{1}{2}$. What are the following ratios?

8. $\frac{b}{c}$ $\frac{1}{2}$ **9.** $\frac{a}{a'}$ $\frac{1}{2}$ **10.** $\frac{d}{e}$ $\frac{2}{1}$ **11.** $\frac{c}{b}$ $\frac{2}{1}$ **12.** $\frac{a'}{a}$ $\frac{2}{1}$

327

Use similar triangles to solve each problem.

13. The sign and the tree cast shadows as shown. How tall is the tree?

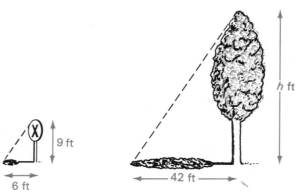

63 ft

h ft

9 ft

6 ft

42 ft

14. How high is the hotel?

240 ft

HOTEL

h ft

40 ft

25 ft

150 ft

15. What is the length of the fairway?

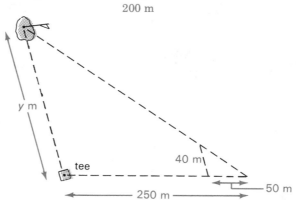

200 m

y m

tee

40 m

50 m

250 m

328

16. How far apart are the lighthouses? 7.5 km

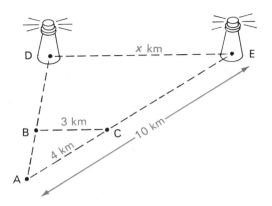

17. Find the height of the flagpole. 29 ft

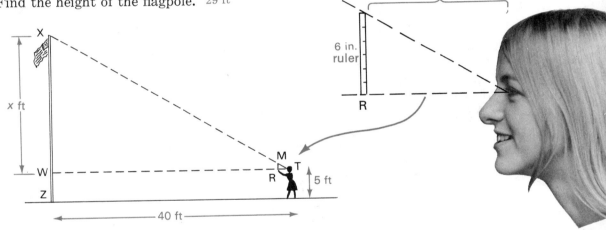

18. Triangles DCE and ABE are similar. Find the width of the lake at AB. 90 m

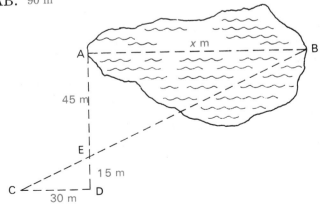

Use a mirror and similar triangles to measure tall objects.

Example : To measure the height of the building, place a mirror a measured distance (10 meters in this case) from the base of the building. Slowly walk toward the mirror until you see the top of the building in the mirror. Measure your distance from the mirror and compute as indicated.

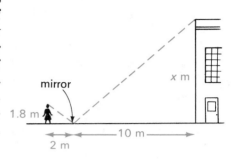

$$\dfrac{\text{your distance from mirror}}{\text{object's distance from mirror}} = \dfrac{\text{your eye-level height}}{\text{object's height}}$$

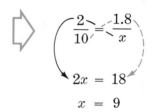

$$\dfrac{2}{10} = \dfrac{1.8}{x}$$

$$2x = 18$$

$$x = 9$$

The building is 9 meters high.

19. What would be the height of the flagpole if your eye-level height is 5 feet? $27\frac{1}{2}$ ft

20–21. **a.** Answers may vary.

20. Use your eye-level height (in inches) and compute the height of the flagpole. (*Note:* It will be necessary to convert 8 ft to inches.)

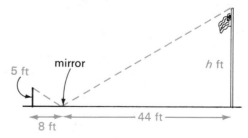

21. Use a mirror to calculate various heights. These might include the height of your classroom, your school building, a tree, and so on.

Similar Triangles in Games

Brent Jones

Courtesy Bally Manufacturing Corp.

In games like pool, miniature golf, air hockey, and many electronic TV games, bank shots can be used. For example, on the miniature golf fairway shown below, you would bank (bounce) the ball off the wall at point B.

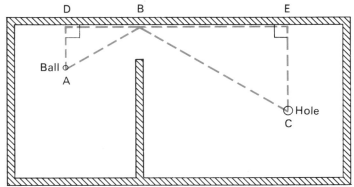

⌐ is the symbol for a right (90°) angle.

There is *only one* point B on the wall. And it is that point where △ABD and △CBE are similar triangles. Notice, therefore, that the angles at which the ball approaches and leaves the wall (angles ABD and CBE) would have the same measure.

Sometimes you can do some quick figuring to find the point where you should bank a shot.

Example: How could you use similar triangles to locate point B in the preceding example?

Step 1: Estimate the distances AD, CE, and DE. Let's say you think:

$$AD = 3 \text{ ft}, CE = 6 \text{ ft, and } DE = 15 \text{ ft.}$$

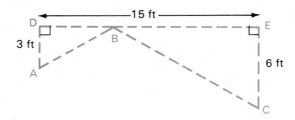

Step 2: Reduce the ratio of the corresponding sides to lowest terms.

$$\frac{AD}{CE} = \frac{3}{6} = \frac{1}{2}$$

Step 3: Find the lengths into which DE must be broken to give the same ratio as found in step 2.

from the ratio in step 2 $1x + 2x = 15$ from the estimate in step 1

$$(1 + 2)x = 15$$

$$3x = 15$$

$$\frac{3x}{3} = \frac{15}{3}$$

$$x = 5$$

So DE must be broken into

$$DB = 1x = 1 \times 5 = 5$$

$$BE = 2x = 2 \times 5 = 10$$

Check: Are the ratios 3 to 6 and 5 to 10 equivalent? ✓

So point B must be 5 ft from point D. Aim at point B.

■ Exercises

Assignment Guide 10.5
Oral: 1–4
Written: Min. 5–9
       Reg. 5–10
       Max. 5–12

A **1.** In the air hockey game below, the puck is at A. Where must the puck be banked to shoot it into the goal at the right?

Between C and D

Courtesy Coleco Industries, Inc.

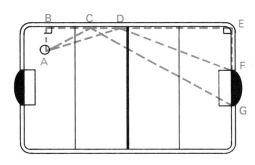

2. Name two pairs of similar triangles above. △ABD and △FED, △ABC and △GEC

Use the pool table shown at right. You want the cue ball at C to bank off the wall at B and hit the eight ball at E.

3. What must be true of △ACB and △DEB? The triangles must be similar.

4. What must be true of the angles at which the cue ball approaches and leaves the wall? The angles must have the same measure.

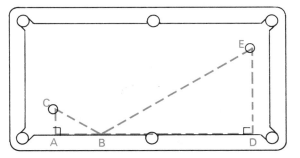

B **5.** Let AC = 10 in., DE = 30 in., and AD = 80 in. Find AB and BD. AB = 20 in., BD = 60 in.

6. Let AC = 8 in., DE = 32 in., and AD = 75 in. Find AB and BD. AB = 15 in., BD = 60 in.

333

Use the miniature golf fairway shown at right. You want the golf ball at G to bank off the wall at B and go in the hole at H.

7. What must be true of △GAB and △HCB? *The triangles must be similar.*

8. What must be true of angles ABG and CBH? *The angles must have the same measure.*

9. Let AG = 2 yd, CH = 1 yd, AC = 6 yd. Find AB and BC. *AB = 4 yd, BC = 2 yd*

10. Let AG = 2 yd, CH = 1 yd, AC = 5 yd. Find AB and BC. *AB = 3⅓ yd, BC = 1⅔ yd*

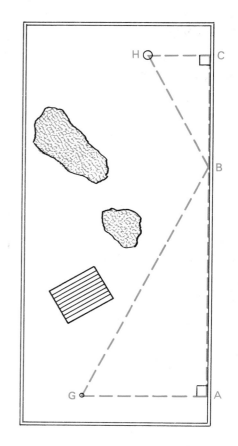

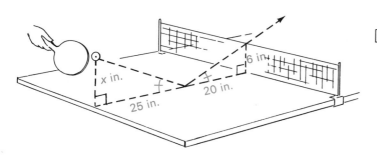

C **11.** Suppose you are practicing table tennis. And you want the ball to just clear the net as shown. How high above the table should you serve? *7½ in.*

12. If you were playing catch against a wall and threw the ball as shown, how high on the wall would the ball hit? *4⅖ ft*

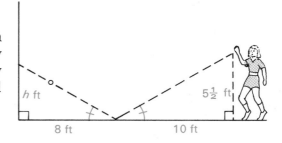

Another Way

Another way to find the point at which to bank a shot follows. Think of flipping (over the wall) the point C, where you want the ball to go. For example,

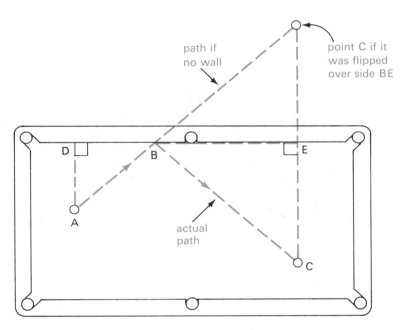

path if no wall

point C if it was flipped over side BE

D

B

E

A

actual path

C

Courtesy Brunswick Corporation

Maps

A map is a reduced drawing of part of the earth's surface. The amount of reduction or scale is usually given by a ratio. For example, on the following map *1 inch represents 50 miles*. That means the ratio of distances on the map to those on earth is 1 inch to 50 miles.

Scale: 1 in. = 50 mi

Example: What is the flight distance from Detroit to Kalamazoo?

Step 1: Measure the distance on the map: $2\frac{3}{4}$ inches

Step 2: Use a proportion to find the actual distance d.

$$\frac{1 \text{ in.}}{50 \text{ mi}} = \frac{2\frac{3}{4} \text{ in.}}{d \text{ mi}} \qquad \frac{1}{50} = \frac{2\frac{3}{4}}{d}$$

$$d = 50 \times 2\frac{3}{4}$$

$$d = 137\frac{1}{2}$$

Check: $\dfrac{1}{50} = \dfrac{2\frac{3}{4}}{137\frac{1}{2}}$

$137\frac{1}{2}$ $\qquad$ $137\frac{1}{2}$ ✓ $\qquad$ The ratios are equivalent.

So the flight distance from Detroit to Kalamazoo is $137\frac{1}{2}$ miles.

■ Exercises

Assignment Guide 10.6
Oral: 1–2
Written: Min. 3–10
Reg. 3–11
Max. 3–12

A By using the map on page 336, tell how you could find the distance between each pair of cities given below.

1. Detroit and Mt. Pleasant $\quad$ Solve $\dfrac{1}{50} = \dfrac{2\frac{1}{2}}{x}$.

2. Flint and Kalamazoo $\quad$ Solve $\dfrac{1}{50} = \dfrac{2\frac{1}{4}}{x}$.

B Use the map on page 336 to find the flight distance between each pair of cities given below.

3. Mt. Pleasant and Lansing $\quad 62\frac{1}{2}$ mi

4. Ann Arbor and Traverse City $\quad 187\frac{1}{2}$ mi

5. Ann Arbor and Detroit $\quad 43\frac{3}{4}$ mi

6. Cadillac and Kalamazoo $\quad 131\frac{1}{4}$ mi

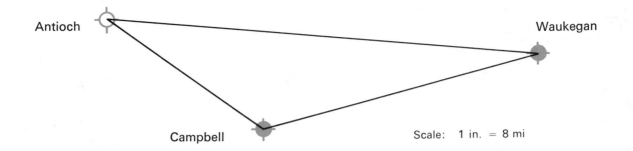

Antioch   Waukegan

Campbell   Scale: 1 in. = 8 mi

Use the map above to complete the following table.

Flight between	map distance (in inches)	actual distance (in miles)
7. Campbell and Waukegan	3	24
8. Waukegan and Antioch	$4\frac{1}{2}$	36
9. Antioch and Campbell	2	16

10. What was the total distance of the trip above? 76 mi

11. If the plane averaged 120 mph, how long would it take for the trip, allowing 5 minutes for the touchdown at Waukegan and 5 minutes for the touchdown at Antioch? 48 min

C   Answer the question.

12. The map below is a reduction of the map above. The scale is missing. What should the scale be? 1 in. = 16 mi

Antioch   Waukegan

Campbell

Scale Drawings and Scale Models

Courtesy Estes Industries,
Penrose, Colorado

A map is one kind of *scale drawing*. But scale drawings can be used to show many other things such as floor plans, building designs, machine parts, or car designs. Sometimes three-dimensional *scale models* are made. Each length on the scale drawing or scale model represents a given distance on the actual object.

Example: The model of a building is $12\frac{1}{2}$ inches tall. The scale is 1 inch = 4 feet. What is the height of the actual building?

You can use a proportion to find the actual height.

$$\frac{1 \text{ in.}}{4 \text{ ft}} = \frac{12\frac{1}{2} \text{ in.}}{h \text{ ft}} \qquad \frac{1}{4} = \frac{12\frac{1}{2}}{h}$$

$$h = 4 \times 12\frac{1}{2}$$

$$h = 50$$

Check: $\qquad \dfrac{1}{4} = \dfrac{12\frac{1}{2}}{50}$

$$50 \qquad\qquad 50 \checkmark$$

So the actual building is 50 feet tall.

■ Exercises

Assignment Guide 10.7
Oral: 1–2
Written: Min. 3–10
    Reg. 3–14
    Max. 3–17

A **1.** The length of the scale drawing is 5 cm. What proportion would you use to find the actual length of the building? $\frac{1}{3} = \frac{5}{x}$

Scale:
1 cm = 3 m

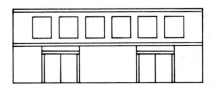

2. The height of the scale drawing is 2 cm. What proportion would you use to find the actual height of the building? $\frac{1}{3} = \frac{2}{x}$

B Copy and complete the following. Refer to the scale drawing above. Measure to the nearest 0.5 centimeter.

Measurement	Scale drawing (in cm)	Actual building (in m)
3. Distance between doorways	1.5	4.5
4. Width of each window	0.5	1.5

Refer to the scale drawing of the car to complete the following. Measure to the nearest 0.5 centimeter.

Scale:
1 cm = 0.6 m

Measurement	Scale drawing (in cm)	Actual car (in m)
5. Height (roof to ground)	2.5	1.5
6. Wheelbase (front-wheel center to rear-wheel center)	4.5	2.7
7. Outside diameter of tires	1	0.6
8. Width of door	1.5	0.9
9. Length of antenna	1	0.6
10. Length of side molding.	6.5	3.9

Complete the following table for a model ship that is based on a 1-to-48 reduction from the original. Thus, the scale is 1 in. = 4 ft.

Measurement	Scale model (in inches)	Actual ship (in feet)
11. Length	18 in.	72 ft
12. Height of mainmast	6 in.	24 ft
13. Height of midmast	$4\frac{1}{2}$ in.	18 ft
14. Height of mainsail	5 in.	20 ft

Photri

C Measure the arrow on each photo. Then use your measurement and the scale below the photo to find the corresponding measurement on the real object.

15.

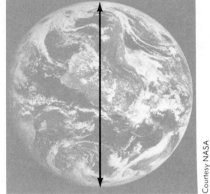
Courtesy NASA

8000 mi   **Scale: 1 in. = 4000 mi**

16.

Courtesy American Airlines

18 m   **Scale: 1 cm = 3 m**

17.

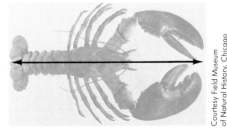
Courtesy Field Museum of Natural History, Chicago

25 cm   **Scale: 1 cm = 5 cm**

Activity 1

Bring a map of your state to class. Use the map to do these exercises.

1. What is the scale of the map?

2. Name the states that border your state.

3. Use the map to plan a trip. Then determine the distance you would travel if you really took the trip.

Activity 2

The floor plan of an apartment is shown below. Use the floor plan to do the following exercises.

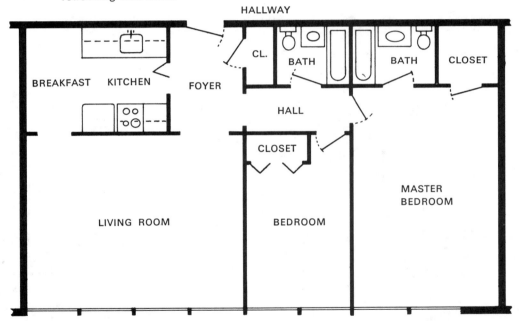

Floor plan scale: 1 inch = 8 feet

1. What are the length and width of the living room? How many square feet of carpeting would be needed to carpet the living room? 18 ft by 15 ft

2. How many 1-foot-by-1-foot tiles would be needed to tile the master bedroom? 228 tiles

3. Make a floor plan of your room at home. Use the same scale as that shown for the apartment above.

MATH AND PIPELINES

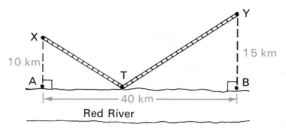

An oil company owns two oil wells. One is located at X and the other at Y. The company wants to connect the two wells by pipeline to a single storage tank T located along the Red River. How far from A should they build the tank so the least amount of pipe is used?

Suppose the distances remained the same, but Y was on the opposite side of riverbank AB. (See drawing below.) Then the shortest distance from X to Y would be on a straight line. You could draw that straight line to locate T.

$\triangle$XAT is similar to $\triangle$YBT.

So, $\dfrac{AT}{TB}$ should equal $\dfrac{AX}{BY}$.

$$\frac{AX}{BY} = \frac{10}{15} = \frac{2}{3}$$

So, use $2x$ and $3x$ for AT and TB and let the sum equal 40.

$$2x + 3x = 40$$

$$5x = 40$$

$$\frac{5x}{5} = \frac{40}{5}$$

$$x = 8$$

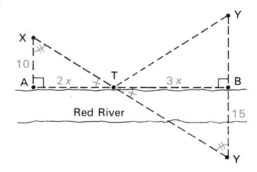

So, AT $= 2 \times 8 = 16$.

Locate the storage tank 16 km from A.

1. Assume the distance from A to B is 60 km. How far from A should the storage tank be built?   24 km

2. Assume the following distances: AX $= 20$ km, BY $= 10$ km, and AB $= 30$ km. How far from A should the storage tank be built?   20 km

Terms and Symbols Review

Suggested Class Time

Course	Min.	Reg.	Max.
Days	2	1	1

Complete each sentence. Choose from these words.

corresponding   *indirect*   *proportional*   *ratio*   *shape*   *size*

1. Similar figures have the same <u>Shape</u>, but may differ in <u>Size</u>.

2. In similar triangles, <u>Corresponding</u> angles have the same measure.

3. In similar triangles, corresponding sides are <u>Proportional</u>.

4. Similar triangles can be used to make <u>Indirect</u> measurements.

5. The scale of a map is usually given by a <u>Ratio</u>.

Chapter 10 Review

10.1   Which pairs of figures are similar?

Assignment Guide Rev.
Oral: Terms & Symbols 1–5
Written:
Min. (day 1) 1–13
    (day 2) 14–21
Reg. 1–13 odd; 14–21
Max. 1–13 odd; 14–21

1. Yes

2. No

3. No

4. Yes

5. Yes

6. No

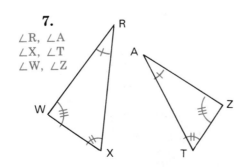

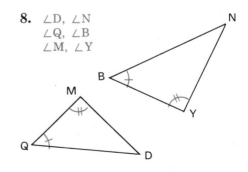

10.2   Name the corresponding angles for each pair of similar triangles.

7.
∠R, ∠A
∠X, ∠T
∠W, ∠Z

8. ∠D, ∠N
∠Q, ∠B
∠M, ∠Y

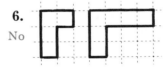

344

Name the corresponding sides for each pair of similar triangles.

9.

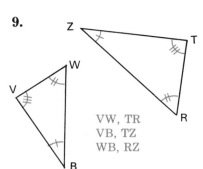

VW, TR
VB, TZ
WB, RZ

10.

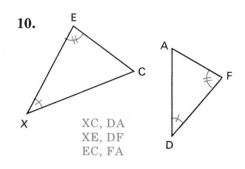

XC, DA
XE, DF
EC, FA

What letter should replace each question mark ?

△RPW is similar to △ZNV.

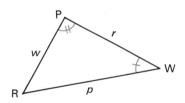

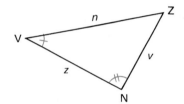

11. $\dfrac{w}{v} = \dfrac{p}{?}$ n

12. $\dfrac{r}{z} = \dfrac{w}{?}$ v

13. $\dfrac{p}{n} = \dfrac{?}{v}$ w

14. Find the values of x and z. $x = 7.6,\ z = 8$

△ABC is similar to △DEF.

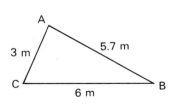

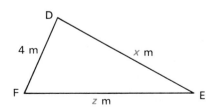

Use similar triangles to solve the problem.

10.4   **15.** What is the height of the tree? (The triangles are similar.) 36 ft

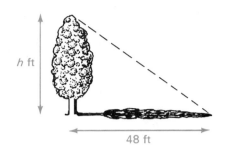
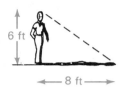

10.5   **16.** You want the cue ball at C to bank off the wall at B and hit the eight ball at E. What is true about △ABC and △DBE? They are similar.

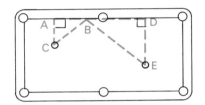

10.6   Use this map to complete the table.

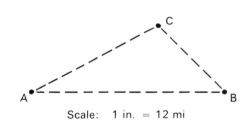

Scale: 1 in. = 12 mi

Distance between	Map distance (in inches)	Actual distance (in miles)
17. A and B	2	24
18. B and C	1	12
19. C and A	$1\frac{1}{2}$	18

10.7   Use the scale drawing to answer the questions.

Scale: 1 in. = 2 ft

20. What is the actual width of the cabinet? 3 ft ·

21. What is the actual height of the cabinet? $1\frac{1}{2}$ ft

Chapter 10 Test

Name the corresponding angles and corresponding sides for each pair of similar triangles.

1. $\angle$D, $\angle$A; $\angle$X, $\angle$Z; $\angle$B, $\angle$W; XD, ZA; XB, ZW; BD, WA

2.

Assignment Guide Test
Written: 1–9

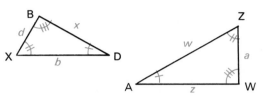

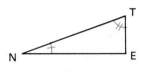

$\angle$N, $\angle$V; $\angle$E, $\angle$F; $\angle$T, $\angle$I; NE, VF; NT, VI; TE, IF

What letter should replace each question mark? Refer to Exercise 1.

3. $\frac{x}{z} = \frac{b}{?}$ w **4.** $\frac{d}{a} = \frac{?}{z}$ x **5.** $\frac{b}{?} = \frac{d}{a}$ w

Solve for x and z in each pair of similar triangles.

6. $x = 4$, $z = 8$

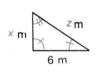

7. $x = 20$, $z = 17.5$

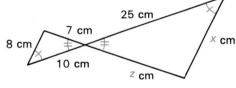

8. What is the actual distance between A and B? Between B and C? Between C and A?

8 mi; 12 mi; 6 mi

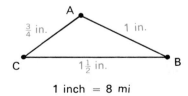

1 inch = 8 mi

9. Find the height of the building. (The triangles are similar.)

12 m

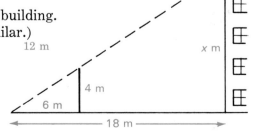

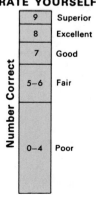
347

Terms and Symbols Review: Chapters 8–10

Which lettered choice best matches each numbered item?

Ch. 8

1. the point at $(0, 0)$ d

2. horizontal axis   e

3. 2 for the point at $(2, {}^-3)$ g

4. positive direction on the y-axis   a

5. negative direction on the x-axis   b

6. the graph of $({}^-1, 0)$ c

Ch. 9

7. the ratio of 2 to 5   n

8. a proportion   h

9. the ratio of 2 to 100   m

10. extremes of $\frac{2}{5} = \frac{4}{10}$ i

11. a cross product for $\frac{2}{5} = \frac{4}{10}$ l

a. up

b. left

c. point

d. origin

e. x-axis

f. y-axis

g. x-coordinate

h. $\frac{2}{9} = \frac{4}{18}$

i. 2 and 10

j. 5 and 4

k. 2×5

l. 20

m. 2%

n. $\frac{2}{5}$

Ch. 10

Complete each sentence. Choose from these words.

angles   *sides*   *scale*   *similar*   *corresponding*

12. _Similar_ _____ figures have the same shape, but may differ in size.

13. In similar triangles, corresponding _Angles_ _____ have the same measure.

14. The _Scale_ _____ of a map is usually given by a ratio.

15. In similar triangles, _Corresponding_ _____ sides are proportional.

Assignment Guide Rev.
Oral: Terms & Symbols 1–15
Written:
Min. (day 1) 1–5; 8–16
     (day 2) 17–25; 29–32
Reg. 1–5; 8–26 even; 29–32
Max. 1–7; 8–32 even

1. Use the rule to complete the table below.

Ch. 8

$y = 2x - 5$

x	$^-2$	$^-1$	0	1	2	3
y	$^-9,$	$^-7,$	$^-5,$	$^-3,$	$^-1,$	1

2. Write the ordered pair for each point on the graph at the right.

a. A   **b.** B   **c.** C   **d.** D
($^-4$, 5) (3, 3) (5, $^-4$) (0, $^-2$)

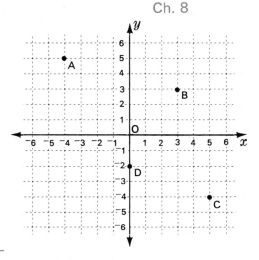

3. Draw a line graph for the table below.

time (hr)	0	1	2	3	4	5	6
temperature (0 °C)	$^-5$	$^-3$	0	1	3	$^-1$	$^-4$

4. Is the set of ordered pairs (1, 3), (1, 4), and ($^-3$, 5) a function?   No

5. A bus is traveling at a rate (r) of 55 mph. How long (t) will it take the bus to go 165 miles (d)? $r \times t = d$ 3 h

Copy and graph the following.

6. a slide 5 units down

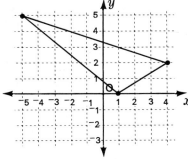

7. a 1-to-2 reduction

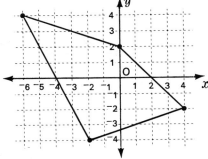

8. Write the ratio of 12 votes to 5 votes. $\frac{12}{5}$, 12 : 5, 12 to 5

Ch. 9

9. Write two ratios equivalent to $\frac{5}{7}$.   Answers will vary.

Solve.

10. $\frac{3}{4} = \frac{n}{24}$ 18

11. $\frac{6}{n} = \frac{60}{37}$ 3.7

Use a proportion to solve.

12. 1 pound of asparagus serves 3 people. How many pounds will serve 15 people? 5 lb

Write as (a) a fraction or mixed number and (b) a decimal.

13. 36%   a. $\frac{9}{25}$ b. 0.36

14. 130%   a. $1\frac{3}{10}$ b. 1.3

15. 17.6%   a. $\frac{22}{125}$ b. 0.176

16. $2\frac{1}{2}$%   a. $\frac{1}{40}$ b. 0.025

Express as a per cent.

17. 0.29   29%

18. 3.5   350%

19. $\frac{2}{5}$ 40%

20. 9   900%

Solve.

21. What is 20% of 92?   18.4

22. 32 is 75% of what? $42\frac{2}{3}$

23. 45 is what per cent of 180?   25%

24. What is $8\frac{1}{2}$% of 100? $8\frac{1}{2}$

25. Morrie averages 14% in tips. How much does he receive in tips on customers' bills of $350? $49

26. Tell how you would round to estimate 29% of 432.   Typical answer: 0.3 × 400

27. An increase from 32 to 40 is what per cent of increase?   25%

28. A decrease from 20 to 18 is what per cent of decrease?   10%

Ch. 10

29. Name the corresponding sides and the corresponding angles.

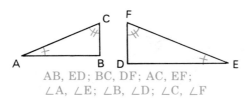

AB, ED; BC, DF; AC, EF;
∠A, ∠E; ∠B, ∠D; ∠C, ∠F

30. Find the values of x and z.

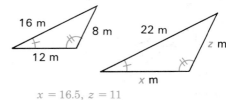

$x = 16.5$, $z = 11$

31. What is the height of the pole?   150 in.

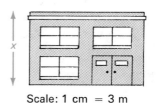

32. Use the scale drawing to find the actual height of the building.   6 m

Scale: 1 cm = 3 m

350

Give the opposite of each number.   6.1

1. 3 $^-3$ **2.** $^-10$ 10 **3.** 25 $^-25$

Give the absolute value of each number.   6.3

4. 12 12 **5.** $^-14$ 14 **6.** 0 0

Compute.

7. $\frac{1}{7} + \frac{3}{7}$ $\frac{4}{7}$ **8.** $\frac{5}{9} - \frac{4}{9}$ $\frac{1}{9}$ **9.** $\frac{3}{4} + \frac{2}{4}$ $1\frac{1}{4}$ 4.7

10. $\frac{1}{2} - \frac{2}{5}$ $\frac{1}{10}$ **11.** $\frac{2}{3} + \frac{1}{6}$ $\frac{5}{6}$ **12.** $\frac{5}{8} - \frac{1}{6}$ $\frac{11}{24}$ 4.8

13. $1\frac{5}{6} - 1\frac{3}{4}$ $\frac{1}{12}$ **14.** $2\frac{1}{2} + 1\frac{7}{8}$ $4\frac{3}{8}$ **15.** $3\frac{1}{2} - 2\frac{2}{3}$ $\frac{5}{6}$ 4.9

16. $0.47 + 0.23$ 0.7 **17.** $6.73 - 2.41$ 4.32 **18.** $2.537 - 1.72$ 0.817 5.3

19. $^-7 + 6$ $^-1$ **20.** $7 + ^-5$ 2 **21.** $^-8 + ^-18$ $^-26$ 6.3

22. $6 - 13$ $^-7$ **23.** $^-7 - 13$ $^-20$ **24.** $8 - ^-26$ 34 6.4

25. $6 \div ^-3$ $^-2$ **26.** $^-6 \div 3$ $^-2$ **27.** $^-6 \div ^-3$ 2 7.3

Solve.

28. $a + 8 = 24$ 16 **29.** $15 = b + 7$ 8 6.5

30. $14 = c + ^-2$ 16 **31.** $d + ^-3 = ^-4$ $^-1$

32. $e - 3 = 6$ 9 **33.** $27 = f - 15$ 42 6.6

34. $7 = g - ^-10$ $^-3$ **35.** $h - ^-6 = ^-3$ $^-9$

Suggested Class Time			
Course	Min.	Reg.	Max.
Days	1	1	0

Assignment Guide GR 11
Written: Min. 1–35
Reg. 1–35

ADDING AND
SUBTRACTING
RATIONAL NUMBERS

11

Earlier, you saw that the numbers called *integers* are just the whole numbers and their opposites.

Integers: $\cdots$, $^-4$, $^-3$, $^-2$, $^-1$, 0, 1, 2, 3, 4, $\cdots$

Now you will see that other numbers, besides whole numbers, also have opposites. And you will add and subtract with such numbers.

Rational Numbers

The quotient of two positive integers can be expressed as a *positive fraction*.

$$3 \div 4 = \frac{3}{4} \qquad\qquad 14 \div 9 = \frac{14}{9}$$

Also, the quotient of two negative integers is *positive* and can be expressed as a *positive fraction*.

$$^-3 \div {}^-4 = \frac{3}{4} \qquad\qquad {}^-14 \div {}^-9 = \frac{14}{9}$$

If two integers have different signs, their quotient is *negative*, and it can be expressed as a *negative fraction*.

$$^-5 \div 2 = \frac{^-5}{2} \qquad\qquad 5 \div {}^-2 = \frac{5}{^-2}$$

$$= -\frac{5}{2} \qquad\qquad = -\frac{5}{2}$$

$$\text{same}$$

So $\quad\boxed{-\dfrac{5}{2} = \dfrac{^-5}{2} = \dfrac{5}{^-2}}$

A **rational number** is any number that can be named by a fraction whose numerator and denominator are integers. (Of course, the denominator cannot be zero.)

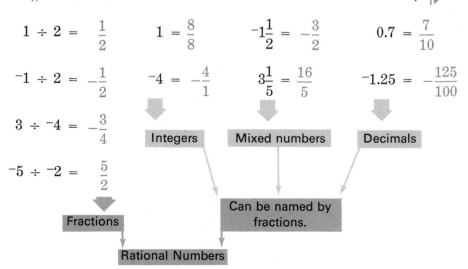

$1 \div 2 = \dfrac{1}{2}$ $\qquad$ $1 = \dfrac{8}{8}$ $\qquad$ $-1\dfrac{1}{2} = -\dfrac{3}{2}$ $\qquad$ $0.7 = \dfrac{7}{10}$

$^-1 \div 2 = -\dfrac{1}{2}$ $\qquad$ $^-4 = -\dfrac{4}{1}$ $\qquad$ $3\dfrac{1}{5} = \dfrac{16}{5}$ $\qquad$ $^-1.25 = -\dfrac{125}{100}$

$3 \div {}^-4 = -\dfrac{3}{4}$ $\qquad\qquad$ Integers $\qquad$ Mixed numbers $\qquad$ Decimals

$^-5 \div {}^-2 = \dfrac{5}{2}$

Fractions $\qquad$ Can be named by fractions.

Rational Numbers

Example 1: How do you read $-\frac{1}{2}$ and $^-1.5$?

$-\dfrac{1}{2}$ is read "negative one-half."

$^-1.5$ is read "negative one and five-tenths."

You know how to draw a number line that shows positive and negative integers. You can show positive and negative fractions on a number line by naming points between the integer points.

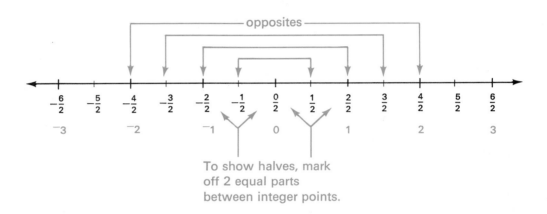

You can draw number lines for thirds, fourths, fifths, and so on, by marking off 3, 4, 5, and so on, equal parts between integer points. The set of all numbers shown on such number lines is called the set of **rational numbers.**

Example 2: What number is the opposite of $\frac{2}{3}$? Of $^-1.5$?

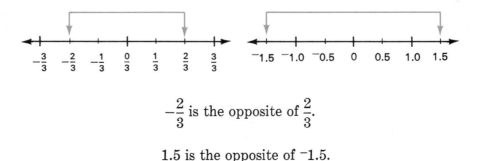

$-\dfrac{2}{3}$ is the opposite of $\dfrac{2}{3}$.

1.5 is the opposite of $^-1.5$.

Example 3: Give the absolute values of $\frac{1}{2}$, 2.6, 0, $^-3\frac{2}{5}$, and $^-1.16$.

Number	Its absolute value	
$\frac{1}{2}$ or $+\frac{1}{2}$	$\frac{1}{2}$	The absolute value of a positive rational number or 0 is the number itself.
2.6	2.6	
0	0	
$^-3\frac{2}{5}$	$3\frac{2}{5}$	The absolute value of a negative rational number is its opposite.
$^-1.16$	1.16	

Assignment Guide 11.1
Oral: 1–7
Written: Min. 8–26
Reg. 8–29
Max. 8–31

■ Exercises

A Use the terms below to complete the following statements.

rational numbers	*positive*	*fraction*
absolute value	*negative*	*opposites*

1. A rational number is any number that can be named by a ＿＿＿ whose numerator and denominator are integers. Fraction

2. $1\frac{5}{8}$ and $^-1\frac{5}{8}$ are ＿＿＿ of each other. Opposites

3. $1\frac{5}{8}$ is the ＿＿＿ of $^-1\frac{5}{8}$ and $1\frac{5}{8}$. Absolute value

4. $\frac{5}{6}$, $^-2$, $^-7\frac{1}{3}$, 0, 9.2, $-\frac{3}{2}$, and $^-2.5$ are ＿＿＿. Rational numbers

5. The quotient of two integers with different signs can be expressed as a ＿＿＿ fraction. Negative

6. The quotient of two negative integers can be expressed as a ＿＿＿ fraction. Positive

7. On a number line, ＿＿＿ fractions are shown to the left of 0. Negative

Give the opposite of each number.

8. $-\frac{1}{2}$ $\frac{1}{2}$ **9.** $\frac{3}{4}$ $-\frac{3}{4}$ **10.** 0.34 $^-0.34$ **11.** $^-0.57$
                                                                                                          0.57

12. $\frac{5}{3}$ $-\frac{5}{3}$ **13.** $3\frac{1}{2}$ $^-3\frac{1}{2}$ **14.** $^-1\frac{2}{3}$ $1\frac{2}{3}$ **15.** $^-4.795$
                                                                                                          4.795

Give the absolute value of each number.

16. $-\frac{1}{3}$ $\frac{1}{3}$ **17.** $\frac{3}{8}$ $\frac{3}{8}$ **18.** 0.96 0.96 **19.** $^-0.34$
                                                                                                          0.34

20. $\frac{7}{5}$ $\frac{7}{5}$ **21.** $4\frac{1}{6}$ $4\frac{1}{6}$ **22.** $^-1\frac{3}{4}$ $1\frac{3}{4}$ **23.** $^-3.159$
                                                                                                          3.159

Graph the following. Use a separate number line for each exercise.

Example: Graph $-\frac{5}{4}$, $-\frac{1}{4}$, $\frac{3}{4}$, and $\frac{7}{4}$ on a number line.

Step 1:   Mark off and label integer points.

Step 2:   Mark off 4 equal parts between integer points and label them.

Step 3:   Graph $-\frac{5}{4}$, $-\frac{1}{4}$, $\frac{3}{4}$, and $\frac{7}{4}$.

24. $-\frac{6}{2}$, $-\frac{1}{2}$, $\frac{3}{2}$, $\frac{5}{2}$ **25.** $-\frac{4}{3}$, $-\frac{1}{3}$, $\frac{1}{3}$, $\frac{4}{3}$

26. $-\frac{9}{5}$, $-\frac{3}{5}$, $\frac{2}{5}$, $\frac{6}{5}$ **27.** $-\frac{8}{6}$, $-\frac{5}{6}$, $\frac{5}{6}$, $\frac{10}{6}$

28. $-\frac{11}{8}$, $-\frac{6}{8}$, $\frac{5}{8}$, $\frac{11}{8}$ **29.** $-\frac{13}{10}$, $-\frac{5}{10}$, $\frac{4}{10}$, $\frac{16}{10}$

30. $-\frac{5}{3}$, $-\frac{1}{2}$, $-\frac{1}{3}$, $\frac{0}{3}$, $\frac{2}{3}$, $\frac{4}{2}$, $\frac{7}{3}$

31. $-\frac{5}{3}$, $-\frac{3}{4}$, $-\frac{2}{3}$, $\frac{0}{4}$, $\frac{5}{4}$, $\frac{4}{3}$, $\frac{6}{4}$

Comparing Fractions

11.2

You can use a number line to compare two rational numbers like $\frac{4}{5}$ and $\frac{2}{3}$.

Since $\frac{4}{5}$ is to the right of $\frac{2}{3}$, $\frac{4}{5} > \frac{2}{3}$ or $\frac{2}{3} < \frac{4}{5}$.

An easier way to compare two rational numbers is to rename them so they have the same *positive* denominator. Then compare the numerators.

Example 1:   Compare $\frac{4}{5}$ and $\frac{2}{3}$.

$$\frac{4}{5} = \frac{4 \times 3}{5 \times 3} = \frac{12}{15}$$

$$12 > 10, \quad \text{so} \quad \frac{12}{15} > \frac{10}{15}$$

$$\frac{2}{3} = \frac{2 \times 5}{3 \times 5} = \frac{10}{15} \qquad \text{and} \quad \frac{4}{5} > \frac{2}{3}.$$

Example 2:   Compare $-\frac{7}{8}$ and $-\frac{5}{6}$.

$$-\frac{7}{8} = \frac{^-7}{8} = \frac{^-7 \times 3}{8 \times 3} = \frac{^-21}{24}$$

Note: To compare negative fractions, think of the numerators as being negative.

$$^-21 < ^-20, \quad \text{so} \quad \frac{^-21}{24} < \frac{^-20}{24}$$

$$-\frac{5}{6} = \frac{^-5}{6} = \frac{^-5 \times 4}{6 \times 4} = \frac{^-20}{24} \qquad \text{and} \quad -\frac{7}{8} < -\frac{5}{6}.$$

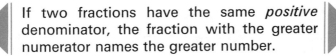

If two fractions have the same *positive* denominator, the fraction with the greater numerator names the greater number.

357

Example 3: Compare $\frac{3}{5}$ and $\frac{6}{10}$.

$$\frac{3}{5} = \frac{3 \times 2}{5 \times 2} = \frac{6}{10}, \quad \text{so} \quad \frac{3}{5} = \frac{6}{10}.$$

■ Exercises

Assignment Guide 11.2
Oral: 1–6
Written: Min. 7–21
      Reg. 7–25
      Max. 7–30

A Tell which fraction in each pair names the greater number.

1. $\frac{5}{12}$ or $\frac{7}{12}$

2. $\frac{9}{16}$ or $\frac{3}{16}$

3. $-\frac{7}{12}$ or $-\frac{5}{12}$

4. $-\frac{11}{20}$ or $-\frac{9}{20}$

5. $-\frac{1}{2}$ or $\frac{1}{2}$

6. $-\frac{2}{3}$ or $\frac{3}{4}$

B Should >, <, or = replace ● to make the sentence true?

7. $\frac{4}{9}$ ● $\frac{7}{9}$ <

8. $-\frac{5}{7}$ ● $-\frac{3}{7}$ <

9. $\frac{3}{4}$ ● $-\frac{2}{3}$ >

10. $\frac{1}{3}$ ● $\frac{1}{2}$ <

11. $\frac{3}{4}$ ● $\frac{5}{2}$ <

12. $\frac{3}{4}$ ● $-\frac{9}{12}$ >

13. $-\frac{7}{24}$ ● $-\frac{3}{8}$ >

14. $\frac{5}{16}$ ● $-\frac{1}{4}$ >

15. $\frac{5}{8}$ ● $\frac{10}{16}$ =

16. $-\frac{10}{12}$ ● $-\frac{5}{6}$ =

17. $-\frac{7}{8}$ ● $-\frac{8}{9}$ >

18. $\frac{9}{16}$ ● $\frac{11}{24}$ >

19. $\frac{7}{4}$ ● $-\frac{5}{3}$ >

20. $\frac{6}{5}$ ● $\frac{5}{4}$ <

21. $-\frac{8}{5}$ ● $\frac{4}{3}$ <

C Use the shortcut below to find whether the first rational number in each pair is greater than or less than the second one.

Examples: a. $\dfrac{3}{4}$ ╳ $\dfrac{1}{2}$ → $4 \times 1 = 4$ - - - - → $6 > 4$, so $\dfrac{3}{4} > \dfrac{1}{2}$.
$3 \times 2 = 6$ - - - - →

b. $\dfrac{-2}{3}$ ╳ $\dfrac{-5}{8}$ → $3 \times {}^{-}5 = {}^{-}15$ - - - → ${}^{-}16 < {}^{-}15$, so $\dfrac{-2}{3} < \dfrac{-5}{8}$.
${}^{-}2 \times 8 = {}^{-}16$ - - →

22. $\frac{2}{3}$, $\frac{1}{2}$ >

23. $\frac{9}{10}$, $\frac{7}{12}$ >

24. $\frac{3}{4}$, $\frac{4}{5}$ <

25. $\frac{-2}{3}$, $\frac{-3}{4}$ >

26. $\frac{-5}{12}$, $\frac{-1}{3}$ <

27. $\frac{-7}{8}$, $\frac{-3}{4}$ <

28. $\frac{4}{5}$, $\frac{-3}{4}$ >

29. $\frac{-3}{8}$, $\frac{2}{5}$ <

30. $\frac{5}{6}$, $\frac{-13}{16}$ >

Changes in 12-Hour Barometer Readings	
Time	Change
6 A.M. Mon.	
	−0.25
6 P.M. Mon.	
	−0.18
6 A.M. Tues.	
	+0.35
6 P.M. Tues.	
	+0.12
6 A.M. Wed.	

Courtesy NOAA

Barometer readings and rainfall amounts are two examples of weather information given with decimals. So weather forecasters must sometimes add and subtract with decimals.

Suggested Class Time			
Course	Min.	Reg.	Max.
Days	1	1	1

Example 1: Add.

a. $^-0.25$ and $^-0.18$

Both addends have the same sign.

$$^-0.25 + {}^-0.18$$

Add their absolute values. $\quad 0.25 + 0.18$

Use the sign of the addends. $\nearrow$ $^-0.43$

$$^-0.25 + {}^-0.18 = {}^-0.43$$

b. $^-0.18$ and 0.35

The addends have different signs.

$$^-0.18 + 0.35$$

$0.35 - 0.18$ $\quad$ Subtract their absolute values.

$+0.17$ $\quad$ Use the sign of the addend with the greater absolute value.

$$^-0.18 + 0.35 = 0.17$$

Example 2: Add 0.12 and ⁻0.12.

The Inverse Property of Addition, stated on page 178, can be used for rational numbers that are opposites.

$$0.12 + {}^-0.12 = 0$$

opposites   sum

Example 3: Subtract ⁻0.18 from 29.72.

$$29.72 - {}^-0.18 = 29.72 + 0.18 \qquad \text{To subtract } {}^-0.18,$$
$$\text{add its opposite.}$$
$$= 29.90$$

▥ Exercises

Assignment Guide 11.3
Oral: 1–12
Written:
Min. 13–32
Reg. 13–27 odd; 28–44
Max. 13–27 odd; 28–46

A Tell whether each sum is positive, negative, or zero.

1. 1.8 + 4.7 Pos.

2. ⁻0.73 + ⁻0.69 Neg.

3. 1.217 + ⁻1.952 Neg.

4. ⁻27.22 + 14.96 Neg.

5. 6.251 + ⁻4.213 Pos.

6. ⁻8.3 + 8.3 Zero

Tell how to change each subtraction to an addition.

7. 1.6 − 1.9
  1.6 + ⁻1.9

8. ⁻4.3 − ⁻5.6
  ⁻4.3 + 5.6

9. 8.27 − ⁻6.28
  8.27 + 6.28

10. ⁻7.234 − 1.732
  ⁻7.234 + ⁻1.732

11. 0.632 − ⁻9.568
  0.632 + 9.568

12. ⁻7.35 − 17.58
  ⁻7.35 + ⁻17.58

B Find each sum or difference.

13. 1.9 + 3.8 5.7

14. ⁻1.6 + ⁻5.9 ⁻7.5

15. 0.834 + ⁻4.675
  ⁻3.841

16. ⁻1.732 + 1.414
  ⁻0.318

17. 6.38 + ⁻6.38 0

18. ⁻4.7 + 4.7 0

19. 4.9 − 1.6 3.3

20. 8.3 − 9.7 ⁻1.4

21. ⁻4.65 − 3.78
  ⁻8.43

22. ⁻1.752 − 2.869
  ⁻4.621

23. 6.5 − ⁻4.8 11.3

24. 7.65 − ⁻10.87
  18.52

25. 2.366 + ⁻1.021
  1.345

26. ⁻8.65 + 9.52 0.87

27. ⁻4.1 − ⁻2.3 ⁻1.8

28. $^-8.751 - {}^-9.914$ 1.163

29. $0.125 - 0.876$ $^-0.751$

30. $0.35 + 0.75$ 1.1

31. $^-0.165 + {}^-0.425$ $^-0.59$

32. $0.438 + {}^-5.76$ $^-5.322$

33. $^-17.3 - 21.4$ $^-38.7$

34. $8.6 - {}^-2.93$ 11.53

35. $^-1.4 - {}^-6$ 4.6

36. $^-2.371 + 4$ 1.629

37. $^-7.41 + {}^-6.9$ $^-14.31$

38. $66.23 + {}^-21.1$ 45.13

39. $^-1.23 - {}^-0.879$ $^-0.351$

40. $^-13 - 11.98$ $^-24.98$

41. $6.28 - {}^-29.52$ 35.8

42. $^-5.68 + 2.591$ $^-3.089$

C Solve each problem.

43. The profits of Ace Distributors for January through March are shown at the right. Find the total profit for the three months.

$541.61

Month	Profit
Jan.	$-$795.48
Feb.	$367.42
Mar.	$969.67

44. During one week, Jesse Floyd wrote checks for $20.95 and $16.49. The next week, he made a deposit of $30.00. What was the change in his bank balance for the two weeks? $^-$7.44

45. The changes in the Dow Jones stock average for one week are given at the right. Find the change for the week. $^-$5.32

Day	Change
Mon.	+1.76
Tues.	+4.38
Wed.	-2.69
Thur.	-5.99
Fri.	-2.78

46. The level of Oxbow Lake was 1.25 meters above normal in the spring. By late fall, it was 0.78 meter below normal ($^-0.78$). What change in water level is given by these two readings? $^-$2.03 m

MANAGING PERSONAL FINANCES

If you get an allowance or you work after school, you might be interested in how to manage your finances. The first step toward managing your finances is to keep a record of how you spend your money. One way is to use a chart like the one below.

Day	Item	Income/ expense	Cash on hand
	Balance from last week		18.94
Mon.	Lunch	⁻1.26	17.68
Tues.	Lunch	⁻1.34	16.34
	School supplies	⁻1.69	14.65
	Extra earnings	10.00	24.65
Wed.	Lunch	⁻1.58	23.07
	Record album	⁻7.71	15.36
Thurs.	Lunch	⁻1.19	14.17
	Gift from Aunt Phoebe	10.00	24.17
	Clothing	⁻21.73	2.44
Fri.	Lunch	⁻1.25	1.19
	Paycheck	65.50	66.69
	Toothbrush and comb	⁻2.64	64.05
Sat.	Deposit to savings	⁻40.00	24.05
	Movie	⁻4.00	20.05

Courtesy Rockwell International

Positive numbers show income amounts, and negative numbers show expenses. As each item is listed, its amount is added to the last number in the cash-on-hand column. So the cash-on-hand column tells you how much money you have at any given time.

Activity 1: Keep a record of your income and expenses for two or three weeks.

Activity 2: List each of your expenses for one week under one of the following six areas: Food, Clothing, Entertainment, Personal needs, Savings, and Other. Find the total for each area. Then find what per cent of your total income for the week was spent for each area. (*Example:* If total income was $60 and total expense for clothing was $15, then per cent of income spent for clothing was $\frac{15}{60} = .25 = 25\%$.) Do this for each week in Activity 1.

Solving Equations With Decimals

You can solve equations with decimals the same way you solve equations with integers.

Example 1: Solve $x + 4.7 = {}^-3$.

Suggested Class Time			
Course	Min.	Reg.	Max.
Days	1	1	1

$$x + 4.7 = {}^-3$$

$$x + 4.7 + {}^-4.7 = {}^-3 + {}^-4.7 \qquad \text{Add } {}^-4.7 \text{ to each side.}$$

$$x + 0 = {}^-7.7$$

$$x = {}^-7.7$$

Check: $\quad x + 4.7 = {}^-3$

$$^-7.7 + 4.7 = {}^-3 \qquad \text{Replace } x \text{ with } {}^-7.7.$$

$$^-3 = {}^-3 \ \checkmark$$

Example 2: Solve $^-3.1 = y - 2.4$.

$$^-3.1 = y - 2.4$$

$$^-3.1 = y + {}^-2.4 \qquad \text{Change } y - 2.4 \text{ to } y + {}^-2.4.$$

$$^-3.1 + 2.4 = y + {}^-2.4 + 2.4 \qquad \text{Add 2.4 to each side.}$$

$$^-0.7 = y + 0$$

$$^-0.7 = y$$

Check: $\quad ^-3.1 = y - 2.4$

$$^-3.1 = {}^-0.7 - 2.4 \qquad \text{Replace } y \text{ with } {}^-0.7.$$

$$^-3.1 = {}^-0.7 + {}^-2.4$$

$$^-3.1 = {}^-3.1 \ \checkmark$$

■ Exercises

Assignment Guide 11.4
Oral: 1–12
Written:
Min. 13–21; Quiz, p. 365
Reg. 13–29 odd; Quiz,
   p. 365
Max. 13–35 odd; Quiz,
   p. 365

A Tell what the first step would be for solving each equation.

1. $m + 6.7 = 9.4$
Add $^-6.7$ to each side.

2. $n + 1.3 = 8.6$
Add $^-1.3$ to each side.

3. $^-2.4 = t + {}^-3.7$
Add 3.7 to each side.

4. $q + 7.8 = 0$
Add $^-7.8$ to each side.

5. $10.5 = s + {}^-9.1$
Add 9.1 to each side.

6. $11.4 = r + {}^-11.4$
Add 11.4 to each side.

Tell what the first *two* steps would be for solving each equation.

7–12. Answers at bottom of page.

7. $d - 1.5 = 3.6$

8. $e - 2.6 = 1.4$

9. $f - {}^-5.9 = 10$

10. $0 = h - {}^-7.1$

11. $^-8.3 = g - {}^-0.3$

12. $^-0.09 = j - 0.09$

B Solve.

13. $n - 6.3 = 9.5$
15.8

14. $n - 7.62 = {}^-6.25$
1.37

15. $k + {}^-4.6 = 4.7$
9.3

16. $0 = t + {}^-1.5$
1.5

17. $6 = h + 2.7$
3.3

18. $n - {}^-4.63 = {}^-10$
$^-14.63$

19. $x - 4.2 = {}^-6.3$
$^-2.1$

20. $y - 3 = {}^-5.95$
$^-2.95$

21. $3.4 = m + {}^-0.16$
3.56

22. $x + 7.5 = {}^-2.5$
$^-10$

23. $n + 0.75 = {}^-0.26$
$^-1.01$

24. $y - {}^-4.7 = 9.7$
5

25. $b - 4.5 = 2.3$
6.8

26. $^-0.7 = t - {}^-3.48$
$^-4.18$

27. $^-5.3 + z = 0.68$
5.98

28. $7.1 + x = 4$
$^-3.1$

29. $^-10.9 = c + {}^-21$
10.1

30. $^-25 = {}^-3.75 + y$
$^-21.25$

C **31.** $1.5 - {}^-a = 8.7$ 7.2

32. $1.6 = {}^-0.77 - {}^-b$ 2.37

33. $(p + {}^-1.9) + 3.41 = 0$ $^-1.51$

34. $25.16 = (q + 7.8) + {}^-9.4$
26.76

35. $6.15 = {}^-3.5 + k + {}^-1.4$ 11.05

36. $^-10.76 = {}^-2.5 + m + {}^-17.4$
9.14

7. Change $d - 1.5$ to $d + {}^-1.5$.
   Add 1.5 to each side.

8. Change $e - 2.6$ to $e + {}^-2.6$.
   Add 2.6 to each side.

9. Change $f - {}^-5.9$ to $f + 5.9$.
   Add $^-5.9$ to each side.

10. Change $h - {}^-7.1$ to $h + 7.1$.
   Add $^-7.1$ to each side.

11. Change $g - {}^-0.3$ to $g + 0.3$.
   Add $^-0.3$ to each side.

12. Change $j - 0.09$ to $j + {}^-0.09$.
   Add 0.09 to each side.

MARKUP AND MARKDOWN

A storekeeper buys an item at the wholesale price and sells the item at the retail price, or sometimes at the sale price.

retail   wholesale   markup   sale   retail   markdown
price   price   price   price   (discount)

$$p = w + m \qquad\qquad s = p - d$$

Use the formulas above to answer the following:

1. The markup on a record album is $1.43. If the retail price is $5.98, what is the wholesale price? $4.55

2. The wholesale price of a sleeping bag is $59.24. If the retail price is $78.99, what is the markup? $19.75

3. A radio is on sale for $35.98. If the markdown is $4.01, what is the retail price? $39.99

4. The sale price of a ten-speed bicycle is $169.95. If the markdown is $84.98, what is the retail price? $254.93

Quick Quiz
Sections 11.1 to 11.4

1. $\frac{2}{3}$, $-\frac{7}{5}$, 8, $^-11$, $-2\frac{3}{4}$, $1\frac{1}{2}$, 0.7, and $^-3.26$ are all ____ numbers.   Rational

2. The opposite of $-\frac{3}{4}$ is ____. $\frac{3}{4}$

3. The absolute value of $^-0.73$ is ____.   0.73

Should $>$, $<$, or $=$ replace ▦ to make the sentence true?

4. $\frac{1}{3}$ ▦ $\frac{2}{3}$ $<$ **5.** $-\frac{3}{4}$ ▦ $-\frac{1}{4}$ $<$ **6.** $-\frac{2}{5}$ ▦ $-\frac{4}{10}$ $=$

Compute.

7. $1.8 + {}^-3.5$ $^-1.7$ **8.** $^-2.6 - {}^-3.15$ 0.55   **9.** $15.12 - 19.25$ $^-4.13$

Solve.

10. $x + 7.4 = 8.1$ 0.7   **11.** $^-10.27 = y - {}^-6.5$ $^-16.77$

365

11.5   Adding and Subtracting With Fractions

Example 1:   Add $-\frac{1}{4}$ and $-\frac{1}{8}$.

Example 2:   Add $\frac{3}{4}$ and $-\frac{1}{2}$.

Suggested Class Time			
Course	Min.	Reg.	Max.
Days	2	1	1

The addends have the same sign.

$$-\frac{1}{4} + \left(-\frac{1}{8}\right)$$

The addends have different signs.

$$\frac{3}{4} + \left(-\frac{1}{2}\right)$$

Rename, using the least common denominator.

$$-\frac{2}{8} + \left(-\frac{1}{8}\right)$$

$$\frac{3}{4} + \left(-\frac{2}{4}\right)$$

Rename, using the least common denominator.

Add the absolute values.

$$\frac{2}{8} + \frac{1}{8}$$

$$\frac{3}{4} - \frac{2}{4}$$

Subtract the absolute values.

Use the sign of the addends.

$$-\frac{3}{8}$$

$$+\frac{1}{4}$$

Use the sign of the addend with the greater absolute value.

$$-\frac{1}{4} + \left(-\frac{1}{8}\right) = -\frac{3}{8}$$

$$\frac{3}{4} + \left(-\frac{1}{2}\right) = \frac{1}{4}$$

Example 3:   Subtract $\frac{5}{6}$ from $\frac{1}{2}$.

$$\frac{1}{2} - \frac{5}{6} = \frac{1}{2} + \left(-\frac{5}{6}\right)$$

Subtracting $\frac{5}{6}$ is the same as adding $-\frac{5}{6}$.

$$= \frac{3}{6} + \left(-\frac{5}{6}\right)$$

$$= -\frac{2}{6}$$

$$= -\frac{1}{3}$$

Simplify.

■ Exercises

Assignment Guide 11.5
Oral: 1–12
Written: Min. (day 1) 13–24
(day 2) 25–36
Reg. 13–35 odd
Max. 13–43 odd

$\boxed{A}$ Tell whether each sum is positive, negative, or zero.

1. $\frac{3}{4} + \frac{2}{3}$ Pos. **2.** $\frac{1}{8} + (-\frac{7}{8})$ Neg. **3.** $-\frac{1}{4} + (-\frac{3}{8})$ Neg.

4. $-\frac{5}{6} + 0$ Neg. **5.** $-\frac{1}{2} + \frac{1}{4}$ Neg. **6.** $\frac{9}{10} + (-\frac{9}{10})$ Zero

Tell how to change each subtraction to an addition.

7. $\frac{1}{8} - \frac{7}{8}$ $\frac{1}{8} + \left(-\frac{7}{8}\right)$ **8.** $-\frac{1}{4} - (-\frac{1}{2})$ $-\frac{1}{4} + \frac{1}{2}$ **9.** $\frac{1}{2} - (-\frac{3}{8})$ $\frac{1}{2} + \frac{3}{8}$

10. $-\frac{1}{6} - \frac{1}{2}$ $-\frac{1}{6} + \left(-\frac{1}{2}\right)$ **11.** $-\frac{2}{3} - (-\frac{1}{2})$ $-\frac{2}{3} + \frac{1}{2}$ **12.** $\frac{1}{8} - (-\frac{2}{3})$ $\frac{1}{8} + \frac{2}{3}$

$\boxed{B}$ Find each sum.

13. $\frac{1}{3} + \frac{1}{2}$ $\frac{5}{6}$ **14.** $\frac{1}{4} + (-\frac{3}{4})$ $-\frac{1}{2}$ **15.** $-\frac{7}{10} + \frac{1}{10}$ $-\frac{3}{5}$

16. $-\frac{1}{5} + (-\frac{2}{5})$ $-\frac{3}{5}$ **17.** $\frac{1}{4} + (-\frac{1}{4})$ 0 **18.** $-\frac{1}{2} + \frac{4}{8}$ 0

19. $-\frac{1}{3} + (-\frac{3}{8})$ $-\frac{17}{24}$ **20.** $\frac{1}{4} + (-\frac{7}{8})$ $-\frac{5}{8}$ **21.** $-\frac{1}{4} + (-\frac{5}{8})$ $-\frac{7}{8}$

22. $\frac{7}{8} + (-\frac{3}{4})$ $\frac{1}{8}$ **23.** $-\frac{1}{2} + \frac{1}{4}$ $-\frac{1}{4}$ **24.** $\frac{3}{4} + (-\frac{1}{2})$ $\frac{1}{4}$

Find each difference.

25. $\frac{7}{8} - \frac{3}{8}$ $\frac{1}{2}$ **26.** $\frac{1}{2} - \frac{2}{3}$ $-\frac{1}{6}$ **27.** $-\frac{1}{6} - \frac{1}{2}$ $-\frac{2}{3}$

28. $\frac{5}{8} - (-\frac{1}{4})$ $\frac{7}{8}$ **29.** $-\frac{3}{5} - (-\frac{1}{5})$ $-\frac{2}{5}$ **30.** $-\frac{1}{4} - \frac{1}{2}$ $-\frac{3}{4}$

31. $-\frac{1}{2} - (-\frac{7}{8})$ $\frac{3}{8}$ **32.** $\frac{2}{3} - \frac{3}{4}$ $-\frac{1}{12}$ **33.** $\frac{1}{2} - \frac{9}{10}$ $-\frac{2}{5}$

34. $\frac{1}{2} - (-\frac{1}{4})$ $\frac{3}{4}$ **35.** $-\frac{7}{8} - (-\frac{1}{2})$ $-\frac{3}{8}$ **36.** $-\frac{1}{4} - (-\frac{2}{3})$ $\frac{5}{12}$

$\boxed{C}$ Compute.

37. $\frac{5}{12} + (-\frac{5}{8})$ $-\frac{5}{24}$ **38.** $-\frac{4}{15} - (-\frac{9}{10})$ $\frac{19}{30}$ **39.** $\frac{5}{9} - \frac{5}{6}$ $-\frac{5}{18}$

40. $-\frac{6}{11} + \frac{2}{3}$ $\frac{4}{33}$ **41.** $\frac{9}{14} + (-\frac{3}{4})$ $-\frac{3}{28}$ **42.** $\frac{1}{9} - \frac{1}{8}$ $-\frac{1}{72}$

43. $(\frac{1}{4} + \frac{1}{8}) + (-\frac{1}{2})$ $-\frac{1}{8}$ **44.** $-\frac{3}{5} + (-\frac{2}{3} + \frac{4}{5})$ $-\frac{7}{15}$

Adding and Subtracting With Mixed Numbers

11.6

Example 1: Add $-1\frac{1}{2}$ and $-1\frac{1}{4}$.

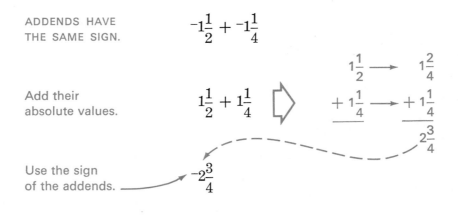

ADDENDS HAVE
THE SAME SIGN.

$$-1\frac{1}{2} + {}^-1\frac{1}{4}$$

Add their
absolute values.

$$1\frac{1}{2} + 1\frac{1}{4}$$

$$\begin{array}{rcl} 1\frac{1}{2} & \longrightarrow & 1\frac{2}{4} \\ + 1\frac{1}{4} & \longrightarrow & + 1\frac{1}{4} \\ \hline & & 2\frac{3}{4} \end{array}$$

Use the sign
of the addends.

$$-2\frac{3}{4}$$

Suggested Class Time

Course	Min.	Reg.	Max.
Days	2	1	1

$$-1\frac{1}{2} + {}^-1\frac{1}{4} = {}^-2\frac{3}{4}$$

Example 2: Add $-1\frac{5}{6}$ and $3\frac{1}{6}$.

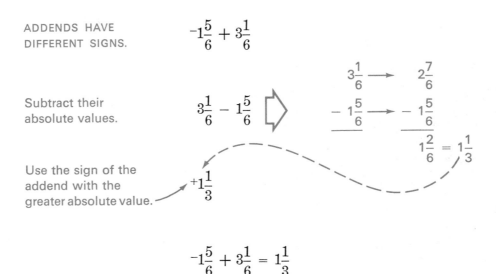

ADDENDS HAVE
DIFFERENT SIGNS.

$$-1\frac{5}{6} + 3\frac{1}{6}$$

Subtract their
absolute values.

$$3\frac{1}{6} - 1\frac{5}{6}$$

$$\begin{array}{rcl} 3\frac{1}{6} & \longrightarrow & 2\frac{7}{6} \\ - 1\frac{5}{6} & \longrightarrow & - 1\frac{5}{6} \\ \hline & & 1\frac{2}{6} = 1\frac{1}{3} \end{array}$$

Use the sign of the
addend with the
greater absolute value.

$$+1\frac{1}{3}$$

$$-1\frac{5}{6} + 3\frac{1}{6} = 1\frac{1}{3}$$

Example 3: Subtract $^-1\frac{3}{5}$ from $^-2$.

$$^-2 - {}^-1\frac{3}{5} = {}^-2 + 1\frac{3}{5}$$

Subtracting $^-1\frac{3}{5}$ is the same as adding $1\frac{3}{5}$.

$$= {}^-1\frac{5}{5} + 1\frac{3}{5}$$

$$= -\frac{2}{5}$$

Assignment Guide 11.6
Oral: 1–12
Written:
Min. (day 1) 13–22
     (day 2) 23–33
Reg. 13–33 odd
Max. 13–37 odd

■ Exercises

$\boxed{A}$ Tell whether each sum is positive, negative, or zero.

1. $1\frac{1}{3} + 2\frac{1}{4}$ Pos.
    2. $-\frac{3}{8} + 1\frac{5}{8}$ Pos.
    3. $^-2\frac{1}{4} + {}^-1\frac{3}{4}$ Neg.

4. $2 + {}^-1\frac{1}{4}$ Pos.
    5. $^-3\frac{1}{2} + 3\frac{1}{2}$ Zero
    6. $1\frac{3}{5} + {}^-3\frac{1}{5}$ Neg.

Tell how to change each subtraction to an addition.

7. $1\frac{1}{3} - 2\frac{2}{3}$ $1\frac{1}{3} + {}^-2\frac{2}{3}$
  8. $3\frac{1}{4} - {}^-1\frac{1}{2}$ $3\frac{1}{4} + 1\frac{1}{2}$
  9. $-\frac{1}{3} - {}^-1\frac{5}{6}$ $-\frac{1}{3} + 1\frac{5}{6}$

10. $^-2\frac{1}{2} - 1\frac{1}{4}$ $^-2\frac{1}{2} + {}^-1\frac{1}{4}$
  11. $\frac{3}{4} - {}^-2\frac{1}{8}$ $\frac{3}{4} + 2\frac{1}{8}$
  12. $^-4 - {}^-2\frac{1}{5}$ $^-4 + 2\frac{1}{5}$

$\boxed{B}$ Compute.

13. $1\frac{3}{4} + {}^-1\frac{1}{4}$ $\frac{1}{2}$
    14. $^-2\frac{1}{3} + {}^-3\frac{2}{3}$ $^-6$
    15. $3 + {}^-1\frac{3}{5}$ $1\frac{2}{5}$

16. $^-1\frac{1}{5} - \frac{2}{5}$ $^-1\frac{3}{5}$
    17. $3\frac{1}{8} - {}^-1\frac{3}{8}$ $4\frac{1}{2}$
    18. $^-1\frac{5}{6} - {}^-3\frac{1}{6}$ $1\frac{1}{3}$

19. $^-5\frac{1}{2} + 1\frac{7}{8}$ $^-3\frac{5}{8}$
    20. $^-1\frac{3}{4} - 4\frac{1}{2}$ $^-6\frac{1}{4}$
    21. $^-1\frac{1}{4} + (-\frac{5}{8})$ $^-1\frac{7}{8}$

22. $2\frac{1}{2} - {}^-1\frac{7}{8}$ $4\frac{3}{8}$
    23. $3\frac{1}{2} - 4\frac{9}{10}$ $^-1\frac{2}{5}$
    24. $^-2\frac{1}{3} + {}^-1\frac{7}{8}$ $^-4\frac{5}{24}$

25. $1\frac{7}{8} + (-\frac{3}{4})$ $1\frac{1}{8}$
    26. $^-3 + 1\frac{4}{5}$ $^-1\frac{1}{5}$
    27. $^-2 - 1\frac{3}{4}$ $^-\frac{1}{4}$

28. $^-2\frac{7}{8} + {}^-1\frac{1}{2}$ $^-4\frac{3}{8}$
    29. $^-7\frac{1}{2} + 3\frac{1}{4}$ $^-4\frac{1}{4}$
    30. $8\frac{3}{4} + {}^-4\frac{1}{2}$ $4\frac{1}{4}$

31. $^-3\frac{1}{4} - (-\frac{2}{3})$ $^-2\frac{7}{12}$
    32. $^-9\frac{1}{2} + 3\frac{1}{4}$ $^-6\frac{1}{4}$
    33. $8\frac{1}{2} - {}^-3\frac{1}{4}$ $11\frac{3}{4}$

$\boxed{C}$ **34.** $^-6\frac{1}{3} + 5\frac{2}{3} + {}^-8\frac{2}{3}$ $^-9\frac{1}{3}$
    35. $1\frac{1}{4} + {}^-3\frac{1}{2} + {}^-5\frac{3}{4}$ $^-8$

36. $^-3\frac{1}{2} + {}^-4\frac{1}{8} + 7\frac{5}{8}$ 0
    37. $^-10\frac{1}{3} + {}^-5\frac{1}{2} + 6\frac{5}{6}$ $^-9$

369

Solving Equations With Fractions

11.7

Example 1: Solve $y + \frac{5}{8} = \frac{1}{8}$.

$$y + \frac{5}{8} = \frac{1}{8}$$

$$y + \frac{5}{8} + \left(-\frac{5}{8}\right) = \frac{1}{8} + \left(-\frac{5}{8}\right)$$ Add $-\frac{5}{8}$ to each side.

$$y + 0 = -\frac{4}{8}$$

$$y = -\frac{1}{2}$$

Check: $y + \frac{5}{8} = \frac{1}{8}$

$$-\frac{1}{2} + \frac{5}{8} = \frac{1}{8}$$ Replace y with $-\frac{1}{2}$.

$$-\frac{4}{8} + \frac{5}{8} = \frac{1}{8}$$

$$\frac{1}{8} = \frac{1}{8} \quad \checkmark$$

Example 2: Solve $-\frac{1}{3} = x - \left(-\frac{1}{4}\right)$.

$$-\frac{1}{3} = x - \left(-\frac{1}{4}\right)$$

$$-\frac{1}{3} = x + \frac{1}{4}$$ Change $x - \left(-\frac{1}{4}\right)$ to $x + \frac{1}{4}$.

$$-\frac{1}{3} + \left(-\frac{1}{4}\right) = x + \frac{1}{4} + \left(-\frac{1}{4}\right)$$ Add $-\frac{1}{4}$ to each side.

$$-\frac{4}{12} + \left(-\frac{3}{12}\right) = x + 0$$

$$-\frac{7}{12} = x$$

Check:
$$-\frac{1}{3} = x - \left(-\frac{1}{4}\right)$$

$$-\frac{1}{3} = -\frac{7}{12} - \left(-\frac{1}{4}\right) \qquad \text{Replace } x \text{ with } -\frac{7}{12}.$$

$$-\frac{1}{3} = -\frac{7}{12} + \frac{1}{4}$$

$$-\frac{1}{3} = -\frac{7}{12} + \frac{3}{12}$$

$$-\frac{1}{3} = -\frac{4}{12}$$

$$-\frac{1}{3} = -\frac{1}{3} \checkmark$$

Assignment Guide 11.7
Oral: 1–14
Written:
Min. (day 1) 15–24
    (day 2) 25–34
Reg. 15–37 odd
Max. 15–43 odd

■ Exercises

Ⓐ Tell what should replace each ?.

1. $a - \left(-\frac{1}{5}\right) = \frac{4}{5}$ **2.** $b + \left(-\frac{1}{6}\right) = -\frac{2}{3}$

  a. $a + ? = \frac{4}{5}$ $\frac{1}{5}$ **a.** $b + \left(-\frac{1}{6}\right) + ? = -\frac{2}{3} + \frac{1}{6}$ $\frac{1}{6}$

  b. $a + \frac{1}{5} + \left(-\frac{1}{5}\right) = \frac{4}{5} + ?$ $-\frac{1}{5}$ **b.** $b + 0 = -\frac{?}{6} + \frac{1}{6}$ 4

  c. $a + ? = \frac{3}{5}$ 0 **c.** $? = -\frac{3}{6}$ b

  d. $a = ?$ $\frac{3}{5}$ **d.** $b = ?$ $-\frac{1}{2}$

Tell what the first step would be for solving each equation.

3. $n + \frac{3}{4} = \frac{1}{4}$ **4.** $m + \frac{1}{8} = -\frac{5}{8}$ **5.** $-\frac{2}{3} = k + \left(-\frac{1}{2}\right)$

6. $-\frac{5}{9} = t + \left(-\frac{1}{9}\right)$ **7.** $x + \frac{3}{7} = -\frac{2}{7}$ **8.** $0 = y + \frac{2}{3}$

3. Add $-\frac{3}{4}$ to each side.   4. Add $-\frac{1}{8}$ to each side.

5. Add $\frac{1}{2}$ to each side.   6. Add $\frac{1}{9}$ to each side.

7. Add $-\frac{3}{7}$ to each side.   8. Add $-\frac{2}{3}$ to each side.

371

Tell what the first *two* steps would be for solving each equation.

9–14. Answers at left below.

9. $b - \frac{1}{4} = \frac{1}{2}$ **10.** $c - \frac{1}{2} = -\frac{5}{8}$ **11.** $\frac{5}{7} = d - (-\frac{4}{7})$

12. $-\frac{1}{3} = f - (-\frac{3}{5})$ **13.** $g - \frac{3}{8} = \frac{1}{4}$ **14.** $0 = h - (-\frac{8}{9})$

B Solve.

15. $a - \frac{1}{3} = \frac{1}{3}$ $\frac{2}{3}$ **16.** $-\frac{5}{6} = c - \frac{5}{6}$ 0   **17.** $b + (-\frac{3}{8}) = \frac{3}{8}$ $\frac{3}{4}$

18. $0 = d + (-\frac{1}{2})$ $\frac{1}{2}$ **19.** $f + \frac{1}{2} = \frac{3}{4}$ $\frac{1}{4}$ **20.** $e - (-\frac{2}{3}) = -\frac{1}{6}$ $-\frac{5}{6}$

21. $-\frac{2}{5} = g - \frac{3}{10}$ $-\frac{1}{10}$ **22.** $i - \frac{1}{3} = -\frac{2}{9}$ $\frac{1}{9}$ **23.** $-\frac{3}{8} = h + \frac{1}{2}$ $-\frac{7}{8}$

24. $j + (-\frac{3}{4}) = -\frac{7}{8}$ $-\frac{1}{8}$ **25.** $-\frac{7}{10} = m + \frac{1}{5}$ $-\frac{9}{10}$ **26.** $\frac{3}{4} = k - (-\frac{1}{4})$ $\frac{1}{2}$

27. $n - (-\frac{1}{3}) = -\frac{5}{9}$ $-\frac{8}{9}$ **28.** $\frac{1}{2} = g - \frac{3}{10}$ $\frac{4}{5}$ **29.** $p + (-\frac{1}{5}) = -\frac{1}{2}$ $-\frac{3}{10}$

30. $\frac{1}{4} + r = -\frac{3}{4}$ -1 **31.** $\frac{4}{9} = \frac{2}{3} + s$ $-\frac{2}{9}$ **32.** $-\frac{5}{8} = -\frac{1}{4} + t$ $-\frac{3}{8}$

9. Change $-\frac{1}{4}$ to $+\left(-\frac{1}{4}\right)$. Add $\frac{1}{4}$ to each side.

10. Change $-\frac{1}{2}$ to $+\left(-\frac{1}{2}\right)$. Add $\frac{1}{2}$ to each side.

11. Change $-\left(-\frac{4}{7}\right)$ to $+\frac{4}{7}$. Add $-\frac{4}{7}$ to each side.

12. Change $-\left(-\frac{3}{5}\right)$ to $+\frac{3}{5}$. Add $-\frac{3}{5}$ to each side.

13. Change $-\frac{3}{8}$ to $+\left(-\frac{3}{8}\right)$. Add $\frac{3}{8}$ to each side.

14. Change $-\left(-\frac{8}{9}\right)$ to $+\frac{8}{9}$. Add $-\frac{8}{9}$ to each side.

Example: Solve $x + 1\frac{1}{5} = {}^-2\frac{3}{5}$.

$$x + 1\frac{1}{5} = {}^-2\frac{3}{5}$$

$$x + 1\frac{1}{5} + {}^-1\frac{1}{5} = {}^-2\frac{3}{5} + {}^-1\frac{1}{5}$$

$$x + 0 = {}^-3\frac{4}{5}$$

$$x = {}^-3\frac{4}{5}$$

Check: $x + 1\frac{1}{5} = {}^-2\frac{3}{5}$

$${}^-3\frac{4}{5} + 1\frac{1}{5} = {}^-2\frac{3}{5}$$

$${}^-2\frac{3}{5} = {}^-2\frac{3}{5} \checkmark$$

33. $a + 3\frac{1}{3} = {}^-7\frac{1}{3}$ ${}^-10\frac{2}{3}$ **34.** $b - 1\frac{5}{8} = {}^-2\frac{1}{8}$ $-\frac{1}{2}$ **35.** $4\frac{1}{5} = c - {}^-5\frac{4}{5}$ ${}^-1\frac{3}{5}$

36. ${}^-3\frac{2}{3} = d - 1\frac{1}{4}$ ${}^-2\frac{5}{12}$ **37.** $3\frac{1}{2} = e - 5\frac{1}{4}$ $8\frac{3}{4}$ **38.** $f - {}^-2\frac{3}{4} = 1\frac{2}{3}$ ${}^-1\frac{1}{12}$

C **39.** $g + 2\frac{1}{8} = 1\frac{5}{6}$ $-\frac{7}{24}$ **40.** $h - 8\frac{2}{3} = {}^-10\frac{4}{5}$ ${}^-2\frac{2}{15}$ **41.** $4\frac{2}{9} = i - 2\frac{3}{8}$ $6\frac{43}{72}$

42. ${}^-5\frac{1}{3} = j + 3\frac{4}{7}$ ${}^-8\frac{19}{21}$ **43.** $k + 10\frac{5}{6} = {}^-4\frac{1}{15}$ ${}^-14\frac{9}{10}$ **44.** $16\frac{1}{4} = t + 12\frac{5}{11}$ $3\frac{35}{44}$

Using Equations to Solve Problems

11.8

Now we can write equations with rational numbers to help solve problems.

Example 1: Mary's earned run average this year was 2.44. This was a change of ⁻0.52 from last year. What was her earned run average last year?

Let x = average last year.

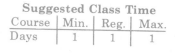

Suggested Class Time			
Course	Min.	Reg.	Max.
Days	1	1	1

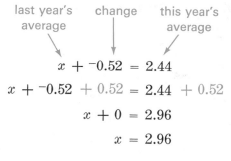

last year's average   change   this year's average

$$x + {}^-0.52 = 2.44$$
$$x + {}^-0.52 + 0.52 = 2.44 + 0.52$$
$$x + 0 = 2.96$$
$$x = 2.96$$

Check: Does an earned run average of 2.96 followed by a ⁻0.52 change give an earned run average of 2.44? ✓

Her earned run average last year was 2.96.

Terry McKoy/The Picture Cube

Terry McKoy/The Picture Cube

373

Example 2: A club at Mary's school sells booster buttons. Last year, the club made a profit of $16\frac{3}{4}$¢ on each button sold. This year the profit was $15\frac{1}{2}$¢ for each button. What was the change in profit from last year to this year?

Let c = change in profit.

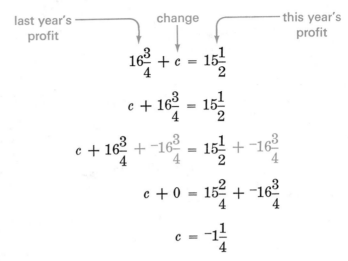

$$16\frac{3}{4} + c = 15\frac{1}{2}$$

$$c + 16\frac{3}{4} = 15\frac{1}{2}$$

$$c + 16\frac{3}{4} + {}^-16\frac{3}{4} = 15\frac{1}{2} + {}^-16\frac{3}{4}$$

$$c + 0 = 15\frac{2}{4} + {}^-16\frac{3}{4}$$

$$c = {}^-1\frac{1}{4}$$

Check: Does going from a profit of $16\frac{3}{4}$¢ to $15\frac{1}{2}$¢ give a change in profit of $^-1\frac{1}{4}$¢? ✓

The change in profit was $^-1\frac{1}{4}$¢. Or we can say this year the club made $1\frac{1}{4}$¢ less on each button than it did last year.

■ Exercises

A Refer to the problem below to answer each question.

Assignment Guide 11.8
Oral: 1–4
Written: Min. 5–15 odd
      Reg. 5–17 odd
      Max. 5–19 odd

Problem: Ms. Willis drove her car from Hilltown to Pine City. Her car used $\frac{1}{4}$ of a tank of gas for the trip. If the gas tank was $\frac{3}{8}$ full when Ms. Willis got to Pine City, how full was the tank before she left Hilltown?

1. What should x represent?

   a. how full the tank was after getting to Pine City

   b. how much gas was used on the trip

   <u>**c.**</u> how full the tank was before leaving Hilltown

2. Which number represents the amount of gas used?

   a. $\frac{3}{8}$ **b.** $-\frac{1}{4}$ **c.** $-\frac{3}{8}$

3. Which number represents the amount of gas left at the end of the trip?

   a. $\frac{3}{8}$ **b.** $-\frac{1}{4}$ **c.** $-\frac{3}{8}$

4. Which equation could you use to help solve the problem?

   a. $\frac{3}{8} + x = -\frac{1}{4}$ **b.** $x + (-\frac{1}{4}) = \frac{3}{8}$ **c.** $-\frac{1}{4} + \frac{3}{8} = x$

B Solve each problem by using an equation. (Use negative numbers whenever they fit.)

5. This morning the barometer reading was 29.96 inches. Now it is 29.82 inches. What was the change in readings? ⁻0.14 in.

6. Ms. Anderson's car has a 40-liter gas tank. If it took 33.7 liters of gas to fill the tank, how much gas was in the tank before it was filled? 6.3 L

7. Yesterday Juan's body temperature was 101.6 °F. Today his temperature is 98.9 °F. What was the change in his temperature readings from yesterday to today? ⁻2.7 °F

8. A smoke detector sells for $27.85. If you use a refund coupon from the company that makes the detector, the cost is only $22.85. How much is the refund? $5.00

9. Sam is a wrestler. On Wednesday he weighed $\frac{3}{4}$ lb over the limit for his weight class. On Friday he weighed $\frac{1}{2}$ lb under the limit. What was his change in weight from Wednesday to Friday? ⁻$1\frac{1}{4}$ lb

10. Mary's chemistry lab is $\frac{3}{4}$ hour long. If she takes $\frac{1}{4}$ hour to read about an experiment, how much time does she have to do the experiment? $\frac{1}{2}$ hr

M. Wannemacher/Taurus Photos

11. At one time during a rainstorm, the water level of a river was $\frac{2}{3}$ ft below the flood line. Three hours later, it was $\frac{1}{2}$ ft above the flood line. What change in the water level is given by these two measurements? $1\frac{1}{6}$ ft

12. At the beginning of February, the inflation rate for the year was $\frac{1}{2}$ per cent. By the end of February the rate rose to $\frac{7}{8}$ per cent. What was the change in the inflation rate during February? $\frac{3}{8}\%$

13. The sale price of a certain record is $4.99. This is $0.98 less than the regular price of the record. How much would you pay for the record at the regular price? $5.97

14. Mr. Conway lives in Cedar City. He drove to Oakville, which is 12.8 miles from Cedar City. If the mileage reading was 18,945.7 after he got to Oakville, what was the reading before he left Cedar City? 18,932.9

15. Last fall a small maple tree was $5\frac{1}{2}$ ft tall. This fall the tree was $6\frac{2}{3}$ ft tall. What was the change in the height of the tree from last fall to this fall? $1\frac{1}{6}$ ft

16. Last year a cherry tree produced $2\frac{1}{2}$ bushels of cherries. This year the same tree produced $2\frac{1}{4}$ bushels. What was the change in number of bushels produced from last year to this year? $-\frac{1}{4}$ bu

C 17. In April the balance of a charge account was ⁻$157.49. In May the balance was ⁻$193.34. What was the change in the balance from April to May? ⁻$35.85

18. Stan borrowed some money and agreed to decrease his debt by $3.25 each month. After one month, his balance was ⁻$22.14. How much money did Stan borrow? $25.39

19. Between January 1 and November 24 of the same year, the prime lending rate of a large New York bank increased by $3\frac{3}{4}$ per cent. The rate on November 24 was $11\frac{1}{2}$ per cent. What was the rate on January 1? $7\frac{3}{4}\%$

20. The price of a share of stock was $24\frac{1}{4}$ dollars at the beginning of the day. At the end of the day, the price was $22\frac{1}{2}$ dollars. What was the change in the price for the day? ⁻$$1\frac{3}{4}$

BOOKKEEPING

Bookkeeping workers keep the records of businesses in an up-to-date and systematic way. They also make up forms that show all amounts taken in and paid out during certain periods.

High-school graduates who have taken business math, bookkeeping, and accounting courses meet the minimum requirements for most bookkeeping jobs. But some employers prefer that applicants also have taken business courses in a community or business college.

A bookkeeping worker might have to find the sum below. The numbers in parentheses are negative. Find the sum.

Account 07359
Monday, Jan. 5, 1981

Received from Acme Tool	$ 1253.75
Received from Harper Welding	576.67
Paid to Phaeton Steel	(2175.00)
Received from Raycon Fabricators	3411.05
Paid to Wilco Aluminum	(575.50)
Total	$2490.97

Courtesy NCR

377

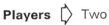

RATS!

Players ▷ Two

Equipment ▷ An ordinary deck of 52 playing cards

Black cards (clubs and spades) stand for positive integers, and red cards (hearts and diamonds) stand for negative integers as follows:

Setup ▷ The deck of cards is placed facedown on a table. This becomes the draw pile.

Play ▷ START: Each player takes two cards from the draw pile.

OBJECT: The cards in your hand make a rational number. One card is the numerator of a fraction, and the other is the denominator. You want to make the greatest number you can with the cards.

Example: You draw the 3 of diamonds and the 9 of clubs. There are two ways you can play the cards.

$-\frac{1}{3} > {}^{-}3$, so you would place your cards on the table as shown on the left above.

WINNING THE HAND: Once the cards have been placed on the table, they cannot be changed. The player whose cards make the greater number wins the hand and picks up all four cards. The cards are placed in the player's point pile.

Example:

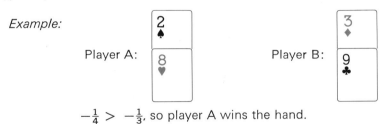

$-\frac{1}{4} > -\frac{1}{3}$, so player A wins the hand.

STARTING A NEW HAND: Each player takes two more cards from the draw pile. The winner of the last hand draws first.

The game is over when there are no cards left in the draw pile and the last four cards have been played. ◁ **End of game**

In case of a tie (when both players' cards make the same number), the cards are left on the table. A new hand is played. The winner of the new hand picks up all the cards on the table. If the game ends before a tie can be broken, the cards stay on the table and are not counted in either player's score. ◁ **Tie hand**

You can take a win from the other player if the player won the hand but you think he/she could have made a greater number with his/her cards. (For example, the play was $\frac{6}{7}$ instead of $\frac{7}{6}$.) You must say "RATS!" before the cards are picked up from the table. If you are right, you get the cards. If you are wrong, the other player gets the cards and you must give the other player 2 points (1 picture card or 2 other cards) from your point pile (or as soon as your point pile has the points if it is empty). ◁ **RATS!**

Each picture card (jack, queen, king) counts 2 points. All other cards count 1 point each. Your score is the total number of points in your point pile. High score wins. ◁ **Scoring**

Terms and Symbols Review

Suggested Class Time

Course	Min.	Reg.	Max.
Days	2	1	1

True or False?

1. $\frac{5}{6}$, $^-2$, $^-7\frac{1}{3}$, 0, 9.2, $-\frac{3}{2}$, and $^-2.5$ are rational numbers. T

2. $-\frac{1}{4}$ is the opposite of $\frac{1}{4}$. T

3. $^-3.61$ is the absolute value of $^-3.61$. F

4. The graph of $-\frac{1}{3}$ is a point on a number line between 0 and 1. F

Assignment Guide Rev.
Oral: Terms & Symbols 1–8
Written:
Min. (day 1) 1–26
(day 2) 27–46
Reg. 1–45 odd
Max. 1–45 odd

5. $^-1 \div {}^-2$ can be expressed as $-\frac{1}{2}$. F

6. Subtracting $^-2.1$ is the same as adding $^-2.1$. F

7. $\frac{5}{8} + (-\frac{7}{8})$ is a negative sum. T

8. $^-1\frac{1}{4} + 3\frac{3}{4}$ is a negative sum. F

Chapter 11 Review

11.1 Give the opposite of each number.

1. $\frac{1}{3}$ $-\frac{1}{3}$ **2.** $^-0.58$ 0.58 **3.** $1\frac{2}{5}$ $^-1\frac{2}{5}$ **4.** $-\frac{9}{10}$ $\frac{9}{10}$

Give the absolute value of each number.

5. 10.49 10.49 **6.** $^-0.68$ 0.68 **7.** $-\frac{4}{9}$ $\frac{4}{9}$ **8.** $1\frac{3}{4}$ $1\frac{3}{4}$

11.2 Should $>$, $<$, or $=$ replace $\bigcirc$ to make the sentence true?

9. $\frac{3}{7} \bigcirc \frac{5}{7}$ $<$ **10.** $\frac{3}{4} \bigcirc \frac{7}{8}$ $<$ **11.** $\frac{3}{4} \bigcirc -\frac{2}{3}$ $>$

12. $-\frac{5}{6} \bigcirc \frac{2}{3}$ $<$ **13.** $-\frac{5}{8} \bigcirc -\frac{1}{2}$ $<$ **14.** $-\frac{7}{8} \bigcirc \frac{14}{16}$ $<$

11.3 Find each sum or difference.

15. $^-5.9 + 3.7$ $^-2.2$ **16.** $^-4.2 + {}^-1.9$ $^-6.1$ **17.** $6.38 + {}^-2.69$ 3.69

18. $^-1.732 - 4.12$ $^-5.852$ **19.** $^-5.7 - {}^-5.2$ $^-0.5$ **20.** $8.3 - {}^-9.6$ 17.9

Solve.

21. $t - 2.4 = 1.6$ ₄ **22.** $v + 1.7 = 10.1$ **23.** $^-1.6 = w - {^-3.1}$ ⁻4.7

8.4

24. $x + {^-1.31} = {^-5.7}$ **25.** $y + 1.9 = 0$ **26.** $^-2.4 = z + 3.35$ ⁻5.75

⁻4.39 ⁻1.9

Find each sum or difference.

27. $-\frac{1}{8} + \frac{3}{8}$ $\frac{1}{4}$ **28.** $\frac{3}{4} + \left(-\frac{1}{8}\right)$ $\frac{5}{8}$ **29.** $-\frac{1}{2} + \left(-\frac{1}{3}\right)$ $-\frac{5}{6}$

30. $\frac{1}{4} - \frac{2}{3}$ $-\frac{5}{12}$ **31.** $-\frac{1}{2} - \frac{1}{4}$ $-\frac{3}{4}$ **32.** $-\frac{3}{8} - \left(-\frac{3}{4}\right)$ $\frac{3}{8}$

33. $^-1\frac{3}{8} + 1\frac{5}{8}$ $\frac{1}{4}$ **34.** $3 + {^-1\frac{1}{2}}$ $1\frac{1}{2}$ **35.** $^-2\frac{3}{4} + {^-1\frac{2}{3}}$ ⁻$4\frac{5}{12}$

36. $^-2\frac{3}{5} - 1\frac{2}{5}$ ⁻4 **37.** $\frac{3}{4} - {^-1\frac{1}{8}}$ $1\frac{7}{8}$ **38.** $^-1\frac{3}{4} - {^-2\frac{1}{4}}$ $\frac{1}{2}$

Solve.

39. $n + \frac{3}{4} = \frac{1}{4}$ $-\frac{1}{2}$ **40.** $p - \frac{3}{8} = -\frac{5}{8}$ $-\frac{1}{4}$ **41.** $\frac{1}{2} = q + \left(-\frac{3}{4}\right)$ $1\frac{1}{4}$

42. $\frac{2}{3} = r - \left(-\frac{5}{6}\right)$ $-\frac{1}{6}$ **43.** $s + \frac{3}{8} = -\frac{1}{4}$ $-\frac{5}{8}$ **44.** $\frac{1}{3} = t + \left(-\frac{1}{2}\right)$ $\frac{5}{6}$

Solve each problem by using an equation.

45. At 8:00 A.M. a water cooler contained $\frac{3}{4}$ gallon of water. At 10:00 A.M. there was $\frac{1}{8}$ gallon of water in the cooler. How much water was used from 8:00 A.M. to 10:00 A.M.? $\frac{5}{8}$ gal.

46. This morning the barometer reading was 30.16. This was a change of $^-0.13$ from last night. What was the reading last night? 30.29

Chapter 11 Test

1. Give the absolute value of $5\frac{1}{3}$. $5\frac{1}{3}$

2. Give the opposite of $^-7.03$. 7.03

Find each sum or difference.

3. $-\frac{3}{4} + \frac{1}{8}$ $-\frac{5}{8}$

4. $\frac{7}{8} + \left(-\frac{1}{2}\right)$ $\frac{3}{8}$

5. $1\frac{1}{2} + \left(-\frac{5}{8}\right)$ $\frac{7}{8}$

6. $^-3\frac{1}{2} + ^-4\frac{1}{2}$ $^-8$

7. $^-3.75 + 4.29$ 0.54

8. $^-8.79 + ^-6.75$ $^-15.54$

9. $-\frac{4}{5} - \frac{1}{10}$ $-\frac{9}{10}$

10. $\frac{1}{4} - \left(-\frac{5}{8}\right)$ $\frac{7}{8}$

11. $^-1\frac{2}{5} - ^-2\frac{1}{3}$ $\frac{14}{15}$

12. $6.7 - 9.6$ $^-2.9$

13. $^-8.9 - 5.2$ $^-14.1$

14. $1.42 - ^-6.75$ 8.17

15. $4 + ^-1\frac{2}{3}$ $2\frac{1}{3}$

16. $-\frac{1}{2} + \left(-\frac{1}{5}\right)$ $-\frac{7}{10}$

17. $^-1\frac{3}{8} - ^-1\frac{1}{4}$ $-\frac{1}{8}$

Solve.

18. $z + \frac{1}{5} = -\frac{3}{5}$ $-\frac{4}{5}$

19. $x + ^-7.2 = 5.3$ 12.5

20. $c - 3.2 = ^-5.7$ $^-2.5$

21. $\frac{3}{4} + f = -\frac{5}{8}$ $^-1\frac{3}{8}$

22. $-\frac{7}{8} + m = 0$ $\frac{7}{8}$

23. $^-4.2 = a + ^-7.3$ 3.1

24. $k - \left(-\frac{1}{2}\right) = -\frac{5}{6}$ $^-1\frac{1}{3}$

25. $\frac{3}{4} = h - \frac{5}{8}$ $1\frac{3}{8}$

26. $b - 6.9 = 8.3$ 15.2

27. $\frac{1}{4} = y - \frac{1}{2}$ $\frac{3}{4}$

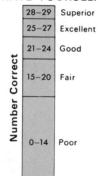
Solve each problem by using an equation.

28. This year's sales for Zee Company were down $1.7 million from last year's sales. If this year's sales were $30.5 million, what were last year's sales? $32.2 million

29. On the first day of a canoe trip, the average speed was $2\frac{1}{2}$ miles per hour. On the second day, the average was $1\frac{3}{4}$ miles per hour. What was the change in average speed from the first day to the second day? $-\frac{3}{4}$ mph

Getting Ready for Chapter 12

Find each product or quotient.

1. $\frac{1}{8} \times \frac{3}{2}$ $\frac{3}{16}$

2. $\frac{3}{4} \times \frac{5}{12}$ $\frac{5}{16}$

3. $\frac{2}{3} \times \frac{9}{16}$ $\frac{3}{8}$ **4.2**

4. $4\frac{1}{2} \times 3$ $13\frac{1}{2}$

5. $\frac{1}{2} \times 2\frac{2}{3}$ $1\frac{1}{3}$

6. $2\frac{1}{2} \times 1\frac{2}{3}$ $4\frac{1}{6}$ **4.5**

7. $\frac{1}{8} \div \frac{2}{3}$ $\frac{3}{16}$

8. $\frac{3}{5} \div \frac{9}{16}$ $1\frac{1}{15}$

9. $1\frac{1}{2} \div 2\frac{3}{8}$ $\frac{12}{19}$ **4.6**

10. 4.3×2.1 9.03

11. 75.3×0.001 0.0753

12. 3.14×65 **5.4**
204.1

13. $0.196 \div 14$ 0.014

14. $4.791 \div 3$ 1.597

15. $0.042 \div 6$ **5.5**
0.007

16. $0.1917 \div 14.2$ 0.0135

17. $9 \div 2.25$ 4

18. $10.24 \div 3.2$ **5.6**
3.2

19. $8 \times {}^{-}7$ ${}^{-}56$

20. ${}^{-}7 \times 8$ ${}^{-}56$

21. ${}^{-}14 \times 9$ **7.1**
${}^{-}126$

22. ${}^{-}14 \times {}^{-}4$ 56

23. ${}^{-}7 \times {}^{-}4 \times 2$ 56

24. $8 \times {}^{-}7 \times 5$ **7.2**
${}^{-}280$

25. ${}^{-}21 \div 7$ ${}^{-}3$

26. ${}^{-}42 \div {}^{-}6$ 7

27. $84 \div {}^{-}12$ **7.3**
${}^{-}7$

Solve each equation.

28. $2n = {}^{-}10$ ${}^{-}5$

29. ${}^{-}35 = {}^{-}5k$ 7 **7.4**

30. $\frac{n}{4} = {}^{-}8$ ${}^{-}32$

31. $17 = \frac{x}{{}^{-}9}$ ${}^{-}153$ **7.5**

32. $17 = {}^{-}2x - 3$ ${}^{-}10$

33. $\frac{z}{6} + 5 = {}^{-}12$ ${}^{-}102$ **7.8**

34. $n - 9.5 = {}^{-}1.3$ 8.2

35. ${}^{-}6.1 = t + {}^{-}4.6$ ${}^{-}1.5$ **11.4**

36. $x - \frac{3}{8} = -\frac{1}{8}$ $\frac{1}{4}$

37. $n + \frac{7}{12} = -\frac{11}{12}$ ${}^{-}1\frac{1}{2}$ **11.7**

Find each value.

38. 10^2 100

39. 10^4 10,000

40. 10^3 1000 **3.8**

41. $25 + 10 \div 5$ 27

42. $(25 + 10) \div 5$ 7 **1.2**

43. Which of the following fractions are equal to $\frac{{}^{-}2}{5}$? **11.1**

    a. $\frac{2}{5}$ **b.** $\frac{{}^{-}2}{5}$ **c.** $\frac{{}^{-}2}{{}^{-}5}$ **d.** $-\frac{2}{5}$

44. Use the formula $t = \frac{d}{r}$ to find how far a skier going 58 feet per **1.9**
second travels in $3\frac{1}{2}$ seconds. 203 ft

12

12

MULTIPLYING AND DIVIDING RATIONAL NUMBERS

Keith Gunnar/Tom Stack & Associates

Air temperature changes about ⁻2.5 °C for every ⁺300 meter change in altitude. So the change that might be expected in climbing from sea level to the top of a mountain 4833.6 meters high is given by this expression.

$$\frac{4833.6}{300} \times {}^{-}2.5$$

To multiply or divide rational numbers, just multiply or divide as you would fractions, mixed numbers, or decimals. Then take care of the sign as you would with integers.

Multiplying and Dividing With Decimals

12.1

For rational numbers expressed using decimals, first multiply or divide the decimals. Then find the sign of the product as you would for integers.

Suggested Class Time

Course	Min.	Reg.	Max.
Days	1	1	1

If two factors have

a. the *same sign*, the product is *positive*.

b. *different signs*, the product is *negative*.

Example 1: Find each product.

a.

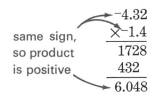

same sign, so product is positive

$$
\begin{array}{r}
-4.32 \\
\times -1.4 \\
\hline
1728 \\
432 \\
\hline
6.048
\end{array}
$$

b.

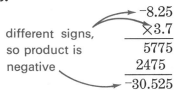

different signs, so product is negative

$$
\begin{array}{r}
-8.25 \\
\times 3.7 \\
\hline
5775 \\
2475 \\
\hline
-30.525
\end{array}
$$

A similar pattern exists for division.

If the divisor and dividend have

a. the *same sign*, the quotient is *positive*.

b. *different signs*, the quotient is *negative*.

Example 2: Find each quotient.

a.

positive quotient because the signs are the same

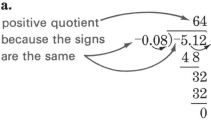

$$
\begin{array}{r}
64 \\
-0.08)\overline{-5.12} \\
48 \\
\hline
32 \\
32 \\
\hline
0
\end{array}
$$

b.

negative quotient because the signs are different

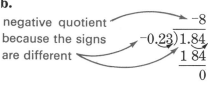

$$
\begin{array}{r}
-8 \\
-0.23)\overline{1.84} \\
1\,84 \\
\hline
0
\end{array}
$$

385

■ Exercises

Assignment Guide 12.1
Oral: 1–12
Written: Min. 13–47 odd
   Reg. 13–57 odd
   Max. 13–65 odd

A Tell whether each product or quotient is positive or negative.

1. 123×4.7 Pos.   **2.** $^-4.3 \times 7.2$ Neg.   **3.** $8.6 \times ^-4.9$ Neg.

4. $^-2.37 \times ^-6.67$ Pos.   **5.** $6 \times ^-1.672$ Neg.   **6.** $^-9.125 \times ^-8$ Pos.

7. $927 \div 7.8$ Pos.   **8.** $628 \div ^-4.8$ Neg.   **9.** $^-9.63 \div 0.037$ Neg.

10. $^-0.69 \div ^-0.03$ Pos.   **11.** $^-8.84 \div 1.25$ Neg.   **12.** $^-1.98 \div ^-9$ Pos.

B Find each product or quotient.

13. 1.7×4.6 7.82   **14.** $^-1.65 \times 46.9$ $^-77.385$ **15.** $0.125 \times ^-48.9$ $^-6.1125$

16. $^-8.6 \times ^-9.2$ 79.12   **17.** $0.25 \times ^-1.95$ $^-0.4875$ **18.** $^-6.75 \times 2.57$ $^-17.3475$

19. $^-2.95 \times ^-4.2$ 12.39   **20.** $1.732 \times ^-5$ $^-8.66$ **21.** $^-1.414 \times 6$ $^-8.484$

22. 6.2×4.7 29.14   **23.** $8.8 \times ^-6.75$ $^-59.4$ **24.** $^-9.99 \times ^-0.55$ 5.4945

25. $3.19 \div 2.9$ 1.1   **26.** $^-0.498 \div 8.3$ $^-0.06$ **27.** $9.99 \div ^-2.7$ $^-3.7$

28. $^-13.69 \div ^-0.37$ 37   **29.** $^-0.1794 \div 0.26$ $^-0.69$ **30.** $19.69 \div 0.11$ 179

31. $855 \div ^-9.5$ $^-90$ **32.** $184.8 \div ^-0.77$ $^-240$ **33.** $^-9.90 \div ^-2.2$ 4.5

34. $158.1 \div 9.3$ 17   **35.** $^-23.8 \div ^-1.4$ 17   **36.** $0.304 \div ^-0.16$ $^-1.9$

Use multiplication or division to answer each question.

37. The height of a weather balloon is changing $^-4.5$ feet per second (ft/sec). What will the change in height be after 15 seconds? $^-67.5$ ft

38. The temperature of a gas is to be lowered from $0\,°C$ to $^-37.5\,°C$ in three stages. If the degree drop is the same in each stage, what will be the temperature of the gas after the first stage? $^-12.5\,°C$

39. The level of the city reservoir is changing $^-1.75$ feet per day, At this rate, what will be the change for a 5-day period? $^-8.75$ ft

40. The depth of an oil well is to be $^-3680$ feet (3680 feet below sea level). The drilling is now 68% complete. At what depth are they now drilling? $^-2502.4$ ft

Find each value.

41. $1.7 \times {}^-2.8 \times 8.3$ ₋39.508

42. $1.26 \times 0.3 \times {}^-0.3$ ₋0.1134

43. $6.5 \div {}^-1.3 \times 4.6$ ₋23

44. $8.7 \div {}^-2.9 \times {}^-9.7$ 29.1

45. $1.4 \times {}^-1.6 \div 0.56$ ₋4

46. $1.96 \div {}^-0.2 \times 0.7$ ₋6.86

47. $1.44 \times {}^-0.9 + {}^-12.6$ ₋13.896

48. ${}^-1.728 \div {}^-1.44 + {}^-12$ ₋10.8

49. $7.2 + 8.3 \times {}^-6.1$ ₋43.43

50. ${}^-11.8 + 4.4 \div 1.1$ ₋7.8

51. ${}^-12.9 - 6.2 \div 3.1$ ₋14.9

52. ${}^-8.7 - 4.5 \times 3.6$ ₋24.9

53. $3.36 \div 6.72 - {}^-5.14$ 5.64

54. ${}^-6.94 \times 5.81 - 2.32$ ₋42.6414

55. $1.6 + 7.1 \div {}^-0.5$ ₋12.6

56. ${}^-0.8 - 1.7 \times 0.09$ ₋0.953

57. $(1.6 + 7.1) \div {}^-0.5$ ₋17.4

58. $({}^-0.8 - 1.7) \times 0.09$ ₋0.225

C **59.** $0.\overline{3} \times 2$ 0.$\overline{6}$

60. $0.\overline{3} \times 3$ 0.$\overline{9}$

61. $0.\overline{3} \times 4$ 1.$\overline{3}$

62. $0.\overline{3} \times 5$ 1.$\overline{6}$

63. Are multiples of repeating decimals also repeating decimals? Yes

For some outdoor activities, it is wise to keep in mind that air temperature changes about ⁻2.5 °C for every ⁺300 meter change in altitude.

64. A sky diver is to leave the plane at an altitude of 2700 meters. About what will the temperature at that altitude be if the temperature on the ground is 10 °C? ₋12.5 °C

65. Mt. Whitney, in California, is about 4400 meters high. If the temperature is 3 °C at the 3500 meter level, about what is it at the top? ₋4.5 °C

Ray Cottingham

387

12.2 Solving Equations With Decimals

Suggested Class Time			
Course	Min.	Reg.	Max.
Days	1	1	1

The fish in the tank shown here eat a total of 13.4 pounds of food daily. They are fed 4 times a day. About how many pounds of food do they eat at each feeding?

The following equation can be used to solve this problem, where n is the number of pounds per feeding.

$$4n = 13.4$$

Authenticated News International

Example 1: Solve $4n = 13.4$.

$$4n = 13.4$$

$$\frac{4n}{4} = \frac{13.4}{4} \qquad \text{Divide each side by 4.}$$

$$n = 3.35$$

Check: $\quad 4n = 13.4$

$$4(3.35) = 13.4$$

$$13.4 = 13.4 \checkmark$$

So the fish eat about 3.35 pounds at each feeding.

■ Exercises

A To solve each equation, what would you do on each side?

Assignment Guide 12.2
Oral: 1–8
Written: Min. 9–25
  Reg. 9–28
  Max. 9–32

1. $4.1n = 25.42 \quad \div 4.1$

2. $\frac{m}{-3.6} = 4 \quad \times -3.6$

3. $\frac{x}{6} = 3.29 \quad \times 6$

4. $-6.8 = 4m \quad \div 4$

5. $\frac{t}{-3.7} = -8.3 \quad \times -3.7$

6. $7.2 = -3x \quad \div -3$

7. $\frac{m}{-4} = 8.7 \quad \times -4$

8. $7.3m = 6.7 \quad \div 7.3$

B Solve.

9. $\frac{x}{6.3} = 5$ 31.5   10. $3.9x = 1.95$ 0.5   11. $\frac{m}{7.2} = {}^{-}8$ ${}^{-}57.6$

12. $3.7 = \frac{x}{4}$ 14.8   13. $6m = 3.6$ 0.6   14. $27.4 = {}^{-}2x$ ${}^{-}13.7$

15. ${}^{-}1.7x = 6.8$ ${}^{-}4$ 16. $\frac{x}{9} = {}^{-}3.3$ ${}^{-}29.7$ 17. $\frac{m}{{}^{-}6.7} = 4.2$ ${}^{-}28.14$

18. $4.5 = \frac{x}{{}^{-}5}$ ${}^{-}22.5$ 19. ${}^{-}2.7x = {}^{-}7.29$ 2.7   20. ${}^{-}3.6 = {}^{-}3b$ 1.2

21. $\frac{t}{{}^{-}4.3} = {}^{-}4.7$ 20.21   22. ${}^{-}5t = {}^{-}5.3$ 1.06   23. ${}^{-}0.16x = {}^{-}1.44$ 9

Write and solve an equation for each problem.

24. The product of a number and ${}^{-}3.6$ is 9. What is the number? ${}^{-}3.6n = 9$; ${}^{-}2.5$

25. When a number is divided by ${}^{-}0.05$, the quotient is 10. What is the number? $\frac{n}{{}^{-}0.05} = 10$; ${}^{-}0.5$

26. A capsule of Brand A cold remedy weighs 0.62 grams. How much do 100 capsules weigh? $0.62(100) = w$; 62 g

A. Devaney, Inc.

27. The total weight of the capsules in a bottle is 64.8 grams. If each capsule weighs 0.9 grams, how many capsules are in the bottle? $0.9x = 64.8$; 72 capsules

28. What would be the weight of 36 of the capsules in Exercise 27? $36(0.9) = w$; 32.4 g

29. A company's profit-and-loss statement for 3 months shows a balance of ${}^{-}\$2169.15$. What was the monthly average? $\frac{{}^{-}2169.15}{3} = a$; ${}^{-}\$723.05$

30. If the temperature changed ${}^{-}8.25\,°C$ in 3 hours, what was the average change per hour? $\frac{{}^{-}8.25}{3} = t$; ${}^{-}2.75\,°C$

C 31. An airplane is flying at 8000 feet altitude. The pilot is told to change altitude at the rate of ${}^{-}400$ feet per minute for the next 15 minutes. What will the plane's altitude be after 15 minutes? $8000 + {}^{-}400(15) = a$; 2000 ft

32. Jay's Auto Sales has a cash reserve of $10,500. This week, subtracting expenses from income gives ${}^{-}\$750$ (a loss of $750). In how many weeks will the reserve be gone if this continues? $10,500 + {}^{-}750w = 0$; 14 wk

Multiplying and Dividing With Fractions

For rational numbers expressed using fractions, multiply or divide the fractions and then find the sign as you would for integers.

Examples: Find each product or quotient.

1. $-\dfrac{3}{8} \times \left(-\dfrac{3}{4}\right)$

Suggested Class Time

Course	Min.	Reg.	Max.
Days	1	1	1

$\dfrac{3}{8} \times \dfrac{3}{4} = \dfrac{9}{32}$ Multiply fractions.

same sign, so product is positive

$-\dfrac{3}{8} \times \left(-\dfrac{3}{4}\right) = \dfrac{9}{32}$

2. $\dfrac{3}{4} \div \left(-\dfrac{1}{2}\right)$

$\dfrac{3}{4} \div \dfrac{1}{2} = \dfrac{3}{\underset{2}{4}} \times \overset{1}{\dfrac{2}{1}}$ Divide fractions.

$= \dfrac{3}{2}$

$= 1\dfrac{1}{2}$

different signs, so quotient is negative

$\dfrac{3}{4} \div \left(-\dfrac{1}{2}\right) = {}^{-}1\dfrac{1}{2}$

3. $-\dfrac{2}{3} \div 6$

$\dfrac{2}{3} \div 6 = \dfrac{2}{3} \div \dfrac{6}{1}$ Write a whole number as a fraction with denominator 1.

$= \dfrac{\overset{1}{2}}{3} \times \dfrac{1}{\underset{3}{6}}$

$= \dfrac{1}{9}$

different signs, so quotient is negative

$-\dfrac{2}{3} \div 6 = -\dfrac{1}{9}$

Assignment Guide 12.3
Oral: 1–15
Written:
Min. 16–30
Reg. 17–45 odd
Max. 17–45 odd;
    46–54

Exercises

[A] Tell whether each product or quotient is positive or negative.

1. $\dfrac{3}{4} \times \dfrac{1}{2}$ Pos.

2. $\dfrac{3}{8}\left(-\dfrac{1}{6}\right)$ Neg.

3. $-\dfrac{3}{8} \times \dfrac{6}{7}$ Neg.

4. $-\dfrac{2}{3}\left(-\dfrac{2}{5}\right)$ Pos.

5. $4\left(\dfrac{3}{7}\right)$ Pos.

6. $-\dfrac{4}{5}(7)$ Neg.

7. $\frac{2}{3} \div \frac{1}{2}$ Pos.   **8.** $\frac{7}{8} \div \left(-\frac{3}{5}\right)$ Neg.   **9.** $-\frac{3}{8} \div \frac{1}{2}$ Neg.

10. $-\frac{5}{8} \div \left(-\frac{2}{3}\right)$ Pos.   **11.** $^{-}4 \div \frac{3}{4}$ Neg.   **12.** $\frac{2}{3} \div {}^{-}10$ Neg.

13. $\frac{1}{3}\left(\frac{2}{7}\right)\left(-\frac{1}{5}\right)$ Neg.   **14.** $\frac{1}{2}\left(-\frac{2}{3}\right)\left(-\frac{1}{5}\right)$ Pos.   **15.** $-\frac{2}{5}\left(\frac{1}{4} \times \frac{2}{3}\right)$ Neg.

B Find each product or quotient.

16. $\frac{2}{3} \times \frac{1}{5}$ $\frac{2}{15}$ **17.** $-\frac{2}{3} \times \frac{7}{8}$ $-\frac{7}{12}$ **18.** $\frac{3}{5}\left(-\frac{7}{9}\right)$ $-\frac{7}{15}$

19. $\frac{5}{9} \div \left(-\frac{1}{6}\right)$ $^{-}3\frac{1}{3}$ **20.** $-\frac{1}{2} \div \frac{1}{4}$ $^{-}2$ **21.** $-\frac{1}{5}(^{-}35)$ 7

22. $\frac{4}{7} \div \left(-\frac{2}{3}\right)$ $-\frac{6}{7}$ **23.** $49\left(-\frac{3}{7}\right)$ $^{-}21$ **24.** $-\frac{5}{6}\left(-\frac{3}{4}\right)$ $\frac{5}{8}$

25. $63 \div \frac{21}{25}$ 75 **26.** $\frac{5}{7}(^{-}84)$ $^{-}60$ **27.** $^{-}18 \div \frac{6}{7}$ $^{-}21$

28. $\frac{3}{4} \div \frac{1}{2}$ $1\frac{1}{2}$ **29.** $-\frac{7}{8} \div \frac{2}{3}$ $^{-}1\frac{5}{16}$ **30.** $\frac{4}{5} \div \left(-\frac{3}{4}\right)$ $^{-}1\frac{1}{15}$

31. $-\frac{1}{2}\left(-\frac{2}{3}\right)$ $\frac{1}{3}$ **32.** $^{-}28 \div \left(-\frac{7}{8}\right)$ 32 **33.** $-\frac{4}{5}\left(\frac{7}{8}\right)$ $-\frac{7}{10}$

34. $^{-}52\left(\frac{3}{4}\right)$ $^{-}39$ **35.** $\frac{5}{6}\left(\frac{3}{10}\right)$ $\frac{1}{4}$ **36.** $\frac{1}{3}\left(\frac{2}{7}\right)\left(-\frac{1}{5}\right)$ $-\frac{2}{105}$

37. $-\frac{2}{5}\left(\frac{1}{4} \times \frac{2}{3}\right)$ $-\frac{1}{15}$ **38.** $\frac{1}{2}\left(-\frac{2}{3}\right)\left(-\frac{1}{5}\right)$ $\frac{1}{15}$ **39.** $\frac{3}{5}\left(-\frac{7}{9}\right)\left(-\frac{3}{7}\right)$ $\frac{1}{5}$

Find each value.

40. $-\frac{3}{5} + \frac{4}{5} \times \left(-\frac{2}{7}\right)$ $-\frac{29}{35}$ **41.** $-\frac{8}{3} + \left(-\frac{4}{5}\right) \div \frac{3}{8}$ $^{-}4\frac{4}{5}$

42. $\frac{1}{6} \times \frac{3}{10} + \frac{1}{5}$ $\frac{1}{4}$ **43.** $\frac{1}{6} \times \left(\frac{3}{10} + \frac{1}{5}\right)$ $\frac{1}{12}$

44. $\frac{3}{7} - \frac{4}{5} \div \left(-\frac{2}{15}\right)$ $6\frac{3}{7}$ **45.** $\frac{9}{16} \times \frac{1}{4} - \frac{3}{32}$ $\frac{3}{64}$

C Determine if the following are true.

46. $\frac{3}{4} \times \left(-\frac{2}{3}\right) = -\frac{2}{3} \times \frac{3}{4}$ T   **47.** $^{-}1.2 \times 4.3 = 4.3 \times {}^{-}1.2$ T

48. $9\left(\frac{2}{3} \times \frac{5}{6}\right) = \left(9 \times \frac{2}{3}\right)\frac{5}{6}$ T   **49.** $(1.2 \times 2.3)3 = 1.2(2.3 \times 3)$ T

50. $-\frac{3}{8} \times 1 = -\frac{3}{8}$ T   **51.** $1 \times {}^{-}7.5 = {}^{-}7.5$ T

Use your answers for Exercises 46–51 to answer the following.

52. Do you think multiplication of rational numbers is commutative? Yes

53. Do you think multiplication of rational numbers is associative? Yes

54. Name the identity number for multiplication of rational numbers. 1

391

Multiplying and Dividing With Mixed Numbers

For rational numbers expressed as mixed numbers, first multiply or divide. Then find the sign of the result as you would for integers.

Examples: Find each product or quotient.

1. $1\frac{1}{4} \times \frac{2}{3}$

$$\frac{5}{\underset{2}{4}} \times \frac{\overset{1}{2}}{3} = \frac{5}{6}$$

> Write a mixed number as a fraction. Then multiply or divide.

same sign, so product is positive

$$1\frac{1}{4} \times \frac{2}{3} = \frac{5}{6}$$

2. $1\frac{1}{4} \div {}^{-}2\frac{2}{3}$

$$\frac{5}{4} \div \frac{8}{3} = \frac{5}{4} \times \frac{3}{8}$$

$$= \frac{15}{32}$$

different signs, so quotient is negative

$$1\frac{1}{4} \div {}^{-}2\frac{2}{3} = {}^{-}\frac{15}{32}$$

3. ${}^{-}4\frac{1}{3} \times 4$

$$4\frac{1}{3} \times 4 = \frac{13}{3} \times \frac{4}{1}$$ Write a whole number as a fraction with denominator 1.

$$= \frac{52}{3}$$

$$= 17\frac{1}{3}$$

different signs, so product is negative

$${}^{-}4\frac{1}{3} \times 4 = {}^{-}17\frac{1}{3}$$

■ Exercises

A Tell whether each product or quotient is positive or negative.

1. $7\frac{5}{8} \times \frac{3}{4}$ Pos.

2. $\frac{2}{5}(-5\frac{1}{4})$ Neg.

3. ${}^{-}2\frac{1}{2} \times 4\frac{2}{3}$ Neg.

4. ${}^{-}6\frac{7}{8}(-1\frac{2}{5})$ Pos.

5. ${}^{-}3\frac{4}{5}(\frac{1}{3})$ Neg.

6. $4(8\frac{3}{16})$ Pos.

7. $9\frac{3}{5} \div {}^{-}1\frac{1}{4}$ Neg.

8. ${}^{-}\frac{2}{3} \div {}^{-}5\frac{3}{5}$ Pos.

9. $7\frac{1}{5} \div {}^{-}1\frac{1}{2}$ Neg.

10. $12\frac{2}{3} \div 4\frac{1}{2}$ Pos.

11. ${}^{-}27\frac{3}{10} \div 6$ Neg.

12. ${}^{-}9\frac{7}{10} \div (-\frac{2}{3})$ Pos.

13. $(-1\frac{1}{2})(-1\frac{2}{3})(-1\frac{4}{5})$ Neg.

14. $2 \times 1\frac{2}{5} \times {}^{-}1\frac{7}{10}$ Neg.

15. $(-3\frac{1}{2})(6\frac{2}{3})(-5)$ Pos.

B Find each product or quotient.

16. $^-3\frac{1}{8} \times \frac{3}{4}$ $^-2\frac{11}{32}$ **17.** $4\frac{1}{2} \div (^-\frac{1}{2})$ $^-9$ **18.** $4\frac{1}{2} \times \frac{2}{3}$ 3

19. $^-3\frac{1}{2}(^-\frac{2}{3})$ $2\frac{1}{3}$ **20.** $^-4\frac{1}{4} \div \frac{2}{3}$ $^-6\frac{3}{8}$ **21.** $2\frac{1}{4}(^-\frac{4}{5})$ $^-1\frac{4}{5}$

22. $^-5\frac{1}{2} \times ^-2\frac{1}{4}$ $12\frac{3}{8}$ **23.** $^-4\frac{1}{2} \div 3\frac{1}{4}$ $^-1\frac{5}{13}$ **24.** $5\frac{2}{3} \times ^-9$ $^-51$

25. $3\frac{1}{7} \div 2$ $1\frac{4}{7}$ **26.** $4\frac{1}{2} \times ^-1\frac{1}{2}$ $^-6\frac{3}{4}$ **27.** $^-1\frac{1}{2} \times 3\frac{3}{4}$ $^-5\frac{5}{8}$

28. $^-5\frac{1}{2} \div 2\frac{1}{4}$ $^-2\frac{4}{9}$ **29.** $\frac{7}{8}(^-3\frac{1}{7})$ $^-2\frac{3}{4}$ **30.** $^-2\frac{1}{2} \div ^-1\frac{1}{4}$ 2

31. $^-\frac{7}{8} \div 3\frac{2}{3}$ $^-\frac{21}{88}$ **32.** $^-6\frac{3}{4} \div \frac{7}{16}$ $^-15\frac{3}{7}$ **33.** $1\frac{1}{4} \div (^-\frac{2}{3})$ $^-1\frac{7}{8}$

34. $^-\frac{3}{4} \times ^-1\frac{7}{8}$ $1\frac{13}{32}$ **35.** $3\frac{1}{2} \div ^-2\frac{1}{4}$ $^-1\frac{5}{9}$ **36.** $^-\frac{3}{8} \div 4\frac{1}{2}$ $^-\frac{1}{12}$

37. $^-3\frac{1}{4} \times 2\frac{1}{2}$ $^-8\frac{1}{8}$ **38.** $^-4\frac{3}{4} \div 8$ $^-\frac{19}{32}$ **39.** $^-7(^-3\frac{5}{14})$ $23\frac{1}{2}$

40. $(^-2\frac{2}{5})(1\frac{1}{3})(^-6\frac{1}{2})$ 26 **41.** $(4\frac{3}{4})(5\frac{1}{5})(^-3\frac{2}{3})$ $^-90\frac{17}{30}$

Find each value.

42. $9\frac{1}{2} \div 2\frac{1}{2} \times ^-4\frac{3}{5}$ $^-17\frac{12}{25}$ **43.** $6\frac{2}{5} \div 3\frac{2}{3} \times ^-5\frac{1}{2}$ $^-9\frac{3}{5}$

C **44.** $\frac{1}{2}(7\frac{9}{10}) + \frac{1}{2}(^-3\frac{3}{10})$ $2\frac{3}{10}$ **45.** $(^-2\frac{3}{10} \times 8\frac{1}{10}) + (\frac{7}{10} \times 8\frac{1}{10})$ $^-12\frac{24}{25}$

46. $(^-4\frac{3}{5})(6\frac{1}{2}) + (^-4\frac{3}{5})(9\frac{1}{4})$ $^-72\frac{9}{20}$ **47.** $(3\frac{1}{2} \times ^-1\frac{1}{4}) - (3\frac{1}{2} \times ^-5\frac{1}{4})$ 14

Use multiplication or division to answer each question.

48. If the temperature changed $^-1\frac{3}{4}$ °F every hour for $3\frac{1}{2}$ hours, what was the total change? $^-6\frac{1}{8}$ °F

49. If the temperature changed $^-12\frac{1}{2}$ °F in $7\frac{1}{2}$ hours, what was the average change per hour? $^-1\frac{2}{3}$ °F

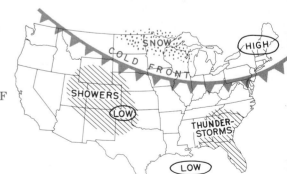

50. The Royster Corporation wants to increase sales $\$3\frac{3}{4}$ million. How long will it take to do this if sales increase $\$1\frac{1}{4}$ million per year? 3 yr

51. Mrs. Wilson's weight changed $^-18\frac{3}{4}$ pounds over a six-week period. What was her average weekly weight change? $^-3\frac{1}{8}$ lb

52. Steel production changed an average of $^-\frac{3}{4}$ ton a day for 5 days. What was the total change for this period? $^-3\frac{3}{4}$ tons

CONSUMER CORNER

Stock Reports

A person who buys shares of a company's stock is buying part ownership in the company. Shares are usually bought and sold through a *stock market* (a group of people, called brokers, whose business is buying and selling stock for others). Many newspapers print daily reports of stock prices. Part of such a report is shown below.

The first column lists some companies. The *Volume* column tells how many of each company's shares were bought and sold that day. The columns labeled *High* and *Low* give the highest and lowest prices paid for a share of the company's stock during the day. (All amounts are in dollars and fractions of a dollar.)

	Volume	High	Low	Close	Chg.
Dictaphone	450,700	26	25	25 ⅝	+5 ⅜
SearsRoeb	333,100	20 ⅛	19 ⅞	20 ⅛	....
TexacoInc	247,700	24 ⅛	23 ⅜	23 ⅝	− ⅛
Boeing	240,200	73 ½	71 ¾	72 ⅛	+ ⅝
HarrisCp	205,500	30 ⅝	29 ¾	30	−1
Exxon	194,200	49 ⅜	48 ½	48 ½	− ½
USSteel	191,900	21 ⅝	21 ½	21 ½	+ ⅛
Chrysler	187,100	8 ⅝	8 ⅜	8 ⅜	....

The *Close* column tells the price of a share at the end of the day. The amount in the *Chg.* column shows how much the closing price of a share went up or down from the closing price of the previous day.

What does the *Chg.* column of the report above tell you about the price of a share of each of the following stocks?

1. Dictaphone It went up $\$5\frac{3}{8}$.

2. Exxon It went down $\$\frac{1}{2}$.

3. Chrysler It stayed the same.

Quick Quiz

Sections 12.1 to 12.4

Find each product or quotient.

1. $2.3 \times {}^{-}1.7$ $^{-}3.91$

2. ${}^{-}4\frac{1}{4} \times {}^{-}2$ $8\frac{1}{2}$

3. $3.42 \times {}^{-}6$ $^{-}20.52$

4. $425 \div {}^{-}1.7$ $^{-}250$

5. ${}^{-}6.39 \div {}^{-}3$ 2.13

6. ${}^{-}12.42 \div {}^{-}0.06$ 207

7. ${}^{-}7 \div \frac{7}{8}$ $^{-}8$

8. $-\frac{2}{3} \times (-\frac{4}{5})$ $\frac{8}{15}$

9. $21(-\frac{3}{7})$ $^{-}9$

10. $\frac{7}{3} \div (-\frac{2}{3})$ $^{-}3\frac{1}{2}$

11. ${}^{-}7\frac{1}{2} \times {}^{-}2\frac{1}{4}$ $16\frac{7}{8}$

12. $-\frac{3}{4}(2\frac{1}{3})$ $^{-}1\frac{3}{4}$

13. $5 \div {}^{-}1\frac{1}{2}$ $^{-}3\frac{1}{3}$

14. ${}^{-}6\frac{2}{3} \div \frac{4}{3}$ $^{-}5$

15. $9\frac{1}{2} \div {}^{-}3$ $^{-}3\frac{1}{6}$

Solve.

16. ${}^{-}2x = 16.2$ $^{-}8.1$

17. $\frac{n}{3.2} = {}^{-}10$ $^{-}32$

18. ${}^{-}4.6 = {}^{-}18.4a$ 18. 0.25

Reciprocals are two numbers whose product is 1.

Example 1: Find the reciprocal of $\frac{2}{3}$.

$$\frac{2}{3} \times \frac{3}{2} = 1$$

So $\frac{2}{3}$ and $\frac{3}{2}$ are reciprocals.

Suggested Class Time

Course	Min.	Reg.	Max.
Days	1	1	1

> To find the reciprocal of a fraction, invert the fraction.

Example 2: Find the reciprocal of $-\frac{3}{5}$.

$$-\frac{3}{5} \times \left(-\frac{5}{3}\right) = 1$$

So $-\frac{3}{5}$ and $-\frac{5}{3}$ are reciprocals.

> The reciprocal of a negative number is negative.

Example 3: Find the reciprocals of **(a)** 6 and **(b)** $3\frac{1}{2}$.

a. $6 = \frac{6}{1}$

$$\frac{6}{1} \times \frac{1}{6} = 1$$

So 6 and $\frac{1}{6}$ are reciprocals.

b. $3\frac{1}{2} = \frac{7}{2}$

$$\frac{7}{2} \times \frac{2}{7} = 1$$

So $3\frac{1}{2}$ and $\frac{2}{7}$ are reciprocals.

> To find the reciprocal of an integer or a mixed number, write the number as a fraction and invert.

Example 4 :   Does 0 have a reciprocal?

You can express 0 as $\frac{0}{1}$. If you invert $\frac{0}{1}$, you get $\frac{1}{0}$. But you know that you can never divide by 0. So 0 has no reciprocal.

■ Exercises

Assignment Guide 12.5
Oral: 1–14
Written:
Min. 15–30; Quiz, p. 394
Reg. 15–32; Quiz, p. 394
Max. 15–39; Quiz, p. 394

Ⓐ Name the reciprocal, if any.

1. $\frac{3}{5}$ $\frac{5}{3}$ or $1\frac{2}{3}$
2. $\frac{5}{3}$ $\frac{3}{5}$
3. $-\frac{4}{7}$ $-\frac{7}{4}$ or $^-1\frac{3}{4}$
4. $-\frac{7}{4}$ $-\frac{4}{7}$

5. 7 $\frac{1}{7}$
6. $\frac{1}{7}$ 7
7. $^-9$ $-\frac{1}{9}$
8. 0 *None*

Find the product.

9. $\frac{7}{8} \times \frac{8}{7}$ 1
10. $-\frac{3}{4} \times (-\frac{4}{3})$ 1
11. $\frac{5}{1} \times \frac{1}{5}$ 1

12. $-\frac{1}{6} \times (-\frac{6}{1})$ 1
13. $\frac{19}{4} \times \frac{4}{19}$ 1
14. $-\frac{21}{5} \times (-\frac{5}{21})$ 1

Ⓑ Name the reciprocal.

15. $\frac{1}{2}$ 2
16. $^-11$ $-\frac{1}{11}$
17. $-\frac{4}{13}$ $-\frac{13}{4}$ or $^-3\frac{1}{4}$
18. $-\frac{1}{10}$ $^-10$

19. 17 $\frac{1}{17}$
20. $\frac{5}{12}$ $\frac{12}{5}$ or $2\frac{2}{5}$
21. $-\frac{13}{3}$ $-\frac{3}{13}$
22. $\frac{12}{5}$ $\frac{5}{12}$

23. $5\frac{1}{2}$ $\frac{2}{11}$
24. $^-7\frac{1}{3}$ $-\frac{3}{22}$
25. $^-6\frac{3}{10}$ $-\frac{10}{63}$
26. $4\frac{7}{8}$ $\frac{8}{39}$

27. $12\frac{3}{4}$ $\frac{4}{51}$
28. $^-11\frac{4}{5}$ $-\frac{5}{59}$
29. 1 1
30. $^-1$ $^-1$

Ⓒ 31. What positive integer is its own reciprocal? (See Exercise 29.) 1

32. What negative integer is its own reciprocal? (See Exercise 30.) $_{-1}$

Find the product.

33. 0.4×2.5 1
34. 0.625×1.6 1

Name the reciprocal in decimal form. (See Exercises 33 and 34.)

35. 0.625 1.6
36. 2.5 0.4
37. 0.4 2.5
38. 1.6 0.625

39. Find the reciprocal of 0.8 in decimal form. 1.25

396

Example 1: Solve $\frac{2}{3}x = -\frac{5}{9}$.

$$\frac{2}{3}x = -\frac{5}{9}$$

$$\frac{2}{3}x \div \frac{2}{3} = -\frac{5}{9} \div \frac{2}{3} \qquad \text{Divide each side by } \tfrac{2}{3}.$$

Dividing by $\frac{2}{3}$ undoes multiplying by $\frac{2}{3}$.

$$x = -\frac{5}{\overset{}{\underset{3}{9}}} \times \frac{\overset{1}{3}}{2}$$

$$x = -\frac{5}{6}$$

Suggested Class Time			
Course	Min.	Reg.	Max.
Days	2	1	1

Check:

$$\frac{2}{3}x = -\frac{5}{9}$$

$$\frac{\overset{1}{2}}{3}\left(-\frac{5}{\underset{3}{6}}\right) = -\frac{5}{9} \qquad \text{Replace } x \text{ with } -\tfrac{5}{6}.$$

$$-\frac{5}{9} = -\frac{5}{9} \;\checkmark$$

Shortcut: To divide by a number, you can multiply by its reciprocal.

Example 2: Use the shortcut to solve $\frac{2}{3}x = -\frac{5}{9}$.

$$\frac{2}{3}x = -\frac{5}{9}$$

$$\frac{3}{2} \times \frac{2}{3}x = \frac{\overset{1}{3}}{2} \times \left(-\frac{5}{\underset{3}{9}}\right) \qquad \text{Multiply each side by } \tfrac{3}{2}.$$

$$1x = -\frac{5}{6} \qquad \text{This step is usually not written.}$$

$$x = -\frac{5}{6}$$

Check: Same as in Example 1.

Example 3: Solve $\frac{n}{8} = -\frac{3}{5}$.

$$\frac{n}{8} = -\frac{3}{5}$$

$$\frac{n}{8} \times 8 = -\frac{3}{5} \times 8$$

$$n = -\frac{3}{5} \times \frac{8}{1}$$

$$n = -\frac{24}{5}$$

$$n = -4\frac{4}{5}$$

Check:

$$\frac{n}{8} = -\frac{3}{5}$$

$$\frac{-4\frac{4}{5}}{8} = -\frac{3}{5}$$

$$-\frac{24}{5} \div \frac{8}{1} = -\frac{3}{5}$$

$$-\frac{\overset{3}{\cancel{24}}}{5} \times \frac{1}{\underset{1}{\cancel{8}}} = -\frac{3}{5}$$

$$-\frac{3}{5} = -\frac{3}{5} \checkmark$$

Assignment Guide 12.6
Oral: 1–9
Written:
Min. (day 1) 10–24
    (day 2) 25–39
Reg. 11–39 odd
Max. 11–47 odd

▪ Exercises

A To solve each equation, what would you do on each side?

1. $\div \frac{2}{3}$ or $\times \frac{3}{2}$

2. $\div -\frac{1}{2}$ or $\times {}^-2$

3. $\div -\frac{3}{10}$ or $\times -\frac{10}{3}$

4. $\div {}^-5$ or $\times -\frac{1}{5}$

5. $\div -\frac{5}{6}$ or $\times -\frac{6}{5}$

6. $\div -\frac{3}{8}$ or $\times -\frac{8}{3}$

1. $\frac{2}{3}x = -\frac{3}{5}$

2. $\frac{3}{14} = -\frac{1}{2}n$

3. $-\frac{3}{10}x = {}^-7$

4. $\frac{4}{5} = {}^-5y$

5. $-\frac{5}{6}m = \frac{4}{9}$

6. $-\frac{4}{9} = -\frac{3}{8}x$

7. $\frac{x}{3} = -\frac{4}{5}$ $\times 3$

8. $\frac{5}{8} = \frac{a}{-6}$ $\times {}^-6$

9. $\frac{x}{-6} = -\frac{3}{2}$ $\times {}^-6$

B Solve.

10. $\frac{4}{5}n = \frac{16}{25}$ $\frac{4}{5}$

11. $-\frac{2}{5} = -\frac{8}{15}t$ $\frac{3}{4}$

12. $\frac{x}{6} = -\frac{13}{4}$ $^-19\frac{1}{2}$

13. $\frac{7}{4} = \frac{a}{4}$ 7

14. $\frac{n}{-9} = -\frac{11}{3}$ 33

15. $\frac{4}{7}r = {}^-5$ $^-8\frac{3}{4}$

16. $\frac{6}{5}n = \frac{12}{10}$ 1

17. $-\frac{7}{3}r = \frac{7}{10}$ $-\frac{3}{10}$

18. $\frac{11}{4} = -\frac{11}{2}x$ $-\frac{1}{2}$

19. $\frac{n}{-3} = 18$ $^-54$

20. $-\frac{3}{5} = \frac{3}{5}s$ $^-1$

21. $-\frac{10}{63} = \frac{a}{3}$ $-\frac{10}{21}$

22. $\frac{n}{3} = -\frac{2}{5}$ $^-1\frac{1}{5}$

23. $12 = -\frac{2}{3}p$ $^-18$

24. $-\frac{13}{20}y = -\frac{39}{100}$ $\frac{3}{5}$

25. $-\frac{1}{3} = {}^-5t$ $\frac{1}{15}$

26. $\frac{d}{-19} = -\frac{1}{38}$ $\frac{1}{2}$

27. $-\frac{9}{10} = {}^-4p$ $\frac{9}{40}$

28. $\frac{15}{2} = {}^-3x$ $^-2\frac{1}{2}$

29. $\frac{2}{5} = \frac{m}{-3}$ $^-1\frac{1}{5}$

30. $^-36 = \frac{9}{7}r$ $^-28$

31. $\frac{c}{5} = -\frac{38}{15}$ $-12\frac{2}{3}$

32. $21n = -\frac{84}{7}$ $-\frac{4}{7}$

33. $\frac{9}{7} = \frac{d}{-56}$ -72

34. $\frac{a}{-13} = -\frac{13}{169}$ 1

35. $0 = \frac{10}{3}x$ 0

36. $-16r = \frac{80}{11}$ $-\frac{5}{11}$

Write and solve an equation for each problem.

37. The product of a number and $-\frac{4}{5}$ is -12. What is the number? $-\frac{4}{5}n = -12;\ 15$

38. The product of a number and $\frac{7}{2}$ is -14. What is the number? $\frac{7}{2}n = -14;\ -4$

39. When a number is divided by 6, the quotient is $-\frac{2}{3}$. What is the number? $\frac{n}{6} = -\frac{2}{3};\ -4$

40. When a number is divided by -3, the quotient is $\frac{5}{12}$. What is the number? $\frac{n}{-3} = \frac{5}{12};\ -1\frac{1}{4}$

C Solve.

Example: Solve $\frac{1}{5}n = -3\frac{1}{3}$.

$$\frac{1}{5}n = -3\frac{1}{3}$$

$$5 \times \frac{1}{5}n = 5 \times -3\frac{1}{3}$$

$$n = -16\frac{2}{3}$$

Check: $\frac{1}{5}n = -3\frac{1}{3}$

$$\frac{1}{5}\left(-16\frac{2}{3}\right) = -3\frac{1}{3}$$

$$\frac{1}{\cancel{5}}\left(-\frac{\cancel{50}^{10}}{3}\right) = -3\frac{1}{3}$$

$$-3\frac{1}{3} = -3\frac{1}{3}\ \checkmark$$

41. $-\frac{2}{5}m = -4\frac{1}{2}$ $11\frac{1}{4}$

42. $-3\frac{1}{2} = 6n$ $-\frac{7}{12}$

43. $6\frac{3}{4} = -1\frac{1}{2}x$ $-4\frac{1}{2}$

44. $-3\frac{2}{3}a = -3\frac{2}{3}$ 1

45. $-4\frac{1}{2} = \frac{x}{8}$ -36

46. $\frac{x}{3} = -5\frac{1}{3}$ -16

Use the formula *d* = *rt* to solve each problem.

47. A diving sphere can move up or down in the water at a rate of $4\frac{1}{2}$ feet per second. At that rate, how long will it take to descend 3150 feet? 700 sec or $11\frac{2}{3}$ min

48. How long would it take the diving sphere in Exercise 47 to rise 405 feet? 90 sec or $1\frac{1}{2}$ min

Courtesy NOAA

399

MATH IN BUILDING TRADES

Carpenters, plumbers, cement workers, plasterers, and many other workers are employed in the building trades. Such workers must often use mathematics in their work.

1. *Plumber:* How many 18-inch lengths of pipe can be cut from three 8-foot lengths of pipe? 15 lengths

2. *Carpenter:* A window opening $3\frac{1}{2}$ feet wide is to be placed in the center of a 12-foot wall. How far from each end of the wall should the opening be? $4\frac{1}{4}$ ft

3. *Plasterer:* About 200 pounds of lime are needed to make enough plaster to cover 45 square yards of wall with a finish coat $\frac{1}{8}$ inch thick. About how much lime is needed to finish 819 square yards of wall? 3640 lb

4. *Cement worker:* Steel bars are used to strengthen parts of concrete buildings. A concrete wall is to have two vertical reinforcing bars at each end and two additional bars every 8 inches of its length. How many reinforcing bars are needed if the wall is 18 feet long? 56 bars

John D. Firestone & Associates, Inc.

C. E. Pefley

Equations With Two Operations

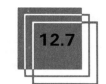
The George Washington Bridge has two end spans of equal length and a center span 0.68 mile long. The overall length of the bridge is 0.9 mile. How long is each end span?

If n is the length in miles of each end span, then

$$2n + 0.68 = 0.9.$$

Authenticated News International

Example 1: Solve $2n + 0.68 = 0.9$.

$$2n + 0.68 = 0.9$$

$$2n + 0.68 + {}^-0.68 = 0.9 + {}^-0.68$$

$$2n + 0 = 0.22$$

$$2n = 0.22$$

$$\frac{2n}{2} = \frac{0.22}{2}$$

$$n = 0.11$$

Check: $2n + 0.68 = 0.9$

$$2\,(0.11) + 0.68 = 0.9$$

$$0.22 + 0.68 = 0.9$$

$$0.9 = 0.9 \checkmark$$

So each end span of the bridge above is 0.11 mile long.

Example 2: Solve $-\frac{1}{3} = \frac{n}{2} + \frac{2}{3}$.

$$-\frac{1}{3} = \frac{n}{2} + \frac{2}{3}$$

$$-\frac{1}{3} + \left(-\frac{2}{3}\right) = \frac{n}{2} + \frac{2}{3} + \left(-\frac{2}{3}\right)$$

$$-\frac{3}{3} = \frac{n}{2} + 0$$

$$^-1 = \frac{n}{2}$$

$$^-1 \times 2 = \frac{n}{2} \times 2$$

$$^-2 = n$$

Check: $-\frac{1}{3} = \frac{n}{2} + \frac{2}{3}$

$$-\frac{1}{3} = \frac{^-2}{2} + \frac{2}{3}$$

$$-\frac{1}{3} = {}^-1 + \frac{2}{3}$$

$$-\frac{1}{3} = -\frac{3}{3} + \frac{2}{3}$$

$$-\frac{1}{3} = -\frac{1}{3} \checkmark$$

401

■ Exercises

A The main steps in the solution of each given equation are shown. Tell how each equation can be found from the equation on its left.

Assignment Guide 12.7
Oral: Reg. & Max. 1–6
Written:
Reg. 7–33 odd
Max. 7–33 odd; 45–55 odd

1. $2.6m + 0.4 = {}^-6.1$ $\Big|$ $2.6m = {}^-6.5$ $\Big|$ $m = {}^-2.5$
   On each side: $\quad + {}^-0.4 \qquad\quad \div 2.6$

2. $-\frac{7}{8} = \frac{4x}{3}$ $\qquad -\frac{21}{8} = 4x$ $\qquad -\frac{21}{32} = x$
   On each side: $\qquad \times 3 \qquad\qquad \div 4$

3. $3.6t - 2.4 = 10.2$ $\Big|$ $3.6t + {}^-2.4 = 10.2$ $\Big|$ $3.6t = 12.6$ $\Big|$ $t = 3.5$
   Change -2.4 to $+{}^-2.4$. $\qquad$ On each side: $\qquad + 2.4 \qquad \div 3.6$

4. $\frac{m}{3} + \frac{7}{9} = \frac{1}{3}$ $\qquad \frac{m}{3} = -\frac{4}{9}$ $\qquad m = -\frac{12}{9}$ $\qquad m = {}^-1\frac{1}{3}$
   On each side: $+\left(-\frac{7}{9}\right) \qquad \times 3 \qquad$ Simplify.

5. ${}^-8 = -\frac{2}{5}n + \frac{6}{5}$ $\qquad -\frac{46}{5} = -\frac{2}{5}n$ $\qquad 23 = n$
   On each side: $+\left(-\frac{6}{5}\right) \qquad \div\left(-\frac{2}{5}\right)$

6. $\frac{x - {}^-3}{4} = 1.2$ $\qquad x - {}^-3 = 4.8$ $\qquad x + 3 = 4.8$ $\Big|$ $x = 1.8$
   On each side, $\qquad \times 4.$ $\qquad$ Change $-{}^-3$ $\quad$ On each side,
   $\qquad\qquad\qquad\qquad\qquad\qquad$ to $+3.$ $\qquad + {}^-3.$

B Solve.

7. $2.7m + 0.4 = 5.8$ ₂ $\quad$ **8.** $3.2k - 4.7 = 4.9$ ₃ $\quad$ **9.** $-\frac{14}{5} = \frac{a}{3} - \frac{4}{5}$ ${}^-6$

10. $\frac{2}{3}n + \frac{5}{6} = \frac{1}{6}$ ${}^-1$ $\qquad$ **11.** $\frac{3x}{4} = 1.8$ ${}^-2.4$ $\qquad$ **12.** ${}^-2 = \frac{a}{3} - \frac{3}{5}$ ${}^-4\frac{1}{5}$

13. ${}^-3y - \frac{3}{4} = \frac{5}{8}$ $-\frac{11}{24}$ $\qquad$ **14.** $2 = \frac{1}{3}x - 1$ ₉ $\qquad$ **15.** $\frac{3}{5}b - \left(-\frac{1}{4}\right) = \frac{2}{3}$ $\frac{25}{36}$

16. $\frac{2x}{{}^-7} = 6.4$ ${}^-22.4$ $\qquad$ **17.** $\frac{k}{4} + 1.5 = {}^-2.7$ ${}^-16.8$ $\qquad$ **18.** $\frac{x - {}^-2.6}{5.2} = 7.3$ 35.36

19. $\frac{y}{6} - 1.5 = {}^-7.2$ ${}^-34.2$ $\qquad$ **20.** $\frac{3}{5}r + \frac{3}{5} = \frac{7}{10}$ $\frac{1}{6}$ $\qquad$ **21.** ${}^-7.6 = \frac{5x}{4.1}$ ${}^-6.232$

22. $3.4k - {}^-4.7 = {}^-8.9$ ${}^-4$ $\quad$ **23.** $\frac{6}{7}d + \frac{2}{5} = \frac{8}{20}$ ₀ $\qquad$ **24.** ${}^-7n + \frac{2}{15} = \frac{5}{6}$ $-\frac{1}{10}$

25. $5m + {}^-2.6 = 3.7$ 1.26 $\qquad$ **26.** $\frac{t}{1.9} + 2 = {}^-1.3$ ${}^-6.27$ $\qquad$ **27.** $\frac{a}{3} + \left(-\frac{4}{7}\right) = \frac{11}{14}$ $4\frac{1}{14}$

28. $\frac{4x}{3} = {}^-6.9$ ${}^-5.175$ $\qquad$ **29.** $-\frac{5}{9} = \frac{2}{3}a + \frac{1}{9}$ ${}^-1$ $\quad$ **30.** $\frac{x + 4.5}{{}^-3.2} = {}^-7.3$ 18.86

31. $\frac{7}{12} = 6n - \frac{5}{12}$ $\frac{1}{6}$ $\qquad$ **32.** $\frac{t}{{}^-4} - 1.5 = 2.7$ ${}^-16.8$ $\quad$ **33.** $-\frac{7}{2}r + \frac{5}{4} = \frac{31}{8}$ $-\frac{3}{4}$

$\boxed{C}$ Use the formula $9C = 5F - 160$ to complete the table. Give each result as a fraction, mixed number, or whole number.

	34.	35.	36.	37.	38.	39.	40.	41.	42.
°C	0	-10	-11.4	-17.77	-17.78	-23	-40	-41	-100
°F	32	14	$11\frac{12}{25}$	$\frac{7}{500}$	$-\frac{1}{250}$	$-9\frac{2}{5}$	-40	$-41\frac{4}{5}$	-148

43. At what temperature are the Fahrenheit and Celsius thermometer readings the same? (See the table above.) Below what temperature are the Fahrenheit readings less than the equivalent Celsius readings? Above what temperature are they more? $-40°; \ -40°; \ -40°$

Solve.

44. $3x + 1\frac{3}{4} = -5\frac{1}{4}$ $-2\frac{1}{3}$ **45.** $2k - 1\frac{1}{2} = 4\frac{1}{3}$ $2\frac{11}{12}$ **46.** $\frac{-4x}{3} = -1\frac{2}{3}$ $1\frac{1}{4}$

47. $\frac{m}{3} + \frac{3}{8} = 4\frac{1}{2}$ $12\frac{3}{8}$ **48.** $\frac{x-3}{4} = -1\frac{2}{3}$ $-3\frac{2}{3}$ **49.** $3x - (-\frac{2}{3}) = 4\frac{1}{2}$ $1\frac{5}{18}$

50. $\frac{2x}{3} = -1\frac{2}{3}$ $-2\frac{1}{2}$ **51.** $5x - 1\frac{2}{3} = -7\frac{1}{2}$ $-1\frac{1}{6}$ **52.** $\frac{t+4}{-7} = 1\frac{2}{3}$ $-15\frac{2}{3}$

53. $2k - 1\frac{2}{3} = -5\frac{1}{2}$ $-1\frac{11}{12}$ **54.** $3x + 1\frac{2}{3} = -2\frac{1}{2}$ $-1\frac{7}{18}$ **55.** $\frac{y}{3} - 1\frac{2}{3} = -5\frac{1}{3}$ -11

Quick Quiz Sections 12.5 to 12.7

Name the reciprocal.

1. $\frac{2}{5}$ $\frac{5}{2}$ or $2\frac{1}{2}$ **2.** $-\frac{7}{8}$ $-\frac{8}{7}$ or $-1\frac{1}{7}$ **3.** 17 $\frac{1}{17}$ **4.** $-4\frac{1}{2}$ $-\frac{2}{9}$

Solve.

5. $\frac{x}{5} = -\frac{3}{16}$ $-\frac{15}{16}$ **6.** $-\frac{6}{7} = \frac{n}{-2}$ $1\frac{5}{7}$

7. $-4t = \frac{12}{13}$ $-\frac{3}{13}$ **8.** $\frac{4}{5} = \frac{3}{10}r$ $2\frac{2}{3}$

9. $2m + 1.2 = -5.6$ -3.4 **10.** $\frac{n}{-3} + \frac{2}{3} = -\frac{5}{2}$ $9\frac{1}{2}$

Using Formulas to Solve Problems

The number of kilowatt-hours you use determines what you pay for electricity.

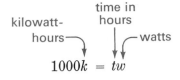

kilowatt-hours ⟶   time in hours   watts

$$1000k = tw$$

Example 1: How many kilowatt-hours are used to run a 200-watt TV for 28 hours?

$$1000k = tw$$

$$1000k = 28 \times 200$$

$$\frac{1000k}{1000} = \frac{5600}{1000}$$

$$k = 5.6$$

Check: Is 1000×5.6 equal to 28×200? ✓

So 5.6 kilowatt-hours are used.

Suggested Class Time

Course	Min.	Reg.	Max.
Days	0	1	1

The approximate horsepower rating of an electric motor is determined by this formula.

horsepower ⟶   watts

$$h = \frac{w}{750}$$

Example 2: How many watts are used by a 2-horsepower lawn mower?

Courtesy Black & Decker

$$h = \frac{w}{750}$$

$$2 = \frac{w}{750}$$

$$2 \times 750 = \frac{w}{750} \times 750$$

$$1500 = w$$

Check: Is $1500 \div 750$ equal to 2? ✓

So the lawn mower uses 1500 watts.

There are many different ways to find the horsepower rating for an automobile. Here is one way.

$$\underset{\underset{h}{\downarrow}}{\text{horsepower}} = 0.4 \times \underset{\underset{n}{\downarrow}}{\overset{\substack{\text{number} \\ \text{of} \\ \text{cylinders}}}{}} \times \underset{\underset{d^2}{\downarrow}}{\overset{\substack{\text{diameter} \\ \text{of piston} \\ \textit{(inches)}}}{}}$$

Example 3: Find the horsepower of a 6-cylinder engine that has a 3.5-inch piston diameter.

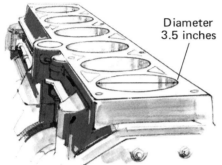

Diameter 3.5 inches

$$h = 0.4 \times n \times d^2$$
$$= 0.4 \times 6 \times (3.5)^2$$
$$= 0.4 \times 6 \times 12.25$$
$$= 29.4$$

Check: In this case, check by redoing your arithmetic. ✓

So the horsepower is 29.4.

Assignment Guide 12.8
Oral: Reg. & Max. 1–5
Written:
Reg. 7–27 odd;
  Quiz, p. 403
Max. 7–27 odd; 28–30;
  Quiz, p. 403

■ Exercises

Ⓐ 1. If your radio uses 2 kilowatt-hours of electricity a month and electricity costs $0.045 per kilowatt-hour, how can you find how much it costs to run the radio each month? Multiply $0.045 by 2.

2. If you know that your 18-watt radio used 1 kilowatt-hour of electricity last month, how can you use the formula from Example 1 to find how many hours it was on last month?
Solve $1000(1) = t(18)$.

3. If you know that your television set was on 50 hours last month and that it used 8.5 kilowatt-hours of electricity, how can you use the formula from Example 1 to tell how many watts it uses?
Solve $1000(8.5) = 50w$.

4. Which formula would you use to find the horsepower rating of a 750-watt vacuum-cleaner motor? $h = \frac{w}{750}$

5. Which formula would you use to find the horsepower rating of a 4-cylinder engine with a 3-inch piston diameter? $h = 0.4 \times n \times d^2$

405

B Use the kilowatt-hour formula from Example 1 to complete this table.

Appliance	t	w	k
6. Hot comb	3	400	1.2
7. Iron	12	1100	13.2
8. Radio	50	15	0.75
9. Sewing machine	28	80	2.24
10. Toaster	10.2	1100	11.22
11. Refrigerator	100	250	25.00
12. Electric range	2.5	12,000	30
13. Hair dryer	20	750	15.00

14. At $0.045 per kilowatt-hour, how much does it cost to run the hot comb in Exercise 6? The radio in Exercise 8? The toaster in Exercise 10? $0.054; $0.03375; $0.5049

15. How long must you use the sewing machine in Exercise 9 to use 1 kilowatt-hour of electricity? 12.5 hr

16. At $0.04 per kilowatt-hour, how much can you save by using a 60-watt bulb instead of a 100-watt bulb for 600 hours? $0.96

Use the horsepower formula from Example 2 to complete this table.

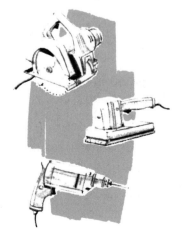

Appliance	w	h
17. Power saw	1500	2
18. Trash compactor	250	$\frac{1}{3}$
19. Power sander	1000	$1\frac{1}{3}$
20. Furnace fan	375	$\frac{1}{2}$
21. Power drill	150	$\frac{1}{5}$
22. Vacuum cleaner	1250	$1\frac{2}{3}$

Use the horsepower formula from Example 3 to complete this table.

	Car	n	d	h
23.	A	6	4.00	38.4
24.	B	8	4.00	51.2
25.	C	8	3.75	45
26.	D	4	3.25	16.9
27.	E	8	4.25	57.8

Courtesy Chevrolet Motor Division, General Motors Corporation

C Stopping distance is the distance the car travels after you notice an obstacle and decide to stop. It depends on your speed. This formula applies to an alert driver whose car has good brakes and is on dry pavement.

stopping distance (*feet*) ⟶   ⟵ speed (*mph*)
$$d = 1.1s + 0.05s^2$$

Example : Find the stopping distance at 20 mph.

$$d = 1.1s + 0.05s^2$$
$$= (1.1 \times 20) + (0.05 \times 20^2)$$
$$= (1.1 \times 20) + (0.05 \times 400)$$
$$= \quad 22 \quad + \quad 20$$
$$= 42 \quad \text{The stopping distance is 42 feet.}$$

28. Use the formula to complete this table.

Speed s	10	20	30	40	50	60	70	80
Stopping distance d	16	42	78	124	180	246	322	408

29. Is the stopping distance at 40 mph double or more than double the stopping distance at 20 mph? More than double

30. Find the difference between the stopping distances for 10 and 20 mph. For 20 and 30 mph. For 30 and 40 mph. Is there a pattern to the differences? Does the rest of the table follow the pattern?
26 ft; 36 ft; 46 ft; yes; yes

Scientific Notation

To talk about the distance to a star and the size of an atom, scientists need very large and very small numbers. Written out in full, these numbers would be hard to work with. But powers of ten can be used to write them in a form that is easier to use.

Suggested Class Time

Course	Min.	Reg.	Max.
Days	0	1	1

You already know what positive exponents mean. The pattern they follow for powers of 10 is shown and extended below.

Yerkes Observatory, University of Chicago

	power of ten	value
Each time the *exponent* is decreased by 1, the *value* is divided by 10.	10^4	10000
	10^3	1000
	10^2	100
	10^1	10
This pattern can be continued to give meaning to 10^0 and to negative exponents.	10^0	1
	10^{-1}	0.1
	10^{-2}	0.01
	10^{-3}	0.001
	10^{-4}	0.0001

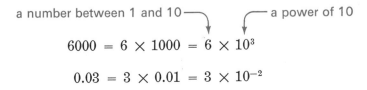

A number is expressed in **scientific notation** by writing it as a number between 1 and 10 multiplied by a power of 10.

Example 1: Express 6000 and 0.03 in scientific notation.

a number between 1 and 10 ⟶   ⟵ a power of 10

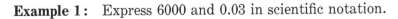

$$6000 = 6 \times 1000 = 6 \times 10^3$$

$$0.03 = 3 \times 0.01 = 3 \times 10^{-2}$$

Example 2: Express 61,000 and 0.00327 in scientific notation.

| First, move the decimal point so it follows the first nonzero digit. | | Then multiply by the power of 10 that gives back the original number. |

6̲1̲0̲0̲0̲,

6.1×10^4

Move the decimal point left 4 places. (This multiplies the number by 10^{-4}.) To undo this, multiply by 10^4.

0̲.̲0̲0̲3̲ 27

3.27×10^{-3}

Move the decimal point right 3 places. (This multiplies the number by 10^3.) To undo this, multiply by 10^{-3}.

Example 3: Express 351.6, 0.0085, 0.0135, and 4065 in scientific notation.

Number	Move decimal point	Multiply by	Scientific notation
351.6	left 2	10^2	3.516×10^2
0.0085	right 3	10^{-3}	8.5×10^{-3}
0.0135	right 2	10^{-2}	1.35×10^{-2}
4065	left 3	10^3	4.065×10^3

■ Exercises

Assignment Guide 12.9
Oral: Reg. & Max. 1–17
Written: Reg. 18–31
Max. 18–35

Ⓐ What exponent should replace each *n* ?

1. $50 = 5 \times 10^n$ 1 **2.** $500 = 5 \times 10^n$ 2 **3.** $5000 = 5 \times 10^n$ 3

4. $3000 = 3 \times 10^n$ 3 **5.** $60 = 6 \times 10^n$ 1 **6.** $400 = 4 \times 10^n$ 2

7. $0.2 = 2 \times 10^n$ ⁻1 **8.** $0.02 = 2 \times 10^n$ ⁻2 **9.** $0.002 = 2 \times 10^n$ ⁻3

10. $0.004 = 4 \times 10^n$ ⁻3 **11.** $0.7 = 7 \times 10^n$ ⁻1 **12.** $0.06 = 6 \times 10^n$ ⁻2

13. $800 = 8 \times 10^n$ 2 **14.** $0.008 = 8 \times 10^n$ ⁻3 **15.** $80 = 8 \times 10^n$ 1

16. To undo moving the decimal point left 8 places, multiply by (*10⁸, 10⁻⁸*).

17. You would multiply by 10^{-6} to undo moving the decimal point (*left, right*) 6 places.

18. 3142 3.142×10^3

19. 34.21 3.421×10^1

20. 546,204
5.46204×10^5

21. 59,603 5.9603×10^4

22. 541.2 5.412×10^2

23. 608
6.08×10^2

24. 0.0134 1.34×10^{-2}

25. 0.00142 1.42×10^{-3}

26. 0.123
1.23×10^{-1}.

27. 0.25 2.5×10^{-1}

28. 0.0004 4×10^{-4}

29. 0.0304
3.04×10^{-2}

Express each measurement using scientific notation.

30. Astronomers use the light-year to measure distance. A light-year is about 6,000,000,000,000 miles. 6×10^{12} mi

31. The earth's atmosphere contains about 1 200 000 000 000 000 000 kilograms of oxygen. 1.2×10^{18} kg

32. One micrometer (or micron) is 0.000 001 meter. 1×10^{-6} m

33. The distance between the sun and the planet Pluto varies from about 2,760,000,000 miles to about 4,600,000,000 miles.
2.76×10^9 mi; 4.6×10^9 mi

C **34.** In living tissue, a typical cell is about 0.000 003 meter long; its volume is about 0.000 000 000 000 000 006 cubic meter.
3×10^{-6} m; 6×10^{-18} m^3

35. A molecule of oxygen weighs 0.000 000 000 000 000 000 000 05 gram. 5×10^{-23} g

Googol

Googol is defined in the cartoon. The word was invented about forty years ago when mathematician Edward Kasner asked his nine-year-old nephew to think of a name for this number.

Now *googol* and *googolplex* are both in the dictionary. A googolplex is 1 followed by a googol of zeros.

1. Write 1 googol in scientific notation.
1×10^{100}

2. Write 1 googolplex as a power of 10.
$10^{10^{100}}$

Terms and Symbols Review

Assignment Guide Rev.
Oral:
Min. Terms & Symbols 1–5
Reg. Terms & Symbols 1–8
Max. Terms & Symbols 1–8
Written: Min. (day 1) 1–18
 (day 2) 19–36
 Reg. 1–49 odd
 Max. 1–49 odd

1. The product of 1.32 and $^-5.7$ is (*positive*, *negative*).

2. The quotient of 5.382 and 8 is (*positive*, *negative*).

3. The product of $^-2\frac{1}{2}$ and $^-4\frac{7}{8}$ is (*positive*, *negative*).

4. The quotient of $\frac{4}{5}$ and $-\frac{2}{3}$ is (*positive*, *negative*).

5. To divide by $-\frac{3}{4}$, you can multiply by its (*opposite*, *reciprocal*).

6. 10^{-3} has a value of (*1000*, *0.001*, *0.0001*).

7. In scientific notation, 7300 is written (73×10^2, 7.3×10^3, 7.3×1000).

8. In scientific notation, 0.006 is written (6×10^{-3}, $6 \div 1000$, 6×10^3).

Chapter 12 Review

Find each product or quotient. 12.1

1. $4.27 \times {}^-1.8$ $_{-7.686}$

2. $^-0.24 \times {}^-3.5$ $_{0.84}$

3. $^-7 \times 5.2$ $_{-36.4}$

4. $^-4.44 \div 1.2$ $_{-3.7}$

5. $^-73.8 \div {}^-6$ $_{12.3}$

6. $123 \div {}^-0.3$ $_{-410}$

Solve. 12.2

7. $\frac{n}{4.3} = {}^-2$ $_{-8.6}$

8. $^-4.3x = 24.08$ $_{-5.6}$

9. $^-5.6 = \frac{a}{4}$ $_{-22.4}$

10. $\frac{m}{^-6} = 8.7$ $_{-52.2}$

11. $^-2.7d = 1.62$ $_{-0.6}$

12. $7r = {}^-12.6$ $_{-1.8}$

Find each product or quotient.

13. $-\frac{4}{5} \times \frac{3}{7}$ $_{-\frac{12}{35}}$

14. $-\frac{2}{3} \times \left(-\frac{7}{8}\right)$ $_{\frac{7}{12}}$

15. $-\frac{5}{9} \times \frac{3}{5}$ $_{-\frac{1}{3}}$ 12.3

16. $-\frac{2}{3} \div \frac{7}{8}$ $_{-\frac{16}{21}}$

17. $\frac{1}{4} \div \left(-\frac{1}{3}\right)$ $_{-\frac{3}{4}}$

18. $-\frac{4}{7} \div 2$ $_{-\frac{2}{7}}$

19. $^-3\frac{1}{7} \times \left(-\frac{3}{4}\right)$ $_{2\frac{5}{14}}$

20. $3\frac{1}{2} \div {}^-2$ $_{-1\frac{3}{4}}$

21. $^-2\frac{1}{4} \times 4\frac{1}{2}$ $_{-10\frac{1}{8}}$ 12.4

22. $^-6\frac{1}{2} \div \frac{1}{8}$ $_{-52}$

23. $^-4\frac{1}{3} \div {}^-3\frac{1}{4}$ $_{1\frac{1}{3}}$

24. $7 \div {}^-1\frac{3}{4}$ $_{-4}$

12.5 Name the reciprocal, if any.

25. $\frac{7}{11}$ $\frac{11}{7}$ or $1\frac{4}{7}$ **26.** $-\frac{4}{9}$ $-\frac{9}{4}$ or $^-2\frac{1}{4}$ **27.** $5\frac{2}{3}$ $\frac{3}{17}$

28. 14 $\frac{1}{14}$ **29.** 0 *None*   **30.** $^-1\frac{3}{4}$ $-\frac{4}{7}$

Solve.

12.6 **31.** $\frac{x}{-4} = \frac{3}{8}$ $^-1\frac{1}{2}$ **32.** $-\frac{3}{5} = \frac{2}{15}r$ $^-4\frac{1}{2}$ **33.** $-\frac{6}{25} = \frac{d}{5}$ $^-1\frac{1}{5}$

34. $-\frac{3}{8}a = -\frac{3}{4}$ 2 **35.** $\frac{5}{8}p = -\frac{25}{64}$ $-\frac{5}{8}$ **36.** $-\frac{6}{11} = 3c$ $-\frac{2}{11}$

12.7 **37.** $\frac{t-3}{6} = -\frac{1}{3}$ 1 **38.** $\frac{n}{3} - \frac{1}{2} = -\frac{5}{6}$ $^-1$ **39.** $0.6x + 8.1 = 5.1$ $^-5$

40. $\frac{3x}{4} = -\frac{5}{8}$ $\frac{5}{6}$ **41.** $^-3.6t - 2.4 = 1.02$ $^-0.95$ **42.** $\frac{x - ^-5.2}{3.7} = ^-3.6$ $^-18.52$

12.8 Solve each problem.

43. Use the formula $k = \frac{tw}{1000}$ to find how long it takes a 25-watt appliance to use 8 kilowatt-hours of electricity. 320 hr

44. Use the formula $h = \frac{w}{750}$ to find the number of watts used by a 3-horsepower motor. 2250 watts

12.9 Express in scientific notation.

45. 300.2 3.002×10^2 **46.** 58.6 5.86×10^1 **47.** 934,000 9.34×10^5

48. 0.673 6.73×10^{-1} **49.** 0.009842 9.842×10^{-3} **50.** 0.01 1×10^{-2}

IT'S OUR NEW 1½ HORSEPOWER LAWN MOWER.

Find each product or quotient.

1. $\frac{3}{4}\left(-\frac{2}{3}\right)$ $-\frac{1}{2}$

2. $-\frac{3}{8} \times \frac{7}{8}$ $-\frac{21}{64}$

3. $1\frac{1}{4} \times {}^{-}2\frac{1}{2}$ $^{-}3\frac{1}{8}$

4. $^{-}2\frac{3}{4} \times {}^{-}1\frac{7}{8}$ $5\frac{5}{32}$

5. 8.13×4.5 36.585

6. $^{-}8.2 \times {}^{-}7.3$ 59.86

7. $\frac{2}{3} \div \frac{7}{8}$ $\frac{16}{21}$

8. $\frac{1}{4} \div \left(-\frac{9}{10}\right)$ $-\frac{5}{18}$

9. $-\frac{1}{2} \div \frac{5}{8}$ $-\frac{4}{5}$

10. $^{-}1\frac{1}{2} \div {}^{-}2\frac{5}{6}$ $\frac{9}{17}$

11. $9.57 \div {}^{-}2.9$ $^{-}3.3$

12. $^{-}19.46 \div {}^{-}1.39$ $_{14}$

13. $-\frac{2}{3} \div 1\frac{1}{3}$ $-\frac{1}{2}$

14. $4 \times {}^{-}6\frac{1}{2}$ $^{-}26$

15. $-\frac{7}{8} \div 4$ $-\frac{7}{32}$

16. $-\frac{3}{17} \times {}^{-}5\frac{2}{3}$ $_1$

17. $\frac{7}{9} \times \frac{9}{7}$ $_1$

18. $12 \times \frac{1}{12}$ $_1$

Solve each equation.

19. $9x = \frac{2}{3}$ $\frac{2}{27}$

20. $5.2x = {}^{-}7.8$ $^{-}1.5$

21. $\frac{x}{6.2} = {}^{-}7.3$ $^{-}45.26$

22. $\frac{x}{8} = -\frac{2}{3}$ $5\frac{1}{3}$

23. $3x + \frac{2}{3} = \frac{1}{2}$ $-\frac{1}{18}$

24. $\frac{3x}{4} = -\frac{2}{3}$ $-\frac{8}{9}$

25. $\frac{x + {}^{-}3.2}{5.7} = {}^{-}6.5$ $^{-}33.85$

26. $3.14x - 5.7 = 10.942$ 5.3

Assignment Guide Test
Written: Min. 1–22
Reg. 1–31
Max. 1–31

Solve each problem.

27. From the formula $k = \frac{tw}{1000}$, find the number of watts used by a bulb that burns 36 kilowatt-hours of electricity in 24 hours. 1500 watts

28. From the formula $h = \frac{w}{750}$, find the horsepower rating of a 3300-watt motor. $4\frac{2}{5}$ horsepower

Express in scientific notation.

29. 67,300 6.73×10^4

30. 980.4 9.804×10^2

31. 0.00036 3.6×10^{-4}

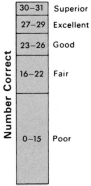

RATE YOURSELF

Number Correct	
30–31	Superior
27–29	Excellent
23–26	Good
16–22	Fair
0–15	Poor

AIR CONDITIONING

Air conditioners are rated by the amount of heat they can remove each hour. The rating is in *British thermal units per hour* (BTU/hr).

An air conditioner for cooling just one room of a house is usually rated between 5000 BTU/hr and 8500 BTU/hr. The number of BTU/hr needed depends on such things as the climate, the size of the room, the location of the room in the house, and the materials the house is made of.

Air conditioners are also rated by how much electricity they use to do their cooling. This rating is called the *energy efficiency ratio* (EER). The EER of an air conditioner is found by dividing its BTU/hr rating by the electrical power, in *watts*, needed to run it. (An air conditioner with an EER of less than 8 is not very efficient.)

Complete the chart. Give each EER to the nearest tenth.

	BTU/hr	watts	EER
	5000	575	8.7 ← $\frac{5000}{575} \approx 8.7$
1.	5100	649	7.9
2.	5300	655.5	8.1
3.	7000	862.5	8.1
4.	8500	862.5	9.9

To find the cost of operating an air conditioner for a certain number of hours, you can use this formula:

$$\text{time in hours} \rightarrow \qquad \leftarrow \text{watts}$$
$$\text{cost} = tew \times 10^{-3}$$
$$\text{cost of electricity per kilowatt-hour} \nearrow$$

Example: What does it cost to run a 690-watt air conditioner for 100 hours if electricity costs 5 cents a kilowatt-hour?

$$\text{cost} = 100 \times 0.05 \times 690 \times 10^{-3}$$
$$= 3.45 \qquad \text{The cost is \$3.45.}$$

If electricity costs 6 cents a kilowatt-hour, find the cost (to the nearest cent) of running each air conditioner in Exercises 1–4 above for 100 hours.

$3.89; \$3.93; \$5.18; \$5.18$

Find the value.

1. 5^2 ₂₅ **2.** 11^2 ₁₂₁ **3.** 21^2 ₄₄₁ **3.8**

4. $^-7 \times\ ^-7$ ₄₉ **5.** $^-1 \times\ ^-1$ ₁ **6.** $^-10 \times\ ^-10$ ₁₀₀ **7.1**

7. $\frac{1}{2} \times \frac{1}{2}$ $\frac{1}{4}$ **8.** $\frac{2}{3} \times \frac{2}{3}$ $\frac{4}{9}$ **9.** $\frac{9}{10} \times \frac{9}{10}$ $\frac{81}{100}$ **4.2**

10. 0.3×0.3 0.09 **11.** 0.7×0.7 0.49 **12.** 1.2×1.2 1.44 **5.4**

Express each fraction in lowest terms. **4.3**

13. $\frac{8}{100}$ $\frac{2}{25}$ **14.** $\frac{10}{25}$ $\frac{2}{5}$ **15.** $\frac{12}{16}$ $\frac{3}{4}$

Express each decimal as a fraction. **5.1**

16. 0.9 $\frac{9}{10}$ **17.** 0.03 $\frac{3}{100}$ **18.** 1.1 $\frac{11}{10}$

Solve each equation.

19. $x + 16 = 25$ 9 **20.** $x + 141 = 315$ 174 **6.5**

21. $y - 15 = 70$ 85 **22.** $z - 81 = 200$ 281 **6.6**

23. The formula for the perimeter of a rectangle is $p = 2l + 2w$. Find **1.9**
the perimeter of a rectangle if $l = 7$ and $w = 5$. 24

Suggested Class Time			
Course	Min.	Reg.	Max.
Days	1	*	0

Assignment Guide GR 13
Written: Min. 1–23
Reg. 1–23

* Combine with Section 13.1.

13

A. Devaney, Inc.

SQUARE ROOTS

Each of the four types of storms (tornado, hurricane, thunderstorm, and cyclone) covers the ground in a roughly circular pattern. Using pictures from weather satellites or radar, weather forecasters can estimate the diameter of a storm. Then with the formula below they can estimate how long the storm will last.

$$t = \sqrt{\frac{d^3}{216}}$$

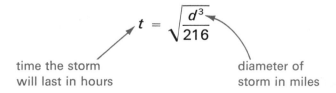

time the storm
will last in hours

diameter of
storm in miles

After you substitute for *d* above, you must find a square root to solve for *t*. In this chapter, you will learn how to find square roots and how to solve problems involving square roots.

You have 81 one-foot-square patio stones. You want to build a square patio and need to find the length of each side.

Suppose you call each side s. Then

$$s \times s = 81$$

or

$$s^2 = 81.$$

Suggested Class Time

Course	Min.	Reg.	Max.
Days	1	1	1

You know $\begin{cases} 9 \times 9 = 81. \\ {}^-9 \times {}^-9 = 81. \end{cases}$

We say: 9 and $^-9$ are **square roots** of 81.

We write: $\sqrt{81} = 9$ and $^-\sqrt{81} = {}^-9.$

The positive square root of 81 is 9.

The negative square root of 81 is $^-9$.

Zefa

Every positive number has two square roots—one positive, the other negative. Zero has only one square root: $\sqrt{0} = 0$.

> The symbol $\sqrt{}$ is used for the non-negative square root of a number, while $^-\sqrt{}$ is used for the negative square root.

Now we know that the patio mentioned above must be 9 feet on each side. (Since we are dealing with a length, we can disregard the negative square root.)

Example 1: Find two solutions for $a^2 = 16$.

$$\text{Since } 4 \times 4 = 16$$

$$\text{and } {}^-4 \times {}^-4 = 16,$$

$$\text{the solutions are 4 and } {}^-4.$$

417

Example 2: Find $\sqrt{400}$ and $^-\sqrt{400}$.

$\sqrt{400}$ is the positive number that gives 400 when squared.

Since $20^2 = 400$, we write $\sqrt{400} = 20$.

$^-\sqrt{400}$ is the negative number that gives 400 when squared.

Since $(^-20)^2 = 400$, we write $^-\sqrt{400} = ^-20$.

■ Exercises

Assignment Guide 13.1
Oral: 1–12
Written: Min. 13–22
      Reg. 13–27
      Max. 13–33

Ⓐ Solve. Find two solutions for each equation if possible.

1. $x^2 = 1$ 1, $^-$1

2. $y^2 = 9$ 3, $^-$3

3. $z^2 = 25$ 5, $^-$5

4. $z^2 = 36$ 6, $^-$6

5. $w^2 = 4$ 2, $^-$2

6. $a^2 = 0$ 0

7. $b^2 = 16$ 4, $^-$4

8. $c^2 = 49$ 7, $^-$7

9. $m^2 = 64$ 8, $^-$8

10. $k^2 = 100$ 10, $^-$10

11. $n^2 = 81$ 9, $^-$9

12. $p^2 = 400$ 20, $^-$20

Ⓑ Find each square root.

13. $\sqrt{4}$ 2

14. $\sqrt{9}$ 3

15. $^-\sqrt{4}$ $^-$2

16. $^-\sqrt{9}$ $^-$3

17. $\sqrt{36}$ 6

18. $\sqrt{25}$ 5

19. $^-\sqrt{49}$ $^-$7

20. $^-\sqrt{16}$ $^-$4

21. $\sqrt{64}$ 8

22. $\sqrt{100}$ 10

23. $^-\sqrt{25}$ $^-$5

24. $^-\sqrt{36}$ $^-$6

25. $\sqrt{81}$ 9

26. $\sqrt{121}$ 11

27. $\sqrt{144}$ 12

Ⓒ **28.** $\sqrt{196}$ 14

29. $^-\sqrt{196}$ $^-$14

30. $\sqrt{225}$ 15

31. $\sqrt{256}$ 16

32. $^-\sqrt{289}$ $^-$17

33. $^-\sqrt{324}$ $^-$18

I HATE BEING A NOTHING! I REFUSE TO GO THROUGH THE REST OF MY LIFE AS A ZERO!

WHAT WOULD YOU LIKE TO BE, CHARLIE BROWN, A FIVE? OR HOW ABOUT A TWENTY-SIX? OR A PAR SEVENTY-TWO?

I KNOW WHAT YOU COULD BE, CHARLIE BROWN.. A SQUARE ROOT!

I THINK YOU'D MAKE A GREAT SQUARE ROOT, CHARLIE BROWN..

I CAN'T STAND IT!

© 1978 United Feature Syndicate

You already know the square roots of many square numbers.

$$1^2 = 1, \quad \text{so } \sqrt{1} = 1.$$

$$2^2 = 4, \quad \text{so } \sqrt{4} = 2.$$

$$3^2 = 9, \quad \text{so } \sqrt{9} = 3.$$

square numbers

Suppose you want to find the square root of a whole number that is not a square number. The following table gives a hint as to how you might begin.

$$\sqrt{1} = 1$$

$$\sqrt{2} = ?$$
$$\sqrt{3} = ?$$
between 1 and 2

$$\sqrt{4} = 2$$

$$\sqrt{5} = ?$$
$$\sqrt{6} = ?$$
$$\sqrt{7} = ?$$
$$\sqrt{8} = ?$$
between 2 and 3

$$\sqrt{9} = 3$$

Suppose you want to estimate $\sqrt{3}$. You know 3 is between 1 and 4, and $\sqrt{3}$ is between $\sqrt{1}$ and $\sqrt{4}$. So $\sqrt{3}$ is between 1 and 2. Since 3 is closer to 4 than to 1, you might estimate $\sqrt{3}$ to be 1.6 or 1.7.

If $\sqrt{3}$ = 1.6, then $(1.6)^2$ should equal 3. But $(1.6)^2$ = 2.56. If $\sqrt{3}$ = 1.7, then $(1.7)^2$ should equal 3. But $(1.7)^2$ = 2.89.

Therefore, both 1.6 and 1.7 are too small as an estimate for $\sqrt{3}$. If you try 1.8, you find $(1.8)^2$ = 3.24. Therefore, $\sqrt{3}$ is between 1.7 and 1.8. You could continue to estimate $\sqrt{3}$ by this process. But there are better methods, and these have been used to compute approximate square roots for tables like the one on page 422. The table also lists the squares of the whole numbers 1–150.

Example 1: Use the table of square roots to find an approximation for $\sqrt{29}$.

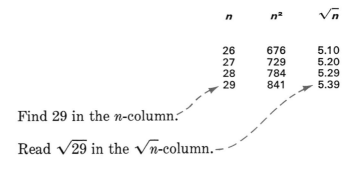

n	n^2	$\sqrt{n}$
26	676	5.10
27	729	5.20
28	784	5.29
29	841	5.39

Find 29 in the n-column.

Read $\sqrt{29}$ in the $\sqrt{n}$-column.

Example 2: Use the table of squares to find 48^2.

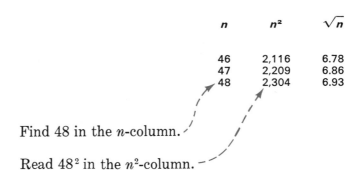

n	n^2	$\sqrt{n}$
46	2,116	6.78
47	2,209	6.86
48	2,304	6.93

Find 48 in the n-column.

Read 48^2 in the n^2-column.

Exercises

Assignment Guide 13.2
Oral: 1–6
Written:
Min. 7–26
Reg. 7–28
Max. 7–29 odd; 31–35

A Tell how to use the table to find the following.

1. $\sqrt{7}$ 2. $\sqrt{79}$ 3. $\sqrt{142}$

4. 15^2 5. 87^2 6. 119^2

1–3. Find 7, 79, or 142 in the *n*-column. Read its square root in the $\sqrt{n}$-column.

4–6. Find 15, 87, or 119 in the *n*-column. Read its square in the n^2-column.

B Use the table to find the following.

7. $\sqrt{18}$ 4.24   8. $\sqrt{42}$ 6.48   9. $\sqrt{94}$ 9.70

10. $\sqrt{110}$ 10.49   11. $\sqrt{128}$ 11.31   12. $\sqrt{149}$ 12.21

13. 14^2 196   14. 37^2 1,369   15. 69^2 4,761

16. 86^2 7,396   17. 108^2 11,664   18. 134^2 17,956

19. $\sqrt{29}$ 5.39   20. 71^2 5,041   21. $\sqrt{63}$ 7.94

22. 92^2 8,464   23. $\sqrt{122}$ 11.05   24. 146^2 21,316

(a) Find each square root in the table. **(b)** Then square that approximation.

Example:

(a) $\sqrt{12} \approx 3.46$ **(b)** $(3.46)^2 = 3.46 \times 3.46$

$$= 11.9716$$

25. $\sqrt{2}$ 26. $\sqrt{3}$ 27. $\sqrt{15}$

28. $\sqrt{41}$ 29. $\sqrt{56}$ 30. $\sqrt{75}$

25. **a.** 1.41 **b.** 1.9881   26. **a.** 1.73 **b.** 2.9929
27. **a.** 3.87 **b.** 14.9769   28. **a.** 6.40 **b.** 40.96
29. **a.** 7.48 **b.** 55.9504   30. **a.** 8.66 **b.** 74.9956

C Square each approximation given for $\sqrt{2}$ below to see how close the result is to 2.

31. $\sqrt{2} \approx 1.414$ 1.999396   32. $\sqrt{2} \approx 1.4142$ 1.99996164

33. $\sqrt{2} \approx 1.41421$ 1.9999899241   34. $\sqrt{2} \approx 1.414213$ 1.999998409369

35. If you square the following decimal, do you think you will get exactly 2? $\sqrt{2} \approx 1.41421356237309504880 3$ No

421

TABLE OF SQUARES AND SQUARE ROOTS

n	n^2	$\sqrt{n}$	n	n^2	$\sqrt{n}$	n	n^2	$\sqrt{n}$
1	1	1.00	51	2,601	7.14	101	10,201	10.05
2	4	1.41	52	2,704	7.21	102	10,404	10.10
3	9	1.73	53	2,809	7.28	103	10,609	10.15
4	16	2.00	54	2,916	7.35	104	10,816	10.20
5	25	2.24	55	3,025	7.42	105	11,025	10.25
6	36	2.45	56	3,136	7.48	106	11,236	10.30
7	49	2.65	57	3,249	7.55	107	11,449	10.34
8	64	2.83	58	3,364	7.62	108	11,664	10.39
9	81	3.00	59	3,481	7.68	109	11,881	10.44
10	100	3.16	60	3,600	7.75	110	12,100	10.49
11	121	3.32	61	3,721	7.81	111	12,321	10.54
12	144	3.46	62	3,844	7.87	112	12,544	10.58
13	169	3.61	63	3,969	7.94	113	12,769	10.63
14	196	3.74	64	4,096	8.00	114	12,996	10.68
15	225	3.87	65	4,225	8.06	115	13,225	10.72
16	256	4.00	66	4,356	8.12	116	13,456	10.77
17	289	4.12	67	4,489	8.19	117	13,689	10.82
18	324	4.24	68	4,624	8.25	118	13,924	10.86
19	361	4.36	69	4,761	8.31	119	14,161	10.91
20	400	4.47	70	4,900	8.37	120	14,400	10.95
21	441	4.58	71	5,041	8.43	121	14,641	11.00
22	484	4.69	72	5,184	8.49	122	14,884	11.05
23	529	4.80	73	5,329	8.54	123	15,129	11.09
24	576	4.90	74	5,476	8.60	124	15,376	11.14
25	625	5.00	75	5,625	8.66	125	15,625	11.18
26	676	5.10	76	5,776	8.72	126	15,876	11.22
27	729	5.20	77	5,929	8.77	127	16,129	11.27
28	784	5.29	78	6,084	8.83	128	16,384	11.31
29	841	5.39	79	6,241	8.89	129	16,641	11.36
30	900	5.48	80	6,400	8.94	130	16,900	11.40
31	961	5.57	81	6,561	9.00	131	17,161	11.45
32	1,024	5.66	82	6,724	9.06	132	17,424	11.49
33	1,089	5.74	83	6,889	9.11	133	17,689	11.53
34	1,156	5.83	84	7,056	9.17	134	17,956	11.58
35	1,225	5.92	85	7,225	9.22	135	18,225	11.62
36	1,296	6.00	86	7,396	9.27	136	18,496	11.66
37	1,369	6.08	87	7,569	9.33	137	18,769	11.70
38	1,444	6.16	88	7,744	9.38	138	19,044	11.75
39	1,521	6.24	89	7,921	9.43	139	19,321	11.79
40	1,600	6.32	90	8,100	9.49	140	19,600	11.83
41	1,681	6.40	91	8,281	9.54	141	19,881	11.87
42	1,764	6.48	92	8,464	9.59	142	20,164	11.92
43	1,849	6.56	93	8,649	9.64	143	20,449	11.96
44	1,936	6.63	94	8,836	9.70	144	20,736	12.00
45	2,025	6.71	95	9,025	9.75	145	21,025	12.04
46	2,116	6.78	96	9,216	9.80	146	21,316	12.08
47	2,209	6.86	97	9,409	9.85	147	21,609	12.12
48	2,304	6.93	98	9,604	9.90	148	21,904	12.17
49	2,401	7.00	99	9,801	9.95	149	22,201	12.21
50	2,500	7.07	100	10,000	10.00	150	22,500	12.25

Extending the Square-Root Table

13.3

The table on page 422 lists the square roots of numbers from 1–150. Often you need to know the square root of a number larger than 150. In some such cases you can use the n^2-column.

Example 1: Find $\sqrt{400}$.

n	n^2	$\sqrt{n}$
19	361	4.36
20	400	4.47
21	441	4.58

400 is given in the n^2-column of the table.

$$400 = 20^2$$

$$\sqrt{400} = 20$$

In many cases, however, you will not find the given number in either the n-column or the n^2-column. In these cases, another method is sometimes useful.

The following examples suggest an important property.

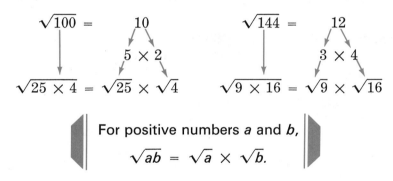

For positive numbers a and b,
$\sqrt{ab} = \sqrt{a} \times \sqrt{b}.$

Example 2: Find $\sqrt{400}$ by using the property just stated.

$$\sqrt{400} = \sqrt{4 \times 100} \qquad \text{or} \qquad \sqrt{400} = \sqrt{16 \times 25}$$

$$= \sqrt{4} \times \sqrt{100} \qquad\qquad\qquad\quad = \sqrt{16} \times \sqrt{25}$$

$$= 2 \times 10 \qquad\qquad\qquad\qquad\quad = 4 \times 5$$

$$= 20 \qquad\qquad\qquad\qquad\qquad\quad = 20$$

423

Example 3: Find $\sqrt{160}$ by using the table on page 422.

160 is not in the n-column or the n^2-column. But 160 can be named as the product of two numbers, each less than 150.

Assignment Guide 13.3
Oral: 1–8
Written:
Min. (day 1) 9–32
(day 2) 33–45 odd;
Quiz, p. 425
Reg. 9–43 odd; Quiz,
p. 425
Max. 9–39 odd; 49–58;
Quiz, p. 425

$$\sqrt{160} = \sqrt{16 \times 10}$$ Find the largest square-number factor.

$$= \sqrt{16} \times \sqrt{10}$$ Both numbers are in the n-column.

$$\approx 4 \times 3.16$$ Find $\sqrt{10}$ in the table

$$\approx 12.64$$

■ Exercises

A Find each square root in the table.

1. $\sqrt{169}$ 13   **2.** $\sqrt{196}$ 14   **3.** $\sqrt{576}$ 24   **4.** $\sqrt{484}$ 22

5. $\sqrt{841}$ 29   **6.** $\sqrt{1296}$ 36   **7.** $\sqrt{2601}$ 51   **8.** $\sqrt{3969}$ 63

B Name each square root as a product of two square roots, one of which has the largest possible square number under the square-root sign.

9. $\sqrt{9} \times \sqrt{2}$
10. $\sqrt{16} \times \sqrt{2}$
11. $\sqrt{25} \times \sqrt{3}$
12. $\sqrt{36} \times \sqrt{2}$
13. $\sqrt{100} \times \sqrt{3}$
14. $\sqrt{100} \times \sqrt{21}$
15. $\sqrt{9} \times \sqrt{11}$
16. $\sqrt{9} \times \sqrt{111}$
17. $\sqrt{81} \times \sqrt{10}$
18. $\sqrt{25} \times \sqrt{10}$
19. $\sqrt{36} \times \sqrt{10}$
20. $\sqrt{144} \times \sqrt{10}$

Example: $\sqrt{200} = \sqrt{100} \times \sqrt{2}$

9. $\sqrt{18}$ **10.** $\sqrt{32}$ **11.** $\sqrt{75}$ **12.** $\sqrt{72}$

13. $\sqrt{300}$ **14.** $\sqrt{2100}$ **15.** $\sqrt{99}$ **16.** $\sqrt{999}$

17. $\sqrt{810}$ **18.** $\sqrt{250}$ **19.** $\sqrt{360}$ **20.** $\sqrt{1440}$

Name each square root as the product of a whole number and a square root. *Hint:* Use your answers from Exercises 9–20.

Example: $\sqrt{200} = \sqrt{100} \times \sqrt{2}$

$$= 10 \times \sqrt{2}$$

21. $\sqrt{18}$ $3 \times \sqrt{2}$ **22.** $\sqrt{32}$ $4 \times \sqrt{2}$ **23.** $\sqrt{75}$ $5 \times \sqrt{3}$ **24.** $\sqrt{72}$ $6 \times \sqrt{2}$

25. $\sqrt{300}$ $10 \times \sqrt{3}$ **26.** $\sqrt{2100}$ $10 \times \sqrt{21}$ **27.** $\sqrt{99}$ $3 \times \sqrt{11}$ **28.** $\sqrt{999}$ $3 \times \sqrt{111}$

29. $\sqrt{810}$ $9 \times \sqrt{10}$ **30.** $\sqrt{250}$ $5 \times \sqrt{10}$ **31.** $\sqrt{360}$ $6 \times \sqrt{10}$ **32.** $\sqrt{1440}$ $12 \times \sqrt{10}$

Find each square root. Use the table on page 422.

33. $\sqrt{640}$ 25.28   **34.** $\sqrt{250}$ 15.8   **35.** $\sqrt{1000}$ 31.6   **36.** $\sqrt{750}$ 27.4

37. $\sqrt{1500}$ 38.7   **38.** $\sqrt{500}$ 22.4   **39.** $\sqrt{189}$ 13.74   **40.** $\sqrt{204}$ 14.28

41. $\sqrt{700}$ 26.5   **42.** $\sqrt{550}$ 23.45   **43.** $\sqrt{168}$ 12.96   **44.** $\sqrt{175}$ 13.25

45. $\sqrt{490}$ 22.12   **46.** $\sqrt{280}$ 16.74   **47.** $\sqrt{630}$ 25.11   **48.** $\sqrt{240}$ 15.48

C Compute.

Examples: **a.** $\sqrt{144 + 25} = \sqrt{169}$ **b.** $\sqrt{144} + \sqrt{25} = 12 + 5$

$$= 13 \qquad\qquad\qquad = 17$$

49. $\sqrt{16 + 9}$ 5   **50.** $\sqrt{16} + \sqrt{9}$ 7   **51.** $\sqrt{64 + 36}$ 10   **52.** $\sqrt{64} + \sqrt{36}$ 14

53. Compare answers for Exercises 49 and 50 and for Exercises 51 and 52. Is $\sqrt{a + b}$ equal to $\sqrt{a} + \sqrt{b}$? No

Compute.

54. $\sqrt{25 - 9}$ 4   **55.** $\sqrt{25} - \sqrt{9}$ 2   **56.** $\sqrt{100 - 36}$ 8   **57.** $\sqrt{100} - \sqrt{36}$ 4

58. Is $\sqrt{a - b}$ equal to $\sqrt{a} - \sqrt{b}$? No

Quick Quiz
Sections 13.1 to 13.3

Find each square root.

1. $\sqrt{25}$ 5   **2.** $\sqrt{49}$ 7   **3.** $\sqrt{81}$ 9

Find two solutions for each equation.

4. $x^2 = 36$ 6, ⁻6   **5.** $m^2 = 100$ 10, ⁻10   **6.** $y^2 = 9$ 3, ⁻3

Use the table on page 422 to find the following.

7. $\sqrt{11}$ 3.32   **8.** 23^2 529   **9.** $\sqrt{139}$ 11.79

Using the table on page 422, find each square root.

10. $\sqrt{300}$ 17.3   **11.** $\sqrt{360}$ 18.96   **12.** $\sqrt{162}$ 12.69

13.4 Square Roots of Rational Numbers

You know that whole numbers have square roots. Now you will see that rational numbers also have square roots.

Example 1:   Find $\sqrt{\dfrac{4}{9}}$.

Here are two ways to do it.

$$\sqrt{\dfrac{4}{9}} = \sqrt{\dfrac{2}{3} \times \dfrac{2}{3}} \qquad\qquad \sqrt{\dfrac{4}{9}} = \dfrac{\sqrt{4}}{\sqrt{9}}$$

$$= \dfrac{2}{3} \qquad\qquad\qquad\qquad = \dfrac{2}{3}$$

For positive numbers a and b,

$$\sqrt{\dfrac{a}{b}} = \dfrac{\sqrt{a}}{\sqrt{b}}.$$

Example 2:   Find $\sqrt{0.64}$.

Here are two ways to do it.

$$\sqrt{0.64} = \sqrt{0.8 \times 0.8} \qquad\qquad \sqrt{0.64} = \sqrt{\dfrac{64}{100}}$$

$$= 0.8 \qquad\qquad\qquad\qquad = \dfrac{\sqrt{64}}{\sqrt{100}}$$

$$= \dfrac{8}{10} \ \text{ or } \ \dfrac{4}{5} \ \text{ or } 0.8$$

■ Exercises

Suggested Class Time

Course	Min.	Reg.	Max.
Days	1	1	1

Ⓐ Name as the square of a fraction. Example: $\frac{4}{100} = \left(\frac{2}{10}\right)^2$

Assignment Guide 13.4
Oral: 1–16
Written: Min. 17–32
  Reg. 17–34
  Max. 17–40

1. $\dfrac{16}{100} \ \left(\dfrac{4}{10}\right)^2$

2. $\dfrac{9}{36} \ \left(\dfrac{3}{6}\right)^2$

3. $\dfrac{1}{4} \ \left(\dfrac{1}{2}\right)^2$

4. $\dfrac{16}{25} \ \left(\dfrac{4}{5}\right)^2$

5. $\dfrac{64}{81} \ \left(\dfrac{8}{9}\right)^2$

6. $\dfrac{25}{100} \ \left(\dfrac{5}{10}\right)^2$

7. $\dfrac{49}{64} \ \left(\dfrac{7}{8}\right)^2$

8. $\dfrac{9}{16} \ \left(\dfrac{3}{4}\right)^2$

426

Name as a fraction. Example: $0.08 = \frac{8}{100}$

9. 0.09 $\frac{9}{100}$ **10.** 0.81 $\frac{81}{100}$ **11.** 0.16 $\frac{16}{100}$ **12.** 0.04 $\frac{4}{100}$

13. 0.25 $\frac{25}{100}$ **14.** 0.36 $\frac{36}{100}$ **15.** 0.01 $\frac{1}{100}$ **16.** 0.0025 $\frac{25}{10,000}$

B Find each square root as a fraction.

17. $\sqrt{\frac{9}{25}}$ $\frac{3}{5}$ **18.** $\sqrt{\frac{16}{49}}$ $\frac{4}{7}$ **19.** $\sqrt{\frac{25}{64}}$ $\frac{5}{8}$ **20.** $\sqrt{\frac{64}{81}}$ $\frac{8}{9}$

21. $\sqrt{\frac{1}{4}}$ $\frac{1}{2}$ **22.** $\sqrt{\frac{49}{100}}$ $\frac{7}{10}$ **23.** $\sqrt{\frac{9}{16}}$ $\frac{3}{4}$ **24.** $\sqrt{\frac{81}{100}}$ $\frac{9}{10}$

Find each square root as a decimal.

25. $\sqrt{0.09}$ 0.3 **26.** $\sqrt{0.81}$ 0.9 **27.** $\sqrt{0.04}$ 0.2 **28.** $\sqrt{0.25}$ 0.5

29. $\sqrt{0.36}$ 0.6 **30.** $\sqrt{0.01}$ 0.1 **31.** $\sqrt{0.0036}$ 0.06 **32.** $\sqrt{1.44}$ 1.2

C Find each square root.

Examples:

a. $\sqrt{\frac{2}{9}} = \frac{\sqrt{2}}{\sqrt{9}}$

$\approx \frac{1.41}{3}$ ← from table

≈ 0.47

b. $\sqrt{\frac{5}{8}} = \sqrt{\frac{5 \times 2}{8 \times 2}}$ → Multiply both numerator and denominator to make the denominator a square number.

$= \sqrt{\frac{10}{16}}$

$= \frac{\sqrt{10}}{\sqrt{16}}$

$\approx \frac{3.16}{4}$ ← from table

≈ 0.79

33. $\sqrt{\frac{5}{16}}$ 0.56 **34.** $\sqrt{\frac{7}{25}}$ 0.53 **35.** $\sqrt{\frac{11}{100}}$ 0.332 **36.** $\sqrt{\frac{5}{36}}$ $0.37\overline{3}$

37. $\sqrt{\frac{1}{2}}$ 0.705 **38.** $\sqrt{\frac{3}{10}}$ 0.548 **39.** $\sqrt{\frac{7}{8}}$ 0.935 **40.** $\sqrt{\frac{3}{50}}$ 0.245

13.5 Square Roots and Equations

To solve some practical problems you have to solve equations like $x^2 = 36$. You already know that this equation has two solutions—one positive and the other negative.

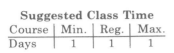

Suggested Class Time

Course	Min.	Reg.	Max.
Days	1	1	1

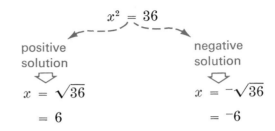

$$x^2 = 36$$

positive solution   negative solution

$$x = \sqrt{36} \qquad\qquad x = {}^-\sqrt{36}$$

$$= 6 \qquad\qquad\qquad = {}^-6$$

In practical problems you are usually interested only in a distance or an amount, and not a direction, so the negative solution does not apply.

Example 1: Find the positive solution of $x^2 = 16$.

$$x^2 = 16$$

$$\sqrt{x^2} = \sqrt{16}$$

$$x = 4$$

Take the square root of each side. (The square root of x^2 is x. The positive square root of 16 is $\sqrt{16}$ or 4.)

Example 2: Find the positive solution of $x^2 = 21$.

$$x^2 = 21$$

$$\sqrt{x^2} = \sqrt{21} \qquad \text{Take the square root of each side.}$$

$$x \approx 4.58 \qquad \text{Use the table.}$$

Example 3: Find the positive solution of $x^2 + 5 = 81$.

$$x^2 + 5 = 81$$

$$x^2 + 5 + {}^-5 = 81 + {}^-5 \qquad \text{Add } {}^-5 \text{ to each side.}$$

$$x^2 = 76$$

$$\sqrt{x^2} = \sqrt{76} \qquad \text{Take the square root of each side.}$$

$$x \approx 8.72 \qquad \text{Use the table.}$$

Exercises

Assignment Guide 13.5
Oral: 1–6
Written: Min. 7–17
    Reg. 7–27 odd
    Max. 7–33 odd

A How would you find the positive solution of each equation?

3–6. Answers at right below.

1. $x^2 = 25$ **2.** $x^2 = 30$ **3.** $x^2 + 9 = 90$

1–2. On each side, take $\sqrt{}$.

4. $x^2 - 5 = 59$ **5.** $x^2 + 2 = 10$ **6.** $x^2 - 4 = 14$

B Find the positive solution of each equation.

7. $x^2 = 9$ 3   **8.** $x^2 = 27$ 5.20   **9.** $x^2 = 42$ 6.48

10. $x^2 + 5 = 30$ 5   **11.** $x^2 + 9 = 42$ 5.74   **12.** $x^2 + 16 = 25$ 3

13. $x^2 - 4 = 60$ 8   **14.** $x^2 - 9 = 81$ 9.49   **15.** $x^2 - 25 = 144$ 13

If an airplane is h miles above the earth, it is approximately d miles from the horizon. The relationship between h and d can be expressed by the following formula.

$$d = \sqrt{8000h}$$

Example: If an airplane is 5 miles high, what is the distance to the horizon?

$$d = \sqrt{8000h}$$
$$= \sqrt{8000 \times 5}$$
$$= \sqrt{40000}$$
$$= 200 \qquad \text{It is 200 miles to the horizon.}$$

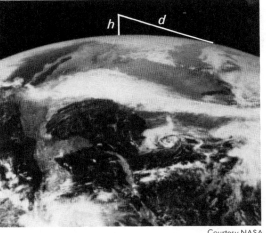

Courtesy NASA

Use the formula above. Copy and complete.

3. On each side: $+ \ ^-9$, take $\sqrt{}$.
4. Change $- 5$ to $+ \ ^-5$. On each side: $+ 5$, take $\sqrt{}$.
5. On each side: $+ \ ^-2$, take $\sqrt{}$.
6. Change $- 4$ to $+ \ ^-4$. On each side: $+ 4$, take $\sqrt{}$.

	Altitude	Distance to horizon		Altitude	Distance to horizon
16.	1 mile	89.6 mi	**17.**	$1\frac{1}{4}$ miles	100 mi
18.	2 miles	126.4 mi	**19.**	$2\frac{1}{2}$ miles	141 mi
20.	3 miles	154.8 mi	**21.**	3.2 miles	160 mi

Solve each equation.

Example: $\sqrt{x} = 5.1$

$(\sqrt{x})^2 = (5.1)^2$ Square each side.

$x = 26.01$

22. $\sqrt{x} = 6$ 36   **23.** $\sqrt{y} = 6.2$ 38.44   **24.** $\sqrt{r} = \frac{4}{7}$ $\frac{16}{49}$

25. $\sqrt{k} = 49$ 2401   **26.** $\sqrt{r} = 25$ 625   **27.** $\sqrt{t} = 128$ 16,384

Example: $\sqrt{x + 3} = 5$

$(\sqrt{x + 3})^2 = 5^2$ Square each side.

$x + 3 = 25$

$x + 3 + {}^-3 = 25 + {}^-3$

$x = 22$

28. $\sqrt{x + 7} = 4$ 9   **29.** $\sqrt{x + 5} = 9$ 76   **30.** $\sqrt{x + 11} = 15$ 214

31. $\sqrt{x - 7} = 7$ 56   **32.** $\sqrt{x - 4} = 6$ 40   **33.** $\sqrt{x - 9} = 14$ 205

Meeting Halley's Comet

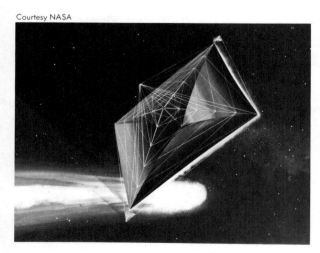

Courtesy NASA

The National Aeronautics and Space Administration is studying plans to launch an unmanned spacecraft to meet with Halley's Comet when it next approaches the sun in 1986. A giant square sail, having an area of 640 000 square meters, would be used to propel the spacecraft by means of sunlight. What would be the length of a side of the sail?

800 m

The Pythagorean Property

13.6

As you probably know, a **right triangle** has one 90° angle (called a *right angle*).

The right triangle shown here has sides that are 5, 4, and 3 units long. If a square is drawn on each side as shown, then it is easy to see that the square of the longest side is equal to the sum of the squares of the other two sides.

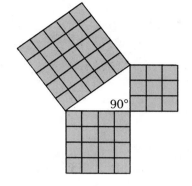

90°

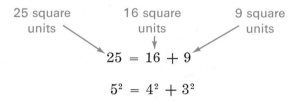

25 square units 16 square units 9 square units

$$25 = 16 + 9$$

$$5^2 = 4^2 + 3^2$$

This illustrates an important property of right triangles.

Pythagorean Property

In a right triangle, the square of the hypotenuse is equal to the sum of the squares of the other two sides. (*Note:* The hypotenuse is the side opposite the right angle, and it is always the longest side.)

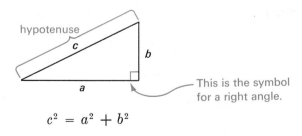

hypotenuse

c

b

a

This is the symbol for a right angle.

$$c^2 = a^2 + b^2$$

This property can be used to find the third side of a right triangle when the other two sides are known.

Example 1: Find the length c of the hypotenuse.

$$c^2 = a^2 + b^2$$

$$c^2 = 8^2 + 6^2$$

$$c^2 = 64 + 36$$

$$c^2 = 100$$

$$\sqrt{c^2} = \sqrt{100}$$

$$c = 10$$

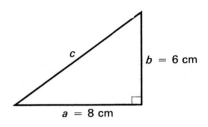

The hypotenuse is 10 cm long.

Example 2: Find the length a of the side.

$$c^2 = a^2 + b^2$$

Hint: Use the table on page 422 to find 25^2 and 24^2.

$$25^2 = a^2 + 24^2$$

$$625 = a^2 + 576$$

$$625 + {}^-576 = a^2 + 576 + {}^-576$$

$$49 = a^2$$

$$\sqrt{49} = \sqrt{a^2}$$

$$7 = a$$

The side is 7 ft long.

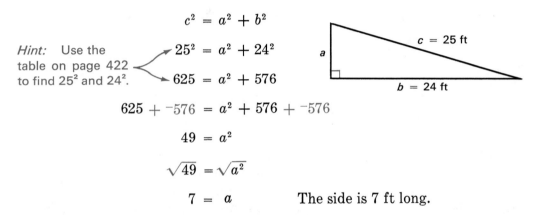

Example 3: Find the length b of the side.

$$c^2 = a^2 + b^2$$

$$17^2 = 15^2 + b^2$$

$$289 = 225 + b^2$$

$${}^-225 + 289 = {}^-225 + 225 + b^2$$

$$64 = b^2$$

$$\sqrt{64} = \sqrt{b^2}$$

$$8 = b$$

The side is 8 m long.

■ Exercises

Assignment Guide 13.6
Oral: 1–8
Written:
Min. 9–19 odd; 21–24;
    Quiz, p. 435
Reg. 9–19 odd; 21–24;
    Quiz, p. 435
Max. 9–19 odd; 21–26;
    Quiz, p. 435

A What equation can you use to find the unknown side in each triangle?

1.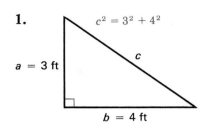
$$c^2 = 3^2 + 4^2$$
$a = 3$ ft c $b = 4$ ft

2.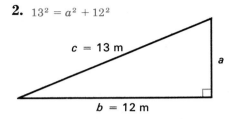
$$13^2 = a^2 + 12^2$$
$c = 13$ m a $b = 12$ m

How would you solve each equation?

3–8. Answers below.

3. $25 = 9 + b^2$ **4.** $100 = a^2 + 64$ **5.** $c^2 = 144 + 25$

6. $5^2 = 3^2 + b^2$ **7.** $10^2 = a^2 + 8^2$ **8.** $c^2 = 12^2 + 5^2$

B Use the right triangle below to help you find each unknown side in the tables.

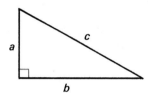

a c b

	a	b	c		a	b	c
9.	3	4	5	**10.**	5	12	13
11.	15	8	17	**12.**	24	7	25
13.	7	24	25	**14.**	21	20	29
15.	9	40	41	**16.**	11	60	61
17.	63	16	65	**18.**	45	28	53
19.	21	20	29	**20.**	8	15	17

3. On each side: $+\ ^-9$, take $\sqrt{\ }$.

4. On each side: $+\ ^-64$, take $\sqrt{\ }$.

5. Add 144 and 25. On each side, take $\sqrt{\ }$.

6. Find 5^2 and 3^2. On each side: $+\ ^-9$, take $\sqrt{\ }$.

7. Find 10^2 and 8^2. On each side: $+\ ^-64$, take $\sqrt{\ }$.

8. Find 12^2 and 5^2. Add 144 and 25. On each side, take $\sqrt{\ }$.

Determine if each triangle is a right triangle.

Examples:

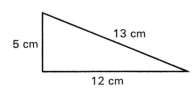

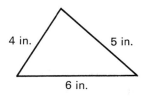

$13^2 = 5^2 + 12^2$

$169 = 25 + 144$

$169 = 169$ True

Yes, it is a
right triangle.

$6^2 = 5^2 + 4^2$

$36 = 25 + 16$

$36 = 41$ False

No, it is not
a right triangle.

21. Yes

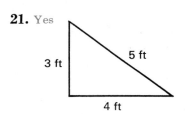

22. No

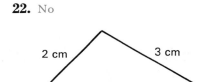

23. Yes

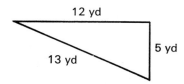

24. Yes

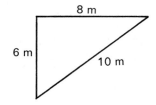

C **25.** Yes

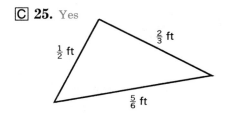

26. Yes

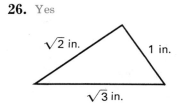

Find each square root as a fraction.

1. $\sqrt{\frac{4}{49}}$ $\frac{2}{7}$ **2.** $\sqrt{\frac{25}{81}}$ $\frac{5}{9}$ **3.** $\sqrt{\frac{1}{100}}$ $\frac{1}{10}$

Find each square root as a decimal.

4. $\sqrt{0.16}$ 0.4   **5.** $\sqrt{0.49}$ 0.7   **6.** $\sqrt{0.09}$ 0.3

Find the positive solution of each equation.

7. $x^2 = 25$ 5   **8.** $x^2 - 4 = 32$ 6   **9.** $x^2 - 9 = 72$ 9

Use the right triangle to help you find each unknown side in the following.

	a	b	c
10.	9	12	15
11.	12	5	13
12.	6	8	10

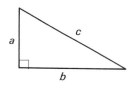

In a Pig's Sty!

A farmer has 250 pigs to sell. How can the pigs be arranged in 8 pens so the farmer can instantly deliver any number of pigs from 1 to 250 by simply opening the right gate or gates and herding the pigs out?

The pens have 1, 2, 4, 8, 16, 32, 64, and 123 pigs in them.

435

13.7 Using the Pythagorean Property

The Pythagorean Property can be used in solving many practical problems.

Example 1: How far is it from point D to point E?

$$c^2 = a^2 + b^2$$

$$14^2 = a^2 + 10^2$$

$$196 = a^2 + 100$$

$$196 + {}^-100 = a^2 + 100 + {}^-100$$

$$96 = a^2$$

$$\sqrt{96} = \sqrt{a^2}$$

$$9.80 \approx a$$

Check: Is 14^2 approximately equal to $(9.8)^2 + 10^2$? ✓

So it is about 9.8 kilometers from D to E.

Example 2: A telephone pole is to be braced by a wire as shown. How high up on the pole should the wire be fastened?

$$c^2 = a^2 + b^2$$

$$39^2 = 15^2 + b^2$$

$$1521 = 225 + b^2$$

$${}^-225 + 1521 = {}^-225 + 225 + b^2$$

$$1296 = b^2$$

$$\sqrt{1296} = \sqrt{b^2}$$

$$36 = b$$

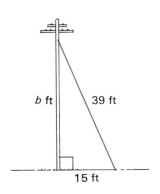

Check: Is 39^2 equal to $15^2 + 36^2$? ✓

So the wire should be fastened 36 feet above the ground.

Exercises

A What equation would you use to find the unknown side in each right triangle?

1.
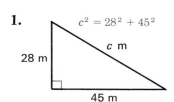
$c^2 = 28^2 + 45^2$
28 m
c m
45 m

2. $61^2 = a^2 + 11^2$
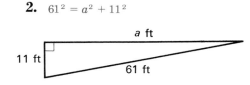
11 ft
a ft
61 ft

3. $85^2 = 77^2 + b^2$
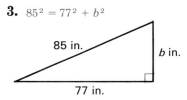
85 in.
b in.
77 in.

4. $c^2 = 90^2 + 90^2$
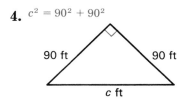
90 ft
90 ft
c ft

B Solve each problem.

5. When Joe had let out 100 yards of kite string, Rita was directly beneath the kite. If Joe is 80 yards from Rita, how high is the kite? 60 yd

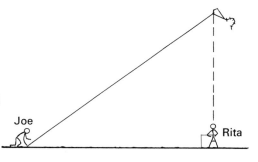
Joe
Rita

6. On a baseball diamond, it is 90 feet between bases. How far is it from home plate to second base? 126.9 ft

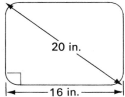
2nd
3rd ? 1st
Ex. 6–7
Home

7. On a softball diamond, it is 60 feet between bases. How far is it from home plate to second base? 84.6 ft

8. What is the height of the TV screen shown at the right? 12 in.

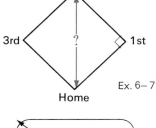
20 in.
16 in.

437

9. The bottom of a 12-foot ladder is placed 3 feet from a building. How high up on the building will the ladder reach? 11.62 ft

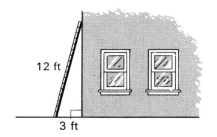

12 ft

3 ft

10. A ship left port and sailed 5 miles west and then 8 miles south. How far was the ship from the port? 9.43 mi

11. A ramp must rise 4 feet over a horizontal distance of 10 feet. What must be the length of the ramp? 10.77 ft

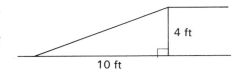

4 ft

10 ft

12. The roof of a house is to be built as shown. How long should each rafter be? 16.48 ft

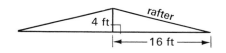

4 ft   rafter

16 ft

C Solve each problem.

Example: The lighthouse at Bernice Point is 16 miles from the lighthouse at Leigh Sound. The point at which the radio beams from these lighthouses make right angles is the same distance from each. What is that distance?

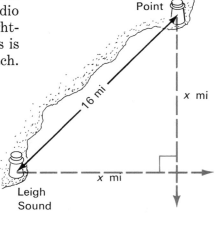

Bernice Point

16 mi

x mi

x mi

Leigh Sound

$$x^2 + x^2 = 16^2$$

$$2x^2 = 256$$

$$\frac{2x^2}{2} = \frac{256}{2}$$

$$x^2 = 128$$

$$\sqrt{x^2} = \sqrt{128}$$

$$x \approx 11.31$$

The point is about 11.31 miles from each lighthouse.

13. How far is point A from each corner of the square window?

16.92 in.

24 in.

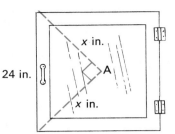

14. If the diagonal of a square is 18 inches long, what is the length of each side? 12.69 in.

15. It is 100 meters from one corner of a square parking lot to the opposite corner. What are the dimensions of the parking lot? 70.5 m by 70.5 m

16. The brace for the square gate shown is 44 inches long. What are the dimensions of the gate?

31.02 in. by 31.02 in.

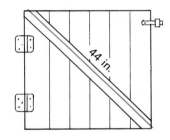

CHECKING RIGHT ANGLES

activities

Builders and surveyors often use the following procedure to check that corners are square (form right angles).

Measure off 3 units along this side.

Measure off 4 units along this side.

If the distance from point A to point B is 5, this angle is a right angle.

If the distance from A to B is not 5, then the angle is not a right angle.

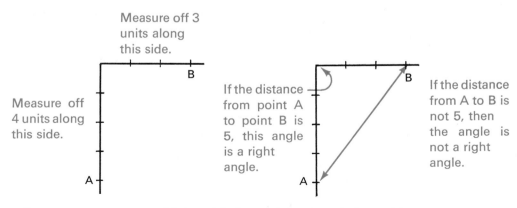

For greater accuracy, multiples of 3, 4, and 5 (such as 6, 8, 10; 12, 16, 20; and so on) are used. Use the above procedure to check the corners of your classroom, a fence, or a tabletop.

13.8 Square Roots and Formulas

To use some formulas, you have to find square roots. Remember the formula from page 416?

time the storm will last in hours $\longrightarrow$ $t = \sqrt{\dfrac{d^3}{216}}$ $\longleftarrow$ diameter of storm in miles

Example 1: How long will a storm last if its diameter is 12 miles?

$$t = \sqrt{\frac{d^3}{216}}$$

$$= \sqrt{\frac{12^3}{216}}$$

$$= \sqrt{\frac{12 \times 12 \times 12}{36 \times 6}}$$

$$= \sqrt{\frac{\overset{2}{\cancel{12}} \times \overset{2}{\cancel{12}} \times \overset{2}{\cancel{12}}}{\underset{1}{\cancel{6}} \times \underset{1}{\cancel{6}} \times \underset{1}{\cancel{6}}}}$$

$$= \sqrt{8}$$

$$\approx 2.83 \quad \triangleleft \quad \text{The storm will last about 2.83 hours.}$$

Example 2: The formula for the area of a circle is $A = \pi r^2$. Find the radius of a circle if its area is 6.28 m². Use 3.14 for π.

$$A = \pi r^2$$

$$6.28 = 3.14 r^2$$

$$\frac{6.28}{3.14} = \frac{3.14 r^2}{3.14}$$

$$2 = r^2$$

$$\sqrt{2} = \sqrt{r^2}$$

$$1.41 \approx r \quad \triangleleft \quad \text{The radius is about 1.41 m.}$$

440

Exercises

A 1. In the formula in Example 1, what does each letter stand for?
t = time storm will last in hours, d = diameter of storm in miles.

2. In Example 2, how would you check the solution 1.41?
See if $6.28 \approx 3.14 \times 1.41 \times 1.41$.

B Solve these problems from various kinds of occupations. Use 3.14 for π.

3. *Weather forecaster:* How long will a storm last if its diameter is 18 miles? 5.20 hr

4. *Tinsmith:* Find the radius of a sheet-metal circle with an area of 28.26 cm². 3 cm

5. *Rescue worker:* A helicopter dropped a survival kit from an altitude of 1024 feet. How long did it take to hit the water? 8 sec

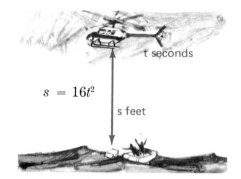

t seconds

$s = 16t^2$

s feet

6. *Pilot:* If a plane's altitude h is $\frac{1}{2}$ mile, how many miles d is it to the horizon? Use $d = \sqrt{8000h}$. 63.2 mi

7. *Tinsmith:* A sheet-metal cylinder is to have a volume V of 15,700 cm³ and a height h of 50 cm. What is its radius r? Use $V = \pi r^2 h$. 10 cm

8. *Plumber:* A drain pipe is to have a circular cross-sectional area A of 50.24 cm². What must its diameter d be? Use $A = \frac{1}{4}\pi d^2$. 8 cm

9. *Carpenter:* Find the length l of a rafter where the horizontal run h is 12 feet and the vertical rise v is 4 feet. Use $l = \sqrt{h^2 + v^2}$. 12.64 ft

Ex. 9

10. *Air-conditioning technician:* Find the diameter D of the main air duct if it feeds three branch ducts with diameters of 8 inches, 7 inches, and 6 inches. Use $D = \sqrt{a^2 + b^2 + c^2}$. 12.21 in.

Ex. 10

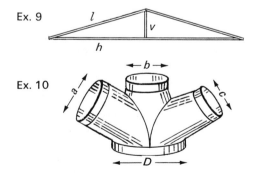

C 11. *Electrician:* The resistance R of a certain 55-watt lamp is 220 ohms. What current I does it require? Use $I = \sqrt{\frac{P}{R}}$, where I is the current in amperes, P is the number of watts, and R is the resistance in ohms. $\frac{1}{2}$ ampere

Square roots can be found with a calculator.

Suppose you want to find $\sqrt{1090}$. You know $30^2 = 900$. So $\sqrt{1090} > 30$. Suppose you make a guess of 32. (Actually, any guess will do.)

① Divide 1090 by 32.

　　　　Press:　1090　$\div$　32　$=$

　　　　Display:　*34.0625*　　(Do not clear the calculator.)

② Average your guess with the result of step 1.

　　　　Press:　$+$　32　$\div$　2　$=$

　　　　Display:　*33.03125* ⟵————— If the calculator has a memory, store this result in the memory and recall in steps 3 and 4. If not, record the result on paper.

③ Divide 1090 by the result of step 2.

　　　　Press:　1090　$\div$　33.03125　$=$

　　　　Display:　*32.999053*　　(Do not clear.)

④ Average the results of steps 2 and 3.

　　　　Press:　$+$　33.03125　$\div$　2　$=$

　　　　Display:　*33.015151*

Notice that the first three digits in the averages from steps 2 and 4 match. So

$$\sqrt{1090} \approx 33.0, \text{ correct to the tenths place.}$$

You could continue to divide and average until the last two averages agree to as many decimal places as you like.

Use the method above to find each square root, correct to the tenths place. If the calculator has a square root key, use it to check your results.

1. $\sqrt{93}$　　**2.** $\sqrt{168}$　　**3.** $\sqrt{264}$　　**4.** $\sqrt{193}$　　**5.** $\sqrt{48}$
　　9.6　　　　　　12.9　　　　　　16.2　　　　　　13.8　　　　　6.9

6. $\sqrt{761}$　　**7.** $\sqrt{1020}$　　**8.** $\sqrt{1500}$　　**9.** $\sqrt{2601}$　　**10.** $\sqrt{1387}$
　　27.5　　　　　　31.9　　　　　　38.7　　　　　　51.0　　　　　37.2

Terms and Symbols Review

Use the terms or symbols to correctly complete the sentences.

Assignment Guide Rev.
Oral: Terms & Symbols 1–5
Written: Min. (day 1) 1–24
(day 2) 25–40
Reg. 1–39 odd
Max. 1–41 odd

square root   *Pythagorean Property* $\sqrt{}$

hypotenuse $-\sqrt{}$

1. Every positive number has a positive and a negative _____. Square root

2. The symbol _____ is used for the nonnegative square root of a number. $\sqrt{}$

3. In a right triangle, the _____ is the side opposite the right angle. Hypotenuse

4. The symbol _____ is used for the negative square root of a number. $-\sqrt{}$

5. The _____ states that $c^2 = a^2 + b^2$, where c is the hypotenuse and a and b are the other sides of a right triangle. Pythagorean Property

Chapter 13 Review

Find two solutions for each equation.   13.1

1. $a^2 = 9$ 3, ⁻3   2. $b^2 = 25$ 5, ⁻5   3. $c^2 = 16$ 4, ⁻4

4. $x^2 = 36$ 6, ⁻6   5. $y^2 = 49$ 7, ⁻7   6. $z^2 = 81$ 9, ⁻9

Use the table on page 422 to find the following.   13.2

7. $\sqrt{2}$ 1.41   8. $\sqrt{3}$ 1.73   9. $\sqrt{7}$ 2.65

10. $\sqrt{15}$ 3.87   11. $\sqrt{26}$ 5.10   12. $\sqrt{89}$ 9.43

13. $\sqrt{21}$ 4.58   14. $\sqrt{45}$ 6.71   15. $\sqrt{96}$ 9.80

16. 27^2 729   17. 52^2 2,704   18. 119^2 14,161

Find each square root by using the table on page 422.   13.3

19. $\sqrt{200}$ 14.1   20. $\sqrt{490}$ 22.12   21. $\sqrt{600}$ 24.5

22. $\sqrt{180}$ 13.44   23. $\sqrt{360}$ 18.96   24. $\sqrt{1700}$ 41.2

13.4   Find each square root as a fraction or decimal, as given.

25. $\sqrt{\frac{1}{4}}$ $\frac{1}{2}$ **26.** $\sqrt{\frac{4}{9}}$ $\frac{2}{3}$ **27.** $\sqrt{\frac{49}{100}}$ $\frac{7}{10}$

28. $\sqrt{0.49}$ 0.7   **29.** $\sqrt{0.36}$ 0.6   **30.** $\sqrt{1.21}$ 1.1

13.5   Find the positive solution of each equation.

31. $x^2 + 5 = 54$ 7   **32.** $x^2 - 4 = 21$ 5

33. $x^2 + 6 = 40$ 5.83   **34.** $x^2 - 12 = 28$ 6.32

13.6   Use the right triangle below to help you complete the following.

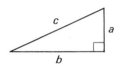

35. $a = 8$, $b = 15$, $c = $ _____ 17   **36.** $a = 3$, $c = 5$, $b = $ _____ 4

37. $b = 24$, $c = 25$, $a = $ _____ 7   **38.** $c = 53$, $b = 28$, $a = $ _____ 45

13.7   Solve each problem.

Ex. 39

39. What is the length of the pond shown at the right? 85 m

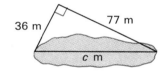

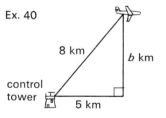

Ex. 40

40. What is the height b of the airplane? 6.24 km

13.8   **41.** A ball is dropped from the top of a cliff that is 64 feet tall. How long will it take the ball to reach the foot of the cliff? Use the formula $s = 16t^2$, where s is the distance in feet and t is the time in seconds. 2 sec

Chapter 13 Test

Find each square root as a whole number, fraction, or decimal, as given.

1. $\sqrt{36}$ 6

2. $\sqrt{81}$ 9

3. $\sqrt{\frac{4}{9}}$ $\frac{2}{3}$

4. $\sqrt{\frac{16}{25}}$ $\frac{4}{5}$

5. $\sqrt{0.64}$ 0.8

6. $\sqrt{0.81}$ 0.9

Assignment Guide Test
Written: Min. 1–20
Reg. 1–20
Max. 1–21

Find each square root by using the table on page 422.

7. $\sqrt{5}$ 2.24

8. $\sqrt{8}$ 2.83

9. $\sqrt{12}$ 3.46

10. $\sqrt{288}$ 16.92

11. $\sqrt{250}$ 15.8

12. $\sqrt{700}$ 26.5

Find the positive solution of each equation.

13. $x^2 = 25$ 5

14. $x^2 = 37$ 6.08

15. $x^2 + 5 = 41$ 6

16. $x^2 - 9 = 40$ 7

17. $x^2 - 7 = 16$ 4.80

18. $x^2 + 9 = 41$ 5.66

Use the Pythagorean Property to solve the following.

19. A 26-foot cable is used to brace an antenna. The cable is anchored 10 feet from the foot of the antenna. How tall is the antenna? 24 ft

Ex. 19

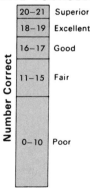

20. A weather balloon is 4000 meters high and directly over a point 900 meters from the weather station. How far is the balloon from the station? 4100 m

Ex. 20

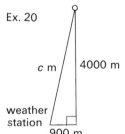

21. The area of a circle is 28.26 square meters. What is the radius of the circle? Use $A = \pi r^2$ and use 3.14 for π. 3 m

RATE YOURSELF

Number Correct	
20–21	Superior
18–19	Excellent
16–17	Good
11–15	Fair
0–10	Poor

MATH AND POLICE WORK

You can determine the speed that a car was traveling by measuring the skid marks.

If all four tires skid and the car comes to a stop without hitting another object, you can use these formulas.

Dry concrete-road	*Wet concrete-road*

$$s = \sqrt{24d}$$ $$s = \sqrt{12d}$$

speed (mph)   distance (ft) car skidded   speed (mph)   distance (ft) car skidded

Example: A car skidded to a stop on a dry concrete-road. The skid marks were 48 feet long. How fast was the car traveling?

$$s = \sqrt{24d}$$
$$= \sqrt{24 \times 48}$$
$$= \sqrt{24 \times 24 \times 2}$$
$$= 24\sqrt{2}$$
$$\approx 33.84 \text{ or } 34 \quad \text{◁ } \textbf{34 mph}$$

Solve these problems.

1. A car skidded to a stop on a dry concrete-road. The skid marks were 120 feet long. How fast was the car traveling?   53.76 or 54 mph

2. A car skidded to a stop on a wet concrete-road. It left skid marks that were 96 feet long. How fast was the car traveling?   33.84 or 34 mph

Suggested Class Time

Course	Min.	Reg.	Max.
Days	0	1	0

Express the following using exponents.   3.8

1. $n \times n \times n \times n$ n^4 **2.** $a \times a$ a^2

Assignment Guide GR 14
Written: Reg. 1–27

3. $y \times y \times y$ y^3 **4.** $b \times b \times b \times b \times b$ b^5

What number should replace each ?   3.4

5. $8(3 + 2) = (8 \times 3) + (? \times 2)$ 8

6. $(4 \times 7) + (4 \times 8) = 4(? + 8)$ 7

Compute.

7. $^-11 + {}^-6$ $^-17$ **8.** $^-9 + 7$ $^-2$ 6.3

9. $^-1.1 + {}^-3.6$ $^-4.7$ **10.** $4.6 + {}^-2.7$ 1.9   11.3

11. $13 - {}^-7$ 20   **12.** $^-16 - 9$ $^-25$ 6.4

13. $\frac{1}{4} + (-\frac{1}{2})$ $-\frac{1}{4}$ **14.** $-\frac{7}{8} + (-\frac{1}{4})$ $^-1\frac{1}{8}$ 11.5

15. $(^-8)(7)$ $^-56$ **16.** $(16)(^-8)$ $^-128$ 7.1

17. $(^-4)(^-8)$ 32   **18.** $(^-3)(^-9)$ 27   7.2

19. $(^-7.2)(0.2)$ $^-1.44$ **20.** $(^-3.4)(^-0.5)$ 1.7   12.1

21. $\frac{1}{2} \times {}^-6$ $^-3$ **22.** $-\frac{3}{4} \times 8 \times \frac{1}{2}$ $^-3$ 12.3

23. $\frac{-8}{-2}$ 4   **24.** $\frac{16}{-8}$ $^-2$ 7.3

Express each fraction in lowest terms.   4.3

25. $\frac{15}{20}$ $\frac{3}{4}$ **26.** $\frac{20}{30}$ $\frac{2}{3}$ **27.** $\frac{18}{24}$ $\frac{3}{4}$

14

Courtesy Rush Presbyterian St. Luke's

14 USING ALGEBRA

All living things are made up of *cells.* The cube is a common shape for plant cells, while the sphere is a common shape for animal cells.

Scientists who study living things might have to find the volume of a cell or its surface area. They could use the following formulas.

Volume of cube $= s^3$ 　　　 Volume of sphere $= \frac{4}{3}\pi r^3$

Surface area of cube $= 6s^2$ 　 Surface area of sphere $= 4\pi r^2$

The right-hand side of each formula is a **polynomial.** In this chapter, you will learn more about polynomials, including how to add, subtract, multiply, and divide polynomials. Also, you'll use algebra to solve more problems.

More About Solving Problems

14.1

Earlier you solved problems that could be translated into equations with one operation. The following problems translate into equations that involve more steps.

Example 1: A punch is made from ginger ale and orange juice. Twice as much orange juice is used as ginger ale. How much of each do you need for 6 quarts of punch?

Let x = amount of ginger ale.

Then $2x$ = amount of orange juice.

amount of ginger ale   amount of orange juice   total amount of punch

$$x + 2x = 6$$

$$3x = 6$$

$$\frac{3x}{3} = \frac{6}{3}$$

$$x = 2 \qquad \text{2 quarts of ginger ale}$$

$$2x = 4 \qquad \text{4 quarts of orange juice}$$

Check: ● Is 4 quarts of orange juice twice as much as 2 quarts of ginger ale? ✓
● Do 4 quarts of orange juice and 2 quarts of ginger ale give 6 quarts of punch? ✓

Example 2: The sum of two consecutive integers is $^-19$. What are the integers?

Let n = some integer.

Then $n + 1$ = next integer.

some integer   next integer   sum

$$n + n + 1 = {}^-19$$

$$2n + 1 = {}^-19$$

$$2n + 1 + {}^-1 = {}^-19 + {}^-1$$

$$2n + 0 = {}^-20$$

$$2n = {}^-20$$

$$\frac{2n}{2} = \frac{-20}{2}$$

$$n = {}^-10 \qquad \text{One integer is } {}^-10.$$

$$n + 1 = {}^-9 \qquad \text{The next integer is } {}^-9.$$

Check: ● Are $^-9$ and $^-10$ consecutive integers? ✓
● Is the sum of $^-9$ and $^-10$ equal to $^-19$? ✓

449

■ Exercises

A 1. If n names an integer, how would you name the next two integers?
$n + 1, n + 2$

2. If n names an even integer, name the next even integer. $n + 2$

3. If n names an odd integer, name the next two odd integers.
$n + 2, n + 4$

B Give an equation for each problem. Then solve the problem.

4. One number is three times a second number. Their sum is 28. What are the numbers? $n + 3n = 28; 7, 21$

5. The sum of two consecutive integers is 65. What are the integers?
$n + n + 1 = 65; 32, 33$

6. The sum of two consecutive even integers is 34. What are the integers? $n + n + 2 = 34; 16, 18$

7. To make dark orange paint, you mix red and yellow paint. You use 5 times as much red as yellow paint. How much of each should you mix to make 18 quarts of dark orange paint?
$x + 5x = 18; 3$ qt yellow, 15 qt red

8. The sum of two consecutive integers is ⁻31. What are the integers?
$n + n + 1 = {}^-31; {}^-16, {}^-15$

9. The sum of three consecutive integers is ⁻57. What are the integers?
$n + n + 1 + n + 2 = {}^-57; {}^-20, {}^-19, {}^-18$

10. One number is 3 more than another. Their sum is ⁻47. What are the numbers? $n + n + 3 = {}^-47; {}^-25, {}^-22$

11. The perimeter of a triangle is 24 inches. Two sides are the same length. The third side is 3 inches longer than each of the other two. How long is each side? $x + x + x + 3 = 24;$
7 in., 7 in., 10 in.

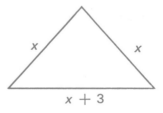

12. The sum of two numbers is 6. One number is 3 times the other. What are the numbers? $n + 3n = 6; 1\frac{1}{2}, 4\frac{1}{2}$

13. Joanne paid $15 for 2 books. One book cost $3 more than the other. How much did she pay for each book? $x + x + 3 = 15; \$6, \$9$

14. One number is $2\frac{1}{2}$ more than 4 times a second number. The sum of the two numbers is $37\frac{1}{2}$. What are the numbers? $n + 4n + 2\frac{1}{2} = 37\frac{1}{2}$; 7, $30\frac{1}{2}$

15. A 124-centimeter board is to be cut into 3 pieces. Two of the pieces should be the same length. The third piece should be 5.5 centimeters longer than each of the other two. How long should each piece be? $x + x + x + 5.5 = 124$; 39.5 cm, 39.5 cm, 45 cm

16. A football field is 40 feet longer than twice its width. Its perimeter is 1040 feet. Find its dimensions.
$2(2w + 40 + w) = 1040$; 160 ft by 360 ft

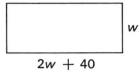

$2w + 40$

|C| **Example:** A store owner took a group of 20 students to an amusement park as a reward for being on the honor roll. Tickets for students under 14 years of age cost \$8, and the other tickets cost \$10. If the store owner spent \$190 on tickets, how many of each kind of ticket were bought?

	number	value
\$10 tickets	x	$10x$
\$ 8 tickets	$20 - x$	$8(20 - x)$

$$10x + 8(20 - x) = 190$$

$$10x + 160 - 8x = 190$$

$$2x + 160 + {}^{-}160 = 190 + {}^{-}160$$

$$\frac{2x}{2} = \frac{30}{2}$$

$$x = 15 \quad \blacktriangleleft \; \text{10-dollar tickets}$$

$$20 - x = 5 \quad \blacktriangleleft \; \text{8-dollar tickets}$$

Courtesy Marriott's Great America®

17. Martha sold 38 albums for a total of \$130. Some albums sold for \$3, and the others for \$4. How many of each were sold?
$4x + 3(38 - x) = 130$; 16 albums at \$4, 22 albums at \$3

18. Twenty-five sacks were placed in a carton. Some weighed 3 pounds, the others 5 pounds. They weighed a total of 89 pounds. How many of each were in the carton?
$5x + 3(25 - x) = 89$; 7 five-pound sacks, 18 three-pound sacks

19. Bill has \$2.25 in dimes and quarters. He has twice as many dimes as quarters. How many of each does he have? *Hint:* Change \$2.25 to 225¢. $25x + 10(2x) = 225$; 5 quarters, 10 dimes

Problems With Too Much or Too Little Information

Sometimes in solving problems, you find that not all the given information is needed. At other times, not enough information has been given to solve the problem.

Suggested Class Time

Course	Min.	Reg.	Max.
Days	0	1	1

Example 1: Marylou is 16 years old, and her sister Carrie is 13 years old. Marylou weighs 108 pounds, and Carrie weighs 96 pounds. How much more does Marylou weigh than Carrie?

You are asked to find how much more Marylou weighs than Carrie. So the information about their ages is not needed.

Example 2: A car traveled from Arlington to Lyons at an average speed of 55 miles per hour. How long did the trip take?

In this case, not enough information is given. You need to know the distance from Arlington to Lyons before you can find how long the trip took.

▪ Exercises

Ⓐ For each problem, tell **(a)** what you are to find and **(b)** whether the problem gives too little, just enough, or too much information for solving the problem.

Assignment Guide 14.2
Oral: Reg. & Max. 1–4
Written: Reg. 5–16
Max. 5–18

1. Frank earns $3.25 per hour at his part-time job. How much did he earn last month?
   a. How much Frank earned last month   b. Too little

2. Marsha sells macrame belts at $5.00 apiece. Each belt costs her $1.27 in materials. The belts range in width from $1\frac{1}{2}$ inches to 2 inches. How much profit does Marsha make on each belt she sells?
   a. The profit on each belt   b. Too much

3. A camera costs $189, and a wide-angle lens for the camera costs $78. How much do both the camera and the wide-angle lens cost?
   a. The cost of both the camera and the lens   b. Just enough

4. At 7 A.M. the temperature was ⁻2°. By noon the temperature had risen 10°. During that period a total of 1.5 inches of precipitation fell. What was the temperature at noon?
   a. The temperature at noon   b. Too much

Ⓑ **5–8.** Solve each problem in Exercises 1–4, if possible.
   5. Not pos.   6. $3.73   7. $267   8. 8°

Solve each problem, if possible.

9. A checking account had a balance of $270. A month later the balance was ⁻$70. What was the change in balance? ⁻$340

10. Sally drove a total of 740 miles on her vacation. Her car used a total of 37 gallons of gasoline. The trip lasted 8 days and cost her a total of $480. How many miles per gallon of gasoline did her car average on the trip? 20 mpg

11. A carpenter sawed two pieces off a board 60 inches long. One piece was $25\frac{1}{2}$ inches long, and the other piece was $16\frac{1}{4}$ inches long. How long was the remaining piece? $18\frac{1}{4}$ in.

12. A tinsmith cut a small circular disk from a 50-centimeter square piece of metal. How much metal was left over? Not pos.

13. A salesperson in a department store receives a 5% commission on all merchandise she sells. Last month she sold $8200 worth of merchandise. She also receives a regular salary of $400 per month, and she received a bonus of $200 for selling the most merchandise for the month. How much was her commission for last month? $410

14. Jerry bought a new watch that cost $119. He also had to pay a sales tax and an excise tax. What was the total cost of the watch? Not pos.

15. The regular price of a coat was $79, but it was marked down 20% from the regular price. How much would you save by buying the coat on sale? $15.80

16. A diver descended from the surface of a lake to the bottom of the lake in $8\frac{1}{2}$ minutes. What was the rate of descent? Not pos.

C **17.** Paul's car has a 13-gallon tank. The car had traveled 206 miles since the last fill-up, and it took 9.8 gallons of gas to fill the tank. How much did it cost to fill the tank? Not pos.

18. An apartment rents for $225 per month. The utilities cost an average of $41 per month, and the garage rent is $25 per month. What is the yearly cost of living in this apartment, including the utilities and the garage rent? $3492

Photo Trends

What Is a Polynomial?

Suggested Class Time		
Course	Min.	Reg.	Max.
Days	0	1	1

Each of the following is a monomial.

$$17 \qquad x \qquad {}^-3y^3 \qquad xy \qquad 8abc^2 \qquad \sqrt{2}$$

Note: In monomials like $^-3y^3$, the exponent applies only to the variable that precedes it. So $^-3y^3 = {}^-3yyy$, and $8abc^2 = 8abcc$.

> A monomial is a number, a variable, or a product of a number and one or more variables.

The following expressions are not monomials. The first is the sum of two monomials. The second is the sum of three monomials.

$$x^2 + 2 \qquad 7x^2 + {}^-3x + {}^-5 \qquad \blacktriangleleft \text{ Usually written } 7x^2 - 3x - 5$$

The expressions above are called polynomials.

> A polynomial is a monomial or the sum of two or more monomials.

Each monomial in a polynomial is called a **term** of the polynomial. Polynomials are named according to how many terms they have. (A polynomial with more than three terms is usually just called a polynomial.)

Monomials (1 term)	Binomials (2 terms)	Trinomials (3 terms)
$2x^3$	$4x^3 - 3x$	$3x^3 + {}^-2x + \sqrt{5}$
$-\frac{1}{2}$	$7x + 6$	$\frac{1}{2}y^2 + 2y - 4$

When two or more monomials have the same variables with equal exponents for the same variables, the monomials are called **like terms.** Otherwise, the monomials are **unlike terms.** (Remember that $x = x^1$.)

Like terms		Unlike terms	
$3x$ and ^-7x		^-4y and $8z$	◀ different variables
$\frac{1}{2}xy^2$ and $7xy^2$	same variables with equal exponents	$3x^2$ and $4x$	
$3x^3y^2$ and $\frac{3}{4}x^3y^2$		$6xy^2$ and $8x^2y$	same variables but different exponents

Exercises

A Which are monomials?

1. 2   **2.** $\frac{2}{3}x + 1$ **3.** $^-7z^2$ **4.** $x + y$

5. xy **6.** $y^3 + 2y - 1$ **7.** $\sqrt{7}$ **8.** a^2bc

9. Can a polynomial have one term? Yes

10. Is a monomial also a polynomial? Yes

Identify each polynomial as a monomial, binomial, or trinomial.

11. $x^3 + 2$ Binomial   **12.** $\frac{1}{2}x^2$ Monomial   **13.** $xy^3 + x^3y + xy$ Trinomial

14. $\sqrt{2}x$ Monomial   **15.** $x + \sqrt{2}$ Binomial   **16.** $\frac{3}{4}x^2 + \frac{1}{2}$ Binomial

B Identify each pair of terms as like terms or unlike terms.

17. $7x, 8x$ L   **18.** $8z, ^-2z$ L   **19.** $\frac{1}{2}xyy, 2xyy$ L

20. $\frac{1}{2}xy^2, 2xy^2$ L   **21.** $^-7xxy, 9xyy$ U   **22.** $^-7x^2y, 9xy^2$ U

23. $4w, ^-8wz$ U   **24.** $-\frac{2}{3}x^3y, x^2y^2$ U   **25.** $8yz, ^-4xz$ U

26. abc, a^2bc U   **27.** $3x^2y^2, \frac{1}{2}x^2y^2$ L   **28.** $2, 2x$ U

29. $^-7x^2, 3x^4$ U   **30.** $^-10s^2t^2, 12s^2t^2$ L   **31.** $3xy, 4yz$ U

32. $3xy, 4yx$ L   **33.** $5mn^2p^2, \frac{1}{2}mn^2p^2$ L   **34.** abc, cba L

Rewrite each polynomial as a sum of monomials.

Example: $7x - 3 = 7x + ^-3$

35. $2x - 5$ $2x + ^-5$ **36.** $^-6y - 1$ $^-6y + ^-1$ **37.** $x^2 - 3x + 2$ $x^2 + ^-3x + 2$

38. $^-2x^2 - 5x$ **39.** $8y^3 - y$ $8y^3 + ^-y$ **40.** $^-2x^3 - 5x^2 - 7x$ $^-2x^3 + ^-5x^2 + ^-7x$
$^-2x^2 + ^-5x$

C Numbers can be expressed in polynomial form, using powers of 10.

Number	Expanded form	Polynomial form
38	$30 + 8$	$3(10^1) + 8$
392	$300 + 90 + 2$	$3(10^2) + 9(10^1) + 2$

Express each number in polynomial form.

41. 79   **42.** 82   **43.** 467   **44.** 896   **45.** 1972

41. $7(10^1) + 9$
42. $8(10^1) + 2$
43. $4(10^2) + 6(10^1) + 7$
44. $8(10^2) + 9(10^1) + 6$
45. $1(10^3) + 9(10^2) + 7(10^1) + 2$

Combining Like Terms

When you replace each variable in a polynomial with a number, the polynomial names a specific number. Then you can *evaluate the polynomial*.

Suppose you evaluate the polynomials $2x + 3x$ and $5x$ for several different replacements.

	$2x + 3x$	Value	$5x$	Value
Replace x with 2.	$2(2) + 3(2)$	10	$5(2)$	10
Replace x with 1.	$2(1) + 3(1)$	5	$5(1)$	5
Replace x with 0.	$2(0) + 3(0)$	0	$5(0)$	0

The polynomials $2x + 3x$ and $5x$ will always give equal values for each replacement of the variable. Such polynomials are called **equivalent expressions.**

By using the distributive property, you can change some polynomials to simpler equivalent expressions.

Examples: **1.** $9a + {}^-3a = (9 + {}^-3)a = 6a$

2. ${}^-7x^2 + 2x^2 + 1 = ({}^-7 + 2)x^2 + 1 = {}^-5x^2 + 1$

Notice that only like terms can be combined.

Examples: Simplify.

3. $7x - 8x = (7 + {}^-8)x = {}^-1x$ or ${}^-x$

Notice that subtraction is rewritten as an addition of the opposite.

4. $4xy^2 - 6xy^2 - 2xy^2 = (4 + {}^-6 + {}^-2)xy^2 = {}^-4xy^2$

5. $\frac{1}{2}y^3 + \underbrace{({}^-\frac{3}{4})y^2 + \frac{1}{2}y^2}_{\text{like terms}} = \frac{1}{2}y^3 + ({}^-\frac{3}{4} + \frac{1}{2})y^2 = \frac{1}{2}y^3 + ({}^-\frac{1}{4})y^2$

Sometimes it is convenient to rewrite a polynomial in column form. For example, $7x - 3x + 4x$ can be written as

$$\begin{array}{r} 7x \\ {}^-3x \\ \underline{4x} \\ 8x. \end{array}$$

■ Exercises

Assignment Guide 14.4
Oral: Reg. & Max. 1–10
Written: Reg. 11–41 odd
Max. 11–49 odd

A What are the missing numbers?

1. $2x + 4x = (2 + 4)x =$ _____x 6

2. $6y + {}^-10y = (6 + {}^-10)y =$ _____y ⁻4

3. _____$z - 9z = (6 + {}^-9)z = {}^-3z$ 6

4. $\frac{1}{3}x + \frac{1}{4}x = (\frac{1}{3} + \underline{\hspace{1cm}})x = \frac{7}{12}x$ $\frac{1}{4}$

5. $2x + 5x - 9x = (2 + 5 + {}^-9)x =$ _____x ⁻2

6. $9y + {}^-8y + {}^-y = (9 + \underline{\hspace{1cm}} + {}^-1)y = 0y$ or 0 ⁻8

7. $1.2x + 2.9x = (1.2 + \underline{\hspace{1cm}})x = 4.1x$ 2.9

8. Which expression is equivalent to $6y + {}^-4y$?

    a. $6y + {}^-4$ **b.** $2y$ **c.** ^-2y **d.** 2

9. Choose all expressions that are equivalent to $10y$.

    a. $8y + 2$ **b.** $7y + 3y$ **c.** $12y + {}^-2y$ **d.** $10y - 1$

10. Choose all expressions that are equivalent to $7y$.

    a. $(5 + 2)y$ **b.** $7y - 1$ **c.** $(10 - 3)y$ **d.** $5y + 2y$

    e. $10y - 3y$ **f.** $6y + y$ **g.** $(4 + 3)y$ **h.** $(8 - 1)y$

B Evaluate each pair of expressions for $x = 0$, $x = 1$, and $x = 2$. Then write *Yes* or *No* to tell if the expressions are equivalent.

11. $5x + 2, 7x$
     2, 7, 12; 0, 7, 14; no

12. $5x + 2x, 7x$ 0, 7, 14; 0, 7, 14; yes

13. $3x^2 + x^2, 4x^4$
     0, 4, 16; 0, 4, 64; no

14. $3x^2 + x^2, 4x^2$ 0, 4, 16; 0, 4, 16; yes

15. $2x - 6x, {}^-4x$
     0, ⁻4, ⁻8; 0, ⁻4, ⁻8; yes

16. $3x^2 - 2x^2, x^2$ 0, 1, 4; 0, 1, 4; yes

17. $^-x + {}^-x, {}^-2x$
     0, ⁻2, ⁻4; 0, ⁻2, ⁻4; yes

18. $x + x^2, 2x^2$ 0, 2, 6; 0, 2, 8; no

Simplify.

19. $8x + 3x$ $\;_{11x}$ **20.** $^-4x^2 + {}^-6x^2$ $\;_{-10x^2}$ **21.** $^-7y + 4y$ $\;_{-3y}$

22. $2m - 5m$ $\;_{-3m}$ **23.** $^-9y^2 + {}^-3y^2$ $\;_{-12y^2}$ **24.** $11xy - 12xy$ $\;_{-xy}$

25. $14m^2n + {}^-6m^2n$ $\;_{8m^2n}$ **26.** $26m^3 - 13m^3$ $\;_{13m^3}$ **27.** $12y^2 + {}^-16y^2 + 8y$ $\;_{-4y^2 + 8y}$

28. $41x + {}^-12x + 12$ $\;_{29x + 12}$ **29.** $^-18n + 30n + 10$ $\;_{12n + 10}$ **30.** $26m + {}^-59m$ $\;_{-33m}$

31. $^-8y - 7y + 11y$ $\;_{-4y}$ **32.** $20z + {}^-10z + 9z$ $\;_{19z}$

33. $6x^2 + 10x^2 + {}^-8x^2$ $\;_{8x^2}$ **34.** $14xy + {}^-19xy + {}^-13xy$ $\;_{-18xy}$

35. $1.8x + 6.4x$ $\;_{8.2x}$ **36.** $-\frac{1}{3}z + (-\frac{2}{3})z$ $\;_{-z}$

37. $\frac{7}{10}m^2 + (-\frac{1}{5})m^2$ $\;_{\frac{1}{2}m^2}$ **38.** $^-3.3y^2 + 2.2y^2$ $\;_{-1.1y^2}$

Add.

39. $11x$ **40.** $1.8x$ **41.** $14ab$ **42.** $7.5y$
    ^-10x $-2.3x$ $-16ab$ $2.5y$
    $9x$ $4.4x$ ^-9ab $^-1.5y$
    ^-3x $\;_{7x}$ $1.5x$ $\;_{5.4x}$ $8ab$ $\;_{-3ab}$ $^-2.8y$ $\;_{5.7y}$

C **43.** $1\frac{1}{2}z$ **44.** $^-6\frac{3}{4}m$ **45.** $^-3\frac{3}{8}a$ **46.** $5\frac{5}{12}x^2$
    $^-2\frac{1}{2}z$ $^-1\frac{1}{2}m$ $1\frac{1}{8}a$ $^-3\frac{1}{2}x^2$
    ^-7z $\;_{-8z}$ $2\frac{1}{4}m$ $\;_{-6m}$ $^-2\frac{1}{4}a$ $\;_{-4\frac{1}{2}a}$ $^-2\frac{1}{6}x^2$ $\;_{-\frac{1}{4}x^2}$

Find the perimeter of each rectangle.

47. ^{6x}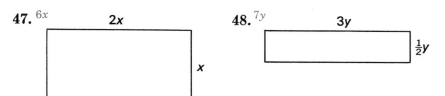

48. ^{7y}

49. Find a monomial for the perimeter of a rectangle where the length is 5 times the width w. $\;_{12w}$

50. Find a monomial for the perimeter of a rectangle where the width is one-half of the length x. $\;_{3x}$

Multiplying Monomials

14.5

You know that a^2 means $a \times a$ and a^3 means $a \times a \times a$.

$$\text{So } a^2 \cdot a^3 = \overbrace{(a \cdot a)}^{\text{2 factors}} \cdot \overbrace{(a \cdot a \cdot a)}^{\text{3 factors}} \quad \blacktriangleleft \quad \text{The } \cdot \text{ can be used for } \times.$$

$$= a \cdot a \cdot a \cdot a \cdot a \quad \blacktriangleleft \quad 2 + 3 \text{ factors}$$

$$= a^5.$$

This example suggests a shortcut we can use when multiplying certain monomials that involve exponents.

Examples: **1.** $x^3 \cdot x^4 = x^{3+4}$ The steps in red can be left out.

$$= x^7$$

2. $y \cdot y^5 = y^{1+5}$ $\blacktriangleleft$ Note that $y = y^1$.

$$= y^6$$

Often a monomial contains both a **constant** (a specific number) and a variable. Notice how such monomials are multiplied.

Examples: **3.** $3x^2 \cdot 5x^4 = (3 \cdot 5) \cdot (x^2 \cdot x^4)$ $\blacktriangleleft$ Rearrange the factors.

$$= 15x^6 \quad \blacktriangleleft \quad \text{Multiply the constants. Then multiply the variables.}$$

4. $(^-3x^2)(2x)(^-4x^3) = (^-3)(2)(^-4) \cdot x^2 \cdot x \cdot x^3$

$$= 24x^6$$

5. $(^-6x^2)(3y)(2x) = (^-6)(3)(2) \cdot x^2 \cdot x \cdot y$

$$= {}^-36x^3y$$

> To multiply monomials containing constants, rearrange the factors so the constants are together and the variables are together. Multiply the constants. Multiply like variables by adding their exponents.

459

▪ Exercises

Assignment Guide 14.5
Oral: Reg. & Max. 1–12
Written: Reg. 13–31 odd;
          Quiz, p. 461
Max. 13–39 odd;
          Quiz, p. 461

$\boxed{\text{A}}$ **1.** Which expression is equivalent to $(x^3)(x^2)$?

a. x^6 <u>**b.**</u> x^5 **c.** $2x^5$ **d.** $2x^6$

2. Which expression is equivalent to $(3x)(2x^2)$?

a. $5x^2$ **b.** $5x^3$ **c.** $6x^2$ <u>**d.**</u> $6x^3$

Replace each ? with the correct exponent.

3. $10^2 \times 10^4 = 10^?$ 6   **4.** $(2^3)(2^4) = 2^?$ 7

5. $5^2 \times 5^5 = 5^?$ 7   **6.** $10^2 \times 10^3 \times 10^4 = 10^?$ 9

7. $(^-6)^3 \times (^-6)^3 = (^-6)^?$ 6   **8.** $7 \cdot x^2 \cdot x^3 = 7x^?$ 5

9. $(2x) \cdot (3x^5) = 6x^?$ 6   **10.** $(3m)(5m^3) = 15m^?$ 4

11. $(3y)(4y) = 12y^?$ 2   **12.** $(2x)(3x)(4x) = 24x^?$ 3

$\boxed{\text{B}}$ Multiply.

13. $a^5 \cdot a^2$ a^7 **14.** $x^2 \cdot x$ x^3 **15.** $y^5 \cdot y^9$ y^{14}

16. $m^6 \cdot m^2$ m^8 **17.** $(2x)3$ $6x$ **18.** $(8y^3)(2)$ $16y^3$

19. $6(^-5x^2)$ $^-30x^2$ **20.** $(^-7)(^-5m)$ $35m$ **21.** $(x^3)(^-4x)$ $^-4x^4$

22. $(^-2c)(^-3c)$ $6c^2$ **23.** $(10x)(20x)$ $200x^2$ **24.** $(7x^2)(3y)$ $21x^2y$

25. $(3m^2)(^-2m^2)(2)$ $^-12m^4$ **26.** $(6x)(^-2x)(\frac{1}{2}x)$ $^-6x^3$ **27.** $(\frac{1}{4}z)(8z^3)(-\frac{1}{2}z^2)$ $^-z^6$

28. $(^-2a)(^-2a)(^-2a)$ $^-8a^3$ **29.** $(21x)(-\frac{3}{7}x^2)(2x^3)$ $^-18x^6$ **30.** $(^-7x^3)(4y^2)(^-5x^2)$ $140x^5y^2$

31. $(0.2cd)(0.01c^2)(10d^3)$ $0.02c^3d^4$ **32.** $(^-5m)(13m^2)(0.001n^3)$ $^-0.065m^3n^3$

$\boxed{\text{C}}$ **33.** $(\frac{1}{4}x^2)(12x)(-\frac{2}{3}y^2)$ $^-2x^3y^2$ **34.** $(^-6x)(-\frac{2}{3}x^3)(7y^2)$ $28x^4y^2$

35. $(a^2)^3$ a^6 **36.** $(b^2)^4$ b^8 **37.** $(3x^3)^2$ $9x^6$

38. $(^-2y^2)^3$ $^-8y^6$ **39.** $(7m)(^-2m)^4$ $112m^5$ **40.** $(x^3)^4(^-7x^2)^5$ $^-16,807x^{22}$

1. Todd bought 2 records for $10. One cost $2 more than the other. How much did he pay for each record? $4 and $6

Identify each pair of terms as *like terms* or *unlike terms*.

2. $8xy^2$, $^-7x^2y$ U

3. $3x^2y^3$, $^-5x^2y^3$ L

4. ^-6y, $4z$ U

Simplify.

5. $9y + 2y$ $11y$

6. $^-17a + ^-3a$ ^-20a

7. $12n + ^-15n$ ^-3n

8. $^-12ab + 18ab + 8ab$ $14ab$

9. $5y^2 + ^-10y^2 + ^-7y^2$ $^-12y^2$

Multiply.

10. $m^3 \cdot m^3$ m^6

11. $x \cdot x^4$ x^5

12. $3(5m^2)$ $15m^2$

13. $(^-4n)(4n^2)$ $^-16n^3$

14. $(2x^3)(8x^4)$ $16x^7$

15. $(4x)(^-8x)$ $^-32x^2$

What's the Catch?

A group on a photograph safari traveled 60 km through swamp and forest, 5 times as far through swamp as through forest. They traveled twice as many kilometers through swamp as the number of crocodiles they saw, and the number of crocodiles they saw was equal to the number of chimpanzees they saw. How far did they travel altogether? 60 km

14.6   Multiplying a Binomial by a Monomial

When you multiply a binomial by a monomial, you can use the distributive property. Remember that the distributive property can be stated as

Suggested Class Time

Course	Min.	Reg.	Max.
Days	0	1	1

$$a(b + c) = a \cdot b + a \cdot c$$

or

$$(b + c)a = b \cdot a + c \cdot a.$$

This can also be illustrated with areas of rectangles.

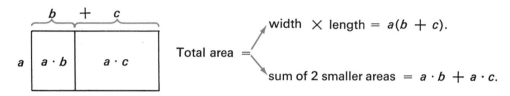

The following examples show how the distributive property is used to multiply a binomial by a monomial.

Examples:

1. $x^2(x + 2) = x^2 \cdot x + x^2 \cdot 2$

$$= x^3 + 2x^2$$

2. $^-2z(z^3 + 2z^2) = {}^-2z \cdot z^3 + {}^-2z \cdot 2z^2$

$$= {}^-2z^4 + {}^-4z^3 \text{ or } {}^-2z^4 - 4z^3$$

3. $(5xy - y^2)2xy = 5xy \cdot 2xy - y^2 \cdot 2xy$

$$= 10x^2y^2 - 2xy^3$$

When multiplying a binomial by a monomial, you can also arrange the work as follows.

$$
\begin{array}{r}
10x^2 + 3x \\
8x \\
\hline
80x^3 + 24x^2
\end{array}
$$
◀ Multiply each term of the binomial by the monomial.

462

Exercises

Assignment Guide 14.6
Oral: Reg. & Max. 1–10
Written: Reg. 11–24
Max. 11–28

A Match each expression in Column A with an equivalent expression in Column B.

A

1. $3x(x + 1)$ d

2. $3x(x^2 + x)$ b

3. $x^2(3x - 1)$ a

4. $3x(x + 3)$ c

B

a. $3x^3 - x^2$

b. $3x^3 + 3x^2$

c. $3x^2 + 9x$

d. $3x^2 + 3x$

5. Which expressions are equivalent to $x^4 - 4x^2$?

  a. $x(x^3 - 4x)$ **b.** $x^2(x^2 - 4)$ **c.** $x(x^4 - 4x^2)$ **d.** $x(x^3 - 4x^2)$

6. Which expressions are equivalent to $8x^3 + 4x$?

  a. $4x(2x^2 + 1)$ **b.** $8x(x^2 + 1)$ **c.** $x(8x^2 + 4)$ **d.** $2(4x^3 + 2x)$

Replace each ? with the correct number.

7. $2x(3x + 4) = 6x^2 + ?x$ 8

8. $9y(2y - 4) = ?y^2 - 36y$ 18

9. $m(m + z) = m^? + mz$ 2

10. $6y(y - 3) = 6y^2 - ?y$ 18

B Multiply.

11. $b^3(9ab + a^2)$ $9ab^4 + a^2b^3$

12. $2a^2(7a + 4b)$ $14a^3 + 8a^2b$

13. $^-3x(3x - 5y)$ $^-9x^2 + 15xy$

14. $5ab(3b^3 + a^2)$ $15ab^4 + 5a^3b$

15. $^-3a(5a + 7b)$ $^-15a^2 - 21ab$

16. $10r(^-4r - 7)$ $^-40r^2 - 70r$

17. $(9x^2 + 3y)2xy$ $18x^3y + 6xy^2$

18. $(8abc + c)c^3$ $8abc^4 + c^4$

19. $(11rs + {}^-8s)10s^2$ $110rs^3 - 80s^3$

20. $(12x^2y^3z + 8xyz)3z$ $36x^2y^3z^2 + 24xyz^2$

21. $\frac{1}{2}m(8m + 5)$ $4m^2 + 2\frac{1}{2}m$

22. $\frac{2}{3}y(12y^2 + 6y)$ $8y^3 + 4y^2$

23. $0.1x(6.8x + 3)$ $0.68x^2 + 0.3x$

24. $0.01y(3.8y + 6)$ $0.038y^2 + 0.06y$

C **25.** $m^3(3m^2 + 3m + 1)$
            $3m^5 + 3m^4 + m^3$

26. $2y(y^3 + 5y^2 + 3)$ $2y^4 + 10y^3 + 6y$

27. $^-7y(11y^2 + {}^-4xy + {}^-7y)$
       $^-77y^3 + 28xy^2 + 49y^2$

28. $x^4(x^3 + x^2 + x + 1)$ $x^7 + x^6 + x^5 + x^4$

FORMULAS AT WORK

Formulas are often used by many kinds of workers. Sometimes the right side of a formula is a polynomial, as in the following examples.

Courtesy Snips Magazine, Inc./ Donald Rich

A metalworker wants to figure the surface area S of a metal container that is shaped like a cylinder. The formula is

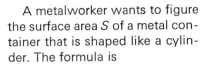

$$S = 2\pi r^2 + 2\pi rh.$$

$\pi \approx 3.14$

A builder may have to figure the force with which water pushes on a window in an aquarium. The formula for the force F in pounds is

$$F = 31h^2w + 62dhw.$$

d = depth, in feet, of window below surface of water

h = height, in feet

w = width, in feet

H. Armstrong Roberts

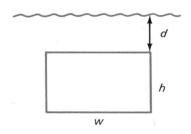

1. Find the surface area of a metal cylinder if $r = 12$ cm and $h = 25$ cm. Use 3.14 for π. 2788.32 cm²

2. Find the force on an aquarium window that is 2 feet below the water surface if the window is 5 feet wide by 4 feet high. 4960 lb

To find the product of 13 and 25, you could use the following method.

$$\begin{array}{r} 10 + 3 \\ 20 + 5 \\ \hline 50 + 15 \\ 200 + 60 \\ \hline 200 + 110 + 15 = 325 \end{array}$$

⟵ 5(10 + 3)
⟵ 20(10 + 3)

Suggested Class Time

Course	Min.	Reg.	Max.
Days	0	1	1

A similar method can be used to find the product of two binomials. For example, the product of $x + 3$ and $2x^2 + 5x$ can be found as shown below.

Example 1:

Like terms are placed in a column, then added.

$$\begin{array}{r} x + 3 \\ 2x^2 + 5x \\ \hline 5x^2 + 15x \\ 2x^3 + 6x^2 \\ \hline 2x^3 + 11x^2 + 15x \end{array}$$

⟵ $5x(x + 3)$
⟵ $2x^2(x + 3)$

 To multiply one binomial by another, you must multiply each term of the first by each term of the second.

The multiplication in Example 1 can also be written as follows. Notice how the distributive property is used.

Example 2:

$$(x + 3)(2x^2 + 5x) = (x + 3)2x^2 + (x + 3)5x$$

Use the distributive property once.

$$= x \cdot 2x^2 + 3 \cdot 2x^2 + x \cdot 5x + 3 \cdot 5x$$

Use the distributive property two more times.

$$= 2x^3 + 6x^2 + 5x^2 + 15x$$

Combine like terms when possible.

$$= 2x^3 + 11x^2 + 15x$$

465

The product of two binomials can be illustrated with areas of rectangles.

Example 3: Multiply $x + 3$ by $x + 2$.

Total area $=$

length $\times$ width $= (x + 3)(x + 2)$.

sum of 4 smaller areas $= x^2 + 3x + 2x + 6$

$= x^2 + 5x + 6$.

Example 4: Multiply $n + 4$ by $n - 6$.

$$(n + 4)(n - 6) = (n + 4)(n + {}^-6)$$

$$= (n + 4)n + (n + 4) \cdot {}^-6$$

$$= n^2 + 4n + {}^-6n + {}^-24$$

$$= n^2 + {}^-2n + {}^-24$$

$$= n^2 - 2n - 24$$

■ Exercises

[A] Replace each ? with the correct number or variable.

1. $(x + 3)(x + 4) = (x + 3)? + (x + 3)4$ $\quad x$

Assignment Guide 14.7
Oral: Reg. & Max. 1–6
Written: Reg. 7–24
Max. 7–30

2. $(y + 5)(y^2 + 6) = (y + 5)y^2 + (y + 5)?$ $\quad 6$

3.

$$7x + 3$$
$$2x + 5$$
$$\overline{35x + 15}$$
$$14x^2 + 6x$$
$$\overline{14x^2 + \ ?x + 15}$$ $\quad 41$

4.

$$y + 6$$
$$y^2 - 3 \quad \langle \text{Think } y^2 + {}^-3.$$
$$\overline{{}^-3y + ?} \quad {}^-18$$
$$y^3 + 6y^2$$
$$\overline{y^3 + 6y^2 + {}^-3y + {}^-18} \text{ or}$$
$$y^3 + 6y^2 - 3y - 18$$

Tell the area of each small rectangle A, B, C, and D. Then tell the total area of the large rectangle.

5.

A: x^2
B: $5x$
C: $2x$
D: 10

$x^2 + 7x + 10$

$(x + 5)(x + 2) = \underline{\quad}$

6.

A: $2y^2$
B: $8y$
C: y
D: 4

$2y^2 + 9y + 4$

$(y + 4)(2y + 1) = \underline{\quad}$

B Find each product.

7. $(x + 2)(x + 5)$ $x^2 + 7x + 10$ **8.** $(y + 1)(y + 6)$ $y^2 + 7y + 6$

9. $(x^2 + 1)(x + 4)$ **10.** $(y + 3)(y^2 + 6)$ $y^3 + 3y^2 + 6y + 18$
$x^3 + 4x^2 + x + 4$

11. $(2y + 1)(y + 6)$ **12.** $(3x + 1)(x + 3)$ $3x^2 + 10x + 3$
$2y^2 + 13y + 6$

13. $(xy + 1)(x - 3)$ **14.** $(4m - 1)(m + 3)$ $4m^2 + 11m - 3$
$x^2y - 3xy + x - 3$

15. $(3x - 5y)(2x + 6y)$ **16.** $(7x - 2y)(2x - 3y)$ $14x^2 - 25xy + 6y^2$
$6x^2 + 8xy - 30y^2$

17. $(2x^2 + 3y)(5x^2 - 2y)$ **18.** $(4y - 2)(3y + 1)$ $12y^2 - 2y - 2$
$10x^4 + 11x^2y - 6y^2$

19. $(4m^2 - 1)(4m^2 - 1)$ **20.** $(^-5a + 1)(^-3a - 2)$ $15a^2 + 7a - 2$
$16m^4 - 8m^2 + 1$

21. $(\frac{1}{2}x + 2)(\frac{1}{2}x + 4)$ **22.** $(\frac{3}{4}y + 1)(\frac{1}{4}y + 2)$ $\frac{3}{16}y^2 + 1\frac{3}{4}y + 2$
$\frac{1}{4}x^2 + 3x + 8$

23. $(1.1m + 3)(0.3m + 6)$ **24.** $(2.8c + 1)(1.5c + 1)$ $4.2c^2 + 4.3c + 1$
$0.33m^2 + 7.5m + 18$

C A shortcut for finding the product of two binomials is simply to add up the products of four pairs of terms.

① *First terms* of the binomials

② *Outside terms* of the binomials

③ *Inside terms* of the binomials

④ *Last terms* of the binomials

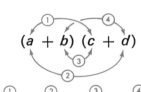

This method for multiplying two binomials is called the FOIL method. Use the FOIL method to find each product below.

25. $(x + 5)(x + 2)$ $x^2 + 7x + 10$ **26.** $(y + 3)(y + 3)$ $y^2 + 6y + 9$

27. $(2x + 1)(3x + 4)$ **28.** $(m + 5)(4m + 2)$ $4m^2 + 22m + 10$
$6x^2 + 11x + 4$

29. $(x^2 + 4)(2x + 3)$ **30.** $(3y^2 + 1)(2y^2 + 1)$ $6y^4 + 5y^2 + 1$
$2x^3 + 3x^2 + 8x + 12$

Adding Polynomials

When you add two or more polynomials, you simply combine like terms.

Example 1: Add $6a + 9$ and $5a + 7$.

Suggested Class Time

Course	Min.	Reg.	Max.
Days	0	1	1

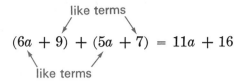

$$(6a + 9) + (5a + 7) = 11a + 16$$

If you want to, you can first rearrange the terms so that like terms are next to each other.

Example 2: Add $9x^2 + 12$ and $^-3x^2 + x + ^-4$.

$$(9x^2 + 12) + (^-3x^2 + x + ^-4) = \underline{9x^2 + ^-3x^2} + x + \underline{12 + ^-4}$$
$$= 6x^2 + x + 8$$

In some cases, you might find the method in the next example helpful. Notice how like terms are arranged in columns. And each polynomial is expressed as a sum of monomials.

Example 3: Add $4x^2 - 6x + 2$ and $^-7x^2 + x + 5$.

$$\begin{array}{r} 4x^2 + {}^-6x + 2 \\ ^-7x^2 + x + 5 \\ \hline ^-3x^2 + {}^-5x + 7 \end{array} \quad \text{or} \quad ^-3x^2 - 5x + 7$$

◀ Notice how $4x^2 - 6x + 2$ was changed.

Example 4: Add $3x^2 - 3xy - 2$, $16y^2 - 3 - 9xy$, and $xy + 4x^2 - 1$.

$$\begin{array}{r} 3x^2 + ^-3xy + {}^-2 \\ 16y^2 + {}^-9xy + {}^-3 \\ 4x^2 + xy + {}^-1 \\ \hline 16y^2 + 7x^2 + {}^-11xy + {}^-6 \end{array}$$
$$\text{or} \quad 16y^2 + 7x^2 - 11xy - 6$$

◀ Express each polynomial as a sum and rearrange the terms, placing like terms in columns.

Exercises

[A] Replace each ? with the correct number.

1. $(7a + 4) + (5a + 6) = ? \cdot a + 10$ 12

2. $(4x^2 + {}^-1) + (8x^2 + {}^-6) = 12x^2 + ?$ ⁻7

3. $(11y^2 + {}^-10y + 2) + (8y + {}^-5) = ? \cdot y^2 + {}^-2y + {}^-3$ 11

4. $(4xy + {}^-2y^2 + 3x^2) + (6xy + 5y^2 + x^2) = 10xy + 3y^2 + ? \cdot x^2$ 4

[B] Add.

5. $(2x + 6) + (3x + 3)$ 5x + 9

6. $(9m + 3) + ({}^-7m + {}^-6)$ 2m − 3

7. $({}^-4y + {}^-2) + (7y + 1)$ 3y − 1

8. $(14w + 3) + ({}^-17w + 8)$ ⁻3w + 11

9. $(9a + 7b) + (4a + 9b)$ 13a + 16b

10. $(x^2 + {}^-8) + ({}^-x^2 + 8)$ 0

11. $(2a + 3b + 3c) + ({}^-1b + 2a + 4c)$ 4a + 2b + 7c

12. $(9y + 8z + {}^-3) + ({}^-9y + {}^-8z + 3)$ 0

13. $(m - n + p) + (m - n + p)$ 2m − 2n + 2p

14. $(y^2 + 3y + 7) + (4y - 9 + 4y^2)$ 5y² + 7y − 2

15. $(7x^2y + 8) + ({}^-9xy + 16)$ 7x²y − 9xy + 24

16. $(3mn - 4m) + (4m^2n + 8m)$ 4m²n + 3mn + 4m

17. $(\frac{1}{2}a + 3) + (\frac{1}{2}a + {}^-2)$

18. $(\frac{2}{3}y - 1) + ({}^-\frac{1}{3}y + 3)$

19. $({}^-\frac{2}{5}x + \frac{1}{10}) + ({}^-\frac{2}{5}x + \frac{3}{10})$

20. $(\frac{5}{8}b + \frac{1}{6}) + (\frac{7}{8}b + \frac{1}{4})$

17. a + 1

18. $\frac{1}{3}y + 2$

19. $-\frac{4}{5}x + \frac{2}{5}$

20. $1\frac{1}{2}b + \frac{5}{12}$

21. 2.1m − 3.1
22. m + 0.2

21. $(1.3m + {}^-1.8) + (0.8m + {}^-1.3)$

22. $({}^-2.4m + {}^-1.7) + (3.4m + 1.9)$

23. $\begin{array}{r} 12x^2 + 14x + {}^-5 \\ 8x^2 + {}^-5x + 1 \\ {}^-2x^2 + 8x + 7 \end{array}$ 18x² + 17x + 3

24. $\begin{array}{r} {}^-6y^2 + {}^-8y + {}^-5 \\ 2y^2 + 3y + 1 \\ {}^-7y^2 + {}^-7y + {}^-6 \end{array}$ ⁻11y² − 12y − 10

[C] **25.** $\begin{array}{r} 5 + 4y + y^2 \\ 8y + 3y^2 + 1 \\ {}^-6y + {}^-5 + 7y^2 \end{array}$ 11y² + 6y + 1

26. $\begin{array}{r} {}^-6xy + 3 + y^2 \\ 2y^2 + 5xy + 1 \\ y^2 + {}^-7 + 8y \end{array}$ 4y² − xy + 8y − 3

27. $(y^4 + 8y - 6y^3 + 5) + (7y + 8y^2 + 3y^4 - 2)$ 4y⁴ − 6y³ + 8y² + 15y + 3

28. $(6a + 2a^3 + 7 - a^2) + (a^3 + 7a^2 - 6a + 1)$ 3a³ + 6a² + 8

469

14.9 Subtracting Polynomials

You know that to subtract an integer, you add its opposite. For example,

$$8 - {}^-5 = 8 + 5.$$

Remember that the sum of an integer and its opposite is 0.

$$7 + {}^-7 = 0 \qquad\qquad {}^-19 + 19 = 0$$

Now consider $2x^2 + 3x$ and $^-2x^2 + {}^-3x$. Notice that the sum of these two polynomials is 0.

$$(2x^2 + 3x) + ({}^-2x^2 + {}^-3x) = 2x^2 + {}^-2x^2 + 3x + {}^-3x$$
$$= 0 + 0$$
$$= 0$$

Therefore, $2x^2 + 3x$ and $^-2x^2 + {}^-3x$ are *opposites*.

 The sum of a polynomial and its opposite is 0.

Example 1: Show that $^-5y^2 + 7y$ and $5y^2 + {}^-7y$ are opposites.

$$({}^-5y^2 + 7y) + (5y^2 + {}^-7y) = {}^-5y^2 + 5y^2 + 7y + {}^-7y$$
$$= 0 + 0$$
$$= 0$$

The example above suggests a way for finding the opposite of a polynomial.

 To find the opposite of a polynomial, change the sign of *each* term of the polynomial.

Example 2: Find the opposite of each polynomial.

a. $^-3x^3 + {}^-5x^2 + 4$ **b.** $7y^2 - 5y + 3$

The opposite is   The opposite is

$3x^3 + 5x^2 + {}^-4.$ $^-7y^2 + 5y - 3.$

You can use the same method to subtract polynomials as you used to subtract integers.

 To subtract a polynomial, you add its opposite.

Example 3: Subtract.

a.
$$
\begin{array}{r}
12x^2 + 5x + 3 \\
-(^-5x^2 + {}^-2x + 1)
\end{array}
\Rightarrow
\begin{array}{r}
12x^2 + 5x + 3 \\
+(\ 5x^2 + 2x + {}^-1) \\
\hline
17x^2 + 7x + 2
\end{array}
$$

b. $(9y^2 - 2y + 1) - (3y^2 - y + 5)$

$\quad = (9y^2 - 2y + 1) + (^-3y^2 + y - 5)$

$\quad = 6y^2 - y - 4$

Exercises

Assignment Guide 14.9
Oral: Reg. & Max. 1–10
Written: Reg. 11–28
Max. 11–36

A Find the opposite of each polynomial.

1. $7x$ $\ ^-7x$ **2.** ^-5y $\ 5y$ **3.** $2x + 1$ $\ ^-2x - 1$

4. $^-7y + 3$ $\ 7y - 3$ **5.** $9y^2 + 2y + 3$ **6.** $^-7a^2 + 5a + 4$ $\ 7a^2 - 5a - 4$
$\qquad\qquad\qquad\qquad\qquad {}^-9y^2 - 2y - 3$

Replace each ? with the correct term.

7. $3x - {}^-2x = 3x + ?$ $\ 2x$ **8.** $^-9y - 3y = {}^-9y + ?$ $\ ^-3y$

9. $(3a + 1) - (2a + {}^-3) = (3a + 1) + (? + 3)$ $\ ^-2a$

10. $(^-x + 4) - (^-3x + 1) = (^-x + 4) + (? + {}^-1)$ $\ 3x$

B Subtract.

11. $14a - {}^-5a$ $\ 19a$ **12.** $^-12y - 3y$ $\ ^-15y$

13. $^-9a - {}^-3a$ $\ ^-6a$ **14.** $16m - {}^-3m$ $\ 19m$

15. $(3x + 1) - (^-5x + 2)$ $\ 8x - 1$ **16.** $(2a + 4) - (3a + 5)$ $\ ^-a - 1$

17. $(11a + {}^-6) - (a + {}^-5)$ $\ 10a - 1$ **18.** $(5m + 4) - (^-5m + {}^-6)$ $\ 10m + 10$

19. $(10y - 7) - (3y - 2)$ $\ 7y - 5$ **20.** $(^-3y^2 - 6) - (5y^2 + 4)$ $\ ^-8y^2 - 10$

21. $(^-15z^2 - 7) - (^-8z^2 - 14)$ **22.** $(13m - 19) - (^-17m + 8)$ $\ 30m - 27$
$\qquad\qquad\qquad\qquad {}^-7z^2 + 7$

471

23.
$$11m^2 + 10m + 8$$
$$\underline{-(9m^2 + {}^-6m + 5)}$$
$${}_{2m^2 + 16m + 3}$$

24.
$${}^-21y^2 + 13y + {}^-9$$
$$\underline{-({}^-8y^2 - 8y - 3)}$$
$${}_{{}^-13y^2 + 21y - 6}$$

25.
$$9x^2 + 8x + 5$$
$$\underline{-(3x^2 - 3x - 7)}$$
$${}_{6x^2 + 11x + 12}$$

26.
$$13m^2 + {}^-7m + {}^-8$$
$$\underline{-({}^-9m^2 + {}^-4m + 12)}$$
$${}_{22m^2 - 3m - 20}$$

27.
$${}^-14a^2 + 13a + {}^-9$$
$$\underline{-({}^-7a^2 + {}^-9a + 8)}$$
$${}_{{}^-7a^2 + 22a - 17}$$

28.
$$20x^2 + 19x + 12$$
$$\underline{-(x^2 + {}^-5x + 10)}$$
$${}_{19x^2 + 24x + 2}$$

C **29.** $({}^-7y + 8y^2 + {}^-10) - (12 + {}^-5y + 2y^2)$ $\ {}_{6y^2 - 2y - 22}$

30. $(5y + 2y^2 + {}^-3) - ({}^-9 + 3y + 2y^2)$ $\ {}_{2y + 6}$

31.
$$17a + 13 + a^3 + {}^-a^2$$
$$\underline{-(15 + {}^-2a^3 + a^2 + {}^-3a)}$$
$${}_{3a^3 - 2a^2 + 20a - 2}$$

32.
$${}^-25 + 10a + a^2 + {}^-14a^3$$
$$\underline{-(18a^3 + 7a^2 + {}^-8a + 12)}$$
$${}_{{}^-32a^3 - 6a^2 + 18a - 37}$$

Simplify.

33. $(7x + {}^-3) + ({}^-3x + 1) - (5x + {}^-4)$ $\ {}^-x + 2$

34. $({}^-4x^2 + 3x) + (6x + {}^-2x^2) - (3x + 7x^2)$ $\ {}^-13x^2 + 6x$

35. $({}^-9x^2 + 3x + {}^-2) + (9x^2 + {}^-6x + 1) - ({}^-8x^2 + {}^-5x + 3)$
$${}_{8x^2 + 2x - 4}$$

36. $(6x^2 + 3) + (x + {}^-6) - ({}^-5x^2 + {}^-3x)$ $\ {}_{11x^2 + 4x - 3}$

Can You Solve It?

7 oz

© 1979 United Feature Syndicate

Dividing by a Monomial

14.10

When you divide monomials, you often use exponents. For example,

$$\frac{x^6}{x^4} = \frac{x \cdot x \cdot x \cdot x \cdot x \cdot x}{x \cdot x \cdot x \cdot x} = x^2. \qquad Shortcut: \; \frac{x^6}{x^4} = x^{6-4} = x^2$$

Notice how the shortcut above can be used to help find the quotient of two monomials. Remember that you can check a division problem by multiplying the quotient by the divisor. The result should equal the dividend.

Examples:

1. $\dfrac{x^5}{x^2} = x^{5-2} = x^3$ $\qquad\qquad$ *Check:* $x^3 \cdot x^2 = x^5$ ✓

2. $\dfrac{\overset{3}{\cancel{15}}x^4}{\underset{1}{\cancel{5}}x^2} = 3x^{4-2} = 3x^2$ $\qquad$ *Check:* $3x^2 \cdot 5x^2 = 15x^4$ ✓

3. $\dfrac{\overset{-4}{\cancel{-48}}m^3n^2}{\underset{1}{\cancel{12}}mn} = {}^-4m^{3-1}n^{2-1} = {}^-4m^2n$ $\qquad$ *Check:* ${}^-4m^2n \cdot 12mn = {}^-48m^3n^2$ ✓

 To divide monomials containing constants, divide the constants. Divide like variables by subtracting their exponents.

When you divide a polynomial by a monomial, you must divide each term of the polynomial by the monomial.

Examples:

4. $\dfrac{20x^3 + 4x^2}{2x} = \dfrac{20x^3}{2x} + \dfrac{4x^2}{2x} = 10x^2 + 2x$

5. $\dfrac{6x^3 + 12x^2 + 18x}{3x} = \dfrac{6x^3}{3x} + \dfrac{12x^2}{3x} + \dfrac{18x}{3x} = 2x^2 + 4x + 6$

■ Exercises

Assignment Guide 14.10
Oral: Max. 1–8
Written: Max. 9–32

A Replace each ? with the correct number or expression.

1. $\dfrac{x^6}{x^3} = x^?$ 3

2. $\dfrac{y^7}{y^4} = y^?$ 3

3. $\dfrac{m^5}{m} = m^?$ 4

4. $\dfrac{25x^2}{5} = ?x^2$ 5

5. $\dfrac{12x^2}{3x} = ?x$ 4

6. $\dfrac{16mn^2}{8mn} = ?n$ 2

7. $\dfrac{8x^2 + 8x}{4x} = \dfrac{8x^2}{4x} + \dfrac{8x}{?}$ 4x
$= 2x + 2$

8. $\dfrac{21x^3 + 14x^2}{7x} = \dfrac{21x^3}{7x} + \dfrac{?}{7x}$ 14x²
$= 3x^2 + 2x$

B Divide.

9. $\dfrac{y^6}{y^4}$ y^2

10. $\dfrac{x^7}{x^3}$ x^4

11. $\dfrac{m^3}{m^3}$ 1

12. $\dfrac{a^3}{a^2}$ a

13. $\dfrac{10x^2}{5}$ $2x^2$

14. $\dfrac{12m^3}{4}$ $3m^3$

15. $\dfrac{16x^4}{4x}$ $4x^3$

16. $\dfrac{20x^3}{5x^2}$ $4x$

17. $\dfrac{36y^5}{4y^3}$ $9y^2$

18. $\dfrac{18c^9}{9c^7}$ $2c^2$

19. $\dfrac{27a^2b^3c^5}{-9ab^2c^4}$ $-3abc$

20. $\dfrac{-16x^3y^2}{4xy}$ $-4x^2y$

21. $4a^2 + 2a$
22. $2x^2 + y^2$
23. $c^4 + c$
24. $12c^2 + 6c$
25. $9x^2 - 8x - 12$
26. $5y^2 - 2y + 3$
27. $^-6x^2y - 3xy + 4$
28. $10x^2 + 5x + 2$

21. $\dfrac{12a^2 + 6a}{3}$

22. $\dfrac{18x^2 + 9y^2}{9}$

23. $\dfrac{c^5 + c^2}{c}$

24. $\dfrac{24c^3 + 12c^2}{2c}$

25. $\dfrac{18x^2 - 16x - 24}{2}$

26. $\dfrac{25y^2 - 10y + 15}{5}$

27. $\dfrac{-36x^3y^2 - 18x^2y^2 + 24xy}{6xy}$

28. $\dfrac{100x^3 + 50x^2 + 20x}{10x}$

C **29.** Use $\dfrac{n^4}{n^2} = n^2$. Let $n = 2$. Substitute and find the powers. Then divide on the left side. Does a true equation result? Yes

30. Repeat Exercise 29, but this time let $n = {}^-3$. Yes

31. Repeat Exercise 29, but this time let $n = 0$. No $\left(\dfrac{0}{0} \neq 0\right)$

32. Which statement is more precise, **(a)** $\dfrac{n^4}{n^2} = n^2$ or **(b)** $\dfrac{n^4}{n^2} = n^2$ if $n \neq 0$? Why? b; $\dfrac{0}{0}$ is not defined.

Terms and Symbols Review

Complete each sentence. Choose from these words.

Assignment Guide Rev.
Oral:
Reg. Terms & Symbols 1–4
Max. Terms & Symbols 1–4
Written: Reg. 1–31
    Max. 1–36

monomial   *binomial*   *trinomial*   *like*   *unlike*

1. A polynomial with 3 terms is called a ____. Trinomial

2. When terms have the same variables with equal exponents, the terms are called ____ terms. Like

3. A polynomial is a ____ or the sum of two or more monomials. Monomial

4. A polynomial with 2 terms is called a ____. Binomial

Chapter 14 Review

Give an equation for the problem. Then solve the problem.   14.1

1. George paid $40 for two sweaters. One cost $12 more than the other. How much did each sweater cost? $x + x + 12 = 40$; $14 and $26

Solve if possible.   14.2

2. On a trip the Wheats traveled 153 miles in 3 hours. They had to pay $3.40 in tolls and used 9.2 gallons of gasoline. What was their average speed for the trip? 51 mph

Which pairs of monomials are like terms?   14.3

3. $3x^2y$, $^-6xy^2$ **4.** $\frac{1}{2}x^3y$, $\frac{2}{3}x^3y$

5. $9x$, ^-7y **6.** ^-3y, ^-10y

Add.   14.4

7. $^-7y + 14y$ $7y$ **8.** $3m + {}^-16m$ ^-13m

9. $9xy^2 + {}^-11xy^2$ $^-2xy^2$ **10.** $^-6x + {}^-10x + 7x$ ^-9x

14.5   **Multiply.**

11. $x^3 \cdot x^5$ x^8

12. $y \cdot y^4$ y^5

13. $(^-3x^2)(2x^2)$ $^-6x^4$

14. $(^-4m)(^-9m^3)$ $36m^4$

14.6   **15.** $2x(^-5x + 1)$ $^-10x^2 + 2x$

16. $(8y + 4)(^-3y)$ $^-24y^2 - 12y$

17. $(3x - 4)(5x^2)$ $15x^3 - 20x^2$

18. $8m(^-4m + ^-2)$ $^-32m^2 - 16m$

14.7   **19.** $(3x + 2)(2x + 4)$ $6x^2 + 16x + 8$

20. $(5y + ^-2)(2y + ^-3)$ $10y^2 - 19y + 6$

21. $(^-8z + 5)(^-3z + 4)$ $24z^2 - 47z + 20$

22. $(7m - 2)(m - 6)$ $7m^2 - 44m + 12$

14.8   **Add.**

23. $(6x + 3) + (5x + 7)$ $11x + 10$

24. $(^-8m + 5) + (^-3m + 7)$ $^-11m + 12$

25. $(^-3x^2 + 7x + 1) + (8x^2 - 8x + 10)$ $5x^2 - x + 11$

26. $13x^2 + ^-25x + 12$
       $^-11x^2 + 9x + 8$
       $2x^2 - 16x + 20$

27. $^-14y^2 + 7y + 1$
       $^-10y + 8 + ^-3y^2$
       $^-17y^2 - 3y + 9$

14.9   **Subtract.**

28. $12a - ^-5a$ $17a$

29. $^-10y - 8y$ ^-18y

30. $9b + ^-7$
       $-(2b + ^-3)$ $7b - 4$

31. $3m^2 + ^-8m + 5$
       $-(2m^2 + ^-2m + 1)$ $m^2 - 6m + 4$

14.10   **Divide.**

32. $\dfrac{24m^2}{8}$ $3m^2$

33. $\dfrac{-36x}{12x}$ $^-3$

34. $\dfrac{-48y^3}{8y}$ $^-6y^2$

35. $\dfrac{27x^3 + 12x^2 + 21x}{3x}$ $9x^2 + 4x + 7$

36. $\dfrac{10y^3 + ^-5y^2 + ^-15y}{^-5y}$ $^-2y^2 + y + 3$

Give an equation for the problem. Then solve the problem.

1. Alana earned \$120 last week at two different jobs. She earned \$20 more at the first job than at the second job. How much did she earn at each job? $x + x + 20 = 120;$ \$70 and \$50

Assignment Guide Test
Written: Reg. 1–13
Max. 1–16

Add.

2. $^-16y^2 + 7y^2$ $_{^-9y^2}$

3. $^-8a + ^-7a + ^-2a$ $_{^-17a}$

4. $9y + ^-8$
$\underline{^-2y + 4}$ $_{7y - 4}$

5. $16x^2 + 10x + ^-5$
$\underline{3x^2 + ^-7x + 4}$ $_{19x^2 + 3x - 1}$

Multiply.

6. $a^2 \cdot a^6$ $_{a^8}$

7. $(^-3m^3)(7m^2)$ $_{^-21m^5}$

8. $5x(4x + ^-7)$ $_{20x^2 - 35x}$

9. $(^-9y^2 + 3y)(^-2y)$ $_{18y^3 - 6y^2}$

10. $(y + 7)(y + 2)$
$_{y^2 + 9y + 14}$

11. $(3x - 4)(2x + 1)$ $_{6x^2 - 5x - 4}$

Subtract.

12. $14y - ^-3y$ $_{17y}$

13. $(^-7x + 6) - (5x + ^-3)$ $_{^-12x + 9}$

Divide.

14. $\dfrac{25x^3}{5x}$ $_{5x^2}$

15. $\dfrac{^-54m^5}{^-6m^2}$ $_{9m^3}$

16. $\dfrac{18a^3 + ^-12a^2 + 15a}{3a}$ $_{6a^2 - 4a + 5}$

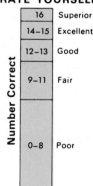

RATE YOURSELF

Number Correct	
16	Superior
14–15	Excellent
12–13	Good
9–11	Fair
0–8	Poor

GOING TO COLLEGE?

Many careers require a college education. To prepare for college, you may have to take two or more years of high-school math. Below are some recommendations of the Mathematical Association of America and the National Council of Teachers of Mathematics.

For each college program listed, the recommended number of years of high-school math is indicated. Reprinted with permission from *The Math in High School . . . you'll need for college,* The Mathematical Association of America, 1978

Agriculture:
Agricultural economics	3
Entomology	3
Environmental sciences	4
Food sciences	3
Forestry	3
Genetics	3
Landscape architecture	3
Plant pathology	3
Rural sociology	3
Wildlife ecology	3
Other areas of agriculture	2

Architecture	3
Art	2

Business:
Accounting	3
Economics	4
Management	4

Communications	2

Education:
Elementary	3
Child development and preschool	3

Engineering	4
History	2
Language and Literature	2
Law	3

Life sciences:
Bacteriology	4
Biochemistry	4
Biology	4

Linguistics	3

Mathematical sciences:
Mathematics	4
Statistics	4
Actuarial sciences	4
Computer science	4

Medicine:
Allied medicine	3
Dental hygiene	3
Dentistry	4
Medical technology	4
Nursing	3
Optometry	4

Medicine: (continued)
Physical therapy	3
Pre-medicine	4
Public health	3

Music	2
Pharmacy	4
Philosophy	2

Physical sciences:
Astronomy	4
Chemistry	4
Geology	4
Physics	4

Social sciences:
Anthropology	2
Asian studies	2
Black studies	3
Geography	3
Political science	3
Psychology	4
Social welfare	2
Sociology	3

Theater	2

This is what a certain number of years of high-school math means.

1 year	First year of *algebra*
2 years	One year of *geometry*
3 years	Second year of *algebra*
4 years	One year of *precalculus mathematics*

You may not have a career in mind right now. But by taking enough high-school math, you'll have more career choices open to you later. And you won't have to take remedial courses in college.

For each number, give **(a)** the hundreds digit, **(b)** the tens digit, and
(c) the ones digit.

1. 3278   **a.** 2   **b.** 7   **c.** 8   **2.** 378   **a.** 3   **b.** 7   **c.** 8   **3.** \$25   **a.** 0   **b.** 2   **c.** 5

Put each set of numbers in order from smallest to largest.

Suggested Class Time			
Course	Min.	Reg.	Max.
Days	0	1	0

4. 15, 36, 10, 25, 9, 16, 2, 5, 36, 25

2, 5, 9, 10, 15, 16, 25, 25, 36, 36

5. 296, 525, 609, 610, 436, 525, 508, 423, 312, 213

213, 296, 312, 423, 436, 508, 525, 525, 609, 610

6. 3.7, 6.8, 2.8, 1.7, 2.1, 5.2, 3.9, 3.3, 9.3, 4.8

1.7, 2.1, 2.8, 3.3, 3.7, 3.9, 4.8, 5.2, 6.8, 9.3

Assignment Guide GR 15
Written: Reg. 1–28

Add.

7. 8, 34, 52, 28, 6, 16, 11, 44, 1   200

8. 5, 19, 12, 18, 0, 18, 14, 26   112

9. 40, 250, 119, 640, 19, 91, 447, 124   1730

Compute.

10. $\frac{1}{2} \times \frac{1}{3}$ $\frac{1}{6}$ **11.** $\frac{2}{5} \times \frac{1}{5}$ $\frac{2}{25}$ **12.** $\frac{5}{12} \times \frac{4}{5}$ $\frac{1}{3}$ 4.2

13. $\frac{1}{2} + \frac{1}{4}$ $\frac{3}{4}$ **14.** $\frac{1}{6} + \frac{1}{3}$ $\frac{1}{2}$ **15.** $\frac{5}{12} + \frac{1}{3}$ $\frac{3}{4}$ 4.8

16. 0.4 + 0.5   0.9   **17.** 0.25 + 0.8   1.05   **18.** 0.58 + 0.33   0.91   5.3

19. \$18.99 + \$19.99 + \$20.95 + \$14.98 + \$15.00 + \$6.00   \$95.91

20. 0.7 × 0.6   0.42   **21.** 0.95 × 0.3   0.285   **22.** 0.5 × 0.75   0.375   5.4

23. 135 ÷ 6   22.5   **24.** 4125 ÷ 12   343.75   **25.** \$100.10 ÷ 10   5.5

                                                        \$10.01

Write as decimals.

26. $\frac{1}{4}$ 0.25   **27.** $\frac{3}{8}$ 0.375   **28.** $\frac{42}{200}$ 0.21   5.5

15 STATISTICS AND PROBABILITY

Statistics and *probability* are two closely related branches of mathematics. As branches of mathematics go, both are rather new.

This chapter begins by looking at *statistics*—the mathematics of organizing and studying sets of numerical facts.

The chapter ends by taking a look at *probability*—the mathematics of chance.

Frequency Tables

15.1

Rita asked 30 classmates how many times they had been to a movie in the last two months. These were the answers:

4, 0, 1, 3, 2, 3, 1, 3, 5, 4, 7, 3, 1, 0, 4,
2, 3, 4, 3, 1, 5, 3, 2, 3, 4, 3, 2, 1, 4, 0

You can usually get a better understanding of a set of numerical facts (like those above) by organizing them in some way. Here's what Rita did. She found the **range** of the answers by finding the lowest answer and the highest answer.

low answer   high answer

0–7

range

Then she made a table that shows how many times each answer was given. This is called a **frequency table**.

Example : Make a frequency table, using Rita's information.

Number of movies	Tally	Number of classmates	
			Count the number of times each answer occurred.
0	|||	3	3 classmates answered 0.
1	ⅢⅡ	5	
2	||||	4	
3	ⅢⅡ ||||	9	
4	ⅢⅡ |	6	
5	||	2	
6		0	No classmates answered 6.
7	|	1	
	Total	30	

Assignment Guide 15.1
Oral: Reg. & Max. 1–6
Written: Reg. 7–18
Max. 7–22

Exercises

A True or False?

1. Making a frequency table is one way to organize information. T

2. The range of 6, 5, 9, 8 is 5–9. T

Use the set of numbers below to complete the frequency table at the right.

4, 5, 5, 6, 6, 5, 8, 4

Number	Tally	Frequency
4	II	2
3. 5	III	? 3
4. 6	? II	2
5. ? 7		0
6. 8	I	? 1
	Total	8

B Find the range.

7. 8, 7, 5, 8, 9, 8, 8, 7, 8, 7, 6 5–9

8. 5, 3, 0, 1, 3, 3, 4, 5, 0, 3, 1 0–5

9. 19, 21, 20, 17, 18, 21, 17, 18, 21, 17 17–21

10. 39, 36, 40, 36, 38, 37, 39, 36, 40, 36 36–40

11.
No.	5	6	7	8	9	Total
Freq.	1	1	3	5	1	11

12.
No.	0	1	2	3	4	5	Total
Freq.	2	2	0	4	1	2	11

13.
No.	17	18	19	20	21	Total
Freq.	3	2	1	1	3	10

14.
No.	36	37	38	39	40	Total
Freq.	4	1	1	2	2	10

Make a frequency table for the set of numbers in each exercise.
11–22. Tally columns have been omitted.

11. Exercise 7   **12.** Exercise 8   **13.** Exercise 9   **14.** Exercise 10

15. *Ratings of a new food product by 50 tasters:* 0, ⁻2, 1, 1, ⁻1, 2, ⁻1, 1, 0, 1, 2, ⁻2, 0, 0, 1, 0, 1, 1, 0, 2, 1, 0, 2, 0, 1, 2, ⁻1, 0, 1, 0, 1, 0, 0, 0, 1, 0, 2, 1, 0, 1, 0, 1, 2, 1, 1, 2, ⁻2, ⁻1, ⁻1, 0 (*Note:* Each rating is given as ⁻2, ⁻1, 0, 1, or 2, with ⁻2 meaning "terrible" and 2 meaning "excellent.")

Rating	⁻2	⁻1	0	1	2	Total
Freq.	3	5	17	17	8	50

16. *Results of tossing a die (singular of dice) 50 times:* 5, 3, 4, 1, 1, 1, 5, 3, 6, 1, 2, 2, 1, 5, 5, 2, 6, 4, 2, 3, 4, 5, 3, 3, 5, 1, 4, 3, 2, 1, 1, 6, 2, 5, 5, 3, 4, 4, 3, 2, 5, 1, 1, 6, 1, 6, 4, 2, 6, 2

No.	1	2	3	4	5	6	Total
Freq.	11	9	8	7	9	6	50

Courtesy Chrysler-Plymouth

17. *Miles-per-gallon ratings of 50 four-cylinder cars:* 26, 24, 22, 22, 22, 24, 24, 21, 20, 22, 25, 28, 20, 20, 24, 24, 24, 23, 26, 26, 20, 28, 23, 23, 26, 20, 21, 23, 24, 20, 28, 22, 22, 21, 28, 24, 21, 25, 20, 21, 25, 25, 20, 20, 20, 23, 26, 22, 21, 24

mpg	20	21	22	23	24	25	26	27	28	Total
Freq.	10	6	7	5	9	4	5	0	4	50

18. *Test scores of 50 students:* 89, 83, 90, 84, 86, 86, 85, 83, 85, 87, 83, 85, 87, 90, 84, 87, 83, 83, 89, 88, 87, 90, 85, 86, 84, 85, 87, 89, 84, 86, 86, 88, 84, 84, 86, 86, 85, 86, 87, 87, 86, 89, 90, 86, 88, 84, 84, 87, 84, 84

Score	83	84	85	86	87	88	89	90	Total
Freq.	5	10	6	10	8	3	4	4	50

C Sometimes the numbers in a set are spread out, and each number appears only once or just a few times. To make the frequency table compact and easy to read, the numbers are *grouped.*

Example: *Number of hours per week 20 students with jobs work:* 25, 30, 12, 20, 40, 15, 23, 24, 24, 20, 35, 35, 28, 30, 26, 31, 19, 25, 11, 28

——— Count the numbers in each group.

Hours per week	Tally	Number of students
11–16	|||	3
17–22	|||	3
23–28	++++ |||	8
29–34	|||	3
35–40	|||	3
	Total	20

There are 3 numbers in the 11–16 group (12, 15, and 11).

19. Copy and complete the frequency table above.

Make a frequency table, using the given groups.

20. *40 test scores:* 87, 43, 78, 75, 87, 93, 68, 58, 59, 86, 40, 80, 68, 92, 90, 60, 65, 73, 78, 71, 64, 62, 85, 68, 71, 57, 88, 99, 82, 71, 85, 79, 80, 85, 73, 73, 87, 76, 73, 77

Groups: 40–49, 50–59, 60–69, 70–79, 80–89, 90–99 Total

2   3   7   13   11   4   40

21. *50 numbers:* 61, 94, 64, 87, 90, 11, 60, 28, 30, 43, 22, 25, 71, 18, 32, 4, 34, 49, 55, 41, 20, 36, 65, 59, 37, 4, 81, 16, 48, 92, 96, 34, 67, 90, 65, 26, 99, 94, 39, 67, 63, 48, 59, 35, 72, 80, 75, 39, 65, 82

Groups: 4–19, 20–35, 36–51, 52–67, 68–83, 84–99 Total

5   10   9   12   6   8   50

22. *50 numbers:* 0.9, 6.6, 5.4, 4.6, 7.2, 7.4, 7.6, 2.3, 3.3, 5.7, 6.7, 3.0, 1.8, 0.5, 4.6, 9.8, 6.5, 9.1, 1.3, 4.8, 7.8, 7.7, 1.4, 5.0, 1.1, 3.4, 7.5, 6.5, 0.4, 0.3, 7.6, 6.3, 4.1, 2.7, 6.7, 3.2, 2.2, 0.3, 4.5, 4.5, 1.8, 1.0, 0.5, 3.5, 1.3, 1.4, 5.2, 1.7, 2.1, 2.0

Groups: 0.3–1.8, 1.9–3.4, 3.5–5.0, 5.1–6.6, 6.7–8.2, 8.3–9.8 Total

15   9   8   7   9   2   50

Bar Graphs

Mr. Davis made a frequency table showing the grades of the 24 students in his pre-algebra class.

Grade	Tally	Number of students
A	ⅣⅠ ⅠⅠⅠ	8
B	ⅣⅠ ⅣⅠ ⅠⅠ	12
C	ⅠⅠⅠ	3
D	Ⅰ	1
F		0
Total		24

This information can also be shown in a **bar graph.** The bars on the graph are all the same width. The heights of the bars represent the frequencies of the grades.

Example 1: How many students received an A in math?

The bar over the "A" column has a height of 8.

Eight students received a grade of A.

Example 2: What grade was the most frequently received?

The bar over the "B" column is the highest.

The grade most frequently received was B.

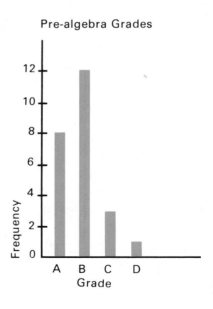

Pre-algebra Grades

The item that occurs most frequently in a set is called the **mode** of the set. The mode of this set is B.

A bar graph that shows frequency and uses only numbers is called a **histogram.** A histogram has no spaces between the bars.

This histogram shows the frequencies with which students received certain scores on a 25-point quiz.

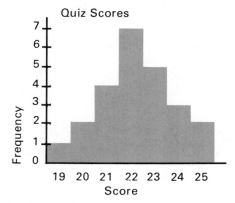

Quiz Scores

Example 3: What is the mode?

The highest bar is over the 22.

The mode is 22.

Example 4: How many students received scores over 22?

Five students received scores of 23, 3 received scores of 24, and 2 received scores of 25.

$5 + 3 + 2 = 10$

Ten students received scores over 22.

Assignment Guide 15.2
Oral: Reg. & Max. 1–8
Written: Reg. 1–15 odd
Max. 1–15 odd;
17–19

Exercises

A Use the bar graph at the right for Exercises 1–8.

Byron's School Buses

1. What is the mode? Buses 35 and 42

2. Which bus brings the least number of students? Bus 57

3. Which bus brings 50 students? Bus 15

4. Which bus brings 60 students? Bus 22

5. Which two buses bring the same number of students? Buses 35 and 42

6. Which bus brings fewer than 50 students? Bus 57

7. The maximum number of students allowed on each bus is 66. Which buses cannot hold 10 extra students? Buses 22, 35, and 42

8. Give two reasons why this graph is not a histogram. The numbers on the bottom scale are the names of the buses and there is space between the bars.

485

Use the histogram at the right for Exercises 9–14.

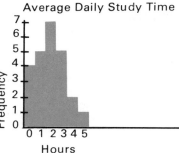

Average Daily Study Time

9. What is the mode? 2 hours

10. What average number of hours a day is spent in study by the least number of students? 5 hours

11. How many students study an average of 3 hours a day? 5 students

12. How many students study an average of 2 hours a day? 7 students

13. How many students average less than 2 hours of study a day?
9 students

14. How many students average more than 2 hours of study a day?
8 students

Make a graph for each frequency table.

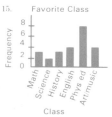

15. Favorite Class

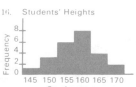

16. Students' Heights

15. Favorite class	Tally	Number of students
Math	|||	3
Science	||	2
History	|||	3
English	||||	4
Phys ed	ℕ |||	8
Art/music	||||	4

16. Height (cm)	Tally	Number of students
145			1
150					3
155	ℕ		6
160	ℕ |||	8
165						4
170				2

Make a frequency table and a graph for the numbers in each exercise.

17. *Test scores of 24 students:* 96, 88, 84, 84, 72, 76, 88, 92, 96, 80, 76, 92, 88, 88, 84, 92, 84, 88, 76, 88, 84, 88, 88, 84

18. *Results of rolling a die 30 times:* 1, 6, 5, 6, 4, 2, 1, 6, 4, 6, 5, 3, 2, 6, 4, 5, 2, 1, 1, 3, 5, 6, 5, 4, 5, 6, 3, 3, 1, 4

17. Test score	Tally	Number of students
72			1
76					3
80			1
84	ℕ		6
88	ℕ |||	8
92					3
96				2
Total		24

Test Scores

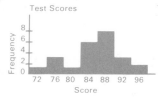

18. Results of die	Tally	Frequency
1	ℕ	5
2					3
3						4
4	ℕ	5
5	ℕ		6
6	ℕ ||	7
Total		30

Die Tossing

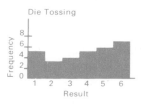

The Median

15.3

Artstreet

The median of a major roadway is the grassy or paved strip in the middle. The **median** of a set of numbers is the number in the middle when the numbers are listed in order.

Example 1: Find the median of these test scores: 80, 90, 85, 75, 80.

Put the numbers in order.

2 numbers   2 numbers

75, 80, 80, 85, 90

median
(middle number)

Find the middle number.

If there is an even number of scores or numbers, there are two middle numbers. To find the median, add the two middle numbers, and then divide by 2.

Example 2: Find the median of 12, 4, 1, 16, 9, 13.

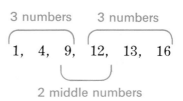

Put the numbers in order.

Find the two middle numbers.

Add, and divide by 2.

$$\frac{9 + 12}{2} = \frac{21}{2} = 10.5$$

median

▨ Exercises

Assignment Guide 15.3
Oral: Reg. & Max. 1–4
Written: Reg. 5–21 odd
Max. 5–25 odd

A 1. The number in the middle of a set of numbers listed in order is called the ____. Median

2. If there are two middle numbers, add them and divide by ____ to find the median. 2

3. The median for 1, 3, 4, 7, 7 is ____. 4

4. The median for 2, 4, 6, 8 is ____. 5

B Find the median.

5. 1, 5, 7, 9, 11 7

6. 2, 4, 6, 8, 10 6

7. 7, 10, 14, 15 12

8. 8, 9, 11, 13 10

9. 11, 14, 23, 27, 28, 34, 36 27

10. 31, 35, 38, 42, 42, 45, 46, 53, 54 42

11. 71, 73, 78, 78,
83, 84, 86, 87,
89, 93, 99, 99   85

12. 54, 55, 57, 58,
61, 63, 65, 68,
72, 77, 79   63

13. 5, 9, 8, 6, 1, 7, 4   6

14. 12, 13, 6, 7, 3, 0, 5   6

15. 4.2, 8.9, 6.1, 1.8, 0.5, 3.4   3.8

16. 3.1, 6.9, 4.3, 3.4, 7.1, 6.3   5.3

17. 144, 221, 320, 320, 183, 128,
32, 121, 330, 371, 364, 274
   247.5

18. 534, 198, 165, 91, 258, 410,
174, 543, 521, 567, 321, 207   289.5

19. 19, 24, 9, 12, 36, 59, 33,
56, 10, 38, 11, 29, 10, 19,
15, 18, 9, 4   18.5

20. 32, 82, 53, 80, 80, 62, 75,
61, 64, 36, 78, 84, 37, 75,
64, 80, 58, 36   64

21. 2:12 (2 minutes, 12 seconds), 4:01, 3:23, 2:46, 1:03, 1:01, 1:46,
1:32, 1:06, 3:21, 2:35, 2:33, 5:25   2:33

22. 1:17 (1 minute, 17 seconds), 2:18, 2:25, 1:46, 3:14, 5:16, 4:39,
3:23, 2:18, 1:11, 4:16, 5:00, 3:06   3:06

C The median can be found by using a frequency table.

Example:

Number	Frequency
1	3
2	2
3	4
4	5
5	4
6	3
Total	21

10 numbers

The middle number is a 4.

10 numbers

The median is 4.

Make a frequency table and then find the median. Use the set in

23. Exercise 7, page 482   8

24. Exercise 8, page 482   3

25. Exercise 17, page 482   23

26. Exercise 18, page 483   86

15.4 The Mean

Suppose someone asked you to find the average of *four* bowling scores. You probably would add the scores and then divide the sum by 4. In statistics, your answer is called the **mean**.

Most averages in sports are means, but other numbers are also called "averages." Many times an "average salary" is the median. A shirt manufacturer may call the size worn by the most people (the mode) the "average shirt size."

Example 1: A bowler's scores for 4 games were 143, 156, 148, and 133. Find the mean score.

Add the scores. $143 + 156 + 148 + 133 = 580$

Divide by the number of scores.

$$\frac{580}{4} = \underset{\text{mean}}{145}$$

Example 2: Find the mean: 1.4, 3.9, 3.7, 2.5.

$$
\begin{array}{r}
1.4 \\
3.9 \\
3.7 \\
+\ 2.5 \\
\hline
11.5
\end{array}
$$

$$
\begin{array}{r}
2.875 \\
4\overline{)11.500} \\
8 \\
\hline
3\,5 \\
3\,2 \\
\hline
30 \\
28 \\
\hline
20
\end{array}
$$

Carry the division out only far enough to give a sensible answer, usually to the same decimal place as (or one more place than) the numbers in the set. In this case 2.88 or 2.9 will do.

If you know the mean and the number of items in the set, you can find the sum of the items, as follows:

Example 3: A paper carrier's mean monthly income for the past year (12 months) was $49. What was the total income for the year?

mean monthly income   number of months in year   total income for the year

$$\$49 \times 12 = \$588$$

Suggested Class Time

Course	Min.	Reg.	Max.
Days	0	1	1

Exercises

Assignment Guide 15.4
Oral: Reg. & Max. 1–4
Written:
Reg. 5–19 odd; Quiz,
p. 493
Max. 5–25 odd; Quiz,
p. 493

A 1. To find the mean of 5, 5, 3, and 7, add the numbers and divide by ____. 4

2. The mean of 5, 5, 3, and 7 is ____. 5

3. If the mean of a set is 5 and there are 6 items in the set, what is the sum of the items? 30

4. The mean number of hours of sunlight the last 7 days was 9. What was the total number of hours of sunlight the last 7 days? 63 hr

B Find the mean.

5. 3, 8, 4, 9 6

6. 7, 5, 6, 10 7

7. 2.1, 2.1, 3.2, 8.9, 1.2 3.5

8. 3.2, 1.6, 2.8, 1.5, 4.4 2.7

9. 12, 15, 21, 35, 6, 17, 10, 9, 11, 15, 0, 12 13.6 or 14

10. 9, 13, 16, 24, 8, 11, 19, 10, 5, 3, 13, 20 12.6 or 13

11. *The costs of 6 gasoline purchases:* $9.70, $11.25, $12.60, $16.60, $10.50, $14.70 $12.558 or $12.56

12. *A basketball player's points per game for 7 games:* 15, 16, 25, 6, 18, 34, 21 19.3 or 19 points

13. *A football team's punt-return yardage for 6 returns:* 37, 19, 28, 17, 5, 12 19.7 or 20 yd

14. *The speeds (miles per hour) recorded by 5 drivers in a qualifying trial for a stock-car race:* 156, 183, 147, 159, 164 161.8 or 162 mph

Solve each problem.

15. For a 26-game season, a basketball team's mean score per game was 79 points. What was the total number of points scored?
2054 points

De Wys, Inc./Rocky Weldon

Courtesy U. S. Navy

16. For a 29-game season, a hockey team's mean goals per game was 4. What was the total number of goals scored? 116 goals

17. In 1846 a sailing ship sailed from Liverpool, England, to New York in 16 days. The mean nautical miles per day was 196.9. How many nautical miles was the trip? 3150.4 naut. mi

18. In 1960 a submarine made an 84-day voyage around the world. The mean number of nautical miles per day was 494. How many nautical miles was the voyage? 41,496 naut. mi

19. Andrea scored a total of 112 points on 16 ten-point quizzes. Felicia scored a total of 96 points on 12 ten-point quizzes. Whose mean quiz score was higher? Felicia's (8 to 7)

20. Juan bowled 6 games and scored a total of 858 points. Ivan bowled 7 games and scored a total of 994 points. Whose mean score was higher? Juan's (143 to 142)

C 21. After the first 6 games of the season, a soccer team's mean goals per game was 3. The team's record for the first 5 games was 2, 5, 0, 1, and 4. How many goals were scored in game 6? (*Hint:* Find the total goals for all 6 games and for the first 5 games.) 6 goals

Use a frequency table to find the mean.

Multiply each number by its frequency.

Example :	Number	Frequency	
	5	1	$5 \times 1 = 5$
	6	3	$6 \times 3 = 18$
	7	4	$7 \times 4 = 28$
	8	2	$8 \times 2 = 16$
	Total	10	67

Add the results.

$$\frac{67}{10} = 6.7$$

mean

Divide by the total frequency.

22. *20 numbers:* 15, 16, 13, 13, 12, 13, 14, 15, 16, 14, 12, 13, 12, 13, 14, 14, 15, 15, 10, 15 13.7 or 14

23. *50 numbers:* 6, 6, 5, 4, 3, 8, 8, 7, 6, 5, 4, 2, 2, 1, 1, 7, 8, 7, 6, 6, 5, 5, 5, 4, 5, 3, 1, 1, 1, 7, 6, 5, 1, 2, 3, 4, 5, 5, 4, 7, 4, 4, 5, 6, 6, 7, 5, 6, 4, 7 4.7 or 5

24. *The life (in months) of 15 storage batteries of a certain make:* 39, 37, 37, 37, 36, 36, 35, 37, 39, 40, 37, 36, 37, 36, 36 37 mo

25. *The strength (pounds per square inch) of 15 samples of a certain kind of wool fabric:* 132, 132, 135, 136, 135, 131, 129, 135, 132, 132, 131, 132, 133, 135, 135 133 lb per sq in.

Quick Quiz
Sections 15.1 to 15.4

Use the following set of numbers in Exercises 1–3.

6, 5, 1, 3, 1, 6, 8, 6

Find

1. the range 1–8

2. the mode 6

3. the median 5.5

4. Make a frequency table for the following set of numbers:

15, 10, 11, 12, 12, 13, 14, 13, 14, 15, 10, 12, 14, 14, 12, 13, 12, 10, 13, 14

No.	10	11	12	13	14	15	Total
Freq.	3	1	5	4	5	2	20

5. Make a graph for the numbers in Exercise 4.

5.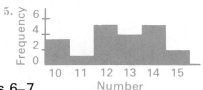

Use the following set of numbers in Exercises 6–7.

23, 38, 21, 20, 40, 36, 10, 21, 17, 31, 41, 21, 33, 44, 25

6. Find the mode. 21

7. Find the median. 25

8. Find the mean for 8, 12, 13, 10, 7. 10

CONSUMER CORNER

In the last few sections you found the range, the mode, the median, and the mean. These four values are called *descriptive statistics.* Each helps describe a set of data (numbers).

The range gives an idea of how spread out the set of data is. And it is called *a measure of variability.*

The mode, the median, and the mean give an idea of the size of the numbers in a set of data. And these three descriptive statistics are called *measures of central tendency.* All three are also sometimes called "averages."

When studying this	A useful "average" is this	Why?
Clothing sizes	Mode	This gives the most-frequently-used sizes and therefore gives a better picture of typical sizes to manufacturers and storekeepers.
Salaries or home values	Median	This middle value is not affected by a few extreme values (like salaries of millionaires) and therefore gives a better picture of typical salaries or home values.
Sports performances	Mean	This value takes into account total performance (extreme scores as well as most-frequent scores) and therefore is a good way to compare teams or individuals.

Talk it over: Which "average" (mode, median, or mean) would probably be best to use in each case?

1. A food packager wants to know the "average" size of a certain product that people will buy.   Mode

2. A racehorse trainer wants to know the "average" time that a certain horse takes to run $1\frac{1}{8}$ miles.   Mean or median

3. A house builder wants to know the "average" income of families in a certain community.   Median

4. A student wants to know the "average" score on a test.   Mean or median

5. A farmer wants to know the "average" yield per acre of a new corn plant.
Mean

If you roll a die (singular of *dice*), there are six possible outcomes—
1, 2, 3, 4, 5, or 6 dots on the top face. If you toss a coin, there are two
possible outcomes—heads or tails. What are the chances of heads on
the toss of a coin? One way to find out is to toss a coin many times,
say 100, and record the results.

Suggested Class Time

Course	Min.	Reg.	Max.
Days	0	1	1

COIN-TOSSING EXPERIMENT

Outcome	Tally	Number of times
heads	⊤⊤⊦ ⊤⊤⊦ ⊤⊤⊦ ⊤⊤⊦ ⊤⊤⊦ ⊤⊤⊦ ⊤⊤⊦ ⊤⊤⊦ ⊤⊤⊦ ⊤⊤⊦ ⊤⊤⊦ II	47
tails	⊤⊤⊦ ⊤⊤⊦ ⊤⊤⊦ ⊤⊤⊦ ⊤⊤⊦ ⊤⊤⊦ ⊤⊤⊦ ⊤⊤⊦ ⊤⊤⊦ ⊤⊤⊦ ⊤⊤⊦ III	53
	Total	100

The table above shows that the outcome was heads 47 times out
of 100 trials (tosses). So the **experimental probability** of the outcome
being heads is $\frac{47}{100}$ or 0.47. A shorter way of writing this is

$$\text{ex pr (heads)} = \tfrac{47}{100} = 0.47.$$
$$\text{Similarly, ex pr (tails)} = \tfrac{53}{100} = 0.53.$$

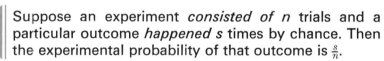

> Suppose an experiment *consisted of n* trials and a
> particular outcome *happened s* times by chance. Then
> the experimental probability of that outcome is $\frac{s}{n}$.

Sometimes a **theoretical probability,** pr, can be found without doing
an experiment.

> Suppose a trial in an experiment *can happen n* equally
> likely ways. If *s* of these ways *would result* in a particular
> outcome, then the **theoretical probability** of that
> outcome is $\frac{s}{n}$.

For the coin experiment, there are 2 ways the coin can land. So the
number of ways a trial (toss) *can happen* is 2. (Assume the coin is
fair and both ways of landing are equally likely.) The number of ways
a trial *would result* in the outcome "heads" is 1. So,

$$\text{pr (heads)} = \tfrac{1}{2} = 0.5.$$
$$\text{Similarly, pr (tails)} = \tfrac{1}{2} = 0.5.$$

There are 10 marbles—7 orange and 3 black— of the same size in a paper bag. They are thoroughly mixed. An experiment was done to find the experimental probability of picking an orange marble from the bag by chance (without looking, and placing the picked marble back into the bag after each trial). The results are below.

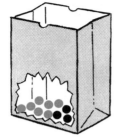

MARBLE EXPERIMENT

Outcome	Number of times
picking an orange marble	53
picking a black marble	27
Total	80

Example 1: Using the table above, find the following *experimental probabilities* for the marble experiment: ex pr (orange) and ex pr (black).

$$\text{ex pr (orange)} = \tfrac{53}{80} \approx 0.66$$
$$\text{ex pr (black)} = \tfrac{27}{80} \approx 0.34$$

Example 2: Find the following *theoretical probabilities* for the marble experiment: pr (orange) and pr (black).

There are 10 equally likely ways a trial *can happen* (because there are 10 marbles in the bag).

There are 7 orange marbles, so the number of ways a trial could result in the outcome "picking an orange marble" is 7.

Therefore, pr (orange) = $\tfrac{7}{10}$ = 0.7.

Similarly, because there are only 3 black marbles,

$$\text{pr (black)} = \tfrac{3}{10} = 0.3.$$

Notice that the experimental probabilities in Example 1 are close to the theoretical probabilities in Example 2. It has been proved that experimental probabilities get very close to theoretical probabilities when the number of trials is very large.

For both experimental and theoretical probabilities,

> Probabilities are never less than 0 or greater than 1.
> An impossible outcome has probability 0.
> An outcome that is sure to happen has probability 1.

Exercises

Assignment Guide 15.5
Oral: Reg. & Max. 1–8
Written: Reg. .9–30
Max. 9–35

A **1.** A(n) (*experimental*, *theoretical*) probability is found without doing an experiment.

There are 10 marbles—5 red, 3 black, and 2 white—all the same size in a bag. One marble is picked from the bag as in Example 1.

2. Name all possible outcomes.
Red, black, white

3. Find pr (red). $\frac{1}{2}$ or 0.5

4. Find pr (black). $\frac{3}{10}$ or 0.3

5. Find pr (white). $\frac{1}{5}$ or 0.2

6. In 100 trials a red marble is picked from the bag 53 times. Find ex pr (red). $\frac{53}{100}$ or 0.53

7. What is the probability of picking a blue marble from the bag? 0

8. Find pr (red) if all the marbles in the bag were red. 1

B The table at the right shows the results of rolling a fair die 100 times. Find **(a)** the experimental and **(b)** the theoretical probabilities for the following outcomes. Express each probability as a fraction reduced to lowest terms.

DIE-ROLLING EXPERIMENT

Outcome	Number of times
1 dot	17
2 dots	14
3 dots	15
4 dots	20
5 dots	16
6 dots	18
Total	100

a. b.

9. 1 dot $\frac{17}{100}$ $\frac{1}{6}$ **10.** 2 dots $\frac{7}{50}$ $\frac{1}{6}$

11. 3 dots $\frac{3}{20}$ $\frac{1}{6}$ **12.** 4 dots $\frac{1}{5}$ $\frac{1}{6}$

13. 5 dots $\frac{4}{25}$ $\frac{1}{6}$ **14.** 6 dots $\frac{9}{50}$ $\frac{1}{6}$

15. 7 dots 0 0 **16.** less than 7 dots

16. 1 1

A spinner like the one at the right has 8 regions—3 orange, 2 white, 2 brown, and 1 black—all the same size. The table at the right shows the results of 80 spins. (The pointer can't stop between regions.) Find **(a)** the experimental and **(b)** the theoretical probabilities for the following outcomes. Express each probability as a decimal.

SPINNER EXPERIMENT

Outcome	Number of times
orange	32
white	16
brown	20
black	12
Total	80

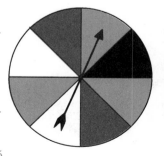

a. b.

17. orange 0.4 0.375 **18.** white 0.2 0.25 **19.** brown 0.25 0.25

20. black 0.15 0.125 **21.** yellow 0 0 **22.** green 0 0

497

A regular deck of 52 playing cards is shown below. There are 13 cards in each of four suits—hearts, diamonds, clubs, and spades. For the experiment of drawing one card from a full, thoroughly shuffled deck, find each theoretical probability as a fraction.

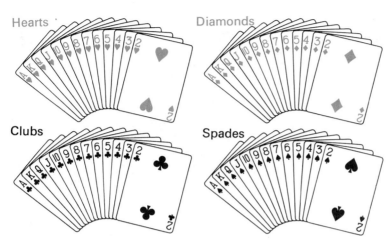

Hearts
Diamonds
Clubs
Spades

23. pr (the 10 of diamonds) $\frac{1}{52}$

24. pr (the 6 of spades) $\frac{1}{52}$

25. pr (a card in clubs) $\frac{1}{4}$

26. pr (a card in hearts) $\frac{1}{4}$

27. pr (a jack) $\frac{1}{13}$

28. pr (a king) $\frac{1}{13}$

29. pr (a black ace) $\frac{1}{26}$

30. pr (a black queen) $\frac{1}{26}$

C To **predict** how many times a particular outcome will happen, you *multiply* the number of trials by the probability of that outcome happening.

31. If you roll a die 240 times, how many times would you expect the outcome to be 4 dots? 40 times

32. If the experiment of drawing one card from a thoroughly shuffled deck is done 260 times, how many times would you expect to draw a card in diamonds? 65 times

33. The probability of recovering from a disease is 75% with treatment and 50% without treatment. If 12,000 people get the disease, how many more would you expect to recover if all had treatment than if none had treatment? 3000 people

34. One baseball player's batting average is .250 (the probability of a hit is .250), and another player's average is .200. How many more hits would you expect the better batter to get if each had 540 official times at bat? 27 hits

35. A supermarket is giving away tickets for cash prizes. There are 100 equal prizes, and the probability of winning a prize with one ticket is $\frac{1}{250,000}$. How many tickets will be given away? (*Hint:* Solve $\frac{1}{250,000} = \frac{100}{t}$.) 25,000,000 tickets

Tree Diagrams and Probability

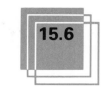

15.6

You are a member of a group that is hosting a meeting. You must be on the setup committee or the cleanup committee and serve as a greeter, a guide, or a food server. Your committee and job are determined by two drawings.

Example 1: To see the different possibilities of duties, you could make a *tree diagram*.

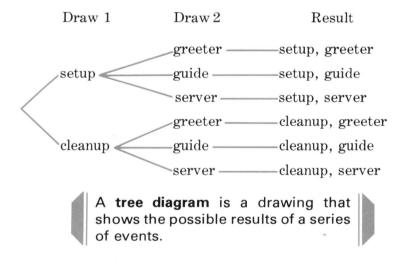

> A **tree diagram** is a drawing that shows the possible results of a series of events.

Example 2: The tree diagram can be used to determine the probability of your being on the cleanup committee and a greeter.

There are 6 possibilities. In only 1 of the possibilities are you on the cleanup committee and a greeter.

$$\frac{\text{desired outcome}}{\text{possibilities}} \rightarrow \frac{1}{6}$$
The probability of being on the cleanup committee and a greeter is $\frac{1}{6}$.

pr (cleanup, greeter) $= \frac{1}{6}$

499

Example 3: Another way to find how many different ways you could work at the meeting is to use multiplication.

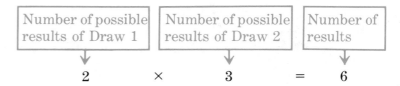

Assignment Guide 15.6
Oral: Reg. and Max. 1–3
Written: Reg. 4–9
  Max. 5–9 odd;
    10–12

▧ Exercises

Ⓐ **1.** What are the possible outcomes if you flip a coin? heads, tails

2. What are the possible outcomes if you roll a die? 1, 2, 3, 4, 5, 6

3. How many possible results are there if you flip a coin and roll a die? 12

Ⓑ **4.** Make a tree diagram that shows all the possible results of flipping a coin and rolling a die.

5. Make a tree diagram that shows all possible results of flipping two coins.

Use the tree diagrams in Exercises 4 and 5 to find each probability.

6. pr (6, heads) $\frac{1}{12}$ **7.** pr (both heads) $\frac{1}{4}$

8. pr (odd number, tails) $\frac{3}{12}$ or $\frac{1}{4}$ **9.** pr (one head, one tail) $\frac{2}{4}$ or $\frac{1}{2}$

Ⓒ **10.** If two dice are rolled, what is the probability that their sum is 7? $\frac{6}{36}$ or $\frac{1}{6}$

11. How many license plates that show 2 letters followed by 3 digits can be made? 676,000 license plates

12. The sports store has 3-speed, 5-speed, and 10-speed bicycles. They come in silver, blue, and black. The handlebars come in standard and racing styles. Make a tree diagram that shows all the possible bicycles.

4. Coin Die Results
```
          1 — heads, 1
          2 — heads, 2
         /3 — heads, 3
heads ⟨  4 — heads, 4
         \5 — heads, 5
          6 — heads, 6

          1 — tails, 1
          2 — tails, 2
         /3 — tails, 3
tails ⟨  4 — tails, 4
         \5 — tails, 5
          6 — tails, 6
```

5. 1st Coin 2nd Coin Results
```
          heads — heads,
heads ⟨           heads
          tails — heads,
                  tails

          heads — tails,
tails ⟨           heads
          tails — tails,
                  tails
```

500

12. Handle- Speed Color Results
bars

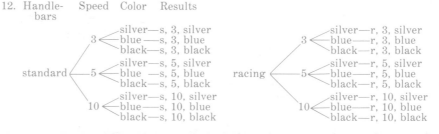

Adding Probabilities

15.7

A bag contains 10 marbles—5 red, 3 white, and 2 blue. You pick one marble from the bag. What is the theoretical probability of picking *"either* a red marble *or* a blue marble"?

Since only one marble is picked at a time, both outcomes—(*1*) picking a red marble and (*2*) picking a blue marble—can't happen on the same trial. They are called **mutually exclusive events.** So we can reason as follows to find pr (red *or* blue):

> There are 5 ways to pick a red marble and 2 ways to pick a blue marble. So there are $5 + 2$, or 7, ways to pick *either* a red *or* a blue marble. There are 10 ways a trial can happen, so pr (red *or* blue) $= \frac{7}{10}$. Notice that

$$\text{pr (red } or \text{ blue)} = \text{pr (red)} + \text{pr (blue)}$$
$$= \tfrac{5}{10} + \tfrac{2}{10}$$
$$= \tfrac{7}{10}$$

> If *A* and *B* are *mutually exclusive events,* then the theoretical probability of outcome *"A or B"* can be found by adding pr (*A*) and pr (*B*).
>
> pr (*A or B*) = pr (*A*) + pr (*B*)

Example : Find the theoretical probability of picking *either* a red *or* a white marble in the experiment above.

$$\text{pr (red } or \text{ white)} = \text{pr (red)} + \text{pr (white)}$$
$$= \tfrac{5}{10} + \tfrac{3}{10}$$
$$= \tfrac{8}{10} \text{ or } \tfrac{4}{5}$$

Assignment Guide 15.6
Oral: Reg. & Max. 1–8
Written: Reg. 9–37 odd
  Max. 9–41 odd

Exercises

A **1.** If two outcomes are mutually exclusive events, then they (*can,* *cannot*) happen at the same time.

2. If *A* and *B* are mutually exclusive events, then pr (*A or B*) = _____.

pr (*A*) + pr (*B*)

3. A and B are mutually exclusive events and pr $(A) = \frac{1}{5}$ and pr (B) $= \frac{3}{5}$, so pr $(A \ or \ B) = $ _____. $\frac{4}{5}$

4. If a coin is tossed once, then pr (heads or tails) $= $ _____. 1

A die is tossed once. Are the following mutually exclusive events?

5. A: throwing a 6; B: throwing a 3 Yes

6. A: throwing a 6; B: throwing an odd number Yes

7. A: throwing a 6; B: throwing an even number No

8. A: throwing an even number; B: throwing an odd number Yes

B A and B are mutually exclusive events. Find pr $(A \ or \ B)$ if

9. pr $(A) = \frac{1}{3}$, pr $(B) = \frac{1}{3}$ $\frac{2}{3}$ **10.** pr $(A) = \frac{1}{5}$, pr $(B) = \frac{2}{5}$ $\frac{3}{5}$

11. pr $(A) = \frac{1}{2}$, pr $(B) = \frac{1}{5}$ $\frac{7}{10}$ **12.** pr $(A) = \frac{2}{3}$, pr $(B) = \frac{1}{4}$ $\frac{11}{12}$

13. pr $(A) = 0.6$, pr $(B) = 0.2$ 0.8 **14.** pr $(A) = 0.3$, pr $(B) = 0.25$ 0.55

There are 12 marbles in a bag—6 red, 3 white, 2 blue, and 1 black. The marbles are thoroughly mixed, and one is picked from the bag. Find the following as fractions.

15. pr (red) $\frac{1}{2}$ **16.** pr (white) $\frac{1}{4}$

17. pr (blue) $\frac{1}{6}$ **18.** pr (black) $\frac{1}{12}$

19. pr (red or blue) $\frac{2}{3}$ **20.** pr (white or black) $\frac{1}{3}$

21. pr (red or white) $\frac{3}{4}$ **22.** pr (white or blue) $\frac{5}{12}$

23. pr (blue or black) $\frac{1}{4}$ **24.** pr (red or black) $\frac{7}{12}$

The integers from 1 to 10 are written on identical pieces of paper that are put into a bowl. They are thoroughly mixed, and one paper is picked from the bowl. Find the following as decimals.

25. pr (a multiple of 3) 0.3 **26.** pr (a multiple of 4) 0.2

27. pr (a multiple of 5) 0.2 **28.** pr (a prime number) 0.4

29. pr (a multiple of 3 *or* a multiple of 5) 0.5

30. pr (a multiple of 4 *or* a prime number) 0.6

31. pr (a multiple of 3 *or* a multiple of 4) 0.5

32. pr (a multiple of 4 *or* a multiple of 5) 0.4

One card is drawn from a thoroughly shuffled deck of 52 playing cards. (See page 498.) Find the following as fractions.

33. pr (a diamond *or* a club) $\frac{1}{2}$

34. pr (a heart *or* a spade) $\frac{1}{2}$

35. pr (a black 3 *or* a face card) $\frac{7}{26}$

36. pr (a black jack *or* a 7) $\frac{3}{26}$

37. pr (an ace *or* a face card) $\frac{4}{13}$

38. pr (a heart *or* a black 5) $\frac{15}{52}$

C To find the probability of an outcome **not** happening, you *subtract* from 1 the probability of that outcome happening.

Example: The probability of rain today is 0.7. What is the probability of no rain today?

$1 - 0.7 = 0.3$. So the probability of no rain today is 0.3.

39. In a particular city, the probability of being involved in an auto accident in a year is 0.2. What is the probability of not being involved in an auto accident in a year? 0.8

40. The probability of Rosemary hitting the bull's-eye of the archery target is 0.48. What is the probability of her not hitting the bull's-eye? 0.52

41. A person who enters a particular contest can win either a first, a second, or a third prize. (They are mutually exclusive events.) The probabilities of winning each prize are as follows: pr (first) = 0.001, pr (second) = 0.005, and pr (third) = 0.02. What is the probability of not winning a prize? 0.974

503

Multiplying Probabilities

Suggested Class Time

Course	Min.	Reg.	Max.
Days	0	1	1

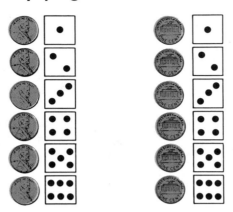

If you toss a coin *and* roll a die, there are 12 possible outcomes. There are two ways the coin can land and six ways the die can land. Notice that

$$2 \times 6 = 12$$

Tossing heads on a coin and rolling 2 dots on a die are called **independent events** because one outcome does not depend on the other outcome. Each can happen independently of the other.

Example 1: What is the theoretical probability of getting heads on the coin *and* 4 dots on the die in the experiment above?

By looking at the outcomes shown above, you can see that 1 of the 12 outcomes is heads *and* 4. So

$$\text{pr (heads } and \text{ 4)} = \tfrac{1}{12}$$

Notice that

$$\text{pr (heads } and \text{ 4)} = \text{pr (heads)} \times \text{pr (4)}$$
$$= \tfrac{1}{2} \times \tfrac{1}{6}$$
$$= \tfrac{1}{12}$$

> If *A* and *B* are *independent events,* then the theoretical probability of the outcome "*A and B*" can be found by multiplying pr (*A*) and pr (*B*).
>
> $$\text{pr } (A \ and \ B) = \text{pr } (A) \times \text{pr } (B)$$

Example 2: What is the theoretical probability of getting heads on the coin *and* a prime number of dots on the die in the experiment above?

$$\text{pr (heads } and \text{ a prime)} = \text{pr (heads)} \times \text{pr (a prime)}$$
$$= \tfrac{1}{2} \times \tfrac{3}{6}$$
$$= \tfrac{3}{12} \text{ or } \tfrac{1}{4}$$

There are 3 primes—2, 3, and 5.

■ Exercises

A **1.** If two outcomes are independent events, then one outcome (*does,* *does not*) depend on the other outcome.

2. If A and B are independent events, then you (*add, multiply*) pr (A) and pr (B) to find pr $(A \text{ and } B)$.

A coin is tossed *and* a die is rolled.

3. How many possible outcomes are there? 12

4. What is the theoretical probability of getting heads on the coin *and* 5 dots on the die? $\frac{1}{12}$

5. What is the theoretical probability of getting tails on the coin *and* 1 dot on the die? $\frac{1}{12}$

A penny is tossed *and* a nickel is tossed.

6. What is the theoretical probability of getting heads on the penny? $\frac{1}{2}$

7. What is the theoretical probability of getting heads on the nickel? $\frac{1}{2}$

8. What is the theoretical probability of getting heads on the penny *and* heads on the nickel? $\frac{1}{4}$

B *A* and *B* are independent events. Find pr (*A and B*) if

9. pr $(A) = \frac{1}{3}$, pr $(B) = \frac{1}{3}$ $\frac{1}{9}$

10. pr $(A) = \frac{1}{5}$, pr $(B) = \frac{2}{5}$ $\frac{2}{25}$

11. pr $(A) = \frac{1}{2}$, pr $(B) = \frac{1}{4}$ $\frac{1}{8}$

12. pr $(A) = \frac{3}{8}$, pr $(B) = \frac{1}{4}$ $\frac{3}{32}$

13. pr $(A) = 0.8$, pr $(B) = 0.58$ 0.464

14. pr $(A) = 0.3$, pr $(B) = 0.83$ 0.249

A spinner has 6 regions of equal size—3 red, 2 white, and 1 blue. (The pointer can't stop between regions.) The spinner is spun once *and* a die is rolled. Find the following as fractions.

15. pr (red *and* 3) $\frac{1}{12}$

16. pr (white *and* 4) $\frac{1}{18}$

17. pr (white *and* an odd number) $\frac{1}{6}$

18. pr (blue *and* an even number) $\frac{1}{12}$

19. pr (blue *and* a prime number) $\frac{1}{12}$

20. pr (red *and* a multiple of 3) $\frac{1}{6}$

A red die and a white die are rolled. Find the following as fractions.

21. pr (red 4 *and* white 1) $\frac{1}{36}$ 　　　　**22.** pr (red 3 *and* white 6) $\frac{1}{36}$

23. pr (red 2 *and* white even number) $\frac{1}{12}$

24. pr (red 5 *and* white odd number) $\frac{1}{12}$

25. pr (red odd number *and* white even number) $\frac{1}{4}$

26. pr (red even number *and* white even number) $\frac{1}{4}$

27. pr (red prime number *and* white multiple of 2) $\frac{1}{4}$

28. pr (red multiple of 2 *and* white multiple of 3) $\frac{1}{6}$

C **29.** Suppose your probability of winning a car in contest A is $\frac{1}{100,000}$ and your probability of winning a TV set in contest B is $\frac{1}{50,000}$. (They are independent events.) What is your probability of winning the car *and* the TV set? $\frac{1}{5,000,000,000}$

30. A basketball player who was fouled in the act of shooting is awarded two free throws. The player's free-throw average is 62% (the probability of making a free throw is 0.62). Find the probability (as a decimal) that the player will make *both* free throws. (They are independent events.) 0.3844

31. In Monopoly, two dice are rolled for each turn. The probability of rolling "doubles" is $\frac{1}{6}$. If doubles are rolled three times in a row, the player goes to "jail." What is the probability (as a fraction) of rolling doubles three times in a row? (They are independent events.)

$\frac{1}{216}$

MATH IN PARAPROFESSIONS

You know that *paramedics* are specially trained helpers who work under a doctor's orders. There are other *paraprofessionals* too. These trained helpers work with some professional like an engineer, a lawyer, or a teacher. Here are just a few:

Agricultural Technician	Ecology Technician
Automotive Technician	Forestry Technician
Chemical Technician	Safety Technician
Child Health Associate	Social Work Aide
Community Aide	Teacher Aide
Dental Assistant	Urban Planning Technician

Most paraprofessions are very new. Some are just getting started. Others are jobs of the future. Probably the best way to become a paraprofessional is to finish high school and then take a special two-year course in a community college.

Some paraprofessions need no more math than you will get in this course. Others need more math in high school or in a community college. Here are some statistics and probability problems from the paraprofessions:

Courtesy E. P. A.

1. Forestry Technician: During the past 75 years a certain tree fungus that occurs in wet, hot summers appeared during 10 summers. A certain shrub blight that occurs in dry, cool summers appeared during 15 summers. What is the probability that either one or the other disease will appear during the next summer? $\frac{1}{3}$

2. Chemical Technician: A certain chemical solution is used to control the growth of bacteria. During 30 tests the solution reduced the number of bacteria by the following per cents: 78, 79, 75, 80, 69, 73, 68, 73, 80, 65, 68, 68, 72, 71, 73, 73, 75, 76, 79, 76, 69, 69, 80, 67, 67, 65, 65, 66, 73, 76. Find the range of the solution's effectiveness. 65–80%

3. Urban Planning Technician: The number of people per day that were in a park during the month of July are as follows: 135, 115, 145, 306, 215, 279, 25, 31, 95, 126, 161, 52, 226, 31, 16, 58, 152, 101, 175, 229, 176, 112, 92, 85, 20, 23, 37, 85, 139, 117, 99. Find the median and the mean.

Median: 112 people; mean: 118 people

Terms and Symbols Review

Suggested Class Time

Course	Min.	Reg.	Max.
Days	0	1	1

1. The _____ gives the low and the high numbers of a set of numbers.
   Range

2. The _____ is the most frequent number in a set of numbers. Mode

3. The _____ is the number in the middle when the numbers in a set are listed in order. Median

4. To find the _____ of 3, 4, 4, 5, add the numbers and divide by 4.
   Mean

Assignment Guide Rev.
Oral:
Reg. Terms & Symbols 1–6
Max. Terms & Symbols 1–6
Written: Reg. 1–29 odd
       Max. 1–29 odd

5. Tossing heads and tossing tails are possible _____ for the experiment of tossing a coin. Outcomes

6. A(n) _____ probability is found by doing an experiment. Experimental

Chapter 15 Review

15.1   Find the range.

1. 1, 5, 7, 8, 2, 10, 6   1–10   2. 125, 113, 104, 113, 184
                                              104–184

Make a frequency table.

3. *25 numbers:* 8, 9, 9, 9, 10, 7, 6, 6, 6, 8, 10, 8, 9, 9, 6, 7, 6, 8, 9, 8, 10, 8, 10, 9, 9

No.	6	7	8	9	10	Total
Freq.	5	2	6	8	4	25

4. *Number of students in 30 classrooms:* 26, 26, 26, 27, 27, 27, 25, 28, 26, 26, 26, 26, 28, 28, 29, 29, 25, 27, 27, 26, 29, 28, 26, 25, 27, 27, 26, 28, 26, 27

No. students	25	26	27	28	29	Total
Freq.	3	11	8	5	3	30

15.2   Use the graph at the right for Exercises 5–7.

5. What is the mode? 9

6. How many students received a score of 7? 4

7. How many students received a score of over 7? 13

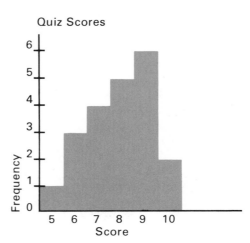

Quiz Scores

508

Find the median. 15.3

8. 6, 9, 11, 15, 21 11 **9.** 5, 12, 16, 24 14

Find the mean. 15.4

10. 12, 15, 16, 13, 10, 5 11.8 or 12 **11.** 1.8, 4.6, 3.9, 8.5, 1.7 4.1

12. For an 18-game season, a soccer team's mean goals per game was 3. Find the total number of goals scored during the season. 54 goals

A spinner has 6 regions—3 red, 2 blue, and 1 green—all the same size. (The pointer can't stop between regions.) Find the following as fractions. 15.5

18. Dime   Quarter   Results

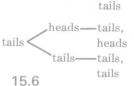

13. pr (red) $\frac{1}{2}$ **14.** pr (blue) $\frac{1}{3}$ **15.** pr (white) 0

16. If *all* the regions of the spinner above were red, find pr (red). 1

17. The pointer was spun 100 times and stopped on a blue region 35 times. Find ex pr (blue) as a decimal. 0.35

18. Draw a tree diagram to show the possible results of flipping a dime and then flipping a quarter. What is the probability that both coins will land showing heads? 15.6

19. If *A* and *B* are mutually exclusive events, you (*add*, *multiply*) pr (*A*) and pr (*B*) to find pr (*A or B*). 15.7

A and *B* are mutually exclusive events. Find pr (*A or B*) if

20. pr (*A*) = $\frac{1}{5}$, pr (*B*) = $\frac{3}{5}$ $\frac{4}{5}$ **21.** pr (*A*) = $\frac{1}{2}$, pr (*B*) = $\frac{1}{4}$ $\frac{3}{4}$

22. For the spinner described above, find pr (red *or* blue) as a fraction. $\frac{5}{6}$

23. If *A* and *B* are independent events, you (*add*, *multiply*) pr (*A*) and pr (*B*) to find pr (*A and B*). 15.8

A and *B* are independent events. Find pr (*A and B*) if

24. pr (*A*) = $\frac{1}{2}$, pr (*B*) = $\frac{1}{3}$ $\frac{1}{6}$ **25.** pr (*A*) = $\frac{2}{3}$, pr (*B*) = $\frac{3}{5}$ $\frac{2}{5}$

The spinner for Exercises 15–17 is spun once, and a die is rolled once. Find the following as fractions.

26. pr (green *and* 5) $\frac{1}{36}$ **27.** pr (blue *and* an odd number) $\frac{1}{6}$

28. pr (red *and* a multiple of 3) $\frac{1}{6}$

Chapter 15 Test

Assignment Guide Test
Written: Reg. 1–17
         Max. 1–17

Use the following set of numbers in Exercises 1–3.

12, 15, 16, 11, 15, 14, 12, 12

Find

1. the range 11–16   **2.** the mode 12   **3.** the median 13

4. Make a frequency table for the following set of numbers: 17, 16, 18, 15, 18, 18, 18, 15, 15, 17, 18, 19, 17, 18, 15, 21, 15, 19, 16, 20.

No.	15	16	17	18	19	20	21	Total
Freq.	5	2	3	6	2	1	1	20

5. Make a graph for the numbers in Exercise 4.

5.
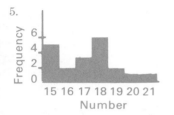

Use the following set of numbers in Exercises 6–7.

40, 23, 34, 10, 28, 11, 12, 31, 25, 29, 11, 34, 23, 47, 34

6. Find the mode. 34   **7.** Find the median. 28

8. Find the mean for 8, 12, 10, 7, 3. 8

9. For a 25-game season, a basketball player's mean points per game was 12. What was the total number of points scored by the player?

300 points

There are 10 marbles in a bag—6 white, 3 red, and 1 blue—all the same size. The marbles are thoroughly mixed and one is picked by chance. Find the following as decimals.

10. pr (white) 0.6   **11.** pr (red) 0.3   **12.** pr (blue) 0.1

13. pr (white *or* red) 0.9   **14.** pr (red *or* blue) 0.4

One marble is picked from the bag in the experiment above, and a die is rolled. Find the following as fractions.

15. pr (white *and* 1) $\frac{1}{10}$ **16.** pr (red *and* an odd number) $\frac{3}{20}$

17. Suppose the bag above contains only three marbles—red, blue, and white. A coin is tossed and a marble is picked. Draw a tree diagram to show the possible results.

17. Marble Coin Results

red
  heads—red, heads
  tails—red, tails

blue
  heads—blue, heads
  tails—blue, tails

white
  heads—white, heads
  tails—white, tails

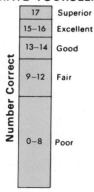

Activity 1: Do each experiment below. Record the results of each experiment in a table like the one on page 495. Then find the experimental probability for each possible outcome.

a. Toss a coin 50 times.

b. Roll a die 60 times.

c. If a cork is tossed, it can land in one of the following ways:

large end up   small end up   on its side

Put five corks in a paper cup and shake the cup. Then turn the cup over quickly, spilling the corks onto your desk. Count the number of corks landing each way. (This is the same as doing five trials with one cork.) Do this 40 times for a total of 200 trials.

Activity 2: Make a top, following the steps below.

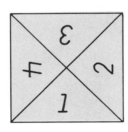
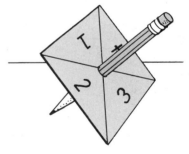

1. Cut a 3- by 3-inch square out of a piece of thin cardboard.

2. Draw a line between each pair of opposite corners. Number the 4 regions.

3. Make a small hole where the lines cross and push a short pencil through it.

To spin the top, hold the pencil straight up and down, and place the sharpened end on your desk top. The piece of cardboard should be "level" with your desk top. Then give the pencil a turn and let go. When the top stops, a side of one of the regions will be resting on the desk top (as shown in step 3 above). The number in that region is the outcome of the spin.

a. Spin the top 60 times, recording the outcomes as in Activity 1. Then find the experimental probability for each of the 4 possible outcomes.

b. Cut a 3- by 4-inch rectangle out of a piece of thin cardboard. Then follow steps 2 and 3 above to make a second top. Repeat part **a,** using the second top.

Terms and Symbols Review: Chapters 8–15

Which term or symbol in parentheses is the best choice?

Ch. 8

1. The x-axis is (*horizontal*, *vertical*, *a point*).

2. The negative direction on the y-axis is (*down*, *up*, *left*).

Ch. 9

3. The equation $\frac{5}{2} = \frac{10}{4}$ is a (*ratio*, *proportion*, *per cent*).

4. For $\frac{2}{3} = \frac{6}{9}$, 2 and 9 are the (*means*, *extremes*, *cross products*).

Ch. 10

5. In similar triangles, corresponding sides are always (*equal in length*, *proportional*, *overlapping*).

6. In similar triangles, corresponding angles have the same (*measure*, *name*, *sides*).

Ch. 11

7. The opposite of $\frac{3}{4}$ is ($\frac{4}{3}$, $-\frac{3}{4}$, $3 \div 4$).

8. Another way to name $^-3 \div {}^-4$ is ($\frac{3}{4}$, $\frac{4}{3}$, $-\frac{3}{4}$).

9. The sum of $-\frac{3}{4}$ and $-\frac{3}{4}$ is (*positive*, *negative*, *zero*).

Ch. 12

10. $^-1\frac{1}{2}$ is the (*reciprocal*, *opposite*, *product*) of $-\frac{2}{3}$.

11. 10^{-2} has a value of ($^-0.02$, *100*, *0.01*).

12. 1.34×10^2 is scientific notation for (*13.4*, *134*, *1340*).

Ch. 13

13. In a right triangle, the side opposite the right angle is the (*hypotenuse*, *square root*, *shortest side*).

14. The nonnegative square root of 9 is ($\sqrt{9}$, $^-\sqrt{9}$, 9^2).

15. Every positive number has (*0*, *1*, *2*) square root(s).

Ch. 14

16. A binomial has (*1*, *2*, *3*) term(s).

17. $2x^2$ and $^-3x^2$ are (*like*, *unlike*, *binomial*) terms.

Ch. 15

18. For 8, 5, 6, 7, 5, the (*range*, *mode*, *median*) is 6.

19. A(n) (*trial*, *experimental*, *theoretical*) probability is found without doing an experiment.

Assignment Guide Rev.
Oral:
Min. Terms & Symbols 1–10;
    13–15
Reg. Terms & Symbols 1–19
Max. Terms & Symbols 1–19

1. Use the rule to complete the table below.

$$y = 3x - 1$$

x	1	2	3	4	5
y	2	5	8	11	14

2. Draw a line graph for the table below.

x	0	1	2	3	4
y	-2	0	2	4	6

Ch. 8

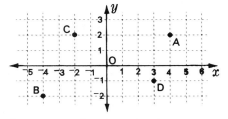

Write the ordered pair for each point on the graph at the right.

3. A (4, 2)   **4.** B (⁻4, ⁻2)

5. C (⁻2, 2)   **6.** D (3, ⁻1)

7. Is the graph for Exercises 3–6 the graph of a function? Yes

8. Is the set of ordered pairs in Exercise 2 a function? Yes

Copy and graph the following.

9. a slide 3 units up

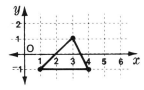

10. a 1-to-2 reduction

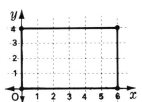

Assignment Guide Rev.

Written:

Min. (day 1) 1–8; 11–26
(day 2) 27–56
(day 3) 57–59; 63;
66–81

Reg. (day 1) 1–8; 11–63 odd
(day 2) 64–91; 94–104

Max. (day 1) 1–10; 11–63 odd
(day 2) 64–104

Copy and complete.

Ch. 9

	per cent	fraction	decimal
11.	40%	$\frac{2}{5}$	0.4
13.	48%	$\frac{12}{25}$	0.48

	per cent	fraction or mixed number	decimal
12.	72%	$\frac{18}{25}$	0.72
14.	130%	$1\frac{3}{10}$	1.3

Solve.

15. $\frac{7}{5} = \frac{n}{35}$ 49   **16.** $\frac{9}{2} = \frac{27}{x}$ 6   **17.** $\frac{6}{a} = \frac{18}{39}$ 13

18. What is 26% of 75?   19.5   **19.** 17 is what per cent of 50?
34%

20. 40% of what number is 10?   25   **21.** 15% of 22 is what number?
3.3

22. A basketball player attempted 15 free throws and made 6 of them. What per cent of attempted free throws did the player make?   40%

23. Name the corresponding sides and the corresponding angles for these similar triangles.

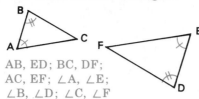

AB, ED; BC, DF;
AC, EF; ∠A, ∠E;
∠B, ∠D; ∠C, ∠F

24. Which letter should replace each question mark?
a. $\frac{a}{e} = \frac{c}{?}$ f **b.** $\frac{c}{f} = \frac{?}{d}$ b

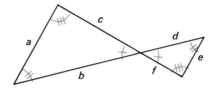

25. What is the actual distance between X and Y? Between Y and Z? Between X and Z?

50 ft; 30 ft; 40 ft

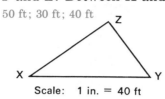

Scale: 1 in. = 40 ft

26. What is the height of the sign? (The triangles are similar.) $7\frac{1}{2}$ ft

Find each sum or difference.

27. $^{-}5.71 + 3.83$ $^{-}1.88$ **28.** $^{-}1.46 + ^{-}3.57$ $^{-}5.03$ **29.** $^{-}3.47 - 8.16$ $^{-}11.63$

30. $2.86 - ^{-}5.14$ 8 **31.** $-\frac{1}{4} + (-\frac{3}{8})$ $-\frac{5}{8}$ **32.** $\frac{3}{5} + (-\frac{1}{10})$ $\frac{1}{2}$

33. $\frac{1}{6} - (-\frac{2}{3})$ $\frac{5}{6}$ **34.** $-\frac{7}{10} - \frac{1}{4}$ $-\frac{19}{20}$ **35.** $^{-}3\frac{1}{4} + ^{-}4\frac{3}{4}$ $^{-}8$

36. $^{-}2\frac{1}{3} + 1\frac{2}{3}$ $-\frac{2}{3}$ **37.** $(-\frac{7}{16}) + 2\frac{5}{8}$ $2\frac{3}{16}$ **38.** $^{-}3\frac{3}{4} - 2\frac{1}{2}$ $^{-}6\frac{1}{4}$

Solve.

39. $z - 5.7 = 7.2$ 12.9 **40.** $y + ^{-}3.6 = 1.2$ 4.8

41. $c - 8.7 = ^{-}11.4$ $^{-}2.7$ **42.** $\frac{7}{10} + a = -\frac{4}{5}$ $^{-}1\frac{1}{2}$

43. $y - (-\frac{2}{3}) = -\frac{1}{6}$ $-\frac{5}{6}$ **44.** $\frac{5}{12} = x - \frac{1}{2}$ $\frac{11}{12}$

45. $n + \frac{1}{4} = -\frac{3}{4}$ $^{-}1$ **46.** $\frac{1}{5} = y - \frac{1}{10}$ $\frac{3}{10}$

Solve this problem.

47. Yesterday Betty's body temperature was 101.2 °F. Today her temperature is 98.6 °F. What was the change in her temperature readings from yesterday to today? $^{-}2.6$ °F

Find each product or quotient.

48. $^-2.3 \times 4.5$ $\quad _{^-10.35}$ **49.** $0.0063 \div {^-0.003}$ $\quad _{^-2.1}$ **50.** $(^-16.2)(^-8.5)$ $\quad _{137.7}$

51. $-\frac{2}{5} \times \frac{3}{5}$ $\quad _{-\frac{6}{25}}$ **52.** $\frac{7}{10} \div \left(-\frac{1}{2}\right)$ $\quad _{^-1\frac{2}{5}}$ **53.** $-\frac{9}{16} \div \left(-\frac{3}{4}\right)$ $\quad _{\frac{3}{4}}$

54. $-\frac{3}{8} \div {^-2\frac{1}{4}}$ $\quad _{\frac{1}{6}}$ **55.** $19\frac{4}{10} \times {^-2\frac{1}{10}}$ $\quad _{^-40\frac{37}{50}}$ **56.** $^-168 \div 5\frac{3}{5}$ $\quad _{^-30}$

Solve.

57. $\frac{x}{6.1} = {^-3}$ $\quad _{^-18.3}$ **58.** $^-25.9 = {^-7.4n}$ $\quad _{3.5}$ **59.** $-\frac{3}{10}y = \frac{3}{5}$ $\quad _{^-2}$

60. $\frac{t-5}{6} = -\frac{7}{18}$ $\quad _{2\frac{2}{3}}$**61.** $^-2.1r + 3.4 = 9.7$ $\quad _{^-3}$ **62.** $-\frac{5}{9} = \frac{2}{3}d$ $\quad _{-\frac{5}{6}}$

63. Name the reciprocal, if any.

    a. $\frac{4}{15}$ $\quad _{\frac{15}{4} \text{ or } 3\frac{3}{4}}$ **b.** $^-1\frac{2}{3}$ $\quad _{-\frac{3}{5}}$ **c.** $^-5$ $\quad _{-\frac{1}{5}}$ **d.** 0 $\quad _{None}$

64. Express in scientific notation.

    a. 7234.7 $\quad _{7.2347 \times 10^3}$ **b.** 0.000378 $\quad _{3.78 \times 10^{-4}}$ **c.** 42.1

    $\quad\quad\quad\quad\quad\quad\quad\quad\quad\quad\quad\quad\quad\quad\quad\quad\quad\quad\quad _{4.21 \times 10^1}$

65. From the formula $1000k = tw$, find the number (w) of watts required by a power tool that uses 21 kilowatt-hours (k) of electricity in 12 hours (t). $\quad _{1750 \text{ watts}}$

Find each square root as a whole number, fraction, or decimal, as given.

66. $\sqrt{25}$ $\quad _{5}$ **67.** $\sqrt{\frac{4}{49}}$ $\quad _{\frac{2}{7}}$ **68.** $\sqrt{0.36}$ $\quad _{0.6}$ **69.** $\sqrt{\frac{81}{100}}$ $\quad _{\frac{9}{10}}$

Find each square root by using the table on page 422.

70. $\sqrt{7}$ $\quad _{2.65}$ **71.** $\sqrt{41}$ $\quad _{6.40}$ **72.** $\sqrt{80}$ $\quad _{8.94}$ **73.** $\sqrt{200}$

$\quad\quad\quad\quad\quad\quad\quad\quad\quad\quad\quad\quad\quad\quad\quad\quad\quad\quad\quad\quad\quad\quad\quad _{14.1}$

Find the positive solution of each equation.

74. $x^2 = 64$ $\quad _{8}$ **75.** $x^2 = 31$ $\quad _{5.57}$ **76.** $x^2 + 3 = 52$ $\quad _{7}$

77. $x^2 - 5 = 76$ $\quad _{9}$ **78.** $x^2 - 4 = 18$ $\quad _{4.69}$ **79.** $x^2 + 20 = 70$

$\quad\quad\quad\quad\quad\quad\quad\quad\quad\quad\quad\quad\quad\quad\quad\quad\quad\quad\quad\quad\quad\quad\quad _{7.07}$

Use the Pythagorean Property to solve.

80. What is the distance from A to B? $\quad _{30 \text{ ft}}$

81. What is the height of the kite? $\quad _{60 \text{ m}}$

Ex. 80

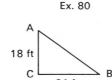

Ex. 81

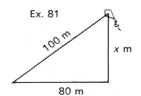

Do the indicated operation.

82. $12x^2 + {}^-10x^2$ $2x^2$ **83.** ${}^-8x + 3x + {}^-5x$ ${}^-10x$

84. $(3y + {}^-1) + ({}^-5y + 7)$ ${}^-2y + 6$ **85.** $12y - {}^-9y$ $21y$

86. $(2x^2 + 1) - ({}^-5x^2 + {}^-3)$ $7x^2 + 4$ **87.** $a^3 \cdot a^4$ a^7

88. $4y^2({}^-5y)$ ${}^-20y^3$ **89.** $(5y^2 + 3y)({}^-2y)$ ${}^-10y^3 - 6y^2$

90. $(x + 5)(x + 3)$ $x^2 + 8x + 15$ **91.** $({}^-5x + 4)({}^-3x + 1)$ $15x^2 - 17x +$

92. $\dfrac{32x^4}{{}^-8x}$ ${}^-4x^3$ **93.** $\dfrac{9y^3 + 15y^2 + {}^-3y}{3y}$ $3y^2 + 5y - 1$

Give an equation for the problem. Then solve the problem.

94. Josh bought two bicycle parts costing a total of $19. One part cost $5 more than the other. How much did he pay for each part?
$x + x + 5 = 19$; $7 and $12

Use the following set of numbers for Exercises 95–99.

3, 3, 5, 1, 4, 2, 1, 3, 2, 3

95. Find the range.   1–5   **96.** Find the mode.   3

97. Find the median.   2.5   **98.** Make a frequency table.

No.	1	2	3	4	5	Total
Freq.	2	2	4	1	1	10

99. Make a graph.

100. Find the mean for 10, 15, 12, 10, 8.   11

There are 10 marbles in a bag—6 red, 3 black, and 1 white—all the same size. They are thoroughly mixed, and one marble is picked by chance.

101. In 100 trials (the picked marble was replaced after each trial), a black marble was picked 32 times. Find ex pr (black). $\frac{8}{25}$ or 0.32

Find these theoretical probabilities for the marble situation above.

102. pr (red) $\frac{3}{5}$ or 0.6   **103.** pr (red *or* white) $\frac{7}{10}$ or 0.7

104. A coin is tossed and a marble is picked from the bag of marbles described above. Find pr (heads *and* black). $\frac{3}{20}$ or 0.15

Complete each sentence.

1. There are __100__ centimeters in one meter.   1.1

2. There are __1000__ millimeters in one meter.

3. There are __12__ inches in one foot.   2.7

4. There are __36__ inches in one yard.

Assignment Guide GR 16
Written: Reg. 1–10

5. There are __3__ feet in one yard.

Use the formula to find each of the following:

6. **Find the area of the parallelogram.**   2.8

   $A = bh$

   30 cm²

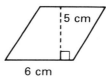

7. **Find the area of the triangle.**

   $A = bh \div 2$

   390 sq in.

8. **Find the perimeter of the triangle.**   3.2

   $p = a + b + c$

   91 in.

9. **Find the area of the circle. Use 3.14 for π.**   5.7

   $A = \pi r^2$

   28.26 sq ft

10. **Find the volume of the prism.**   2.8

    $V = area\ of\ base \times h = Bh$

    24 m³

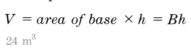
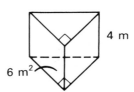

517

16 GEOMETRY

Geometry is a branch of mathematics that studies the size, shape, and location of objects in space.

Many occupations require a knowledge of geometric figures. They also require an ability to find perimeter, area, and volume.

Points, Lines, and Planes

16.1

A **point** is a location in space. It is named with a capital letter. A point has no dimensions.

•A   point A

A **line** is a set of points that extends indefinitely in two opposite directions. A line is named by using two points on the line. Since only one line passes through two points, you could say that two points determine a line. A line has only one dimension, length.

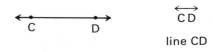

$\overleftrightarrow{CD}$

line CD

A **line segment** is part of a line with two *endpoints*. A line segment is named by using both endpoints.

$\overline{GH}$

segment GH

A **ray** is a part of a line that includes one endpoint and extends indefinitely in one direction. A ray is named by using the endpoint and one other point on the ray.

$\overrightarrow{EF}$

ray EF

An **angle** is formed by two rays with a common endpoint called a *vertex*. An angle is named by using the vertex or by using a point on one ray, then the vertex, and then a point on the other ray.

∠S or ∠RST

angle S

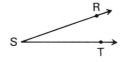

A **right angle** looks like a square corner.

An **acute angle** is smaller than a right angle.

An **obtuse angle** is larger than a right angle.

Intersecting lines meet in a point. When two lines intersect, four angles are formed. If the angles are right angles, the lines are called *perpendicular lines.*

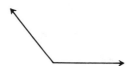

Parallel lines are lines in a plane that do not intersect.

A **plane** is a set of points that is "flat" and extends without end in all directions. A plane is named by using any three *noncollinear* (not on the same line) points on the plane. Since only one plane passes through three noncollinear points, you could say that three noncollinear points determine a plane.

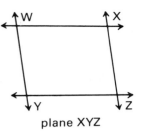

plane XYZ

A **half plane** is determined by one line in the plane and the part of the plane on only one side of that line.

Space is the set of all points and has three dimensions—length, width, and thickness.

Assignment Guide 16.1
Oral: Reg. & Max. 1–19
Written: Reg. 21–29 odd
Max. 21–29 odd;
31–40

Exercises

[A] Tell whether each of the following best describes a point, a line, or a plane.

1. a desk top plane

2. a corner of a box point

3. a tip of a pencil point

4. an edge of a box line

Name a physical object that suggests each of the following:
5 –13. Accept any reasonable answers.

5. a point

6. a line

7. a plane

8. a ray

9. a line segment

10. parallel lines

11. a right angle

12. space

13. perpendicular lines

Tell whether each of the following is acute, right, or obtuse.

14. obtuse

15. acute

16. right

Using the angle in Exercise 14, give the

17. name.

18. vertex. U

19. sides. UT or $\overrightarrow{UV}$

∠U, ∠TUV, or ∠VUT

520

B Use the figure at the right for Exercises 20–26. (Remember, the lines can be extended.)

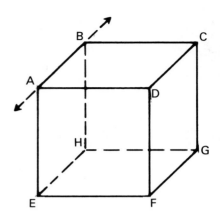

20. Are $\overleftrightarrow{AB}$ and $\overleftrightarrow{EH}$ parallel lines? yes

21. Are $\overleftrightarrow{BH}$ and $\overleftrightarrow{CG}$ perpendicular lines? no

22. Name three lines that meet at point F.

23 –25. Other names are possible. $\overleftrightarrow{FG}$, $\overleftrightarrow{DF}$, and $\overleftrightarrow{EF}$

23. Name a plane that is parallel to plane ABE.

plane CDF

24. Name two planes that intersect to form $\overleftrightarrow{DF}$.

planes CDF and ADE

25. Name three planes that contain point H.

planes ABE, BCG, and EFG

26. Name a line that intersects plane ABC in only one point.

$\overleftrightarrow{AE}$, $\overleftrightarrow{BH}$, $\overleftrightarrow{DF}$, or $\overleftrightarrow{CG}$

Draw each figure.

27 –32. See pupils' drawings

27. a line segment

28. a pair of perpendicular lines

29. a ray

30. a pair of parallel lines

C 31. two perpendicular rays with the same endpoint

32. two perpendicular rays that do not have the same endpoint

Skew lines are lines in different planes that are not parallel and that will never intersect. Use the figure above for Exercises 33–40.

33. Are $\overleftrightarrow{BH}$ and $\overleftrightarrow{EF}$ skew lines?   34. Are $\overleftrightarrow{DC}$ and $\overleftrightarrow{BH}$ skew lines?

yes   yes

Tell whether each pair of lines is parallel, perpendicular, or skew.

35. $\overleftrightarrow{HG}$ and $\overleftrightarrow{FG}$ 36. $\overleftrightarrow{EA}$ and $\overleftrightarrow{BC}$ skew   37. $\overleftrightarrow{AD}$ and $\overleftrightarrow{GH}$ parallel

perpendicular

38. $\overleftrightarrow{DF}$ and $\overleftrightarrow{EH}$ skew   39. $\overleftrightarrow{EF}$ and $\overleftrightarrow{HE}$ 40. $\overleftrightarrow{DF}$ and $\overleftrightarrow{BH}$ parallel

perpendicular

Polygons, Perimeter, and Circumference

Many figures are formed by joining the endpoints of line segments. If the line segments do not cross and the figure is closed, the figure is a **polygon**.

Suggested Class Time

Course	Min.	Reg.	Max.
Days	0	1	1

triangle **quadrilateral** **pentagon** **hexagon** **octagon**

A regular polygon has all sides *congruent* (the same length) and all angles congruent (the same measure).

Triangles may be classified according to their sides.

scalene triangle
no sides congruent

isosceles triangle
at least two
congruent sides

equilateral triangle
all sides congruent

Triangles may also be classified according to their angles.

acute triangle
all acute angles

right triangle
one right angle

obtuse triangle
one obtuse angle

Some special quadrilaterals are shown.

  trapezoid
exactly one
pair of
parallel sides

  parallelogram
two pairs of
parallel sides

rhombus
parallelogram
with four
congruent sides

rectangle
parallelogram
with four right
angles

square
rectangle with
four congruent
sides

To find the perimeter of a polygon, add the lengths of the sides.

Example 1: Find the perimeter.

1.3 cm $2.5 + 1.3 + 2.5 + 1.3 = 7.6$

2.5 cm

The perimeter is 7.6 cm.

Sometimes you may have to measure a side of a polygon.

Example 2: Find the length of $\overline{AB}$ to the nearest $\frac{1}{8}$ inch.

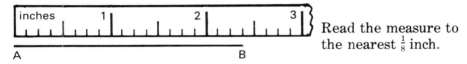

Read the measure to the nearest $\frac{1}{8}$ inch.

Be sure to align the end of the ruler or the zero mark with the endpoint of the segment.

$\overline{AB}$ is $2\frac{3}{8}$ in. long.

Example 3: Find the length of $\overline{CD}$ to the nearest centimeter.

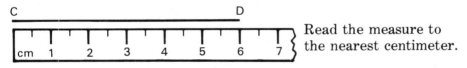

Read the measure to the nearest centimeter.

$\overline{CD}$ is 6 cm long.

The circumference of a circle is the distance around. You can use the following two formulas to find the circumference.

$C = \pi d$ The circumference is equal to π times the diameter.
$C = 2\pi r$ The circumference is equal to 2 times π times the radius.

Example 4: Find the circumference. Use 3.14 for π.

10 cm

$C = \pi d$
$= 3.14 \times 10$
$= 31.4$

5 cm

$C = 2\pi r$
$= 2 \times 3.14 \times 5$
$= 31.4$

The circumference is 31.4 cm.

■ Exercises

A Match each name with the letter of the figure.

 a
 b
 c
d
 e
 f

1. triangle ᵉ **2.** quadrilateral ᵇ **3.** hexagon ᶜ **4.** octagon ᶠ

Classify each triangle according to its sides.

5. 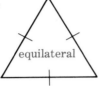 equilateral

6. 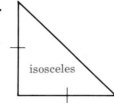 isosceles

7. 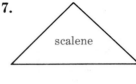 scalene

Classify each triangle according to its angles.

8. 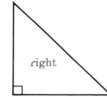 right

9. 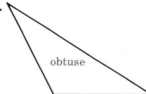 obtuse

10. 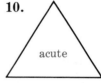 acute

Measure each segment to the nearest $\frac{1}{8}$ inch.

11. ———— $1\frac{1}{8}$ in.   **12.** ———— $\frac{7}{8}$ in.   **13.** —— $\frac{3}{8}$ in.

14. ——————— $2\frac{2}{8}$ in.   **15.** ——————— $1\frac{6}{8}$ in.

Measure each segment to the nearest centimeter.

16. ———— 3 cm   **17.** —— 1 cm   **18.** ———— 2 cm

19. ————————— 5 cm   **20.** ———— 4 cm

B Draw line segments with the following lengths.

21–30. See pupils' drawings.

21. $4\frac{3}{8}$ in.   **22.** $2\frac{5}{8}$ in.   **23.** 3 cm   **24.** 4 cm   **25.** $5\frac{1}{2}$ in.

26. $1\frac{1}{4}$ in.   **27.** 12 cm   **28.** 15 cm   **29.** $\frac{7}{8}$ in.   **30.** $\frac{3}{4}$ in.

Find each perimeter.

31. 10 m · 14 m · 10 m

32. 3 cm · 3 cm · 3 cm

33. 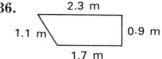 6 ft · 21 ft

31. 34 m
32. 9 cm
33. 54 ft
34. 68 in.
35. 8.6 cm
36. 6 m

34. 17 in.

35. 2.2 cm · 1.2 cm · 1.8 cm · 1.2 cm · 2.2 cm

36. 2.3 m · 1.1 m · 0.9 m · 1.7 m

37. a regular hexagon, where each side is 24 cm 144 cm

38. a rectangle with a length of 12 m and a width of 8 m 40 m

39. a square, where each side is $5\frac{3}{8}$ ft $21\frac{1}{2}$ ft

40. a parallelogram with a length of $9\frac{1}{2}$ in. and a width of 6 in. 31 in.

Find each circumference. Use 3.14 for π.

41. 7 cm

42. 9 m

43. 3.2 m

44. 6.5 cm

41. 21.98 cm
42. 28.26 m
43. 20.096 m
44. 40.82 cm

45. a diameter of 3.6 m 11.304 m **46.** a radius of 15.6 cm 97.968 cm

C Measure each side of the polygons to the nearest $\frac{1}{8}$ inch and give the perimeter for each polygon.

47. 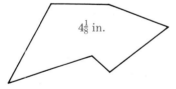 $4\frac{1}{8}$ in.

48. 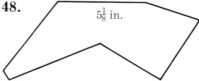 $5\frac{1}{8}$ in.

49. The distance between bases on a baseball diamond is 90 ft. How far does a batter run when he hits a home run? 360 ft

50. What distance do you ride in one turn of a Ferris wheel when you sit 20 ft from the center? 125.6 ft

51. Are all squares rectangles?
yes
52. Are all rectangles squares?
no
53. Are all rhombuses squares?
no
54. Are all squares rhombuses?
yes

16.3 Area

Example 1: Find the area of the rectangle.

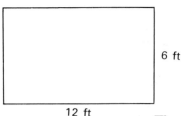

6 ft

12 ft

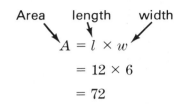

Area $\quad$ length $\quad$ width

$A = l \times w$

$= 12 \times 6$

$= 72$

The area is 72 sq. ft.

Example 2: Find the area of each triangle.

4 m

3 m

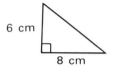

6 cm

8 cm

Area $\quad$ base $\quad$ height

$A = bh \div 2$

$= 3 \times 4 \div 2$

$= 6$

The area is 6 m².

Note that the height is perpendicular to the base. If the triangle is a right triangle, the sides of the right angle are the base and the height.

$A = bh \div 2$

$= 8 \times 6 \div 2$

$= 24$

The area is 24 cm².

Example 3: Find the area of the circle. Use 3.14 for π.

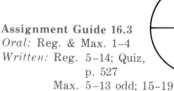

16 in.

Area $\quad$ radius

$A = \pi r^2$

$= 3.14(8)^2$

$= 200.96$

The diameter is given as 16 in. Divide by 2 to find the radius because the formula uses *r*.

The area is 200.96 sq in.

Assignment Guide 16.3
Oral: Reg. & Max. 1–4
Written: Reg. 5–14; Quiz,
$\quad$ p. 527
$\quad$ Max. 5–13 odd; 15–19
$\quad$ Quiz, p. 527

■ Exercises

A **1.** How many square feet are in one square yard? 9 sq ft

2. How many square centimeters are in one square meter? 10 000 cm²

3. How many square meters are in one square kilometer? 1 000 000 m²

4. How many square inches are in one square foot? 144 sq in.

B Find the area of each figure. Use 3.14 for π.

5.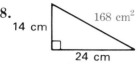
96 sq ft   8 ft
12 ft

6.
196 m² 14 m

7.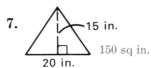
15 in.
150 sq in.
20 in.

8.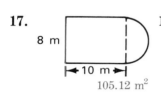
168 cm²
14 cm
24 cm

9.
3 ft
28.26 sq ft

10.
18 cm
1017.36 cm²

11. The official U.S. flag is 4 ft wide and $7\frac{1}{2}$ ft long. What is the area of the flag? 30 sq ft

12. The screen of a television set is $18\frac{1}{2}$ in. wide and 14 in. high. What is the area of the screen? 259 sq in.

13. What is the area of a circular skating rink that has a 140-ft diameter? 15,386 sq ft

14. How much felt is used in a pennant with a base of 12 in. and a height of 30 in.? 180 sq in.

C **15.** Find the cost of carpeting a floor that is 15 ft by 12 ft at $24.95 per square yard. $499

16. To the nearest foot, what is the area of the floor space that remains uncovered if a rug with a 42-in. diameter is placed on a floor that is 14 ft by 10 ft? 130 sq ft

Find the area of each figure.

17.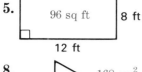
8 m
10 m
105.12 m²

18.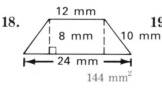
12 mm
8 mm   10 mm
24 mm
144 mm²

19.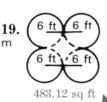
6 ft   6 ft
6 ft   6 ft
483.12 sq ft

Draw each of the following:
1 –3. See students' drawings.

1. $\overline{AB}$ **2.** $\overleftrightarrow{CD}$ **3.** $\overrightarrow{EF}$

Quick Quiz
Sections 16.1 to 16.3

Find the perimeter of each figure.

4.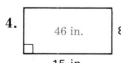
46 in.   8 in.
15 in.

5. 12 m 48 m 20 m
16 m

6. 12 cm   13 cm
8 cm   54 cm   6 cm
15 cm

7. Find the area of the figure in Exercise 4. 120 sq in.

8. Find the area of the figure in Exercise 5. 96 m²

Surface Area

rectangular prism

triangular prism

hexagonal prism

The solids shown above are **polyhedrons.** The faces (top, bottom, and sides) are all polygons.

> The surface area of a prism is the sum of the areas of the faces.

Example 1: Find the surface area of the following prism:

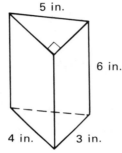

5 in.

6 in.

4 in.   3 in.

Face		Area
Top	$A = 3 \times 4 \div 2$	6
Bottom	$A = 3 \times 4 \div 2$	6
Right side	$A = 3 \times 6$	18
Left side	$A = 4 \times 6$	24
Back side	$A = 5 \times 6$	30
		84

The surface area is 84 sq in.

triangular pyramid

rectangular pyramid

cylinder

Other three-dimensional objects are pyramids and cylinders.

> The surface area of a pyramid is the sum of the areas of the faces.

If a cylinder were cut apart, you would see that the bases (top and bottom) are circles and the other surface is a rectangle. The length of the rectangle is the circumference of the base, and its width is the height of the cylinder.

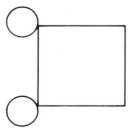

Example 2: Find the surface area of the cylinder.

Area of each base

$A = \pi r^2$

$\quad = 3.14(9)^2$

$\quad = 254.34$

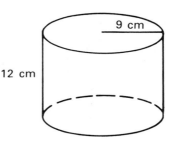

12 cm

9 cm

Area of the rectangle

$A = lw$

$\quad = 2 \times 3.14 \times 9 \times 12$

$\quad = 678.24$

Length of the rectangle
$l = 2\pi r$

Surface area $= 254.34 + 678.24 + 254.34$

$\quad = 1186.92$

The surface area is 1186.92 cm^2.

■ Exercises

Assignment Guide 16.4
Oral: Reg. & Max. 1–10
Written: Reg. 11–20
Max. 11–19 odd;
21–28

A̲ Match each figure with its name.

1. triangular prism c

2. rectangular pyramid d

3. cylinder f

4. pentagonal pyramid e

Tell the number of faces each of the following figures has:

5. rectangular prism 6 faces

6. hexagonal prism 8 faces

7. triangular pyramid 4 faces

8. hexagonal pyramid 7 faces

9. What is the shape of the sides of a prism? parallelograms

10. What is the shape of the sides of a pyramid? triangles

B Find the surface area of each figure. Use 3.14 for π.

11. 2736 cm²
12. 408 sq in.
13. 156 sq ft
14. 486 m²
15. 904.32 mm²
16. 2543.4 sq ft

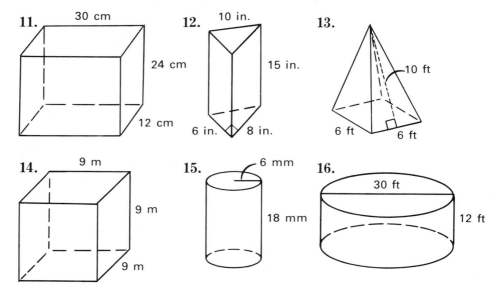

11. 30 cm, 24 cm, 12 cm

12. 10 in., 15 in., 6 in., 8 in.

13. 10 ft, 6 ft, 6 ft

14. 9 m, 9 m, 9 m

15. 6 mm, 18 mm

16. 30 ft, 12 ft

17. How much paper is needed to make a box 20 cm long, 12 cm wide, and 6 cm high?
864 cm²

18. A small can has a radius of 3 cm and a height of 7 cm. About how much metal was used to make the can?
188.4 cm²

19. How many square inches of wire mesh are needed to make a cage 36 in. long, 30 in. wide, and 15 in. high?
4140 sq in.

20. How many square feet of asbestos are needed to cover the curved surface and the ends of a water tank that is 4 ft in diameter and 6 ft high? 100.48 sq ft

C **21.** How many square feet of paper are needed to make 1000 labels for cans, each 7 in. high and 4 in. in diameter? (Round your answer to the nearest square foot.) 611 sq ft

The formula for the surface area of a sphere is $A = 4\pi r^2$. Find the surface areas of spheres with the following radii. Use 3.14 for π.

22. 5 in.   **23.** 22 ft   **24.** 4.5 m   **25.** 6.2 cm   **26.** 120 mm
314 sq in.   6079.04 sq ft   254.34 m²   482.8064 cm²   180 864 mm²

27. The radius of the earth is about 4000 miles. Find its surface area. Use 3.14 for π.
200,960,000 sq mi

28. The circumference of a basketball is about 30 in. Find its surface area. Use 3 for π.
300 sq in.

The volume (V) of a prism or a cylinder is equal to the area of the base (B) times the height (h).

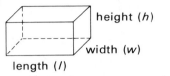

height (h)

width (w)

length (l)

radius (r)

height (h)

$V = Bh$ or

$V = lwh \quad (B = lw)$

$V = Bh$ or

$V = \pi r^2 h \quad (B = \pi r^2)$

Suggested Class Time			
Course	Min.	Reg.	Max.
Days	0	1	1

Example 1: Find the volume of this triangular prism.

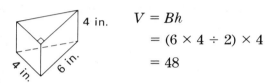

4 in.

4 in.

6 in.

$V = Bh$

$= (6 \times 4 \div 2) \times 4$

$= 48$

The volume of the prism is 48 sq in.

Example 2: Find the volume of this cylinder. Use 3.14 for π.

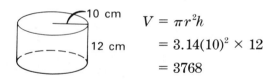

10 cm

12 cm

$V = \pi r^2 h$

$= 3.14(10)^2 \times 12$

$= 3768$

The volume of the cylinder is 3768 cm³.

The volume (V) of a pyramid is equal to one third of the area of the base (B) times the height (h).

Example 3: Find the volume of this pyramid.

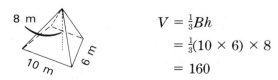

8 m

10 m

6 m

$V = \frac{1}{3}Bh$

$= \frac{1}{3}(10 \times 6) \times 8$

$= 160$

The volume of the pyramid is 160 m³.

■ Exercises

Assignment Guide 16.5
Oral: Reg. & Max. 1–6
Written: Reg. 7–17
　　　Max. 7–17 odd; 18–25

A 1. How many cubic feet are in one cubic yard? 27 cu ft

2. How many cubic inches are in one cubic foot? 1728 cu in.

3. How many cubic centimeters are in one cubic meter? 1 000 000 cm³

4. How many cubic millimeters are in one cubic centimeter? 1000 mm³

5. How many cubic inches are in one cubic yard? 46,656 cu in.

6. How many cubic meters are in one cubic kilometer? 1 000 000 000 m³

B Find the volume of each figure. Use 3.14 for π.

7. 36 cu ft
8. 15⅝ cu in.
9. 132 cu ft
10. 1.56 m³
11. 141.3 m³
12. 508.68 cm³
13. 1413 mm³
14. 336 cu ft
15. 1440 m³

7.

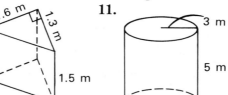

8.

9.

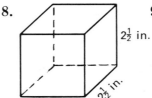

10.

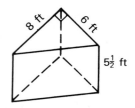

11.

12.

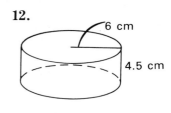

13.

14.

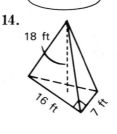

15.

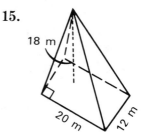

16. A pound of butter will fit into a container having the shape of a rectangular prism 8 in. long, 1 in. wide, and 4 in. high. Find the volume of this container. 32 cu in.

17. A pound of cement will fit into a container having the shape of a rectangular prism 3 in. long, 1 in. wide, and 3 in. high. Find the volume of this container. 9 cu in.

⚆ **18.** One cubic foot of water weighs about 62.4 lb. What is the weight of the water in a water bed that is 8 ft long, 6 ft wide, and 8 in. high? 1996.8 lb

19. Three hundred fourteen cubic feet of water was put into a cylindrical pool. If the pool had a radius of 5 ft, what was the height of the water? 4 ft

20. What happens to the volume of a cylinder when you double its height? It doubles.

21. What happens to the volume of a cylinder when you double its radius? It quadruples.

22. What happens to the volume of a cylinder when you double its height and its radius? It is 8 times as big.

23. What happens to the volume of a rectangular prism when you double its length? It doubles.

24. What happens to the volume of a rectangular prism when you double its length and its width? It quadruples.

25. What happens to the volume of a rectangular prism when you double all three of its dimensions? It is 8 times as big.

Liters of Fun

1 cm
1 cm
1 cm

The box shown above has a capacity of 1 milliliter.

1. What is the capacity in milliliters of a box with a volume of 1000 cm³? 1000 mL

2. What is the capacity in liters of a box with a volume of 1000 cm³? 1 L

3. A liter of water has a mass of 1 kilogram. What is the volume of a container that holds 1 kilogram of water? 1000 cm³

A
3 liters

B
8 liters

Tell how you could carry the following amounts of water, using only the containers shown above.

4. 5 liters

5. 2 liters

6. 4 liters

4. Fill B. From B pour 3 L into A. There are 5 L left in B.

5. Fill B. From B pour 3 L into A. Empty A. From B pour 3 L into A. There are 2 L left in B.

6. Fill B. From B pour 3 L into A. Empty A. From B pour 3 L into A. Empty A. Pour the remaining 2 L from B into A. Fill B. Fill A from B (1 L from B). Empty A. From B pour 3 L into A. There are 4 L left in B.

533

TANGRAMS

An ancient Chinese puzzle called a **tangram** consists of 7 pieces that form a square.

Trace the tangram shown below.

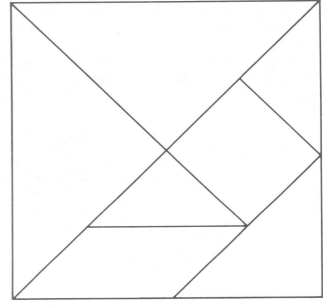

1.

2.

3.

4.

5.

From these seven pieces you can make geometric figures and various pictures.

A. a right triangle

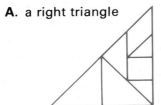

B. a rooster

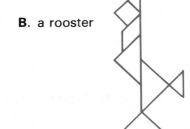

6.

7.

8.

9.

Can you make these figures? (Remember, you must use all seven pieces for each figure.)

1. a rectangle	**2.** a trapezoid	**3.** a parallelogram
4. a hexagon	**5.** a pentagon	**6.** an isosceles triangle
7. a cat	**8.** a dog	**9.** a whale

H. Armstrong Roberts

MATH ON THE FARM

On page 478 there is a list of the numbers of years of high-school math recommended as preparation for various college programs. Notice that one of the longer lists of college programs can be found under Agriculture. Many farmers find a college education essential. Others do not have even a high-school education. Yet all find that math is required in operating a farm.

Farmers must know how to find perimeter, area, and volume. They also must use computation to figure yields, prices, income, and expenses.

In the United States the size (area) of a farm is measured in acres.

◀ 1 acre = 43,560 sq ft   1 sq mi = 640 acres ▶

1. A farmer has a rectangular field that is 1980 feet long and 1100 feet wide. What is the area of the field in acres?   50 acres

2. For irrigation in a field a farmer uses a center-pivot irrigation system. The pipeline carries water and rotates in a circle with a radius of 290 feet. To the nearest acre, how many acres does the irrigation system water?   6 acres

3. If the farmer wants to fence the circular area irrigated in Exercise 2, how much fencing will be needed?   1821.2 feet

4. A bale of hay is 14 inches tall, 18 inches wide, and 38 inches long. What is the volume of a bale of hay?   9576 cu in.

5. The part of the loft shown in color will be filled with hay. What is the volume of that part of the loft?
    6048 cu ft

6. When baled hay is stored, there must be "breathing room," or air space. If 80% of the space in Exercise 5 can be used for storing baled hay, how many bales (to the nearest whole bale) can be stored?
    873 bales

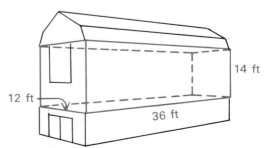

14 ft

12 ft

36 ft

Terms and Symbols Review

Match each name with the letter of a symbol and with the letter of a figure.

Assignment Guide Rev.
Oral:
Reg. Terms & Symbols 1–14
Max. Terms & Symbols 1–14
Written:
Reg. 1–5 odd;
   6–21
Max. 1–5 odd;
   6–21

1. angle MNP D., f   **A.** $\overleftrightarrow{RS}$

2. line RS A., h   **B.** $\overrightarrow{RS}$

3. line segment RS   **C.** $\overline{RS}$

                C., g

4. ray RS B., j   **D.** $\angle MNP$

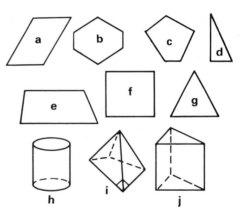

Match each name with the letter of a figure.

5. c
6. f
7. j
8. i
9. b
10. h
11. e
12. d
13. a
14. g

5. pentagon   **6.** square

7. prism   **8.** pyramid

9. hexagon   **10.** cylinder

11. trapezoid

12. right triangle

13. parallelogram

14. isosceles triangle

Chapter 16 Review

16.1   Tell whether each pair of lines is parallel, perpendicular, or neither.

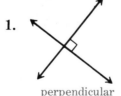

1.

perpendicular

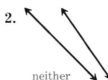

2.

neither

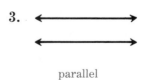

3.

parallel

16.2   Find the measure of each line segment to the nearest $\frac{1}{8}$ inch and to the nearest centimeter.

4. _____ $4\frac{3}{8}$ in., 11 cm

5. _____ $3\frac{1}{2}$ in., 9 cm

Find the perimeter of each figure.

6.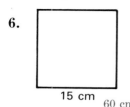
15 cm   60 cm

7.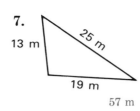
13 m   25 m   19 m   57 m

8.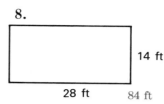
14 ft   28 ft   84 ft

9. Find the circumference of a circle with a diameter of 4 m. Use 3.14 for π.   12.56 m

Find the area of each figure. Use 3.14 for π.   16.3

10.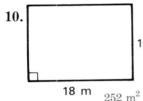
14 m   18 m   252 m^2

11.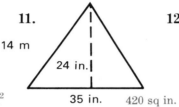
24 in.   35 in.   420 sq in.

12.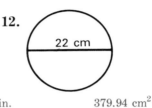
22 cm   379.94 cm^2

13. Bart mowed a rectangular lawn that was 60 ft long and 48 ft wide. What was the area of the lawn?   2880 sq ft

Find the surface area of each figure. Use 3.14 for π.   16.4

14.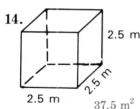
2.5 m   2.5 m   2.5 m   37.5 m^2

15.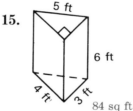
5 ft   6 ft   4 ft   3 ft   84 sq ft

16.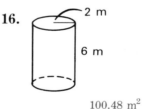
2 m   6 m   100.48 m^2

17. How much wood was used to make a crate that is 7 ft long, 3 ft wide, and 3 ft high?   102 sq ft

Find the volume of each figure. Use 3.14 for π.   16.5

18.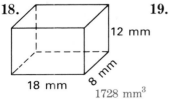
12 mm   18 mm   8 mm   1728 mm^3

19.
7 in.   16 in.   2461.76 cu in.

20.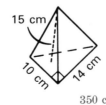
15 cm   10 cm   14 cm   350 cm^3

21. Ann rented a storage unit that was 12 ft long, 15 ft wide, and 10 ft high. What was the volume of the storage unit?   1800 cu ft

Chapter 16 Test

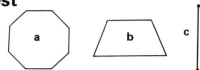 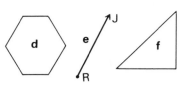

Assignment Guide Test
Written: Reg. 1–21
Max. 1–21

Match each name with the letter of a figure above.

1. $\overline{RJ}$ c

2. $\overleftrightarrow{RJ}$ g

3. $\overrightarrow{RJ}$ e

4. triangle f

5. hexagon d

6. trapezoid b

Find the perimeter or circumference of each figure. Use 3.14 for π.

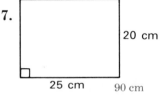

7. 20 cm 25 cm 90 cm

8. 10 in. 6 in. 8 in. 24 in.

9. 6 m 37.68 m

Find the area of the figure in

10. Exercise 7. $500\ cm^2$ **11.** Exercise 8. $24\ sq\ in.$ **12.** Exercise 9. $113.04\ m^2$

Find the surface area of each figure. Use 3.14 for π.

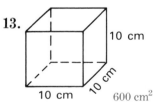 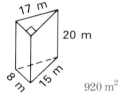 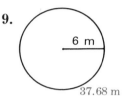

13. 10 cm 10 cm 10 cm $600\ cm^2$

14. 17 m 20 m 8 m 15 m $920\ m^2$

15. 4 ft 12 ft $401.92\ sq\ ft$

Find the volume of the figure in

16. Exercise 13. $1000\ cm^3$ **17.** Exercise 14. $1200\ m^3$ **18.** Exercise 15. $602.88\ cu$

19. Nadia is refinishing a circular tabletop with a radius of 60 cm. What is the area of the tabletop? (Use 3.14 for π.) $11\,304\ cm^2$

20. How much cardboard is needed to make a box with a lid if the box is to be 12 in. long, 9 in. wide, and 6 in. high? $468\ sq\ in.$

21. A pool is 12 ft long, 10 ft wide, and 5 ft deep. How many cubic feet of water is needed to fill the pool? $600\ cu\ ft$

Getting Ready for Chapter 17

Solve and graph each inequality.   2.4

1. $n - 3 < 2$ $n < 5$,

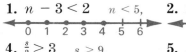

2. $2x > 6$ $x > 3$,

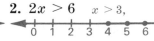

3. $12 < 6 + m$ $m > 6$,

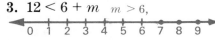

4. $\frac{s}{3} > 3$ $s > 9$,

5. $5 > r + 1$ $r < 4$,

6. $16 < 8p$ $p > 2$,

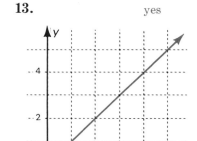
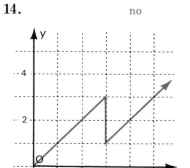
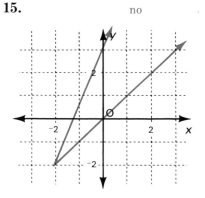

Solve each equation.   2.6

7. $2x - 3 = 81$ $x = 42$ **8.** $21 = 3n + 6$ $n = 5$ **9.** $52x + 5 = 109$ $x = 2$

10. $6 + 10x = 86$ $x = 8$ **11.** $4y - 30 = 130$ $y = 40$ **12.** $16 = 12 + 4x$ $x = 1$

Tell whether each of the following is a function.   8.5

13.   yes   **14.**   no   **15.**   no

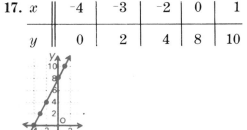

Draw a line graph for each table.   8.4

16.

x	0	1	2	3	4	5
y	3	4	5	6	7	8

17.

x	-4	-3	-2	0	1
y	0	2	4	8	10

17 More Algebra

In the seventeenth century René Descartes combined algebra and geometry to solve problems. In chapter 8 you studied the ideas of graphing and functions. In this chapter you will use those ideas in new ways to solve problems.

Graphing Equations in the Coordinate Plane

To draw the graph of an equation, make a table, plot enough points to determine the shape of the graph, and then sketch the graph. The graph of the equation shown at the right is a straight line.

There are many forms of equations whose graphs are straight lines. One of the most common is the *standard form* of an equation, $ax + by = c$. The letter a is the *coefficient* of x. That is, a stands for a number that will be multiplied by the value of the variable x. In the same way, b is the coefficient of y. The letter c represents a number. Note that the values of a, b, and c can be positive, negative, or zero.

$2x + y = 6$

x	0	-2	4
y	6	10	-2

 The **standard form** of an equation is $ax + by = c$.

Suggested Class Time			
Course	Min.	Reg.	Max.
Days	0	1	1

Example 1: Sketch the graph of $3x + {}^-4y = 12$.

Make a table. Choose values of x that make it easy to compute y. Compute y.

x	0	2	4
y			

$$3x + {}^-4y = 12$$
$$3(0) + {}^-4y = 12$$
$$0 + {}^-4y = 12$$
$${}^-4y = 12$$
$$y = {}^-3$$

$$3x + {}^-4y = 12$$
$$3(2) + {}^-4y = 12$$
$$6 + {}^-4y = 12$$
$${}^-4y = 6$$
$$y = {}^-1\tfrac{1}{2}, \text{ or } {}^-1.5$$

$$3x + {}^-4y = 12$$
$$3(4) + {}^-4y = 12$$
$$12 + {}^-4y = 12$$
$${}^-4y = 0$$
$$y = 0$$

Complete the table.
Plot the points.
Sketch the graph.

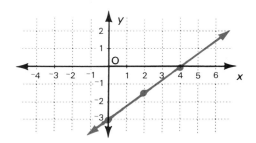

x	0	2	4
y	-3	-1.5	0

541

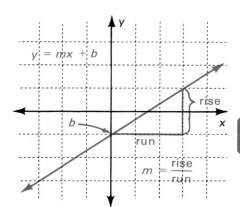

$y = mx + b$

Another form of an equation is the *slope-intercept form*. The **slope** of a line is the ratio of its *rise* to its *run*. The coefficient m stands for the slope. The letter b stands for the number where the graph of the equation crosses the y-axis, called the y-intercept.

> The **slope-intercept form** of an equation is $y = mx + b$, where m is the slope and b is the y-intercept.

If the slope is negative, either the rise **or** the run will be in a negative direction—that is, to the left or down.

Example 2: Find the slope of the graph of each equation.

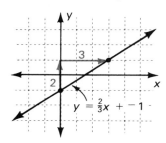

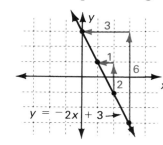

Notice that you can use any two points on the graph.

$$\frac{6 \text{ up}}{3 \text{ left}} \longrightarrow \frac{6}{-3} \quad m = {}^-2$$

$$\frac{\text{rise}}{\text{run}} \longrightarrow \frac{2 \text{ up}}{3 \text{ right}} \quad m = \frac{2}{3}$$

$$\frac{\text{rise}}{\text{run}} \longrightarrow \frac{2 \text{ up}}{1 \text{ left}} \quad \frac{2}{-1} \quad m = {}^-2$$

Example 3: Sketch the graph of $y = 0.5x - 3$.
Make a table. Compute y.
Complete the table.

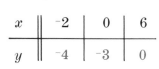

x	$^-2$	0	6
y	$^-4$	$^-3$	0

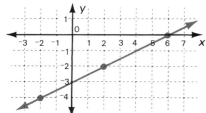

Sketch the graph.

A standard-form equation can be changed to slope-intercept form.

Example 4: Change $2x + {}^-3y = 6$ to slope-intercept form.

Use the slope-intercept form to name the y-intercept and the slope.

$$2x + {}^-3y = 6$$
$$^-3y = {}^-2x + 6$$
$$\frac{^-3y}{^-3} = \frac{^-2x}{^-3} + \frac{6}{^-3}$$
$$y = \tfrac{2}{3}x + {}^-2$$

Exercises

Assignment Guide 17.1
Oral: Reg. & Max. 1–6
Written: Reg. 7–15 odd;
16–18
Max. 7–23 odd

A Tell whether each equation is in standard form or in slope-intercept form. If it is in slope-intercept form, give the slope and the y-intercept.

1. $-2x + y = 3$ **2.** $y = 9x - 3$ **3.** $2x + 9 = y$
standard form   slope-intercept form, $m = 9$, $b = -3$ slope-intercept form, $m = 2$, $b = 9$

4. $1 = -\frac{2}{3}x + y$ **5.** $8 = 2x + -y$ **6.** $y = -2x + -\frac{1}{2}$
standard form   standard form   slope-intercept form, $m = -2$, $b = -\frac{1}{2}$

B Graph each equation.

7. $3x + y = 6$ **8.** $y = -3x + -1$ **9.** $2x + 3 = y$

10. $x + -2y = 3$ **11.** $9x + 2y = 12$ **12.** $y = -0.5x + -2.5$

Change each equation to slope-intercept form. Then name the slope and the y-intercept.

13. $2x + 5y = 10$ **14.** $-8 = 3x + 4y$ **15.** $6x + -3y = 4$
$y = -\frac{2}{5}x + 2$, $m = -\frac{2}{5}$, $b = 2$ $y = -\frac{3}{4}x + -2$, $m = -\frac{3}{4}$, $b = -2$ $y = 2x + -\frac{4}{3}$, $m = 2$, $b = -\frac{4}{3}$

16. $3y + 2x = 0$ **17.** $0 = -2x + y$ **18.** $3x = 2y$
$y = \frac{2}{3}x + 0$, $m = \frac{2}{3}$, $b = 0$ $y = 2x + 0$, $m = 2$, $b = 0$ $y = \frac{3}{2}x + 0$, $m = \frac{3}{2}$, $b = 0$

C Equations like $y = 3$ and $x = -4$ have only one variable. You can think of these as being equations with two variables where one coefficient is zero. Notice how the equations are graphed.

$y = 3$
or
$0x + y = 3$

x	-2	0	3
y	3	3	3

$x = -4$
or
$x + 0y = -4$

x	-4	-4	-4
y	-1	0	2

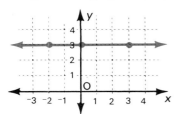

Draw the graph of each equation.

19. $y = -2$ **20.** $x = 5$ **21.** $x = -7$ **22.** $y = 8$

23. What equation describes the set of ordered pairs whose x-coordinates are zero? Draw the graph of that equation. $x = 0$

24. What equation describes the set of ordered pairs whose y-coordinates are zero? Draw the graph of that equation. $y = 0$

7.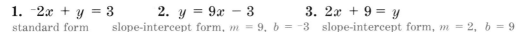
8.
9.
10.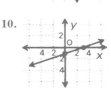
11.
12.
22.

9.   20.   21. 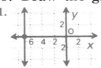   23.   24.

543

17.2 Graphing Inequalities in the Coordinate Plane

Suggested Class Time			
Course	Min.	Reg.	Max.
Days	0	1	1

The graph of the $2x + y = {}^-4$ is shown by the solid line. The shaded part of the graph shows the solution for $2x + y > {}^-4$.

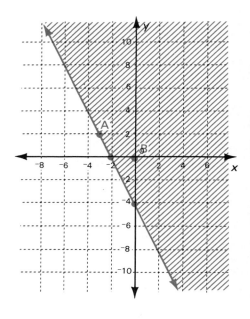

The entire graph (the solid line and the shaded area) shows the solution to $2x + y \geq {}^-4$. The symbol $\geq$ means "is greater than or equal to."

You can check the solution by choosing two or three points in the shaded area and substituting in the equation to see if the ordered pair for each point makes the inequality true. Suppose you choose points A and B.

Point	$A({}^-3, 2)$	$B(0, 0)$
Inequality	$2x + y \geq {}^-4$	$2x + y \geq {}^-4$
Substitute	$2(-3) + 2 \geq {}^-4$	$2(0) + 0 \geq {}^-4$
	This is true $\longrightarrow$ $\,{}^-4 \geq {}^-4$	This is true $\longrightarrow$ $\,0 \geq {}^-4$
	because ${}^-4 = {}^-4$. True	because $0 > {}^-4$. True

Example 1: Show the graph of $x + {}^-2y \leq {}^-2$.
$\leq$ means "is less than or equal to."

Make a table for
$x + {}^-2y = {}^-2$

x	0	${}^-2$	4
y	1	0	3

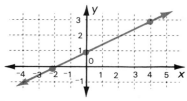

Graph the equation. Decide whether to shade above or below the line. An easy point to check is $(0, 0)$.

$$x + {}^-2y \leq {}^-2$$
$$0 + {}^-2(0) \leq {}^-2$$
$$0 \leq {}^-2$$

False. Shade the part that does not contain $(0, 0)$—above the line.

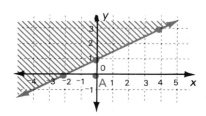

Example 2: Show the graph of $y > 0.5x - 1.5$.

Make a table for $y = 0.5x - 1.5$.

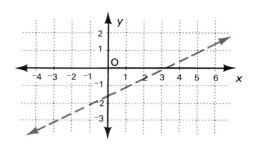

x	0	5	-3
y	-1.5	1	-3

Use a dotted line for the graph of the equation. Notice that the inequality "is greater than" and does not include "is equal to." The dotted line shows that the equation is the boundary for the graph but is not included in the solution for the inequality.

Decide whether to shade above or below the dotted line. Use (0, 0) as the test point.

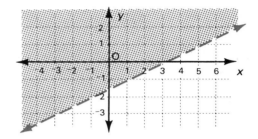

$$y > 0.5x - 1.5$$

$$0 > 0.5(0) - 1.5$$

$$0 > -1.5$$

True. Shade the part containing (0, 0).

■ Exercises

A Tell whether each of the following would use a solid line or a dotted line on the completed graph.

1. $y < -2x + 3$ dotted line   **2.** $x + 2y \le 0$ solid line

3. $5x + 2y \ge 0.5$ solid line   **4.** $x - y > 2$ dotted line

Tell whether to shade above or below the line to complete each graph.

5. $y < -2x + 3$ below   **6.** $x + 2y \le 0$ below

7. $5x + 2y \ge 0.5$ above   **8.** $x - y > 2$ below

Assignment Guide 17.2
Oral: Reg. & Max. 1–8
Written: Reg. 9–19 odd; Quiz,
p. 547
Max. 9–25 odd;
27–30; Quiz,
p. 547

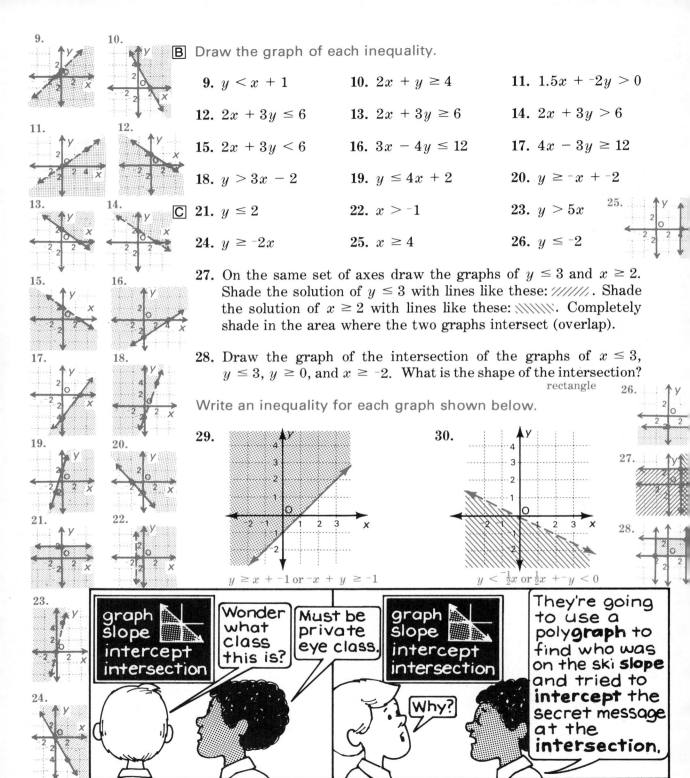

9. 10.

11. 12.

13. 14.

15. 16.

17. 18.

19. 20.

21. 22.

23.

24.

B Draw the graph of each inequality.

9. $y < x + 1$ **10.** $2x + y \geq 4$ **11.** $1.5x + {}^-2y > 0$

12. $2x + 3y \leq 6$ **13.** $2x + 3y \geq 6$ **14.** $2x + 3y > 6$

15. $2x + 3y < 6$ **16.** $3x - 4y \leq 12$ **17.** $4x - 3y \geq 12$

18. $y > 3x - 2$ **19.** $y \leq 4x + 2$ **20.** $y \geq {}^-x + {}^-2$

C **21.** $y \leq 2$ **22.** $x > {}^-1$ **23.** $y > 5x$

24. $y \geq {}^-2x$ **25.** $x \geq 4$ **26.** $y \leq {}^-2$

25.

27. On the same set of axes draw the graphs of $y \leq 3$ and $x \geq 2$. Shade the solution of $y \leq 3$ with lines like these: ///////. Shade the solution of $x \geq 2$ with lines like these: \\\\\\\. Completely shade in the area where the two graphs intersect (overlap).

28. Draw the graph of the intersection of the graphs of $x \leq 3$, $y \leq 3$, $y \geq 0$, and $x \geq {}^-2$. What is the shape of the intersection?

rectangle

26.

Write an inequality for each graph shown below.

29.

30.

27.

$y \geq x + {}^-1$ or ${}^-x + y \geq {}^-1$

$y < \frac{{}^-1}{2}x$ or $\frac{1}{2}x + {}^-y < 0$

28.

546

Tell whether each equation is in standard form or slope-intercept form.

1. $7x + 2 = y$
slope-intercept form

2. $x + 2y = {}^-2$
standard form

3. $y = 2x + 1$
slope-intercept form

Change each equation to slope-intercept form. Give the slope and the y-intercept.

4. $2x + y = 3$
$y = {}^-2x + 3$, $m = {}^-2$, $b = 3$

5. $x + 2y = 3$
$y = {}^-\frac{1}{2}x + \frac{3}{2}$, $m = {}^-\frac{1}{2}$, $b = \frac{3}{2}$

6. $12 = 4x + {}^-3y$
$y = \frac{4}{3}x + {}^-4$, $m = \frac{4}{3}$, $b = {}^-4$

Draw the graph of each inequality.

7. $2x + y < 3$

8. $x + 2y \geq 3$

9. $12 \leq 4x + {}^-3y$

7.

8.

9.

Hitting the Slopes

1. On the same set of axes draw the graphs of $3x + 2y = 6$ and $3x + 2y = 2$.

2. Do you notice anything special about these lines?
Yes, the lines are parallel.

3. What is the slope of each line?
$m = {}^-\frac{3}{2}$

4. Draw the graphs for $y = 3x + 4$ and $6x + {}^-2y = {}^-4$. Find the slope for each line. $m = 3$

Mount Snow Ski Resort

5. If the slopes of two lines are the same, the lines are _____.
parallel

6. Draw the graphs for $2x + y = 3$ and $x + {}^-2y = {}^-2$.

7. Do you notice anything special about these lines?
Yes, the lines are perpendicular.

8. What is the slope for each of these lines? Are the slopes the same? What product do you get if you multiply the slopes?
$m = {}^-2$, $m = \frac{1}{2}$, no, ${}^-1$

9. Draw the graphs for $y = {}^-3x + 1$ and $x - 3y = 3$. Find the slope for each line. $m = {}^-3$, $m = \frac{1}{3}$

10. If the product of the slopes is ${}^-1$, the lines are _____.   perpendicular

1.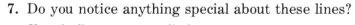

4.

6.

9.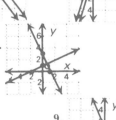

547

17.3 Direct Variation

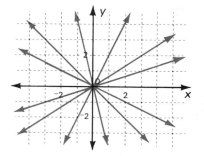

Each of the graphs shown at the right has a y-intercept of 0. Each line is a function—a set of ordered pairs whose first numbers are different.

The equation for each graph is of the form

$y = mx + b$, where $b = 0$ or $y = mx$

Since the slope of each line is constant, this equation is more often written $y = kx$. This function is called a *direct variation.*

 A **direct variation** is a function in which the ratio of two variables is constant.

The constant k is called the **constant of variation.** As either variable, x or y, changes in value, the value of the other variable also changes, so that the ratio between the variables remains the same. The relationship between the variables is stated, "y varies directly with x" or "y is directly proportional to x."

If you know the value of k and the value of one variable, you can find the value of the other variable.

$C = \pi d$ is a direct variation.

Example 1: Complete the table. Use 3.14 for π.

Circumference	diameter	$C = \pi d$
6.28	2	$\longrightarrow 6.28 = 3.14d \longrightarrow d = 2$
12.56	4	$\longrightarrow C = 3.14(4) \longrightarrow C = 12.56$
0	0	$\longrightarrow 0 = 3.14d \longrightarrow d = 0$

Example 2: Find the constant of variation for the graph at the right.

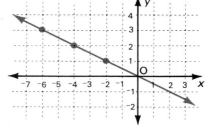

$$y = kx$$

Choose any points on the graph. Substitute the values in the equation and solve for k.

$(^-4, 2)$	$(2,\ ^-1)$	$(^-6, 3)$
$y = kx$	$y = kx$	$y = kx$
$2 = k(^-4)$	$^-1 = k(2)$	$3 = k(^-6)$
$^-\frac{1}{2} = k$	$^-\frac{1}{2} = k$	$^-\frac{1}{2} = k$

The constant of variation is $^-\frac{1}{2}$.

(0, 0) is also a point on the graph. Why is (0, 0) a poor choice for finding the value of k?

Example 3: The distance (d) a spring stretches varies directly with the force (f) applied. If 30 pounds of force stretches a spring 2 inches, how far will the spring be stretched by a 40-pound force?

Make a table.

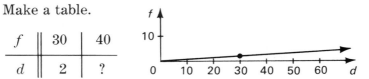

f	30	40
d	2	?

Find the value of k.

$d = kf$

$2 = k(30)$

$\dfrac{1}{15} = k$

$d = \dfrac{1}{15}f$ Write the formula.

$d = \dfrac{1}{15}(40)$ Substitute 40 for f.

$d = 2\dfrac{2}{3}$ Solve for d.

The spring will stretch $2\frac{2}{3}$ inches.

■ Exercises

Assignment Guide 17.3
Oral: Reg. & Max. 1–5
Written: Reg. 7–15 odd
   Max. 7–15 odd;
   16–18

A Complete each sentence.

1. A direct variation is a function in which the ratio of two numbers is ____.   constant

2. The constant k is called the ____.   constant of variation

3. In $y = kx$, if y increases in value, x will (increase, decrease) in value.   increase

4. The perimeter (p) of a square varies directly with the length (s) of a side. The value of k is 4. The equation that expresses this direct variation is ____. $p = 4s$

5. The total cost (c) of carpeting varies directly with the number of square yards (n) purchased. If $c = 200$ and $n = 10$, $k =$ __20__ .

B Each table shows a direct variation. For each table, find k, write the equation for the variation, and complete the table.

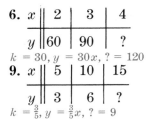

6.
x	2	3	4
y	60	90	?

$k = 30, y = 30x, ? = 120$

7.
x	2	4	?
y	1	2	5

$k = \frac{1}{2}, y = \frac{1}{2}x, ? = 10$

8.
x	10	100	200
y	1	10	?

$k = \frac{1}{10}, y = \frac{1}{10}x, ? = 20$

9.
x	5	10	15
y	3	6	?

$k = \frac{3}{5}, y = \frac{3}{5}x, ? = 9$

10.
x	2	4	5
y	$4n$	$8n$	?

$k = 2n, y = 2nx, ? = 10n$

11.
x	1	3	4	?
y	12	36	?	60

$k = 12, y = 12x,$

	4	5
	48	60

Draw a graph for each direct variation.

12. $p = 4s$ 13. $d = 5t$ 14. $m = \frac{1}{6}e$ 15. $C = 6.28r$

C Solve each problem.

16. The time (t) needed to cook a roast varies directly with the weight (w) of the roast. If a 3-pound roast requires 54 minutes to cook, how long should a 5-pound roast be cooked?   90 minutes

17. The number of bags (b) of cement needed varies directly with the number of cubic yards (n) of concrete to be made. If 25 bags of cement are needed to make 4 cubic yards of concrete, how many bags of cement are needed to make 18 cubic yards of concrete?   112.5 bags

18. The amount (a) of simple interest earned varies directly with the amount saved (s). If $13.75 in interest is earned on $250, find the amount of interest earned on $600. $33.00

12.

13.

14.

15.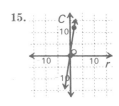

550

Inverse Variation

Pete and Melissa would like to buy a stereo that costs \$360. They made a table to see how long it would take to save enough to buy the stereo. The amount saved per week is represented by r, and the number of weeks by t.

r	10	20	25	30	40	50
t	36	18	14.4	12	9	7.2

Notice that as r increases, t decreases. Furthermore, $r \times t = \$360$. The \$360 is the constant in the equation. This relationship is called an *inverse variation*.

> An **inverse variation** is a function in which the product of two variables is a constant.

The equation for an inverse variation is of the form $xy = k$, where k is the constant of variation.

Example 1: Sketch the graph of $rt = \$360$.

Use the table at the top of the page to locate points.

Notice that the points do not form a straight line. They form a curve.

What happens when $r = \$130$?

When $r = \$720$? When $t = 36$?

When $t = 72$? When $t = 720$?

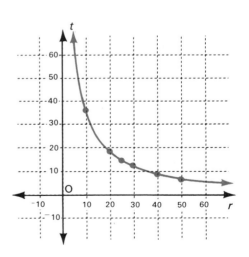

What happens if r or t has a negative value?

Generally, physical amounts can only be positive. Mathematics, however, deals with both positive and negative numbers. If Example 1 were extended to include negative numbers, the table and the graph would look like these.

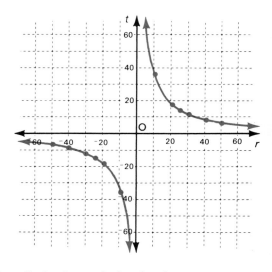

r	-10	-20	-25	-30
t	-36	-18	-14.4	-12

The graph has two sections and is called a hyperbola. As the negative values of r increase, the values of t decrease.

Example 2: The time (t) it takes to travel a certain distance varies inversely with the average rate (r). If it takes 6 hours to travel a certain distance at 50 miles per hour, how long will it take to travel the same distance at 75 miles per hour?

Make a table.

r	50	75
t	6	?

Find the constant of variation.

$$rt = k$$
$$(50)(6) = k$$
$$300 = k$$

$rt = 300$	Write the formula.
$75t = 300$	Substitute 75 for r.
$t = 4$	Solve for t.

It will take 4 hours.

■ Exercises

[A] Which of the following are inverse variations?

1. $ST = 300$
inverse variation

2. $y = 10x$
not an inverse variation

3. $y = \frac{x}{5}$
not an inverse variation

4. $y = \frac{16}{x}$
inverse variation

5.

x	2	4	6
y	1	2	3

not an inverse variation

6.

p	12	18	24
q	6	4	3

inverse variation

7.

I	10	20	40
W	100	50	25

inverse variation

8.

not an inverse variation

9.

inverse variation

10.

inverse variation

17. $xy = 48, ? = 24$

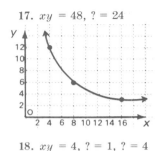

[B] Given the tables below, find each constant of variation k, and complete each table. Each table shows an inverse variation.

11.

x	9	?
y	2	3

$k = 18, ? = 6$

12.

t	10	?
r	50	25

$k = 500, ? = 20$

13.

x	$^-6$	9
y	$^-3$	?

$k = 18, ? = 2$

14.

m	10	15
n	4.5	?

$k = 45, ? = 3$

15.

t	2.5	20
r	100	?

$k = 250, ? = 12.5$

16.

x	$^-18$	12
y	$^-18$	?

$k = 324, ? = 27$

18. $xy = 4, ? = 1, ? = 4$

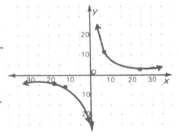

19. $xy = 72,$

x	$^-2$	24	72	144
y	$^-36$	3	1	0.5

Write the inverse variation for each table. Complete each table and sketch the graph of the variation. $(x > 0, y > 0)$

17.

x	16	8	4	2
y	3	6	12	?

18.

x	16	8	4	2	1
y	0.25	0.5	?	2	?

[C] **19.**

x	$^-36$	$^-18$	$^-12$	$^-2$	2	6	24	72	144
y	$^-2$	$^-4$	$^-6$	?	36	12	?	?	?

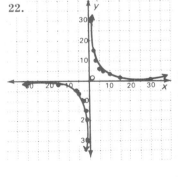

Solve each problem.

The current (I) in an electrical circuit is inversely proportional to the resistance of the circuit (P). Suppose the current is 12 amperes when the resistance is 10 ohms.

22.

20. Find the current when the resistance is 20 ohms.
60 amperes

21. Find the resistance when the current is 4 amperes.
30 ohms

22. Given the equation $xy = 30$, make a table and sketch the graph of the inverse variation. Use both positive and negative values for x and y.

(sample table)

x	$^-30$	$^-15$	$^-5$	1	3	30
y	$^-1$	$^-2$	$^-6$	30	10	1

Systems of Equations

Rolanda asked Chuck if he could guess the number of spots showing on the hidden dice. She gave him two clues: "The total number of spots showing is 7" and "Twice the number of spots on the first die minus the number of spots on the second die is 8."

Chuck said he could use algebra to solve the puzzle. He let x represent the number of spots showing on the first die and y represent the number of spots showing on the second die. He then wrote the following two equations:

$$x + y = 7 \text{ and } 2x - y = 8$$

To find an answer to the puzzle, find an ordered pair for which both equations are true.

Example 1: Find an answer to the dice puzzle.

Draw the graphs of the equations on the same set of axes.

$x + y = 7$

x	1	3	6
y	6	4	1

Label the graph for this equation "line m."

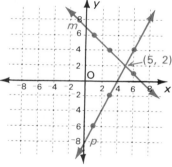

$2x - y = 8$

x	1	3	6
y	-6	-2	4

Label the graph for this equation "line p."

Lines m and p appear to intersect at (5, 2). Check to see if both equations are true for this ordered pair.

$x + y = 7$ $2x - y = 8$

$5 + 2 = 7$ $2(5) - 2 = 8$

     $7 = 7 ✓$ $10 - 2 = 8$

                            $8 = 8 ✓$

The answer is 5 spots and 2 spots.

A pair of equations like $x + y = 7$ and $2x - y = 8$ is called a **system of equations.**

> A solution of a system of equations is an ordered pair (*x, y*) for which both equations are true.

The graphing method for solving a system of equations is useful, but not always exact. For that reason, it is necessary to check a solution. To check, substitute the ordered pair in each equation.

Example 2: Find the solution that satisfies both of these equations:
$x - y = 2$ and $2x + y = 1$

Make a table for each equation.

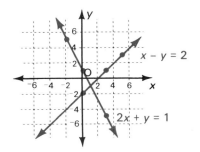

$x - y = 2$

x	0	3	5
y	-2	1	3

$2x + y = 1$

x	0	3	-2
y	1	-5	5

Draw the graphs and locate the point of intersection. Check that each equation is true for $(1, {}^-1)$.

$$x - y = 2 \qquad\qquad 2x + y = 1$$
$$1 - ({}^-1) = 2 \qquad\qquad 2(1) + ({}^-1) = 1$$
$$1 + 1 = 2 \qquad\qquad 2 + ({}^-1) = 1$$
$$2 = 2 \checkmark \qquad\qquad 1 = 1 \checkmark$$

A system of equations that has one solution (the graphs intersect at one point) is **consistent.**

Example 3: Study the graphs of each system of equations.

Sometimes there are no solutions.

$$x + y = 6$$
$$x + y = 2$$

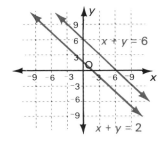

Other times there are many solutions.

$$x + y = 6$$
$$2x + 2y = 12$$

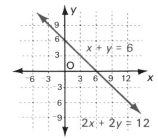

Since the lines are parallel, no ordered pair is the solution. This system is **inconsistent.**

Since the equations have the same graph, there are many solutions. This system is **dependent** and consistent.

555

■ Exercises

Assignment Guide 17.5
Oral: Reg. & Max. 1–3
Written: Reg. 4–10; 11–15 odd
Max. 3–15 odd; 17–26

$\boxed{A}$ Pick the system that could be used to solve each problem.

1. The sum of two numbers is 8. Three times the first number minus twice the second number is 9. Find the numbers. ᵇ·

a. $x - y = 8$
$3x - 2y = 9$

b. $x + y = 8$
$3x - 2y = 9$

c. $xy = 8$
$3x + 2y = 9$

2. April has $0.55 in nickels and dimes. There are 8 coins. How many dimes does she have? (n = nickels, d = dimes) ᶜ·

a. $0.05n + 0.10d = 0.55$
$n - d = 8$

b. $0.05n - 0.10d = 0.55$
$n + d = 8$

c. $0.05n + 0.10d = 0.55$
$n + d = 8$

d. $0.05d - 0.10n = 0.55$
$n - d = 8$

3. The difference between Jo's house number and Ed's house number is 12. The sum of their house numbers is 86. Find the house numbers. ᵃ·

a. $x - y = 12$
$x + y = 86$

b. $x + y = 12$
$x - y = 86$

c. $x - y = 12$
$x - y = 86$

$\boxed{B}$ Determine whether the given ordered pair is a solution of the system of equations.

4. $(3, ^-2)$ $2x - y = 2$ no
$x + y = 1$

5. $(^-1, 0)$ $x - y = ^-1$ yes
$3x + 2y = ^-3$

6. $(1, ^-4)$ $x + 2y = ^-7$ yes
$2x - y = 6$

7. $(^-5, ^-3)$ $^-x + y = 2$ yes
$x - 3y = 4$

Tell whether each of the following systems is consistent, inconsistent, or dependent.

8. $3x - y = ^-1$
$6x - 2y = 4$
inconsistent

9. $2x + y = 3$
$4x + 2y = 6$
dependent and consistent

10. $x + 2y = 5$
$x + 3y = 6$
consistent

Solve each system by graphing.

11. $x + y = 10$ (8, 2)
$x - y = 6$

12. $^-x + y = 3$ ($^-6, ^-3$)
$x - 2y = 0$

13. $2x + y = 5$ (2, 1)
$3x - y = 5$

14. $x + 3y = 4$ (1, 1)
$x - 3y = ^-2$

15. $3x - y = 7$ (3, 2)
$x + y = 5$

16. $3x - y = 4$ (2, 2)
$2x - y = 2$

556

Here is an algebraic method, called the substitution method, for solving a system of equations.

Solve this system by substitution: $3x - 4y = 8$ and $2x - 4y = 4$.

$2x - 4y = 4$	Solve either equation for one
$2x = 4y + 4$	variable in terms of the other.
$x = 2y + 2$	Solve the second equation for *x*.
$3x - 4y = 8$	Substitute $2y + 2$ for *x*
$3(2y + 2) - 4y = 8$	in the first equation.
$6y + 6 - 4y = 8$	
$2y = 2$	Solve for *y*.
$y = 1$	
$3x - 4(1) = 8$	Substitute *y* in either
$3x = 12$	equation to find *x*.
$x = 4$	

$$
\begin{array}{ll}
Check: \quad 3x - 4y = 8 & \quad 2x - 4y = 4 \\
\quad\quad 3(4) - 4(1) = 8 & \quad 2(4) - 4(1) = 4 \\
\quad\quad 12 - 4 = 8 & \quad 8 - 4 = 4 \\
\quad\quad 8 = 8 \ \checkmark & \quad 4 = 4 \ \checkmark
\end{array}
$$

Solve each system by substitution.

17. $x - 2y = 5$
$2x - y = 10$
(5, 0)

18. $4x + {}^-2y = 8$
${}^-2x + 5y = 20$
(5, 6)

19. $2x - y = 30$
$6x + {}^-3y = 90$
many solutions, dependent system

Solve the following exercises on page 556.

20. Exercise 1
(5, 3)

21. Exercise 2
3 dimes

22. Exercise 3
Jo's—49, Ed's—37

23. Change both equations in Exercise 8 to slope-intercept form. What is true about the slopes of the lines? They are the same.

24. Change both equations in Exercise 9 to slope-intercept form. What is true about the slopes and the *y*-intercepts? They are the same.

25. Rosa was thinking of two numbers. The sum of the numbers was 50. Twice the first number plus the second number was 90. What were the numbers? 40 and 10

26. Bill and Gloria have 95 cents between them. Bill has 7 cents more than Gloria. How much money does each one have? Bill has 51¢ and Gloria has 44¢.

MATH AND SCIENCE

Many equations and formulas are used by scientists. Since it often is not safe or convenient to perform experiments under varying conditions, experiments are often carried out at room temperature and pressure. Results are then adjusted mathematically to different conditions.

Pfizer Inc.

There is a law that says that for gas confined in a container,

$PV = k$, where P is pressure, V is volume, and k is a constant

1. Is $PV = k$ an example of a direct variation or an inverse variation? inverse variation

2. As the volume increases, what happens to the pressure? It decreases.

3. Find the constant k for a gas that has a volume of 242 mL at a pressure of 657 mm Hg. 158 994

A given sample of gas has a pressure of P_1 and a volume of V_1. If the pressure exerted upon the gas sample is changed to P_2, the volume becomes V_2. According to Boyle's Law,

$$P_1 V_1 = k$$
$$\text{and } P_2 V_2 = k \text{ (the same constant);}$$
$$\text{therefore, } P_1 V_1 = P_2 V_2$$

4. A gas has a volume of 500 mL when a pressure of 760 mm Hg is exerted upon it. What is the volume if the pressure is reduced to 730 mm Hg? (Round to the nearest whole number.) 521 mL

5. The pressure on 952 mL of gas is changed from 561 mm Hg to the standard pressure (760 mm Hg). What is the new volume of the gas? (Round to the nearest whole number.) 703 mL

Suggested Class Time

Course	Min.	Reg.	Max.
Days	0	1	1

Assignment Guide Rev.
Oral:
Reg. Terms & Symbols 1–6
Max. Terms & Symbols 1–6

Terms and Symbols Review

Match each of the following.

1. standard form of an equation h

2. slope-intercept form of an equation g

3. is less than a

4. is greater than or equal to c

5. inverse variation f

6. direct variation e

a. $<$ **b.** $>$

c. $\geq$ **d.** $\leq$

e. $y = kx$

f. $xy = k$

g. $y = mx + b$

h. $ax + by = c$

Assignment Guide Rev.
Written:
Reg. 1–37 odd
Max. 1–37 odd

Chapter 17 Review

Draw the graph of each equation. 17.1

1. $3x + y = 2$ **2.** $y = x - 2$ **3.** $7 = 2y + x$

4. $x = y + 3$ **5.** $2x + 3y = 6$ **6.** $^-2x + 4 = y$

Change each equation to slope-intercept form. Then name the slope and the y-intercept.

7. $6x + 3y = 10$ **8.** $2y - 4x = 8$ **9.** $7x - y = {}^-3$
$y = -2x + 3\frac{1}{3}, \ m = -2, \ b = 3\frac{1}{3}$ $y = 2x + 4, \ m = 2, \ b = 4$ $y = 7x + 3, \ m = 7, \ b = 3$

10. $x - 2y = 4$ **11.** $3y + 4x = 12$ **12.** $^-2x + {}^-3y = 6$
$y = \frac{1}{2}x + {}^-2, \ m = \frac{1}{2}, \ b = -2$ $y = \frac{-4}{3}x + 4, \ m = \frac{-4}{3}, \ b = 4$ $y = \frac{-2}{3}x + {}^-2, \ m = \frac{-2}{3}, \ b = -2$

Draw the graph of each inequality. 17.2

13. $y > x + 1$ **14.** $2x + y < 3$ **15.** $3x + 2y \geq 6$

16. $8 \leq 2x - y$ **17.** $4x > 2y + 2$ **18.** $y \leq {}^-2x - 3$

Each table shows a direct variation. For each table, find k, write the equation for the variation, and complete the table.

19.

x	4	6	12
y	2	3	?

$k = \frac{1}{2}$, $y = \frac{1}{2}x$, ? = 6

20.

x	$^-2$	4	8
y	$^-8$	16	?

$k = 4$, $y = 4x$, ? = 32

21.

x	$^-6$	2	?
y	30	$^-10$	$^-25$

$k = ^-5$, $y = ^-5x$, ? = 5

Draw a graph for each direct variation.

22. $d = 6t$ **23.** $v = \frac{2}{3}x$ **24.** $a = ^-0.5m$

22.

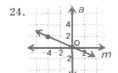

Each table shows an inverse variation. For each table, find k, write the equation for the variation, and complete the table.

25.

x	6	8	?
y	4	3	2

$k = 24$, $xy = 24$, ? = 12

26.

x	8	18	36
y	72	32	?

$k = 576$, $xy = 576$, ? = 16

27.

x	$^-3$	6	?
y	12	$^-6$	$^-18$

$k = ^-36$, $xy = ^-36$, ? = 2

23.

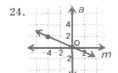

Use each equation to complete the table. Then sketch the graph. ($x > 0$, $y > 0$)

24.

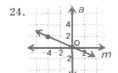

28. $xy = 5$

x	5	1	0.25
y	1	5	20

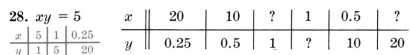

x	20	10	?	1	0.5	?
y	0.25	0.5	1	?	10	20

29. $xy = 40$

x	8	20	80
y	5	2	0.5

x	0.5	1	4	8	10	?	40	80
y	80	40	10	?	4	2	1	?

28.

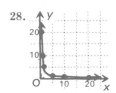

Determine whether the given ordered pair is a solution of the system of equations.

30. $(2, 0)$
$3x - y = 6$
$x + 6y = 2$
yes

31. $(^-5, 2)$
$3x + y = ^-12$
$^-2x + y = 12$
no

29.

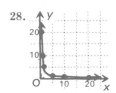

Tell whether each of the following systems is consistent, inconsistent, or dependent.

32. $3x + y = 7$
$x + 3y = 7$
consistent

33. $2x - 5y = 6$
$6x - 15y = 18$
dependent and consistent

34. $4x + 2y = 9$
$2x + y = ^-9$
inconsistent

Solve each system by graphing.

35. $x + y = 3$
$x - y = 5$
$(4, ^-1)$

36. $3x - y = ^-2$
$x + 2y = 4$
$(0, 2)$

37. $2x - 3y = 4$
$4x - y = ^-2$
$(^-1, ^-2)$

1.   2.   3.

Chapter 17 Test

Draw the graph of each equation or inequality.

4. 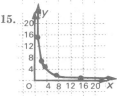 5.

1. $2x + y = 3$ **2.** $x - 3y = {}^-1$ **3.** $y = 2x - 1$

4. $6x + 3y < 0$ **5.** $y \geq 4$ **6.** ${}^-3x + 2y \leq {}^-6$

6. 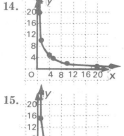 7.

7. $y = 4x$ **8.** $d = \frac{1}{5}x$ **9.** $r = {}^-3x$

Change each equation to slope-intercept form. Then name the slope and the *y*-intercept.

8.  9.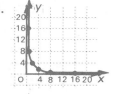

10. $y = \frac{-4}{3}x + 2,\ m = \frac{-4}{3},\ b = 2$ 11. $y = \frac{3}{5}x - 2,\ m = \frac{3}{5},\ b = {}^-2$

10. $4x + 3y = 6$ **11.** $3x - 5y = 10$ **12.** $6x + y = 2$

12. $y = {}^-6x + 2,\ m = {}^-6,\ b = 2$

13.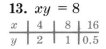

Use each equation to complete the table. Then sketch the graph. ($x > 0,\ y > 0$)

13. $xy = 8$

x	4	8	16
y	2	1	0.5

x	0.5	1	2	4	?	16
y	16	8	4	?	1	?

14.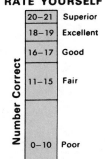

14. $xy = 20$

x	4	5	20
y	5	4	1

x	1	2	?	5	10	?
y	20	10	5	?	2	1

15.

15. $xy = 15$

x	5	7.5	15
y	3	2	1

x	1	2	3	5	?	?
y	15	7.5	5	?	2	1

Tell whether each of the following systems is consistent, inconsistent, or dependent.

16. $x + 3y = 4$
   $3x + 9y = 12$
dependent and consistent

17. $2x + 4y = 5$
   $4x + 2y = 5$
consistent

18. $x + y = 3$
   $2x + 2y = 3$
inconsistent

RATE YOURSELF

Number Correct	
20–21	Superior
18–19	Excellent
16–17	Good
11–15	Fair
0–10	Poor

Solve each system by graphing.

19. $x + y = 3$
   $x - 2y = 0$
(2, 1)

20. $2x + y = 8$
   $2x - y = 4$
(3, 2)

21. ${}^-x + y = 4$
   $x + 3y = 0$
(${}^-3$, 1)

Terms and Symbols Review: Chapters 16–17

Suggested Class Time

Course	Min.	Reg.	Max.
Days	0	1	1

Ch. 16 Which term or symbol in parentheses is the best choice?

Assignment Guide Rev.
Oral:
Reg. Terms & Symbols 1–16
Max. Terms & Symbols 1–16

1. The symbol for line XY is ($\overline{XY}$, $\overrightarrow{XY}$, $\overleftrightarrow{XY}$). $\overleftrightarrow{XY}$

2. The symbol for line segment RS is ($\overline{RS}$, $\overrightarrow{RS}$, $\overleftrightarrow{RS}$). $\overline{RS}$

3. The symbol for ray AB is ($\overline{AB}$, $\overrightarrow{AB}$, $\overleftrightarrow{AB}$). $\overrightarrow{AB}$

4. (*Intersecting, Parallel, Perpendicular*) lines never meet. Parallel

5. A(n) (*right, acute, obtuse*) angle is smaller than a right angle. acute

6. A triangle with three sides of different lengths is (*equilateral, scalene, isosceles*). scalene

7. A polygon with five sides is a (*hexagon, trapezoid, pentagon*). pentagon

8. A (*trapezoid, parallelogram, rhombus*) has four congruent sides. rhombus

9. A (*square, trapezoid, rhombus*) is a rectangle with four congruent sides. square

10. $V = lwh$ is the formula for the (*area, surface area, volume*) of a rectangular prism. volume

Ch. 17 11. The equation $ax + by = c$ is in (*standard form, slope-intercept form*). standard form

12. The symbol that means "is less than or equal to" is ($\leq$, $<$, $\geq$). $\leq$

13. In a direct variation, as x increases, y (*increases, decreases*). increases

14. The graph of an inverse variation is a (*straight line, curve*). curve

15. In the equation $y = 5x$, (y, 5, x) is the constant of variation. 5

16. If the graphs of a system of equations are parallel, the system is (*consistent, inconsistent, dependent*). inconsistent

Use the figure at the right for Exercises 1–6.

1. The length of $\overline{AB}$ is __3__ cm.

2. The length of $\overline{BC}$ is __4__ cm.

3. The length of $\overline{AC}$ is __5__ cm.

4. The perimeter of triangle ABC is __12 cm__.

5. $\overline{AB}$ and $\overline{BC}$ are (*perpendicular*, *parallel*).

6. The area of triangle ABC is __6 cm²__.

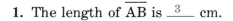
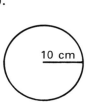

7. Find the circumference of the circle.
   62.8 cm

8. Find the area of the circle. 314 cm²

Find the surface area of each figure.

9.
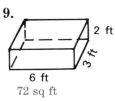
6 ft
2 ft
3 ft
72 sq ft

10.
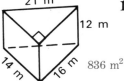
21 m
12 m
14 m
16 m
836 m²

11.
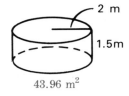
2 m
1.5m
43.96 m²

Find the volume of the figure in

12. Exercise 9.
   36 cu ft

13. Exercise 10.
   1344 m³

14. Exercise 11.
   18.84 m³

Change each equation to slope-intercept form. Then give the slope and the *y*-intercept.

15. $2x + y = {}^-3$ 16. $6x + {}^-2y = 15$ 17. $3y - 2x = 12$

15. $y = -2x - 3$, $m = -2$, $b = {}^-3$ 16. $y = 3x - 7\frac{1}{2}$, $m = 3$, $b = {}^-7\frac{1}{2}$

Graph each equation or inequality.

17. $y = \frac{2}{3}x + 4$, $m = \frac{2}{3}$, $b = 4$

18. $2x + y = {}^-3$ 19. $y = x + 2$ 20. $3x - y \leq 3$

21. $y > x - 1$ 22. $y = 2x$ 23. $xy = 16 \, (x > 0, y > 0)$

Solve each system by graphing.

24. $x - y = 4$ and $2x + y = 2$ 25. $2x + 3y = 6$ and $3x + 2y = {}^-1$
   (2, ${}^-$2)   (${}^-$3, 4)

18.
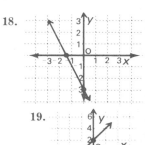

19.
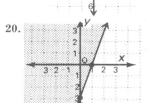

20.
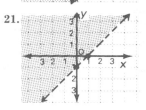

21.
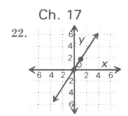

22.
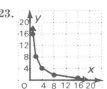

23.

INDEX

A

Absolute value, 178, 355
Adding
decimals, 150–152, 359–361
fractions, 108–110, 126–132, 366–367
integers, 176–180
mixed numbers, 127–129, 133–134, 368–369
polynomials, 468–469
probabilities, 501–503
rational numbers, 359–361, 366–369
zero, 73
Addition
inverse operation of, 35
on number line, 176–177
properties of, 66, 69, 73, 178
Angles
acute, 519
corresponding, 318
obtuse, 519
right, 431, 519
Area, 53–55, 164–166, 526–527
Associative properties, 69–72
Averages, 490, 494
Axes, 243

B

Bar graphs, 484–485
Base of a power, 88
Binomials, 454
multiplying, 462–467

C

Capacity
metric units of, 4, 533
U.S. units of, 50
Celsius degree, 4, 52
Central tendency
measures of, 494
Checking solutions
of equations, 23, 554–555

of inequalities, 42–43
of problems, 190
Circle, 138, 152, 164–165, 523, 526
Circumference, 523
Commutative properties, 65–68
Composite number, 85
Constant, 459
Coordinates, 244
Corresponding angles, 318–321
Corresponding sides, 318–321
proportional, 322–325
Cross products, 283
Cubic units, 53–55
Cylinder, 528–529, 531

D

Decimals
adding, 150–152, 359–361
dividing, 157–162, 385–387
fractions or mixed numbers as, 145–146
multiplying, 153–155, 385–387
opposites of, 354
per cents as, 290
reading and writing, 145–146
rounding, 147–149
subtracting, 150–152, 359–361
Denominator, 107
least common, 130
Direct variation, 548–549
Distributive property, 76–79
Dividing
decimals, 157–162, 385–387
fractions, 123–125, 390–391
integers, 205–207
mixed numbers, 123–125, 392–393
number by itself, 74
by one, 107
polynomials, 473–474
rational numbers, 385–387, 390–393
square roots, 426
into zero, 74
not by zero, 74, 107, 207, 396

Divisibility, 80–84
Division
    inverse operation of, 35

E

Equations, 14–22
    with addition or subtraction, 37–39, 183–187, 363–364, 370–372
    on balance beam, 23–25
    checking solutions of, 23, 554–555
    graphing, 541–542, 548–557
    with multiplication or division, 40–41, 208–213, 388–389, 397–399
    proportions as, 283–285
    slope-intercept form, 542
    solving by substitution, 557
    solving problems with, 190–192, 373–376, 449–453
    square roots and, 428–430
    standard form, 541
    systems of, 554–555
    with two operations, 47–49, 220–221, 401–403, 449–451
Estimating
    per cents, 302–303
    products of decimals, 153–154
    quotients of decimals, 162
    sums and differences of decimals, 150–151
    whole-number computations, 148–149
Exponents, 88–90, 408–410
Extremes of a proportion, 283

F

Factor(s), 80
    divisibility and, 80–84
    greatest common, 91–92
    prime, 85–90
Fahrenheit degree, 50, 52
Formulas, 26–27, 222–224, 404–407, 523, 526, 528–529, 531

Fractions, 107–110
    adding, 108–110, 126–132, 366–367
    comparing, 357–358
    decimals as, 145–146, 353
    dividing, 123–125, 390–391
    equivalent, 108
    integers as, 353
    like, 126, 130
    in lowest terms, 113–115
    in measurement, 523
    mixed numbers as, 116–118, 353
    multiplying, 111–112, 390–391
    negative, 353
    opposites of, 354
    per cents as, 290
    ratios as, 275
    reciprocals of, 395–396
    simplifying, 113–115
    subtracting, 126–132, 366–367
    unlike, 130
    whole numbers as, 107
Frequency tables, 481–483
Functions, 250–257
    graphing, 251–253, 541–542, 548–552

G

Geometry, 519–539
    plane figures, 519–527
    three-dimensional figures, 528–533
Graphing
    functions, 251–253
    ordered pairs, 240–245
    solutions of open sentences, 42–46, 188–189, 214–219
Graphs
    bar, 484–485
    histograms, 484–485
    line, 246–249
    misleading, 269
    used to enlarge and reduce, 258–261
    used to slide, 262–264

Greatest common factor (GCF), 91–92

H

Histograms, 484–485
Hyperbola, 552
Hypotenuse, 431

I

Identity properties, 73
Indirect measurement, 326–330
Inequalities, 14–22, 544–545
  with addition or subtraction, 42–46, 188–189
  checking solutions of, 42–43
  graphing solutions of, 544–545
  with multiplication or division, 42–46, 214–219
  with two operations, 49
Integers, 173–175
  absolute values of, 178
  adding, 176–180
  dividing, 205–207
  multiplying, 201–204
  reciprocals of, 395–396
  subtracting, 181–182
Inverse operations, 35–36
Inverse property of addition, 178
Inverse variation, 551–552

L

Least common denominator, 130
Least common multiple (LCM), 93–95
Length
  metric units of, 3, 523
  U.S. units of, 50, 523
Line graphs, 246–249
Lowest terms, 113, 117

M

Maps, 336–338
Mean, 490–494
Means of a proportion, 283
Measurement
  metric system of, 3–5, 523, 533
  U.S. system of, 50–52, 523
Median, 487–489, 494

Metric units, 3–5, 53–55
  changing, 154–155, 158–159, 164–166
Mixed numbers
  adding, 127–129, 133–134, 368–369
  decimals as, 145–146
  dividing, 123–125, 392–393
  fractions as, 116–118
  multiplying, 119–121, 135, 392–393
  per cents as, 290
  reciprocals of, 395–396
  subtracting, 127–129, 133–134, 368–369
Mode, 484, 494
Monomials, 454
  dividing by, 473–474
  multiplying, 459–463
Multiplication
  inverse operation of, 35
  properties of, 66, 69–70, 73
Multiplying
  decimals, 153–155, 385–387
  fractions, 111–112, 390–391
  integers, 201–204
  mixed numbers, 119–121, 135, 392–393
  by one, 73
  polynomials, 459–463, 465–467
  probabilities, 504–506
  rational numbers, 385–387, 390–393
  square roots, 423
  by zero, 74, 202

N

Number line
  addition on, 176–177
  opposites on, 173, 354
  solutions on, 42–46, 188–189, 214–219
Numerator, 107

O

One
  as exponent, 88–89
  properties of, 73–75, 107

Manual and Tests
PREPARING TO USE ALGEBRA

Fourth Edition

Albert P. Shulte

Director, Mathematics Education
Oakland Schools
Pontiac, Michigan

Robert E. Peterson

Chairman, Mathematics Department
Fraser High School
Fraser, Michigan

Manual

LAIDLAW BROTHERS • PUBLISHERS
A Division of Doubleday & Company, Inc.
RIVER FOREST, ILLINOIS

Sacramento, California   Chamblee, Georgia   Dallas, Texas   Toronto, Canada

Contents

Manual

* Permission is given to teachers of PREPARING TO USE ALGEBRA to reproduce these performance objectives and tests entirely or in part. This includes permission to make photocopies and to develop duplicating masters for classroom use.

Introduction to Teacher's Edition

The teacher's edition of PREPARING TO USE ALGEBRA contains an annotated student's text and a bound-in teacher's manual with tests.

Annotated Student's Text. The full-size student's pages are over-printed with the following teacher's information:

- **Suggested Class Times** for each section and for each review and self-test give time allotments for three course levels—minimum, regular, and maximum. A summary of these class times appears on page T6.

- **Assignment Guides** are given for each exercise set, as well as for each review and self-test. This information facilitates adapting daily exercise assignments to the three course levels.

- **Answers** to exercises are also overprinted on the student's pages.

Manual and Tests. Special teacher's pages are bound with the annotated student's text. These pages include the following:

- **Overview of Student's Text** is a brief summary of the organization and special features of the text.

- **Notes to the Teacher** provide an overview of each chapter and teaching suggestions regarding each section.

- **Performance Objectives** for the entire text are given in a separate list that may be reproduced for classroom use.

- **Tests** include chapter pretests and posttests, as well as cumulative tests. See page T37 for an overview of the tests. Like the performance objectives, the tests may be reproduced for classroom use.

Manual

Overview of Student's Text

PREPARING TO USE ALGEBRA is a prealgebra text designed to get students ready for the successful study of algebra. Practical content also makes this a very effective text for nonalgebra students who need to develop more than minimum competencies in mathematics. The teacher will find the following features particularly useful.

Practical content is emphasized throughout the text. There are three main content areas:

- **Computational skills** with fractions, mixed numbers, decimals, and per cents are carefully developed to ensure that students have the background necessary for success in algebra and for daily living. See Chapters 3, 4, 5, 9, 11, and 12.

- **Introductory concepts of algebra** are gradually developed and are used to reinforce the work with computational skills. This material includes working with variables, simplifying and evaluating expressions, solving equations, graphing, using formulas, and operating with positive and negative numbers. See Chapters 1, 2, 3, 6, 7, 8, 11, 12, 13, 14, and 17.

- **Problem solving and applications** are interwoven with all other topics in the text to help teach and to motivate. Special attention is given to this content area in Sections 1.4, 2.9, 4.10, 5.7, 6.8, 7.9, 8.6, 9.4, 9.8, 9.10, 10.4–10.7, 11.8, 12.8, 13.7, 13.8, 14.1 and 14.2.

Concise, readable explanations in every section employ step-by-step examples that students can readily follow.

Three course levels—minimum, regular, and maximum—are built into the flexible textbook design. A summary of suggested class times for the three levels appears on page T6. Teacher's annotations on the student's pages give section-by-section class times as well as daily exercise assignment guides for all three course levels.

Abundant exercises in each section are graded as follows:

- **"A" exercises** are for oral classwork (though some or all of them may be assigned as written work for slower classes).

- **"B" exercises** are for individual written practice. Whenever possible, the odd- and even-numbered "B" exercises are equivalent in content and difficulty, with the "odds" providing the regular practice and the "evens" remaining as backup exercises.

- **"C" exercises** are optional for enrichment and student discovery.

Frequent review material is organized as follows:

- **Getting Ready.** Each chapter begins with a "Getting Ready" page. The exercises on this page review material that will be used or extended in the chapter. Reference numbers direct students to earlier sections for any additional review that may be needed.

- **Quick Quiz.** These self-quizzes cover a few sections at a time, making possible the early detection of trouble spots.

- **Chapter Review.** The review exercises (which include a review of terms and symbols) are grouped by sections for easy omission of optional material. Reference numbers key the exercises to the respective sections.

- **Chapter Test.** In these self-tests the items are not grouped by sections in order to approximate a realistic test situation. Optional topics are restricted to the last few test items.

- **Cumulative Review.** Comprehensive reviews appear after Chapters 3, 7, 10, 15, and 17. Each contains a review of terms and symbols.

Optional special features in each chapter provide an occasional change of pace. This material falls into the following categories (see page viii for a complete list):

- **Career Corner.** These special topics relate mathematics to career information and to on-the-job applications.

- **Consumer Corner.** These special topics relate mathematics to consumer information and to everyday applications.

- **Activities.** Special pages involve students in experiments, games, and other "hands on" activities that explore new topics or reinforce earlier work.

- **Other Special Topics.** A variety of brief optional features stimulates student interest.

Homework Handbook is a unique end-of-book aid that provides model solutions and answers to selected exercises. Answers are given for the *odd-numbered items* in the "A" and "B" exercises and in the Chapter Reviews, as well as for *all items* in each Quick Quiz and Chapter Test. A model solution is given for each major exercise type in the text. The Homework Handbook will be especially helpful when the student has had to miss some class time or when the teacher has had to shorten a class session for some unscheduled activity. (The Homework Handbook appears in the student's text only since the teacher's edition already contains a complete set of answers.)

Summary of Suggested Class Times*

Chapter or Cumulative Review	Time Allotments in Days for			Possible Omissions
	Minimum Course	Regular Course	Maximum Course	These sections may be omitted from the course(s) indicated in parentheses.
Ch. 1	11	11	10	
Ch. 2	13	11	10	
Ch. 3	13	12	11	
Cum. Rev. 1–3	2	1	1	
Ch. 4	13	11	11	4.10 (min.)
Ch. 5	9	8	8	
Ch. 6	9	10	9	6.7 (min.)
Ch. 7‡	7	11	10	7.6–7.9 (min.)
Cum. Rev. 1–7	3	2	2	
	80	**77**	**72**	◀ **1st Sem. Totals†**
Ch. 8	8	7	9	8.7–8.8 (min. & reg.)
Ch. 9	14	11	11	9.9 (min.), 9.10 (min. & reg.)
Ch. 10	10	8	8	
Cum. Rev. 8–10	2	1	1	
Ch. 11	14	10	9	
Ch. 12	10	11	10	12.7–12.9 (min.)
Ch. 13	11	8	9	13.8 (min. & reg.)
Ch. 14	—	11	11	Ch. 14 (min.), 14.10 (reg.)
Ch. 15	—	10	9	Ch. 15 (min.)
Cum. Rev. 8–15	3	2	2	
Ch. 16	—	7	6	Ch. 16 (min.)
Ch. 17	—	7	6	Ch. 17 (min.)
Cum. Rev. 16–17	—	1	1	
	72	**94**	**92**	◀ **2nd Sem. Totals†**

* See annotations on student's pages for section-by-section suggestions.
† Some free time has been allowed for testing and flexibility.
‡ For the minimum course, the teacher may prefer to shift Chapter 7 to the second semester and omit parts of Chapter 13.

Notes to the Teacher

Overview: The first section introduces metric units so that measurements can be used in problem situations as early as possible (for example, see Exercises 33–40 on page 11 and Exercises 26–31 on page 15). The rest of the chapter is concerned with important basic concepts about mathematical phrases and sentences. Here, the groundwork is laid for evaluating phrases, solving open sentences, and using formulas. All of these skills will be reviewed and extended in later chapters.

The content of this chapter will be new to many students, and it represents a welcome change of pace from arithmetic topics of earlier courses.

1.1 This section introduces only the most commonly used metric units. Conversions and computations with these metric measurements will be developed later.

Parts of the body can be used to help students remember the sizes of a *meter*, a *centimeter*, and a *millimeter*. A meter is approximately half of an adult arm span, a centimeter about the width of the smallest finger, and a millimeter about the thickness of a front tooth.

The *gram* and the *kilogram* should be related to weights of such objects as a paper clip and a pair of gym shoes. The *liter* is a little more than a quart (the equivalency of 1 L to a volume of 1000 cm^3 is developed in the C exercises of Section 2.8). The *Celsius temperatures* that will mean the most to the students are 0°C—temperature at which water freezes; 37°C—normal body temperature; and 100°C—temperature at which water boils.

1.2 To demonstrate the need for the rule for order of operations, have the students evaluate the phrase

$$3 + 4 \times 7 - 2$$

and share their answers. Point out that a phrase cannot have more than one value. There is a need for some standard of evaluation—the rule for order of operations.

Proficiency needs to be developed in the application of the rule for order of operations to phrases that do not contain grouping symbols as well as to those that do. Both kinds of phrases will occur later in open sentences.

1.3 Emphasize the three ways to indicate multiplication (the raised dot as a symbol for multiplication is introduced in Chapter 14). Example 1 affords students a chance to discover the need for ( ) when $12h$ is changed to 12(2).

To emphasize that a variable is a place-holder, demonstrate the following manipulative aid:

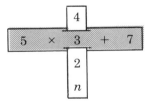

This aid can also be constructed to demonstrate the same variable used in two places and two different variables:

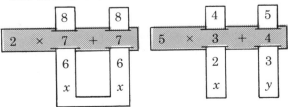

You might point out that in Exercises 17, 18, and 25–27 when the same variable occurs more than once in a phrase, it represents the same number; when different variables occur (as in the C exercises), they may represent the same or different numbers.

1.4 This section is the introduction to solving verbal problems. Concentrate on developing the vocabulary for $+$, $-$, $\times$, and $\div$. This vocabulary will increase as future sections are encountered.

Another point of importance here is order. The phrases that seem to confuse students most in this sense are *subtracted from, more than,* and *less than.* A good activity for helping with this difficulty is to have the students work backward. Have the students make all appropriate translations for simple mathematical phrases such as $5 + x$ and $x - 9$ using the vocabulary on page 12.

1.5 Point out that inequalities may be interpreted two ways. It should be understood, for example, that $4 < x$ means both "four is less than x" and "x is greater than four." This will be helpful when solving inequalities later.

1.6 For some students you may want to point out that the presence of a variable is *not* the sole criterion for an open sentence; the *neither-true-nor-false* criterion must also be satisfied. To demonstrate this, have the students consider the following:

1. $x + 6 = 1 + x + 5$

2. $x + 5 = x + 7$

The first sentence is called an *identity*—no matter what value is chosen for x, the statement is true. The second sentence is false for any replacement of x. Although both sentences contain variables, neither is *open.*

1.7 Point out that replacing the variable, in turn, by each member of the replacement set yields all possible sentences for a given open sentence.

Emphasize that the solution set for an open sentence is dependent upon the replacement set as well as upon the sentence itself. For a given open sentence it is possible that from one replacement set no solutions may be obtained, whereas from another replacement set there may be several solutions.

You may wish to point out that $\{\varnothing\}$ is *not* a symbol for the empty set.

1.8 Emphasize the importance of keeping the beam in "balance"—whatever is done on one side must also be done on the other. This is an intuitive generalization of the properties for solving equations.

Students who can solve the equations without using the balance beam should be encouraged to do so. In some exercises the variable is on the right. Students may simply subtract the same number from both sides, or they may interchange sides before solving.

Activities 1, 2, and 3 on page 32 may be used with this section (or Activity 3 can be postponed for use with Section 2.4).

1.9 This section introduces work with formulas, a topic that will appear in later chapters. Have the students verbally state a rule or principle and then translate it into mathematical symbols. Start with common relationships like the number (p) of pennies in a certain number (d) of dimes is ten times the number of dimes. Use tables if necessary. Translate this into $p = 10d$.

Overview: In this chapter, the solution of open sentences, handled informally in Chapter 1, is formalized. Sentences involving addition, subtraction, multiplication, or division are solved by performing the inverse operation with the same number on both sides of the sentence. Many formulas are included, providing practical applications of the work with sentences. Practice in translating verbal statements into mathematical sentences is also included.

A secondary emphasis in this chapter is on measurement. U.S. units are presented. Area and volume formulas are included, and areas and volumes are calculated, using either metric or U.S. units.

2.1 The work done here with inverse operations prepares students for solving equations and inequalities formally.

2.2 This is a good time to stress the importance of the check in solving an open sentence (or any problem).

Since the C exercises involve more than one variable, you may wish to remind students that *solving for x* means we must get *x* alone on one side of the equation or inequality.

2.3 Through the use of inverse operations the students are developing an informal knowledge of the addition and multiplication properties of equality. With this in mind, it should be stressed than when an operation is to be "undone," the inverse operation must be done to *both* sides of the equation.

2.4 The use of the dot to indicate a number in the solution set and a solid arrowhead ▶ to indicate the continuation of a solution set should be thoroughly reviewed. It should be noted that since the replacement set is the set of whole numbers, zero is the smallest number satisfying any inequality. Thus, the present use of the ◀ refers only to the *whole numbers* less than a given number. Later, when solving inequalities with an integer replacement set, ◀ will mean the same as ▶

2.5 This section affords an opportunity to summarize the basic methods for solving open sentences involving one operation. It is also an excellent time to work on individual student difficulties.

2.6 Discuss the examples in detail so that students recognize the use of two operations in each solution process.

A class discussion of the A exercises is an important step toward student success in this section.

2.7 In spite of the increasing move to metrication, U.S. units are still used extensively in everyday situations. This will continue to be true in the foreseeable future. Thus students need this practice in using U.S. units.

The conversion formula changing Celsius temperatures to Fahrenheit is probably the most relevant of all the conversion formulas to the students. Many signs are flashing Celsius as well as Fahrenheit temperatures at them every day. Travelers from the U.S. to Canada frequently feel the need to make such conversions.

2.8 Point out that length is measured in linear units such as meters and inches, whereas area is measured in square units and volume in cubic units.

2.9 Depending upon your class, you might find it advisable to do several of the B exercises as a class discussion. Require that students write a variable or a phrase to represent each unknown in the problem and that each variable or phrase is clearly defined as to what it represents.

With regard to the *Universal Product Code,* page 62, you might want to point out that libraries use a similar code to keep track of books and that department stores use such a code for inventory control.

Chapter 3   Important Properties   Pages 63–101

Overview: This chapter deals with important structural properties of addition and multiplication, including the commutative, associative, and distributive properties as well as properties of 0 and 1. Students are shown how these properties can be used to simplify computation and to solve equations.

The chapter also deals with exponential notation, greatest common factor (GCF), and least common multiple (LCM). The GCF and LCM play important roles in simplifying, adding, and subtracting fractions.

This is a key chapter and all sections should be thoroughly taught.

3.1 Students should realize that we *assume* (accept without proof) the commutative properties of addition and multiplication. However, as shown by Example 2, you need only one *counterexample* (a result that shows a case when the property fails) to prove that subtraction and division are not commutative. Use Examples 3 and 4 to emphasize some purposes for knowing the properties— to extend equation-solving skills and to make computation easier.

3.2 Addition and multiplication are *binary* operations—that is, operations on *pairs* of numbers. When three numbers are to be added (or multiplied), two must be chosen to add (or multiply) first. The result is then added to (or multiplied by) the third number. The associative property simply tells us that

whatever choice is made for the first two, the resulting answer to the computation is still the same.

Students should realize that computation is easier when multiples of ten are involved. Thus, when adding or multiplying three or more numbers, the students should be encouraged to use the properties to obtain multiples of ten whenever possible.

3.3 This section is primarily a review of the properties of zero and one. Reinforcement of these properties is always beneficial to students, especially the difference between division *of* zero by a nonzero number (getting a 0 answer) and division *by* zero (no answer).

3.4 The distributive property plays a key role in algebra. Techniques of finding special products and factoring special types of expressions take advantage of the distributive property.

Example 2 shows how the distributive property may be used to add $2x$ and x by first expressing x as $1x$. Exercises 1–10 mix various forms in which the distributive property may be viewed, and these exercises help prepare students for use of the distributive property in solving equations.

Exercises 25–32 illustrate that multiplication is also distributive over subtraction.

3.5 Students tend to overlook the fact that 1 is a factor of every number and that every number is a factor of itself. Emphasizing these points now will help students understand the GCF in Section 3.9.

Operation Decode, page 82, should be interesting for better students.

3.6 The divisibility rules introduced in this section are a valuable aid to factoring whole numbers. Their use should be encouraged throughout the chapter.

The C exercises introduce the rule for divisibility by 6. Most students can be encouraged to try these exercises.

A Shorter Shortcut, page 84, provides both a shortcut for divisibility by 3 and a possible lead-in to the process of *casting out nines.* Casting out nines is a check for computational accuracy. It is discussed in many books on the teaching of arithmetic.

3.7 Encourage students to use the divisibility rules for finding prime factorizations in this section.

Students sometimes wonder why 1 is not considered to be a prime. Like the primes, 1 contains no factors other than itself and 1. Actually, 1 is excluded from the primes by definition for convenience of stating the following property, often called the *fundamental theorem of arithmetic*: A composite number can be factored into primes in only one way except for the order of the factors. For example, the unique factorization of 36 is $2 \times 2 \times 3 \times 3$. If we allowed 1 to be a prime, then 36 could have many other prime factorizations, such as $1 \times 2 \times 2 \times 3 \times 3$ or $1 \times 1 \times 2 \times 2 \times 3 \times 3$. Since 1 plays no significant role in factoring numbers, mathematicians chose to exclude it from the primes.

3.8 Some students erroneously interpret exponential form as multiplication. That is, 3^5 is seen as 3×5. To preclude such an error, emphasize that an exponent acts as a counter to tell how many times the base is used as a *factor.*

3.9 This section is a prerequisite for Section 4.3, *Simplifying Fractions,* in which students need to find the GCF of the numerator and denominator. You may restrict this lesson to the GCF of two numbers without disrupting the continuity of later content. In that case, you may omit Example 4 and Exercises 19–20 and 22–26.

3.10 Students should develop a good understanding of LCM. It will be applied later (Sections 4.8 and 4.9) when adding and subtracting with fractions. Point out that the LCM of two numbers might be (1) the greater of the two numbers (Example 2), (2) the product of the two numbers (Example 3), or (3) a number between the greater number and their product (Example 1). Unlike the GCF concept, the LCM concept should *not* be restricted to two numbers, since students will later be required to find sums of more than two fractions. Use Exercises 11 and 24 to show that the LCM of prime numbers is always their product.

LCM's Around You, page 95, provides applications of the LCM for better students.

Math in Landscaping, page 100, applies a formula using exponents to find the weight of balled trees. Many students will be surprised that mathematics is used in this manner.

Try a New Twist, page 101, provides an excellent change of pace for enrichment. The activities give students a taste of topology. Results of the scissor cutting will surprise students (and teachers, if they have not done this previously).

The *Cumulative Review* on pages 102–104 is one of five cumulative reviews in this text. These cumulative reviews provide a midsemester review and an end-of-semester review for each semester.

Chapter 4   Fractions and Mixed Numbers   Pages 105–142

Overview: This chapter provides the opportunity for students to develop and practice computational skills for the four basic operations with fractions and mixed numbers. Students will have opportunities to review and use these skills in later chapters.

4.1 This section is a quick review of some elementary fraction concepts. Most students should be able to master these concepts with little or no teacher guidance.

4.2 This section reviews the basic skills of multiplying with fractions. Demonstration of the physical model on page 111 for multiplying with fractions will be helpful to those students who want to know how, for example, $\frac{2}{3} \times \frac{4}{5}$ can equal $\frac{8}{15}$. Emphasize that the word *of* translates to multiplication.

4.3 Students simplify a fraction (to lowest terms) by dividing the numerator and the denominator by the GCF. When finding a product, the simplifying can be done before or after multiplying (see Example 3). Emphasize dividing out common factors *before* multiplying for those students who will continue taking algebra courses.

Another Way, page 115, gives a convenient form for showing the work both of finding the GCF and of dividing both numerator and denominator by it.

4.4 Standard procedures are used to change mixed numbers to fractions and vice versa. Emphasize that the sentence following Example 3 means that from now on fractional answers should be changed to mixed numbers in lowest terms whenever possible.

You might wish to consider *Math and Typing,* page 142, for additional practice.

4.5 This section combines the uses of skills presented previously in the chapter. Example 3 and Exercises 10–12 and 34–39 apply multiplication with mixed numbers to converting measurements in the U.S. system to smaller units.

Using Recipes, page 122, applies multiplication of fractions and mixed numbers to changes necessary for increasing and decreasing the number of servings prepared.

4.6 You may wish to give a short rationale for the "invert and multiply" algorithm. A brief explanation along the following lines should suffice:

$$\frac{1}{3} \div \frac{2}{5} = \frac{\frac{1}{3}}{\frac{2}{5}} = \frac{\frac{1}{3}}{\frac{2}{5}} \times \frac{\frac{5}{2}}{\frac{5}{2}} = \frac{\frac{1}{3} \times \frac{5}{2}}{\frac{2}{5} \times \frac{5}{2}} = \frac{\frac{1}{3} \times \frac{5}{2}}{1} = \frac{1}{3} \times \frac{5}{2}$$

Point out that $\dfrac{\frac{5}{2}}{\frac{5}{2}}$ is another name for 1, and since 1 is the identity number for multiplication, this multiplication does not change the problem.

To help students avoid errors, stress that simplification is done only after the division problem is changed to a multiplication problem.

Example 3 and Exercises 5–6 and 31–36 apply division with mixed numbers to converting measurements in the U.S. system to larger units.

4.7 Sections 4.7–4.9 form a unit on addition and subtraction with fractions and mixed numbers. The present section deals only with cases where the denominators are the same number.

When discussing the examples on page 127, carefully consider how the answers are expressed in lowest terms.

4.8 You might begin the lesson with a review of LCM's. Students who have difficulty finding the least common denominator (the LCM of the denominators) can be allowed to find any common denominator. Show these students that they can always use the product of the two denominators as their common denominator.

4.9 This section combines the skills taught in Sections 4.7 and 4.8. The method shown for finding the products in Exercises 30–35 prepares students for multiplication of two binomials in Chapter 14.

4.10 Discuss the examples, emphasizing that the answers require a whole number of bars and boxes. Then help students interpret the fractional answers accordingly.

Depending upon your class, you may want to read several of the problems and discuss the kinds of answers required before making an assignment. This section may be omitted from the minimum course.

Overview: This chapter is, for most students, a review of the operations with decimals. The emphasis is on computing just as with whole numbers—the difference being in the location of the decimal point. Operations with decimals are then applied to solving verbal problems and equations and to working with metric units.

Estimating answers by rounding to a convenient place and then computing is used to check on the correctness of a computation and to aid in placing the decimal point.

5.1 In this text decimals less than 1 are written with a lead zero to the left of the decimal point (for example, 0.75). This notation calls attention to the decimal point and is in agreement with the notation used for decimals in scientific work and in the metric system.

Answers to the B exercises are given in lowest terms. This is consistent with the agreement about fractional answers made in Chapter 4 and with the reminder given in Example 1. However, you may wish to accept other answers. If so, be sure students realize that the answers are equivalent.

5.2 After discussing the attendance example, have students describe other situations in which an approximation is sufficient or appropriate.

Review rounding techniques by discussing each example in detail. In this text rounding is carried out by looking at the digit

Manual

to the right of the place to which the number will be rounded. The rounding scheme used is the common one of rounding up if the digit examined is 5 or greater, rounding down if the digit is 4 or less.

5.3 In adding or subtracting decimals, the decimal points should be aligned. Many students, faced with decimals having different numbers of decimal places, find it helpful to write 0's on the right to make the number of places the same for each number.

Examples 1 and 2 and Exercises 4 and 5 show students different uses of 0's in decimals. An initial 0 as in 0.17 merely calls attention to the decimal point and may be omitted. Final 0's as in 31.900 may be inserted or omitted and are often used in addition and subtraction. Other 0's, as in 2.059, must not be omitted, since they help establish place values for other digits.

Notice that 0.40, 0.4, .40, and .4 are all acceptable answers for Exercise 10. As noted previously, we consistently retain the initial 0 and give the answer as 0.4.

5.4 Some students may want to know why there is one, two, three, or more digits after the decimal point. A brief explanation along the following lines should suffice:

$$0.1 \times 0.1 = \frac{1}{10} \times \frac{1}{10} = \frac{1}{100} = 0.01$$

$$0.1 \times 0.01 = \frac{1}{10} \times \frac{1}{100} = \frac{1}{1000} = 0.001$$

Math and Diving, page 156, shows an application of decimals in sports.

5.5 Sections 5.5 and 5.6 form a unit on division of decimals. In this section the divisor is always a whole number. Discuss examples in detail, including the comments with arrows, to indicate the key points.

5.6 The example in the opening paragraph explains why the decimal point can be moved the same number of places in both the divisor and the dividend. As shown in that example, we are merely multiplying both divisor (denominator) and dividend (numerator) by the same power of ten. All exercises in this section will result in terminating decimals as quotients. However, the students may have to include 0's in the dividend to continue the division in some cases.

Unit Pricing, page 163, is an important consumer application of decimals.

5.7 As Examples 2 and 3 are discussed, point out how easy it is to change all the metric measurements to the same unit.

The *Career Corner,* page 170, shows the industrial use of tolerance limits for acceptable dimensions of machined parts.

Chapter 6   Adding and Subtracting Integers   Pages 171–198

Overview: This chapter serves as an introduction to the integers. Techniques are developed for addition and subtraction of integers and for the solution of open sentences involving these operations on integers. Also, a method for solving verbal problems by using equations is considered.

6.1 Emphasize that a positive number can be named with or without a positive sign, for example, $^+16$ or 16. In this text, the positive sign is used only when extra emphasis is needed. Notice that the signs for positive and negative numbers ($^+$ and $^-$) are raised, and they are slightly smaller than the signs used to indicate addition and subtraction (+ and −). This helps students distinguish between the uses of these signs and eliminates the need for using parentheses or brackets in some cases.

Weather Reports, page 193, provides students with an application of integers and requires them to interpret tables and to evaluate formulas. This may be used in conjunction with Section 6.1.

6.2 Sections 6.2 and 6.3 form a unit on addition of integers. Students should understand they need not draw number lines for the exercises. Merely thinking of moves along a number line can be helpful.

The activities on pages 194–195 can be used with this section or with Section 6.3.

6.3 The concept of absolute value gives some students trouble. For these students, you may wish to interpret absolute value on a number line. The absolute value of any integer is its distance from zero on a number line, without regard to direction from zero. Since only distance and not direction is involved, the absolute value is not a signed number.

For students who have difficulty adding integers of different signs, physical interpretations such as temperature, profit and loss, and game scores will help.

Example 3 and Exercises 37–45 can be used to point out that addition of integers is associative.

6.4 Emphasize that subtracting an integer by adding its opposite allows us to change every subtraction exercise to an addition exercise. Once that is done, all students need to know is how to add integers.

6.5 Solution of addition equations can be introduced by the "undoing" approach. Emphasize that the addition of an integer to a variable can be "undone" by adding its opposite as well as by subtracting the original integer.

Make sure students check their answers by substitution into the *original* equation.

6.6 Previously students changed subtraction problems to equivalent addition problems. Now they will solve subtraction equations by changing them to equivalent addition equations.

6.7 Emphasize that an inequality involving addition or subtraction can be solved by the same methods as those used to solve equations.

This section may be omitted from the minimum course.

6.8 Here, students are required to apply their skills with integers to solving verbal problems. Have students follow the steps as outlined in the text for finding solutions. Encourage students to draw diagrams for the problems whenever visualization would be helpful.

Chapter 7   Multiplying and Dividing Integers   Pages 199–229

Overview: This chapter extends the students' knowledge of integers to finding products and quotients. These operations are then applied to solving equations, inequalities, and verbal problems.

7.1 The intuitive approach used in this section enables students to find the required products. A more rigorous treatment can be given to some students.

7.2 Here is another way to make the rules for multiplying integers seem plausible.

water running in at 3 gallons per minute	water running out at 3 gallons per minute
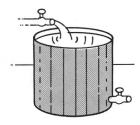	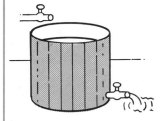

1. 4 min from now there will be 12 gal. more in the tank.

$$^+4 \times {}^+3 = {}^+12$$

2. 4 min ago, there were 12 fewer gal. in the tank.

$$^-4 \times {}^+3 = {}^-12$$

1. 4 min from now there will be 12 fewer gal. in the tank.

$$^+4 \times {}^-3 = {}^-12$$

2. 4 min ago, there were 12 gal. more in the tank.

$$^-4 \times {}^-3 = {}^+12$$

Emphasize that it is the associative property of multiplication that allows the choice of which integers to multiply first in Example 2.

7.3 Discuss each example in detail, including the comments, to emphasize the key points of the section. Refer to the rules in Sections 7.1 and 7.2 to help students see the similarity between multiplication and division of integers.

Students will benefit from a review of the order of operations before doing Exercises 34–43. The C exercises remind students of the properties of zero previously discussed in Section 3.3.

7.4 Emphasize that the techniques used to solve the equations in this section are the same as those used to solve equations with whole numbers.

The C exercises illustrate how the distributive property can be used to solve some types of equations.

7.5 Again, stress that the techniques used to solve equations here are the same as those used to solve equations with whole numbers.

7.6 It cannot be emphasized too strongly that multiplying both sides of an inequality by a negative number changes the sense, or direction, of the inequality. Many students find this a difficult concept to grasp.

This section and the remainder of the chapter may be omitted from the minimum course.

7.7 Compare this section with Section 7.6 to show that the same rule applies for both multiplication and division by a negative number when solving inequalities.

7.8 Discuss each example in detail. If difficulties arise, students should refer to or review Section 2.6.

7.9 This section applies the techniques learned in the chapter to solving verbal problems involving multiplication or division of integers.

Watts the Limit?, page 225, provides a practical application of formulas to electric circuits. Another application is provided in *Power Lines and Pipelines*, page 229, which discusses expansion and contraction of such lines.

The *Cumulative Review* on pages 230–234 can be used as an end-of-semester review for the first semester.

Overview: This chapter informally develops the concepts of *ordered pair* and *function,* enabling students to interpret and construct graphs. The chapter also relates functions and graphing to the physical world and reinforces skills in computing with integers, in using the metric system, and in solving verbal problems.

8.1 Emphasize the two forms for writing ordered pairs in Example 1—a table and a listing. Stress the importance of the order of the numbers in an ordered pair. Student desks can be assigned column and row numbers to illustrate ordered pairs.

8.2 This section deals with graphing ordered pairs of *whole numbers* only. Again, stress the importance of order—the first number indicates a move to the right, and the second number indicates a move up. Illustrate this by graphing two ordered pairs like (2, 3) and (3, 2).

All students can be assigned the C exercises.

8.3 This section extends graphing to ordered pairs of integers. Students should understand that the *x*-coordinate indicates a move to the right or the left, while the *y*-coordinate indicates a move up or down.

Treasure Hunt, page 272, may be used as an activity with this section.

8.4 A discussion of the *Consumer Corner* topic, *Misleading Graphs,* page 269, should give students ideas as to the daily uses of graphs. Emphasize that graphs must be titled and neatly labeled for easy reading and interpretation.

8.5 Relationships in the physical world are very often described by sets of ordered pairs. The intent of this section is for students to recognize when such a set is a function. Do not strive for a sophisticated interpretation or for a thorough understanding of functions.

Many students find that graphing ordered pairs and applying the "vertical line" test is the easiest method for recognizing a function. Though not required, such a practice is permissible.

8.6 This is a very important section for students. The variety of problems enables them to make practical applications of what they have learned. Students are required to bring together in a purposeful way what might otherwise appear to be isolated topics—variables, open sentences, solving equations, order of operations, and functions. This section points out the importance of learning mathematics.

"*Magic Number 30*" *Formula,* page 270, is suitable for use with this section.

8.7 The material in Sections 8.7 and 8.8 provides an enjoyable and interesting reinforcement of computational and graphing skills as well as an introduction to similar figures, a topic that will be presented in Chapter 10. Both of these sections may be omitted from the minimum or regular course.

8.8 Discuss the examples in detail to help students discover how to make a slide to the right, to the left, up, or down. Exercises 13 and 14 tie together the ideas of this and the preceding sections.

Overview: This chapter deals with three important and interrelated topics: (1) ratios, (2) proportions, and (3) per cents. These topics are practical and useful to most people.

Many students will probably have a relatively weak background in these topics. Also, the approach, particularly to per cent, is likely to be somewhat different from the students' previous background. This is an important chapter and mastery of the topics by most students is a reasonable goal.

9.1 Point out the many practical applications of ratios. Emphasize that a fraction is usually the most convenient way to express a ratio. Encourage all students to try the C exercises.

9.2 Be sure students interpret the drawings on page 279 as three ways of comparing the same pair of sets—not as three different pairs of sets. Stress that a ratio is in lowest terms if the fraction for that ratio is in lowest terms.

Gear Ratios, page 278, and *Ratios in Advertising,* page 282, are practical applications of this section.

9.3 You may want to use an example such as the following to show why the cross-product pattern works:

$$\frac{2}{3} = \frac{34}{n}$$

$$\frac{2}{3} \times 3 = \frac{34}{n} \times 3 \qquad \text{Multiply both sides by 3.}$$

$$2 = \frac{34 \times 3}{n}$$

$$2 \times n = \frac{34 \times 3}{n} \times n \qquad \text{Multiply both sides by } n.$$

$$2n = 34 \times 3$$

Postal Ratios, page 285, applies proportions to determining the permissible range of lengths of an envelope of given width.

9.4 When setting up proportions from verbal problems students must be consistent in their use of units. That is, an example comparing pounds of meat to minutes required to cook must be set up in a proportion as *either*

$$\frac{a \text{ pounds}}{b \text{ minutes}} = \frac{c \text{ pounds}}{d \text{ minutes}}$$

or

$$\frac{a \text{ pounds}}{c \text{ pounds}} = \frac{b \text{ minutes}}{d \text{ minutes}}$$

9.5 Per cent is presented here as a ratio comparing a number to 100. The section is intended to make students skillful in changing freely from per cent form to fraction or decimal form.

Ratios at Work, page 293, shows the use of ratios and per cents in describing grades.

9.6 Discuss each example in detail. Point out that when a decimal is changed to a per cent, the decimal point is moved two places to the right. To achieve success in the remainder of this chapter, students need to become skilled in changing these expressions from one form to another.

9.7 This section deals with the three basic types of per cent problems. Stress that all three types may be solved using the proportion

$$\frac{a}{b} = \frac{p}{100}$$

Two other types of per cent problems, per cent of increase and per cent of decrease, are presented in Section 9.10.

9.8 Stress the steps used to solve a per cent problem, and point out how they are used in each example. The verbal problems in this section give numerous applications of the three types of per cent problems developed in Section 9.7.

9.9 Students are presented with a method of estimating per cents. In Exercises 25–32, students can see how close their estimates come to exact answers.

Point out to students how estimating per cents allows them to mentally check sales tax, tips in restaurants, finance charges, interest payments, and other money-related matters.

Both this section and Section 9.10 may be omitted from the minimum course.

9.10 Students should be reminded that the per cent of increase (or decrease) is always based on the original amount, and calculated as a per cent of that amount.

This section may be omitted from the regular course.

Chapter 10   Indirect Measurement   Pages 311–347

Overview: This chapter introduces similar figures and their properties. Emphasis is given to similar triangles and to the use of proportions in finding missing lengths and in making indirect measurements. Practical uses are given of indirect measurements in games, in maps, and in scale drawings and scale models.

10.1 Illustrate similar figures by using a magnifying glass, a photograph and its enlargement, or any suitable examples. Emphasize that similar figures have the same shape but may differ in size.

Students can trace the figures in this section and move the tracings as needed to help determine similar figures.

10.2 To emphasize that corresponding angles of similar triangles have the same measure, have students trace one of the triangles on paper and superimpose it on the other, angle by angle. This could also be done via an overhead projector.

Point out to students the usefulness in naming similar triangles by listing corresponding vertices in the same order. This method makes it easy to pick out corresponding angles and sides from the names of the triangles.

10.3 Draw two similar triangles on the board—one with sides 10″, 14″, 18″ and the other with sides 15″, 21″, 27″ (do not include dimensions with drawings). Have students measure the sides and determine the ratios of the lengths of corresponding sides. Make sure that the numerators of all ratios are chosen from the sides of one triangle and the denominators from the corresponding sides of the other triangle. When similar triangles are in different relative positions, remind students that corresponding sides are opposite corresponding angles.

10.4 Discuss the examples in detail, emphasizing the steps used to solve the problems. In step 3, you may allow students to skip the first proportion and go directly to the proportion that omits units.

10.5 To help students set up proper ratios, make sure they name the similar triangles with corresponding vertices in the same order. Point out that in the example the ratio AD : CE must be the same as the ratio DB : BE, so DB is represented by $1x$ and BE by $2x$ ($1x : 2x = 1 : 2$). Ask students what they would use to represent DB and BE if the ratio AD : CE had been 2 : 3, 3 : 5, 1 : 4, and so forth.

Another Way, page 335, and *Math and Pipelines,* page 343, may be used as enrichment with this section.

10.6 You might have students bring local maps to compute distances meaningful to them. Using a street map, you might have students set up a route (using whatever guidelines you wish) for a 30-mile or 50-kilometer marathon (using units that match the map scale).

Activity 1 on page 342 may be used with this section.

10.7 This section could be introduced by demonstrating a scale drawing or a scale model of a car, a plane, or a building. Discuss occupations that might require such models or drawings and how they might be used. Have students compute lengths, widths, or heights from the scale of the drawing or the model.

Activity 2 on page 342 is a suitable extension of this section.

The *Cumulative Review* on pages 348–350 can be used as a midsemester review for the second semester.

Chapter 11   Adding and Subtracting Rational Numbers   Pages 351–382

Overview: This chapter extends the available set of numbers to the entire set of rational numbers. Since the integers have already been studied, the techniques used for operating with integers can be applied to operations on positive and negative fractions, mixed numbers, and decimals.

The opportunity is provided here for a thorough review of addition and subtraction with integers, decimals, fractions, and mixed numbers. These operations are then applied to solving equations and verbal problems.

11.1 It would be beneficial to discuss again with students the reason why the denominator of a fraction may not be zero. You might also review the concepts of *opposite* and *absolute value* in Chapter 6. See Examples 2 and 3.

11.2 Point out that (1) when comparing fractions, *any* positive fraction is greater than *any* negative fraction and (2) when two

negative fractions are compared, the fraction with the *larger* absolute value is farther to the left of 0 on the number line and thus is the lesser of the two fractions.

The activity *Rats!*, pages 378–379, provides practice in comparing fractions.

11.3 This section brings together the skills and concepts learned in Section 5.3 (adding and subtracting decimals) and Sections 6.3 and 6.4 (adding and subtracting integers). You may want to review the important ideas from those sections prior to discussing the present section.

Managing Personal Finances, page 362, provides activities involving addition of positive and negative decimals and practice in computing per cents. A similar application of positive and negative decimals is provided in *Bookkeeping,* page 377.

11.4 Remind students to change subtraction to addition of the opposite. Once they have done this, the problems can be solved as with integers (Sections 6.5 and 6.6).

Markup and Markdown, page 365, provides application of the kinds of equations solved in this section.

11.5 This section correlates with Section 11.3. You may want to review the important ideas from Sections 4.7 and 4.8 (adding and subtracting like and unlike fractions) as an introduction to the lesson.

11.6 The same approach as that presented in Sections 11.3 and 11.5 is used here to introduce addition and subtraction of positive and negative mixed numbers. Again, you may wish to review (Section 4.9) with students before discussing the lesson.

11.7 Remind students to use the same methods here as when solving equations involving the addition or the subtraction of integers. Stress that all answers should be reduced to lowest terms.

11.8 This section requires students to use addition and subtraction of rational numbers in equations for solving verbal problems. In the examples, emphasize the use of a variable to represent the unknown quantity. Be sure students include units of measure in their answers when necessary. Some teachers also prefer that each answer be stated in a complete sentence, as in the example.

Chapter 12   Multiplying and Dividing Rational Numbers   Pages 383–414

Overview: This chapter provides review for multiplication and division of integers, fractions, mixed numbers, and decimals through the extension to rational numbers. These operations, along with addition and subtraction of rational numbers, are then applied to equations and formulas involving one or two operations. Scientific notation is introduced as a shorthand for writing rational numbers that would otherwise be difficult to read (for example, 0.000 000 000 036).

12.1 To determine products and quotients of positive and negative decimals, students combine (1) algorithms for multiplying and dividing decimals and (2) rules for the signs of products and quotients of integers. Refer students to Sections 5.4–5.6 and 7.1–7.3 for review as needed. Remind students of the rule for order of operations to prepare them for Exercises 41–58.

12.2 Remind students of the methods used to solve equations involving multiplication and division as presented in Sections 2.3, 7.4, and 7.5. In Exercises 26–32, students' answers should include proper units.

12.3 Briefly review the rules for determining the sign of a product or a quotient of positive and negative numbers. Students should have no problem applying this to products and quotients of positive and negative fractions. For those students who have difficulty remembering how to find products and quotients of fractions you might suggest a review of Sections 4.2 and 4.3.

12.4 By now, students should be proficient in determining the sign of a product or a quotient of rational numbers. Briefly review Sections 4.4 and 4.5 with students having difficulties with the mixed numbers.

Stock Reports, page 394, provides the opportunity to start students on a possible project. You might "give" students $5000 to invest in the stock market. They should invest exactly that amount and watch the papers for a period of time, perhaps one month. Several times during this period, you could have students compute and report on their gain or loss to date. This would give the students a chance to see the usefulness of working with mixed numbers.

12.5 The concept of *reciprocal,* which can be used to solve equations involving fractions in Section 12.6, should be thoroughly understood. Stress the statements written in the colored boxes and the fact that the product of a pair of reciprocals is 1.

12.6 The equations in this section involve only one operation. Stress the fact that division by a number can be replaced by multiplication by the reciprocal. The A exercises can be used to reinforce this. Students should also be reminded to be careful in determining signs of the products.

Math in Building Trades, page 400, could be discussed as enrichment with this section.

The following sections of this chapter may be omitted from the minimum course.

12.7 Discuss the examples in detail, having students tell what is done in each step.

You may want to review Sections 2.6 and 7.8 if students reveal the need.

12.8 The formulas in this chapter do not need to be memorized. Encourage students to read formulas by substituting words for mathematical symbols. This demonstrates that formulas are complete sentences.

Air Conditioning, page 414, helps students become educated consumers and can be used here.

12.9 The following examples may prove helpful in explaining to students how the decimal point is "moved" in scientific notation:

$$6000 = \frac{6000}{1} \times \frac{1000}{1000} = \frac{6000}{1000} \times \frac{1000}{1}$$

$$= 6 \times 1000 = 6 \times 10^3$$

$$0.03 = \frac{0.03}{1} \times \frac{100}{100} = \frac{0.03 \times 100}{1} \times \frac{1}{100}$$

$$= 3 \times \frac{1}{100} = 3 \times 10^{-2}$$

Scientific notation can also be explained as a doing-undoing operation on a number: the moving of the decimal point being the "doing" and the multiplication by a power of 10 being the "undoing."

Chapter 13   Square Roots   Pages 415–446

Overview: This chapter provides a basis for working with square roots in later courses. Simple quadratic equations are solved, the Pythagorean Property is developed and used, and rules for multiplication and division of square roots are introduced.

13.1 Emphasize that *the* square root of 0 is 0. All other whole numbers have two square roots—one positive and the other negative. Stress the meanings of the symbols $\sqrt{}$ and $^-\sqrt{}$.

In Exercises 1–12 point out that two answers are required—one positive and one negative. In Exercises 13–33, only one answer should be given, since $\sqrt{}$ requires a positive answer and $^-\sqrt{}$ requires a negative answer.

13.2 Point out that the table on page 422 is actually two tables—a table of squares and a table of square roots. Emphasize that the square roots listed in the table (except for perfect squares) are approximations to the nearest hundredth. For that reason we use $\approx$ instead of $=$ in statements like $\sqrt{29} \approx 5.39$. Students can check that 5.39^2 is not exactly equal to 29.

The activity on page 442 enables students to use hand-held calculators to approximate square roots. The method described is the divide-and-average method.

13.3 Example 3 indicates that the *largest* square-number factor should be found. If students do not follow this procedure (or if they use a calculator), slightly differing results may be obtained in some cases. For example,

$$
\begin{array}{ccc}
\sqrt{810} & \text{or} & \sqrt{810} \\
\sqrt{81} \times \sqrt{10} & & \sqrt{9} \times \sqrt{90} \\
9 \times 3.16 & & 3 \times 9.49 \\
28.44 & & 28.47
\end{array}
$$

You may prefer to allow these slight variations (caused by rounding error in the table). However, the answers given in the text for all such square roots have been computed by following the procedure of Example 3.

To help in finding the largest square-number factor, you might encourage prime factorization. For example,

$$
\begin{aligned}
\sqrt{700} &= \sqrt{2 \times 2 \times 5 \times 5 \times 7} \\
&= \sqrt{(2 \times 5) \times (2 \times 5) \times 7} \\
&= \sqrt{10 \times 10} \times \sqrt{7}
\end{aligned}
$$

13.4 This section considers square roots of rational numbers that when written as fractions have square-number numerators and denominators. When computing square roots of decimals, some students may find it easier to change the decimals to fractions first and then use the rule for finding square roots of fractions. (See the second method in Example 2.) Remind students that the fractional answer for this type of problem should be converted to a decimal.

The C exercises consider square roots of rational numbers that cannot be expressed exactly by fractions or decimals.

13.5 Since most practical problems students will encounter require only the positive solution, the positive square root is emphasized in this section.

The C exercises introduce a property for solving equations that may be verbalized as "You can square both sides of an equation" and may be symbolized as "If $\sqrt{a} = b$, then $a = b^2$." Most students will be able to do these exercises.

Meeting Halley's Comet, page 430, requires use of an equation of the type $x^2 = a$ and could be used with this section.

13.6 Point out that by using the Pythagorean Property, if the lengths of *any* two sides of a right triangle are given, the length of the third side can be found. Also, stress that since the measures of the sides of a triangle are positive numbers, we only need to find the positive solutions for the equations.

13.7 This section emphasizes practical applications of the Pythagorean Property. You might have students suggest situations in their daily lives where this property would prove helpful.

You might use the activity on page 439, *Checking Right Angles,* in conjunction with this section.

13.8 This section applies square roots to formulas used by persons in various occupations. In a minimum or regular course you may wish to omit this section.

Math and Police Work, page 446, gives yet another application of formulas involving square roots.

Overview: This chapter considers two fundamental algebra topics—verbal problems and polynomials. Verbal problems have been studied throughout the book. But here students determine if the information provided in a verbal problem is necessary and sufficient for its solution. They also solve verbal problems requiring equations with more than one operation. Polynomials are formally introduced and methods for their addition, subtraction, multiplication, and division are discussed.

Both this chapter and Chapter 15 may be omitted from the minimum course.

14.1 Some students are confused by the fact that both odd and even consecutive integers may be represented by x, $x + 2$, $x + 4$, and so forth. To help these students you might have them write a sequence of even integers and a sequence of odd integers on their paper. Have them determine the difference between each consecutive pair in their sequences. Point out that this difference will always be 2. Given an even (or odd) integer x, the next even (or odd) can be found by adding 2 to get $x + 2$.

Encourage students to draw diagrams when suitable. Labeling the diagrams will help in setting up the corresponding equations.

14.2 In your class discussion of Exercises 1–4 have students determine what else is needed if there is not enough information and what is *not* needed if too much information is given. You might help students set up equations, when possible, for the A exercises.

What's the Catch?, page 461, may be used with this section, or after Section 14.5 as a quick reminder of information needed in verbal problems.

14.3 The purpose here is to introduce students to vocabulary they will need in the remainder of the chapter. Point out that the order of variables in a term is unimportant, since by the commutative property $xy = yx$. However, to facilitate the use of operations on polynomials, you might have students write the variables in each term in alphabetical order.

As pointed out in the text, negative terms of a polynomial are usually indicated by subtraction as, for example, $7x^2 - 3x - 5$. This notation will be used consistently in algebra courses. However, students of this course may find the equivalent form $7x^2 + {}^-3x + {}^-5$ more helpful.

14.4 Explain that the substitution of numbers for variables in two expressions does not prove that they are equivalent. However, it can prove that two expressions are *not* equivalent. Emphasize that the substitution of more than one or two numbers is often necessary. For example, $x + 10$ and $x^3 + 10$ will produce the same results for x values of ${}^-1$, 0, and 1 even though the expressions are not equivalent.

14.5 Point out that the rearrangement of variables and constants is possible because of the commutative and associative properties. The raised dot, ·, is introduced as another symbol indicating multiplication. Encourage students to use this symbol instead of the $\times$ to avoid confusion with the variable x in handwritten work.

Emphasize the last two sentences in the rule given at the bottom of page 459. Some students may start adding the constants as well as the exponents when multiplying, thinking that they can use the addition shortcut for each part of a multiplication.

14.6 Success in this section relies heavily on skills mastered in Section 14.5 and the students' ability to use the distributive property. Allow students to work vertically or horizontally, whichever way is more comfortable. For students continuing in an algebra course, you might stress the horizontal method.

Formulas at Work, page 464, reviews the use and evaluation of formulas in a polynomial setting.

14.7 Again, you may allow students to use either the vertical or the horizontal method, as they wish. Discuss each example thoroughly. Remind students to combine any like terms, but point out that there may, at times, be no like terms to combine (for example, Exercises 9, 10, and 13).

Most students will enjoy the FOIL method of multiplying two binomials and should be encouraged to try this method as outlined in the C exercises.

14.8 Discuss each example in detail. At this point some students may be confusing $x + x = 2x$ with $x \cdot x = x^2$. Remind them of the differences. When adding, exponents remain the same. Only when multiplying (or dividing, as in Section 14.10) do they add (or subtract) exponents.

14.9 You might introduce this section by reviewing subtraction of integers, emphasizing the importance of opposites. To assist students in finding opposites of polynomials, thoroughly discuss Examples 1 and 2. Once they feel comfortable in doing this, subtraction of the polynomials should follow with ease. Again, remind students that *to subtract,* they *add the opposite.*

The cartoon in *Can You Solve It?,* page 472, poses a problem with just enough information for students to solve. It serves as a quick review of problem solving and may be assigned as enrichment.

14.10 As in Section 14.5, strongly emphasize the rule given for division. This will avoid the possible mistake, for example, of

$$\frac{12x^3}{4x} = 8x^2$$

Also, when students are dividing polynomials by monomials, have them *first* change the problem to a sum of monomials divided by monomials, as in Examples 4 and 5. This will avoid mistakes such as

$$\frac{\overset{10}{20x^3} + 4x^2}{\underset{1}{2x}} = \frac{10x^3}{x} + \frac{4x^2}{x} = 10x^2 + 4x$$

as well as many others.

This section may be omitted for the regular course.

Going to College?, page 478, should be discussed with all students, as it may affect the future plans of many of them.

Overview: This chapter discusses some of the basic concepts of statistics and probability. Methods of organizing sets of numbers, of determining measures of central tendency, and of computing probabilities are presented. The chapter offers a change of pace in the students' study of mathematics while requiring the use of concepts learned in previous chapters.

15.1 In making a frequency table students should first determine the range of the set of numbers. Have them list the numbers in the *Number* (or otherwise appropriately labeled) column in ascending order, skipping *no* integers between the low and high numbers. The *Tally* column will be helpful to students in determining the frequency of each number. You may allow students to omit this column if they wish.

For students working the C exercises point out that the groups are all the same size. You might let these students suggest other appropriate sizes for the groups and make frequency tables using the new groupings.

15.2 Discuss the labels on each graph. Point out that since there is no one correct scale for the frequency, the scale can vary. When drawing a graph, students should choose a scale that is appropriate for the numbers that they are showing on the graph. Point out that the scale for the frequency for the graph for Exercise 1–8 jumps from 0 to 45. This is shown using a jagged line.

15.3 Discuss the meaning of median as the middle number of a list that is arranged in order of size. Point out that the median is not necessarily the same as the average.

15.4 Point out in Example 3 how the total of the numbers in a set can be found by simply multiplying the number of items by the mean value.

Exercises 15–21 require students to determine whether they are looking for the mean of a set of numbers or its total. You might point out that when the total of a set is given along with the number of items in the set, part of the work has already been done—the only operation left is the division.

What's Average?, page 494, lets the students apply what they have learned in Sections 15.3 and 15.4 to situations where the

best measure of central tendency is to be determined. This could be used as a class discussion with the present section.

15.5 Sections 15.5–15.9 form a unit on probability. Here students are introduced to experimental and theoretical probabilities of certain events.

The statements at the bottom of page 496 should be thoroughly discussed. You might have students suggest outcomes that would have probabilities of 0 and 1.

15.6 Be sure that students understand how a tree diagram is made. Point out that multiplication can be used to check that a tree diagram has the correct number of results.

15.7 This section requires students to add fractions. For this reason you may wish to give a short review of addition with fractions or have students refer back to Sections 4.7 and 4.8 when they feel the need.

15.8 Make sure students understand the difference between independent events and mutually exclusive events. Since students are required to multiply fractions to obtain probabilities in this section, you may find the need to review Sections 4.2 and 4.3.

Math in Paraprofessions, page 507, introduces students to some applications of statistics and probability. It also suggests paraprofessions as possible careers to consider.

The two activities in *Experiments With Chance*, page 511, provide the opportunity for students to do experiments for themselves. If time allows, you might wish to have students work these experiments in class.

The *Cumulative Review*, pages 512–516, can be used as an end-of-semester review for the second semester for the minimum course.

Overview: This chapter discusses basic geometric figures, both two-dimensional and three-dimensional. The relationships of figures and parts of figures are examined. Finding the perimeter, the circumference, the area, the surface area, and the volume of geometric figures uses many previously learned skills.

16.1 Point out that in speaking, "line AB" may mean "line segment AB." Draw ray GH and ray HG on the board. Be sure that students understand that they are not the same ray. However, line HG is the same as line GH and line segment HG is the same as line segment GH.

Have a large rectangular prism available for discussion and examination by students while Exercises 20–26 are completed. It would also be useful for demonstrating skew lines.

16.2 Point out the difference between polygons and figures that are not polygons. A polygon is a simple (no sides crossing) closed figure. The names reflect the number of sides: tri—three, quad—four, pent—five, hex—six, oct—eight. Be sure to discuss regular polygons and other special polygons.

Measuring is an essential skill. Students should have little difficulty with Exercises 11–30. If they do, review the basic skills of using rulers—both customary and metric— and have students measure and draw many line segments.

Exercises 51–54 are expected to raise some thoughts involving logical reasoning. These could be completed orally in a small-group setting.

16.3 After students have completed Exercise 18, encourage them to find the area of other trapezoids and then find a general formula for the area. They should find $A = (b_1 + b_2) \div 2 \times h$, where b_1 and b_2 are the bases and h is the height.

16.4 Make sure that students understand that the bases of a prism are congruent and parallel. In this lesson, only right prisms are considered. Encourage students to use a step-by-step approach in finding surface area: Find the area of each base, find the area of each side (lateral face), and then find the sum of the measures.

16.5. Be sure that students understand that the volume of a prism or a cylinder is found by multiplying the area of the base by the height. Some students may need review in finding the area of the base.

Liters of Fun, page 533, is intended to extend the student's understanding of the metric system while providing some fun. Students may wish to use suitable containers for Exercises 4–6.

Tangrams, page 534, can be used as an independent activity. It is a tool that can be used to see geometric relationships and to build visual perception skills. There are more than 300 possible designs. Students who enjoy this activity should be encouraged to use their imagination to find some of the other designs.

Math on the Farm, page 535, provides practical applications of finding perimeter, area, and volume to the career of farming.

Overview: In this chapter linear equations are graphed in the coordinate plane. Point out that if any equation has two variables, the solution set must be an ordered pair where the value of x is written first, regardless of where it appears in the equation.

Students will learn that the graph of every equation in the form $Ax + By = C$ is a straight line. They will change equations from standard form to slope-intercept form.

17.1 Equations that have a straight-line graph are called linear equations. Be sure to discuss the beginning paragraphs of this lesson in detail. Also discuss each example in a step-by-step method. Emphasize that in the slope-intercept form, y must be positive. For students assigned the C exercises, you may wish to extend the discussion of horizontal and vertical lines by asking what the slope is for equations like $y = 3$ ($m = 0$) and $x = {}^{-}4$ (m is undefined).

17.2 Students must understand the meaning of the symbols $<$, $>$, $\leq$, and $\geq$. To challenge more capable students, extend Exercise 28 by having the students make up similar exercises.

Hitting the Slopes, page 547, shows students how to tell if two lines are parallel or perpendicular by simply looking at the equations in slope-intercept form.

17.3 Direct variations and their graphs are easily understood if students realize that they have worked with many such equations. Caution students not to try to use a short-cut with the suggested methods.

17.4 Emphasize that inverse variations do not have a straight line for a graph. For Exercises 17 and 18 students need only show the first-quadrant (positive) branch of the hyperbola.

17.5 Guide students through the process of solving systems of equations graphically. Emphasize the need to check all solutions found by using graphs.

Example 3 illustrates two types of systems that often give students problems: those with no solutions and those with many solutions. If students did not complete *Hitting the Slopes* on page 547, now would be a good time to assign this topic.

Advanced students should be given the opportunity to solve a system of equations by substitution, as shown in the C exercises.

Math and Science, page 558, uses Boyle's Law as an example of using mathematics in laboratory experiments.

The *Cumulative Review*, pages 562–563, can be used with the *Cumulative Review* on pages 512–516 as an end-of-semester review for the second semester.

Performance Objectives

This list of course goals includes objectives for
every section of PREPARING TO USE ALGEBRA.

Chapter 1

The student can do the following:

1.1 ☐ Recognize the common metric units
for measuring length, mass (weight),
temperature, and capacity.

☐ Know the meanings of the metric
prefixes *kilo-*, *centi-*, and *milli-*.

1.2 ☐ Determine the value of a numerical
phrase by using the rule for order of
operations or by following the order
indicated with parentheses.

1.3 ☐ Recognize a variable as a place-
holder.

☐ Evaluate a phrase by replacing the
variable(s) with the given number(s).

1.4 ☐ Translate simple verbal phrases into
numerical phrases.

1.5 ☐ Write numerical sentences using
the verbs =, <, and >.

☐ Translate simple verbal sentences
into equations and inequalities.

1.6 ☐ Classify a sentence as true, false,
or open.

☐ Find whole-number replacements
to make an open sentence true or false.

1.7 ☐ Determine the solution set of an
open sentence by replacing the variable
with each member of a limited replacement set.

1.8 ☐ Solve and check equations of the
form $n + 3 = 5$ or $12 = n + 7$ by using
the balance beam as a model.

1.9 ☐ Determine the value of one variable
of a formula by substituting the given
value(s) for the other variable(s).

Chapter 2

The student can do the following:

2.1 ☐ Select the inverse of a given
operation.

☐ Simplify given expressions involving inverse operations.

☐ Check subtraction and division by
using inverse operations.

2.2 ☐ Solve an addition or subtraction
equation by using the inverse operation.

2.3 ☐ Solve a multiplication or division
equation by using the inverse operation.

2.4 ☐ Solve an inequality involving only
one operation by using the inverse
operation, and then graph the solutions
on a number line.

2.5 ☐ Solve and graph an open sentence
involving only one operation.

2.6 ☐ Solve an equation involving two
operations by using the inverse operations in reverse order.

2.7 ☐ Use multiplication and division of
whole numbers to convert common
U.S. measurements to equivalent U.S.
measurements.

2.8 ☐ Use formulas to find areas and volumes of geometric figures in either metric or U.S. units.

2.9 ☐ Use symbols to represent quantities.
☐ Translate verbal sentences into equations.

Chapter 3

The student can do the following:

3.1 ☐ Apply the commutative properties of addition and multiplication to solving equations and to making computation easy.

3.2 ☐ Apply both the commutative and associative properties to solving equations and to simplifying computation.

3.3 ☐ Recognize and use the properties of zero and one in computation and equation solving.

3.4 ☐ Use the distributive property in equation solving and in computation.

3.5 ☐ Find the factors of a whole number.

3.6 ☐ Use the rules for divisibility to decide whether a whole number is divisible by 2, 3, 5, or 10 and to help find the factors of a whole number.

3.7 ☐ Determine whether a whole number is prime or composite.
☐ Give the prime factorization of a whole number.

3.8 ☐ Express a power by using an exponent.
☐ Find the value of a power that is expressed with an exponent.

3.9 ☐ Find the greatest common factor of two or more whole numbers by using prime factorization.

3.10 ☐ Find the least common multiple of two or more whole numbers by using prime factorization.

Chapter 4

The student can do the following:

4.1 ☐ Find equivalent fractions by using diagrams.
☐ Add fractions that have a common denominator.

4.2 ☐ Multiply with fractions.

4.3 ☐ Express a fraction in lowest terms.

4.4 ☐ Express a mixed number as a fraction and a fraction as a mixed number.

4.5 ☐ Multiply with mixed numbers.
☐ Convert a U.S. measurement from one unit to a smaller one by multiplying.

4.6 ☐ Divide with fractions and mixed numbers.
☐ Convert a U.S. measurement from one unit to a larger one by dividing.

4.7 ☐ Add and subtract with fractions and with mixed numbers that have a common denominator.

4.8 ☐ Add and subtract with fractions that have different denominators.

4.9 ☐ Add and subtract with mixed numbers that have different denominators.

4.10 ☐ Solve verbal problems that involve U.S. units of measurement.

☐ Decide whether the fractional result or the next larger or smaller whole number is the best answer.

Chapter 5

The student can do the following:

5.1 ☐ Correctly read a decimal.

☐ Change a decimal to an equivalent fraction or mixed number.

☐ Change a fraction or mixed number whose denominator is 10, 100, or 1000 to a decimal.

5.2 ☐ Round a number to the place indicated.

☐ Estimate the answer to a whole-number computation by rounding.

5.3 ☐ Add or subtract decimals.

☐ Estimate the answer to an addition or a subtraction involving decimals.

5.4 ☐ Multiply decimals.

☐ Estimate the answer to a multiplication involving decimals.

☐ Convert a metric measurement from one unit to a smaller one by multiplying.

5.5 ☐ Divide decimals by whole numbers.

☐ Change a fraction or mixed number to an equivalent decimal.

☐ Convert a metric measurement from one unit to a larger one by dividing.

5.6 ☐ Divide decimals.

5.7 ☐ Solve problems involving decimals and metric units.

Chapter 6

The student can do the following:

6.1 ☐ Identify the opposite of any integer.

6.2 ☐ Use a number line to find the sum of two integers.

6.3 ☐ Find the absolute value of an integer.

☐ Add integers without using a number line.

6.4 ☐ Subtract an integer by adding the opposite.

6.5 ☐ Solve equations involving addition of integers.

6.6 ☐ Solve equations involving subtraction of integers.

6.7 ☐ Solve and graph inequalities involving addition or subtraction of integers.

6.8 ☐ Use equations to solve verbal problems involving integers.

Chapter 7

The student can do the following:

7.1 ☐ Find the product of two integers when both are positive or when one is positive and one is negative.

7.2 ☐ Find the product of any two or three integers.

7.3 ☐ Find the quotient of any two integers (no fractional results).

☐ Use the rule for order of operations with integers.

7.4 □ Solve equations involving multiplication of integers.

7.5 □ Solve equations involving division of integers.

7.6 □ Solve and graph inequalities involving division of integers.

7.7 □ Solve and graph inequalities involving multiplication of integers.

7.8 □ Solve equations involving two operations with integers.

7.9 □ Solve verbal problems involving multiplication or division of integers.

Chapter 8

Th student can do the following:

8.1 □ List a set of ordered pairs for a given rule.

8.2 □ Graph a set of ordered pairs of whole numbers using graph paper.

8.3 □ Graph a set of ordered pairs of integers using graph paper.

8.4 □ Draw a line graph for a table of ordered pairs.

8.5 □ Determine whether a set of ordered pairs is a function by inspecting the ordered pairs or their graph.

8.6 □ Use formulas to solve verbal problems.

8.7 □ Make an enlargement (or a reduction) of a figure by multiplying (or dividing) both coordinates of each given point and graphing the new ordered pairs.

8.8 □ Slide a figure by adding to or subtracting from one or both coordinates of each given point and graphing the new ordered pairs.

Chapter 9

The student can do the following:

9.1 □ Use ratios to make comparisons.
□ Name ratios in three ways.

9.2 □ Find ratios equivalent to a given ratio.

9.3 □ Use cross products to solve proportions.

9.4 □ Use proportions to solve problems.

9.5 □ Express ratios as per cents.
□ Express per cents as decimals, fractions, mixed numbers, or whole numbers.

9.6 □ Change decimals, fractions, mixed numbers, or whole numbers to per cents.

9.7 □ Solve the three kinds of per cent problems.

9.8 □ Solve verbal problems involving per cents.

9.9 □ Estimate the answers to calculations involving per cents.

9.10 □ Solve problems involving per cent of increase or per cent of decrease.

Chapter 10

The student can do the following:

10.1 ☐ Identify similar figures.

10.2 ☐ Identify the corresponding angles and the corresponding sides of similar triangles.

10.3 ☐ Write proportions for the corresponding sides of similar triangles.

☐ Use proportions to find the length of a side of a triangle in a pair of similar triangles.

10.4 ☐ Use the proportions between the sides of similar triangles to make indirect measurements.

10.5 ☐ Use the proportions between the sides of similar triangles to solve problems about objects bouncing off a surface.

10.6 ☐ Compute distances using map scales and proportions.

10.7 ☐ Find measurements using scale drawings or models, and proportions.

Chapter 11

The student can do the following:

11.1 ☐ State the opposite and find the absolute value of a rational number.

☐ Graph rational numbers on a number line.

11.2 ☐ Determine for a pair of rational numbers like $\frac{4}{5}$ and $\frac{2}{3}$ whether $\frac{4}{5} < \frac{2}{3}$, $\frac{4}{5} = \frac{2}{3}$, or $\frac{4}{5} > \frac{2}{3}$.

11.3 ☐ Add and subtract positive and negative decimals.

11.4 ☐ Solve equations involving addition or subtraction of positive and negative decimals.

11.5 ☐ Add and subtract positive and negative fractions.

11.6 ☐ Add and subtract positive and negative mixed numbers.

11.7 ☐ Solve equations involving addition or subtraction of positive and negative fractions or mixed numbers.

11.8 ☐ Use equations involving addition or subtraction of rational numbers to solve verbal problems.

Chapter 12

The student can do the following:

12.1 ☐ Multiply and divide positive and negative decimals.

☐ Use the rule for order of operations in computing with positive and negative decimals.

12.2 ☐ Solve equations involving multiplication or division of positive and negative decimals.

12.3 ☐ Multiply and divide positive and negative fractions.

☐ Use the rule for order of operations in computing with positive and negative fractions.

12.4 ☐ Multiply and divide positive and negative mixed numbers.

12.5 ☐ Find the reciprocal of a rational number expressed as a fraction, a mixed number, or an integer.

12.6 ☐ Solve equations involving multiplication or division of positive and negative fractions.

12.7 ☐ Solve equations involving two operations with rational numbers.

12.8 ☐ Use formulas to solve problems.

12.9 ☐ Express numbers in scientific notation.

Chapter 13

The student can do the following:

13.1 ☐ Determine the positive and negative square roots of square numbers (perfect squares).

13.2 ☐ Use a table to find squares and approximate square roots of whole numbers.

13.3 ☐ Find square roots of numbers greater than 150 by using the property $\sqrt{ab} = \sqrt{a} \times \sqrt{b}$ and the table.

13.4 ☐ Find square roots of rational numbers written in fraction or decimal form.

13.5 ☐ Solve equations that involve taking the square root of each side.

13.6 ☐ Determine the length of a side of a right triangle by using the Pythagorean Property.

13.7 ☐ Use the Pythagorean Property to solve indirect-measurement problems.

13.8 ☐ Solve problems by using formulas involving square roots.

Chapter 14

The student can do the following:

14.1 ☐ Solve verbal problems using equations involving more than one operation.

14.2 ☐ Determine if a verbal problem gives too much, too little, or just enough information for solving it.

☐ Solve problems with just enough or too much information.

14.3 ☐ Identify monomials, binomials, and trinomials as special polynomials.

☐ Distinguish between like and unlike terms.

14.4 ☐ Simplify polynomials involving addition and subtraction of like terms.

14.5 ☐ Multiply monomials.

14.6 ☐ Multiply a binomial by a monomial.

14.7 ☐ Multiply two binomials.

14.8 ☐ Add two or more polynomials.

14.9 ☐ Find the opposite of a polynomial.

☐ Subtract one polynomial from another.

14.10 ☐ Divide a polynomial by a monomial.

Chapter 15

The student can do the following:

15.1 ☐ Find the range of a set of numbers.

☐ Make a frequency table for a set of numbers.

15.2 ☐ Read, interpret, and make bar graphs and histograms.

☐ Determine the mode of a set of numbers.

15.3 ☐ Find the median of a set of numbers.

15.4 ☐ Find the mean of a set of numbers.

☐ Find the sum of the items in a set when given the mean and the number of items.

15.5 ☐ Determine the experimental and theoretical probabilities of a particular outcome.

15.6 ☐ Use a tree diagram to show possible outcomes and to determine the probability of a particular result.

15.7 ☐ Determine the theoretical probability of outcome *A or B* where *A* and *B* are two mutually exclusive events.

15.8 ☐ Determine the theoretical probability of outcome *A and B* where *A* and *B* are two independent events.

Chapter 16

The student can do the following:

16.1 ☐ Identify basic geometric figures and classify angles.

16.2 ☐ Identify polygons and classify triangles.

☐ Measure a line segment to the nearest $\frac{1}{8}$ inch and to the nearest centimeter.

☐ Find the perimeter of a polygon and the circumference of a circle.

16.3 ☐ Find the area of a polygon or a circle.

16.4 ☐ Identify three-dimensional figures and find their surface areas.

16.5 ☐ Find the volume of three-dimensional figures.

Chapter 17

The student can do the following:

17.1 ☐ Identify standard and slope-intercept forms of equations and draw their graphs.

17.2 ☐ Graph inequalities in the coordinate plane.

17.3 ☐ Identify direct variations and draw their graphs.

17.4 ☐ Identify inverse variations and draw their graphs.

17.5 ☐ Solve a system of equations by graphing.

Notes

Manual

T36

Overview of Tests

Chapter tests. The following tests contain a pretest and a posttest for each of the 17 chapters in PREPARING TO USE ALGEBRA. Since the pretests are parallel in content and difficulty to the posttests, they can also be used as alternate posttests.

Cumulative tests. Also included are five cumulative tests covering Chapters 1–3, 1–7, 8–10, 8–15, and 16–17. On the following pages, each cumulative test is inserted at the proper place in the sequence of chapter tests (for example, Cumulative Test for Chapters 1–3 follows Posttest for Chapter 3). The cumulative tests provide a midsemester test and an end-of-semester test for each semester. There is also an End-of-Year test.

Test times. Each chapter pretest and posttest is designed to be completed in about 40 minutes. Each cumulative test will require approximately 80 minutes. The End-of-Year Test will require approximately 160 minutes.

Pretest for Chapter 1   Symbols and Sentences

1–5. Match each term or symbol with the best description.

1. kilo-

2. milli-

3. meter

4. gram

5. 7(5)

a. metric unit of weight

b. prefix meaning "thousandth"

c. divide 7 by 5

d. prefix meaning "thousand"

e. metric unit of length

f. multiply 7 by 5

6–7. Find each value.

6. $16 + 5 \times 3$

7. $(17 - 4) \times 2$

8–9. Replace each variable with 6. Find the value.

8. $6y + 4$

9. $n(n - 2)$

10–13. Classify each sentence as *True*, *False*, or *Open*.

10. $n + 7 = 2$

11. $6 > 4 + 2$

12. $32 - 6 \times 2 = 20$

13. $7x = 35$

14–15. Solve. Use {3, 4, 5, 6, 7} as the replacement set.

14. $28 = 3x + 7$

15. $2y + 1 < 12$

16–17. Solve.

16. $x + 5 = 12$

17. $16 = n + 7$

18–19. Use the formula $m = c \div 100$ to find the number of meters (*m*) equal to the given number of centimeters (*c*).

18. 700

19. 45 000

20. *Translate into symbols:* Eight is less than some number *n* decreased by five.

Posttest for Chapter 1   Symbols and Sentences

1–5. Match each term or symbol with the best description.

1. centi-

2. degree Celsius

3. cm

4. $\frac{3}{4}$

5. liter

a. symbol for centimeters

b. divide three by four

c. three is less than four

d. prefix meaning "hundredth"

e. metric unit of temperature

f. metric unit of capacity

6–8. Find each value.

6. $21 - 10 \div 2$

7. $(6 + 7) \div (15 - 2)$

8. $(17 + 9)2$

9–10. Replace each variable with 5. Find the value.

9. $3x + 7$

10. $7(y + 2)$

11–14. Classify each sentence as *True, False,* or *Open*.

11. $25 - 4 \times 3 = 13$

12. $x + 6 = 8$

13. $10 < 6 - 1$

14. $3(6) > 15$

15–16. Solve. Use $\{0, 1, 2, 3, 4\}$ as the replacement set.

15. $2 + n < 6$

16. $15 = 4x - 1$

17–18. Solve.

17. $n + 9 = 14$

18. $17 = x + 12$

19. Use the formula $d = rt$ to find the distance flown by a plane that travels 480 kilometers an hour for 3 hours.

20. *Translate into symbols:* Fourteen is greater than some number n increased by twelve.

Pretest for Chapter 2   Solving Open Sentences

1–8. Solve.

1. $x + 17 = 36$

2. $12 = n - 3$

3. $\frac{n}{6} = 11$

4. $24 = 6z$

5. $2x + 5 = 23$

6. $\frac{r - 6}{2} = 7$

7. $9 = 4s - 7$

8. $7 = \frac{t}{8} - 3$

9–12. Solve and graph.

9. $3x = 18$

10. $n + 4 < 7$

11. $25 > t - 7$

12. $\frac{r}{6} < 10$

13–18. Complete.

13. 300 in. = _?_ ft

14. 11 yd = _?_ ft

15. 5 lb = _?_ oz

16. 28 qt = _?_ gal.

17. A rectangle with length 17 in. and width 9 in. has area _?_ .

18. A rectangular solid 12 cm long, 8 cm high, and 5 cm wide has volume _?_ .

19–20. Translate into symbols.

19. Sixteen is two less than six times a number n.

20. A "scientific" calculator costs $9 more than twice as much as a "student" calculator from the same company. The scientific calculator costs $59.

Posttest for Chapter 2   Solving Open Sentences

1–8. Solve.

1. $x + 11 = 18$

2. $18 = n - 4$

3. $\frac{z}{3} = 15$

4. $35 = 7y$

5. $4x + 1 = 33$

6. $\frac{t - 5}{3} = 6$

7. $12 = 5x - 3$

8. $5 = \frac{n}{12} - 3$

9–12. Solve and graph.

9. $24 = 6n$

10. $x + 5 < 9$

11. $y - 3 > 17$

12. $\frac{a}{3} > 9$

13–18. Complete.

13. 64 oz = _?_ lb

14. 17 ft = _?_ in.

15. 14 qt = _?_ pt

16. 42 ft = _?_ yd

17. The area of a rectangle 18 inches long and 8 inches wide is _?_ .

18. The volume of a rectangular solid with length 15 cm, width 12 cm, and height 9 cm is _?_ .

19–20. Translate into symbols.

19. Thirty-seven is two more than seven times a number.

20. A \$175 pocket camera with automatic exposure costs \$25 more than three times as much as another pocket camera from the same company.

Pretest for Chapter 3   Important Properties

1–4. Compute.

1. $5 \times (20 \times 37)$

2. $(6 + 43) + 4$

3. $(9 \times 17) + (1 \times 17)$

4. $3(10 + 4)$

5–7. Solve.

5. $(6x)4 = 96$

6. $11n + 2n = 39$

7. $14y - y = 78$

8–13. Find the value.

8. 12×0

9. $16 \div 16$

10. $0 \div 17$

11. 6^2

12. 1^7

13. the square of 5

14. Is the given number prime or composite?

  a. 11

  b. 14

15. Find all the factors you can for each number.

  a. 18

  b. 30

16. Write the prime factorization.

  a. 25

  b. 40

17. Is 1620 divisible by the given number?

  a. 2

  b. 5

  c. 10

  d. 3

18. Write, using exponents.

  a. $6 \times 6 \times 6 \times 6 \times 6$

  b. $1 \times 1 \times 1$

19. Find the GCF of each set of numbers.

  a. 8 and 18

  b. 9, 12, and 15

20. Find the LCM of each set of numbers.

  a. 7 and 12

  b. 9, 12, and 15

Posttest for Chapter 3   Important Properties

1–4. Compute.

1. $(16 \times 4) \times 25$

2. $(19 + 198) + 2$

3. $(8 \times 27) + (2 \times 27)$

4. $7(100 + 4)$

5–7. Solve.

5. $(9y)6 = 108$

6. $15x + 5x = 100$

7. $18z - z = 85$

8–13. Find the value.

8. 1×14

9. $92 + 0$

10. $0 \div 12$

11. 3^4

12. 5^3

13. the square of 8

14. Is the given number prime or composite?

    a. 15

    b. 13

15. Find all the factors you can for each number.

    a. 32

    b. 16

16. Write the prime factorization.

    a. 50

    b. 20

17. Is 165 divisible by the given number?

    a. 2   **b.** 5   **c.** 10   **d.** 3

18. Write, using exponents.

    a. $2 \times 2 \times 2$

    b. $4 \times 4 \times 4 \times 4 \times 4$

19. Find the GCF of each set of numbers.

    a. 12 and 28

    b. 6, 18, and 33

20. Find the LCM of each set of numbers.

    a. 9 and 10

    b. 6, 18, and 33

Cumulative Test for Chapters 1–3

1–2. Which term in parentheses is the best choice?

1. The (*liter, gram, meter*) is a metric unit of weight.

2. The prefix (*kilo-, centi-, milli-*) means "thousandth."

3–11. Find each value.

3. $4 + 2 \times 5$

4. $(5 \times 3) + (12 \div 2)$

5. 4^3

6. $9 + 5 - 14$

7. $(18 + 6) \div (23 - 17)$

8. $3^2 \times 2^4$

9. $(7 \times 1) + (14 \div 14)$

10. $(9 + 5) - 14$

11. $2^2 \times 3 \times 5$

12–19. Solve each equation.

12. $y + 9 = 31$

13. $x - 11 = 18$

14. $5n = 45$

15. $\frac{x}{3} = 16$

16. $4y + 9 = 41$

17. $\frac{n + 7}{2} = 9$

18. $^-19 + y = ^-19$

19. $18x - 6x = 24$

20–22. Solve each inequality.

20. $n - 5 < 9$

21. $6y > 18$

22. $\frac{x}{11} < 4$

23. Use the formula $c = m \div 10$ to find the number of centimeters (*c*) equal to 5200 millimeters (*m*).

24. *Translate into symbols:* Fourteen divided by some number n is less than five.

25–29. Complete.

25. 7 ft = __?__ in.

26. 63 ft = __?__ yd

27. 48 oz = __?__ lb

28. 12 gal. = __?__ qt

29. A rectangle with length 19 in. and width 7 in. has area __?__ .

30. Write the prime factorization of 105.

31–34. Is the given number prime or composite?

31. 19   **32.** 28   **33.** 22   **34.** 29

35–37. Find the GCF of each set of numbers.

35. 18 and 42   **36.** 11 and 20   **37.** 7, 35, and 49

38–40. Find the LCM of each set of numbers.

38. 6 and 30   **39.** 12 and 15   **40.** 5, 6, and 10

1–5. Express as a fraction.

1. $5 \div 7$ **2.** 41 **3.** $2\frac{1}{2}$ **4.** 0 **5.** $2 \div 3$

6–9. Express in lowest terms.

6. $\frac{10}{25}$ **7.** $\frac{48}{64}$ **8.** $\frac{9}{6}$ **9.** $3\frac{5}{3}$

10–24. Compute.

10. $\frac{1}{3} \times \frac{4}{5}$ **11.** $\frac{2}{3} \times \frac{3}{8}$ **12.** $7 \times \frac{1}{2}$

13. $2\frac{1}{2} \times \frac{1}{3}$ **14.** $3\frac{1}{2} \times 2\frac{1}{5}$ **15.** $\frac{3}{7} \div \frac{1}{3}$

16. $\frac{3}{8} \div 6$ **17.** $1\frac{1}{4} \div 2$ **18.** $4\frac{1}{9} \div 2\frac{1}{3}$

19. $\begin{array}{r} \frac{5}{12} \\ +\frac{3}{12} \\ \hline \end{array}$ **20.** $\begin{array}{r} 3\frac{5}{8} \\ -1\frac{3}{8} \\ \hline \end{array}$ **21.** $\begin{array}{r} 7 \\ -3\frac{5}{16} \\ \hline \end{array}$

22. $\begin{array}{r} 5\frac{1}{2} \\ +7\frac{5}{6} \\ \hline \end{array}$ **23.** $\begin{array}{r} \frac{1}{5} \\ +\frac{3}{4} \\ \hline \end{array}$ **24.** $\begin{array}{r} 6\frac{5}{8} \\ -3\frac{7}{8} \\ \hline \end{array}$

25. How many $2\frac{1}{2}$-gallon buckets can be filled from a 20-gallon tank?

Tests

Posttest for Chapter 4   Fractions and Mixed Numbers

1–5. Express as a fraction.

1. $7 \div 9$ **2.** 29 **3.** 1 **4.** $5\frac{1}{3}$ **5.** $2\frac{1}{2}$

6–9. Express in lowest terms.

6. $\frac{12}{40}$ **7.** $\frac{14}{72}$ **8.** $\frac{15}{10}$ **9.** $4\frac{8}{5}$

10–24. Compute.

10. $\frac{1}{2} \times \frac{7}{8}$ **11.** $\frac{3}{4} \times \frac{4}{9}$ **12.** $\frac{2}{3} \times 6$

13. $4\frac{3}{8} \times \frac{1}{6}$ **14.** $9\frac{1}{3} \times 3\frac{3}{8}$ **15.** $\frac{5}{8} \div \frac{1}{5}$

16. $\frac{5}{8} \div 10$ **17.** $2\frac{1}{2} \div 4$ **18.** $3\frac{1}{3} \div 1\frac{1}{9}$

19. $\begin{array}{r} \frac{1}{14} \\ +\frac{5}{14} \\ \hline \end{array}$ **20.** $\begin{array}{r} 5\frac{4}{7} \\ -1\frac{1}{7} \\ \hline \end{array}$ **21.** $\begin{array}{r} 9 \\ -2\frac{1}{2} \\ \hline \end{array}$

22. $\begin{array}{r} 5\frac{2}{3} \\ +9\frac{3}{6} \\ \hline \end{array}$ **23.** $\begin{array}{r} \frac{1}{3} \\ +\frac{3}{4} \\ \hline \end{array}$ **24.** $\begin{array}{r} 4\frac{7}{10} \\ -2\frac{9}{10} \\ \hline \end{array}$

25. The Smiths' car goes $17\frac{1}{3}$ miles on a gallon of gas. How far does it go on 5 gallons?

Pretest for Chapter 5   Decimals and Estimating

1–3. Write as a fraction or a mixed number.

1. 0.008   **2.** 0.03   **3.** 13.7

4–6. Write as a decimal.

4. $\frac{3}{8}$ **5.** $4\frac{3}{5}$ **6.** $\frac{9}{1000}$

7–8. Round to the nearest (a) ten, (b) one, and (c) hundredth.

7. 438.619   **8.** 22.073

9–14. (a) Estimate the value;
      (b) then compute the value.

9. 23.8 + 7.2   **10.** 9.683 − 4.79   **11.** 3.7 × 1.8

12. 3.24 × 6.5   **13.** 4.78 + 3.901 + 6.4   **14.** 4.97 × 1.8

15–20. Compute.

15. 6.5 ÷ 0.05   **16.** 9.6 ÷ 16   **17.** 6.98 × 100

18. 437.8 ÷ 100   **19.** 53 cm × 20 cm   **20.** 4 km × 1.9 km

21–24. Complete.

21. 3.6 km = _?_ m   **22.** 12 cm = _?_ m

23. 42 mm = _?_ cm   **24.** 12.4 kg = _?_ g

25. If five people are served equal portions from a bottle
holding 950 mL of milk, how much is in each portion?

Posttest for Chapter 5   Decimals and Estimating

1–3. Write as a fraction or mixed number.

1. 0.68   **2.** 0.007   **3.** 24.3

4–6. Write as a decimal.

4. $\frac{5}{8}$ **5.** $8\frac{1}{5}$ **6.** $\frac{7}{100}$

7–8. Round to the nearest (a) ten, (b) one, and (c) hundredth.

7. 618.824   **8.** 14.185

9–14. (a) Estimate the value;
         (b) then compute the value.

9. 18.7 + 4.3   **10.** 12.704 − 3.86   **11.** 7.18 × 3.9

12. 2.9 × 3.2   **13.** 3.64 + 6.934 + 1.3   **14.** 43.8 × 1.3

15–20. Compute.

15. 12.8 ÷ 0.04   **16.** 2.25 ÷ 15   **17.** 8.49 × 100

18. 8342.5 ÷ 1000   **19.** 6 cm × 81 cm   **20.** 3.5 km + 0.7 km

21–24. Complete.

21. 7.1 km = _?_ m   **22.** 43 cm = _?_ m

23. 98 mm = _?_ cm   **24.** 28.6 kg = _?_ g

25. If 960 mL of a liquid is divided into four equal
portions, how much is in each portion?

Pretest for Chapter 6   Adding and Subtracting Integers

1–3. Name the opposite of each number.

1. ⁻19   **2.** 7   **3.** 0

4–6. State the absolute value of each number.

4. 32   **5.** ⁻4   **6.** ⁻16

7. Arrange the numbers in order from least to greatest.

⁻15, 12, 0, 15, 7, ⁻3

8–15. Compute.

8. ⁻8 + 15   **9.** ⁻35 + 20   **10.** ⁻72 + ⁻11

11. 9 + ⁻18 + 2   **12.** 15 − ⁻7   **13.** ⁻30 − ⁻45

14. ⁻6 − 13   **15.** ⁻12 − (⁻3 + 3)

16–19. Solve.

16. ⁻20 = x − 10   **17.** n − ⁻3 = 12

18. 5 = x − ⁻10   **19.** 6 = y − 2

20–23. Solve and graph.

20. x + ⁻4 > 10   **21.** x + 2 < ⁻7

22. y − ⁻4 > 10   **23.** n + ⁻7 < 16

24–25. Solve these problems.

24. A number minus ⁻9 is 12. What is the number?

25. The regular price of a television is $573. The sale price is $495. What is the change in price?

Posttest for Chapter 6 Adding and Subtracting Integers

1–3. Name the opposite of each number.

1. 62   **2.** $^-4$ **3.** 23

4–6. State the absolute value of each number.

4. $^-105$ **5.** 0   **6.** 14

7. Arrange the numbers in order from least to greatest.

4, $^-1$, 16, 3, $^-7$, $^-15$

8–15. Compute.

8. $^-16 + 9$ **9.** $^-92 + 147$ **10.** $(14 - 21) + {}^-5$

11. $^-21 - {}^-14$ **12.** $40 - {}^-38$ **13.** $7 - 17$

14. $^-12 + 63$ **15.** $^-4 - 11$

16–19. Solve.

16. $^-3 = 9 + x$ **17.** $n - 21 = {}^-40$

18. $^-21 = y + 7$ **19.** $^-14 + x = 2$

20–23. Solve and graph.

20. $x + 9 < {}^-14$ **21.** $n - {}^-4 < {}^-2$

22. $y - 6 > {}^-14$ **23.** $x + 23 < {}^-12$

24–25. Solve these problems.

24. 10 added to a number equals $^-17$. What is the number?

25. The balance in an account goes from $^-250$ to $^+1000$. What is the change in the account?

Pretest for Chapter 7   Multiplying and Dividing Integers

1–8. Find the product or quotient.

1. $^-2 \times ^-16$

2. $11 \times ^-12$

3. $^-13 \times 3$

4. $24 \div ^-3$

5. $^-125 \div ^-25$

6. $^-63 \div 9$

7. $\frac{15}{^-3}$

8. $\frac{^-12}{^-4}$

9–14. Solve.

9. $2x = ^-12$

10. $^-9y = 54$

11. $8x = 56$

12. $\frac{w}{4} = ^-6$

13. $^-63 = 7x$

14. $1 = \frac{x}{7}$

15–20. Solve and graph.

15. $8n > ^-56$

16. $35 < 7x$

17. $^-80 > ^-16y$

18. $\frac{w}{6} > ^-8$

19. $5 < \frac{x}{^-7}$

20. $^-20 > \frac{m}{^-2}$

21–24. Solve.

21. $2x + 7 = ^-29$

22. $^-19 = ^-5x - 4$

23. $\frac{y}{6} + ^-4 = 9$

24. $\frac{x + ^-2}{5} = 3$

25. A hot-air balloon changed its altitude $^-75$ feet every minute for 15 minutes. What was the total change in altitude?

Posttest for Chapter 7   Multiplying and Dividing Integers

1–5. Find each product or quotient.

1. $^-8 \times 3$

2. $^-16 \times {}^-4$

3. $24 \div {}^-3$

4. $^-72 \div {}^-8$

5. $\frac{49}{^-7}$

6–13. Solve.

6. $^-4x = 48$

7. $^-33 = 3y$

8. $49 = {}^-7n$

9. $9x = 63$

10. $\frac{w}{5} = 2$

11. $^-3 = \frac{x}{^-7}$

12. $\frac{m}{8} = {}^-6$

13. $\frac{y}{^-4} = {}^-32$

14–19. Solve and graph.

14. $6n > {}^-48$

15. $42 < 7x$

16. $^-72 > {}^-18y$

17. $\frac{x}{3} < {}^-24$

18. $^-14 > \frac{w}{^-3}$

19. $2 > \frac{y}{2}$

20–23. Solve.

20. $4x + 7 = {}^-29$

21. $^-23 = 6y - 5$

22. $\frac{x}{8} + {}^-5 = 6$

23. $\frac{n + {}^-4}{3} = 9$

24–25. Solve these problems.

24. An airplane changes its altitude $^-12{,}000$ feet in 8 minutes. What is the rate of change in altitude?

25. A checking account shows a change of $^-\$12$ each week for 16 weeks. What has been the total change in the checking account?

T53

Cumulative Test for Chapters 1–7

1–15. Find each value.

1. $5 + 3 \times 6$

2. $(7 - 7) \div 2$

3. $2^3 + 3^2$

4. $4\frac{1}{2} \div 1\frac{1}{5}$

5. $46 \div 46$

6. $\frac{1}{2} \times 3\frac{1}{4}$

7. $^-9 - ^-7$

8. $3.5\overline{)2.1}$

9. $^-8 + ^-3$

10.
$$\begin{array}{r} \frac{5}{6} \\ +\frac{1}{4} \\ \hline \end{array}$$

11.
$$\begin{array}{r} 42.37 \\ +6.05 \\ \hline \end{array}$$

12.
$$\begin{array}{r} 7 \\ -5\frac{2}{3} \\ \hline \end{array}$$

13.
$$\begin{array}{r} 0.042 \\ \times\ 3.4 \\ \hline \end{array}$$

14. $15 \times ^-4$

15. $^-81 \div ^-9$

16. *Translate into symbols:* Forty-two is three less than five times a number.

17–26. Solve each equation.

17. $x + 14 = 32$

18. $\frac{n}{3} - 8 = 7$

19. $\frac{x + 6}{4} = 1$

20. $1 \times 32 = x$

21. $775 + 0 = n$

22. $7x + 2x = 108$

23. $n - 4 = ^-12$

24. $3x = ^-21$

25. $5y + ^-3 = 27$

26. $\frac{x + 5}{4} = ^-7$

27–32. Solve each inequality.

27. $4x > 24$

28. $y + 6 < 17$

29. $\frac{n}{3} > 1$

30. $n - 7 < 2$

31. $5x > 40$

32. $x + 15 < 37$

33–36. Solve and graph.

33. $x - {}^-2 > 17$ **34.** $n + 3 < {}^-8$ **35.** $\frac{x}{-2} > 21$ **36.** ${}^-56 < 4y$

37–41. Complete.

37. 6 qt = ___?___ pt   **38.** 24 oz = ___?___ lb

39. 4.5 cm = ___?___ mm   **40.** 61 L = ___?___ mL

41. The volume of a rectangular solid with length 13 cm, width 10 cm, and height 7 cm is ___?___ .

42–44. Find the GCF of each pair of numbers.

42. 18 and 42   **43.** 7 and 35   **44.** 11 and 20

45–47. Find the LCM of each pair of numbers.

45. 12 and 15   **46.** 6 and 30   **47.** 9 and 10

48–50. Solve these problems.

48. Use the formula $d = rt$ to find the average speed of a car that traveled a 324-mile course in 6 hours.

49. A recipe calls for $1\frac{1}{2}$ ounces of shortening for each serving. How many ounces are needed for 7 servings?

50. The sale price of a stereo is $472. The regular price is $545. What is the change in price?

Pretest for Chapter 8   Graphing

1–2. Use the rule to complete the ordered pairs. x is given first.

1. $y = {}^-3x + 2$

x	$^-4$	$^-1$	0	$^-5$
y				

2. $y = 2x + 4$

$(0, \underline{\ ?\ }), (1, \underline{\ ?\ }), (^-3, \underline{\ ?\ })$

3–8. Write the ordered pair for each point on the graph at the right.

3. A   **4.** B   **5.** C

6. D   **7.** E   **8.** F

9. Draw a line graph for the table.

x	0	1	2	3	4
y	$^-3$	$^-1$	1	3	5

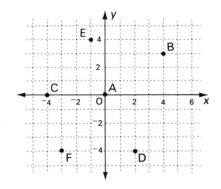

10. Is the graph for Exercises 3–8 the graph of a function?

11. Is the set of ordered pairs $(^-1, 2)$, $(1, 2)$, and $(1, 3)$ a function?

12. For the ordered pair $(^-9, 3)$, the x-coordinate is ___?___ .

13. To reach its destination on time, a plane must make a ground speed g of 147 mph. What airspeed a should it maintain? $g = a - 43$.

14–15. Use the drawings to graph the following:

14. a 1-to-2 reduction

15. a slide 3 units down.

14.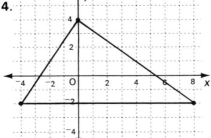

15.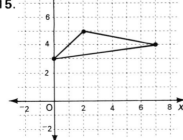

Posttest for Chapter 8   Graphing

1–2. Use the rule to complete the ordered pairs. x is given first.

1. $y = x$

($^-7$, $\_\overset{?}{\_}\_$), (0, $\_\overset{?}{\_}\_$), (10, $\_\overset{?}{\_}\_$)

2. $y = x + 2$

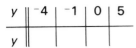

x	$^-4$	$^-1$	0	5
y				

3–8. Write the ordered pair for each point on the graph at the right.

3. A   **4.** B   **5.** C

6. D   **7.** E   **8.** F

9. Draw a line graph for the table.

x	0	1	2	3	4
y	$^-3$	$^-2$	$^-1$	0	1

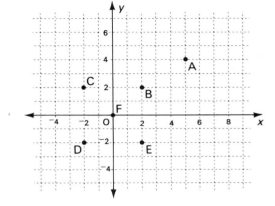

10. What are the coordinates of the origin?

11–12. Tell whether each graph is the graph of a function.

11.

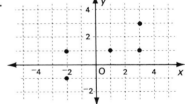

12.

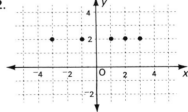

13. Mary saw lightning strike a tree that was 3300 feet away. How long after that did she hear the noise? $d = 1100t$

14–15. Use the drawings to graph the following:

14. a slide 3 units left

15. a 1-to-2 enlargement.

14.

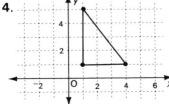

15.

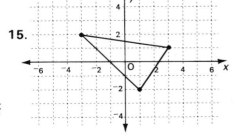

Pretest for Chapter 9   Ratios, Proportions, and Per Cents

1–4. Change each ratio to lowest terms.

1. $\frac{20}{70}$

2. $\frac{24}{48}$

3. $\frac{20}{400}$

4. $\frac{15}{75}$

5–9. Solve each proportion.

5. $\frac{4}{n} = \frac{20}{25}$

6. $\frac{3}{7} = \frac{15}{n}$

7. $\frac{9}{10} = \frac{n}{80}$

8. $\frac{6}{n} = \frac{42}{49}$

9. $\frac{8}{11} = \frac{72}{n}$

10–15. Solve.

10. 4% of 180 is what number?

11. 3.2% of 60 is what number?

12. 16 is what per cent of 80?

13. 7 is what per cent of 20?

14. 60% of what number is 120?

15. 25% of what number is 90?

16–21. Complete the following tables:

	Fraction or mixed number	Decimal	Per cent		Fraction or mixed number	Decimal	Per cent
16.	$\frac{3}{5}$	?	?	**17.**	?	0.375	?
18.	?	0.7	?	**19.**	$\frac{5}{8}$	?	?
20.	?	?	72%	**21.**	?	?	190%

22. Estimate 43% of 594.

23–25. Use a proportion to solve each problem.

23. If a cricket chirps 20 times in 15 minutes, how many times will it chirp in an hour?

24. A restaurant meal cost $24 for 2. How much is a 15% tip for the waiter?

25. If a tire sells for $60 after a 25% reduction, what is the regular price?

T58

Posttest for Chapter 9   Ratios, Proportions, and Per Cents

1–4. Change each ratio to lowest terms.

1. $\frac{30}{80}$

2. $\frac{18}{24}$

3. $\frac{60}{420}$

4. $\frac{30}{75}$

5–9. Solve each proportion.

5. $\frac{3}{9} = \frac{n}{54}$

6. $\frac{4}{7} = \frac{32}{n}$

7. $\frac{7}{10} = \frac{n}{110}$

8. $\frac{5}{n} = \frac{45}{63}$

9. $\frac{5}{13} = \frac{60}{n}$

10–15. Solve.

10. 8% of 240 is what number?

11. 1.9% of 80 is what number?

12. 35 is what per cent of 200?

13. 11 is what per cent of 20?

14. 20% of what number is 17?

15. 80% of what number is 160?

16–21. Complete the following tables:

	Fraction or mixed number	Decimal	Per cent		Fraction or mixed number	Decimal	Per cent
16.	$\frac{4}{5}$	?	?	**17.**	?	$0.16\frac{2}{3}$	?
18.	?	0.9	?	**19.**	$\frac{3}{4}$	?	?
20.	?	?	59%	**21.**	?	?	175%

22. Estimate 32% of 783.

23–25. Use a proportion to solve each problem.

23. If an airplane uses 18 gallons of fuel in cruising for 2 hours, how much fuel will it use in cruising for 5 hours?

24. How much is the 4% sales tax on a $50 video game?

25. If a bathing suit sells for $30 after a 40% reduction, what is the regular price?

Pretest for Chapter 10   Indirect Measurement

1–2. Name the corresponding angles and corresponding sides for each pair of similar triangles.

1.

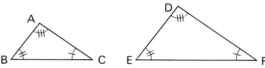

2.

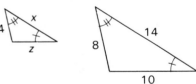

1. ∠A and ∠ ?   **2.** ∠T and ∠ ?

∠B and ∠ ?   ∠U and ∠ ?

∠C and ∠ ?   ∠V and ∠ ?

AB and ?   TV and ?

BC and ?   TU and ?

AC and ?   WV and ?

3–4. What letter should replace each question mark?

3. $\frac{b}{e} = \frac{a}{?}$ **4.** $\frac{c}{f} = \frac{?}{e}$

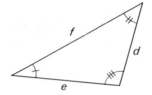

5–6. Solve for *x* and *z* in each pair of similar triangles.

5.

6.

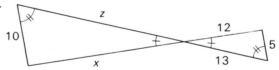

7. What is the actual length of the boat?

Scale: 1 cm = 2 m

8. Find the height of the kite.
(The triangles are similar.)

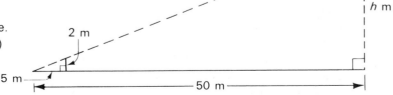

Posttest for Chapter 10   Indirect Measurement

1–2. Name the corresponding angles and corresponding sides for each pair of similar triangles.

1.
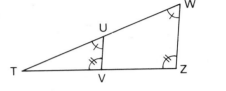

2.
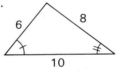

1. ∠A and ∠ ?   **2.** ∠T and ∠ ?

∠B and ∠ ?   ∠U and ∠ ?

∠C and ∠ ?   ∠V and ∠ ?

AB and ?   TV and ?

BC and ?   TU and ?

AC and ?   WZ and ?

3–4. What letter should replace each question mark?

3. $\frac{a}{d} = \frac{c}{?}$ **4.** $\frac{b}{?} = \frac{c}{f}$

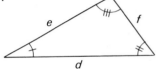

5–6. Solve for *x* and *z* in each pair of similar triangles.

5.   **6.**

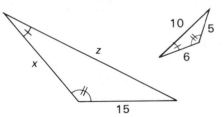

7. What is the actual distance between A and B?

Scale: 1 in. = 12 mi

$1\frac{1}{2}$ in.

8. Find the width of the pond.
(The triangles are similar.)

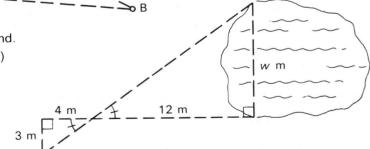

4 m   12 m   *w* m

3 m

T61

Cumulative Test for Chapters 8–10

1–2. Use the rule to complete the ordered pairs.

1. $y = 3x - 2$

    (4, _?_) (5, _?_) (6, _?_) (7, _?_)

2. $y = x - 1$

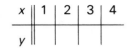

3–6. Write the ordered pair for each point on the graph at the right.

3. R   **4.** S

5. T   **6.** U

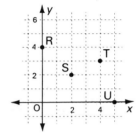

7. Is the graph for Exercises 3–6 the graph of a function?

8–11. Write each ratio as a fraction in lowest terms.

8. 8 losses to 21 wins   **9.** 72 votes to 32 votes

10. 17 nurses to 4 doctors   **11.** 5 teachers to 175 students

12–14. Solve each proportion.

12. $\frac{3}{5} = \frac{9}{n}$ **13.** $\frac{8}{14} = \frac{n}{21}$ **14.** $\frac{n}{7} = \frac{15}{21}$

15–18. Solve.

15. 40% of 85 is what number?   **16.** 6 is what per cent of 75?

17. 80% of what number is 52?   **18.** 115% of 200 is what number?

19. During an economy test, a car traveled a 162-mile course in 3 hours. What was the average speed? ($rt = d$)

20. A report states that 70% of the 2440 families in Playville own their homes. How many families own their homes?

21. Name the corresponding sides and the corresponding angles.

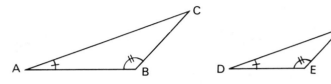

∠A and ∠ ?   AB and ∠ ?

∠B and ∠ ?   BC and ∠ ?

∠C and ∠ ?   AC and ∠ ?

22. Find the height of the tower. (The triangles are similar.)

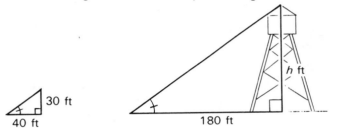

23–25. Complete the following table:

Fraction or mixed number	Decimal	Per cent
23. $\frac{6}{10}$	?	?
24. ?	0.25	?
25. ?	?	150%

26. Use the drawing to graph a slide 3 units down.

27. What is the actual distance between A and B?

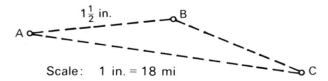

Scale: 1 in. = 18 mi

Pretest for Chapter 11   Adding and Subtracting Rational Numbers

1. Give the absolute value of $^-5\frac{1}{3}$.

2. Give the opposite of 6.95.

3–13. Find each sum or difference.

3. $-\frac{3}{8} + \frac{1}{4}$

4. $^-4\frac{1}{3} + ^-8\frac{1}{3}$

5. $1\frac{1}{4} + \left(-\frac{7}{8}\right)$

6. $^-11.32 + ^-8.09$

7. $-\frac{2}{5} - \frac{3}{10}$

8. $\frac{2}{3} - \left(-\frac{4}{9}\right)$

9. $^-1\frac{3}{4} - ^-2\frac{1}{3}$

10. $9.7 - 6.6$

11. $^-7.3 - 4.7$

12. $3.02 - ^-1.97$

13. $6 + ^-1\frac{5}{8}$

14–23. Solve.

14. $z + \frac{2}{3} = -\frac{1}{3}$

15. $x - ^-3.9 = 8.2$

16. $c - 4.6 = ^-5.9$

17. $\frac{2}{3} + f = -\frac{1}{4}$

18. $k - \left(-\frac{1}{3}\right) = -\frac{2}{9}$

19. $^-6.1 = a + ^-8.2$

20. $-\frac{4}{5} + n = 0$

21. $\frac{2}{3} = h - \frac{3}{5}$

22. $x - 9.8 = 3.6$

23. $\frac{2}{3} = y - \frac{1}{12}$

24–25. Solve each problem by using an equation.

24. Buy-Quik Company sold $1.2 million more this year than last year. This year they sold $17.4 million. What were last year's sales?

25. A train averaged $29\frac{3}{4}$ miles per hour in the morning. In the afternoon, it averaged $26\frac{1}{8}$ miles per hour. What was the change in average speed from the morning to the afternoon?

T64

1. Give the absolute value of $4\frac{3}{8}$.

2. Give the opposite of $^-11.02$.

3–13. Find each sum or difference.

3. $\frac{2}{3} + \left(-\frac{1}{9}\right)$

4. $2\frac{1}{5} + \left(-\frac{3}{10}\right)$

5. $^-5\frac{2}{5} + {}^-9\frac{2}{5}$

6. $^-6.03 + 4.71$

7. $-\frac{3}{8} - \frac{1}{2}$

8. $\frac{1}{5} - \left(-\frac{7}{10}\right)$

9. $3.6 - 7.2$

10. $^-4.8 - 3.9$

11. $1.98 - {}^-5.58$

12. $-\frac{1}{4} + \left(-\frac{2}{5}\right)$

13. $^-3\frac{2}{3} - 4\frac{1}{9}$

14–23. Solve.

14. $x + \frac{1}{5} = -\frac{3}{5}$

15. $z + {}^-2.4 = 6.5$

16. $c - 3.3 = {}^-4.7$

17. $\frac{1}{5} + y = -\frac{1}{8}$

18. $-\frac{1}{9} + n = 0$

19. $^-8.4 = a + {}^-3.7$

20. $k - \left(-\frac{2}{5}\right) = -\frac{3}{10}$

21. $\frac{1}{5} = h - \frac{2}{3}$

22. $x - 8.6 = 4.7$

23. $\frac{4}{9} = y - \frac{2}{3}$

24–25. Solve each problem by using an equation.

24. The opening stock-market averages showed Electro Utilities at $9\frac{7}{8}$. The closing averages showed Electro Utilities at $8\frac{3}{4}$. What was the change in the stock?

25. Calloway Cookies showed a profit of $3.9 million. If they spend $2.7 million on a new factory, how much of the profit is left?

1-12. Find each product or quotient.

1. $-\dfrac{5}{6} \times \dfrac{3}{5}$

2. $\dfrac{7}{8}\left(-\dfrac{2}{3}\right)$

3. $1\dfrac{3}{8} \times \,^-2\dfrac{1}{3}$

4. $\dfrac{1}{6} \times 6$

5. $^-14 \times 5.12$

6. $\dfrac{3}{2} \div \dfrac{2}{6}$

7. $\dfrac{1}{3} \div \left(-\dfrac{4}{7}\right)$

8. $0.78 \div \,^-2.6$

9. 1.02×2.4

10. $2\dfrac{1}{3} \div \,^-3$

11. $^-2 \times \,^-1\dfrac{3}{4}$

12. $^-12.15 \div \,^-2.5$

13-20. Solve each equation.

13. $^-4x = \dfrac{8}{3}$

14. $1.3x = \,^-3.12$

15. $\dfrac{x}{^-1.56} = 45.3$

16. $-\dfrac{9}{10}x = \dfrac{1}{4}$

17. $-\dfrac{1}{2} = \dfrac{3}{4}x + \dfrac{1}{8}$

18. $0.6x + 8.1 = 5.1$

19. $\dfrac{x + \,^-4.2}{6.3} = 5.1$

20. $3x + \dfrac{2}{3} = \dfrac{1}{2}$

21-22. Solve each problem.

21. What is the horsepower of a 125-watt electric motor? $h = \dfrac{w}{750}$

22. How many hours must you use a 200-watt television to use 2.3 kilowatt-hours of electricity? Express your answer by using a mixed number or a decimal. $k = \dfrac{tw}{1000}$

23-25. Express in scientific notation.

23. 41   **24.** 10,000   **25.** 0.0001

1–12. Find each product or quotient.

1. $-\frac{3}{8} \times {}^-2\frac{1}{2}$

2. $4\left({}^-3\frac{1}{3}\right)$

3. ${}^-7.3 \times 6.2$

4. $-\frac{1}{4} \div \frac{5}{6}$

5. ${}^-1\frac{1}{2} \times {}^-2\frac{1}{2}$

6. ${}^-7.8 \div 5.2$

7. $16\frac{2}{3} \div {}^-9$

8. $\frac{4}{9} \times \frac{9}{4}$

9. ${}^-5\frac{1}{4} \div {}^-1\frac{3}{4}$

10. ${}^-4.3 \times {}^-7.2$

11. $5 \div {}^-2.5$

12. ${}^-7.8 \div {}^-5.2$

13–20. Solve each equation.

13. $-\frac{7}{8}x = \frac{2}{3}$

14. ${}^-0.1794 = 1.3x$

15. $\frac{x}{{}^-4.5} = {}^-8.13$

16. $\frac{x}{6} = -\frac{1}{7}$

17. $2x - \frac{3}{4} = \frac{1}{4}$

18. $-\frac{9}{10}x = \frac{1}{4}$

19. $\frac{x}{{}^-7.2} + 2.1 = 6.4$

20. $\frac{x - 0.5}{{}^-7.2} = 3.8$

21–22. Solve each problem.

21. How many kilowatt hours are used when you run a 2500-watt electric heater for 24 hours? $k = \frac{tw}{1000}$

22. How many watts would be used by a $\frac{1}{2}$-horsepower electric motor? $h = \frac{w}{750}$

23–25. Express in scientific notation.

23. 19.75

24. 3000

25. 0.02

Pretest for Chapter 13   Square Roots

1–6. Find each square root as a whole number, fraction, or decimal as given.

1. $\sqrt{64}$

2. $\sqrt{225}$

3. $\sqrt{\dfrac{1}{4}}$

4. $-\sqrt{\dfrac{16}{49}}$

5. $\sqrt{0.0049}$

6. $\sqrt{0.0001}$

7–12. Find each square root by using the table.

7. $\sqrt{8}$

8. $\sqrt{13}$

9. $\sqrt{65}$

10. $\sqrt{106}$

11. $\sqrt{256}$

12. $\sqrt{196}$

13–18. Find the positive solution of each equation. Use the table when necessary.

13. $x^2 = 36$

14. $x^2 = 63$

15. $x^2 - 2 = 98$

16. $x^2 - 6 = 42$

17. $x^2 + 4 = 71$

18. $x^2 + 7 = 35$

19–20. Solve each problem.

19. The gate is 4 feet long and 3 feet high. How long must the brace be?

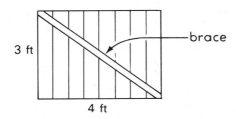

20. How long will a storm last if it has a diameter of 6 miles?

Use $t = \sqrt{\dfrac{d^3}{216}}$.

Posttest for Chapter 13   Square Roots

1–6. Find each square root as a whole number, fraction, or decimal as given.

1. $\sqrt{49}$ **2.** $\sqrt{121}$ **3.** $\sqrt{\frac{9}{16}}$

4. $\sqrt{\frac{36}{81}}$ **5.** $\sqrt{0.25}$ **6.** $\sqrt{0.64}$

7–12. Find each square root by using the table.

7. $\sqrt{7}$ **8.** $\sqrt{14}$ **9.** $\sqrt{67}$

10. $\sqrt{105}$ **11.** $\sqrt{324}$ **12.** $\sqrt{676}$

13–18. Find the positive solution of each equation. Use the table when necessary.

13. $x^2 = 49$ **14.** $x^2 = 52$ **15.** $x^2 + 6 = 31$

16. $x^2 + 5 = 20$ **17.** $x^2 + 3 = 39$ **18.** $x^2 - 4 = 22$

19–20. Solve each problem.

19. A television screen has a height of 9 inches and a 15-inch diagonal. What is the width of the screen?

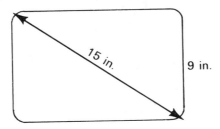

20. The area of a circle is 50.24 square meters. Find the radius. Use $A = \pi r^2$ and use 3.14 for π.

1. The sum of two consecutive odd integers is $^-28$. What are the integers?

2–6. Add.

2. $14x^2 + {}^-6x^2$

3. $4y + 5y + 8y$

4. $(2xz + 4) + ({}^-3xz - 7)$

5. $\begin{aligned} 8a + {}^-7 \\ {}^-3a + \ \ 5 \\ \hline \end{aligned}$

6. $\begin{aligned} 24x^2 + {}^-13x + \ \ 2 \\ {}^-5x^2 + \ \ \ \ 9x + {}^-5 \\ \hline \end{aligned}$

7–13. Multiply.

7. $y^3 \cdot y^4$

8. $(9n^2)({}^-5n^5)$

9. $6a(2a + {}^-4)$

10. $(6x^2 + {}^-3x)({}^-3x)$

11. $(n + 4)(n + 8)$

12. $(2y + {}^-5)(y + 7)$

13. $\begin{aligned} 5x^2 + \ \ 2 \\ 3x \ \ + {}^-4 \\ \hline \end{aligned}$

14–17. Subtract.

14. $7x - {}^-4x$

15. $(a + 2) - (3a + 4)$

16. $({}^-12y^2 - 3) - (4y^2 - 5)$

17. $\begin{aligned} 18n^2 + {}^-6n + 4 \\ -(2n^2 - \ \ 3n - 1) \\ \hline \end{aligned}$

18–20. Divide.

18. $\dfrac{56x^4}{8x^3}$

19. $\dfrac{36x^3y^2}{{}^-6xy}$

20. $\dfrac{24y^3 + {}^-16y^2 + 8y}{4y}$

1. The sum of two numbers is $^-10$. One number is 4 times the other. What are the numbers?

2–6. Add.

2. $^-6xy + 2xy$

3. $12a + {}^-4a + {}^-7a$

4. $(5x + {}^-3) + ({}^-3x + 6)$

5. $\begin{array}{r} {}^-11y + 4 \\ 7y + {}^-8 \\ \hline \end{array}$

6. $\begin{array}{r} {}^-19x^2 + {}^-11x + 4 \\ 13x^2 + 6x + {}^-9 \\ \hline \end{array}$

7–13. Multiply.

7. $n^5 \cdot n^2$

8. $(3x^2)({}^-15x^3)$

9. $({}^-5a^2 + 3a)2a$

10. $({}^-8y^3 + 3y^2)({}^-2y)$

11. $(x + {}^-6)({}^-x + 3)$

12. $(4a + 2)(3a + {}^-6)$

13. $\begin{array}{r} 7x^2 + 3 \\ {}^-2x + 2 \\ \hline \end{array}$

14–17. Subtract.

14. $^-9x - {}^-3x$

15. $(5n - 2) - (3n + 6)$

16. $(13y^2 + 5) - (9y^2 - 3)$

17. $\begin{array}{r} 25x^2 + 7x + 5 \\ -(15x^2 + 3x - 3) \\ \hline \end{array}$

18–20. Divide.

18. $\dfrac{49x^5}{7x}$

19. $\dfrac{72x^3y^4}{9xy^2}$

20. $\dfrac{24a^4 + 18a^3 + 12a^2}{6a}$

T71

Pretest for Chapter 15   Statistics and Probability

1–3. Use the following set of numbers:
11, 10, 15, 11, 18, 17, 11, 15.

1. Find the range.   **2.** Find the mode.   **3.** Find the median.

4. Make a frequency table for the following
set of numbers: 21, 20, 17, 20, 16, 17, 19, 23, 18, 21,
19, 23, 20, 19, 20, 17, 20, 18, 16, 22.

5. Make a graph for the numbers in Exercise 4.

6–8. Use the following set of numbers:
22, 33, 39, 27, 10, 10, 30, 33, 11, 10, 33, 29, 46, 33, 22.

6. Find the range.   **7.** Find the mode.   **8.** Find the median.

9. Find the mean for 10, 5, 7, 13, 15.

10. The mean number of hours of sunlight per day for the last 14 days
was 11. What was the total number of hours of sunlight
for the last 14 days?

**11–16. There are 10 marbles—5 white, 3 red, and 2 blue—all
the same size in a bag. The marbles are thoroughly mixed, and
one is picked by chance.**

11. Name all possible outcomes.   **12.** Find pr (red).

13. Find pr (white).   **14.** Find pr (blue).

15. Find pr (blue *or* red).   **16.** Find pr (white *or* blue).

17. A bag contains 4 marbles—red, blue, green, and yellow. A coin is tossed
and a marble is picked. Draw a tree diagram to show the possible
results.

**18–20. A die is rolled, and one card is picked from a thoroughly
shuffled deck of 52 playing cards. Find the following
probabilities as fractions.**

18. pr (6 *and* a diamond)   **19.** pr (even number *and* a face card)

20. pr (5 *and* a black card)

Posttest for Chapter 15   Statistics and Probability

1–3. Use the following set of numbers:
   15, 22, 19, 18, 18, 21, 19, 19.

1. Find the range.   **2.** Find the mode.   **3.** Find the median.

4. Make a frequency table for the following
   set of numbers: 18, 17, 14, 17, 13, 14, 16, 20, 15, 18,
   16, 20, 17, 16, 17, 14, 17, 15, 13, 19.

5. Make a graph for the numbers in Exercise 4.

6–8. Use the following set of numbers:
   72, 55, 69, 71, 70, 80, 53, 69, 51, 53, 67, 55, 69, 71, 80.

6. Find the range.   **7.** Find the mode.   **8.** Find the median.

9. Find the mean for 12, 2, 9, 5, 7, 11, 3.

10. For a 42-game season a basketball player's
   mean points per game was 15. What was the
   player's total number of points scored?

11–16. A die is tossed once.

11. Name all possible outcomes.   **12.** Find pr (6).

13. Find pr (3).   **14.** Find pr (an even number).

15. Find pr (6 *or* an odd number).   **16.** Find pr (5 *or* 2).

17. One bag contains 3 marbles—red, blue, and green. Another bag
   contains 3 marbles—white, yellow, and purple. A marble is picked
   from each bag. Draw a tree diagram to show the possible results.

**18–20. A die is rolled, and a coin tossed. Find the following
   probabilities as fractions.**

18. pr (6 *and* heads)   **19.** pr (5 *and* tails)   **20.** pr (an even number *and* tails)

Cumulative Test for Chapters 8–15

1. Use the rule to complete the ordered pairs.

$y = 3x + 2$

x	1	2	3	4
y				

2. Write the ordered pair for each point on the graph at the right.

   a. R   **b.** S   **c.** T

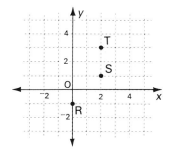

3. Is the graph for Exercise 2 the graph of a function?

4. Use the drawing to make a 1-to-3 reduction.

5–7. **Complete the following table.**

Fraction or mixed number	Decimal	Per cent
5. $\frac{6}{10}$	?	?
6. ?	0.25	?
7. ?	?	150%

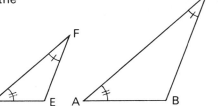

8–9. **Solve.**

8. 115% of 200 is what number?

9. 6 is what per cent of 75?

10. Name the corresponding angles and the corresponding sides.

   ∠D and ∠ ?   DE and ?

   ∠E and ∠ ?   EF and ?

   ∠F and ∠ ?   DF and ?

11. What is the actual distance between A and B?

Scale: $\frac{3}{4}$ in. = 6 mi

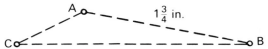

12. Find the height of the tree. (The triangles are similar.)

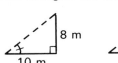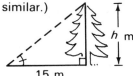

8 m

10 m

15 m

h m

13–21. Find each value.

13. $-\frac{2}{5} + \frac{3}{10}$

14. $\frac{5}{6} - \left(-\frac{1}{6}\right)$

15. $-\frac{3}{4} \times 5$

16. $-2\frac{2}{3} \div -1\frac{7}{9}$

17. $^-7.68 + 5.37$

18. $^-9.83 - 5.842$

19. $0.038(5.2)$

20. $3.51 \div ^-1.3$

21. $^-1\frac{2}{3}\left(-\frac{3}{5}\right)$

22–31. Solve.

22. $x + \frac{1}{2} = \frac{3}{4}$

23. $x - 4.3 = ^-6.7$

24. $9x = ^-8.1$

25. $\frac{x}{3} = \frac{1}{2}$

26. $x - \frac{3}{4} = \frac{1}{2}$

27. $^-5x = \frac{3}{4}$

28. $\frac{x}{^-7.2} = 4.3$

29. $\frac{x + 6}{^-3} = ^-8$

30. $\frac{3}{8} = \frac{n}{24}$

31. $\frac{6}{14} = \frac{x}{21}$

32–33. Write in scientific notation.

32. 453,000

33. 0.0602

34–35. Use the table to find an approximation of each square root.

34. $\sqrt{7}$

35. $\sqrt{20}$

n	n^2	$\sqrt{n}$	n	n^2	$\sqrt{n}$
1	1	1.00	6	36	2.45
2	4	1.41	7	49	2.65
3	9	1.73	8	64	2.83
4	16	2.00	9	81	3.00
5	25	2.24	10	100	3.16

36–37. Find the positive solution.

36. $x^2 - 0.36 = 0.28$

37. $\frac{x^2}{2} = 8$

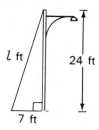

l ft   24 ft

7 ft

38. Use the Pythagorean Property to find the length of the support wire.

39–42. Simplify.

39. $19x^2 + 2y + {}^-6x^2 + 6y$

40. $({}^-24xz + 6) - ({}^-8xz + 12)$

41. $(n - 12)(n + 3)$

42. $\frac{21x^3 - 14x^2 + 7x}{7x}$

43–45. Solve these problems.

43. 55% of the 5380 eligible voters in a precinct registered as Democrats. How many voters registered as Democrats?

44. A plumber's bill was $95.75. This included $49.25 for materials and $15.50 an hour for labor. How many hours of work were charged for?

45. A company makes 2 black-and-white TV sets for every 5 color sets. This month, 480 black-and-white sets were made. How many color sets were made?

46–47. Use the following set of numbers: 33, 31, 35, 34, 30, 32, 35, 43, 33, 33, 33, 31.

46. Find   **a.** the mean   **b.** the median   **c.** the mode   **d.** the range

47. Make a frequency table.

48–50. There are 10 marbles in a bag—5 white, 3 red, and 2 black—all the same size. They are thoroughly mixed, and one marble is picked by chance.

48. a. Find pr (white).   **b.** Find pr (white *or* black).

49. In 50 trials (the picked marble was replaced after each trial), a red marble was picked 16 times. Find ex pr (red).

50. A coin is tossed, and a marble is picked from the bag of marbles described above. Find pr (tails *and* white).

Pretest for Chapter 16   Geometry

    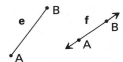

1–6. Match each name with the letter of a figure above.

1. $\overrightarrow{AB}$

2. $\overline{AB}$

3. $\overleftrightarrow{AB}$

4. octagon

5. square

6. scalene triangle

7–9. Find the perimeter or circumference of each figure. Use 3.14 for π.

7. 12 cm, 16 cm

8. 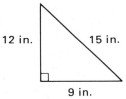 12 in., 15 in., 9 in.

9. 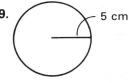 5 cm

10–12. Find the area of the figure in

10. Exercise 7.

11. Exercise 8.

12. Exercise 9.

13–15. Find the surface area of each figure. Use 3.14 for π.

13. 18 cm, 6 cm, 14 cm

14. 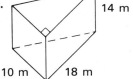 21 m, 14 m, 10 m, 18 m

15. 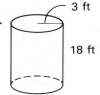 3 ft, 18 ft

16–18. Find the volume of the figure in

16. Exercise 13.

17. Exercise 14.

18. Exercise 15.

19. Bill is refinishing a circular tabletop with a radius of 70 cm. What is the area of the tabletop? (Use 3.14 for π.)

20. How much cardboard is needed to make a box with a lid if the box is to be 16 in. long, 8 in. wide, and 4 in. high?

21. A pool is 16 ft long, 12 ft wide, and 6 ft deep. How many cubic feet of water are needed to fill the pool?

Posttest for Chapter 16 Geometry

 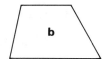 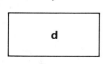 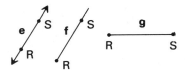

1–6. Match each name with the letter of a figure above.

1. $\overrightarrow{RS}$ **2.** $\overleftrightarrow{RS}$ **3.** $\overline{RS}$

4. rectangle **5.** rhombus **6.** isosceles triangle

7–9. Find the perimeter or circumference of each figure. Use 3.14 for π.

7.
24 cm
24 cm

8.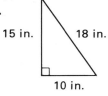
15 in. 18 in.
10 in.

9.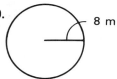
8 m

10–12. Find the area of the figure in

10. Exercise 7. **11.** Exercise 8. **12.** Exercise 9.

13–15. Find the surface area of each figure. Use 3.14 for π.

13.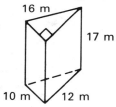
20 cm
12 cm
8 cm

14.
16 m
17 m
10 m 12 m

15.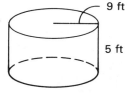
9 ft
5 ft

16–18. Find the volume of the figure in

16. Exercise 13. **17.** Exercise 14. **18.** Exercise 15.

19. Marcia is refinishing a tabletop with a radius of 80 cm. What is the area of the tabletop? (Use 3.14 for π.)

20. How much cardboard is needed to make a box with a lid if the box is to be 15 in. long, 5 in. wide, and 3 in. high?

21. A pool is 15 ft long, 10 ft wide, and 5 ft deep. How many cubic feet of water are needed to fill the pool?

Tests

Pretest for Chapter 17   More Algebra

1–9. Draw the graph of each equation or inequality.

1. $3x + y = 6$

2. $2x - y = {}^-2$

3. $y = 3x - 1$

4. $4x + 2y < 0$

5. $y \geq 3$

6. ${}^-3x + y \leq {}^-3$

7. $y = 3x$

8. $d = \frac{1}{3}x$

9. $r = {}^-2s$

10–12. Change each equation to slope-intercept form. Then name the slope and the y-intercept.

10. $5x + 2y = 10$

11. $4x - 6y = 12$

12. $4x + y = 2$

13–15. Use each equation to complete the table. Then sketch the graph. $(x > 0, y > 0)$

13. $xy = 6$

x	0.5	1	2	3	?	12
y	12	6	3	?	1	?

14. $xy = 16$

x	1	2	4	?	8	?
y	16	8	4	1	?	0.5

15. $xy = 21$

x	1	2	3	7	?	?
y	21	10.5	7	?	2	1

16–18. Tell whether each of the following systems is consistent, inconsistent, or dependent.

16. $2x + 3y = 5$
    $4x + 6y = \frac{1}{5}$

17. $x + 4y = 3$
    $4x + y = 3$

18. $2x + 2y = 4$
    $x + y = 2$

19–21. Solve each system by graphing.

19. $x + y = 5$
    $x - y = 1$

20. $2x + y = 8$
    $2x - y = 4$

21. $3x + y = 10$
    $3x + 8y = {}^-4$

1–9. Draw the graph of each equation or inequality.

1. $2x + y = 5$ **2.** $3x - 2y = {}^-6$ **3.** $y = 2x - 3$

4. $2x + 4y > 0$ **5.** $y \leq 3$ **6.** $^-x + 2y \geq {}^-4$

7. $y = 2x$ **8.** $d = \frac{1}{4}x$ **9.** $r = {}^-5s$

10–12. Change each equation to slope-intercept form. Then name the slope and the y-intercept.

10. $3x + y = 6$ **11.** $2x - 3y = 6$ **12.** $^-x + 2y = 4$

13–15. Use each equation to complete the table. Then sketch the graph. ($x > 0$, $y > 0$)

13. $xy = 10$

x	20	10	5	2	?	0.5
y	0.5	1	2	?	10	?

14. $xy = 18$

x	18	9	6	3	?	1
y	1	2	3	?	9	?

15. $xy = 24$

x	24	12	6	4	?	?
y	1	2	4	?	12	24

16–18. Tell whether each of the following systems is consistent, inconsistent, or dependent.

16. $x + y = 5$
$\quad\;\; x - y = 5$

17. $\;\; x + 2y = 5$
$\quad\;\; 3x + 6y = 15$

18. $\;\; 5x - 2y = 1$
$\quad\;\; 10x - 4y = 5$

19–21. Solve each system by graphing.

19. $x - y = 2$
$\quad\;\; x + y = 6$

20. $2x + 3y = 2$
$\quad\;\;\; x + y = 0$

21. $2x - 3y = {}^-3$
$\quad\;\; 2x + 3y = 15$

Cumulative Test for Chapters 16–17

 a

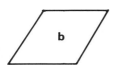 b

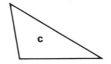 c

 d

 e

 f g

1–6. Match each name with the letter of a figure above.

1. $\overleftrightarrow{MN}$

2. $\overline{MN}$

3. $\overrightarrow{MN}$

4. parallelogram

5. hexagon

6. obtuse triangle

7–9. Find the perimeter or circumference of each figure. Use 3.14 for π.

7.
12 cm
21 cm

8.
20 in. 26 in.
17 in.

9.
10 m

10–12. Find the area of the figure in

10. Exercise 7.

11. Exercise 8.

12. Exercise 9.

13–15. Find the surface area of each figure. Use 3.14 for π.

13.
16 cm
8 cm
14 cm

14.
13 m
6 m
8 m 10 m

15.
8 ft
14 ft

16–18. Find the volume of the figure in

16. Exercise 13.

17. Exercise 14.

18. Exercise 15.

19. Barbara is refinishing a tabletop with a radius of 90 cm. What is the area of the tabletop? (Use 3.14 for π.)

20. How much cardboard is needed to make a box with a lid if the box is to be 12 in. long, 6 in. wide, and 2 in. high?

21. A pool is 16 ft long, 12 ft wide, and 6 ft deep. How many cubic feet of water are needed to fill the pool?

Tests

22–30. Draw the graph of each equation or inequality.

22. $3x + y = 6$ **23.** $4x - 2y = {}^-4$ **24.** $y = 3x - 4$

25. $3x + y < 0$ **26.** $y \leq {}^-2$ **27.** $x - 2y \geq {}^-6$

28. $y = 6x$ **29.** $d = \frac{1}{3}x$ **30.** $r = {}^-2x$

31–33. Change each equation to slope-intercept form. Then name the slope and the y-intercept.

31. $2x + y = 5$ **32.** $3x - 6y = 18$ **33.** ${}^-x + 3y = 9$

34–36. Use each equation to complete the table. Then sketch the graph. $(x > 0, y > 0)$

34. $xy = 12$

x	12	6	4	3	?	1
y	1	2	3	?	6	?

35. $xy = 15$

x	15	7.5	5	3	?	1
y	1	2	3	?	7.5	?

36. $xy = 36$

x	36	18	9	4	?	?
y	1	2	4	?	18	36

37–39. Tell whether each of the following systems is consistent, inconsistent, or dependent.

37. $2x + 3y = 5$ **38.** $x + 3y = 5$ **39.** $x - y = 8$
      $4x + 6y = 10$ ${}^-x + 3y = {}^-5$ ${}^-x + y = 4$

40–42. Solve each system by graphing.

40. $x + y = 3$ **41.** $x - y = 4$ **42.** $x + 2y = 14$
      $x - y = 7$ $4x - y = {}^-2$ $x - 3y = {}^-11$

Tests

End-of-Year Test

Choose the best answer.

1. Find the value of $10 + 6 \times 3$.

  A 48   **C** 28

  B 22   **D** 18

2. Translate into symbols: the sum of twice n and eight.

  A $8n + 2$ **C** $2n - 8$

  B $2n + 8$ **D** $2(n + 8)$

3. Find the value of $2n + 3$ when n is replaced with 4.

  A 11   **C** 5

  B 14   **D** 27

4. Solve $x + 4 = 9$. Use the replacement set $\{3, 4, 5, 6\}$.

  A 3   **C** 5

  B 4   **D** 6

5. Solve $2n + 1 > 5$. Use the replacement set $\{0, 2, 4, 6\}$.

  A 0, 2, 4   **C** 2, 4, 6

  B 0, 2   **D** 4, 6

6. Solve $16 = b + 9$.

  A $b = 9$ **C** $b = 3$

  B $b = 7$ **D** $b = 25$

7. Solve $36 = 4a$.

  A $a = 9$ **C** $a = 40$

  B $a = 8$ **D** $a = 144$

8. Solve $\frac{n}{12} = 6$.

  A $n = 2$ **C** $n = 72$

  B $n = 18$ **D** $n = 6$

9. Solve $4z > 8$.

  A $z > 2$ **C** $z < 2$

  B $z > 32$ **D** $z < 32$

10. Solve $3(m + 2) = 15$.

  A $m = 3$ **C** $m = \frac{13}{3}$

  B $m = 5$ **D** $m = \frac{17}{3}$

11. Which graph shows the solution to $x - 2 < 5$?

12. 2 gal = _____ qt

  A 4   **C** 8

  B 16   **D** $\frac{1}{2}$

13. Dan is 6 feet tall. How many inches tall is he?

A 12 **C** $\frac{1}{2}$

B 216 **D** 72

14. Find the area of the rectangle shown at the right.

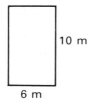

10 m

6 m

A 60 m

B 32 m

C 60 m²

D 32 m²

15. Which shows the commutative property of addition?

A $(a + b) + c = a + (b + c)$

B $a + b = b + a$

C $a + 0 = a$

D $a(b + c) = ab + ac$

16. Which shows the associative property of multiplication?

A $(a \times b) \times c = a \times (b \times c)$

B $a \times b = b \times a$

C $a \times 0 = 0$

D $a(b + c) = ab + ac$

17. Which of the following shows the prime factorization of 20?

A $2 \times 2 \times 5$

B $2 \times 5 \times 5$

C $2 + 2 + 2 + 2 + 2 + 5 + 5$

D 4×5

18. Solve $5w + 3w = 120$.

A $w = 40$ **C** $w = 60$

B $w = 8$ **D** $w = 15$

19. What is the GCF of 12 and 28?

A 2 **C** 4

B 3 **D** 7

20. What is the LCM of 4 and 6?

A 2 **C** 8

B 24 **D** 12

21. Find $\frac{2}{3} \times \frac{3}{5}$ in lowest terms.

A $\frac{6}{15}$ **C** $1\frac{1}{3}$

B $\frac{2}{5}$ **D** $\frac{5}{8}$

22. Find $\frac{3}{4} \div \frac{1}{3}$ in lowest terms.

A $2\frac{1}{4}$ **C** $\frac{1}{4}$

B $1\frac{1}{12}$ **D** $\frac{4}{9}$

23. Find $6 \times 2\frac{1}{2}$ in lowest terms.

A $\frac{1}{15}$ **C** 15

B $2\frac{2}{5}$ **D** 12

24. Find $\frac{1}{2} + \frac{2}{3}$ in lowest terms.

A $\frac{1}{3}$ **C** $\frac{3}{5}$

B $\frac{2}{5}$ **D** $1\frac{1}{6}$

25. Find $2\frac{3}{5} - \frac{9}{10}$ in lowest terms.

   A $1\frac{7}{10}$ **C** $2\frac{7}{10}$

   B $2\frac{1}{2}$ **D** $3\frac{1}{2}$

26. Jill worked $4\frac{2}{3}$ hours one day and $6\frac{1}{2}$ hours the next day. How many hours were worked?

   A $10\frac{1}{6}$ hr   **C** $10\frac{3}{5}$ hr

   B $11\frac{1}{6}$ hr   **D** $10\frac{1}{6}$ days

27. Express $5\frac{4}{5}$ as a decimal.

   A 5.45   **C** 5.08

   B 5.4   **D** 5.8

28. Round 35.5845 to the nearest hundredth.

   A 35.6   **C** 35.58

   B 35.59   **D** 35.585

29. Estimate 25.1×9.7.

   A 25   **C** 180

   B 30   **D** 250

30. Find the product of 3.6 and 0.04.

   A 0.144   **C** 14.4

   B 1.44   **D** 144

31. Find the sum of 21.2, 5.39, and 28.06.

   A 44.65   **C** 54.65

   B 54.55   **D** 414.515

32. Divide 0.832 by 3.2.

   A 0.26   **C** 26

   B 2.6   **D** 260

33. Jennifer is 175 cm tall. Andrea is 1.88 m tall. How much taller is Andrea than Jennifer?

   A 186.25 cm   **C** 1.3 m

   B 13 m   **D** 13 cm

34. Find $^-35 - 23$.

   A $^-12$ **C** 58

   B 12   **D** $^-58$

35. Find $^-24 \div ^-4$.

   A 8   **C** $^-6$

   B 6   **D** $^-8$

36. Solve $s - 4 = ^-2$.

   A $s = 2$ **C** $s = ^-2$

   B $s = 6$ **D** $s = ^-6$

37. Solve $\frac{m}{8} = ^-16$.

   A $m = ^-128$ **C** $m = ^-2$

   B $m = 2$ **D** $m = -\frac{1}{2}$

38. Solve $^-12 = 4x$.

   A $x = ^-48$ **C** $x = 48$

   B $x = ^-3$ **D** $x = 3$

39. Use the rule to complete the table: $y = 3x + 4$.

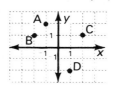

x	0	2	4	5
y	4	10	?	?

A 12, 15   **C** 16, 19

B 11, 12   **D** 16, 22

40. Which letter is at $(^-2, 1)$?

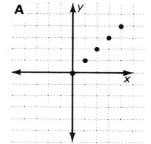

A A   **C** C

B B   **D** D

41. Which graph does not show a function?

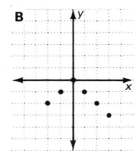

42. Find n in $\frac{8}{3} = \frac{n}{12}$.

A $n = 32$ **C** $n = 96$

B $n = 4.5$ **D** $n = 2$

43. A plane's airspeed (a) is 200 mph, and the speed of the wind directly against the plane is 40 mph. Find the plane's ground speed (g). $g = a - 40$

A 50 mph   **C** 160 mph

B 150 mph   **D** 240 mph

44. Al won an election by a 4 to 3 margin. His opponent got 1200 votes. How many votes did Al get?

A 900 votes   **C** 3600 votes

B 1600 votes   **D** 4800 votes

45. Write $\frac{7}{8}$ as a per cent.

A 114.3%   **C** 87.5%

B 8.75%   **D** 0.875%

46. 30 is what per cent of 75?

A 40   **C** 25

B 30   **D** 250

47. How much is 80% of 5600?

A 700   **C** 7000

B 448   **D** 4480

48. A baseball player got 12 hits. That was 40% of the number of times at bat. How many times did the player bat?

A 24   **C** 36

B 30   **D** 48

49. Which pair of angles are corresponding angles for these similar triangles?

A $\angle ABC$, $\angle GHJ$

B $\angle ACB$, $\angle GHJ$

C $\angle CBA$, $\angle GJH$

D $\angle BAC$, $\angle HGJ$

50. $\triangle MNP$ is similar to $\triangle RST$. Find x.

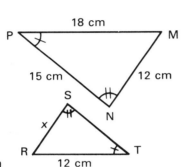

A 8 cm

B 10 cm

C 18 cm

D 14.4 cm

51. The map distance between Kent and Shannon is $2\frac{1}{2}$ inches. The scale is 1 in. = 20 mi. Find the actual distance between towns.

A 500 miles

B $2\frac{1}{2}$ miles

C 16 miles

D 50 miles

52. Find $^-3\frac{2}{3} - (^-1\frac{1}{2})$.

A $^-2\frac{1}{6}$

B $2\frac{1}{6}$

C $^-5\frac{1}{6}$

D $5\frac{1}{6}$

53. Find $^-0.82 + 2.1$.

A 2.92

B $^-2.92$

C $^-1.28$

D 1.28

54. Solve $n + {}^-3\frac{2}{5} = {}^-2\frac{1}{10}$.

A $n = {}^-1\frac{3}{10}$

B $n = 1\frac{3}{10}$

C $n = 5\frac{1}{2}$

D $n = {}^-5\frac{1}{2}$

55. Find $^-3.5 \times 7$.

A $^-0.5$

B 0.5

C 24.5

D $^-24.5$

56. Find $^-8.1 \div {}^-0.3$.

A 2.7

B $^-27$

C $^-2.7$

D 27

57. Solve $6t = {}^-12.72$.

A $t = {}^-2.12$

B $t = 2.12$

C $t = {}^-212$

D $t = {}^-21.2$

58. Solve $^-12 = \frac{r}{0.06}$.

A $r = {}^-200$

B $r = {}^-2$

C $r = {}^-72$

D $r = {}^-0.72$

59. If the temperature changed $^-12.6°C$ in 4 hours, what was the average change per hour?

A $^-8.6°C$

B $^-3.15°C$

C $^-50.4°F$

D $^-50.4°C$

60. Pat's weight change was $\frac{-3}{4}$ pound each week for 12 weeks. What was the total weight change?

A $^-9$ pounds

B $11\frac{1}{4}$ pounds

C $^-16$ pounds

D $^-\frac{1}{4}$ pound

61. Solve $x^2 = 64$.

   A $x = 4$ or $^-4$ **C** $x = 8$ or $^-8$

   B $x = 2$ or $^-4$ **D** $x = 10$

62. How far is it from M to N?

   A 10 ft   **C** 12 ft

   B 13 ft   **D** 15 ft

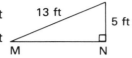

63. Which expression equals ^-18y?

   A $(^-10y)8$ **C** $10y - 8y$

   B $^-10y - {}^-8y$ **D** $3(^-6y)$

64. Find $(2x - 1) - (3x - 5)$.

   A $5x - 6$ **C** $^-x + 4$

   B $^-x + {}^-4$ **D** $5x + 4$

65. Find $(^-5a + 3)(a + {}^-2)$.

   A $^-5a^2 - 7a - 6$ **C** $^-2a - 6$

   B $^-5a^2 + 13a - 6$ **D** $^-5a - 6$

66. Find the median of this set of numbers: 8, 4, 9, 9, 5.

   A 9   **B** 7   **C** 5   **D** 8

67. Find the mean of this set of numbers: 16, 11, 9, 8, 16.

   A 12   **B** 5   **C** 16   **D** 11

68. You throw a die. What is pr (even number)?

   A $\frac{1}{6}$ **B** 1   **C** $\frac{1}{3}$ **D** $\frac{1}{2}$

69. You toss two coins. What is pr (heads, heads)?

   A $\frac{3}{4}$ **B** $\frac{1}{2}$ **C** $\frac{1}{4}$ **D** 0

70. The perimeter of $\triangle$STV is ____.

   A 21 in.

   B 12 in.

   C 18 in.

   D 18 sq in.

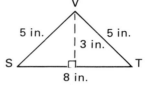

71. The area of $\triangle$STV is ____.

   A 25 sq in.   **C** 24 sq in.

   B 12 sq in.   **D** 18 sq in.

72. Find the volume of a cylinder with a radius of 4 cm and a height of 10 cm. Use 3.14 for π.

   A 251.2 cm^3 **C** 2512 cm^3

   B 502.4 cm^3 **D** 3516.8 cm^2

73. Give the slope of this equation: $3x - 2y = {}^-12$.

   A 3   **B** $^-2$ **C** 6   **D** $\frac{3}{2}$

74. Which ordered pair is a solution of $2x + {}^-6 = 5y$?

   A $(0, {}^-1)$ **C** $(2, {}^-2)$

   B $(2, 2)$ **D** $(^-2, {}^-2)$

75. The sum of two numbers is 10. Three times the smaller number is equal to twice the larger number. What are the numbers?

   A $(4, 6)$ **C** $(10, 0)$

   B $(8, 4)$ **D** $(8, 2)$

Answers to Tests

Pretest   Chapter 1

1. d   **2.** b   **3.** e   **4.** a   **5.** f   **6.** 31   **7.** 26   **8.** 40
9. 24   **10.** Open   **11.** False   **12.** True   **13.** Open   **14.** {7}   **15.** {3, 4, 5}
16. 7   **17.** 9   **18.** 7   **19.** 450   **20.** $8 < n - 5$

Posttest   Chapter 1

1. d   **2.** e   **3.** a   **4.** b   **5.** f   **6.** 16   **7.** 1   **8.** 52
9. 22   **10.** 49   **11.** True   **12.** Open   **13.** False   **14.** True   **15.** {0, 1, 2, 3}
16. {4}   **17.** 5   **18.** 5   **19.** 1440 kilometers   **20.** $14 > n + 12$

Pretest   Chapter 2

1. 19   **2.** 15   **3.** 66   **4.** 4   **5.** 9   **6.** 20   **7.** 4   **8.** 80
9. $x = 6$ **10.** $n < 3$ **11.** $32 > t$
12. $r < 60$ **13.** 25   **14.** 33   **15.** 80   **16.** 7
17. 153 square inches   **18.** 480 cubic centimeters   **19.** $16 = 6n - 2$ **20.** $59 = 2x + 9$

Posttest   Chapter 2

1. 7   **2.** 22   **3.** 45   **4.** 5   **5.** 8   **6.** 23   **7.** 3   **8.** 96
9. $4 = n$ **10.** $x < 4$ **11.** $y > 20$
12. $a > 27$ **13.** 4   **14.** 204   **15.** 28   **16.** 14
17. 144 square inches   **18.** 1620 cubic centimeters   **19.** $37 = 7n + 2$ **20.** $175 = 3c + 25$

Pretest   Chapter 3

1. 3700   **2.** 53   **3.** 170   **4.** 42   **5.** 4   **6.** 3   **7.** 6   **8.** 0
9. 1   **10.** 0   **11.** 36   **12.** 1   **13.** 25   **14.** a. Prime b. Composite
15. a. 1, 2, 3, 6, 9, 18   b. 1, 2, 3, 5, 6, 10, 15, 30   **16.** a. 5^2 b. $2^3 \times 5$
17. a. Yes   b. Yes   c. Yes   d. Yes   **18.** a. 6^5 b. 1^3 **19.** a. 2   b. 3
20. a. 84   b. 180

Posttest   Chapter 3

1. 1600   **2.** 219   **3.** 270   **4.** 728   **5.** 2   **6.** 5   **7.** 5   **8.** 14
9. 92   **10.** 0   **11.** 81   **12.** 125   **13.** 64   **14.** a. Composite   b. Prime
15. a. 1, 2, 4, 8, 16, 32   b. 1, 2, 4, 8, 16   **16.** a. 2×5^2 b. $2^2 \times 5$
17. a. No   b. Yes   c. No   d. Yes   **18.** a. 2^3 b. 4^5 **19.** a. 4   b. 3
20. a. 90   b. 198

Cumulative Test   Chapters 1–3

1. *gram*   **2.** *milli-*   **3.** 14   **4.** 21   **5.** 64   **6.** 0   **7.** 4   **8.** 144
9. 8   **10.** 0   **11.** 60   **12.** 22   **13.** 29   **14.** 9   **15.** 48   **16.** 8
17. 11   **18.** 0   **19.** 2   **20.** $n < 14$ **21.** $y > 3$ **22.** $x < 44$ **23.** 520 centimeters
24. $14 \div n < 5$ **25.** 84   **26.** 21   **27.** 3   **28.** 48   **29.** 133 square inches   **30.** $3 \times 5 \times 7$
31. Prime   **32.** Composite   **33.** Composite   **34.** Prime   **35.** 6   **36.** 1   **37.** 7   **38.** 30
39. 60   **40.** 30

Pretest Chapter 4

1. $\frac{5}{7}$ 2. $\frac{41}{1}$ 3. $\frac{5}{2}$ 4. $\frac{0}{1}$ 5. $\frac{2}{3}$ 6. $\frac{2}{5}$ 7. $\frac{3}{4}$ 8. $1\frac{1}{2}$

9. $4\frac{2}{3}$ 10. $\frac{4}{15}$ 11. $\frac{1}{4}$ 12. $3\frac{1}{2}$ 13. $\frac{5}{6}$ 14. $7\frac{7}{10}$ 15. $1\frac{2}{7}$ 16. $\frac{1}{16}$

17. $\frac{5}{8}$ 18. $1\frac{16}{21}$ 19. $\frac{2}{3}$ 20. $2\frac{1}{4}$ 21. $3\frac{11}{16}$ 22. $13\frac{1}{3}$ 23. $\frac{19}{20}$ 24. $2\frac{3}{4}$

25. 8 buckets

Posttest Chapter 4

1. $\frac{7}{9}$ 2. $\frac{29}{1}$ 3. $\frac{1}{1}$ 4. $\frac{16}{3}$ 5. $\frac{5}{2}$ 6. $\frac{3}{10}$ 7. $\frac{7}{36}$ 8. $1\frac{1}{2}$

9. $5\frac{3}{5}$ 10. $\frac{7}{16}$ 11. $\frac{1}{3}$ 12. 4 13. $\frac{35}{48}$ 14. $31\frac{1}{2}$ 15. $3\frac{1}{8}$ 16. $\frac{1}{16}$

17. $\frac{5}{8}$ 18. 3 19. $\frac{3}{7}$ 20. $4\frac{3}{7}$ 21. $6\frac{1}{2}$ 22. $15\frac{1}{6}$ 23. $1\frac{1}{12}$ 24. $1\frac{4}{5}$

25. $86\frac{2}{3}$ miles

Pretest Chapter 5

1. $\frac{1}{125}$ 2. $\frac{3}{100}$ 3. $13\frac{7}{10}$ 4. 0.375 5. 4.6 6. 0.009 7. a. 440 b. 439

c. 438.62 8. a. 20 b. 22 c. 22.07 9. a. 31 b. 31 10. a. 5 b. 4.893
11. a. 8 b. 6.66 12. a. 21 b. 21.06 13. a. 15 b. 15.081 14. a. 10 b. 8.946
15. 130 16. 0.6 17. 698 18. 4.378 19. 1060 cm² 20. 7.6 km² 21. 3600 22. 0.12
23. 4.2 24. 12 400 25. 190 milliliters

Posttest Chapter 5

1. $\frac{17}{25}$ 2. $\frac{7}{1000}$ 3. $24\frac{3}{10}$ 4. 0.625 5. 8.2 6. 0.07 7. a. 620 b. 619

c. 618.82 8. a. 10 b. 14 c. 14.19 9. a. 23 b. 23 10. a. 9 b. 8.844
11. a. 28 b. 28.002 12. a. 9 b. 9.28 13. a. 12 b. 11.874 14. a. 44 b. 56.94
15. 320 16. 0.15 17. 849 18. 8.3425 19. 486 cm² 20. 4.2 km 21. 7100 22. 0.43
23. 9.8 24. 28 600 25. 240 milliliters

Pretest Chapter 6

1. 19 2. $^-7$ 3. 0 4. 32 5. 4 6. 16 7. $^-15$, $^-3$, 0, 7, 12, 15
8. 7 9. $^-15$ 10. $^-83$ 11. $^-7$ 12. 22 13. 15 14. $^-19$ 15. $^-12$
16. $^-10$ 17. 9 18. $^-5$ 19. 8 20. $x > 14$ [number line: 13, 14, 15, 16]
21. $x < ^-9$ [number line: $^-11$, $^-10$, $^-9$, $^-8$] 22. $y > 6$ [number line: 5, 6, 7, 8] 23. $n < 23$ [number line: 21, 22, 23, 24]
24. 3 25. $^-\$78$

Posttest Chapter 6

1. $^-62$ 2. 4 3. $^-23$ 4. 105 5. 0 6. 14 7. $^-15$, $^-7$, $^-1$, 3, 4, 16
8. $^-7$ 9. 55 10. $^-12$ 11. $^-7$ 12. 78 13. $^-10$ 14. 51 15. $^-15$
16. $^-12$ 17. $^-19$ 18. $^-28$ 19. 16 20. $x < ^-23$ [number line: $^-25$, $^-24$, $^-23$, $^-22$]
21. $n < ^-6$ [number line: $^-8$, $^-7$, $^-6$, $^-5$] 22. $y > ^-8$ [number line: $^-9$, $^-8$, $^-7$, $^-6$] 23. $x < ^-35$ [number line: $^-37$, $^-36$, $^-35$, $^-34$]
24. $^-27$ 25. $^+1250$

Pretest   Chapter 7

1. 32   **2.** ⁻132   **3.** ⁻39   **4.** ⁻8   **5.** 5   **6.** ⁻7   **7.** ⁻5

8. 3   **9.** ⁻6   **10.** ⁻6   **11.** 7   **12.** ⁻24   **13.** ⁻9   **14.** 7

15. $n > ⁻7$ [number line ⁻8 ⁻7 ⁻6 ⁻5]   **16.** $5 < x$ [number line 4 5 6 7]   **17.** $5 < y$ [number line 4 5 6 7]

18. $w > ⁻48$ [number line ⁻49 ⁻48 ⁻47 ⁻46]   **19.** $⁻35 > x$ [number line ⁻37 ⁻36 ⁻35 ⁻34]   **20.** $40 < m$ [number line 39 40 41 42]

21. ⁻18   **22.** 3   **23.** 78   **24.** 17   **25.** ⁻1125 feet

Posttest   Chapter 7

1. ⁻24   **2.** 64   **3.** ⁻8   **4.** 9   **5.** ⁻7   **6.** ⁻12   **7.** ⁻11

8. ⁻7   **9.** 7   **10.** 10   **11.** 21   **12.** ⁻48   **13.** 128

14. $n > ⁻8$ [number line ⁻9 ⁻8 ⁻7 ⁻6]   **15.** $6 < x$ [number line 5 6 7 8]   **16.** $4 < y$ [number line 3 4 5 6]

17. $x < ⁻72$ [number line ⁻74 ⁻73 ⁻72 ⁻71]   **18.** $42 < w$ [number line 41 42 43 44]   **19.** $4 > y$ [number line 2 3 4 5]

20. ⁻9   **21.** ⁻3   **22.** 88   **23.** 31   **24.** ⁻1500 feet per minute   **25.** ⁻$192

Cumulative Test   Chapters 1–7

1. 23   **2.** 0   **3.** 17   **4.** $3\frac{3}{4}$ **5.** 1   **6.** $1\frac{5}{8}$ **7.** ⁻2

8. 0.6   **9.** ⁻11   **10.** $1\frac{1}{12}$ **11.** 48.42   **12.** $1\frac{1}{3}$ **13.** 0.1428   **14.** ⁻60

15. 9   **16.** $42 = 5n - 3$ **17.** 18   **18.** 45   **19.** ⁻2   **20.** 32

21. 775   **22.** 12   **23.** ⁻8   **24.** ⁻7   **25.** 6   **26.** ⁻33   **27.** $x > 6$

28. $y < 11$ **29.** $n > 3$ **30.** $n < 9$ **31.** $x > 8$ **32.** $x < 22$

33. $x > 15$ [number line 14 15 16 17]   **37.** 12   **38.** $1\frac{1}{2}$ **39.** 45   **40.** 61 000

34. $n < ⁻11$ [number line ⁻13 ⁻12 ⁻11 ⁻10]   **41.** 910 cubic centimeters   **42.** 6   **43.** 7

35. $x < ⁻42$ [number line ⁻44 ⁻43 ⁻42 ⁻41]   **44.** 1   **45.** 60   **46.** 30   **47.** 90

36. $⁻14 < y$ [number line ⁻15 ⁻14 ⁻13 ⁻12]   **48.** 54 miles per hour   **49.** $10\frac{1}{2}$ ounces   **50.** ⁻$73

Pretest   Chapter 8

1. 14, 5, 2, ⁻13   **2.** 4, 6, ⁻2   **3.** (0, 0)   **4.** (4, 3)   **5.** (⁻4, 0)   **6.** (2, ⁻4)   **7.** (⁻1, 4)

8. (⁻3, ⁻4)   **9.** See graph below.   **10.** Yes   **11.** No   **12.** ⁻9   **13.** 190 miles per hour

9. 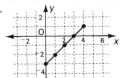   **14.** 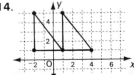   **15.**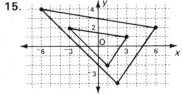

Posttest   Chapter 8

1. ⁻7, 0, 10   **2.** ⁻2, 1, 2, 7   **3.** (5, 4)   **4.** (2, 2)   **5.** (⁻2, 2)   **6.** (⁻2, ⁻2)   **7.** (2, ⁻2)

8. (0, 0)   **9.** See graph below.   **10.** (0, 0)   **11.** No   **12.** Yes   **13.** 3 seconds

9. [graph]   **14.** [graph]   **15.** [graph]

Pretest Chapter 9

1. $\frac{2}{7}$ **2.** $\frac{1}{2}$ **3.** $\frac{1}{20}$ **4.** $\frac{1}{5}$ **5.** 5 **6.** 35 **7.** 72 **8.** 7

9. 99 **10.** 7.2 **11.** 1.92 **12.** 20% **13.** 35% **14.** 200 **15.** 360 **16.** 0.6, 60%

17. $\frac{3}{8}$, 37.5% **18.** $\frac{7}{10}$, 70% **19.** 0.625, 62.5% **20.** $\frac{18}{25}$, 0.72 **21.** $1\frac{9}{10}$, 1.9 **22.** 240

23. 80 times **24.** $3.60 **25.** $80

Posttest Chapter 9

1. $\frac{3}{8}$ **2.** $\frac{3}{4}$ **3.** $\frac{1}{7}$ **4.** $\frac{2}{5}$ **5.** 18 **6.** 56 **7.** 77 **8.** 7

9. 156 **10.** 19.2 **11.** 1.52 **12.** 17.5% **13.** 55% **14.** 85 **15.** 200 **16.** 0.8, 80%

17. $\frac{1}{6}$, $16\frac{2}{3}$% **18.** $\frac{9}{10}$, 90% **19.** 0.75, 75% **20.** $\frac{59}{100}$, 0.59 **21.** $1\frac{3}{4}$, 1.75 **22.** 240

23. 45 gallons **24.** $2 **25.** $50

Pretest Chapter 10

1. ∠D, ∠E, ∠F, DE, EF, DF   **2.** ∠Z, ∠W, ∠V, ZV, ZW, UV
3. d **4.** b **5.** $x = 7$ **6.** $x = 24$ **7.** 5 meters **8.** 20 meters
                             $z = 5$ $z = 26$

Posttest Chapter 10

1. ∠D, ∠E, ∠F, DE, EF, DF   **2.** ∠T, ∠W, ∠Z, TZ, TW, UV
3. f **4.** e **5.** $x = 12$ **6.** $x = 18$ **7.** 18 miles **8.** 9 meters
                             $z = 15$ $z = 30$

Cumulative Test Chapters 8–10

1. 10, 13, 16, 19 **2.** 0, 1, 2, 3 **3.** (0, 4) **4.** (2, 2) **5.** (4, 3) **6.** (5, 0)

7. Yes **8.** $\frac{8}{21}$ **9.** $\frac{9}{4}$ **10.** $\frac{17}{4}$ **11.** $\frac{1}{35}$ **12.** 15 **13.** 12

14. 5 **15.** 34 **16.** 8% **17.** 65 **18.** 230 **19.** 54 miles per hour

20. 1708 families **21.** ∠D, ∠E, ∠F, DE, EF, DF **22.** 135 feet **23.** 0.6, 60% **24.** $\frac{1}{4}$, 25%

25. $1\frac{1}{2}$, 1.5 **26.** 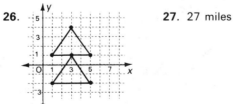 **27.** 27 miles

Pretest Chapter 11

1. $5\frac{1}{3}$ **2.** ⁻6.95 **3.** $-\frac{1}{8}$ **4.** $-12\frac{2}{3}$ **5.** $\frac{3}{8}$ **6.** ⁻19.41 **7.** $-\frac{7}{10}$

8. $1\frac{1}{9}$ **9.** $\frac{7}{12}$ **10.** 3.1 **11.** ⁻12 **12.** 4.99 **13.** $4\frac{3}{8}$ **14.** ⁻1

15. 4.3 **16.** ⁻1.3 **17.** $-\frac{11}{12}$ **18.** $-\frac{5}{9}$ **19.** 2.1 **20.** $\frac{4}{5}$ **21.** $1\frac{4}{15}$

22. 13.4 **23.** $\frac{3}{4}$ **24.** $16.2 million **25.** $-3\frac{5}{8}$ miles per hour

Posttest   Chapter 11

1. $4\frac{3}{8}$ 2. 11.02 3. $\frac{5}{9}$ 4. $1\frac{9}{10}$ 5. $-14\frac{4}{5}$ 6. -1.32 7. $-\frac{7}{8}$

8. $\frac{9}{10}$ 9. -3.6 10. -8.7 11. 7.56 12. $-\frac{13}{20}$ 13. $-7\frac{7}{9}$ 14. $-\frac{4}{5}$

15. 8.9 16. -1.4 17. $-\frac{13}{40}$ 18. $\frac{1}{9}$ 19. -4.7 20. $-\frac{7}{10}$ 21. $\frac{13}{15}$

22. 13.3 23. $1\frac{1}{9}$ 24. $-1\frac{1}{8}$ 25. \$1.2 million

Pretest   Chapter 12

1. $-\frac{1}{2}$ 2. $-\frac{7}{12}$ 3. $-3\frac{5}{24}$ 4. 1 5. -71.68 6. $4\frac{1}{2}$ 7. $-\frac{7}{12}$ 8. -0.3

9. 2.448 10. $-\frac{7}{9}$ 11. $3\frac{1}{2}$ 12. 4.86 13. $-\frac{2}{3}$ 14. -2.4 15. -70.668 16. $-\frac{5}{18}$

17. $-\frac{5}{6}$ 18. -5 19. 36.33 20. $-\frac{1}{18}$ 21. $\frac{1}{6}$ horsepower   22. 11.5 or $11\frac{1}{2}$ hours

23. 4.1×10^1 24. 1×10^4 25. 1×10^{-4}

Posttest   Chapter 12

1. $\frac{15}{16}$ 2. $-13\frac{1}{3}$ 3. -45.26 4. $-\frac{3}{10}$ 5. $3\frac{3}{4}$ 6. -1.5 7. $-1\frac{23}{27}$ 8. 1

9. 3 10. 30.96 11. -2 12. 1.5 13. $-\frac{16}{21}$ 14. -0.138 15. 36.585 16. $-\frac{6}{7}$

17. $\frac{1}{2}$ 18. $-\frac{5}{18}$ 19. -30.96 20. -26.86 21. 60 kilowatt hours   22. 375 watts

23. 1.975×10^1 24. 3×10^3 25. 2×10^{-2}

Pretest   Chapter 13

1. 8 2. 15 3. $\frac{1}{2}$ 4. $\frac{4}{7}$ 5. 0.07 6. 0.01 7. 2.83

8. 3.61 9. 8.06 10. 10.3 11. 16 12. 14 13. 6 14. 7.94

15. 10 16. 6.93 17. 8.19 18. 5.29 19. 5 feet   20. 1 hour

Posttest   Chapter 13

1. 7 2. 11 3. $\frac{3}{4}$ 4. $\frac{2}{3}$ 5. 0.5 6. 0.8 7. 2.65

8. 3.74 9. 8.19 10. 10.25 11. 18 12. 26 13. 7 14. 7.21

15. 5 16. 3.87 17. 6 18. 5.1 19. 12 inches   20. 4 meters

Pretest   Chapter 14

1. $-15, -13$ 2. $8x^2$ 3. $17y$ 4. $-xz - 3$ 5. $5a - 2$ 6. $19x^2 - 4x - 3$
7. y^7 8. $-45n^7$ 9. $12a^2 - 24a$ 10. $-18x^3 + 9x^2$ 11. $n^2 + 12n + 32$ 12. $2y^2 + 9y - 35$
13. $15x^3 - 20x^2 + 6x - 8$ 14. $11x$ 15. $-2a - 2$ 16. $-16y^2 + 2$ 17. $16n^2 - 3n + 5$
18. $7x$ 19. $-6x^2y$ 20. $6y^2 - 4y + 2$

Posttest   Chapter 14

1. $-2, -8$ 2. $-4xy$ 3. a 4. $2x + 3$ 5. $-4y - 4$ 6. $-6x^2 - 5x - 5$
7. n^7 8. $-45x^5$ 9. $-10a^3 + 6a^2$ 10. $16y^4 - 6y^3$ 11. $-x^2 + 9x - 18$ 12. $12a^2 - 18a - 12$
13. $-14x^3 + 14x^2 - 6x + 6$ 14. $-6x$ 15. $2n - 8$ 16. $4y^2 + 8$ 17. $10x^2 + 4x + 8$
18. $7x^4$ 19. $8x^2y^2$ 20. $4a^3 + 3a^2 + 2a$

Pretest   Chapter 15

1. 10–18   **2.** 11   **3.** 13

4.

No.	16	17	18	19	20	21	22	23	Total
Freq.	2	3	2	3	5	2	1	2	20

5.

6. 10–46   **7.** 33

17.

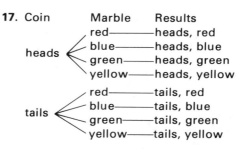

8. 29   **9.** 10   **10.** 154 hours

11. white, blue, or red   **12.** $\frac{3}{10}$ **13.** $\frac{1}{2}$

14. $\frac{1}{5}$ **15.** $\frac{1}{2}$ **16.** $\frac{7}{10}$

18. $\frac{1}{24}$ **19.** $\frac{3}{26}$ **20.** $\frac{1}{12}$

Posttest   Chapter 15

1. 15–22   **2.** 19   **3.** 19

4.

No.	13	14	15	16	17	18	19	20	Total
Freq.	2	3	2	3	5	2	1	2	20

5.

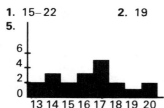

6. 51–80   **7.** 69

17.

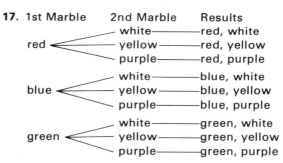

8. 69   **9.** 7   **10.** 630 points

11. 1, 2, 3, 4, 5, or 6   **12.** $\frac{1}{6}$ **13.** $\frac{1}{6}$

14. $\frac{1}{2}$ **15.** $\frac{2}{3}$ **16.** $\frac{1}{3}$

18. $\frac{1}{12}$ **19.** $\frac{1}{12}$ **20.** $\frac{1}{4}$

Cumulative Test   Chapters 8–15

1. 5, 8, 11, 14   **2. a.** $(0, ^-1)$ **b.** $(2, 1)$ **c.** $(2, 3)$ **3.** No   **4.**

5. 0.6, 60%   **6.** $\frac{1}{4}$, 25%   **7.** $1\frac{1}{2}$, 1.5   **8.** 230   **9.** 8%

10. $\angle A$, $\angle B$, $\angle C$, AB, BC, AC   **11.** 14 miles   **12.** 12 m   **13.** $^-\frac{1}{10}$

14. 1   **15.** $^-3\frac{3}{4}$ **16.** $1\frac{1}{2}$ **17.** $^-2.31$ **18.** $^-15.672$

19. 0.1976   **20.** $^-2.7$ **21.** 1   **22.** $\frac{1}{4}$ **23.** $^-2.4$

24. $^-0.9$ **25.** $1\frac{1}{2}$ **26.** $1\frac{1}{4}$ **27.** $^-\frac{3}{20}$ **28.** $^-30.96$ **29.** 18

30. 9   **31.** 9   **32.** 4.53×10^5 **33.** 6.02×10^{-2} **34.** 2.65   **35.** 4.48   **36.** 0.8

37. 4   **38.** 25 feet   **39.** $13x^2 + 8y$ **40.** $^-16xz - 6$ **41.** $n^2 - 9n - 36$ **42.** $3x^2 - 2x + 1$

43. 2959 voters   **44.** 3 hours   **45.** 1200 color sets   **46. a.** 32.75   **b.** 33   **c.** 33   **d.** 30–35

47.

No.	30	31	32	33	34	35	Total
Freq.	1	2	1	5	1	2	12

48. a. $\frac{1}{2}$ **b.** $\frac{7}{10}$ **49.** $\frac{8}{25}$ **50.** $\frac{1}{4}$

Pretest   Chapter 16

1. g **2.** e **3.** f **4.** a **5.** d **6.** b **7.** 56 cm **8.** 36 in. **9.** 31.4 cm
10. 192 cm^2 **11.** 54 sq in. **12.** 78.5 cm^2 **13.** 888 cm^2 **14.** 1064 m^2 **15.** 395.64 sq ft
16. 1512 cm^3 **17.** 1260 m^3 **18.** 508.68 cu ft **19.** 15 386 cm^2 **20.** 448 sq in. **21.** 1152 cu ft

Posttest   Chapter 16

1. f **2.** e **3.** g **4.** d **5.** c **6.** a **7.** 96 cm **8.** 43 in. **9.** 50.24 m
10. 576 cm^2 **11.** 75 sq in. **12.** 200.96 m^2 **13.** 992 cm^2 **14.** 766 m^2 **15.** 791.28 sq ft
16. 1920 cm^3 **17.** 1020 m^3 **18.** 1271.7 cu ft **19.** 20 096 cm^2 **20.** 270 sq in. **21.** 750 cu ft

Pretest   Chapter 17

1.   **2.**   **3.**

4.   **5.**   **6.**

7.   **8.**   **9.**

10. $y = -\frac{5}{2}x + 5, m = -\frac{5}{2}, b = 5$ **11.** $y = \frac{2}{3}x - 2, m = \frac{2}{3}, b = {}^-2$ **12.** $y = {}^-4x + 2, m = {}^-4, b = 2$

13.   **14.**   **15.**

16. inconsistent   **17.** consistent   **18.** dependent and consistent
19. (3, 2)   **20.** (3, 2)   **21.** (4, ⁻2)

Posttest   Chapter 17

1.   **2.**   **3.**   **4.**   **5.**

T95

6.

7.

8.

9.

10. $y = {}^-3x + 6$, $m = {}^-3$, $b = 6$

11. $y = \frac{2}{3}x - 2$, $m = \frac{2}{3}$, $b = {}^-2$

12. $y = \frac{1}{2}x + 2$, $m = \frac{1}{2}$, $b = 2$

13.

x	2	1	0.5
y	5	10	20

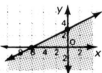

14.

x	3	2	1
y	6	9	18

15.

x	4	2	1
y	6	12	24

16. consistent

19. (4, 2)

17. dependent consistent

20. (⁻2, 2)

18. inconsistent

21. (3, 3)

Cumulative Test   Chapters 16–17

1. g   **2.** f   **3.** e   **4.** b   **5.** a   **6.** c   **7.** 66 cm   **8.** 63 in.   **9.** 62.8 m
10. 252 cm² **11.** 170 sq in. **12.** 314 m² **13.** 928 cm² **14.** 266 m² **15.** 1105.28 sq ft
16. 1792 cm³ **17.** 240 m³ **18.** 2813.44 cu ft **19.** 25 434 cm² **20.** 216 sq in. **21.** 1152 cu ft

22. **23.** **24.** **25.** **26.**

27. **28.** **29.** **30.**

31. $y = {}^-2x + 5$, $m = {}^-2$, $b = 5$

32. $y = \frac{1}{2}x - 3$, $m = \frac{1}{2}$, $b = {}^-3$

33. $y = \frac{1}{3}x + 3$, $m = \frac{1}{3}$, $b = 3$

34.

x	3	2	1
y	4	6	12

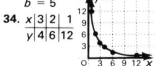

35.

x	3	2	1
y	5	7.5	15

36.

x	4	2	1
y	9	18	36

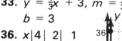

37. dependent and consistent

40. (5, ⁻2)

38. consistent

41. (⁻2, ⁻6)

39. inconsistent

42. (4, 5)

End-of-Year Test

1. C   **2.** B   **3.** A   **4.** C   **5.** D   **6.** B   **7.** A   **8.** C   **9.** A   **10.** A   **11.** D   **12.** C   **13.** D
14. C   **15.** B   **16.** A   **17.** A   **18.** D   **19.** C   **20.** D   **21.** B   **22.** A   **23.** C   **24.** D   **25.** A   **26.** B
27. D   **28.** C   **29.** D   **30.** A   **31.** C   **32.** A   **33.** D   **34.** D   **35.** B   **36.** A   **37.** A   **38.** B   **39.** C
40. B   **41.** D   **42.** A   **43.** C   **44.** B   **45.** C   **46.** A   **47.** D   **48.** B   **49.** C   **50.** B   **51.** D   **52.** A
53. D   **54.** B   **55.** D   **56.** C   **57.** A   **58.** D   **59.** B   **60.** A   **61.** C   **62.** C   **63.** D   **64.** C   **65.** B
66. D   **67.** A   **68.** D   **69.** C   **70.** C   **71.** B   **72.** B   **73.** D   **74.** D   **75.** A